An Anthropologist at Work

Writings of Ruth Benedict

Eucharist.

Light the more given is the more denied.
Though you go seeking by the naked seas,
Each cliff etched visible and all the waves
Pluming themselves with sunlight, of this pride
Light makes her sophistries.

You are not like to find her, being fed
Always with that she shines on. Only those,
Storm-driven down the dark, see light arise,
Her body broken for their rainbow bread
At late and shipwrecked close.

An
Anthropologist
at Work

Writings of Ruth Benedict

BY MARGARET MEAD

ILLUSTRATED WITH PHOTOGRAPHS

HOUGHTON MIFFLIN COMPANY BOSTON

The Riverside Press Cambridge

Acknowledgments

THE PREPARATION of this book has depended upon the hard work and devoted interest of many individuals, beginning with those who kept the files, many years ago, for Franz Boas, Edward Sapir, and Ruth Benedict. I have been able to draw on published materials on their life and work — on Melville J. Herskovits' *Franz Boas: The Science of Man in the Making*, and on *Selected Writings of Edward Sapir in Language, Culture, and Personality*, edited by David G. Mandelbaum, which includes the bibliography of his poetry prepared by his son, Philip Sapir. I have also to thank the American Philosophical Society for permission to use the Boas files. The final sorting and ordering of Ruth Benedict's papers and their selection and editing for this book have depended upon contributions of time and interest by Ruth Valentine, Sula Benet, Mary E. Chandler, Marie Eichelberger, Geoffrey Gorer, and Rhoda Métraux. I am indebted to the Boas family for permission to use Franz Boas' letters, to Reo Fortune for permission to include his letters about the Dobuan chapter of *Patterns of Culture*, to the Sapir family for permission to use Edward Sapir's letters, to Erik H. Erikson and to the Viking Fund — which, in 1949, published *Ruth Fulton Benedict, a Memorial* — for permission to reproduce the drawing he made of her, and to her sister, Margery Fulton Freeman, for permission to use family pictures and for supplying a wealth of biographical material. Finally, I am indebted to Ruth Benedict herself for the selections she made among her early papers.

vii

For permission to reproduce previously published work by Ruth Benedict and others, I have to thank the *American Anthropologist*, the *American Journal of Orthopsychiatry*, *The Annals* of the American Academy of Political and Social Science, *The Atlantic Monthly*, the Bernice P. Bishop Museum, Columbia University Press, the *Journal of American Folk-Lore*, the *Journal of General Psychology*, William Morrow and Company, *The Nation*, Charles Scribner's Sons, and the *University of Toronto Quarterly*. Also for permission to reproduce poems by Ruth Benedict ("Anne Singleton"), Edward Sapir, and myself, I have to thank *The Canadian Forum*, *The Measure*, *The Nation*, *The New Republic*, *New York Herald Tribune Books*, *Palms*, *Poetry*, and *Voices*. I am indebted to the Boston Museum of Fine Arts for permission to reproduce El Greco's portrait of Fray Felix Hortensio Paravicino.

After the formation of the Institute for Intercultural Studies, Ruth Benedict used it as an instrument for the expenditure of the residue of the Quain Fund, which had been left to her to use for the benefit of anthropology. Since her death, the Institute has received substantial contributions from her executors which have been used in Benedict Grants made to individuals with whose special circumstances and needs, as well as with whose scholarship, we have felt she would have been in sympathy. The ordering of her papers for their deposit in the Vassar College Library and the preparation of this book have been done through the Institute for Intercultural Studies, and any royalties the book may earn will be used for Benedict Grants in the future.

MARGARET MEAD

New York
March 15, 1958

Contents

PART VI

Illustrations

Introduction

WHAT HAPPENS on the growing edges of life is seldom written down at the time. It is lived from day to day in talk, in scraps of comment on the margin of someone else's manuscript, in words spoken on a street corner, or in cadences which lie well below the words that are spoken. Later it lives on, reshaped and reinterpreted, in the memories of those who were part of it and finally slips, like a child's leaf boats after a long journey down a stream, into the unrecognizing hands of one's spiritual descendants who do not know the source of the water-soaked treasures which have landed on the shores of their lives. In any generation there may be a group of people who find meaning in just these unrecorded parts of life, who can read a book the better for knowing what the author meant to write while writing something else, or who even catch a glimpse of excitement from a first edition if they know also how the writer felt on the day those crisp fresh pages first met his eye. Particularly today there is great interest throughout the world in "becoming" rather than in completed form, in the latent image and in the counterpoint between almost forgotten words and new, unimagined meanings. And so it seems a possible enterprise to try to set down such a piece of oral history as lies back of the work of Ruth Benedict, who came, unexpectedly, into a young science and shaped her thought into a book which for a generation has stood as a bridge between those who cherish the uniqueness of individual achievement and those who labor to order the regularities in all human achievement. *Patterns of Culture* has gone through eleven printings, has been translated into fourteen languages, and has become as timeless as the lives of the peoples on which it is based.

In this collection of Ruth Benedict's published and hitherto unpublished short papers, I do not propose to evaluate her work but only to try to describe how and why it was done the way it was done. She wrote so little and so infrequently that it would be hard for the student to piece together the background of each period — why certain problems were selected, why some point was stressed with seemingly undue emphasis, why sometimes boredom and sometimes laughter weigh down or lift a sentence or a paragraph. So I have interspersed through the papers background chapters which draw, especially in the earlier years, also on the parts of her thought which originally were kept separate from her anthropological work and were put instead into poems, some of which were published under the *nom de plume* of Anne Singleton. There will be least about the years of teaching and administration at Columbia University, between 1931 and 1939, for I was out of the country for five of those years and have only letters to fill them in. Toward the end of her life her anthropological writing became a sufficient vehicle; there were no more poems, but unashamedly lovely passages of prose placed precisely as she felt and wished them to be. The need for describing the background of each paper grows less and less, until finally her last paper stands alone.

She saw her work in a context of three other anthropologists: Franz Boas, her teacher, for whom she assumed an increasing professional burden in his old age (she was thirty-three and he was sixty-three when she came to study with him); Edward Sapir, who was the contemporary whose work she valued most highly, whom she knew best when she was just beginning her work in anthropology, and when both he and she were writing a great deal of poetry and he was also writing music; and myself, her first student, fifteen years younger but anthropologically almost a contemporary, for I began my anthropological work in the year in which she took her Ph.D. I was both her student and the student of Franz Boas; I shared her interests in anthropology and in poetry, and the interests of Edward Sapir.

She was the mediator in my relationship to both; it was her interpretation of what "Professor Boas" hoped for from his students that
became mine, and her vividly relayed conversations and letters from
Sapir became part of my thinking before I came to know him.
Behind and beyond us both lay the longer and stormy relationship
of Boas and Sapir, each embittered but still cherishing his recognition
of the other as the theoretical adversary most worth crossing swords
with. (Part of our tradition of this relationship was the story that
Boas once went to extraordinary lengths to arrange for Sapir's expensive travel to an international congress to hear a linguistic paper
which Boas would read and with which Sapir would then certainly
disagree.) The specific interests of linguistics and music which
Sapir shared with Boas were both closed to Ruth Benedict and myself, while our adventures in poetry were kept as much as possible
from Boas, who would, so Ruth Benedict believed, have disapproved
of them. Sapir used no *nom de plume* but relied simply on the
pleasant obscurity of the small poetry journals for which we used to
carry our friends' manuscripts in our pockets. As for mine, they
were hardly ever good enough to submit even to such tiny magazines,
and besides my formal work as a graduate student, I presented for
the professorial eye an appearance of orderly and objective behavior
— editorial work on the *Journal of the American Statistical Association* and an assistantship to William Fielding Ogburn, its editor.
The circumstance that I filled his office with working poets —
Louise Bogan, Léonie Adams, and Louise Townsend Nicholl — was
not advertised too widely. And in this way, Ruth Benedict and
Sapir came to know them too.

We were at the end of an epoch — an epoch in which anthropology had been written for specialists in technical language and, when
it happened to concern the Kwakiutl or the Hopi, a good bit of it *in*
Kwakiutl or Hopi. Almost all of Boas' efforts were being put into
getting more grammars of American languages completed, more
folklore collected and collated, more details of Siberian native behavior set down by the aging Russian refugee, Jochelson — groundwork, spadework, highly technical work, work so technical that it
tempted no humanist within its pages. Those who looked to anthropology for materials for one kind of thought looked to England and

The Golden Bough; specialists in *Geisteswissenschaft* still looked to
Germany; students of religion looked to England and France. But
Americans had been held firmly to the basic tasks of collecting
masses of vanishing materials from the members of dying American
Indian cultures, and it was in terms of the urgency of this salvage
task that I decided to become an anthropologist. In the spring of
1933, there was no indication that the poetry and *belles lettres* that
lay hidden among linguistic texts and forbidding kinship diagrams
in Ruth Benedict's papers would be blended, within the American
anthropological tradition of precise and untiring field work, into
books which would be read as often by future poets as by future
anthropologists. True, Boas had written *The Mind of Primitive Man,*
published first in English in 1911 and then in German in 1914. But
its polemical character, its awkward and unendearing style, and the
lack of reference to any particular primitive man, meant that its
importance was successfully concealed from most of the students
who were ordered to read it. (I had read it for a book report in a
course in elementary psychology and received a C for the dullness
of my comment.) We needed some sense of whole cultures, of
whole ways of life to bring home to us what anthropology was really
about.

Meanwhile we lived, in a sense, lives in which the arts and the
sciences fought uneven battles for pre-eminence. Boas would leave
his office and his labor over the particularities of some nearly extinct
American Indian language to spend the evening improvising at his
piano. Sapir would let his Nootka texts lie half-finished while he
wrote:[1]

> Distant strumming of strings, vague flutings, drum
> Give mood a surer voice and fancy wings more fleet
> Than declarations positive and sweet
> Of orchestras; I hear song fragments come
> From the far end of the cornfields with the wind
> Which bring me magic, inarticulate,
> More than the studied ecstasy of great
> Singers in gesture

Or he would work at a piece of music which someone "had thought as good as Richard Strauss." And Ruth Benedict firmly continued to keep the parts of her life separate, signing her married name ("which I always think of as a *nom de plume*," she used to say) to such papers as "A Matter for the Field Worker in Folklore" in the *American Journal of Folk-Lore*,[2] and not publishing her poems at all.

The materials which I have used for this book are first of all the corpus of Ruth Benedict's work, which is now deposited in the library of her college, Vassar. The early experiments in writing, going back to schoolgirl essays, the journal entries, and the diaries are those which she herself elected to keep. I have used no unpublished papers of hers which were not in her own files. Her executrix, Ruth Valentine, returned some letters to those who had been close to her and were still alive, including my letters to her, so that all the letters she herself kept as a record have not been drawn on.

I have also her letters to me, and Sapir's letters to her, and her correspondence with Boas (from the Boas files in the American Philosophical Society). As all of us were frequently in the field and so were separated, some of these letters are very important. I have her poems, both published and unpublished, and Sapir's poems, published and unpublished — which he had sent to her — and the poems I wrote within their writing, to serve as a mnemonic for the ways in which we felt. Where dates are given, they have been checked; where publications are mentioned, they also have been checked. I have tried to provide the necessary and sufficient documentation essential to future scholars — especially in the chronological life history — but this is an incidental, not the primary, purpose of this book.

What she herself kept as a record is essentially her view of what was important in her life, here ordered by my understanding growing out of a friendship of twenty-five years. Any other of her close friends would undoubtedly have placed the accents differently, for she responded selectively to each one of us.

During the last quarter of a century, anthropologists have had to learn a great deal about how to combine descriptions of another culture with a due respect for the living and future members of the society who embodied that culture. Once we thought we could combine a sufficient respect for the culture — as a coherent and viable way of life of a very different people — without any reference to the feelings or life histories of those on whose lives our material was based. They would never read what was written, nor would the lay world. Safely buried in technical journals, embalmed in jargon, remarks on the polygamous marriages of a prominent chief or the publication of esoteric and carefully guarded religious secrets of a particular priesthood seemed harmless enough. But this situation has been slowly changing, particularly in the Southwest, as interested lay people have come to live near the Indian pueblos and have become involved in their political fate, and as with increasing literacy and participation in the wider world many of the Indians have become concerned with what was written about them. There are many references in Ruth Benedict's letters from Zuñi to the Indians' distrust and reserve.

It remained for us in later years to come fully to grips with the problem, and to realize that the description of any culture whose members had been identified as individuals involved writing a description to which they themselves would agree and which would not, furthermore, outrage the sensibilities of members of other cultures who would read the account. These ethical premises were worked on in the Columbia University Research in Contemporary Cultures, which Ruth Benedict inaugurated and directed, and were discussed at a meeting of the American Orthopsychiatric Association in 1947.[3] It was discussed in this context because we felt it affected the way in which a physician discussed a patient, a lawyer a client, or a teacher a pupil.

In this book I have tried to carry this principle one step further to consider not only those who are still living and their children as likely to be affected by this picture of a sister, a friend, a teacher, a colleague, and a representative of the discipline which they hold dear, but also the question of whether it is not possible to include the past itself in the criteria of presentation. I have tried to put nothing in this account which Ruth Benedict herself would not have found appropriate. She never learned to accept compliments very easily, and it is possible that she would have made a wry disowning face over some of the glowing things which have been said about her. But I have tried to write so that there would be nothing which she would delete as harmful to another person or as alien to herself. It may be that such a standard of biography can only be attempted at first by those who knew the subject well, but possibly if we practice hard and self-consciously, we may come in time to be able to understand the individuality, the culture, and the period of those who died long ago well enough so that we can phrase their lives in such a way that no matter how many centuries have transpired, the phrasing would make sense to them.

This is not a detective story, and it can be read in any order; a finished life can be seen as simultaneous, each detail as illuminative prospectively as it is illuminative retrospectively. Unfortunately, writing is a sequential art and cannot, like painting, give us the entire landscape at once. But I have tried to arrange this book so that it will suit the preferences of different readers, those who prefer reading the last pages first, those who prefer to digest their own raw materials before glancing at someone else's interpretive statement. These materials are presented in chunks, not woven through with little snippets of half sentences and half lines of poems as is done in so many biographical studies, because she and I both believed in the importance of presenting materials in sufficient bulk so that the cadence and pattern could be perceived. (Her two volumes of Zuñi materials are the best example of this method of presentation of original materials.)[4] I have placed the bulk of the illustrative materials from letters, journals, poems, or articles as separate sections which can be treated as documentation of my introductory statement or as introductory to my comments, which may be read as added. It has been possible only in rare instances to give chapter and verse for the moment at which any given relationship between the materials dawned upon me. But my own memory has woven back and forth like an embroidery needle threading together parts of a tapestry as I have reread the materials.

Ruth Benedict devoted the first years of her marriage to a serious attempt to write an analysis of the lives of three women of the past — Mary Wollstonecraft, Olive Schreiner and Margaret Fuller — in the hope that through such studies she would find a key to the meaning of creativity for human beings who happened also to be women. While she worked on these essays, she lamented the absence of vivid and intimate materials which would bring the lives of contemporary women more fully to life. Lacking these, she wrote about Mary Wollstonecraft "whose life story . . . makes her our contemporary." Then she laid aside these studies, only one of which — the essay on Mary Wollstonecraft — was completed, though it remained unpublished, to enter instead upon long years of disciplined and responsible scientific work. Her own life and the records she kept of it — her journals and letters and early work — have made it possible for me to write the life of a contemporary, gifted woman which she had believed could be written only about a woman of the past.

Here I want to set down what will otherwise be lost about how Ruth Benedict became a figure of transition, binding the broken sureties of a past age, to which she was full heir, to the uncertainties which precede a new integration in human thinking, for we shall not look upon her like again.

An
Anthropologist
at Work

Writings of Ruth Benedict

Part I

Search: 1920–1930

Margaret Mead

"I HAVEN'T strength of mind not to need a career," Ruth Benedict used to say, with a rueful smile, during her first years in anthropology. And anthropology provided dignified busy work for a married woman without children who needed something significant to fill her time, but something which did not make too great claims on her dedication or her imagination. Although this attitude toward a career was never to disappear entirely, it was strongest at the beginning. She brought only one part of her life with her when, at the age of thirty-three, she began to do graduate work, and in her late thirties she could still write in one of her casually kept journal notes, "I gambled on having the strength to live two lives, one for myself and one for the world."

Necessarily, any account of her life, either before she entered anthropology or afterwards, when told from any one point of view is unusually incomplete. She kept us all in separate rooms and moved from one to another with no one following to take notes. I visited her once at her summer home in New Hampshire, and I saw her husband three times. I never saw the family farm in the Shenango Valley. Before her death, I had met her mother and her sister only twice. Several of her closest friends I have never even seen. These all belonged in another part of life — as anthropology and poetry were separate worlds into which these others did not come in person.

I met her first in the autumn of 1922, when I was a senior at Barnard College. Professor Boas still taught a large undergraduate class there, and Ruth Benedict was the assistant who took us on trips to the American Museum of Natural History to illustrate the materials on the course. Although in the period between graduating from Vassar College in 1909 and marrying Stanley Benedict in 1914, she had taught English literature in a girls' school, this was her first experience of college teaching. In the early weeks of that course, anthropology began to come alive for me. Professor Boas, with his great head and slight frail body, his face scarred from an old duel and one eye drooping from a facial paralysis, spoke with an authority and a distinction greater than I had ever met in a teacher. He believed in encouraging in his students the very kinds of behavior which his authoritative and uncompromising sense of what was right and just also tended to discourage. Characteristically, after a semester spent asking us rhetorical questions which we hardly ever ventured to answer — though I would write the answer down in my notebook and would glow with pleasure when it turned out to be right — he excused me and one other student from taking an examination, because of "helpful participation in classroom discussion."

Marie Bloomfield [1] and I set out to get acquainted with his assistant, "Mrs. Benedict," while most of the class fretted against her inarticulate shyness and her habit of wearing always the same dress — and that not a very becoming one. Yet even for the two of us who were becoming excited by the material, the Museum classes were painful. After a particularly exciting — and halting — explanation of the model of the Sun Dance in the Plains Indian Hall, I asked for more references and was brushed aside with inexplicable asperity. When I persisted, the lecturer blushed scarlet and said she would give me something next time. This was a reprint of her own first published article, "The Vision in Plains Culture." [2] The fact of publication, having her name in print, mentioning that she had written anything were all almost too difficult to manage. Enthusiastic as Marie and I were about what we felt she was saying, when she invited us to the seminar at which she was to report on *Human Nature and Conduct*,[3] we found her combination of shyness and inarticulateness devastating. It was years before she conquered this shyness and could speak with fluency and authority, and she was always a little surprised at herself when she succeeded and more than a little likely to add a touch of mischief to whatever she was saying successfully.

By the end of the first semester I was so enthusiastic and talked so much about the course on the campus that the registration doubled. Ruth Benedict's vivid delight in the details of Northwest Coast art and of the Toda kinship system gave life to the clarity and order of Professor Boas' presentation of man's development through the ages. I could move from the sense of his grasp of the materials, through the sudden excitement of finding a picture of a reconstructed prehistoric man holding a bundle of firewood in his slightly too prehensile arms, to discussions with Ruth Benedict about both anthropology and poetry. She herself had just found Professor Boas and "sense," and she conveyed to me a double feeling of urgency: the need to learn everything that he had to teach at once because this might be his last year of lecturing, and to rescue the beautiful, complex patterns that people had contrived for themselves to live in that were being irrevocably lost all over the world. So I began to attend all the graduate courses, little groups of five or six students under a professor who had no time for administrative red tape and who was perfectly willing to let an undergraduate go where an undergraduate wished.

I gradually learned how Ruth Benedict had found anthropology after seven years of childless marriage to a husband whose increasing distinction as a biochemist had been matched by his increasing withdrawal from any contacts except with his immediate laboratory assistants. None of the "causes" which had occupied her college generation had enlisted her interest. Woman's suffrage, as a great issue, had bored her; education for women was a battle won, as far as she was concerned, in her mother's day. Social work meant that somehow a life symbolized by "the suburbs" was to be promoted among the unfortunate. "But," she would add hastily, "of course I don't want people to live in slums." The World War was for her an example of how ruthlessly man's bright hopes could be destroyed — a feeling she expressed in the poem, "Rupert Brooke, 1914–1918":[4]

Now God be thanked who took him at that hour,
Who let him die, flushed in an hour of dreaming.
Nothing forever shall have any power
To strip his bright election of its seeming.
He is most blest. There was great splendor dying
Then when our faith made all man's hell a cleanness,
Then when our vision flashed like strong birds flying,
Before we had known victory and its meaning.

We are wise now and weary. Hopes he knew
Are perished utterly as a storm abated.
One mockery yet shall leap as flame wind-taken
Down dreadful years: unknowing what they do,
Our sons shall chant his words, and go elated,
Dying like him; like him with faith unshaken.

She had written poetry and under a pseudonym began to publish some poems, but no one was allowed to see her writing. "The poems were just saying 'ouch' because someone had stepped on one's foot," she would say. Community activities in the suburb of Douglas Manor, where she lived during the first years of her marriage, meant very little. She had tried teaching Sunday school but was dismissed when she gave her class the assignment of looking up Jesus in the Encyclopaedia Britannica. The long summers in New Hampshire — for Stanley believed in long vacations[5] — were delightful for the first two weeks and much too long thereafter. As she was physically strong and easily competent, housework in a summer cottage barely filled an hour. But the hours of depression must be masked; the day must be got through somehow until the depression lifted. In the winters she tried various expedients. She worked on a book of biographies of famous women, beginning with Mary Wollstonecraft.[6] She spent one winter working quite hard at rhythmic dancing. Through Sophie Theis, a college friend, she worked as a volunteer for the State Charities Aid Association analyzing case histories. One after another, in these years, she watched her friends — the friends she had chosen for their special intensities — vanish into the maw of some completely accepted orthodoxy: Christian Science, high church Anglican missions, progressive education, psychoanalysis. And no child was born to her.

When she first encountered anthropology, she was looking not for a real career but rather for some new expedient to get through the days which would be less meaningless than the others had proved to be. As Stanley had become increasingly intolerant of close neighbors and of urban living, they had moved to a little house in Bedford Hills, where he slept soundly despite the whistling trains. Psychoanalysis was just becoming known; the pressure, intensified through the years, to make each deviant person submit to it as a duty was fully embodied in advice given her by a college friend, who was well equipped with a knowledge of how depressed and desperate she often felt and who wrote to her:[7]

I am glad you are enjoying solitude in the woods, and reading. And I hope you are taking care of yourself, and playing and being outdoors. The trouble is, both you and Stanley have too much brain power, and you tend to work too hard. Don't be old before your time. I hope you will move to the village and have a good time, and several love affairs, next year. Of course, there is no stake in life, only a series. That's why living in the moment is so important. I shall always feel that you'd get a good deal out of analysis. You are, in many ways, a very suppressed person. You have built up two personalities, more or less consciously, a public and a private, and the strain is rather heavy. It isn't that you can't do it, but that it will wear you out to do it. And scholarship may become too great a retreat, much as it may benefit the world! However, any expression carries its wreckage, and intellectual achievement must be worth a good deal to you. Life is vacuous, and you cannot have the sense of utility every moment. . . .

In 1919, she decided to attend some lectures at the New School for Social Research, an institution which was still in a ferment of new ideas taught by brilliant people who were disqualified from teaching elsewhere by some act of social or political nonconformity. The young middle-aged, those who had been delayed or sidetracked in choosing a career, went there to explore, to taste the possibilities of kinds of learning about which they knew nothing. Among those teaching at the New School were Alexander Goldenweiser, the most picturesque of the generation of anthropologists who came to maturity before the first World War, and Elsie Clews Parsons, who had once written books of broad and provocative speculation — *Social Rule* and *The Old Fashioned Woman* and, under a male pseudonym (John Main), a book on ceremonial license.[8]

Goldenweiser, mercurial, excited by ideas about culture, but intolerant of the petty exactions of field work,[9] was working on the first book by an American anthropologist which was to present cultures briefly as wholes. His *Early Civilization*[10] appeared in the autumn of 1922. In his lectures the bold strokes, the vivid partial characterizations with which he sketched in "the red paint culture of Melanesia" or described the rise and fall of Gothic architecture in Europe, the magnificent flare that outshone the lack of detailed information caught the imagination of students, whom he treated as potential captives of his charm.

Goldenweiser interested both Ruth Benedict and Melville Herskovits, who entered anthropology from the New School at the same period. His book was the first one that undergraduates could read to get a sense of what a culture was, and he had a quick, imaginative response to the enthusiasm which his brilliance inspired in others. Ruth Benedict valued what she learned from him and writhed at his naive sense of self-importance, a quality for which she had little charity.[11]

Mrs. Parsons was lecturing out of her discovery of anthropology as a matter made up of the very careful assemblage and analysis of details, and her presentation contrasted sharply with Goldenweiser's lazy brilliance. From her, students learned that anthropolgy consisted of an enormous mass of little bits of material, carefully labeled by time, place, and tribe — the fruits, arid and bitter, of long, long hours of labor and devotion.

Anthropology made the first "sense" that any ordered approach to life had ever made to Ruth Benedict. Her fellow students at the New School knew her as "Mrs. Benedict," whose husband never was present. She appeared to them a gentle, wraithlike figure, her hair going prematurely gray and never staying in place, dressed with a kind of studied indifference, just deaf enough to miss a great deal of what was being said before others recognized it, and painfully shy — the beauty which had been hers as a young girl misted over by uncertainty and awkwardness. Though she took some part in student activities at the New School, these were mentioned in later years only in connection with the name of someone she had known there, Frank Tannenbaum or Lawrence K. Frank. Essentially she was isolated from any milieu, meeting others only at occasional dinners with colleagues of her husband or at lunches or dinners alone with individual old friends.

Then, in 1921, she came to Columbia University. Professor Boas, with his customary disregard for administrative rules, succeeded in giving her graduate credit for her work at the New School, and she rapidly completed her doctoral dissertation on "The Concept of the Guardian Spirit in North America." [12] The years in which she studied under Boas and those in which I studied under him were essentially the same, but I had her mediation to his remote reserve. The excitement which she felt about his mind broke through the austerity of his fundamentally paternal relationship to his students, and the rest of us became grandchildren to a professor whom a year later we began to call "Papa Franz." Ruth Benedict continued to come to his classes from 1923 to 1925. She was an active participant in seminars, where I acquired a very useful speed in writing by sitting beside her and writing down the parts of the discussion which she was unable to hear. In discussing what she learned at Columbia that became the basis for her further work, I have drawn both upon my notes from 1922 to 1925 and upon her own interpretations during that period of what she was still learning or had just learned.

The Columbia University Department of Anthropology was, in the early 1920's, a small embattled group. During the war Franz Boas' pacifism had made him, because of his German origin, a target for the enflamed feelings of the period.[13] He had no sympathy with the issues of World War I, he repudiated bitterly the use of scientific work as "cover" for intelligence operations, and his relations with colleagues and students were stormy. There were violent scenes in the meetings of the American Anthropological Association. Other difficulties arose when a young anthropologist, a returned soldier, appeared in the department in uniform.

By 1922, although much of the rancor of the wartime period had cooled, Boas was still virtually a professor without a department, his work pared to the bone. Although he taught an undergraduate course at Barnard College, there was no undergraduate work at Columbia College, and after Goldenweiser, who had had a lecturer's appointment, lost his job in 1919, Boas was the only full-time faculty member of the department. Bruno Oetteking, an old-style German anatomist who was located at the Heye Museum, taught one course in physical anthropology. Pliny Earle Goddard of the American Museum of Natural History, who was Boas' sentimentally devoted admirer, nominally taught a class in technology at the Museum. Otherwise, whatever courses were given, Boas himself had to give, and he taught theory and linguistics and biometrics in dreadful concentration and with no quarter given to beginners or to those with a defective background. In the biometrics course, I remember his saying one day, "I am embarrassed. Some of you do not know the calculus. I will teach you the calculus." In the twenty minutes left of the hour he did! Linguistics, after a brief general course in the science of language, meant plunging directly into the analysis of difficult American Indian languages.

In his lectures, Boas referred to tribes all over the world without placing them in time or space or by author, and even when one sat "on the right side of his mouth" his very German pronunciation was hard to understand. He always gave references first in German and only then in English, and there were rumors that, on two weeks' notice, he would demand seminar reports based on sources in such languages as Dutch or Danish. The student struggled with the clear, higher-level abstractions and the unintelligible details in lectures and with reading, most of which was specialized, technical, and not organized to any point of current interest. The few students in the department took courses more than once because each time they were almost completely different. For in spite of the intolerable load of teaching, which he combined with the direction of great bodies of research in folklore and linguistics, Boas always prepared each lecture as if it were to be given for an audience of a hundred of his peers. Nevertheless, for a whole field of anthropology, such as primitive art or primitive religion, the student might have one or two lectures on "method," and that was all.

Ruth Benedict came into the department during the period when Boas was still interested in diffusion and in having his students laboriously trace a trait or a theme from culture to culture, showing the changes which the trait or the complex of traits underwent. The student read every scrap of material, annotated and analyzed, and plotted distributions and integrations. Meanwhile in lectures Boas spent a great deal of his time pointing out the errors of all single explanations of the origins, forms, or changes in human cultures. With great rigor he discussed the nineteenth century English evolutionists, who had arranged cultural forms in an ascending series with nineteenth century England at the top; the geographical determinists, like Ratzel and Huntington; the German diffusionist school, which claimed the existence of age-old *Kulturkreise* stretching from Tasmania to Tierra del Fuego, in which similarities in the form of a tool, the shape of a house, or the arrangement of social groups were regarded as evidence of a single, widely spread earlier stage of culture; the English diffusionist school of Rivers, Perry, and Elliot Smith, which postulated a single origin — in Egypt — of all high civilizations and followed the Children of the Sun around the world; theories of religion, Bastian's *Elementargedanken* or Durkheim's concept of a mystic of collectivity; and psychological theories, which postulated an essential difference between the mentality of "the primitive" and that of modern man or else, in the manner of Freud, a "psychological determinism which left no room for the concept of accident." [14]

Out of the discussions students selected themes for investigation. So, for instance, as problems emerging from the seminars — where what we learned could be summarized in the statement that "everything is related to everything else" — Herskovits chose the cattle culture of East Africa and I selected the question of the relative stability of different elements of culture in Polynesia. In the work that was done, culture was to be studied as "culture" in all its complexity of historical origins and within the physical environment — which could limit or implement but was not of itself creative — within which human beings of any race and speaking any language could learn to live. By mapping out culture areas, which included all those primitive cultures whose relationships to one another were due to historical contact, geographically defined, the student learned to place any particular problem in context. So a comparison between two North American Indian tribes was different from a comparison between a North and a South American Indian tribe, and was completely different from a comparison between a tribe in the Americas and another in Africa. Forms — the shape of an ax, or a way of classifying a man and his son together, or the theme of a myth — had always to be looked at in the light of similar forms in neighboring societies. Where such contact had to be ruled out, explanations were sought in the common working of men's minds, in the similarity of human emotions ("What man anywhere would not respond with anger if his picture was spat upon?" [15]), and in common problems deriving from the need to survive and persist as a group. The ability of the human child to learn any human culture by imitation was emphasized, but little attention was given to *how* the child learned except for some recognition of what Boas called "automatic behavior" — behavior which lies below verbal consciousness and so is beyond the possibility of question or challenge. Forms of marriage were assumed to be limited by the nature and differing constitutions of the two sexes, tools by the shape of man's hand and by the structure of his brain, gestures by the form of the body and by the needs of communication.

Each culture — the learned ways of behavior characteristic of a group — was treated as having equal dignity with every other culture. Boas, although he had been friendly to the development of the idea of cultural centers — tribal groups which had been centers of integration and of the diffusion of some special or generalized cultural form — nevertheless always emphasized that those tribes, which we, looking toward the center, called "marginal," were not marginal from their own point of view.

Culture change was treated as a problem calling for the detailed analysis of specific forms — the design on the border of a pot, a particular way of making basketry, a shift from nomadic to settled existence — and any tendency to see direction or progress was rigorously checked. Instead, there was an emphasis on possible reversibility — on the possibility that representational designs could become geometric and geometric designs representational — on deterioration, on resistance to an innovation even though it might represent an improvement, and on the conservatism of cultural forms associated with religion. The individual Indian or African appeared primarily as the concrete locus of cultural information, or he might only be implicit in the tone in which Boas spoke of the Kwakiutl as "my dear friends." He might be the hero of an anecdote or the teller of a tale, but he was placed so precisely only in order that we might know more about cultural process as a whole.

Students were given, on the one hand, an exceedingly critical examination of all the theoretical formulations which had been presented to date — this was called Methods; and, on the other hand, we were given concrete, highly specialized demonstrations of studies in a great variety of fields, such as human growth, language, art, mythology, or religion — this was Subject Matter. And we were made aware of the need to test and evaluate the assumptions which lay back of the unsatisfactory theories by making comparative studies or by doing field work. Above and beyond it all was a vast possible panorama, a landscape with only tiny points of illumination *yet*, in which each small study, each theoretical problem had a place in the strictest relationship to every other study and theoretical problem. Someday, when we knew enough about how culture changed, how human genetics worked, how religious ideas were embodied in culture . . . someday all that vast landscape would be filled in. But this filling in seemed so far in the future and Boas was so unwilling to commit himself prematurely on a single point, that it was all the more remarkable that he was also able to conceive of the period when those laws which would be found to hold for human behavior would be obvious and would seem commonplace.

Ruth Benedict's doctoral thesis was the fifteenth dissertation in anthropology at Columbia University. The titles of the fourteen that preceded hers and of the forty-three succeeding ones during the years up to World War II show the same emphasis.[16] Only in the case of Ruth Bunzel's *The Pueblo Potter: A Study of Creative Imagination in Primitive Art*[17] did Boas' emerging interest in the individual reveal itself in these dissertations. Taken as a whole they reveal a pattern of small, isolated segments of content and problem out of which a structure was being built.

At the same time, Robert Lowie was beginning to systematize the developing insights about social organization. *Primitive Society*[18] was published in 1920, and Ruth Benedict took one course with him before he left his Museum post to teach at the University of California. When, after the publication of "The Vision in Plains Culture," she met the incorrigible Jaime de Angulo for the first time, he explained delightedly, "You don't talk the way you write!" And she replied, "I wrote that for Dr. Lowie. Do you know Dr. Lowie?"

Yet there were signs of change. Haeberlin's thesis on "The Idea of Fertilization in the Culture of the Pueblo Indians" [19] was pointed out to us, and the phrase "the best graduate student since Haeberlin" was a ready one to several tongues. In the summer of 1924, Boas sent Ruth Bunzel on a preliminary field trip to Zuñi to study the creative imagination and the role of the individual in art. In 1925, Boas chose as my field-work problem the study of adolescence among a primitive people. Later he told Ruth Benedict, "When I sent Margaret Mead to Samoa, I had decided that diffusion was done. It was time to attack a new set of problems." Twenty-five years earlier, Alfred Kroeber, who had entered anthropology from the study of literature, had written on the "Decorative Symbolism of the Arapaho," [20] and Leslie Spier had made a study of the dimensions of Plains Indian painted leather pouches (*parfleches*) to demonstrate that each tribe had a slightly different esthetic preference, relating his theory to the Weber-Fechner studies of proportion.[21] But as Boas had strict, puritanical views about the sequence in which problems should be investigated, these ventures into new fields had not been followed up. So when the problem I was to work on in Samoa was announced, Alfred Kroeber, in New York on a visit, exclaimed, "I'd have given anything in the world to have worked on a problem like that."

The idea of pattern was already in use among anthropologists, but most frequently with reference to the set of universals such as technology, religion, social organization, art, language, and so on, which characterize every human society, rather than with reference to a particular culture. Pattern was also used to describe the way any part of cultural behavior was organized. I remember walking down Amsterdam Avenue with a fellow student in the spring of 1925, and seeing two people meet, each greeting the other in passing, "Good evening! Isn't it a lovely evening?" And we two students turned to each other and said in one breath, "Pattern!"

There was then, however, no emphasis upon society or upon the study of a culture in which individuals or groups, rather than items of behavior, were the appropriate units. Individuals were identified so that the pattern of the culture could be explicated. Resistance and acceptance of new traits from other peoples were seen to be related to the existing pattern within which an idea could be integrated readily, with difficulty, or not at all. So the plot of a myth could be shown to have been altered to suit the different patterns of social organization in different cultures — the hero could shift from being the youngest to the eldest son, the villain from father-in-law to mother's brother — and the new version would be congruent in patterning with other parts of the culture. Or in a new context bits of one tale — incidents or characterizations such as "the advisory dung" or the "star husband" — could be detached from one plot and added to another. In terms of living myth-makers, the people of each culture worked with whatever materials they had, their own traditional tales, and the ways in which their lives were organized in relation to kin and clan. When they were confronted with a new tale, they reorganized it in familiar ways or took it to pieces and redistributed the bits in different tales.

To demonstrate how this process worked, we were taught to use the kinds of materials that seemed objectively the most verifiable: texts of myths and folktales recorded verbatim in the original language and attributed to specific informants, art styles which could be photographed or drawn so that each detail could be reproduced for analysis, languages which, of course, were also based upon texts, and kinship systems which could be considered against the biological background of sex and age, birth, and marriage.

The whole method had developed out of the study of the broken cultures of tribes which had long since given up hunting the buffalo or pouring great vats of olachen oil upon their feasting fires. The anthropologist worked with a few informants, one at a time, his knowledge sometimes mediated by an interpreter. The anthropologist had no access to living events, for the actual life that the Indians were then living — as pensioners of the Federal government, casual crop-gatherers, followers of rodeos, or sellers of curios to tourists — held only fragments of the picture of life that could be reconstructed of earlier days when costume and house, the means of livelihood, and the ways of relating themselves to one another and to the universe were congruent and esthetically satisfying wholes.

Boas was first of all a scientist. He wanted a real corpus of materials to work on, large bodies of material which would make possible the cross-checking of each detail and would provide a basis for making certain kinds of negative statements. For the absence of a trait such as the use of a hammock, or torture in the vision-quest, or a detail of pottery making, was as important in this kind of analysis as the presence of a trait, and to make significant negative statements a very large corpus — ideally an exhaustive collection of every known myth or of every decorative design in a given culture — is necessary.

There was then no body of psychological theory by which smaller amounts of materials could be interpreted. The use of psychoanalytical theory, learning theory, Gestalt psychology, or ethology was all in the future. Cultural materials had to be analyzed with an assumption of a common humanity and of common potentialities for all human beings; there was nothing else. The kind of instinct psychology used by Shand and MacDougal, on which Radcliffe-Brown had drawn in his study of the Andaman Islanders,[22] based on a listing of instincts, had not proved satisfactory. At Columbia University, William Fielding Ogburn was giving lectures on psychological aspects of culture, in which early psychoanalytic writing was presented to students.[23] Historical controversies over "the origin of the blood feud" or "the function of the mother-in-law taboo" were discussed. But the final summary statement was always, "Never look for a *psychological* explanation unless every effort to find a *cultural* one has been exhausted." "Psychological" referred to the innate, generic characteristics of the mind; "cultural" referred to the behavior learned as a member of a given society. Without any psychological theory which could both include and supplement cultural theory, the nature of man had to be derived from cultural materials. In 1923, the alternative seemed to be endless projections of man as he behaved in our own culture onto mankind as a whole.

Ruth Benedict formed her own view of the contribution of anthropology before the first steps were taken in the study of *how* individual human beings, with their given potentialities, came to embody their culture. In her later work she came to accept and sometimes to use the work in culture and personality which depended as much upon dynamic psychology as upon cultural anthropology, and she came to recognize that society — made up of persons organized in groups — was as important as a subject of study as was the culture of a society. But her primary learning took place in the early 1920's, was grafted upon the kind of perceptive study of literature which was based upon the study of literary *products,* and was grounded in no psychobiological theory of man.

"The Vision in Plains Culture," her first publication, already uses the basic conceptions which were to inform all her work. In the years that followed, she read and prepared abstracts of mythology for the Southwest folklore concordance,[24] taught, and did field work all within this framework. This was scholarly, scientific work, a respectable and sensible way of spending one's time if one didn't "have strength of mind not to need a career." She had tried busy work that did not make sense to her; now she had found busy work with high standards set by someone for whom she had great respect, among materials that delighted her to the extent that they were bizarrely different and esthetically satisfying.

The Vision
in Plains Culture*

THE INDIANS of the Plains share with the tribes to the east and the west an inordinate pursuit of the vision. Even certain highly formalized conceptions relating to it are found on the Atlantic Coast and on the Pacific. Thus, in spite of all diversity of local rulings, the approach to the vision was, or might always be, through isolation and self-mortification. More formally still, the vision, over immense territories, ran by a formula according to which some animal or bird or voice appeared to the suppliant and talked with him, describing the power he bestowed on him, and giving him songs, mementoes, taboos, and perhaps involved ceremonial procedure. Henceforth for that individual this thing that had thus spoken with him at this time became his "guardian spirit."

Not only the means of obtaining the vision, however, and the events of the vision itself, were standardized over thousands of miles, east and west, and north and south; the sanctions derived from it were as widely formalized. Ceremonial procedure, pre-eminently, was derived from it, but, almost as widely, healing powers, success in battle, and control of the weather. Even trivial connections have crossed the continent; so that, not only on the Plains, but on Puget Sound [1] and on Chesapeake Bay[2] the person who confers a name upon another chooses some phrase descriptive of something his guardian spirit said or did in his vision.

* American Anthropologist, XXIV, No. 1 (1922), 1–23.

In spite of such widespread uniformities, however, the vision-quest of the Plains has a character very distinct from that of the Plateau Salish on the one hand, and of the Woodland Algonkian on the other. In regard to one fundamental conception, the Plains lie like a wedge thrust up and separating these two widely separated areas, each more like one another than either is like the neighboring Plains. For both to the east and the west of the Plains the pursuit of the vision is definitely an affair of adolescence, a ritual at entrance to maturity. Among the Winnebago and Central Algonkian, boys trained for fasting from the age of eight or nine[3] — even from the age of five[4] — and were expected to persevere in it at intervals until puberty. In theory at least, after intercourse with women, the pursuit of visions was discontinued for life. To the west, among the Plateau Salish, this fasting for a guardian spirit is combined with a puberty training lasting for years, during which the boy seeks to acquire skill by magical means for his chosen profession in life.[5] The vision of the guardian spirit is by no means the culmination of the period of probation; it has become almost incidental in the strong local development of a professional apprenticeship during adolescence.

On the Plains, however, it is mature men who characteristically seek the vision. Among the Arapaho[6] and the related Gros Ventre,[7] Dr. Kroeber long ago pointed out that the custom of puberty fasting is not known at all. According to the myths and recorded experiences, this generalization holds good for all the Western Plains, north and south. At the east, especially among the Assiniboine,[8] the Hidatsa,[9] and the Omaha,[10] the puberty convention of the Woodlands is known and practiced in varying degrees; but it is always in addition to the characteristic Plains maturity fast. That is, we find even among the Omaha, who most definitely link the securing of a guardian spirit with puberty, that the vision is sought also for all kinds of recurring experiences throughout maturity, as it is all over the Plains, and is not in the Eastern Woodlands.

This one generalization — that the pursuit of visions on the Plains is an affair of maturity and not of adolescence — is probably, however, the only blanket description that is possible in the personal *wakan* experiences of this area. Each tribe has its own distinctive version, a pattern so distinct that any random reference to fasting and vision in the native texts could almost without fear of mistake be assigned to the one particular tribe from which it was collected — at most to two or three which are in some way closely associated.

The truth of this assertion can most readily be tested by an examination (I) of certain patterns which are rather commonly assumed to be characteristic of the vision-quest of the Plains; and (II) of certain tribal patterns, which, though they have universally traveled in weakened form beyond the limits of any one tribe, are yet strongly localized.

1

Three patterns of wide distribution are sometimes taken to characterize the vision-quest of the Plains: (1) The infliction of self-torture; (2) the lack of a laity-shamanistic distinction; (3) the attaining of a guardian spirit. Are these indeed integral parts of the vision-idea of the Plains as a whole; or are they rather distinct patterns existing sometimes side by side with the vision-quest without ever amalgamating with it, and at all times combining with it in different proportions and with different connotations?

Let us examine first the relation in which self-inflicted torture stood to the visionary experiences. In such a typical Plains tribe as the Blackfoot, torture was of course well-known. They practiced the sun dance, and those who entered the ordeal tore loose the skewers inserted in the muscles of the back, as was done in all Plains tribes where the sun dance was observed, with the sole exception of the little known Kiowa. Self-torture was practiced also in a variety of other connections. Maximilian[11] specifically contrasts the Blackfoot custom of cutting off finger joints in mourning, with the Mandan convention of making the same offering in the pursuit of a vision. Dr. Wissler mentions also among the Blackfoot another widespread Plains torture-pattern known as "Feeding-the-sun-with-bits-of-one's-body." [12] The skin is pricked up with a splinter or sharp knife, and a coin-shaped piece cut from beneath. The precise procedure is reported for the Dakota, the Cheyenne, and the Arapaho. But in all these cases the idea is of a sacrifice to the sun, for the Blackfoot on the occasion of a war party. The idea, so far as we know, among the Blackfoot is never associated with guardian-spirit experiences.

In fact no one of these torture customs has become associated with the vision practices. We have an enormous literature for the Blackfoot, and nowhere, in their bulky traditions,[13] or in the vision-stories collected by Dr. Wissler,[14] or in the observant records of McClintock[15] or Grinnell,[16] is the use of any self-torture other than hunger and thirst even hinted at.

This same disassociation of torture- and vision-patterns holds also, though in lesser degree, for the Arapaho to the south. Torture for mourning,[17] for votive offerings for success,[18] and in the sickness of relatives,[19] is marked in Arapaho culture. In not one of the vision experiences collected by Dr. Kroeber, however, is torture used in connection with the securing of visions.[20] The disassociation is not so complete as among the Blackfoot, for in one of the three recorded variants for the origin of the Buffalo Lodge[21] the supplicant "not only abstained from food and drink, but inflicted pain upon himself. Then he saw a vision." Mooney also, in his history of the ghost dance,[22] relates that Black Coyote had been told in a mourning vision to make exaggerated use of the offering of coin-shaped bits of skin to insure the lives of his remaining children. This "vision" command, however, is an almost perfect combination of all three of the usual Arapaho nonvisionary uses of laceration.

The Cheyenne have been very closely associated with the Arapaho for generations; yet their practices in this regard differ strongly. We lack any synthetic account of their culture and any large body of traditions, but in the fragments that we have there is abundant emphasis upon self-torture. Thus G. A. Dorsey states in 1905 that "the Cheyenne probably practiced torture to a greater extent for all purposes than any other tribe so far as is known. Wherever Cheyenne came together, it was a common sight to see men torturing themselves around the camp circle." [23] They would also retire to a lonely hill where they were tied suspended from poles, seeking a vision. Recently, in his *When Buffalo Ran*, G. B. Grinnell has given us the only concrete description of a Cheyenne vision-quest.[24] In the experience he describes, the supplicant goes out to a lonely part of the prairie on the day selected, accompanied by the person who is to tie the thongs for him. The pins and knife are consecrated by prayer and held toward the sun and sky, and laid upon the earth. He is then tied to the pole by means of wooden pins driven through the flesh. All day long, after he is left alone again, he must walk back and forth on the sunward side of the pole, praying constantly, and fixing his eyes on the sun, trying to tear the pins loose from the torn flesh. At night the helper returns, and pieces of the torn skin are held toward the sun and sky and the four directions and buried. That night he sleeps on the prairie and gets his power.

In recent practice, therefore, the use of torture in the vision-quest is strongly established among the Cheyenne. We have in addition to these descriptions, however, two fragmentary collections of traditions containing five references to fasting and vision,[25] and not one of these connects torture with the experience. It may well be, therefore, that the association of torture and vision even for the Cheyenne is not rooted very far back in their history. We know that even in 1850 they were living in territory contiguous to the Dakota and Hidatsa,[26] among whom if anywhere we must look for a strongly rooted association of torture and religious experiences. Taken in connection with the well-known instability of Cheyenne culture[27] in the century preceding our knowledge of them, it seems possible that the vigorous association of torture with the vision is a recent phenomenon among the Cheyenne.

This fragmentary evidence from the Cheyenne of a recent use of torture in the pursuit of the vision is greatly strengthened by the very full data from the Crow, where we find precisely the same contrast between ancient tradition and more modern usage. There is an entire omission of self-torture from the very numerous accounts of vision experiences in their mythology.[28] In recent practice, however,[29] the sacrifice of finger joints, the cutting of strips of skin from arms and legs, and all the variants of the sun dance torture are resorted to in obtaining the vision.

Throughout all the tribes of the Western Plains we find, then, a marked disassociation, either in the present or the past, of the two patterns of torture and the pursuit of visions. Among the tribes of the Southern Plains, the torture pattern hardly exists at all. The Omaha cut their arms and legs in mourning,[30] and the Pawnee, at least the Pawnee women, on similar occasions did the like.[31] The one possible reference to any use of torture in religious experiences — for neither the Omaha nor the Pawnee observed the sun dance — is in J. O. Dorsey's description of the accessories of prayer among the Cegiha,[32] where, as the sixth feature, he mentions "offerings of goods or pieces of the suppliant's flesh"; but he is including here cognate tribes such as the Kansa and Ponca which had adopted the sun dance and certain tortures. Certainly nowhere in his own many specific descriptions in the same volume, nor in his native texts,[33] nor in Miss Fletcher's work, is there any other mention of laceration.

For the Pawnee we have a voluminous body of myths and traditions and the concept of self-torture in any connection is conspicuously absent.

There remain, then, the tribes of the Eastern and Northern Plains, more especially the western Dakota and the Mandan-Hidatsa. These tribes do in fact present an almost complete picture of the amalgamation of the two patterns, self-torture and the vision-quest.

For the village tribes, De Smet says in 1852 that he "could not discover a single man at all advanced in years whose body had not been mutilated, or who possessed his full number of fingers." [34] And Maximilian had before remarked (1833) that these offerings were not made as among the Blackfoot, but in intercession with the spirits.[35]

Among the neighboring Assiniboine we find recorded these same modes of self-torture in the pursuit of the vision. One description[36] records how men fasting for visions on Snake Butte were attacked by snakes, till at last one in his frenzy cut off strips of his flesh and fed them. "None of the other men have done this before," the snakes tell him. "Come with us, grandchild! We pity you." Thus he was successful.

The one vision story of the Gros Ventre traditions duplicates this same situation, and adds more specific details; the suppliant cuts his flesh, his ears, and his little finger — this last considered an especial deprivation according to Catlin, at least among the Mandan.[37]

But it is among the Dakota that, according to our data, the vision was most often sought by torture. It is true that even in describing the western Dakota, Dr. Walker[38] confines any mention of the torture strictly to the sun dance. But all other authorities emphasize the part played by lacerations in the securing of any sort of vision among the Dakota. J. O. Dorsey in his "Siouan Cults" has gathered together the older descriptions. Riggs, writing in 1869, describes the sun dance form of tying, and continues: "Thus they hang suspended only by those cords without food or drink for two, three, or four days, gazing into vacancy, their minds fixed intently upon the object in which they wish to be assisted by the deity, and waiting for a vision from above. Once a day an assistant is sent to look upon the person thus sacrificing himself. If the deities have vouchsafed him a vision or revelation, he signifies the same by motions, and is released at once; if he is silent, his silence is understood, and he is left alone to his reverie." [39] Lynd describes those "who pass knives through the flesh in various parts of the body, and wait in silence, though with fixed mind, for a dream or revelation." [40]

In the process of qualifying as a shaman the vision-by-torture played an equally important part. The final tortures of the sun dance, here as nowhere else, were reserved for those who desired to become shamans,[41] and the ultimate purpose of the ordeal was the obtaining of the vision which was granted at any time before the dispersal for the next winter's camp. Or a candidate might go to an individual shaman, who accompanied him to an isolated spot and tied him as in the sun dance; or he might himself cut off and offer bits of flesh in the presence of the shaman.[42]

It seems, then, that the association between self-torture and the vision centered in the Dakota-Mandan area. The geographical continuity of the distribution of the practice, the gradual shading-off of the torture, especially in connection with the vision-quest, make it seem probable that the connection originated only once and was diffused from that center.

One outstanding consideration points to the Dakota as the center from which it was distributed, if not necessarily the tribe where the connection originated. This consideration is the otherwise fortuitous association existing everywhere throughout the Plains between torture and an offering to the sun. The Blackfoot feeds the sun with the coin-shaped bits of his body; the Cheyenne, in the guardian-spirit vigil, consecrates his knives and torn flesh to the sun and keeps his eyes fixed upon it. Everywhere where we find torture we find that the sun, for no apparent reason, is especially involved. Now it is just here among the Dakota where the sun does really play a pre-eminent and much emphasized part in their ceremonial practices and in their cosmology. So far as our data go no other Plains tribe separated out the sun and raised it to the supreme place, as did the Dakota. Their sun dance, unlike that of most tribes, was in large part a veritable worship of the sun. When, therefore, from the study of geographical distribution, we find evidence that the greatest and most deeply rooted development of self-torture in the vision-quest was just here among the Dakota, is it not also probable that the connection with the sun was diffused along with the torture practices from this center?

The infliction of self-torture, therefore, is a Plains pattern distinct from that of the vision-quest and combined with it in different proportions in each different tribe. The center of association between the two was in the Dakota-Mandan region, and in recent practice was strongly developed among the Cheyenne and Crow, though in their mythologies such practices have no place. The Blackfoot never resorted to lacerations in the pursuit of visions; and the Arapaho, perhaps, as Dr. Kroeber suggests, influenced by the tortureless ghost dance, almost as absolutely divorce the two. On the Southern Plains, moreover, among the Omaha and Pawnee laceration was not practiced in any connection, except as it was incumbent upon women in mourning. It was never a means of obtaining visions.

The second generalization concerning the vision which requires examination is that from it there resulted, as in many other parts of North America, the absence of any laity-shamanistic distinction. Logically it seems that such a loss must follow in a culture that holds it more or less obligatory for every man to go out at least once in his life and obtain power from the spirits. And this logical corollary is indeed common on the Western Plains. Among the Arapaho "a distinct profession of medicine men or shamans can not be spoken of with any approximation to correctness, any more than can a caste of warriors. The differences between individuals in kind and degree of supernatural powers were apparently not greater than in matters of bravery or distinction in war." [43] And the absence of a special spiritually sanctified profession is emphasized in Dr. Lowie's statement concerning the Assiniboine:

> It depended wholly on the nature of the revelation whether they became founders of dancing societies, wakan practitioners, owners of painted lodges, fabricators of war-shirts, or prophets. In every case implicit obedience was required.[44]

But on the Eastern Plains this simple logic of a common access for all men to supernatural power was overlaid in a variety of ways, notably among the Dakota and the Pawnee.

The Dakota make a sharp break between the laity and the shamans; their preliminary experiences, special knowledge, and relations to the supernatural were all differentiated. The shamans possessed an esoteric vocabulary; they were organized in cults where initiation was wholly on the basis of supernatural experience; they alone had guardian spirits won by fasting and vision. Those entering the sun dance enrolled in different grades and endured different tortures according as they were candidates for the shamanistic class or not.

So far has this classification gone that guardian spirits were obtained by diametrically different methods by the two classes. Shamans fasted for their visions in the ordinary way;[45] on the contrary, the guardian spirits of those not so numbered were assigned at puberty by the shamans.[46] The old writers, whose descriptions make up J. O. Dorsey's account of the cults of the Dakota, go so far as to say that individual guardians were here never revealed in vision; but in this they were certainly ignorant of the necessary qualifications of the shaman.

Among the Dakota we have still no fixed and hierarchal priestly class. The Pawnee, however, while supposedly sharing the same guardian-spirit ideas as the Arapaho, for instance, have found it possible to superimpose a ranked and vested College of Cardinals. A vision by no means in itself gave right of entrance into this priestly hierarchy. A shaman was made not by any momentary experience, however essential, but by prolonged training. In the myths this necessity is most often formalized somewhat after this fashion in the

spirits' instructions: "There [in your lodge] you must stay by yourself, so that I may appear to you in your dreams, and teach you the
songs and also my powers." [47] In practice, candidates were instructed
by the shaman or priest whom they would succeed at his death.[48]
For since the number was practically fixed, vacancies could occur
only in this way.

But the Pawnee not only fixed a gulf between the laity and the
nonlaity; this latter class was also strongly subdivided.[49] Highest in
prestige, authority, and esoteric knowledge stood the priests, guardians of the sacred tribal bundles, to whom even the chiefs were
subordinate. Separated from these, but also from the laity, were the
medicine men, whose powers came more especially from visions and
whose functions were healing and sleight-of-hand. In theory, at
least, these two groups did not enter each other's ceremonies.

This differentiation of priest and medicine man corresponded to
the division of their cosmology, so that the priestly class derived
their power from the gods above (chiefly the stars) and the medicine
men from the gods below (chiefly the animal lodges).

While, therefore, the guardian-spirit idea carried with it over the
greater part of the Plains the idea of a common exercise by all men
of spiritual powers, sharp separations between laity and nonlaity had
nevertheless arisen in certain tribes, notably the Dakota and Pawnee.

The third generalization concerning the vision-quest which requires
examination is that which makes it synonomous with the attaining
of a guardian spirit. However it may be in other areas of North
America, on the Plains there is no tribe where the vision-quest was
not a much more general phenomenon than the acquiring of a
guardian spirit. Everywhere, even in those tribes where every man
was expected to fast once in his life specifically for an individual
guardian, the vision was sought also by the same means on continually recurring occasions — that is in mourning; as an instrument
of revenge on one's enemies; on account of a vow made in sickness
or danger for oneself or one's relative; on initiation into certain
societies; and as a preliminary to a war party. On all these occasions,
the seeker ordinarily received his power or commands directly, without specifically acquiring a guardian spirit.

Besides this invariable usage, moreover, there is an immense divergence among the tribes of the Plains in the degree to which they associate the formula of the guardian spirit with even the primary or "great" vision — the one, that is, almost always, according to their traditions, more or less distinguished from all others, and which was the Plains equivalent of the surrounding practice of the puberty fast for a guardian spirit.

With certain tribes the primary vision was indeed very closely bound up with the securing of a guardian spirit. This was true among the Blackfoot and the Crow, but the association was according to an entirely different formula. Crow ceremonialism in very many different phases — initiation into the Tobacco Planting Ceremony, the Medicine Pipe ritual, even in certain cases into war party leadership — is formalized as an "adoption" by a ceremonial "father." So in the vision-quest. The power that appears to the Crow addresses him in set words, "I make you my son." Afterwards throughout the myths he will be referred to as "the dwarf-adopted one," the "one the Sun adopted," etc.; the guardian spirit is addressed as "father." It is significant that this same form of address is found only among the Hidatsa, the Gros Ventre, and the Arikara, who are all in territory contiguous to that of the Crow. None of these tribes, however, follow out the implications of this intimate relationship as the Crow do, for example, in the following myth. A dwarf-adopted boy is held captive by Red-Woman and the dwarf goes out searching for him. "He came up to the place. 'I think this witch has my boy in there.' He sent an eagle to scout for his son." That failed, and he sent the smallest ant, who came back with word of his son.[50] That is, under the influence of this nomenclature, at least in certain cases, the Crow conceive a sort of paternal responsibility on the part of the "father" that is quite foreign to the thought of the other tribes.

The Blackfoot have also a strong sense of an intimate and peculiar relation obtaining between the suppliant and the animal or thing that has blest him in this fast, but they have not the Crow formula. They have followed another line of thought, and in the overwhelming majority of the experiences both in the myths and in the shamanistic biographies they conceive a man's guardian spirit to be some animal or bird or thing seen by him in some everyday connection that for some reason stands out in consciousness. Their vision-stories, therefore, describe actual and rather minor occurrences without any particular formula. Medicine comes from the skunk who follows and is fed; from the eagle when one has unwittingly made camp at the foot of a particularly tall tree holding a particularly large eagle's nest; from the swollen white woodworm which crawls out of the decaying log as it begins to burn on the hearth. When we compare this with the complicated formula of the Dakota, or, better still, the cosmic visions of the heavens that an Ojibwa requires,[51] we recognize the strong individuality of this Blackfoot trait.

In contrast to this insistence upon securing at the time of this vision a guardian spirit with intimate and personal relations to oneself, we may consider the Cheyenne vision described above. Here, as is common where torture is predominant, the associated idea of the sun is stressed throughout in the details of preparation, in the walking on the sunward side of the pole, in the fixation of the eyes upon the sun, and finally in the offering of the torn flesh. When finally the wolf appears in a vision the following night it is hardly more than a postscript.

The Cheyenne story is only an indication of a tendency which we find logically carried out among the Dakota. As we have already noted in the discussion of the differentiation of laity and nonlaity in this tribe, for the majority of the people the guardian spirit was assigned at puberty by the shamans — the "armor gods" [52] — and the subsequent seeking of visions had no relation whatever to this acquisition. The object in these was to secure supernatural communication with the sun or with lesser of the *wakan tanka*. "If an Oglala contemplates any important undertaking, he ought to seek a vision." [53] But these visions did not raise any question of guardian spirits.

Even for the shamans, who sought guardian spirits in vision more nearly according to the usual Plains pattern, there was nothing comparable to the simple rapport of the Blackfoot with his individual spirit guardian. The Dakota shaman, if he was successful, obtained a highly complex dream involving four sets of actors, and the metamorphosis of at least two of these sets. Which one of these actors in this highly artificial dream constituted the man's guardian spirit was

a purely formal matter, but one inexorably fixed by tribal usage.[54]
Among the Dakota, therefore, the guardian-spirit formula was all
but struck out of the vision-quest.

Among the Pawnee the separation of the vision-quest and the
guardian-spirit idea has proceeded along another line. The Pawnee,
to judge by the voluminous collected *Traditions*, present a number
of marked points of contrast to the rest of the Plains. We have
already had occasion to mention several. But at no point, in relation
to the visions, are they so sharply at variance with all Plains ideas
whatsoever as in their substitution of the "animal lodges" for the
guardian-spirit formula. The Pawnee, as we have seen, separate the
spirits into two great groups — of the "above," and the "below."
The above-gods were the source of their star cult, the basis of their
tribal bundle scheme, and the patrons of the priests (as distinct
from the medicine men). The below-gods were presided over by the
four (or five) definitely localized "animal lodges," [55] and were the
source of the power of the medicine men or shamans. The stories of
these animal lodges make up sixteen of the twenty-six tales of *wakan*
experiences recorded in the volume of Pawnee *Traditions*. These
lodges were not abodes of groups of buffalo or flocks of eagles, such
as were rather commonly seen by vision-seekers of other tribes; they
were lodges which were supposed to exist under various well-known
hills and rivers where *all* the animals gathered together for sleight-of-
hand performances and to teach their powers. These animal medicine lodges are present in just two other Plains bodies of myths, the
Wichita[56] and the Arikara;[57] that is, the other two Caddoan tribes
of the Plains for which we possess collections of traditions. It is
therefore an old and persistent Caddoan conception, and its analogies
are not with the Plains region but with the Southwest. It is in the
legends of the Navaho[58] that we find again the division into upper
and lower gods, their separate and rival powers, even the abodes of
the animal gods in lodges under the water, "Water-monster, Frog,
Fish, Beaver, Otter, and others." One element only of the common
Pawnee story is lacking in the Navaho legend, the conception of
personal power acquired in the animal lodge. We may assume that
the Pawnee easily associated that typical Plains idea with a familiar
conception of animal lodges, and in so doing, inhibited the develop-

ment among them of the guardian-spirit formula. For it is obvious from the whole mass of Pawnee mythology that the idea of the individual guardian as generally understood has no place whatever in their vision-quest. Their medicine men learned the mysteries of "*all the animals*"; if one animal sometimes stands out prominently in some such capacity as that of messenger, it is still a far cry to the Crow or Blackfoot relationships. Where we do find a conception of an individual rapport with a definite animal or thing, in the myths, it is traced to a relationship at birth or before. That this is indeed a fundamental Pawnee conception seems the more probable from Murie's note appended to "Pawnee Indian Societies" [59] to the effect that every child while in the womb, through the mediumship of one or other parent, was brought under the power of an animal; though sometimes trees, stars, or the thunder might take the place of the animal.

On account, therefore, of the universal Plains usage of seeking a vision on many constantly recurring occasions, and also on account of the characteristic practices of tribes such as the Dakota and Pawnee, where the guardian-spirit formula hardly exists at all, the vision-quest on the Plains was a much more general phenomenon than the acquisition of a guardian spirit.

2

We have, then, examined three patterns rather commonly held to be descriptive of the vision-quest of the Plains as a whole, and found that tribal practices in each instance run the whole possible range of variation. Besides this, moreover, there are certain other patterns definitely localized in certain tribes or groups of tribes on the Plains which contribute still more to the complexity.

Most striking of these is the concept of purchase among the Blackfoot. The visions themselves could be bought and sold. Every man went out at least once in his life seeking a vision on his own account. Many failed, so the Blackfoot repeatedly assert. But whether he met with success or failure, he must also buy other men's visions for his social prestige. They were the basis of the tribal economic system; the greater proportion of Blackfoot capital was invested in these readily salable commodities. Investment in them, as Dr. Wissler puts it, was equivalent to money in the savings bank. Tribal dandies purchased them also as a means of parading their wealth. Just as all the Plains tribes had gatherings where they publicly rehearsed their war deeds, so the Blackfoot had also occasions where each recounted the visions he had owned and the property he had paid for them. And his recital was met with jeers or approval according as it was short or long.[60]

I have called it buying the vision, for to the Blackfoot that is what it meant. In telling his story he makes absolutely no distinction in the use of the first person between those visions he has bought and those he has fasted for. Its designation in the literature is "purchasing the medicine bundle," but commonly the purchaser makes up his own bundle anew, according to the specifications; what he has really bought being the songs, the taboos, the "power," and the right of performing the ceremony that goes with it.

The number of such bundles among the Blackfoot is practically countless, all conforming to a definite tribal ritualistic pattern. This pattern also has determined tribal usage in a host of miscellaneous connections: shields, headdresses, songs, painted tipis, shirts of ordinary Plains type, even vows of self-torture, and many of the industrial arts are transferred exactly as is a medicine bundle. Even the sun dance has adapted itself to this pattern, and its annual celebration is strictly the transfer of a bundle according to the usual conditions of such transfer.[61] The ritualistic system of the Blackfoot, then, offers a perfect example of the enormous formative power of a once-established pattern and its tendency toward indefinite self-complication.

The idea that the blessing of the spirits may be bought and sold we find also among the Crow,[62] the Arapaho,[63] the Hidatsa,[64] as also among the Winnebago.[65] But nowhere does this concept take the prominent place in tribal life that it does among the Blackfoot. Among the Winnebago it is merely a weak substitute for the real vision provided for those who fail to get one on their own account. Among the Hidatsa, as we shall see, it is combined with their idea of inheritance.

For quite as the Blackfoot have developed the concept of purchase, the Hidatsa have elaborated a definitely localized pattern of inheritance. The Hidatsa are matrilineal; but medicine bundles are inherited in the father's line. It was a strangely uncoordinated process by which rights to visions were perpetuated, for though it was obligatory that it descend in the male line, one must also have the same vision before one inherited, and one must likewise pay a purchase price.[66] Since an inheritor must have a vision from the family bundle, the function of the father in preparing the mind of the suppliant for this particular spirit-visitant became important. Not only was supervision exercised by the father over fasting, but ceremonies had to be performed under the superintendence of duly qualified bundle owners. Formerly people made dances on the initiative of visions, but they were found to die soon after.[67]

The practice of transferring the vision or the medicine bundle in the male line is found with varying intensity in several tribes — the Crow, the Arapaho, the Pawnee (for shamans), the Arikara, the Omaha, and most strongly among the Central Algonkian.[68] In fact this concept of inheritance of visions, closely associated with the necessity of having also the same vision, a coincidence brought about by an effort of family supervision, seems to be primarily an Algonkian trait, and possibly intrusive on the Plains. It is only one of the characteristic Algonkian procedures that are found in detail on the Eastern Plains.

It is from this point of view, i.e., its close parallelism with Woodlands culture, that it is most profitable to examine the vision practices of the Omaha. We have already noted the parallelism of this tribe to the Algonkian in absence of torture, in the connection they maintained between the acquiring of a guardian spirit and puberty fasting, and in the practice of inheritance coupled with the requirement of dreaming the family dream. The catchwords of the vision are also alike among the Omaha and the Algonkian. Thus the invariable form of address to their individual spirit is, for both, "Grandfather," a term used nowhere else on the Plains except among the Kiowa, and again among the Navaho.[69] Just as invariable is the formula of the vision: "I have had compassion upon you." This also is common to the Algonkian and Omaha, and has a very limited distribution in the rest of the Plains area.

The hierarchy into which the Omaha grouped their visions is also interesting from this point of view.[70] Animals could bestow only the lowest degree of power; above these were ranged a cloud-appearance and an eagle-winged human shape; above these again, the mere sound of a voice. The abstraction of mundane form from the apparition of the vision is in various forms one of the most distinctive characteristics of the Central Algonkian experiences.

We have few relevant myths from the Omaha, but one of them describes a fasting experience with another very marked Algonkian characteristic — the use of the fasting tent made for the occasion by father or mother. It is almost a formula. "At length he said, 'Father, let my mother make a tent for me.' And his mother made a tent for him." That is, he announced that he intended to fast, and the family complied.[71]

The Pawnee and the related Arikara stand alone in an exuberant development of sleight-of-hand, which was the prerogative and passport of the shaman. It is sleight-of-hand first and foremost that is taught the initiate in the animal lodges of the *Traditions*. The great Twenty Day Ceremony of the shamans was one long legerdemain.

But any survey of the Pawnee vision complex must be inadequate unless we take also into account a difference in psychological attitude which places them at the opposite pole, for instance, from the Crow. For the Crow attitude, the following text is typical: "Medicine Crow fasted and prayed for four days. He cut off a finger joint and offered it to the Sun. 'Sun, look at me. I am poor. I wish to own horses. Make me wealthy. That is why I give you my little finger.' " [72] Or in an old man's phrase: "I was going to be poor; that is why I had no vision." [73] But the Pawnee have made the transition from this view of the vision as a mechanistic means of controlling forces and events, to a view of it as a means of spiritual contact. That is, a certain transfer of emphasis has taken place from material to spiritual values.

Take the story of the warriors who appealed to the keeper of a bundle. "The owner of the bundle spoke as each man passed his hands over his head and arms, and said, 'My friends, I take pity on you; but it is not I, it is these things before me, although they are dead, and the Sun, who must help you.' " [74] Or this advice of a shaman to a candidate about to fast for a vision: " 'Be sure to be poor in heart. Talk to the stone, and let all your wishes be known. Say that you are poor, and keep nothing back.' " [75]

The Omaha, as well as the Pawnee, have discovered this special spiritual significance in *wakan* experiences. The old men counseled their grandsons thus: "Walk ye in remote places, crying to Wakanda. Neither eat nor drink for four days. Even though you do not gain the power, Wakanda will aid you. If you are as poor men, and pray as you cry, he will help you." [76]

The very great diversity of the vision-pattern even in one culture area such as the Plains is therefore evident. Not only are the general traits unevenly distributed and even entirely lacking in certain tribes, but local developments of one kind and another have overlaid the common pattern till it is at times hardly recognizable. A blanket classification under some such head as the "acquiring of guardian spirits" leads us nowhere. Correlated with the use or disuse of torture; with the existence of a shamanistic caste, or the free exercise of supernatural powers by all men; with the conception of visions as savings-bank securities or as contact with the compassion of Wakanda — are and must be psychological attitudes of the utmost diversity which make of Plains "religion" a heterogeneity which defies classification. Animism, magic, mana-ism, mysticism — all the known classifications of religion — jostle each other in this one area; and after all these headings were tabulated, the real diversities would still remain outside. For this reason, topical studies of religion must lack the rich variety of actuality and imply a false simplicity. Is it not our first task to inquire as carefully as may be in definite areas to what things the religious experience attaches itself, and to estimate their heterogeneity and their indefinite multiplicity?

A Matter for the Field Worker
in Folklore*[1]

THE MORE intimate our knowledge of folklore the more conscious we become of the part played in it by traditional material, as distinguished from the role of firsthand observation, definite recording of tribal custom, tribal history and the like. We no longer make painstaking analyses of the migration legends of southern North America, and the absence of such traditions is not regarded as proof of a prehistoric origin at that spot.

This same skepticism concerning the face-value of folkloristic material holds also in the matter of custom and of belief. It is easy to point out instances. The Zuñi in common with the Hopi have courting stories of the suitors who offer bundles in sign of courtship. But this is not a Zuñi custom. In the "Hoodwinked" Dancer story of the Kaibab Paiute, Rat sends home those of the mountain sheep and deer that he has not killed, promising to cremate their dead companions at sunset; but he makes a fire to cook their meat which he has prepared. However, the Paiute never burn their dead; it is traditional material.

It is equally true with regard to mythological concepts. Among the Serrano of Southern California I was repeatedly told that they knew nothing of the fate of the soul and had no concepts of an afterlife. But on the same afternoon they might tell the story of Orpheus with considerable detail of the habits and food and life of the people

* Journal of American Folk-Lore, XXXVI, No. 139 (1923), 104.

of the dead. I am convinced that there was no contradiction in their minds.

This lack of correspondence between the statements of folklore and the customs and beliefs of the people is often of great importance in the correct understanding of the material, but at present we are under great difficulties in estimating it. The point which is essential to emphasize is that this is a matter which can be recorded only by the field worker. No research or theory is likely to supply the omission. Such annotations of tales by the recorder do not mean an intrusion of his point of view into the data, but on the contrary add another dimension to our understanding of the meaning of the story to the people who tell it, and make possible an otherwise impossible study of the hold which traditional material has upon mankind.

Cups of Clay *

A CHIEF of the Digger Indians, as the Californians call them, talked to me a great deal about the ways of his people in the old days. He was a Christian and a leader among his people in the planting of peaches and apricots on irrigated land, but when he talked of the shamans who had transformed themselves into bears before his eyes in the bear dance, his hands trembled and his voice broke with excitement. It was an incomparable thing, the power his people had had in the old days. He liked best to talk of the desert foods they had eaten. He brought each uprooted plant lovingly and with an unfailing sense of its importance. In those days his people had eaten "the health of the desert," he said, and knew nothing of the insides of tin cans and the things for sale at butcher shops. It was such innovations that had degraded them in these latter days.

One day, without transition, Ramon broke in upon his descriptions of grinding, mesquite and preparing acorn soup. "In the beginning," he said, "God gave to every people a cup, a cup of clay, and from this cup they drank their life." I do not know whether the figure occurred in some traditional ritual of his people that I never found, or whether it was his own imagery. It is hard to imagine that he had heard it from the whites he had known at Banning; they were not given to discussing the ethos of different peoples. At any rate, in the

* From "The Diversity of Cultures," *Patterns of Culture* (Boston, Houghton Mifflin, 1934), Ch. II, 21–22.

mind of this humble Indian the figure of speech was clear and full of meaning. "They all dipped in the water," he continued, "but their cups were different. Our cup is broken now. It has passed away."

Our cup is broken. Those things that had given significance to the life of his people, the domestic rituals of eating, the obligations of the economic system, the succession of ceremonials in the villages, possession in the bear dance, their standards of right and wrong — these were gone, and with them the shape and meaning of their life. The old man was still vigorous and a leader in relationships with the whites. He did not mean that there was any question of the extinction of his people. But he had in mind the loss of something that had value equal to that of life itself, the whole fabric of his people's standards and beliefs. There were other cups of living left, and they held perhaps the same water, but the loss was irreparable. It was no matter of tinkering with an addition here, lopping off something there. The modeling had been fundamental, it was somehow all of a piece. It had been their own.

Counters in the Game*

In the Genesis of the Ojibwa, the great Brother-Gods are creating the earth. Male and female, they created the Ojibwa.

"And now," the Elder said to the Younger, "let us make the white people."

Great care did they take in creating the white people. Male and female, they created them.

And then, foreknowing the future, and reading therein all the checkered career of the white man, the Ojibwa Brother-Gods pass but one remark upon their creature. Merely this:

"Now no matter who one of them may be, nor how poor, they shall purchase land one from another."

To purchase land! The Brother-Gods of the Ojibwa were not above having their joke at the outlandish ways of the foreignborn. And, of course, richer material was never yet furnished ready to hand to an old-established people. How blundering they were, these white people! — whose very presence mysteriously denuded the land of the buffalo that were its wealth, and who befouled rivers that were the homes of great spirits. Worse things than blundering, too, the Brother-Gods knew of the white men; were they not people who abrogated to themselves the right to kill? Did they not honor the commander who massacred an Indian post, and put to death shamefully the Indian who scalped his enemy in traditional warfare? Strange people indeed!

* Unpublished manuscript, *circa* 1925.

But, after all, this was the crowning paradox: they bought and sold the land. Some mysterious association of ideas connected the little metal disks they carried, or the beads and cloth they knew how to procure, with certain strangely limited squares and triangles of land along the riverbanks or out on good prairie. There was more to this matter than one saw at first: to the white man, when those metal disks, or the cloth, or the beads, had once changed hands, it was not the use of the ground for the time being that passed to them, the earth itself was theirs forever. There was no logic to that. The cloth wore out, and the beads dropped off and were broken, and the money passed back in barter to the white people; but the land was there as it was at first, and the white man owned it still.

Clearly there was no reasonableness in it. Did not the land belong to anyone who had the will or the need to work it? What had they to fear from that? Did they think anyone would insist on more than his share? But why would one seek to own more ground than one needed? Was it not enough to have land on which to plant the Indian corn and trap hare which one's own family could eat each year? Who would accumulate land he could not use? It was inconceivable. When one worked, one worked to some end; and here there was no end.

No, it was for some other reason than a livelihood that the white man "purchased land one from another." It was for prestige.

Now the Indian understood the high cost of prestige quite as comprehensively as the latest aspirant to the fold of the socially elect. The idea he could not attain to was that cornerstone of civilization — the value of more land than one can use. He did not perceive that one can show one's wealth in land.

Were there not other things to buy that one must be always dispossessing others of their ground-space in order to prove himself of great prestige? A song for instance. In far-removed areas of North America, in tribes whose handicraft and whose rules of life differed as Chinese from Egyptian, a man's song was private property. It may have cost twenty horses, or many beaded robes, or a heaped-up pile of blankets. Originally it had been imparted in a vision as a climax of fasting and perhaps self-torture. To sing it was to please the spirit who gave it, and to cause him to fulfill his promise of assistance.

Men have come unscathed from the arrows of twenty enemies by the aid of a song. Poor boys have become chiefs through possessing one powerful song. Are they not worth good horses and beaded robes and blankets?

But land? Were the white men protected in battle by the square miles they owned, and had not even tilled? Or how could one become great through owning what was free as the water or the air?

Or, again, there were the visions themselves which one could acquire for prestige. One fasted, and perhaps cut off a finger, and prayed till one's spirit revealed himself. And if one was a Blackfoot, for instance, one also bought these sacred dreams. One must have many visions, important visions, to be a chief; and the way to get these was by purchase. There were formal "smokers" for the married men, where each tribesman rehearsed in turn the visions he had owned and the property he had paid for them, and the recital was met with jeers or approbations according to whether it was short or long. It was a great hour for the man who had paid many horses for many visions.

But it was reasonable to buy a vision to signify one's prestige. To own a vision was to keep its medicine bundle hanging from its tripod in one's tipi, to perform its rite, to sing its songs; did not all of these things make one transcendentally important to the welfare of the tribe? But the white man bought land he could not even overlook from his cabin — if indeed he lived there at all. No rite went with his purchase; his "tribe" had no stake in his acquisition. Clearly there was no reasonableness in it.

Up on the Northwest Coast they played the game with different rules and different counters. All the zest of life lay in a cutthroat competition in the giving away of goods. All the piles of blankets you could levy, you gave to your rival at a great "potlatch." He could not refuse them or he admitted bankruptcy; and before he could receive them, he must top them with an equal pile. In his turn, with this hundred per cent interest he must bestow the whole upon you again at the feast he was now obliged to make. So endlessly the game went on, among all people according to their rank and ability. And the honors went to the chief who most recklessly crowded his rival to the wall in this duel of gift-making.

For, to the Kwakiutl, one showed one's wealth by amassing it for public transfer. And wealth, in any case, was of value only as it passed through your hands. It was an object of desire only because it whipped up the game of potlatches, making one able to provide endless feasts in due succession.

But no man sees the logic of another's symbols. After all, the Indian was foolishly bewildered by the white man's mania. They played, both of them, the identical game — the game of prestige. One played it with songs and visions and the giving of goods for counters; the other played it with land. And if the red man's counters were harmless and dispossessed no one of food or shelter, on the white man's counters have hung progress, and the glories of civilization.

The Uses
of Cannibalism*

WE HAVE done scant justice to the reasonableness of cannibalism. There are in fact so many and such excellent motives possible to it that mankind has never been able to fit all of them into one universal scheme, and has accordingly contrived various diverse and contradictory systems the better to display its virtues.

The present decade, indeed, is likely to appreciate to an unusual degree the advantages that attach to cannibalism so soon as the matter may be presented. We have already had recourse to many quaint primitive customs our fathers believed outmoded by the progress of mankind. We have watched the dependence of great nations upon the old device of the pogrom. We have seen the rise of demagogues, and even in those countries we consider lost in a mortally dangerous idealism we have watched death dealt out to those who harbor the mildest private opinions. Even in our own country we have come to the point of shooting in the back that familiar harmless annoyance, the strike picketer. It is strange that we have overlooked cannibalism.

Mankind has for many thousands of years conducted experiments in the eating of human flesh, and has not found it wanting. Especially it has been proved to foster the feeling of solidarity within the group and of antipathy toward the alien, providing an incomparable means of gratifying with deep emotion the hatred of one's enemy. Indeed, all the noblest emotions have been found not only com-

* Unpublished manuscript, *circa* 1925.

patible with it, but reinforced by its practice. It would appear that we have here rediscovered that specific and sovereign remedy for which we have long perceived statesmen to be groping. It will be well, therefore, to pass the known facts briefly in review.

It is necessary first to place beyond doubt the high moral sentiments with which the custom has been allied. It has been unfortunate that in our solicitude lest heroism, endurance, and self-control should perish from a world so largely devoted to commerce and the pursuit of wealth, we should have overlooked the matter of cannibalism. Certain valiant tribes of the Great Lakes and the prairies long ago made use of it to this purpose. It was to them their supreme gesture of homage to human excellence. It is told by old travelers that of three enemies whose death made the occasion for such a celebration of their valor, two were eaten with honor, while the one remaining was passed over and untouched. For at the death, this one had marked himself a coward, and cried out under torture. Of such flesh no one would eat. In the old papers of the Jesuit Fathers we find it stated: "When then the captive had been slain, if so be that he had looked with laughter upon the thongs, the knives and the fire, and had sung songs continually in his torture, they took his heart and divided it among the warriors, that they might imbibe a portion of so great a valor." By this device, therefore, they made certain that nobility should not perish from the earth.

This is of course not the only excellent ethical use to which cannibalism has been put among the peoples of the world. There are tribes to whom it is an expression of tenderness to the most nearly related dead so to dispose of their discarded bodies — a supreme cherishing of those for whom there can be no other remaining act of tenderness. But, indeed, it is not necessary to look upon it in this particular light; eating the dead has also been regarded as sharing in the identical qualities of marriage, and those among whom the relations of lawful wedlock were prohibited were denied also the intimacy of cannibalism. It was incest not only to marry from among them, but also to eat their flesh.

Cannibalism has proved also to be extraordinarily well qualified to provide the excitement of an ultimate aggression. This has proved recently to be by no means the frivolous subject that it may appear.

Indeed we have been confronted by the problem on such a large scale that, in the interests of progress, it is difficult not to press the matter. Without the infantile ostentations and unfortunate appeals to the hatred of one's fellow beings which characterize our Black Shirts and our Red Shirts, the Indians of Vancouver Island found a heightened excitation, disciplined in endless ritual and taboo, in a ceremonial show of cannibalism. Secret societies of the men were all-important on Vancouver Island; the whole winter was given over to their rites. And they were sufficiently aristocratic; membership was limited to first sons of noble birth. When it was time for such a one to become a member of this society, he retired to the forests or the graveyard, and it was said that the spirits had taken him. Here an almost mummified corpse was prepared and smoked, and at the appointed time, in the midst of great excitement, the noble youth returned to the village with the Spirit of the Cannibal upon him. A member of the society carried the corpse before him, while with violent rhythms and trembling of his tense body, he rendered in dance his seeking for human flesh. He was held by his neck-ring that he might not attack the people, and he uttered a terrible reiterated cannibal cry. But when he had bitten the corpse, the ecstasy left him, and he was "tamed." He drank the emetic, and retired again to solitude in a state of great sacredness, where for months he observed the endless taboos of the newly initiate.

It is obvious that nothing could be more harmless to the community; one useless body per year satisfactorily satisfied the craving for violence which we have clumsily supplied in modern times in the form of oaths, blood-and-thunder, and vows to undertake the death of industrious households. They achieved the highest tension of excitement and aggression without advocating malice toward the minority or arrogantly claiming the prerogatives of a Chosen People.

All these uses of cannibalism are, however, of small moment in comparison with the one we must now consider. It is its service in the cause of patriotism. Nothing, we are well aware, will so hold in check the hostile elements of a nation as a common purpose of revenge. This may be raised to a high degree of utility by various well-known phrases and figures of oratory which picture our determination to "drink the blood of our enemies." It has however been held essential that we pursue this end by the death, in great numbers and with distressing tortures, of young men in sound health and vigor. Nothing could show more lamentably our ignorance of previous human experiments. It is this aspect of cannibalism that has appealed most widely to the human species; it has enabled them to derive the most intense emotional satisfaction from the death, even the accidental death, of one solitary enemy, allowing them to taste revenge in a thoroughgoing and convincing manner, ministering to their faith in his extirpation, root and branch, body and soul.

This practice was perhaps best understood by the head-hunters of certain parts of the Malay Archipelago. They carried on their negotiations of warfare with ritualistic formality; with great punctilio they refrained from seeming to dictate to their honored adversaries either the time or the manner of fighting. They slept peacefully side by side, and whiled away the time in ancient ritual. But at the hour agreed, they joined forces with the fierceness of males in breeding season, hurling their vilest taunts each at the other, till bodies had been secured. All the excitement of the engagemnt was only the preliminary. When a modest feast had been secured, the fires were lighted, and the angry passion which uncurbed might have killed a hundred enemies was humanely employed in the disposal of a few.

The Maoris of New Zealand, before the feast, took from their enemies the exquisitely tattooed heads which were their incomparable pride, and setting them on posts about them, taunted them after this fashion:

> "You thought to flee, ha? But my power overtook you.
> You were cooked; you were made food for my mouth.
> Where is your father? He is cooked.
> Where is your brother? He is eaten.
> Where is your wife? There she sits, a wife for me!"

No one who is familiar with the breakdown of emotional satisfaction in warfare as it is recorded in postwar literature of our time can fail to see in all this a hopeful device for the re-establishment of an emotional complex which shows every sign of disintegration among us. It is obvious that something must be done, and no suggestion seems more hopeful than this drawn from the Maoris of New Zealand.

The serviceability of cannibalism is therefore well established. In view of the fact that ends now so widely sought in modern war and its aftermaths can thus be attained by the comparatively innocent method of cannibalism, is it not desirable that we consider seriously the possibility of substituting the one for the other before we become involved in another national propaganda? Our well-proved methods of publicity give us a new assurance in the adoption even of unfamiliar programs; where we might at one time well have doubted the possibility of popularizing a practice so unused, we can now venture more boldly. While there is yet time, shall we not choose deliberately between war and cannibalism?

Selections from the Correspondence
of Edward Sapir with Ruth Benedict
1922–1923

Ottawa, Ont.
June 25, 1922

Dear Mrs. Benedict,

I read your paper yesterday[1] in one breath, interrupted by supper, most necessary of distractions, only. Let me congratulate you on having produced a very fine piece of research. It makes a notable addition to the body of historical critiques that anthropology owes to Boas. I put it with such papers as Goldenweiser's "Totemism" [2] and Waterman's "Exploratory Element in American Mythology" [3] except that it impresses me as being decidedly more inspiring than either of these. A logical sequel (but one never works logically) is another paper on the historical development of the guardian spirit in a particular area, the idea being to show how the particular elements crystallized into the characteristic pattern. This "how" would involve consideration of some of the more general behavior patterns of the area or tribe and should perhaps show, unless you balk at psychology under all circumstances, how the crystallization could form a suitable frame for adequate individual expression. There is room somewhere for psychology — not so much as cultural determinant as incidental, but important, cultural content (or, better, utilization). Or do you take the extreme view (perhaps justifiable enough) that no matter what patterns rise, no matter how unsuitable they seem *a priori* for the guidance of human behavior, human psy-

49

chology can and does accommodate itself to them as it accommodates itself to practically any physical environment? Culture then becomes merely environment for the individual psyche and can be made as much or as little of as this psyche pleases (or is allowed by its nature). And, conversely, culture, being historically moulded "environment" for individual living, can take no account whatever of the facts and theories of psychology. If you take this view, you need never discuss psychology as student of culture, but how then can you "evangelize" either? You would have to be a kind of culture fatalist. I should like to see the problem of individual and group psychology boldly handled, not ignored, by some one who fully understands culture as a historical entity. I hope you will do just this one of these days in connection with a concrete problem, whether guardian spirit or something else. By the way, a slight error should be corrected: the Pit (not Pitt) River Indians, also known as Achomawi, are in northern California, not southern Oregon. You might change Takelma gō yō′ to go yò (or goyò); this is the standard form used in my Takelma Texts[4] and Takelma Grammar[5] (or simply goyo, perhaps best of all).

You might get a hint or two for Nootka from my article in "Vancouver Island Indians," just published in the last volume of Hastings' Encyclopedia.[6] I lazily confined myself to Nootka in it and merely gave bibliographical references for the other tribes of the island. It seems to me that for Nootka it would be quite inadequate to look upon the "Wolf Ritual" initiation as the equivalent of the typical American guardian spirit experience. (Even in Kwakiutl I am inclined to doubt if Boas' formulation is quite adequate.) Unless I am greatly mistaken, the individual manitou complex is broken up in Nootka into 3 distinct and only partly equivalent patterns. First of all, we have the actual individual experience in the woods or other secluded place. Power is obtained for doctoring (from bird or fish class) or for hunting, fishing, or other pursuit. The aberrant features in Nootka are: a vision is not necessary, but rather actual and accidental waking contact; the manitou is an individual, not a class, and is practically always an abnormal object or folk-loristic being (ranging from a blind snake or mysterious hand jutting up out of the ground to centaur-like beings, lightning serpent, wood nymph, or spirit canoe bearing many beings, one for each desirable blessing); the finder is in no way personally identified in a mystical manner with the visitation (even in the case of the doctor, who places his guardian in his breast); the being or phenomenon does not as a rule *grant* a blessing, properly speaking, but is generally killed or grabbed or in some manner physically handled, some part (e.g. half the dried body or the mucus from the nose or what not) being carefully preserved as a kind of amulet. This whole complex is a very much more material, fetichistic sort of thing than the regular guardian spirit experience. Emphasis is placed on the amuletic gift or booty rather than on the mystical power of the blesser. But the complex is reminiscent none the less of your guardian spirit spirit adventure. In both, specific power is gained; in both, the individual acts, on the whole, apart from society; the Nootka fetish is clearly related to the eastern token or bundle (indeed, wrapping and hiding the fetish is essential); both types of experience involve taboos; and, perhaps most interesting of all, neither experience can be safely rejected (if a Nootka refuses the "gift" of a mysterious object or being, he and his children are liable to suffer misfortune). All in all, the Nootka complex may be looked upon as a materialized or fetichistic degradation of the more typical manitou complex or, possibly, as a more archaic, non-visional form of it. (Surely, the Kwakiutl have equivalent experiences.) The second pattern is the ancestral experience, which is a more "poetic," less secretive, variety and concerns itself, as a rule, with more god-like beings (whale, thunder-bird, wolf, shark, sea-otter). These experiences are often associated with visions (or dreams) and constitute the legendary warrant for *topatis* (privileges). Names, songs, legends, paintings, are handed down by virtue of them. Often the whale or other supernatural being is heard singing in its vision and this song becomes a blessing or privilege. A link between the first and second pattern is constituted by the fact that the ancestor often gets a material token (water of life, war-club, piece of lightning serpent's tail), which is handed down in his family, but, alas! has generally been lost some time in the less remote past. One suspects that the old and typical guardian spirit complex has here become split into two patterns: a legendary and sociologized sublimation, under the stress of ideas of rank and privilege and under the stimulation of

Northern ideas of crest, and a magical, underground version that keeps its character as individual experience. The third pattern is the "Wolf Ritual" initiation and specific dances (these dances are impersonations of folk-loristic beings, of actual animals, and of occupations). These dances correspond to the Kwakiutl Winter Feast performances. What affiliates the Wolf Ritual with the guardian spirit complex is not any blessings the novices obtain (unless the *tro·-kwa·-na<* or "ecstacy" be considered a blessing) but the origin legend of the ritual, which is a decidedly typical manitou-ritual legend. This third pattern, for the Nootka, is certainly the most aberrant of all as a guardian spirit experience, as religious formalism and privilege have taken the individual aspect out of it. However, it is significant that certain of the Wolf Ritual beings are identical with beings from whom amulets may be obtained according to my first pattern, though I doubt if the performance of the dances is actually connected with individual fetish experiences. There is another point which is probably of the greatest historical importance. Among many tribes of the Columbia River valley (e.g. Wasco-Wishram) there are ceremonials in which each dancer represents, without specifically mentioning, his own manitou ("tam —"); there are special songs and pantomimic performances. Now it is not at all unlikely that the Nootka Wolf Ritual dances and the Kwakiutl Winter Feast dances are a highly specialized or petrified form of such group-manitou performances, the individually acquired manitou being changed into a ritualized and hereditarily owned being. To summarize, pattern 1 is a fetichistic manitou complex; pattern 2, a crest or privilege manitou complex; pattern 3, a ritualized manitou complex. Another offshoot of the group-manitou performance is the contest of rival doctors, who show off their familiars. This type is particularly common among the Washington Coast Salish, and has traveled north from this area to the Nootka (a fourth, shamanistic, manitou complex). The Midewiwin is the most complicated ritual that has grown up on this basis. From the point of view of your guardian spirit-vision complex, one may say the token or bundle is specialized in pattern 1; the vision in pattern 2; the mystic relationship ("ecstacy") and public ritualization, where present, in pattern 3. — But I did not intend to write an article on Nootka manitous. Only, your paper has stimulated me and when it is published, I may overcome my indolence sufficiently to write a brief article for the Anthropologist along the lines of my present remarks.

One of the by-products of your paper is a depressive mood induced in me by the realization how little I have fulfilled my duty in making public the various materials I have gathered, much of them of real interest. I hope that within the next 5 or 10 years I may do a little to make good. Harcourt would not make a contract for "Whale and Thunderbird" because of his uncertainty of what sort of book it would turn out to be, but suggested my submitting 2 or 3 specimen chapters. I don't know whether to do this later on or to approach some other publisher. You are very flattering about the Culture book, but I have not yet taken myself seriously enough to actually prepare a plan. Perhaps later, when I am in the field.

No, I have not written any poems lately. Liveright returned the MS. He says he desires to publish only great or near great poetry. I am afraid that my MS, good or bad, is neither one nor the other. I have pretty well decided that my attempt to make public a volume is premature. Perhaps, slowly, in 5, 10, or 15 years, enough meritorious verse may accumulate to make up a really worth while volume. One *really good* book of verse would be an achievement. Why work for quantity? "The King of Thule" has not yet appeared in The Nation,[7] so I am enclosing you a copy. It is a bit long for its quality. Did you see my little write-up of Maxwell Bodenheim in The Nation (June 21st)? The New Republic is to have an unsigned paragraph on the same book from my pen — you may be annoyed to see how I dodged saying precisely the same things.[8]

Are you anthropologizing hard these days? My second reason for wanting to do Sarcee (really Athabaskan — I take Sarcee merely because it is most accessible) is decidedly startling. All in good time. All I shall say now is that, for me, the Nadene (Haida-Tlingit-Athabaskan) problem does not stop with Nadene itself. It fills me with something like horror and melancholy both to see how long and technical a road I must travel in linguistic work, how fascinating its prospect, and how damnably alone I must be. There is practically no one to turn to for either assistance or sympathetic interest.

Good luck to you!

Sincerely,
E. Sapir

Ottawa, Ont.
Sept. 10, 1923.
Dear Mrs. Benedict,

I enjoyed very much your letter of just a month ago and feel we are going to get a really fruitful treatment of American mythology from you. I wish I knew enough about it to discuss it intelligently. I am sure you are right about the overwhelmingly historical or traditionally moulded character of mythology in all cases. Jung would get small comfort from you, I'm afraid. What about his "primordial images," of which I am reminded once again in his "Psychological Types"? [9] I am sending you by registered mail excerpts from my MS "Texts of the Kaibab Paiutes and Uintah Utes," [10] i.e. carbon copies of the title page, contents, introduction, translations of Paiute and Ute narratives, and notes to translations. The texts themselves you will not need. The material is rather scanty but may help to eke out your Shoshonean collectanea. I have no idea when Dr. Gordon intends to publish the volume. He has also Ute grammar and Ute dictionary. *Resquiescant in pace!* . . .

. . . The summer's work was quite successful, I believe. The high and low tones of Kutchin correspond very nicely to those of Sarcee. Should this fact be featured in the press? I am sorry I could not get a great volume of text, but my Indian was pretty busy at the camp and not well acquainted with native lore. However, the linguistic material is really good, it seems to me, far better than would have been Anvik data from T. B. Reed.

My leg is getting on pretty well, but it is unexpectedly tiring to hobble with the cane. I had the naive idea that as soon as the crutches were discarded I should be able to function as a normal specimen of Homo erectus. Now I see I must be content with the other label, Homo sapiens. What's the gossip? Do you know if Theresa Mayer (I do not know her husband's name) is safe in Japan?

Cordially,
E. SAPIR

Two Diaries

ONLY TWO diaries were found among Ruth Benedict's papers, each covering a few winter months — the first written in 1923, when she was just becoming acquainted with anthropologists as a professional group, and the second in 1926, after she had also come to know a group of poets. Taken together, they provide a small but precise diagram of the different aspects of her life in the early 1920's. In contrast to her journal, the diaries record the small events of day-to-day life, but as each runs for no more than a few weeks, they suggest a habit of commencing the New Year with a resolution to keep track of events, personal and professional, which always lapsed as other preoccupations intervened.

These two little diaries were handwritten in small bound volumes, each page of which is headed with a printed date. In the 1923 diary, the poem "New Year" is written in — with many emendations — on the last page, with the notation, "on buying this diary," and the date, December 12, 1922. Also written in the back are four other poems, all dated 1925.

* * *

DIARY: 1923

New Year

I shall lie once with beauty,
Breast to breast;
Take toll of you, year;
Once be blessed —

I'll walk your desert quite
Self-possessed;
~~Never~~ Nor once cry pity
At ~~your worst~~ any jest;

All ~~your~~ thousands of hours, year,
Be undistressed —
~~So I couch~~ When I lie once with beauty
Breast to breast.

Monday, January 1
The New Year in with sheets of rain, and a southeast wind. S. gave up going into city to see if Clarke was arriving. A good day to sit by one's own fire and look out at the rain and at the whipping trees. Toward sunset, cleared under gale from northwest — Walked in its teeth as far as sleeting roads allowed, past farm house and to Switz. House and played Go bang! — A good day.

Tuesday, January 2
S. to city. I, odd jobs to put my best foot forward in my house-keeping for Mrs. Powers — who came for first time P.M. A long visit — Mrs. Zeriol, Mrs. Murphy and the village — I'm thankful I have her! — Worked some on Cups of Clay, but gave over and length-ened S's blankets. — Clarke and Minnie *did* come in yesterday. S—

to take Clarke to Dr. Foster tomorrow. — Saw coalman — ½ ton tomorrow, nut and pea.

Wednesday, January 3
In to city. 9 AM class; Aunt Mamie's coat; shopped for curtains but unsuccessful. Back for 1 PM class and Goldenweiser till 4 — Down again to 32nd in sleet and storm to see Clarke and Minnie — . . . Home in thick wet snowfall — beautiful — Depression. Edge of cliff; sensation of falling; vacuum. Later M.I.A. in — Her visit home a great success — out to impress them.

Thursday, January 4
9 AM section — all of them apparently unable to stand. Barbeau in tower room, and read his notes. Anthrop. lunch — ES there, and walked to Museum with him. His wife . . . physically very ill. Talked of Esther and Mrs. Parsons; relationship terms. Bought jam and cards! I must remember afterwards how simple happiness is — I don't want anything more or different at such times — I'm just at ease. Another section 3:30; M. Mead waited afterward. Dentist at five — Clarke at hotel at 7:30. "Rain" with M.I.A. — excellent. I shall remember Sadie in her glory — she

Friday, January 5
9 AM class. Up to "Rochester" for room for Clarke — Telephone — and Dr. Boas' remark I'd better take his class — grip. Lunch with N. Kellner, and taught class Diffusion. Stumbled into anti-evolution. N.B. — never argue that point again; it's dead. Section at Museum and back to E.S. Lecture — met M.I.A. Played with Helen[1] till M was ready to leave — invited her to play with me Tuesday. Up on street car to 125th. Out to Bedford Hills on 6:15.

Saturday, January 6
A lazy day — though I meant to work. Tried a pot boiler a la Batuala. Go Bang till 11 P.M.!! I beat two to one.

We'll have no crumb in common
In all our days
We shall not make
A dream come true by naming it together;
Nor go full-fortified
From touch of lips.

These are sweet things.
To us they are as words
Rhymed in proud cadence
By a jesting fool.

We have but this: an hour
When the life-long aimless stepping of our feet
Fell into time and measure
Each to the other's tune.

Sunday, January 7
S— slept A.M. and worked at papers P.M., but a good day. Comfortable. At 4, walk to Switz. 19° above. Read Matthew Arnold — he is astonishingly fresh; I like him, for all he takes life so heavily.

Monday, January 8
In at 8 in sleet storm. Train half hour late. Worked on thesis. Lunch with M. Mead. Two sections. At 7 Clarke and Minnie at the Rochester.

Tuesday, January 9
Rain slush and water. Helen Sapir's day — paper dolls in my room; lunch from "printed menu"; wardrobe of dolls; swimming pool; and typewriter. E.S. in seminar at 4, and ice cream across the street. Talked of Ogburn's book.[2] He made fun of Helen which she quite properly resented. Took Helen home; saw Mrs. Boas, and back to dinner with Esther Cornell and Agnes de Lima. Met E.S. at Stark Young's lecture — horribly competent. Agnes and her baby and her

spotty rug! A good time. 248 W. 11th Street. — Refused dinner with E.S. — he lectured tonight at Cooper Union.

Wednesday, January 10

Class 9 AM. Thesis till 12 — Classes till 6. Dinner with Boas and Herskovits at Faculty Club. To "Rochester": found Clarke and Minnie satisfied and comfortable. To M.I.A. for clothes — I've a notion I can apply myself to turning out a piece of work better than for a long time. I feel so remarkably undistraught. Heaven send it lasts!

Thursday, January 11

Wrote Swanton about thesis. Met E.S. and Helen in hall, but only in passing. Shall not meet again. Worked in Library 10–6. Missed lunch till too late. Weary. Dinner with Miss Gordon in "Methods" class. Rochester.

Friday, January 12

Class at nine — Library — Lunch with N. Kellner — Class — Back to Seminar room; exhaustion. The spirit is willing . . . Out to Rochester; Clarke out at doctor's since ten; Minnie much worried; fever. Stayed an hour and left S's telephone. Down to see Rodin exhibit — A "Despair [?] clasping one foot"; figures from Bourgeois de Calais. Out to Bedford Hills. S. went to E.S.'s lecture at Cooper Union!!

Saturday, January 13

A good day at relationship systems — not Mohave however. Out to Mrs. Powers (Mrs. Zeriol two months off yet!); coal man (500 lbs. first of week). Back with S.R. express (blankets, dishpans) and much groceries, in taxi; S— already there. Dinner, and papers; Go bang till ten. Together over the matches! + . Mail — Aunt Myra planning to sell farm. Stanley's secret idea of buying.

Sunday, January 14

Shut in with snowfall. Beautiful. Up for papers A.M. and out at twilight, plowing as far as Sanatarium hill top. Haze of snowfall. Working on relationship terms and Melanesia.

Monday, January 15

In at 8 with S—. To Rochester to see Clarke and Minnie. Minnie in bed over weekend — fever and uprootedness. Museum to get South Sea hall in hand for afternoon sections. Class at Columbia. Letter from Swanton — discouraging. Two sections at Museum. Call on Esther Goldfrank: I don't envy her. Met Jeanette B . . . for dinner — Pirate's Den, and Jolly Friars! "Will Shakespeare." Excellent. Haidie Wright as Queen Elizabeth; Otto Kruger, W.S.; Winifred Lenihan, Anne Hathaway; Katherine Cornell, Mary Fitton. I'll always have the set of Queen E's shoulders to remember standing in the doorway protecting S— at his writing. One could go far with that behind one's back!

Tuesday, January 16

In Library. Relationship systems, and Serrano for seminar. Section at Museum at 3:30 — Got Gifford's Relationship Systems for Goddard. Up to Rochester — Uncle Will in town — Typed Cups of Clay[3] in evening.

Wednesday, January 17

Classes — Lunch with M. Mead, tea with N. Kellner; dinner and theater with Uncle Will. "Loyalties." Discussed Aunt Myra and the farm.[4] Poor Aunt Myra! and she must work herself into a breakdown over the losses when no one cares a penny how large the mortgage grows.

Seminar — *Contra* Dr. Boas on culture areas. He's such a godsend. Argued with him again about the Races book.

Thursday, January 18

Call from Miss Kissell at 7 AM! Agreed to: Feb. 17 SW; Mar. 10, Peru; Apr. 21, Mexico; May 12, Mound builders. M.I.A. increasingly

impossible at breakfast. "Always had let people walk all over her;
Dr. S— said that was the trouble." — "Wished I'd ever have had
bad luck once"!! Classes at Museum. Translated Barbeau's songs —
Lunch — Mrs. Canon remarked on missing me last week! Up to
Rochester — not in. Chilkot blankets from storeroom. Section, and
M. Mead to tea till 5.30. Dentist — Downtown for "Tidings brought
to Mary" — to be withdrawn Sat. L. I. Grimby in Library — Ran
into "Mercury," and with her to theater. Beautiful pageant.

Friday, January 19
   Classes and section at Museum. Took 5 o'clock train out to B.H.
— A good evening.

Sunday, January 21
   Downpour all day. Burned soft coal. Worked on relationship
terms and played Go-bang with S—. A good day.

Monday, January 22
   Couldn't sleep — Went downstairs and shut drafts of fire — which
went out by morning. Ran for train from telephone — Library for
relationship terms. Class and sections. Asked —— Pedwiza for tea
at Fichl's. Here's someone who still believes in Paradise on earth —
she enters it on Friday, day after examination week! It's a pleasure
to see such burning confidence — and terrible too. But some people
are happy.

Tuesday, January 23
   Worked, and saw Dr. Boas. Downtown to bank and Hill Club —
to inspect — Felt very isolated tonight, and sent check for membership.

Wednesday, January 24
   Worked in seminar A.M. Barnard attendance report. 2 P.M.
Goldenweiser — on the Egyptian mummy and crumbling of primi-

tive civilization. Bored!! How could he! Down in pouring rain, gale
and slush to Museum and found Clarke and Minnie punctual to the
dot. Minnie and the fur piece. Clarke and "high ideals in art."
Down on surface car to Civic Club with Daniels — Dinner with the
Marquesa and the blanket broker! Gloating — C.D. "M.I.A.
doesn't want you come down here. She thinks you'd be shocked
. . . Yes she thinks of you as part of all that background she's trying
to break away from"!!! A long and egotistic but reassuring letter
from M.I.A.

Thursday, January 25
   Out to B.H. on ten o'clock to get coal put in. Stopped on errand
at Mrs. Powers and stayed to lunch. Nice people — Mrs. Zeriol has
refused to let Dr. Adams make examination, and he has refused to
treat her unless she does: — they think there's nothing the matter.
   Translated and typed Indian Lit. — quite nice — Quarter ton pea
coal from Young and Halsted.

Friday, January 26
   Struck snag in Serrano paper[5] and put it aside — 5 P.M. Worked
at S's desk all day. Beautiful snowy weather.

Saturday, January 27
   Working on Wintun systems of kinship — Uptown for 6 o'clock
and met S— Evening played Go Bang.

Sunday, January 28
   Waked up at 5:30 and began to write Wintun paper. At it all
day and almost finished. Good sport. S— slept AM and wrote
papers PM. More Go Bang, and stockings, evening.

>   "For when by night the May wind blows
>   The lilac blooms apart,

The memory of his first love
Is shaken on his heart" —

L. I. G. . . .[6]

— "Faileth nothing that was to thee eternal."

Monday, January 29
In on 8 o'clock and finished typing Wintun paper in seminar
[room]. Call on Clarke and Minnie — discouraged and helpless.
. . . Met Dr. Boas for dinner at Esther's. . . . Business meeting at
the Ethnological Society and Dr. Jochelson. Walk up with Nelsons
and Esther.

Tuesday, January 30
Typing all day on Cups of Clay and working on papers. Weary.
M.I.A. for dinner and her room afterwards. An undiscussed reconciliation. Walked an hour at 9:30 — cold night with moon;
peculiar blue sky. — For lunch had invited Clarke and Minnie, and
they missed the directions. Called PM, and found note telling of
their sudden decision to leave tomorrow. Invitation from Agnes
Benedict for lunch tomorrow.

Wednesday, January 31
Examination 9–12. Worked on seminar report. Lunch with
Agnes — I and Clarke are similar natures! From her opinion of
Clarke should be a compliment — . . . A guarded but amicable
occasion. Back to examination papers, and a summons from Dr.
Boas for discussing Wintun rel. terms — Discouragement; took
Gifford's on faith, and it isn't right — I'll learn! Rushed down to
Penn station to see Clarke off — too early! Missed Stanley. Dense
dark boredom. — Called Mrs. Rohde Pedwiza. Too tired for
theater. Home and exam papers till 10:30.

Thursday, February 1
Better. Corrected papers all day and to Moscow Art Theater at
night. I wasn't stirred — "Three Sisters" — and I knew the play and

it had stirred me. Perhaps I was repelled by Masha's lack of reserve, her childishness in her love affair. Anyway I think it's time somebody said that we have as good acting as the Russians.

Friday, February 2

At home — 119 Street — with my papers — P.M. missed Dr. Boas and out on 5 P.M. train. Depression after telephoning S—; "against which all these years her lifted life had splintered." — But it's just mannerism; all right at home. Fire out, but fortunately warm weather and ½ ton coal from BH Coal Co.

Saturday, February 3

A lazy day. Papers finished, and not much else to show. Uptown at 5 — Go bang with S— night.

Release

She said: since all that ever shall
Lift up its face to mine
Shall bear these features, let me tell
Them clearly, line by line.

Let my slow finger trace the curve
Above your curtained eye
Know the lift of your lips: preserve
The clasp of hand and cheek and thigh.

Then I shall go ahead again,
Armed now from ultimate fear,
Always in some casual crowd of men,
I know you near.

Sunday, February 4

A touch of grip — a bug on top of being tired, and . . . . In house all day — bed most of it. Misery night. But a good time with S—

Thursday, February 8
Marie Bloomfield's suicide in papers. It's unbearable that life should be so hard for them. I know it's all wrapped up with my wish for children — and dread that they might not want the gift. — It bowls me over completely. Wrote M. Mead — She came to my room before bed time. Lillian Milgram too I shall remember meeting in the hall; evidently she'd been to Ogburns. Couldn't go to lunch. — Someday I hope I'll be able to go through with things just in the way Dr. Boas does.

Monday, February 12
Dr. Boas talked to me about a fellowship in SW folklore. He'd had a letter from Mrs. Parsons falling in with his suggestion.

Tuesday, February 13
Worst sick headache I've had in years. I know my subconscious staged it — But really I suppose it's hanging on to the idea that I can teach at Barnard — which my conscious self has known I couldn't do, always.

Thursday, February 15
Said nothing to Mrs. Parsons at lunch — nor she to me. Dr. Boas said I was to approach her. Oh well — Discussed it with M.I.A. P.M. — it seemed more possible.

Friday, February 16
Couldn't
/Wrote Mrs. Parsons I'd take the job. Wrote Mrs. Parsons I was interested.

Saturday, February 17
Miss Kissel's class at Museum. Quite fun. Worked on art, etc., museum all day. Lunch with Dr. Goddard. He settled scores for my

lack of attention to him this winter. Began with my felicitations on
Gladys' job.[7] He took up Dr. Boas' worry about me for me. "He
said he supposed there'd always be these driblets of research but that
was all he could see ahead for me." — I feel some capacity for
making a place for myself, thank you! but on the elevated I was
weary, and plain wept with vexation. Not that I credit the thrust to
Dr. Boas.

Monday, February 19
   Found a letter from Mrs. Parsons with details — $1000 and a
study of SW mythology.

Tuesday, February 20
   Wrote Mrs. Parsons I'd take the job.

Thursday, February 22
   The longest day I ever remember. Holiday — Worked in locked-
up Barnard library on art all AM — The window cleaners reading
Shakespeare — No one at lunch. Evening to Hill Club — Stupid
and painful. Mrs. Alice Duer Miller on movie problems.

Saturday, February 24
   In city to work on art for sections and for class Monday. Got out
of money!

Sunday, February 25
   It's as if we inhabited the opposing poles — He kept talking about
a job for him at California, or for me at Wellesley. S— "It isn't any
laws people need [for divorce]; just the nerve" — He has a fixed
idea, and he'll drive me to it — maybe.

Monday, February 26
Taught Barnard class on art — then two museum sections. All with handicap. M. lunch. Sleet and wind — Home and to bed in spite of ethnological meeting — M.I.A. in evening.

Saturday, March 3
A headache and couldn't work — But a not unpleasant day. Spring weather; mud under foot.

Wednesday, March 7
After A. A. G's class — Totemism, Heaven defend us — went down to lunch with him. Cut Barnard class for the purpose! A pleasant time; he's easy to please — After seminar talk with M. Mead about her future — She rests me like a padded chair and a fire place. I say it's the zest of youth I believe in when I see it in her. Or is it that I respond understandably to admiration?

Thursday, March 8
Finished off thesis and mailed it; Anthropology lunch. To Museum for Peru with Goddard — great help. Downtown and bought a suit! Weary — too weary to stay for theater. Home and read Many Marriages and Faint Perfume. Quickening of the spirit is pain almost to madness. And in spite of all I say, pain is not indifferent to me! I can't exclude the knowledge of pain from my choices. I dread intense awareness. — And yet it comes with such ghastly frequency. I had one today, buying stamps at the underground Library post office — inconceivable that such a thing as life existed — such a thing as my power to look out and be conscious of these other people. The whole thing an arrangement of lines and dots in a kaleidoscope. — Again reading Many Marriages. Only that was an awareness of a life one could exist in without distaste — And then it seems to me terrible that life is passing, that my program is to fill the twenty-four hours each day with obliviousness, with work — And oh, I am lonely —

Friday, March 9

I out to Leonia for night with Hallers. Dr. Sapir expected today. Wife is leaving hospital. . . .

Saturday, March 10

Rain and sleet. In from Leonia, and to Museum for Miss Kissel's class — Home to Bedford Hills.

Monday, March 12

Classes, sections and library. Dr. Sapir, with Michael,[8] in hall — "At least there's something else to think of besides life and death," he said when I said how glad I was his wife was well again. . . . Theatre with Mrs. Rohde — Ethel Barrymore in the "Laughing Lady" — terrible bore.

Tuesday, March 13

Sections — at Barnard. Lunch with M. Mead — discussed her going into anthropology. I hope she does it. I need a companion in harness! Downtown in pouring rain to dinner with Jeannette B—— and Wild Animals in Africa — Snow expedition. Almost as good as being surrounded by trumpeting wild elephants yourself.

Wednesday, March 14

Dr. Sapir came to ask about country boarding places. He wanted me to come to see his wife today — and I went at three — . . . All she's willing to do is to fend for herself in this city — and she not able to walk a block.

Thursday, March 15

Anthropology lunch, and I stayed afterwards to talk to Dr. Sapir who came very late. I spoke of Miss R——'s paranoic trend, and he said, "It's very easy for me to understand that type of person. It comes naturally." Downtown and bought lamp and sweater for S's birthday. Home weary.

Friday, March 16
Classes and sections and Miss Mayer's Indian yogi party. Pouring rain. The Rochester after 12 — . . . .

Saturday, March 17
Worked on texts AM. Out to Bedford Hills. Saw Dr. Sapir ahead of me at noon, but suddenly I didn't care whether he looked up or not. He didn't, and I went on to the train. Stanley's birthday; he got out at six. The cliff tonight. Nothing could bring life to it. But he's got a beautiful new Zeiss lens Kodak and it ought to be fun.

Monday, March 19
Worked in seminar and at classes all day. No word from Dr. Sapir though I know he's still here. Typed and mailed Cups of Clay to Century. Here's hoping!

Tuesday, March 20
Tonight message from Dr. Sapir to me through Michael. He's been ill with grip and he'd like to have me come to see them. The room is just across from mine now. A much less depressing cell than the first one; the room's much better and quieter. He looks dreadful. How do we ever escape the upper and the nether millstones? Anyway he's between them. . . . Evening with M.I.A. — M. Mead told Dr. Boas today about PhD in Anthropology — He poured cold water but she arose.

At Ending*

At ending when the world is done
And the dead air lets fall the ash

* Lines 17–18 have been deleted and lines 19–20, which are substituted, are on a separate slip of paper. These lines and line 7 differ from later versions of the poem.

Upon the blackened plain no flash
Shall light henceforth forever, none
Of all the wandering breezes kiss
Again to loveliness like this —

There can be silence always. Riven,
Infertile, charred as any star
Thick sown at evening, they are
That were mythology of heaven
To our sight: arbutus bed,
And the dark pines, thick-carpeted.

And down the burnt-out air shall come
No hurt upon the night, no cry
Our hearts must rise to satisfy,
No portent of delirium.
~~God and his ending down this night~~
~~Lest I hear you cry this candle light.~~
Silence will lie upon your weeping,
O dear, most dear! and you be sleeping.

The Worst is not our Anger*

The worst is not our anger, Hearts
Grown icy with the bitterness
Of calculated hurt redress
Somehow their ruin. Love departs

Thus numbly always, nor leaves behind
One red-lipped fagot of the fire
Of her incredible and dear desire.
Weep but for this: that we are blind

---

* After line 9, three lines have been deleted:
                              "and weary
            Of all the woodnotes of that veery
            We heard in love's lost countryside."

With passion who have been clear-eyed
As planets after rain: and know
No longer any grief, who go
Just to see love crucified.
Down the vain ways where love has died.

For Seed Bearing

No longer, cool within the soil her roots shall draw
Milk of earth's tenderness, or press ecstatic lips
To breasts of passing showers. Blossomtime shall flaw
To arid seed-bearing, and the hard alien pips
Be weary consummation of the ecstacy
She knew on summer mornings. All her scope shall be

Maturing of their sapless entity for ends
Unloved and hidden. Press no comfort on her grief
Of that oncoming June when the warm sap distends
A garden ripened in her bitterness, whose leaf
Is moulded of her leaf, whose ecstacy no less
Than she has known. She would escape from God's largess.

Of a Great Love

The proud and instant lightening patterning
The else-unlovely heaven she had made
Her soul in pride of splendor, who would fling
White love unleashed to all men, blacken blade
Past our far reckoning.

How shall we drink the torment of the storm
That has laid waste our hills? how bear to know
Them cradled safe from every other form
The sky can take, save this, that strikes and lo!
Cinders and blackened corn.

DIARY: 1926

Friday, January 1
New Year's Eve with Edward — Fichl's and Women's Faculty
Club! I've never seen him more alive; all his turmoil has gone like
a last week's thunderclap, nor even bitterness for a residue. It's
evaporated. . . . He put me on the 1:55 train at Hoboken, and I
wrote to MM for two hours. Norwich[9] at 10 A.M. and Margery and
Bobby at 5 P.M. Margery is better than I'd suppose.

Saturday, January 2
Lunch at the Newtons. Slept from 8:30 P.M.

Sunday, January 3
Took 12:25 back for New York. In the A.M. explored attic and
reaped two grandfather's wall shelves, and a doll's chair. Mrs. Penny
showed me. Diary — good 1776 pessimist pages.
Proof and Zuñi books on train. Missed train at Penn. and out to
Lowie's for evening party — inhabited by soulful females and maiden
uncles and aunts, also Radin. Lowie read aloud forty page skit on
Deutsche verein! Night at Westminster, whither conveyed by Lowie
in taxi!

Monday, January 4
Tea with Radin in Faculty Club. . . . Lunch with Boas at Fac.
Club for Michelson — poor dear! . . . [In margin:] A.M. Léonie.

Tuesday, January 5
Tea with Lowie at Faculty Club. He quarreled with Edward's
classification of him as extravert — he's an introvert of course, and
mystic. "Behaviorism is a bad sign post to follow" and *he* knows

how hard won his poised manner is. That will make us all introverts by auto-definition: Goldie, Lowie, Radin and Sapir. And Edward thinks all the rest extraverts — even so!

Class at 4; they were more nearly asleep than I've ever seen them. Dinner with Gene Weltfish and letters off for next boat to M. M.

Wednesday, January 6
Out after dinner to Bedford Hills. Found Stanley with his arm in a sling — an infection.

Letter at 10 AM from Mrs. Mead referring to tornado in Samoa. Telephoned everywhere and could find no news. Then Mrs. Bunzel found it in Monday's paper — Manua especially razed. Wrote Mrs. Mead and sent last letter to M. M. for this boat. Sent cable for Dr. Boas to M — asking for reply.

Thursday, January 7
Worked proof reading Cochiti Tales.[10] No word from M — Helen and Ginger to call, and paste "meds" on yellow paper.

Friday, January 8
More tales.

Saturday, January 9
More tales — Still no word from M —

Sunday, January 10
Finished Cochiti box.
Walk — Nice day.

Monday, January 11
Shopping for earphones!
Still no word from M. M. Four telegrams to date from Marie.

Lunch with Radin. He gives me his RBAE *set* out of storage!! Tea with Jeannette Nichols and dinner and much conversation with E. MacKinstry. . . . Home at 1:30 AM.

Tuesday, January 12

A telephone from Dr. Boas when I got home at 10:30 — Margaret cables "Well." I sent telegrams to the Meads and to Marie, and took hot bath like a ritual.

Got earphone from Western Electric for trial and didn't have nerve to take it out in class!

Took M. Ashley to lunch for birthday celebration — Class good. Dinner with Eda Lou. Work in seminar with Olbrechts.

Wednesday, January 13

Lunch with Goddard and meet his daughter of FPA verse fame. Dr. Boas joined us for dessert — "He'd rather have written a good poem than all the books he'd ever written — to say nothing of a movement in a symphony." It was his answer to Goddard's veiled attempt to betray my poetic inclinations — whereat he guesses merely.

Ran off — when I went down to return the earphones! — to Quinn's Memorial Exhibit. — One clear inspiration of Davies' "Palladium"; and beyond everything Picasso's "Sad Mother" — a study in blues with a mother shut-eyed in an ecstacy of foreboding (?) holding an old-faced, indifferent child. Went with Fan and Melville. Dinner at Russian Bear with the Radins.

Thursday, January 14

Lunch with F—. Lost my way and got there an hour late. She makes a religion of efficiency so it was difficult. But a good time. A sweet baby, excellently brought up and cared for. . . . They've struck it rich — very rich — just lately, and now she can afford two more babies. . . . Home at 5 to superintend the fireplace.

Friday, January 15
Struggles with Spaziano,[11] but aided by Mr. Reynolds. The house in turmoil. Worked at Zuñi proof reading [MS] — A ton of queer looking coal.

Saturday, January 16
More fireplace, but as members of the union they couldn't work in the afternoon. Cleaned cellar.

Sunday, January 17
An exile day — Spaziano at the fireplace. We worked upstairs — I at Winnebago tales, Stanley at "Friendly Arctic." At 4 Spaziano withdrew, leaving fireplace all bricked — only waiting for tiles. Spanish.

Monday, January 18
. . . Verse AM.
Lunch with Bunny — and her ironic dilemma. Session with Elsie — she's providing an anthropological haven in the Sub!
. . . Letter to MM.

Tuesday, January 19
Last class on myth. Dr. Boas talked to me about the seminar on mythology for next term — he wants me to take charge, and he'll attend. Ouch! But I have a feeling for doing it too. — Lunch with Dr. Boas and Gladys. I imparted news of Radin's course — not badly received on the whole.
Dinner with Eda Lou. . . .

Wednesday, January 20
Another cart load of books from Radin. I had lunch with him and spent the afternoon putting them in order — indexed all my

own old reprints and sets too. E. MacKinstry broke the date for dinner tonight, and I ate milk and zwieback in the office and wrote many letters.

Thursday, January 21
Tea with Miss Sturtevant at A. Lincoln's. . . . Ran for dinner at Hazel's — She'd telephoned "they were having a distinguished guest — would I care to join them." . . . Back to Radin's lecture. Not so bad. All about Winnebago things he knows and loves. He and Olbrechts home with me at midnight.
Anthropology lunch — Elsie sails for "Abyssinia" Sat.

Friday, January 22
Lunch with M. M.'s engineer who left her Dec. 10th or something like that.[12] . . . A nice person too. Home, and a cable from Margaret "Love."

Monday, January 25
Out at Bedford Hills. More Zuñi and Cochiti tales.

Tuesday, January 26
Letters from Margaret — even one since the hurricane. . . . I'm more at ease about Margaret than before — heaven knows whether I have any reason — but her letters seemed to me to have a better ring. — At Stanley's suggestion took Goddard on my guest ticket to *Goat Song*. Tower had died today and Goddard was very blue — He held my hand through two acts! and brought me home and had chocolate at Fichl's at midnight.

Wednesday, January 27
Lunch with Radin — much anthropological divergence. "If I convinced him, he'd lose all his interest in anthropology." Just so.

— Work on Religion book to send to Social Research application.
— Dinner with E. MacKinstry, with Dorothy Lathrop and [*sic*]
illustrators and Miss Massey and her friend in the evening. Drinks
and cigarettes and showed my — Bunny's — Katcina pictures to
admiring audience.

Thursday, January 28
   Margaret's pictures came and I mailed them according to directions. It's quite good. — Miss Beckwith with me to anthropology
lunch. Down to tea with Louise Bogan at Brevoort. . . . Back to
Bunny's for Radin's lecture — COLD!

Friday, January 29
   Lunch with Gladys.
   Down to hospital to see Esther Schiff with Bunny — and down to
Hazel's for tea. Met Eda Lou for dinner with Louise Bogan,
Raymond, Leonie, and — van Slyke and her husband. Then to
Poetry group to Louise's reading. . . . Edmund Wilson, Rolfe
Humphries, Genevieve Taggard, Robert W. . . . (?). . . . Louise
was a lovely figure — read with an accent of disdain, very becoming.

Saturday, January 30
   Shopping and theater for Louise and Leonie — a matinee. Hedda
Gabbler with Emily Stevens. A botched reading to my mind — it's
ridiculous making Hedda *care*. Someday Mrs. . . . . . will be played as
the complete idiot — enough to ruin any man. The MS symbol just
won't get by any more.
   Tea at Huyler's afterwards. Louise may be abroad with Maidie
while we are. She isn't happy, but that would be a miracle. She's
one of the most lovable beings. Out to Bedford Hills.

Sunday, January 31
   A quiet rainy sleeting Sunday.

Monday, February 1

Expected Spaziano, but he didn't come — too dangerously slippery! All the quieter. Tried an "Ethics" paper and settled down to Cochiti tales. Luxury before the fireplace. Stanley out at 5.

Tuesday, February 2

In to city. Lunch with Leonie. . . .

Miss R . . . says, "Her husband is living, did you know? And she has men friends. That's so broad. I think it's just fine don't you?" — What shall we do with the creature?

Ruth Sawtell to dinner. A very good sort. Work in room in evening.

Thursday, February 4

A great snowstorm. Cut lunch and we all had sandwiches and tea in seminar room. Dinner at Bunny's and Radin's course afterwards.

Friday, February 5

Lunch with Oetteking (!) and audited Goddard's books afterwards. Home at 5. Stanley had brought me my arctics and we climbed the snow fields to the house.

Saturday, February 6

Too snowy for the mason to come to finish the fireplace. Stanley stayed out and we had a snowed-in, busy day. Worked through my Scalp Dance MS.

Monday, February 8

Letter from Mrs. Mead of another cable "Well." (F. 3rd) Lunch with Jeannette Nichols, and provender-visit to Thelma Adamson who has been ill. Back to Seminar room and dictated to Miss Rodgers into machine, evening. Melville is late — Fan had appendicitis operation Saturday.

Tuesday, February 9

. . . First session of SW course — Spanish explorers. 9 registrants. Dinner with Sophie Theis — Tales of Roumania — the use of the extra railroad tiles; the parting gift of the live hen; the history of Evelyn Scott.

Wednesday, February 10

Typed at War Dance MS. Got lunch for Thelma and ate mine with Radin. Seminar on Environmental factors, Jacobs. Good, but dull. Typed, evening.

Part II

Anne Singleton

1889–1934

Margaret Mead

"THESE TWO worlds that I knew as a child stretched out in all directions. Happiness was a world that I lived in all by myself and for precious moments. These moments were my pearls of great price." Ruth Benedict wrote this of herself in "The Story of My Life . . ."

The sense of living different lives, of meeting predetermined ways of life which were not intrinsically her own, of incompatibility between her own temperament and any particular version of American culture, never left her. Long ago, as a small child, she had learned the inadvisability of sharing with anyone what she really felt. An episode when a servant girl on a nearby farm committed suicide, and her religious grandparents, while sending her to school to read about the noble Cato, condemned the girl out of hand left a triple imprint. It did not make sense to her that suicide should be applauded among the ancient Romans and at the same time be execrated in northern New York State. Yet if one tried to say this to the people one loved most in the world, they not only would not agree but would be hurt and shocked and alienated. The world was so ordered that one must at whatever cost live up to the ethical standards not of ancient Rome but of modern America. It was better to fold one's long legs under a cotton print dress, smile with distant sweetness, and retire into a world of one's own, one's hands dutifully busy with household chores, one's eyes turned to the changing beauty of the shifting light outside on springing peach bloom or to the hard flash of sunlight on sleet-laden trees. It was far better to be silent than to grieve the grandfather who was all the father she knew, or to sadden further the heart of her mother who continued in deep widowhood and, on each anniversary, revived with frightening emotion the death of her husband who had been prematurely cut off when his two daughters were twenty months and three months old. It was better not to pucker the brow of the little grandmother who always "gave you a kiss if she passed you in the hall" and about whom she wrote in the poem "Of Graves":[1]

> My grandmother was slim and white,
>   And idle as can be,
> And sometimes in the bright sunlight
>   She'd shiver suddenly.
>
> She always laughed a little laugh
>   And nodded down to me:
> "The rabbit nibbled at the grass
>   Will someday cover me."
>
> And days I shiver swift and strange,
>   This still is what I see:
> Sunlight and rabbit in the grass.
>   And peace possesses me.

It was better, too, not to get into fruitless arguments with her sister who was almost close enough to be a twin, whose beauty was as sunny as her own was somber, and whom she always saw as untroubled by demons.

Ruth Benedict loved the minutiae of real life, and we spent hours telling each other stories about people whom the other had never met, wondering and speculating why they had done or felt or thought what they seemed to have. But in all the stories she told there was no one whom she had really hated or even feared. Her own feeling of being different she saw as a threat to the happiness and the incomprehensible contentment and involvement of the people around her. Her inappropriate gay laughter at some incongruity which no one else recognized was read by her sister as "liking to see people put on a griddle," and in later life it frightened serious young male students who felt uncomfortable studying under a woman who had so much power to hinder or to help them. As late as 1925, Edward Sapir, replying to a letter from her about the loveliness of individuality, protested: "There is something cruel, Ruth, in your mad love of psychic irregularities. Do you not feel that you extract your loveliness from a mutely resisting Nature who will have her terrible revenge?" [2]

The violent temper of her early years was subdued summarily by an event which, as she described it, had an almost medieval quality — when her mother forced her to kneel with a candle on a cold floor until God granted her prayer that she would never again so completely lose control of her temper. And she never did.

The beauty of her father's face in death, only indirectly remembered, survived for her in the inexplicable captivation of El Greco's Fray Felix Hortensio Paravicino,[3] a portrait which she found in the Boston Museum (and which her mother later said resembled her father more than any photograph), in her strong sense of the beauty of the dead, and in the terrible gap which she felt between what any living human being was and what a human being might be. In later years a lecture which she was trying to give would become a torture of fading attention as before her eyes there would move a procession of eidetic figures of bedraggled, half-human creatures, straggling like dust-covered fowl into a poultry house, fit only for the food of more glorious beings. And one of the most violent disagreements she and I ever had was over the ceiling of the Sistine Chapel — whose outsized demigods repelled me and delighted her — as she smiled mischievously, saying, "I knew you wouldn't like it."

Deeply religious, the orthodoxy of her childhood soon lost any power except as a pattern that had meaning for others. I can still recall the passionate repudiation in her voice as she looked at the towers of Notre Dame, across the Seine from where we were sitting in a little churchyard, and said, "Isn't it unbearable that that is all about nothing?" This feeling comes out in the bitterness of such a poem as "Ripeness Is All":[4]

> The star that loosed this arrow down the dark
> Is centuries-long extinguished, and its ray
> Clean as a pinpoint, perfect to the mark,

Shivers not yet to void. Bodies decay,
Life being put asunder, and sweet sound
No longer holds the air where streams are bound,

Only this gleam is fathered of the dead,
A goblin birth, having no source in heaven
Nor in men's eyes, a disinherited
And phantom thing, that soon shall scatter even
Its slight and tapered essence, and the dark
Close down at length over its gutted spark.

Preposterous years, held taut in nothingness
To carry so a futile beam to earth,
Though night be nothing profited, no less
Outstare our trivial doubting. Death and birth
Are whimsies of the wind; nothing avails;
Yet till its term is spent, no star beam fails.

Her deep, cut-off melancholy was accentuated by a deafness in
one ear, so that her detached smile was often a smile of gentle in-
comprehension as well as one of equally gentle estrangement. Yet
combined with this strain of almost unmanageable depression went a
sensuous delight in life — in swimming and dancing, in the heat and
sting of the changing seasons, in startlingly sharp kinesthetic perceptions, as in a dream "where I couldn't see the shroud, but I felt the
scissors cold against my skin as the cloth was slit down the back." [5]
The long summers on the farm and the later summers at the lake
in New Hampshire kept clear and alive the imagery which she used
first in her poetry and later in her prose writing. In an early, unpublished poem she wrote:

The maple buds are scarlet on the sky
Again — warm clustering rubies wedded of the sun —
Spring has come back to winter-famished places . . .

And in another version of this poem she tried a shift of imagery:

The maples lift the brightening of their life
Drop by red drop against the sky again.

It was always real maple buds, real streams, actual sleet-covered trees about which she wrote; the words came and went in an effort to capture the image. Bred on the King James Bible and on early American poetry with its hemlocks and fringed gentians and rabbits, she was seldom tempted to echo words rather than to attempt to reproduce images.

Later, the stuff of Indian myth and ritual, drawing as it did on the same landscape, became one of the doorways through which the separated parts of her life began to be united.

But in 1921, when Ruth Benedict entered anthropology, she still believed that it was safest to keep most of her personal imaginative life to herself. The poems which she wrote under the pseudonym of Ruth Stanhope she showed to no one. Under another pseudonym, Edgar Stanhope, she had planned to write "chemical detective stories" for which Stanley would supply the plots.[6] Her long struggle with the manuscript on the fate of outstanding women born before their time was also conducted in strict privacy,[7] punctuated by periods of too great immediate delight in life or of despair, when she wrote nothing. When later she began to publish poems, these appeared under still another pseudonym — Anne Singleton.[8]

The year 1923 marked not only the publication of her doctoral thesis, "The Concept of the Guardian Spirit in North America," [9] but also the beginning of a series of friendships in which the old taboos on confidence could be dropped. Characteristically, however, she buried the past. She never told me what her original pseudonym had been nor did she ever show me any of the drafts of the life of Mary Wollstonecraft, although she kept them carefully. A few of the earlier poems were slowly produced, but with no word as to whether they had ever been published.

Chief among these relationships which, for the first time, made her interest in writing poetry a lively, shared preoccupation was her friendship with Edward Sapir, which began in formal anthropological terms but soon overflowed into an interchange of poems and discussions of poetry. As she came to know Léonie Adams and Louise Bogan and Eda Lou Walton, she had their poems, too, to enjoy in manuscript and as part of the lives of people she knew. Many of our poems grew out of our relationships to one another, and the intensities of the contemporary human plots were discussed and rediscussed against the background of the childhood experience and special temperament of each. Sapir dedicated "Zuñi" [10] and "Signal" [11] to Ruth Benedict, and "Ariel" [12] to me. She wrote "Lift Up Your Heart" [13] and "This Gabriel" [14] for me. I wrote "Misericordia" [15] and "Absolute Benison" [16] for her, and "For a Proud Lady" [17] for Louise Bogan.

Zuñi

Edward Sapir

I send you this. Through the monotony
Of mumbling melody, the established fall
And rise of the slow, dreaming ritual,
Through the dry glitter of the desert sea
And sharpness of the mesa keep the flowing
Of your spirit, in many branching ways,
Be running mirrors to the colored maze,
Not pool enchanted nor a water slowing.

Hear on the wing, see in a flash, retreat!
Beauty is brightest when the eye is fleet.
And priests are singing softly on the sand
And the four colored points and zenith stand;
The desert crawls and leaps, the eagle flies.
Put wax into your ears and close your eyes.

Ariel (to M.M.)

Edward Sapir

Of the heedless sun are you an Ariel,
Rising through cloud to a discovered blue,
The windy, rocking landmarks travel through
And clamber up a crazy pinnacle.
Be wild, oblivious, nor think how fell
One mocking angel and a frightened crew
Through all the sunny pools of air into
The dark and wondrous ritual of Hell.

For you have footing poised and in your breast
The interchange of breath, both quick and slow.
Reckless, be safe. The little wise feet know
Sun-way and cloud's and sudden earthen aim,
And steps of beauty quicken into flame
Wherein you burn up wholly in arrest.

Misericordia

Margaret Mead

Summer, betray this tree again!
Bind her in winding sheets of green;
With empty promises unlock her lips;
Sift futile pollen through her finger-tips.
Curve those tense hands so tightened in disdain,
To eager chalices for falling rain.
Break and elaborate that frozen line
With golden tendril and swift sinuous vine.
Summer, in mercy blur this bare delight
Of chiseled boughs against the winter night.

Absolute Benison

Margaret Mead

Those who delighted feed on difference
Measure the larkspur head-higher than the rose,
Can find no benison in burials,
The only absolute that summer knows.

But those who weary of this variance
Which only an impertinence can name,
Weary of matching petal with pale petal
To find them similar but not the same,

Turn with nostalgia to that darkened garden
Where all eternal replicas are kept,
And the first rose and the first lark song
Since the first springtime have slept.

For a Proud Lady

Margaret Mead

Yours is a proud and fearful heart
That snares the weather in its mood,
As once you snatched the morning mists
All veils for your one maidenhood.

The snow is but a banner white
Run up by God for your defeat;
You take cold winter days to read
Fate patterned in indifferent sleet.

And sweeter weathers have no art
To dull this prophecy of harm;
You only watch the hare-bell's tilt
To hear instead its belled alarum.

Each of us made a different contribution. The poems of Léonie
Adams gave her pure delight and a measure of her own slender gift.
Long, intricate discussions with me marked the beginning of the
self-awareness that made it possible for her to write "The Story of
My Life . . ." in 1935. But it was in the vivid, voluminous correspondence with Edward Sapir that her own poetic interest and
capacity matured. Only one side of their correspondence — his
letters to her — survive. Between 1923 and 1925 they both wrote
continually, sometimes several times a week, exchanging and com-
menting on almost every poem. Each planned a book of verse, with
the other's comments in mind, and as a sort of daily fare they also
planned a special anthology.

In 1928, Harcourt Brace turned down her manuscript of verse in
an unsigned letter:[18]

Mr. Louis Untermeyer has turned over your manuscript to us
and we have held it for a more careful reading. This poetry has
a definite quality and is far more distinctive than most of the
manuscripts we see. Unfortunately, however, there is so small a

market for poetry that we hesitate to publish even what might be considered "appealing" verse. In the case of your own grave and highly thoughtful work, that potential market would be still small. We have come to the regretful conclusion that publishing this manuscript would be a doubtful venture and, much as we admire it, we are compelled to return it to you.

Although she continued to write poetry and to send around poems which had not yet been accepted by one or another of the little poetry magazines, the rejection of this manuscript really ended her aspirations as a poet. In a letter from Paris, Léonie Adams wrote to her,[19] "I am sorry Harcourt didn't take the poems but I feel more and more that such things are accidents and of no mortal consequence." But she said, "They aren't good enough to give one's life to," for she never had any doubt that publication is the validation of the work of a poet.

Harcourt Brace also rejected Sapir's manuscript, and Ruth Benedict describes his reaction in a letter to me:[20]

A rotten thing happened about the poems. . . . He suggested taking his poems to Louis Untermeyer if he was back, and I encouraged him of course. I said I'd call Harcourt and see if Untermeyer was expected back. I called one morning at 9 AM and was put right on Untermeyer's wire and he answered the call. I introduced myself and he asked me down to lunch. I couldn't and he made the appointment for next Monday. I told him Sapir was in town for the week and would like to bring in his volume of poems. He said, "No, tell him to send them in the regular channels. The proposition of printing verse has its difficulties down here, and I can't take but one volume to Harcourt with my enthusiastic endorsement." — I'd hoped it would never come to a direct issue between these two volumes in this way, and of course there was nothing to do but to tell Edward just what happened. He said it was only the first dodge Untermeyer thought of, and he congratulated me on the good auguries for my book; he took it altogether well, but he was much depressed. He took the volume away from me, and said he'd bury it. I had a feeling that he'd put a bigger stake on recognition through his verse than I had on mine and if I could, I'd have turned the publication over to him in a minute.

Her own manuscript was rejected a week later.

As she gained in assurance in anthropology and came to be known as an anthropologist also among those who were interested in poetry, poetry journals and other publications carried remarks that broke the barrier between "Anne Singleton" and Ruth Benedict. On one of these, she herself commented:[21]

> Léonie had Untermeyer's new *American* poetry there.[22] He announces "Anne Singleton — the pseudonym under which a well-known anthropologist writes her poems — " and says she's "interesting but influenced; her cadences do not conceal the accents of Léonie Adams and Louise Bogan. Her metaphysics are her own." "The Son of Man" and "Unshadowed Pool" are there. — When he gets out another edition they'll be under the name of Ruth Benedict; I won't be so bepseudonymed.

From the beginning, Sapir chafed against the concealment as nonsensical. In 1924, when she was sending out poems, he wrote to her:[23]

> By the way, you mustn't dare use a nom de plume. No tricks of the protective coloration type. Better develop a hide if you're going to lose your conscience.

In 1925, when Frances Herskovits questioned the authorship of poems which appeared in *The Measure*, he wrote again:[24]

> She . . . was told it was an unknown person who wrote in, apparently, from Texas. But apparently Melville and she know you are writing verse. It seems absurd to make such an ado about concealment, don't you think?

And in 1926, he again chided her:[25]

I rather sympathize with Eda Lou Walton about your pen name. You know how I feel about ever toying with the idea of dissociation of personality. I hate it. Lie outright if you have to, but for God's sake don't stylize the lie into a pretty institution.

Gradually she came closer to being willing to merge the two identities. The real climax came in the late summer of 1925, when she returned from Zuñi to find Stanley brooding over a chance remark overheard about her poems. He had her take a copy of a poetry magazine which contained a group of her poems and paste new postage stamps over the name of every author; then he set himself the task of identifying the poems that were hers. She wrote me triumphantly: "He got every one right." This episode inaugurated the best years of their marriage.

This was a temporary state, however, for the things she said in her verse were uncongenial to him. But it made it possible for her to work toward the publication of a book which would have appeared as the work of Ruth Benedict. However, the early years of the depression were particularly unfavorable for getting poetry published, and in the end she published only very few poems as Ruth Benedict. By this time, 1933, the manuscript of *Patterns of Culture* had been accepted. After the book's conspicuous success, she was caught in an unwillingness to trade on her success in one field to bolster up a much more minor success in another.[26]

At the same time that she gave up working seriously at writing poetry, she also stopped work on a book on religion, a book to which Sapir frequently refers in his letters to her. In the summer of 1928, she drafted a chapter on religion for a textbook that Boas was preparing,[27] and did not return again to the subject except in lectures.

During the whole period in which she was publishing in the poetry magazines, she kept careful card records of each poem's circulation:

Ways Not Winds' Ways

NR
Dial   Feb. 28
Century   March 7

Scribners   April 23
"Books"   Nov. 25
Sat. Review   Jan. 29
Nation or Poetry   3/10/30
Harpers   4/10/30
Nation   taken

The year usually is lacking, for one can remember — for a while —
when one has written and submitted a poem. Gradually her comments on Anne Singleton became more and more detached:[28]
"Won't an editor ever print a line of mine without knifing poor
Anne Singleton?" In letters to me she began to use an older name,
"Sally," for the self who came and went and who would "dictate"
lines only when it suited her.

In 1929, she wrote to me, in comment on a small book of rumina-
tions which I had left behind when I went to the field:[29]

I save the little manuscript book like a too scant water supply
on a voyage in an open boat. But this morning I waked hours
ago with a back and forth rocking restlessness and I took out
my flagon. I've been reading the first pages, about the making
of symbols, and the figure you use of the held-breath suspense
till, it may be after a long time, the symbol is perfected, moved
me like a universal, newly discovered clue. We talked of it last
spring and perhaps it was only incubating all the time. It seemed
to me yours was the right phrasing, the breaking of the chrysalis
fact into the butterfly significance and that we wasted time
combing experience (fact) for symbols (significance). The part
of wisdom is, as you say, the hushed watching of experience till
it takes on the form it will wear, the wings it will fly with.
That's congenial, very, to my feeling about the process of verse
— incubation, gestation. And I'd never made half enough of it.

Sapir turned against poetry rather than giving it up, and as he
became immersed in the hustle of everyday anthropological administration and politics — in which he and Boas were often on opposite
sides — Ruth Benedict's comments on meetings with him reflected

an increasing exasperation. In a letter describing the American Anthropological Association meeting in 1928, she wrote:[30]

Christmas meetings have been feeble editions of the Congress — terribly feeble. Edward's here and Radin and Mel and Papa Franz is at all meetings though he looks old and grey. But I've been flatly bored. Out of the evening I spent with Edward there was one hour of free reciprocity and a couple of excellent moments and five hours was on the ogre of THE AGE and the piffle of mental activity. He's singing hymns to the noble business man — four square and operating with the solid materials of existence. The way for us to follow in his footsteps is to serve on committees and importance will descend upon us. Why, THE AGE has no need of books of verse — that finished off poetry. It was pitiful. The good side of it is his enjoyment of the lectures I heard him give at the meetings — and the charm and assurance he has in them. Nobody but Gladys could resist him.

Radin is in Edward's good graces in the old degree and basks in it as if the sun had selected his garden plot out of all the world. Edward remarked that he'd always choose Paul and Ogburn (my divinities didn't suit him — meaning Papa Franz — we were talking about Ogburn). He says you must lower your voice and breathe a little sigh before you mention Ogburn's name for he's in the forefront of power — dispenses the money for the Social Research Council etc.

The "Woods Hole" for Anthropology, at Santa Fe, went through with flying colors. Kidder administers everything. They have a budget of $40,000 a year of which $7000 goes for fellowships — predoctorate for work under instruction in the SW, Southern Plains, and Mohave region. There are to be three leaders in charge this summer — Kidder, Kroeber and Sapir. . . . He'll do Navaho language. — It's all taking the region out of the Papa Franz-Gladys combination, and I imagine that problem will be still further in the background by the time Gladys is ready to revert to Navaho again. Father Bernard too is making a stand that his manuscript, the big one Gladys was

working on, should go to Edward for editorial work, not to
Gladys.

The professional interests which had first brought Ruth Benedict
and Sapir together and then had been interwoven with their interest in poetry now slowly moved them somewhat apart.

The years between the commencement of her work on *Patterns of
Culture* and the outbreak of the war were trying and difficult. There
was no money for students and no jobs for them. There was great
uncertainty about the future of the department. She worried, too,
about how Stanley was making out after she had helped him to buy
a new house and had set it up for him. But a new integration came
out of these years which gathered up the part of herself which had
always wanted to be committed to an absorbing moral purpose, as
she became involved in working for better race relations and for a
more democratic society. In this context, the themes she had hoped
to find in Mary Wollstonecraft and the passion she had expressed
in her early satires were woven back into her contemporary life.
Sapir, in the same world climate, turned his back in the end upon
administration and anthropological politics to plunge into a passionate study of Semitics.

But Ruth Benedict did not find as complete absorption until,
toward the end of the war, she did her work on Japan, when all the
themes — anthropological "sense," delight in the beauty of a pattern, overwhelming pity for human suffering, and a hope that something might be done about it by an increase in scientific knowledge
of human behavior — came together.

The Story of My Life . . .*

THE STORY of my life begins when I was twenty-one months old, at
the time my father died. That March my father came back from
Trinidad where he had gone in a vain attempt to throw off the fever
that was killing him, and ten days later he died. He had been ill for
the year before, and they think now that he had been infected with
an obscure disease during a certain operation. He was a young
surgeon with a passionate love of his work and of research,[1] and nine
months before his death he had had to give up his practice in New
York and come home with my mother and me to her father's farm.
I have very little idea what he was really like, but the part he played
in my childhood, and still plays, was none the less great for that. It
may even be that I kept some memory of him, for they tell me that
all through my childhood I called one chair in the house my father's
chair, a chair no one else associated with my father. They do not
know, but they think it was the chair he sat up in the one time
during the last ten days of his life when they got him up out of bed.
If I did keep this memory of my father's face, it would explain
many things that puzzle me, for certainly these glimmerings have
nothing to do with his pictures, which were taken in full health and
with the round beard and whiskers that were the fashion of the
times. My memories have to do, instead, with a worn face illu-

* Uncompleted, partly typewritten, partly handwritten manuscript, prepared
for MM in 1935, at a time when life histories were becoming a matter of
anthropological interest.

97

minated with the translucence of illness, and very beautiful. There is no dispute that my father was beautiful. The power that such faces had over me I never associated with my father till the day I took my mother to the Boston Museum to see my favorite of all such faces, El Greco's Fray Felix Hortensio Paravicino.[2] Ever since I had first discovered that picture I had found ways and means of getting to Boston to see it; my feeling for it was over and above my appreciation of the superb finality of the painter's art. My visits were acts of friendship and love for the man painted. I always called him "mine." One day many years after I was married my mother was in Boston with me. She knows little of painting, and an El Greco I liked meant nothing to her. But when we went into the large gallery where it hangs she went at once to the portrait, not knowing it was "mine." I could not understand. Finally she turned to me and said, "It is your father. It is your father just before he died. There are no pictures of him as he looked then, but now you know what he looked like."

My aunt told me not many months ago something that, though I remember nothing of it, makes it the more likely that this memory of my father's face is real, but that the transfiguration I attribute to it was the transfiguration of death and not of illness. My mother was crushed by my father's death. She was left with two babies, one three months old, and she wanted desperately to have me remember my father. She took me into the room where he lay in his coffin, and in an hysteria of weeping implored me to remember. Nothing is left to me consciously of this experience, but if it is suppressed it would go a long way to explain the effect my mother's weeping has always had upon me. She made a cult of grief out of my father's death, and every March she wept in church and in bed at night. It always had the same effect on me, an excruciating misery with physical trembling of a peculiar involuntary kind which culminated periodically in rigidity like an orgasm. It was not an expression of love for my mother, though I often pitied her. The affect was devastating, an affect that would be intelligible if it were a calling up of my "primal scene," the forgotten hour when my mother had implored me to remember, and, loving my father's face, I had violently repudiated her and her grief.

Certainly from my earliest childhood I recognized two worlds, whether or not my knowledge was born at that tragic scene at my father's coffin — the world of my father, which was the world of death and which was beautiful, and the world of confusion and explosive weeping which I repudiated. I did not love my mother; I resented her cult of grief, and her worry and concern about little things. But I could always retire to my other world, and to this world my father belonged. I identified him with everything calm and beautiful that came my way. One of the first scenes I remember in detail was in the living room at my grandfather's with all the family about. I had just said that the Christ on the wall — the big "Christ before Pilate" — was my father, and my mother's face was set for the scene of grief any mention of my father always called up, and my grandparents' faces were shocked with the blasphemy, or perhaps only the naïveté, of my illusion.

My reaction to death was, I think, just another aspect of my feeling about my father. When I was four, my grandmother took me, in the casual neighborhood custom of that farming country, to a tenant house on the hill where the baby had just died, and we saw the dead child as a matter of course. She was laid out in the stiff parlor, and I remember vividly her transparent beauty. She seemed to me the loveliest thing I had ever seen, and I remember contrasting her with the ragamuffin brothers and sisters and the bedraggled mother. If they had died, mightn't they have been beautiful like that? But they hadn't.

This feeling about physical death has never left me. I used to think more often than I do now about lying dead myself. It was a deeply felt sanction for living decently, for even death couldn't make that special transformation out of a face filled with loathing and pettiness. Even now I feel I've been cheated or unfaithful if I can't see the dead face of a person I've loved. Sometimes they're disappointments, but often not. Stanley's father I never saw in my life except broken and querulous and in an institution. But in his coffin I really saw him, and it was more than all the rest. It seemed wanton that I was the only one who could be glad that he had won a face like that.

These two worlds that I knew as a child stretched out in all directions. Happiness was in a world I lived in all by myself, and for precious moments. These moments were my pearls of great price. There were quite a number of ways I could put myself in order for them; I associate them especially with holding a sleeping kitten on my lap on the woodhouse steps looking out over the east hills, and with shelling peas for the family — there were thirteen or fourteen to feed and it was a long job — at peace on the front porch while everybody else was busy in the kitchen. The transition back again into the mundane world and all its confusions was likely to be stormy. The family were constantly exercised about my ungovernable tantrums. They came on for no reason the family could fathom, and they swept on thereafter without my feeling that I had any participation in them. I was violent either to myself or to anyone else within reach. Of course I was always punished and wept over, but I can't remember any guilt about the tantrums. What I was guilty about was the spoiling of my moments, my bogging myself down in violence so that they didn't come again. I was guilty enough about that, but it was a guilt toward myself, not a social guilt.

In this happy world I lived in by myself I had several different games. The one I remember best was the beautiful country on the other side of the west hill where a family lived who had a little girl about my age. This imaginary playmate and her family lived a warm, friendly life without recriminations and brawls. So far as I can remember I and the little girl mostly explored hand in hand the unparalleled beauty of the country over the hill. About the time I was five my mother thought I was old enough to stand the climb up the west hill, and one day I went up with her and my aunts. I had been promised that we'd go up to the top and look over. It was a long climb for my legs, and I was very hot and tired when at last we came to the edge of the pasture and looked down into the rolling hills beyond — and *Uncle George's farm.* Instead of the wonderland I'd pictured, it was all familiar and anything-but-romantic territory. We had driven through the ravine to Uncle George's every holiday since I could remember. And that was all. I never played again with my little playmate over the hill.

I never ran away again either. During my babyhood running away figured as my family crime along with my tantrums. I remember only twice, but they were both great occasions. The earliest I remember chiefly for my dilemma afterwards. Mother had gone away for a few days' visit when I was three or four, and had asked for my promise that I wouldn't run away while she was gone. But I did. When she got back she questioned me about my promise, and I refused to answer. She ruled that I should stay in the house till I'd told her. But having me cooped up in the house didn't work very well, and I was prolonging it day by day. I couldn't tell her. As I think of it now, I imagine that running away and all that concerned it belonged to my "other" world, and I couldn't bring myself to talk to Mother about it. Certainly there was no question of staving off punishment in my refusal, for the punishment would end as soon as I told. The whole family were hard put to it, and after I'd experimentally turned on the spigot of the kerosene can in the woodhouse and let out the whole contents on the floor, Mother decided to change her ruling. I could think of a great many things to do, and they were just as inconvenient as if they had been malicious. So one morning Mother took me into the downstairs bedroom and said that I must stay there without anything to eat till I'd told. I remember very well my efforts all that day. The family ate dinner at noon, and the afternoon wore on. They ate supper and the lights were lighted. Mother sat with me most of the day waiting. At last I got it out. My relief was like physical drunkenness. I had achieved one of the most difficult tasks I've ever been set. Mother took me out to the dining room and we ate together alone by the lamplight.

It wasn't till I was about six that I remember thinking out this reluctance to tell about the things that concerned me most nearly. I had gone out into the barn to jump in the hay, but instead I went to a retreat of mine in the haymow. Under a big beam one could make a cavern in the hay completely concealed in the dark. It was a hiding place we used in hide-and-seek in the haymows, but I used to go there alone and lie in the hot dark, the hayseeds sticking to my wet skin. The family could always understand jumping in the hay, but they could never have understood lying in the dark in the hay if there wasn't a hide-and-seek game going on. (I suppose I liked my hiding place because it was my "grave," and they certainly would have disapproved if they'd known that.) That day it came to me with a brilliant flash of illumination that I could always without fail have myself for company, and that if I didn't talk to anybody about the things that mattered to me no one could ever take them away. I think that was the fundamental knowledge that I lived on till I was thirty-five. I added to it then that being oneself was too big a job to keep the seal of secrecy on always, and other people could take it or leave it. But until I was thirty-five I believed that the things that mattered must always hurt other people to know or make them interfere, and the point was to avoid this. My feeling about my verse and my nom de plume, my relations to Stanley, all are unintelligible without the rule of life I discovered in the haymow.

The second running away I remember added a codicil to my rule of life, and it was a codicil I phrased explicitly before I phrased the main proposition. Mother thought that I was playing in the elder patch, which was allowed, but I had set off for the flat, which was a long excursion across the railroad tracks. When I got down there, I found Grandfather was haying on the flat, and he did not know I had run away. Now my grandfather was the one person who stood out for me above all others. He was a grand old man with strong, calm movements, a patriarch who led us all in family prayers on our knees every morning around the breakfast table. The one phrase he used in every prayer was that the Lord should lead us toward "the light that shineth more and more unto the perfect day." The punishments the rest of the family administered when I had tantrums never registered in my consciousness, but Grandfather's rising from his chair and going to the barn was a terrible memory. I did not have tantrums after that when he was in the house.

That day on the flat Grandfather welcomed me royally. He took me on the haywagon to load the hay, and into the barn while he threw over the sweet-smelling load. When they came up for milking I rode up on the empty wagons. But here was a difficulty, and I had to tell Grandfather that Mother didn't know I'd gone to the flat. He smiled down at me and said, "Well, if she doesn't ask, we won't tell her." It was a high point in my life. I had a secret with Grandfather, and I could see that he liked it as well as I did. Pretty soon I strolled into the house from the elder patch, and Mother asked me, "Were you playing in the elder patch all this time?" I said yes, and it didn't bother me at all; why should it? But that evening after milking, when Grandfather came in for supper, he lifted me up to his face and whispered to me, "Did Mother ask?" What could I do? I said no, and he smiled at me again. But I ate no supper. I had lied to my grandfather, and that was a different matter. My grandfather, I suppose, belonged to "my" life; anyway he was one of my self-elected loyalties, and I'd been false to it. Life was more complicated than I had supposed, and somehow, somehow after that I must plan so that I wouldn't have to *lie to Grandfather.*

In this education in the complexities of ethics I was forced into one step which I thought very important. Margery and I said the Lord's prayer every night at Mother's knee, and the phrase that bothered me was the "Forgive us our debts." I understood it very literally as meaning that everything I had done would be wiped out as if it had not been. Every night, then, I started over again with a sheet as clean as I thought Margery's was. I do not remember what sin I had on my conscience the night I first got out of bed and said the prayer over again omitting the "Forgive us our sins." It was certainly before I was six. I was at least twelve years old and full grown before I ever said it again. I had no Puritan load on my conscience about my unforgiven sins, and no obsession about them. It was merely that by not saying the prayer I made myself responsible for them. I always said the part, "as we forgive our debtors," for that was a human forgiveness and was quite different from wiping the slate clean. I never discussed the matter with anyone, and it never occurred to me to consider that all authority was on the other side. I hadn't discovered that there could be any authority over and above the fact that it didn't seem right to me.

It is curious how small a part in my real life my sister played. We were always together. She was only eighteen months younger than I, a cherubically beautiful child with no behavior problems. As a playmate she cried easily and could be teased, and I rather scorned these things, but usually I played a decent enough role of elder sister. In my tantrums I sometimes hit her, and Mother was always worrying about my hurting her. But I think I never did. I was certainly not jealous of her, though she was the family favorite and pet and they always talked of her beauty. I remember when I was fourteen how odd I thought a visitor's comment that I was beautiful. It is the single comment of the sort I ever heard till I was thirty. I hated reference to myself, and it was quite irrelevant to me whether I was ugly or beautiful. It just didn't belong to "my" world.

I can remember very little about the outer events of my first years of school. When I was five Mother began teaching in Norwich, three miles from the farm, and we lived in town during the week with one or other of my aunts as housekeeper. The only event I remember vividly from that year is my horror at myself for breaking the doll of the little girl who lived next door. We were playing amicably enough, when on an unaccountable impulse I dashed her doll to the sidewalk and it broke into smithereens. Her mother called me into her house. How could I explain to her mother? Obviously I couldn't; I couldn't even guess myself why I had done it. I was horrified and humiliated; I had done something without the slightest will of my own, something that made no sense. For years I used to dream about it.

For the next two years Mother taught in Missouri. The train trips were new experiences, and I still have a notebook chiefly concerned with the scenery, like: "The sun came up over the Mississippi like this: ◿," with red chalk painting in the sun. There were verses too. But my models in verse were execrable. I had *The Child's Book of Verse*, or something like that, but it wasn't the custom to read anything but doggerel to children. When I could read — and I read anything I could find at seven — I made a favorite of Jean Ingelow, one of the volumes around Grandfather's house. "Bregenz" and "The Judas Tree" were my prime favorites.

All through my childhood I had to cope with various disabilities. My deafness was a consequence of babyhood measles, and it wasn't until I was five that anyone discovered that I couldn't hear as well as other children. The theory was that I didn't choose to answer — which was true too. I used to get a penny for every day when I answered each time at the first word. And I usually earned the penny. But my hearing was pretty bad at this time, and doctors began taking out my tonsils and trying by various means to help keep my eardrums intact.

The sickness that followed me all through my childhood was "bilious attacks." No one can date when these began, but I did not have them before my father died. From the time I was two or three until I began to menstruate I always had them, and at least by the time I was seven or eight had settled down into a rhythmic recurrence. For years and years they descended upon me about every six weeks, and curiously enough for the first ten years my menstrual periods had the same six-weekly rhythm. Menstruation superseded them. I had a great deal of menstrual pain as a child, but never once did it induce another bilious attack.

During these attacks, I lay in bed prostrated with vomiting for a couple of days. I always took these descents into complete misery with a very good grace, and was an excellent and uncomplaining patient. The third day, when I sat up in bed for my first poached egg, was always a high watermark of felicity, a day I think of with greater pleasure than any of the days when I was well.

The tantrums continued all this time, and when they were bad I often vomited. But I did not connect the two. Everything about the two was different. Nevertheless there may well have been in both a common symbolism of rejection.

I had two deeply felt tabus that are among my earliest memories and have continued through most of my life; certainly they were established before we left the farm the fall that I was six. One of these was against crying before anyone. It was a final humiliation which was devastating to me. It never occurred except in the terrible aftermaths of my tantrums when the sin of violence to "my" world overwhelmed all other tabus. But I dreamed of it. My common exposure dreams were minutely detailed experiences of bursting into tears in a room filled with attentive well-known faces. This tabu continued in full force until long after I was married. One day then when I was very low I had one of the most beautiful daydreams of my life — I am using "daydream" for that peculiar experience that has often been so much more actual than any dream — and all the later changes in my tabu on weeping are tied up with that day-dream. I was alone on a great desert that was dominated by a magnificent Egyptian sphinx. Nothing can describe the wisdom and irony of that sphinx's face, and I went to it and buried my face on its paws and wept and wept — happily and with confidence. And the paws of the sphinx were soft and furry like a kitten's. (I had wept before "my" world, and the tabu was never so compulsive after that.)

The other tabu of my childhood was against the expression of pain. At seven or eight in Missouri I remember lying awake all night with a toothache and not calling anyone. At five I remember jumping off a beam in the barn and fainting with a sprained ankle. But I crawled into the hay afterward to try to prevent anyone's finding me and seeing my pain. Both these tabus I remember vividly when I was old enough to wash the dishes at the farm. I was about nine or ten, and there were always thirteen or fourteen in the family. It was my share of the work to wash the breakfast and dinner dishes while Margery dried, and I think I have never since been so tired as I used to be when I finished. I would look at the aunts and think how terrible it was that everyone was as tired as I was. I had two techniques to keep from crying with my weariness. One was to keep a glass of water on the shelf and drink down the lump in my throat, and the other was to go to the privy and wait till I'd dried my eyes. After the dishes were done I used to go to the attic and let the tears come in solitude. But I never told or begged off or wept in public.

Looking back on it, it seems likely enough that these tabus — they were my most stringently required virtues — grew out of my "primal scene" too. They belonged to the half of the picture I repudiated, and to be guilty of these breaches was to ally myself to the "other" world. There is a certain amount of evidence of this in the vividness with which I remember early scenes of my mother's pain — certainly it was in her that I minded such experiences most. She had a great deal of dentistry done before we left the farm when I was six, and she had no tabu on expressing pain. My feeling at these times was nearest to humiliation — and repudiation. Even when I was fourteen I vomited when she burned herself with hot candy, but it was her groans that upset me, not pity for her pain.

After two years in Missouri, Mother went to a town in Minnesota to be "lady principal" of a coeducational academy. For the first time people began to play some real part in my life — not very real, but at least occupying. At school I was the leader of the little group of the élite, and curiously all the professors' children were girls and those we took in were also girls. Boys did not figure at all. Even so, the person I remember most warmly out of these years was the janitor of the school, a nice-looking man of perhaps forty who used to make wonderful purple illuminated title pages for us and who was subsequently discharged under a cloud — for soliciting young girls, though at the time I did not understand. He was certainly very kind to me, and the warmest person I knew. I liked to have him stroke back my hair and know how well he liked me.

Ever since I had stopped playing with my little playmate who lived over the hill, "my" world had been one I made up mostly out of my Bible. I was brought up in the midst of the church: my grandfather whom I loved was a Baptist deacon and a pillar of the religious community; we went to church and Sunday school as a matter of course. Nevertheless my religious life had nothing to do with institutional Christianity nor with church creeds. I loved the story of Christ, and I knew it better than the ministers before I was ten. I had thought the picture of Christ on the wall *was* my father, and I think I never stopped believing it as far as my emotions went. The story of Jesus was "my" world. I liked that part of my Bible better than any other book I had. I can't disentangle now how much or how little I understood, but it was a way of life that made sense to me — that I "recognized" in a way I did not recognize my mother's world. I never identified my "religion" with the authority of the family, any more than I identified it with any dogmas, so that I never had to throw off a yoke of religious submission. Theological doubts never raised their head against me. For me, the gospels described a way of life, and Christ, who had lived that life. Besides, the church taught me to pray, and I took it at its word. Prayer was better than the playmate over the hill, but still it was much the same. Christ was a real person to me, and my favorite company. I learned most of what I knew about life from the Bible. I can't remember when I did not know about position in intercourse and about semen — I think I knew almost everything except menstruation, for I learned it all in the Bible stories, and it was all part of a great and good reality that held, too, the best things I knew.

Nevertheless the tantrums persisted. They were outside invasions of my person, and it seemed to me that devils swept down upon me. By this time I was full grown as far as stature was concerned — I was as tall as I am now at eleven — and Mother was doubly worried about my hurting Margery. Besides, the year we moved to Buffalo — I was eleven — I was unusually unaccountable. At last there was a time when I was having a seizure every day or so. After an especially bad week Mother summoned all her forces. I had had one going to bed. It was late and I was crying myself to exhaustion after one had passed. Mother talked to me solemnly and dictated a promise, which I repeated after her, never to have another tantrum. She went out of the room and brought back a Bible and a candle, and gave it to me to read at a verse which invoked the aid of Jehovah. Afterwards I slept the sleep of utter exhaustion. I never had another tantrum. Not that I was strengthened to repel them; I have never from that day to this had the familiar impulse.

What succeeded them were depressions. Until I thought about it carefully a year or so ago I'd always dated my depressions from my first years of menstruation, and indeed I menstruated for the first time the following year. But certainly all my ideology connects my tantrums and my depressions as two different manifestations of the same kink, one supplanting the other. Both I have always called my "devils," not realizing until now that I had slipped into the same usage about my depressions that I had always had for my tantrums. Both of them were protests against alienation from my Delectable Mountains, and both of them thrust me further from them and were therefore sins. I don't think during all these years I've ever loved and luxuriated in my fits of depression. They were always set over against my beautiful country, but they were more acceptable than unwanted participation in the "other" world that was not "mine."

All during these years no person had ever really mattered to me. I think I was a warm little girl, and I felt protective toward my mother and my sister, but the world was all a very strange place inhabited exclusively by alien people. I was considered very "touchy" about physical contacts, and Aunt Mamie used to play a game with me when I could hardly more than run around, which consisted in threatening to hug me while I ran and hid behind chairs and sofas. The big scene of the kind I remember was with Uncle Justin. Uncle Justin was my father's uncle and a Fundamentalist, Tremont Temple, Baptist parson. He was a big, cocksure man, and perhaps one of the reasons I hated him was that he always made my mother sad. (He had had a revelation from God that my father would not die.) When he came to our house he always prayed on his knees with the whole family, and I was afraid my mother would weep. He gave Margery a fifty cent piece on one visit for kissing him, and then tried to give me mine. But I ran in terror from room to room and finally hid on the treadle under the sewing machine.

No one in my childhood really got past my physical and emotional aloofness. They never got into "my" world. I began about this time to fantasy a world all inhabited by people of a strange dignity and grace. They moved about as I afterwards discovered Blake's figures move — not walking, but skimming the ground in one unbroken line, and they lived on a lovely hill where I used to go and watch them. I knew their faces, and I never admitted there any faces that I knew. Their world was something I called up voluntarily, never something that was obsessive, and as I grew older I added to it out of Blake's figures and out of the figures on the roof of the Sistine Chapel. But no one I knew was ever there.

The first person I ever saw who, I knew, belonged somewhere else than in the world I stood so aloof from was, amusingly enough, Mabel Dodge. It was when I was fourteen and she was an unmarried girl, five or six years older, living in the Becker family. The youngest Becker daughter was one of the first of those people who have been romantically devoted to me, and I used to see her older sister's friend around the house. I remember knowing that she lived for something I recognized, something different from those things for which most people around me lived. I am sure she never knew I existed, but I carried a very vivid image of her in my mind without being attracted to her emotionally at all.

Nothing seems to me more striking in my whole childhood than this small role that warm human relations played. I can't remember any longing to have any person love me, or any sense of frustration that I wasn't chosen. People did not figure even in matters of mere popularity; I can't remember any impulse to put myself across, or any recognition of inferiority if I was not a leader. In Owatonna I was very much the leader; in Buffalo, not at all. But it made no difference to me which way it was.

Just as striking is the small role that material things played. This is particularly curious because, from my childish point of view, we had everything in Owatonna, and in Buffalo from the time I was eleven we were very poor. This change was not so much a change in Mother's salary, as it was due to living conditions in a city and to the relative economic status of the people we knew. Still it was in part a matter of lesser salary. Mother elected to take the position of librarian in charge of the large staff because of its greater security as compared with the teaching jobs she had had in the Middle West. Library salaries could be depended upon to advance at a regular amount each year, and the job was permanent until retirement age. She went on a salary of sixty dollars a month — fifteen dollars a week for a family of four. I remember the momentous occasion of spending one dollar and fifty cents for a hat. Each year in rotation one of us could have a new coat. Margery's art lessons are the only nonessential expenditure I remember. One of the stories Mother still tells with feeling is of Margery describing the meat they'd had for dinner when she was invited to a friend's house: "It was a brown on the outside and red in the middle. *It was good.*" She had never seen roast beef before.

But I was never conscious of my clothes or of poverty.[3] Much, much later when we graduated from high school I remember being humiliated because I hadn't known enough to select the proper dress for an afternoon party and had worn a white one — white wasn't a daytime color then. But even then I can't remember any rebellion against the skimpy wardrobe we could afford.

By the time we went to Buffalo we were making some of our own clothes, and the process of learning to use paper patterns and making "simulated box plaits" was terribly trying to me. Margery had learned by making doll's dresses, but I'd never cared how my dolls were dressed. Margery had even made my doll a dress once because she had been distressed about her, but it wasn't a distress I could appreciate. When I was expected to keep myself in underwear and shirtwaists as Margery did, it came very hard. I don't doubt the family suffered. But I think I never spoiled a piece of material, and I fulfilled the family requirements after a fashion. They didn't expect me to be "handy" anyway; Margery was the "handy" one. It was all of a piece with my execrable handwriting; Margery wrote a neat round hand, but mine was hen tracks.

Even before we went to Buffalo I had "written things." One summer we were home at the farm from Owatonna and Uncle Will was counting my mint. He offered me a dollar if I would copy ten "pieces" into a notebook for him, and I guess he still has it. I don't remember anything in it, but it gave me a great sense of pride and responsibility. Mother, I know, thought it wasn't a good idea to give the child an inflated sense of what her scribblings were worth, but I think it was only fair to counterbalance for the moment my abiding sense of Margery's "handiness."

When Margery began to go to art school on Saturdays in Buffalo I stayed home and wrote pieces for Mother to correct. One description of an April snowstorm I still remember. It began: "Through numberless days of sunshine and spring the sun had made love to the earth, and lovely, lovely had been the days." It distressed me that it had a beat like verse — the whole description had — but I didn't know how else to say it.

By this time I had read a good deal — Dickens, especially *David Copperfield*, and Scott, especially *Ivanhoe*. But I don't think I got much education from them. They didn't make a fantasy world for me at all, and no book even at this time ever competed with the Bible. The story of Ruth was better than *Ramona*, and the poetry of Job was better than Longfellow. I still have my first big Bible, carefully underlined through with red and black ink, and interleafed with painfully written manuscript pages. From the time we went to Buffalo, Margery and I earned our five cents a week for church and a penny for Sunday school by learning three verses of the Bible a day and six on Sunday. We learned dozens and dozens of chapters. I supposed "Evangeline" and "Hiawatha" were better poetry, but I didn't like them so well.

It was probably this habit of Bible learning that gave me the idea of learning poems. Margery and I washed the dishes always, and I made a cloth-covered rack to set up over the dish pan. I copied out the poems and strapped them in the rack and we learned them aloud as we washed. I remember especially choosing "Thanatopsis" and "To a Waterfowl" and "To a Skylark" and the "Ode to the West Wind" and "Swiftly, walk over the waves, Spirit of Night."

The Sense
of Symbolism *[1]

MAN IS always reaching out beyond the world he sees and hears. In every age since history began, he has tried to express, even amid the confusions of his thought and the crudities of his language, something of that other world he only feels and does not touch or see — the world of thoughts and ideals. Yet the tools man works with are only crude, and this world of aspirations and ideals demands perfection; and so there must necessarily remain much that transcends the thought and language of man. It is with the sense of this limitation that he has fashioned symbols. He has looked at Nature and seen in its bountiful sky, in its life-giving sun, and in its majestic storms, the embodiment, the symbol of his aspirations. He has gone further — he has created his own myths of the gods of Olympus, he has fashioned his own Ark of the Covenant, and then he has filled the work of his own hands with the intensity of symbolic meaning which, as abstract truth, was beyond his power to express. Symbolism therefore is a great inherent demand of mankind for the expression of the intangible world of his ideals.

As the ideals of man, moreover, have varied in different civilizations and in different ages, so the symbolism which nations have vitalized has developed in widely different ways; and the most fas-

* Undated manuscript with marginal notations in a later style of writing. Style of handwriting suggests that this essay was written *circa* 1909, when RFB was a college student.

cinating study of the ideals of different nations is through the revelations of their peculiar sense of symbolism.

There is something irresistibly suggestive in the persistence and the marked modifications of symbolism in all ages. To the Greek artist and the Roman statesman, to the Hebrew prophet and the medieval schoolman, symbolism was necessary to express his own peculiar racial ideals. The most influential and vital expressions of symbolism among the ancient nations were those developed among the Greeks and among the Hebrews.

To the Greeks the absorbing ideal was beauty. They lived under a stainless sky, in a land of blue seas and white mountains. They drank in beauty as their birthright, and it is not strange that it was for the expression of the beautiful that they fashioned their symbols. All the actual world about them they peopled with the symbols of beauty — Helicon and Parnassus were the abodes of their Muses; Cythera was the loved haunt of Aphrodite and from its waters she had arisen, born of the foam; the gate of clouds about Olympus welcomed the great gods themselves to the banquet of nectar and ambrosia. For it is in their myths that we feel most strongly the desire of the Greek to express under forms his sense of the ideal world. Into these tales he put the wealth of his inspiration from the rising of the sun and the flowering of the hyacinth, the abandon, also, of mere loveliness of *description* and incident that distinguishes them from the symbolic literature of all other nations.[2] The Greeks required even of their symbolism that it be beautiful.

Not so the Hebrews. Their great racial aspiration was towards holiness, towards God. Pictorial beauty hardly existed for them. Their arts of painting and of sculpture were strangled by their religion and without these the sense of visual beauty was also lost. They developed, instead, a peculiarly analytic sense of symbolism. They had analyzed every object into a conventional symbol, and its appeal to them was not through its beauty, but through this peculiar significance. In these lines from the Song of Solomon,[3] —

> Thy nose is like the tower of Lebanon,
> which looketh towards Damascus,

they saw no farcical picture before their eyes; their minds only recognized the tower of Lebanon as the symbol of dignity giving character to the landscape as the nose gives character to the face. So too they could write: —

> Thy neck is like the tower of David builded for an armory
> Whereon there hang a thousand bucklers
> All the shields of the mighty men.

To them it was not a picture, only a conventional association of ideas. It appealed not to the emotions but to the analytical interest. This same keen analytical sense of symbolism called into being also their elaborate system of temple worship — all the complicated ceremonial rites of their religion. No race has ever possessed so strongly developed a sense of symbolism as the Hebrews.

For centuries after the decadence of the Greek and Hebrew civilizations, all sense of symbolism was but a modification either of the Greek consciousness of it, directed toward the seen, the pictorial, or of the Hebrew, directed toward the unseen, the spiritual. The Romans, during the period of their growth and greatest native strength, produced no literature, vitalized no symbolism. In their later glory they consciously imported that of the Greeks and attempted to naturalize it. But the genius of the Romans was naturally material or logical, and they only succeeded in externalizing and *crudifying* the symbolism they had imported.

The Middle Ages, on the other hand, adapted not the Greek but the Hebrew symbolism. If in the age of Solomon this had no pictorial beauty, in the age of the Church Fathers it became unspeakably grotesque. Their feeling of awe and inspiration in symbolism seemed heightened in proportion to the insignificance or ugliness of the sign itself. Their grotesque even ludicrous representations of the "four living creatures" of Revelations were to them supremely satisfying symbols of the four Evangelists. No word of the Scriptures, moreover, seemed to them complete till they had wrenched from it some spiritual symbolism; even the simplest words of Job and Esther they overweighted with doctrinal significance. Everywhere, in art, in literature, in life, symbolism was developed to hide and stifle the true beauty, the real life. The Middle Ages shows us indeed the caricature of Hebrew symbolism.

It was not until the age of the Renaissance and the Reformation that the two great expressions of ancient symbolism became in any real sense *welded* together. The Renaissance gave back to the world the ancient Greek ideals; the Reformation stripped the Hebrew symbols of their veil of caricature. So in the earlier modern literature and in the works of the Old Masters we discover the first blending of Greek and Hebrew symbolism.

The Modern Age, however, has turned from symbolism to extreme realism. In its nature there must be in symbolism revelation and yet concealment. Our modern civilizations have lost, however, the charm of concealment — the aim of all effort, in science, in literature, in life is complete revelation. All the tendencies of the modern world have been in keeping with this development — the growing emphasis on the active life, the spread of education, and especially the development of modern science. It is inevitable, however, in this effort after exact realism of detail that the sense of the larger unity of things should be obscured. It is inevitable also in this restless inquiry into all things for the sake of complete understanding that the sense of reverence and awe should also be lost. So in our modern reaction from the symbolic we have lost somewhat of the old sense of unity, the old reverence. For symbolism is, in its highest aspect, a reverential search after the highest truth, an acknowledgment of the broad unity of things.

In literature, however, the tendency towards symbolic expression is becoming more and more marked. There is indeed a French "School of Symbolists," but it seems hard to justify the appropriation of the term "symbolists." Their work is not rich in symbols; it is rather on suggestion than on symbolism that they lay stress. In any case, the symbolism of Verlaine's verses, and of Maeterlink's dramas is not the sane, healthy half revelation, half concealment whose essentials are reverence and the sense of unity. There are, however, many influences which are tending toward the development of a true, sane modern symbolism. Such is the modern insight into the beautiful fullness of purpose in Nature. It is an attitude essentially new, and yet holding within itself both the Greek sense of the beautiful and the Hebrew sense of the divine; and it is coming to recognize the intangible significance of the world about us that can be expressed only through the symbols of Nature.

But chief, perhaps, among these modern influences towards symbolism is the growing effort to embody the Idea in the novel or the drama. Under this influence the characters and situations of modern art are becoming, in their original conception in the artist's mind, more and more only the essential symbols for the expression of a pervading truth.

Journals

BEGINNING AT the time when she was teaching in a girls' school, in California, two years before her marriage, Ruth Benedict kept a journal in which she wrote only intermittently, but over a long period of years. The "Journal: 1912–1916" was kept in a black bound notebook. The entries, written in ink, have been much corrected. Three passages, written on odd sheets of paper and dated November and December, 1915, have been interpolated.

At the back of the bound journal and in envelopes with early poems, she had put a collection of other journal fragments, written on many kinds of paper, all but one handwritten. While some are dated, others are undated, and the sequence is therefore largely conjectural. A good many fragments, so heavily revised as to be unintelligible, some copied-out quotations, and many tentative notes in outline form have been omitted here.

JOURNAL: 1912–1916

Oct., 1912. Sunday.[1]

The faithfulness of this old notebook is touching. It has travelled across half of Europe and all of America without once learning the object of its existence. It was given to me to write my home letters in while I was abroad so that they could be neatly preserved for posterity between suitable covers. The idea shocked my modesty — also my sense of proportion — and the notebook shared the scorn I heaped on the purpose it was intended for.

Three years have gone by since then. Dresden and Rome seem very far in the distance; I had forgotten until I opened these pages just now that this notebook was meant to hold gems of travel for posterity. I want it now for a very different purpose.

I want it now for my very own; I want it to help me to shake myself to rights during the next few months. I've just come through a year in which I have not dared to think; I seemed to keep my grip only by setting my teeth and playing up to the mask I had chosen. I have not dared to be honest, not even with myself. I could only try to live through day after day, day after day, and not dishonor them overmuch. In spite of myself bitterness at having lived at all obsessed me; it seemed cruel that I had been born, cruel that, as my family taught me, I must go on living *forever*. Life was a labyrinth of petty turns and there was no Ariadne who held the clue.

I tried, oh very hard, to believe that our own characters are the justification of it all. Bob believes it, and I think Margery would if she ever felt it mattered. But the boredom had gone too deep; I had no flicker of interest in my character. What was my character anyway? My real *me* was a creature I dared not look upon — it was terrorized by loneliness, frozen by a sense of futility, obsessed by a longing to *stop*. No one had ever heard of that Me. If they had, they would have thought it an interesting pose. The mask was tightly adjusted.

I could see no way out. All my cheerfulness, my gaiety were part and parcel of the mask — the Me remained behind. I longed to be old — sixty or seventy — when I fancied the Me might have been strangled by the long-continued tight-lacing of the mask. I only wanted my feelings dulled — I wanted to be just placidly contented when I saw the full moon hang low over the ocean. And the weary years seemed unendurable.

I am not afraid of pain, nor of sorrow. But this loneliness, this futility, this emptiness — I dare not face them.

So much of the trouble is because I am a woman. To me it seems a very terrible thing to be a woman. There is one crown which perhaps is worth it all — a great love, a quiet home, and children. We all know that is all that is worth while, and yet we must peg away, showing off our wares on the market if we have money, or manufacturing careers for ourselves if we haven't. We have not the motive to prepare ourselves for a "life-work" of teaching, of social work — we know that we would lay it down with hallelujah in the height of our success, to make a home for the right man.

And all the time in the background of our consciousness rings the warning that perhaps the right man will never come. A great love is given to very few. Perhaps this make-shift time filler of a job *is* our life work after all.

It is all so cruelly wasteful. There are so few ways in which we can compete with men — surely not in teaching or in social work. If we are not to have the chance to fulfil our one potentiality — the power of loving — why were we not born men? At least we could have had an occupation then. . . .

They laugh at home about my "course in old maids" this winter. It really isn't a joke at all. It's quite tragically serious. There were three at school. They retold all their twenty-year old conversations with men — conversations that of course *might* have developed into love affairs *if* they'd allowed the liberty — so that you might be led to realize that they were not old maids by necessity. — All except Miss Van W——. No one had ever even let her suspect that he "was interested in her." It was she who was really tragic. She kept her cook books in the bottom of her trunk and took them out and fingered them lovingly. Her primary children adored her, and yet she had no charms of person or manner. She had one gift — she could love. But in her barren thirty-six years even that passionate necessity had grown so thick-coated with mannerisms, so padlocked with reticence that there were few to whom she discovered it. She was so tragically alone. All her brothers and sisters were married or dead. Her father and mother lived in Colorado and it was sure breakdown for her to be in the high altitude. She had not seen them in three years. As we walked the streets of lighted bungalows at night, she would drink them in one after another, and as we neared the school, she sighed once, "There are so many homes! There ought to be enough to go around."

I shall never forget one of her confidences. We had been talking over our lives, and with a little catch in her breath and a downward flutter of her eyes, she asked hesitatingly, "Have I ever told you of Mr. Dodge? I had meant to, someday. He had a ranch near Claremont — a good ranch. And he wanted a wife. He tried to get my best friend, Miss Allen. He would have taken anyone. But I — I never encouraged him."

It was as if she had said: "Behold, I too am brave; I too will not stop short of the ideal." It was so pitiful — so terrible. The horror of the revelation struck deep.

Then there are the girls I know in Pasadena. They are most of them ten years older than I. They are no longer young; they will probably never marry. They are fighting the ennui of a life without a purpose. Some of them are studying shorthand, some are taking music lessons, one just embroiders. They are doing their best — to trump up a reason for living. And within a year they'll find that there is no virtue even in a pay envelope to make life seem worth living.

The trouble is not that we are never happy — it is that happiness is so episodical. A morning in the library, an afternoon with someone I really care about, a day in the mountains, a good-night-time with the babies[2] can almost frighten me with happiness. But then it is gone and I cannot see what holds it all together. What is worth while? What is the purpose? What do I *want*?

And yet, why should I care? The people I love best do not. But always I know that is not the question. It is "Why do I *have* to care?" If I shut my eyes to it, it pounces upon me from the dark, and my weapons are not ready.

For two weeks now I have been interested. I have not seriously, fiercely, wanted to stop. I can think quite calmly about last year. And the thought of the future does not obsess me. I am glad to put my effort into my English classes — glad to have the girls like their work and like me. I hope, I *hope* that I can feel my way this year to a safer foothold where I shall dare to look all about me and take my bearings. I think more clearly with a pen in my hand — therefore the help of this book.

What is it that holds these episodes together? Much as I have rebelled against it, I cannot hit on any answer but the old one of self development. Perhaps my trouble comes from thinking of the end as my *present* self, not as a possible and very different future self. It is hard never to fall into the way of thinking that now you are ready to use your hard-won experience. Of course you mean to go on learning, but from a certain vantage point of attainment; it is always very hard for me to feel that year after year is just added *preparation* — and for what? The great instinctive answer is for Motherhood — yes, I think I could accept that with heart and soul — so much do our instincts help us out in our problems — but no girl dares count on Motherhood. Ethically, if Motherhood is worth while, it ought to be also worthy to have a hand in the growth of a child or a woman. The difference is just a question of instinct.

Oct. 25, 1912. (Rewrite)
I saw a quotation from Stevenson the other day. I cannot quote it, but it concerned aspirations. "Aspirations are the riches of the soul," he said. "The man who has an abundance and a variety of them is spiritually rich." And it might be true. Why not?

My aspirations this year have been so many agony points. My longing for understanding has been a bitter cry against blindness; my longing for expression, an impatient contempt of any word I could utter; my longing for service, a dull ache of knowledge of our isolation from each other, and of the futility of our helpfulness; my longing for friendship, a "blanching, vertical eye-glare" of loneliness. And as I thought I hated all negative things! I was putting flood tides of emotion into pure negatives every day.

It's all wrong. Little by little, in the long run, aspirations *can* realize themselves. Work for that. We must count it our wealth. Why must we rebel as passionately against the blindness, the futility, the loneliness? It is nobler to be thankful, even, for the vision of what might be, and pray — try to pray — that we may keep the dream even if all our whole lives long we may never have one ecstacy of realization. Perhaps that is what Carlyle means when he says, "We can do without happiness and instead thereof find blessedness." I'm sure it's what Christ meant when he said, "The kingdom of heaven is within you."

And this culture of the aspirations is "self-development," isn't it? It is strange how long we rebel against a platitude until suddenly in a different lingo it looms up again as the only verity.

Nov. '12

I have been reading Walt Whitman, and Jeffries' *Story of My Heart*. They are alike in their superb enthusiasm for life — for actual personal living. To Jeffries nothing, literally nothing, is of worth except as it feeds his "soul-life, his psyche," and as a fantastic appendage, his fevered, exotic dream of the soul-life of future generations. Whitman is far sturdier and more healthful; but it is their common ground that impresses me: their unwavering, ringing belief that the *Me* within them is of untold worth and importance. I read in wonder and admiration — in painful humility. Does this sense of personal worth, this enthusiasm for one's own personality, belong only to great self-expressive souls? or to a mature period of life I have not yet attained? or may I perhaps be shut from it by eternal law because I am a woman and lonely? It seems to me the one priceless gift of this life: — of all blessings on earth I would choose to have a man-child who possessed it.

It seems as I read their outbursts that I could attain to a like enthusiasm by a process of mental discipline. For it is not that I cannot enjoy — I can stand on the dizzy heights and behold the nations of the world. But the instinctive thought that comes to crown the experience is just, "If only, if *only* everything might stop with this." It is a far cry to their enthusiasm for living, — I strive and strive but I cannot compass it.

Their thoughts of death too are strange to me — their horror and repudiation of annihilation in dying, their discomfort in the thought that the world goes on without them. Oh, I *want* to stop! If there is any discomfort in the thought it's that there would be some left who would suffer. But they would feel it was "the will of God," and,

after all, everything would go on as before. The only pity is that
no one would know me well enough to be glad.

Nov. '12

The burden of all moralizers is the praise of the present — I think
I need to think far more about the future. If one cannot see any
virtue in the present, at least one can firmly resolve never to put
any mortgage on a future which may perhaps be more significant —
never to allow any boredom to throw away a chance for a friendship,
nor any bitterness to wreck the carrying out of a plan one has
reckoned good. There is no reason why even rather excessive boredom should injure one's health or one's intellect — and they're perhaps the only essentials.

The only thing you can give the world is what you *are* — yourself.
And it really does count to be a Miss Orton rather than a Miss
D——. Therefore, go in for character building with all Mary P——'s
crudeness and enthusiasm!

Thanksgiving, '12

I am puzzled about Thanksgiving. The only warm, whole-hearted
thanksgiving I can attain is that "the dog-orned year's behind me
not before!" And yet I'm intellectually thankful for food and drink,
health, education, for my position, my family, my friends. In that
sense I've everything to be thankful for; — why doesn't it make me
glad to go on? Is it true that the lack of zest comes from the
superabundance rather than from the lack? It can't be, for I'd do
without every one of them to throw off this loneliness and to believe
in my work. I'm not afraid of pain or of sorrow — but this loneliness,
this emptiness of life —

Jan. 7 [1913]

All my humor and philosophy seem to have deserted me. There's
just a foolish little rhyme that runs over and over in my head for
comfort:

Serene I fold my arms and wait
  Nor care for wind, nor tide, nor sea;
I have no more gainst time and fate
  For Lo! mine own shall come to me. —
I stand amid the eternal ways
  And what is mine shall know my face.

I suppose it's fatalism and nerveless acquiescence, it's quite certainly a lie for I haven't found that mates are paired off automatically in this universe nor that great souls feel any fullblooded satisfaction. And yet all the time its rhythm brings to me something of the patience and the dignity that what little philosophy I can muster does not bring me.

And what is mine shall know my face.

("If we hope for that which we see not, then do we with patience wait for it.")

Faith is the sturdiest, the most manly of the virtues. It lies behind our pluckiest, blindest, most heartbreaking strivings. It is the virtue of the storm just as happiness is the virtue of the sunshine. It is a mistake to feel that it has to do only with the future; faith in the present too has the weight of all authority behind it. "The results of life are uncalculated and uncalculable. The persons who compose our company converse, come and go, and design and execute many things, and somewhat comes of it all, but an unlooked for result." Who can tell? Something *may* come of all this fumbling in the dark — Need it be so hard to accept the blindness? God give us the faith that looks unflinchingly at the day before us and accepts it, even lovingly, as an opportunity to be faithfully, squarely lived up to God, that is the faith we need!

But there is more. Our faith in the present dies out long before our faith in the future. There may come a time significant enough to retrieve all our boredoms and our pains. We'll put no mortgages on that future!

The trouble with life isn't that there is no answer, it's that there are so many answers. There's the answer of Christ and of Buddha, of Thomas à Kempis and of Elbert Hubbard, of Browning, Keats and of Spinoza, of Thoreau and of Walt Whitman, of Kant and of Theodore Roosevelt. By turns their answers fit my needs. And yet, because I am I and not any one of them, they can none of them be completely mine. There is a certain egotism that is not born with us, nor achieved, but which is at length thrust upon us — the stinging knowledge that for ourselves we must build up our own answer, that not even a Kant or a Christ can answer it for us.

It is strange in looking over other people's answers to the great riddle, how little it seems to signify whether or not they felt they had solved it. Keats and Ibsen stand to me for as definite answers as Browning or Schopenhauer. And yet I suppose Keats died gasping in the thick fog of the unanswerable, and Ibsen never really left off playing the Sphinx. What we call "answers" are, rather, attitudes taken by different temperaments toward certain characteristic problems — even the interrogation may be an "answer."

May 20.

It is almost the end of the school year — the tableaux, the innumerable themes, the *Mustard Seed*, the senior essays, even final examinations will be done within two weeks. My utter thankfulness has only one cloud, — next year. I wince at the thought of it; and hate myself for a coward in doing it. — If I felt that there were no question about my duty in going on conventionally, I'd square my shoulders and march to the music of course. But it doesn't seem very clear. In a world that holds books and babies and canyon trails, why should one condemn oneself to live day-in, day-out with people one does not like, and sell one's life to chaperone and correct them? The only trouble is that there may not be any better way of realizing the good things of life than right here. Stanley's[3] ruled out; the farm is attractive but very pious; Buffalo[4] is impossible; I cannot go vagabonding for that costs money. Besides, I have some grains of my family's common-sense, and I know the trouble is not primarily in the environment. "America is here or nowhere." I can learn to

manage myself here as well as at the farm.— And yet it seems sometimes as if it would help famously to exchange chaperoning and
study-hours for a garden of hollyhocks and pansies against the old
apple trees and lilacs at Grandfather's. I'll do it yet!

June 15.

It was almost a month ago that the night-mare began. Suddenly,
when Bertrice[5] seemed the strongest, she was sick as few babies can
be and live. And it lasted, not one day but ten. We dared not
think of Margery's and Bob's homecoming; and they, on their side
of the continent, had the trials of absence and uselessness to add to
their despairing anxiety.

It is all like a bad dream. It came just at the time when I was
working from 6 A.M. till 11 P.M. at school; I'll never do it again, never.
But the night-mare ended, as night-mares do if we give them time;
and the baby is slowly gaining, and Commencement is passed and
done with. Mother and I are on the East-bound train — with four
months of vacation ahead of me.

After school was over, I went to Miss Orton; I told her how I
hated the meals and the chaperoning, and asked if I might have a
conditional engagement for next year. And when I came away I'd
even promised I wouldn't dread coming back next year, "for it would
break my heart to have you." She promised some very definite things,
too, but it wasn't those that made the differences. She gave me a
self-respect I had not had for months — years — and I think it was
because she never once implied that it is our business to live placidly
through *anything*. Apparently it never occurred to her that I had
whimpered. Even Mother always tells me somewhere in the conversation that life isn't all cake. Instead, she said that if any part
of life seemed so hard as to neutralize all the rest, it was the most
natural thing in the world to try to change it if it were in any way
possible. As I left I told her about the farm and how they would
love to have me there, and she still held my hand and said, "But
they'll have to wait. We want you too." Then and there I would
have done anything for that woman; coming back next year seemed
too small a test.

She said the younger teachers naturally felt the strain of the life most keenly; the older ones had a more satisfying interest in their work. "What is it?" I asked her. "Perhaps I can grow into it." — "Oh, no," she answered quickly and soberly, "I wouldn't want you to. We narrow our interests until we grow fossilized, as — as I am. And then we have to make our teaching fill our lives. We have to, to live. I want you to have many interests. You have much to expect of life."

And so I left her. But that hour had made an unbelievable difference in my thoughts of next year. She hadn't treated me as if I were a child and expected to find life planned for my private enjoyment; she hadn't even implied that I wasn't game to take all that was coming to me without a whimper; she didn't ask if I were troubled by love affairs: she talked with me as with an equal who had a right to his own distastes, and tried to help me to plan my year more pleasantly. God bless her!

July 27

Yes, I am coming back to the farm. I'll make something off the garden and the orchard — perhaps in time it will be a prosperous business. And except for my four months' vacation in the winter, I shall not need much money. I'm coming primarily because I *want* to — because I can't believe that joyless life is significant life. I want to plan and manage and learn and work among the out-door elemental things of life. I don't delude myself with any "unselfish" motives, though if I could give Aunt Myra the good times she's missed, that would have its place too.

Social work, teaching, farming: — it's rather an undignified array for three years. It bespeaks floundering and mismanagement. Is it playing the weathercock? Most people would only half-veil this common-sense judgment in their surprised questionings. Left to myself I should hardly have thought of it perhaps. My jobs have never been an end in themselves, always just a means, and a rather subordinate means. They have never been the essential. That, I think, has never wavered much: to find a way of living not utterly incongruous with certain passionate ideals: to attain to a zest for life, an enthusiasm for the adventure which will forever deliver me from my shame of cowardice, to master an attitude toward life which will somehow bind together these episodes of experience into something that may conceivably be called life.

I *will* succeed; I *will* love the journey itself and the commonplace experiences of it. I cannot do it in boarding school without endless waste and friction. This home is waiting for me with the out-door life I love, the leisure, the home-life. Why should I not accept it and thank God?

There is only one argument that troubles me. It is the fear of being a quitter, of having run away from the fight for my own private enjoyment. The faith this world needs is the faith that can hold its own in the rub and irritating contact of the world. I plan large work among the farmers and their children to salve my conscience. But I do not know —

Aug. 20.

How shall I say it? That I have attained to the zest for life? That I have looked in the face of God and had five days of magnificent comprehension? — It is more than these, and better. It is the greatest thing in the world — and I have it. Is it not incredible? It happened when Stanley came down last week. He had been here one week in July — a glorious week of tramping and rowing and reading, of lying on the hilltops and dreaming over the valleys. But I let him go again.

And last week he came down for two days on his way to Europe. And Oh I was so glad to see him! I think I knew it that night. But he did not see it. We went down to the Collins' Woods in the boat, and still he did not see. It was afternoon when I told him — I had hoped he would see for himself. But it had happened, and I'd rather be with him than anywhere else in God's universe.

He had been lying on the ground. He sat up and moved toward me, and said with a tenderness and awe I had never heard before, "Oh, Ruth, is it true?" And then he put his arms around me, and rested his head against me. In the long minute we sat there, he asked in the same hushed voice, "Ruth, will you marry me?" And

I answered him, "Yes Stanley." After that we did not speak. Later it was I who told him first that I loved him. — And so the whole world changed. Is it not awesome — wonderful beyond expression? Every day I have grown surer, happier. Nothing in all my life would be worth setting over against our Sunday afternoon drive through Lyon Brook or our last afternoon together on the towpath.

We turn in our sleep and groan because we are parasites — we women — because we produce nothing, say nothing, find our whole world in the love of a man. — For shame! We are become the veriest Philistines — in this matter of woman's sphere. I suppose it is too soon to expect us to achieve perspective on the problem of woman's rights — but surely there is no other problem of human existence where we would be childish enough to believe in the finality of our little mathematical calculations of "done" or "not done." But here in the one supremely complicated relation of man and woman which involves the perpetual interchange of all that is most difficult to be reckoned — here we thrust in "the world's coarse thumb and finger," here we say "to the eyes of the public shalt thou justify thy existence." — Oh no! do we care whether Beatrice formed clubs, or wrote a sonnet? In the quiet self-fulfilling love of Wordsworth's home, do we ask that Mary Wordsworth should have achieved individual self-expression? In general, — a woman has one supreme power — to love. If we are to arrive at any blytheness in facing life, we must have faith to believe that it is in exercising this gift, in living it out to its fullest that she achieves herself, that she "justifies her existence."

What are moods? Are they the grace and perfume of existence, or are they the uncertain shoals on which we run aground and perish? Are they to be cultivated as the finest flowers of existence, or are they to be rooted out as the weeds "that choke the true Word"? The Romanticists based their whole scheme of life on the ideal unfolding of moods; they treated them royally.

We *must* believe in the nobility of man — how can we help it? Can it be that we were blind to it because the exterior was warped or mean? — because the plump worried face of the elderly little school ma'am hid from us her lifelong honest strivings to do her duty, strivings forever unrewarded, held to unwaveringly when the last hope of love or happiness is gone; is it because the dust of theological combat has dimmed our eyesight that we cannot see the sturdy insistence upon truth that leads men to give up their reliance on divine help, their hopes of the joys of heaven — What is truth? — a mere concept, an intellectual norm: and yet for this, men, not the picked and noblest souls, but thousands to whom flattering and prizes still appeal, for this love of what they call the "truth," they will give up a conception of creation which appeals to every human instinct — where man lives the center of the affectionate interests of the hierarchy of heaven, goes attended by guardian angels, and finally ascends to take his public reward for all the strivings of his life, and compensation for all its sorrows.

Life lays a compelling hand upon us women. We thought once, in college perhaps, that we were the artificers of our own lives. We planned our usefulness in social work, in laboratories, in schools — Perhaps we thought we considered marriage as a possible factor in our lives. And all the time we did not yet know we were women — we did not know that there lay as certain a moral hindrance to our man-modelled careers as to a man-modelled costume of shingled hair and trousers. — We learn it at last — that the one gift in our treasure house is love — love — love. If we may not give it, if no one looks into our eyes and asks our gift — we may indeed collect ourselves and offer our second-best to the world, and the world may applaud. But the vital principle is gone from our lives.

Douglaston[6] — Nov. '14.

I have hardly written here for a year and more. Last winter I had Stanley to write to, my work to do, my small busyness of preparation to fill my time. This year I have Stanley to talk to, to play with, to passionately love, but no longer to write to. With all my duties of housekeeping and cooking and clothes providing and visiting, I have such abundant leisure as I never dreamed of except in my year abroad. And that was barren leisure — leisure that mocked at my scant happiness, at the pressing terror behind. My leisure now pulses with content, with eager desires.

I have so much, so much—life seems so incomparably rich these days. I have been happy, happy this summer, as I did not think it was given to be unless one were very young or very blind. We have had love and companionship that have given us all of heaven that men have bodied forth out of their longings — its satisfactions and its ecstacies. Five months ago, with all my consciousness of the power of loving that was the greatest part of me, with all the hunger and thrust of my love, I had no notion of its strength and depth and power of healing. No wonder the days seemed dreary and empty enough, without this satisfying comradeship, this ardent delight, this transforming love — now that I have it, it is what gives meaning to all of life.

Until we are once happy, the longing for happiness must be, I suppose, the preoccupation of life. Our instincts keep telling us that there we shall find reality — a reality that will be *per se* convincing — not because authority or arguments have established it. And it is true. What need has a happy woman to "justify her existence"? This pre-occupation with happiness is almost wholly bad: the greater the possibilities in the person, perhaps, the more intensely he longs for what must grow to seem an unattainable harmony. It seems to me that it is only when he has once been happy that his faculties are liberated — that he is "for aye out of destruction's reach."

— The winter is before me to accomplish anything I wish. I have difficulty only in concentrating on something: for amusement and for Stanley I shall try to write out the chemical detective stories[7] for which he supplies the plots — it might be for profit also; then there are the "social work" stories; I want to study Shakespeare and keep a book of notes; I'd like to read Goethe intelligently; my pet scheme is to steep myself in the lives of restless and highly enslaved women of past generations and write a series of biographical papers from the standpoint of the "new woman." [8] My conclusion so far as I see it now is that there is nothing "new" about the whole thing except the phraseology and the more independent economic standing of recent times — that the restlessness and groping are inherent in the nature of women and this generation can outdo the others long since past only in the frankness with which it acts upon these; that nature lays a compelling and very distressing hand upon woman, and she struggles in vain who tries to deny it or escape it, — life loves the little irony of proving it upon the very woman who has denied it; she can only hope for success by working according to Nature's preconceptions of her make-up — not against them. This in general — in particular, women are the most individualistic of God's creatures, and the "woman problem" is a lazy man's expression of a . . .

Nov. '15 —

There is no one of our radiant faiths that seems more surely planted and reared in us by a mocking Master of the Revels than that which shines out from all of us in our radiant faith in "our children." — The dreams that slipped from us like the sand in the hour glass, the task we laid aside to give them birth and rearing, — all this they shall carve in the enduring stone of their achievements — The master stroke of the irony, the stabbing hurt of it, is that it is all so noble and self-less a dream; it is truly, "that last infirmity of noble minds."

Nov. '15 —

I am puzzled about my intellectual bearings; I have a sense of unswept mussiness in my incentives. I believe in high endeavor, in motives that lead us far afield from our circumscribed selves; yet my imagination circles round and round, as if mesmerized, above the uselessness of it all: above the long travail that brings only change, change not to be dignified as progress; above the passionate sacrifice that only damns the loved one it would save. Endeavor I must believe in; its effectiveness, I cannot.

The point might be, then, with Marcus Aurelius and Epictitus, to make the spiritual effort *per se* worthwhile, to divorce it from all attempt to prevail. It is useless: you get unfailingly to Epictitus's brazen egotism, to his fleshless brutalities. No, high endeavor cannot be divorced from the world of results — yet the world of results can never justify it. There is the crux of the difficulty. You must care passionately that those results should come — yet you must be able to surmount not only the collapse of that which you have struggled for, but even of those passionate beliefs that have nerved you for the struggle.

Well, it can be done. Mine may seem a nerveless inspiration to those "who hold so fast by God's infinity"; to those, too, who believe in the magic efficacy of service to mankind; but it is something, some firm ground from which to reconnoitre these warning beliefs in endeavor and in its uselessness.

It is only a kind of scrupulousness, perhaps — a scrupulousness like that which drives us to a bodily cleanliness that has no thought of measuring itself by the requirements of health; — a scrupulousness lest any forces of life that have, for the generation, become ours shall "return unto the void" — that that level of life which we glimpse in the future of our friends, which we catch our dregs of inspiration from in highly disciplined writers and thinkers, which, supremely, we covet for our children — that that level of life we have it for our consummate duty to attain — and not in these friends, these children of ours; in ourselves. — It is only against such a background that it has meaning for me; as an isolated striving for the perfection of a personal self it is paltry; as one impulse in the universal striving toward the dignity of rich personality which gives meaning to all life — as such it is a cause to which I can give my loyalty.

Dec. '15

On this first dazzling snow-frosted morning of the winter, I have read again those few pages whose words still seem to slip into my consciousness not from the printed page but from my memory — Pater's Conclusion to his *Renaissance*.

It belongs to the very texture of my life. — How it brings back that old passionate blank despair when I was so very young — that old fevered tossing of my startled brain in the clutch of its first perplexity at the aims of living. The hours had a hopeless abandon that does not come again in all our wiser gropings. We grow in time to trust the future for our answers —

And then came Pater. Every instant of that late afternoon is vivid to me. I even know that I had to creep to the windowseat to catch the last dim light in that bare tower room of my Freshman days. The book fell shut in my hands at the end, and it was as if my soul had been given back to me, its eyes wide and eager with new understanding. — I leaned my arms on the window ledge; across the green-black of the campus pines in the dusk, the Catskills, their horizon line diamond-cut against the sky, glowed with all the colors of sundown — I remember two crows flapped heavily westward, following the sun . . .

Afterwards, I disbelieved. I had much in me to contradict Pater; my early religion which tried so hard to make me a moral being, my pity for others that almost made me an efficient one. But I was not run into either mould. And it is Pater's message that comes back to me as the cry of my deepest necessity: "to burn with this hard gem-like flame" — to gain from experience "this fruit of a quickened, multiplied consciousness," to summon "the services of philosophy of religion, of culture as well, to startle us into a sharp and eager observation" —

And surely the world has need of my vision as well as of Charity Committees; it is better to grow straight than to twist myself into a doubtfully useful footstool; it is better to make the most of that deepest cry of my heart: "Oh God let me be awake — awake in my lifetime."

Oct. 1916 —

Again another winter. It is hard for me to look with any satisfaction on the two winters that are passed — and now another. "Mary Wollstonecraft" I do believe in — but will she ever be published? I doubt it, and more and more I know that I want publication.

JOURNAL FRAGMENTS: 1915–1934

Sorrow — (for Mary Wollstonecraft)[9]

It is the poverty of sorrow that haunts me. Why can't I *feel* it? I should be so utterly content if I could press it in till it was utterly mine — till it literally became me. Then I should be living again. Anything to live! To have done with this numbness that will not let me feel. Someday it will come perhaps — unless all our powers of feeling are a lie, and we can never feel. Perhaps that is the truth — perhaps all we can do is to be pathetic.

Distractions —

All our ceremonies, our observances, are for the weak who are cowards before the bare thrust of feeling. How we have hung the impertinent panoply of our funeral arrangements over the bleak tragedy of death! And joy too. What are our weddings, from the religious pomp to the irrelevant presents and the confetti, but presumptuous distractions from the proud mating of urgent love?

[Undated][10]

. . . the place where he works, nor meet the men he knows best. I must have my world too, my outlet, my chance to put forth my effort.

And never did desires dovetail more neatly — for I don't want a "position," heaven forbid! nor a committee chairmanship — All I want I can do here at home in my ready-to-hand leisure. The only necessity is that I should realize my purposes seriously enough and work at writing with sufficient slavishness.

— If I had children or were expecting one, it would call a truce to these promptings, I suppose. But surely it would be only a truce — it would sign no permanent terms of peace with them. . . .

There is no misreading of life that avenges itself so piteously on men and women as the notion that in their children they can bring to fruition their own seedling dreams. And it is just as unjust to the child, to be born and reared as the "creation" of his parents. He is *himself*, and it is within reason that he may be the very antithesis of them both. — No, it is wisdom in motherhood as in wifehood to have one's own individual world of effort and creation.

[Undated]

I have always tried to get some sort of idea of what I really mean by the spiritual life. It's not easy. I think I divide the riches of the mind into two kingdoms: the kingdom of knowledge, where the reason gives understanding, and the kingdom of wisdom, where detachment gives understanding. This detachment is the life of the spirit, and its fruit is wisdom. That would cover it fairly well — the life of the artist and the life of the mystic. Its essence is its immediacy — without the distractions of belief or anxiety. It has no dogmas, it has no duties. It is a final synthesis of knowledge, and it is also a laying aside of knowledge. — But it remains a kingdom of the mind, and as indivisible as the kingdom of reason.

All circumstances in the history of the world that for any reason have favored detachment have kept the spiritual life in existence, accidentally, as it were: religion, because it was oriented toward "another" world; grief, because it swept away the preoccupying landmarks of this world; artistic creativeness, because it has always demanded a withdrawal. The wisdoms that have been born of these experiences are not necessarily to be trusted, for wisdoms of this order need not less but greater discipline than wisdoms of other orders, and they have not often had that. But such wisdoms are, nevertheless, the wisdoms man has always been wise enough to attribute to his gods, and when we have achieved it the myth of divinity will have come true on earth.

The Lake,[11] Dec. 23, 1916

checking up

These Christmas days at the Lake each year have been a taking of stock and a plan of campaign. It isn't *time* to do it that the Lake has given me — it's the perspective, the calmness. The Fall is always a hectic season — a time when "things" seem to rise in the might of their manifold pettiness, when the broken days seem to accomplish nothing and I lose my head — my worst mood gets the upper hand, and the only rule to which I steadfastly hold then is never to decide anything till I've ceased being an idiot.

But up here I'm no idiot. I'm strong and eager and in love with life. And Stanley's presence day by day — the ecstacy of it, and the quiet satisfaction — is like a great sweet light around me — a light from which no darkness looks fearsome.

The particular problem of this winter is how I may cut through the . . . and entanglements of our order of life and make good in my writing. I would like to simplify our living down to the level of Francis and Martha Fulton's — cut away the incubus of a house and coal fires and course dinners that is so surely swamping Mrs. Slaughter's talent in mere amateurness. But that would trouble Stanley's work — perhaps less than I think — but for that reason it isn't fair to begin with that. Anyway, he cares little enough for the complexities of domesticity, bless his heart! I'd be quite free to take an editorial job if I could get one. At home that had seemed the roughest, surest way of rousing me to a sharp, professional attitude. Now, perhaps it's because I don't seem to need such drastic medicine as I did two weeks ago — two days ago! — that solution seems less satisfactory. I'd like to get my "women" done. I felt then that they'd never "get across" till I'd acquired a better sense of an audience. That's what "Mary" lacks. But I deliberately decided to write her to please myself, with no aim but to satisfy my own requirements. And I think practice with models would give me an even more definite sense of what my "women" require than work on a ten-cent magazine. Yes. I'm going back to write Margaret Fuller for an audience — to write my "introduction" — to attempt Olive Schreiner. On the practical side, I must get a publisher back of me, and that may mean rewriting "Mary" before I'm willing to send her out. It's a big job — and begory I'll do it!

New Women of Three Centuries.

Christmas, '16. — Snowbound at the Lake.

I've pledged my word to a "business in life" now. Last night Stanley and I talked. We hurt each other badly, for words are clumsy things, and he is inexorable. But, at any rate, he does not baby me, and honesty helps even when it is cruel.

I said that for the sake of our love — our friendship, rather — I must pay my way in a job of my own. I would not, would not drift into the boredom, the pitiableness of lives like —— or ——. He said that, whatever the job, it would not hold me; nothing ever had, social work or teaching. Children might for a year or two, no more.

As for the question of success in such a thing having any value in our relations with each other, it was nonsense; it only meant that I'd discovered now that marriage in its turn did not hold me. If I'd found we lacked friendship now, there was no solution possible — neither of us could change our personalities. He had no faith in the future.

I told him he should see. My past list of jobs proved nothing: until I loved him nothing had ever seemed to me worth the effort of attaining. I could lay hold of no motive. Now I understood; I cared and cared deeply, and for what I wanted I was willing to pay high. I should prove that I could do better than to drift into a meaningless routine. I should prove that I was no rolling stone. I should prove too that whatever I could achieve in my own life was something added to our relationship with each other.

— And now I must prove my word. I must bind it to me till it is closer than breathing, nearer than hands and feet. It means that for the first time in my life, I have committed myself to the endeavor for *success* — success in writing. It means that before summer I shall have completed "Adventures in Womanhood" — and found a publisher for them. It means that what I can do to get them into the magazines, I will do. It means that with all the force within me, I will write, this winter.

Jan., 1917.

I read the *Real Adventure*[12] the other day — some year or so late. Of course it stirred me. Less, perhaps, for its story of a very understandable revolt against a play-thing existence, than for the motives it *left out*. Rose is to me an eminently satisfying and rounded person, the kind it's good to have in the world — morally healthy And she would have recoiled in displeasure from a motive of "justifying her existence" — from "doing good." On the other hand, she could never conceivably sink to wanting to "chuck it." She didn't mean to miss "the big things of life" — for her, the finest possible relation with her husband. For her, her elimination of motives was the natural result of her education and her temperament — with me it's all back breaking weeding out. The "big things of life"? — of course they include service, but they are love, friendship, beauty, clear thinking, honest personality —

I long to speak out the intense inspiration that comes to me from the lives of strong women. They have made of their lives a great adventure; they have proved that out of much bewilderment of soul, steadfast aims may . . .

The Great Affirmation of any honest mind implies also the power of rejection — In actual experience the greater, the more pivotal the Affirmation, the more devastating the rejection. Take Ellen Key. With her whole soul she affirms what our dirty-minded Puritan-bred society discounts in any private conversation: monogamy. She believes greatly and sincerely that (without the need of threat and punishment) without the double handcuffs of the marriage ceremony, without the threat of the vulgarity of the divorce court, men and women are capable of giving themselves to one another simply, completely, permanently, are capable of seeing in that permanency the dignity and beauty of their love. It is an affirmation of the attainability of a spiritual act our most spiritual leaders hesitate to make; yet they stand appalled before the negations it implies.

How much hunger for a focussed.   for effective action eats inward and leaves only a waste barrenness because no pivotal issues are articulated — because these hungerers and thirsters after righteousness are yet of that great class who cannot formulate their own issues, their own goals. And as their lives go barren — for they have the capacity for loyalty, for generous desire, but have not the capacity for that concentrated, pitiless analysis that divides the complicated sheep from the complicated goats of our modern issues.

[Undated]
I have always used the world of make-believe with a certain desperation. It has never been much an affair of daydreams — a useful pair of spectacles, rather, to color in some endurable fashion an unendurable mood. I remember the keen excitement of finding that I could create the perfect illusion that I was (doing this thing) for the *last time*. Tomorrow I would be dead; surely I could go thru' it

once even with a dash of zest. Days, weeks, almost years I wore those spectacles. They are inimitable for producing an illusion of vivacity and even gusto in the most melancholic.

But the necessity for that particular make-believe doesn't last always — for years I've spurned it. My spectacles now have nothing of the grim about them, but they're wonderfully effective. It's very simple: this is my daughter's life that's posing as mine. It's my daughter's love life which shall be perfect; it's my daughter's abilities which shall find scope; it's my daughter's insight that shall be true and valid; it is she who owes it to speak out her beliefs. It is she who shall not miss the big things of life. . . . — The efficacy of such spectacles I suppose no man could understand — how many women could, I wonder? Practically a great many women act all thru' their adult life in an un-make-believe version of the same underlying notion: the passionate belief in the superior worth-whileness of our children. It is stored up in us as a great battery charged by the accumulated instincts of uncounted generations. When there are no children, unless the instinct is somehow employed, the battery either becomes an explosive danger or at best the current rapidly falls off, with its consequent loss of power.

The highest endowments do not create — they only discover. All transcendent genius has the power to make us know this as utter truth. Shakespeare, Beethoven — it is inconceivable that they have *fashioned* the works of their lives; they only saw and heard the universe that is opaque and dumb to us. When we are most profoundly moved by them, we say, not "O superb creator" — but "O how did you *know!* Yes it is so." Lesser men may give us a very keen pleasure through "creation," as Poe does, as Stevenson does, but even they are caught at times up into that realm where they too discover the uncredited; — and then we pause in our tribute to their skill, and for the moment are simply one with them in their discovery. And those moments are all their glory.

May, 1917.
How far awry my plans have gone this year! I was to make good in writing — I've not touched it. I thought I had done with the med-

dling of social work — I've spent my whole year at it. In a sense I'm satisfied with the job. I've called an organization into being that's doing good work, and needed work; we've got Day Nurseries in sight. A dozen other women are working well who otherwise wouldn't have had a niche to work in. And with that I compare my writing — those "women" that nobody believes in, the falsetto note I'm so conscious of, the strain and turmoil that writing means for me; — why shouldn't I give it up? There are a half dozen positions I'm wanted in, and at will I can induce [?] one self or the other — the writer's self, or the worker's self. If only at the same time I could strangle the discarded self! It's the rub. The other day when I was getting up an open meeting and spending the day at the telephone, I wept because I came across a jumbled untouched verse manuscript. Yet I suppose I'd reverse the cause of tears if I were to pin my next decade to writing alone. And yet oh, I long to prove myself by writing! The best seems to die in me when I give it up. It is the self I love — not this efficient, philanthropic self. And isn't that the test? I need something to give me faith in my writing — some success, some point gained. But if I go on without heroics, just patiently believing in the part of me I dare to love — wouldn't that be worth while? Just to vegetate this summer, and write in this book, and, if I can, write "Margaret Fuller" — isn't that best, without being so wordy about my conflicting selves? And how useless to attempt anything but a steady day-by-day living with this tornado of world-horror over our heads —

Aug. 15, 1919 —

I wouldn't have missed Camp,[13] I find now; but it didn't answer my questions in the way I'd planned. It wasn't an answer at all; it was a challenge to prove my inspirations as good as theirs. Unless I can do that, it's my part to sink my irritations and rebellions and go after *their* inspirations. For they've got them, and there's an unencumbered ease and a "lit"-ness about their work that is most worth learning from. But oh! the muddleheadedness, the false exclusions, the holier-than-thou-ness that one must will oneself blind to, minute by minute.

Their very exclusions have emphasized the riches they cast over-board — hard thinking, concern with the life and organization of this world, sensitiveness to art values other than movement.

Oct. 1920.

There is good in me, and Oh! there is great good in Stanley. And we've both of us a decent measure of self-control. Why must we go on hurting each other so cruelly? I feel about it as I might if we were two children I've never had. I think I've no more resentment than if he *were* my child — and I wonder sometimes if I'm not just as powerless to right things as if I were the mother. For it isn't a question of greater self-control — the more I control myself to his requirements, the greater violence I shall do my own — kill them in the end. I know so well what he needs: — he's taken me once for all — the intimacy is proved, established; all he asks is to keep an even tenor. And, knowing this, for years I can keep away from sub-jects which disrupt the quiet — my own ambitions; my sense of futility; children — chiefly children. But I'm made on the exactly antithetical scheme — it is my necessary breath of life to understand and expression is the only justification of life that I can feel without prodding. The greatest relief I know is to have put something in words, no matter if it's as stabbing as this is to me; and even to have him say cruel things to me is better than an utter silence about his viewpoint, year in and year out. — And so it's insoluble — a wanton cruelty to him no less than to me. So we grow more and more strangers to the other — united only by gusts of feelings that grow to seem more and more emptiness in our lives, not part and parcel of them; and by an intolerable pity for each other as human beings cruelly tortured.

[Undated]

"Choose the best, and custom shall render it easy and agreeable." There's a lot of comfort in that. It's been known for a couple of thousand years — I believe Bacon quotes it out of Seneca — and William James has dinned it in the ears of this generation. But we can't seem to count on it. Now my best, my thing "that in all my years I tend to do" is surely writing.

[Undated]

America's Coming of Age, Van Wyck Brooks.[14]

The happiest excitement in life is to be convinced that one is fighting for all one is worth on behalf of some clearly seen and deeply felt good, and against some greatly scorned evil. . . . The exhilarating sense of conflict and of rest from conflict which together make up the meaning of life, no longer universally possible on the plane of instinct, have largely come to exist in the more contagious, more gregarious, more interdependent world of the intelligence. In that world the majority are lost and astray unless the tune has been set for them, the key given them, the lever and the fulcrum put before them, the spring of their own personalities touched from the outside.

It is of no use to talk about Reform. Society will be very obedient when the myriad personalities that compose it have, and are aware that they have, an object in living. . . . The stench of atrophied personality.

[Undated]

A Defining of the Issues

A red-blooded person, if he is to find any satisfaction in the conflict of life, must sense an opposition of values, a conflict of issues to one side or the other of which he keeps himself loyal. From this attainment of his loyalty he privately instinctively measures his virtues; from his short-comings in its service, his sins. The issues may be a million-fold; they grade the man only as they correspond to a worthy distinction in reality, according as they really cut deep. No matter how vital the man, he cannot rise to any great significance so long as his conflict of issues is between failure and success measured in dollars; nor his wife, so long as her opposition of values is measured by the dust on the rounds of the chairs. That goes without saying.

In the progress of feminism the issues have been drawn usually on some variation of parasitism vs. labor — Mrs. Gilman claimed it for the sake of woman's economic independence, Olive Schreiner for the sake of her self-fulfillment. I think conditions are rapidly falsifying these issues: the vast majority have the right to labor now — wartimes have seen to that — in the great war-game no one is exempted. And it is a necessary emancipation; without it there would be no further step. But it is only initial. Our factories are filled with women and girls, and their experience is as nothing — nothing — in their development. They get from it no sense of the dignity of associated labor, no sense of the contributive value of their product, no experience in organized self-government. It is along these lines, through trades organizations, that this pointless labor must be made a factor in the onward march of women.

Practically all the "labor" open to the majority of women is open to the same objection; something must be done to it before it can have any value. That value can be gained quite as surely off a pay roll as on it. No, I do not believe that the modern conditions require any longer the issue of labor — paid labor vs. parasitism. Personally, it means nothing to me, what do I care where the money comes from? And don't I know that I can use my time to better advantage myself than an employee could? — Of course every woman should have it as a resource: when money is essential she should be able to market her time and abilities, when love is a curse she should be economically able to escape from it, when years are a long ennui, she should take up an exciting career. But these are all special problems and in this generation need only rough commonsense for their solution. The deeply-sundering issue in feminism doesn't lie any longer in paid labor vs. parasitism.

What is it then? Initiative to go after the big things of life — not freedom *from* somewhat; initiative *for* somewhat. Now for some women the big things of life include political activity and it is abundantly right that they should seek their place there. For the great majority of women, however, the big things of life are love, children, social activity according to their abilities. And in the matter of love and children there is no initiative, liberty of conscience, permitted. But it is necessary that we have some voice in the conditions under which these big things of our lives shall be realized, that we have the freedom for their achievement. The emotional part of woman's life — that part which makes her a woman — must be brought up out of the dark and allowed to put forth its best. . . .

. . . Issue: It is not political recognition, it is not economic independence: the goal could never be reached without these — without dress reform, also readjustment of conventional marriage and the abolition of the stigma on divorce, the honest facing of prostitution and illegitimacy, without the economic compensation of women's services in childbearing; all these are a part of the great objective. But the ultimate objective, the high goal remains an inward affair, a matter of attitude.

. . . We have gained no real victory yet. What of our social life, our economic life, our physical life? Still we shrink in terror from freedom of conscience there: (illustrate, Ibsen, *Ghosts*). Our wise men tell us the danger is unthinkable. There are sanctities that must be preserved.

Why have these fields been so backward? Because women were backward. They are the fields where women have the great stakes. Her role to bring freedom of conscience into the complexities of our social life, so to govern freedom that liberty of conscience may come in social relationships.

. . . The issue really and truly is fine free living in the spirit world of socialized spiritual values — for men as for women. But owing to artificial actual conditions their problems are strikingly different.

[Undated]

Goals for Women

In respect to their purposes in living, women defy classification. For most of them goals do not exist; the goals are confusing to think of, they are vaguely felt to be subversive of many comfortable customs. At most, a goal exists for her in and thru' the person of some one else: for her husband she must perform vicarious leisure, must indicate his bank account by her outer wraps; for her children she must achieve or maintain a social circle to which they may be "presented." Or, on a higher plane, she may desire to become the perfect complement to her particular mate, or the adequate potter of her children's spiritual clay. Now selflessness, on either plane, must be judged, in common sense, by its social utility. And the verdict, in every case where it means a lack of responsibility for achievement of a four-square personality, the verdict must be that such selflessness is both futile and wasteful — futile in that any elementary recognition of the facts of experience . . . any kindergarten recognition of the psychology of personality must force down our throats the fact that in every family the most loving meddling with other people's personalities is still meddling and [is] rewarded as meddling always is, by frustration; wasteful, in that at that point the dignity of robust personality has been denied.

"Goals for Women" is based on the recognition of thoroughgoing differences between men and women — differences of the mind and of the body. These differences are both deeper in some respects and shallower in others than are today generally recognized. A great accumulation of data is necessary — of unfettered discussion, of unfettered pioneering in action — before much that is can be achieved. (The accumulation of this social data, we may consider, I think, a duty.) All that can be deduced now is that granting these thoroughgoing differences between the man and the woman, it is only by thoroughgoing cooperation on an equal plane, in thought and in action, that the potentialities of society can be realized.

[Undated]
We do not trust love. We have never trusted love. How should we? Born of Puritan distrust of the senses, of its disgust at the basic manifestations of life, brought up from our youth to think sacred and indispensable the perpetual lock and key of marriage — how should we have faith in love? For us, a working faith in the power for good of love is a reversal of our whole attitude toward society: can anyone who believes that love can be trusted to make every self-respecting effort after permanence argue fanatically that an extension of the legal right to have done with loveless co-habitation will

deluge the world with immorality? To one who has glimpsed a vision of faith in love it is the first step toward any morality of any worth whatever. Or can one who honors love so much that it is inconceivable that a husband or wife should hold one another by any other created bond, can he grow hot and insulted at the mere idea that causes for divorce should be widened beyond a proof of adultery and cruelty?

It seems impossible as one reads the words of these self-styled "upholders of morality" that they have ever known love or had one vision of its ideal — could they ever have dreamed love's dear dream of permanence, could they ever have seen that only in this dream love attains dignity? Could they have seen the burning bush and removed their shoes from off their feet, knowing that the ground whereon they stood was holy ground? Could they have known love's passion to give itself new and new and new, never as something promised and expected, as a glorious free-willed flood tide at morning.

If we trusted love it would not obsess us. For that reason above all — that we may go on to something else — oh, we need so desperately to learn, syllable by syllable this new faith in love. It is the great new motivation that is coming — the motivation that will open the next great horizons for the world. We have never glimpsed what those horizons will reveal, or only in rare homes have we caught the hint, the hint that must necessarily be intimate and revealed as the sap coming in the spring trees that we know only thru' the ever returning miracle that enables them after the sterility of winter at last to put forth and bud.

It will mean faith of such a sort that it will refuse to be satisfied with less than its own counsels of perfection, and will have strength to achieve them not in promiscuity but in the loyalty of one woman and one man. It will mean faith of such sort that a career without love, a denial of love that a glib success may be attained, will seem the great refusal, and we will draw no lines outside of which our experience of love is punishable. It will mean such a faith and open-eyed understanding of relationships that we will no longer think it worth while to buy the merely physical chastity of our young girls by maintaining the cause of prostitution. It will mean that we definitely believe the message of the long evolution of love: that it has added to its dynamic intensity a fineness of incomparable worth, . . .

. . .[15] can't get food, that fact's got to be the limit of your horizon. It's just as bad with this other hunger; and the worst of it is that both hungers paint a lie. It seems that the satisfaction of the craving will give you inspiration such as you've never known and strength for increased achievement. It's utterly false; satisfaction is a soporific. It's an end in itself, and its culmination is — sleep. Oh, I know that's enough — those tortured years don't ask for any more. My only point is that, in saving ourselves from the human waste heap, it's necessary to satisfy the craving so THAT *we'll be free to go on to something else.* — You ask if I can suggest anything. It's something for personal decision; but I know H. G. carefully examines the case against what's characteristically known as "self abuse" and can't make out any verdict against it except when it violates any law of. . . . I can't believe that "free love" is a way out — it seems to me that every chance love's got for dignity and distinction depends on a *belief* in its permanency. It is repulsive to me to think of blunting its possibilities by casual shiftings. That's why I can't swallow the solution in Plato's Republic — otherwise it has its attractions. — There must be a way out, for future generations if not for ours: the whole question of the effect on health and sanity is so absolutely untouched by investigation — practically — that who knows what an unsuperstitious study might uncover? Perhaps we'll find out that in women of this type a conscientious regard for conventional purity has bred more bitterness and disgust of life than prostitution has at the other end, in *its* victims.

[Undated]

Three years ago I went one Sunday in New Hampshire to a big Second Advent camp meeting. The impression was one of the most vivid I have ever had. It seemed the *reductio ad absurdum* of the religion even of those I respected. The great outdoor camp ground was filled with close-lipped people to whom the universe was about as rich and various as it is to a cat after mice. It seemed to me that their minds and souls were knotted and tied against the very notion of infinity. And yet the whole object that had brought them together was to claim for themselves and to testify to each other, personal and intimate consolations and championship from the Almighty that staggered imagination. No stretch of sympathy could conceive that finite man was here rising toward the infinite — No. It seemed to me that now I understood such in its essence was even the religion I respected — it was always fundamentally a paralyzing, a limiting, a mocking finite, of the Infinite.

It was not a time when I was desperate. Love had seen to that, and happiness was every morning fresh and amazing. I could leave the Infinite alone rather easily for myself and for other people. For the first time in my life I could go among people without wondering how and why they endured living. I wished now that I might have known then what I knew now so that I could have been glad with them instead. For now it was almost ecstacy to march . . . this funny parade with a thousand people, and know that any or all of them understood and had been lit by this bonfire of love and delight I knew. And I had thought their lives meaningless!

But in the years that followed I found myself thinking often of that camp meeting, and with envy. I was amazed at the time, for my original feeling of repulsion had seemed too strong to allow of any easy transition to desire. But the old fight was on again — I understood that it was *necessary*, necessary not as any exposition or embroidery of life, but for the continuance of living itself, to (link up) finite and infinite. It seemed to me that life could not be lived otherwise —

Oh, but you are no preacher, you see! you are my play fellow, you
    lifting, falling, laughing water!
I let you maul me about in your tumbled, white-haired breakers —
You are the strong, careless-handed Sport of God,
You, the sun-flooded, you the storm-exultant.
Here, here I join your laughing carousels —
Here where I cut arrow-like your solid up-right wave,

Here where I lie quiet in the long-drawn undulations of your tidal
    risings —
Here I give myself up to your age-long frolic.

[Undated]
   The goal of intelligence in human relations would very likely be
to secure relationships of loving enough, starting with sufficient
dignity and intensity to allow something to come of them. But
when I look at the people who can boast [of] intelligence over
against those who can't, they don't fall into any classification of the
sheep and the goats. Wouldn't being able to keep out of brawls
with one's closest intimates be an obvious point at issue? And look
at the brawls that are the classic feature of the modern sophisticated
menage! I'd rather risk my grandmother's techniques, that never
once were on the level of conscious scrutiny to make her "shaper of
her fate" than . . .

[Undated]
   There can be nothing half so self-evident as the absurdity of maintaining the general *rightness* of any set of conclusions, and consequent wrongness of the rest. Thanks be unto the Lord, I suppose,
righteousness was never patented. It exists wherever and in whatever human being any idea kindles to light genuine enthusiasm. It
is merely an academic problem whether Shelley was *right*, or the
Tolstoi of the later years — Dante or Montaigne — Nietzsche or
Emerson. How easy it is [to] pile up the absurd contrasts! And
coming down to the conflicts where the dust is not yet laid, it follows that validity goes both . . . with Stanley and with Bob, with
a whole nation at war and with Bertrand Russell. It is only a question of the degree in which the conviction answers to the hungers
of that one and only soul, and of the quality of the loyalty that it
commands in that soul.

   I wonder if any philosopher ever tried to pair off the basic ideas
of different cultures with their emotional contexts in specific societies. The Christian world believes in immortality; does it bring

us peace and comfort? Oh no! probably dread of death and incon-
solable grief for the departed have never been carried to greater
lengths than in this same Christian world. The Stoics and Epi-
cureans built on the fundamental conviction that all is material
and relative, they were intellectual skeptics; yet the ethical context
of their systems can give pointers in the virtues to most, no, to all,
revealed religions of the world. The Cyrenaics would be an even
more extreme example. Their starting point is that all life is a shadow,
that all existence is merely at the pinpoint of the present, that knowledge is illusory and virtue without intrinsic value — and their teaching, derived from all this, is of the scrupulously honorable life — Do
we look curiously enough into the strange clashes in history when
new ideas are put forward? Why did Natural Selection rouse such
a furor, except for the illogical fact that a belief in out-of-hand
creation had got itself wrapped up into a religious bundle of ethics
and theology and emotional responses? The sudden association of
poor old Marxian socialism with "red peril" today is of the same
order. And who could make out a case in logic for the orthodox
identification of capitalism and democracy? No — in politics, in
religion, in marriage, in every department even in the most advanced
cultures, the basic fortuitous associations persist; things just "are
so." — And what a beautiful pyramid of analogies one could pile
up from anthropology! I'd like to make out the case for identity
between civilized man and savages in respect to fortuitous association
of ideas. All anthropologists nowadays admit it.

Contiguous to our lives on one side there exists a life of the spirit
— a world wherein we are as babes, and yet have to learn to stand
upright. O, I do not mean ministerial commonplaces! I mean
something so strenuous that the quests of the Grail are but faint
shadows of a reality, something so costly that there are few indeed
who dare reckon on paying that price. And yet that is the only
thing in life that interests me. The growth of the world in that
direction alone is able to excuse its existence. And that can only
come about by individual quest.

The unendurable dregs of every spasm of bitterness is always the
same — "Faugh! it's all melodrama! melodrama!" — Quite dispas-

sionately, I think the sting is largely undeserved, for I think I can stand as much bitterness as another man, and that when I give way it's because at the moment it's the only way out: Or perhaps I write that out of desperation because I know I sat down here to nerve [?] myself and I can't do that without the rudiments of self-respect. There you are! Am I my own dupe, or am I an honest melancholiac at these times who needs doctor's advice? Damn!

The secret of art is a love of the *medium*. The medium is only the outwardness thru' which the spirit at the moment works, yet to love it in itself and for itself is the indispensable prelude to achievement. It must be a love for it that makes easy submission to its limitations and insight into its possibilities. So that a wood-cut page from an old 15th century Book of Hours, with its honest limitation to the nature of the wood it worked in, can give us a quality of pleasure which the superfluous craftsmanship of Timothy Cole can never touch. And a dozen lines of an etching by Rembrandt, each line bitten visibly into the metal, conjures up a joy and a sense of finality that the whole 19th century does not communicate.

So with words.

St. Paul sur Nice
August, 1926

This mood that haunts me with such persistency has nothing to do with any nihilism. It passes for such, but it's really a refuge from it. I know to the bottom of my subconsciousness that no combination of circumstances, no love, no well-being, will ever give me what I want. But death will. Passion is a turn-coat, but death will endure always; life is a bundle of fetters or it isn't worth living, and for all our dreaming of freedom, only death can give it to us. Life must be always demeaning itself, but death comes with dignity we don't have even to deserve. We all know these things, but in me it's bred a passionate conviction that death is better than life. Why do people fear and resent it? Shouldn't they hanker for it? Isn't it good to know that we'll be the plowed earth of this planet through hot human generations that will disport themselves as we did, millions of ants upon their ant hill?

And my mood has nothing to do with suicide. It's a cheap way of attaining death, and death at least need not come cheap. I shall come by it honestly, and I wish I could think that people would feel that same honor for me that I feel first at any news of death — the honor for anyone who has held out to the end.

[Undated][16]

There is only one problem in life: that fire upon our flesh shall burn as a knife that cuts to the bone, and joy strip us like a naked blade. There are no other problems. We live instead, our passions we fling at the sure lies and trumperies if perhaps by these we may buy one burning moment. We cast about always searching with what coin we shall purchase it. Some by incest have broken the crust and travelled to this earth-core of aliveness; some have made pain the bedfellow of their imagination and licked blood from the welts they have laid upon the flesh of their most loved. Some have laid hold on fear; in other generations men feared hell and quivered, and they feared death too before scales fell from their eyes and they saw that within is death a bogey. But we, caught between the accident of birth and the desirability of death, how shall we set stars in heaven? We shall wither to our death as in a dream, knowing all things are folly, phantoms, shadows.

June 9, 1934

What is this need I have so strongly and which comes over me only the more overwhelmingly after I've been faithful for a while to my jobs and duties? It's nothing that I can recognize in the other people I see much of; their needs could all be met by certain adjustments in the external world or in their own thinking. They set up various kinds of relationships with work and things and people — love relationships or experiences of a will to power — and it's in these relationships that their life flowers or goes to waste. I can't get hold of either attitude really; work even when I'm satisfied with it is never my child I love nor my servant I've brought to heel. It's always busy work I do with my left hand, and part of me watches grudging the waste of lifetime. It is always distraction — and from what? It's hard to say. From contemplation and detachment, from an impersonal candor that knows work and people in their proper proportions — that sees existence under the form of eternity, maybe. I wish I had lived in a generation that cultivated the spiritual life; perhaps then I wouldn't have felt so frustrated. Perhaps, though, in having this life traditionally channelled for me, I'd have been content with the fortuitous degree that was provided, that seems intolerable to me, for the great reward that my temperament has ever given me is detachment and unconcern. That can't by definition come in the course of traditional participation, even in a cult of spiritual life. As it seems to me now there is no way to achieve these rewards if one has signed on a dotted line. And if one has not, the way is painful and erratic. Perhaps one day the right environment will be hit upon and a culture will arise that by its very nature fosters spiritual life that is nevertheless detached and adventurous — something of the sort that Spinoza or Christ achieved in certain flashes. It's nothing that has appeared on earth yet.

What might it be like? Chiefly a great sureness, experience out of which belief and existing had passed with all the other traits of temporality, love that could recognize no private motive in its glad acceptance of whatever was unrolled before it. Work could not be alien to it, certainly not friendship, but to work or to live would not be distraction but largess of its own prodigal security. It would be so amply foundationed upon verities that are not the sport of time and chance that incidents of faithlessness, of failure, of death, would not touch its being. The many changes would all have departed and these to whom the life of the spirit was a reality could pass in and out of the temple at will, their smallest acts lit with the radiance of their knowledge. It's a dream.

Preface to
an Anthology

I LOVE some of my printed books as much as anyone can. Just the same, my heart always beats faster at a book of blank pages than it does at any book filled with printing.

> Heard melodies are sweet but those unheard
> Are sweeter,

and opening a dummy I almost think I hear them. Therefore because this one is so pleasant and so handily shaped, I shan't copy my own verses in it but something nearer celestial singing. I have always needed to have all in one place the poems I know by heart; even when I know them well a word or a verse may slip me, and even sometimes I forget for years on end to recall some poem I've learned. This book shall hold the poems I know by heart.

It will be pleasant to write them down, one an evening, at the end of the day. I shall write them in from memory and correct afterwards any wrong words or omissions. If I want to include any poem here, there'll be only one way to do it — to learn it. But I have no quarrel with that. There is only one way to have citizenship without let or hindrance in the country of Poetry and that is to know poems by heart. Anyone's days have waste stretches in them — subway rides, speeches, sleepless nights — but if one has poems by heart these may be the best moments of the day. I have found it so.

The order of the verses means only that on that particular night

156

I wanted to write out that particular poem. And they are not Best Poems; many poems — "The Ancient Mariner" and many passages of Shakespeare or of Blake — that I think belong in any such selection I happen never to have learned. But these are poems I have lived with.

Selections from the Correspondence
of Edward Sapir with Ruth Benedict
1923–1938

THESE LETTERS are a very small selection from the voluminous correspondence which Edward Sapir carried on with Ruth Benedict, mainly in the early years of their friendship. None of her letters survive, but the poems she sent him and his responses to them provide a sense of her side of the exchange. Almost all of Sapir's letters were written by hand, in a fine, precise script as if for publication, and when she once typed a letter to him he protested, "Use the typewriter for scientific MS but not for correspondence, please! Things don't look right in type."

The years from 1923 to 1925, in which they wrote most frequently — sometimes several long letters a week — were troubled ones for both of them. For Sapir this was the period of the illness and death of his first wife, of his increasing sense of isolation in his position in Ottawa before it was decided that he should go to the University of Chicago. For Ruth Benedict it was the period in which she tried to reconcile the demands of a professional commitment with those of her marriage. For both, the letters were an escape into the world of poetry — the poetry they wrote and the poetry of others of which they planned ideal anthologies. The friendship, begun in anthropology (see the earlier letters in Part I), was primarily informed by their aspirations as poets, and when each turned to other interests, the letters became less frequent. For each of them, poetry and writing about poetry was only a small fragment of their complex lives, but through it both were rescued from the isolation in which they were living, he in Ottawa and she in New York.

Ottawa, Ont.
Oct. 22, 1923

Dear Mrs. Benedict, . . .

. . . Thanks for your too kind remarks about the poems. I shall let you have the verse you speak of. The "Gypsy" poem[1] was for children and has not been published as yet. I never wrote about a falcon. You either mean "The Jackal" or "A Pair of Tricksters" (bluejay and raven). I believe I understand the latter, but the former does not seem quite naturally to mean what was in my mind when I wrote it, so it is a kind of vagabond thing now, looking for a kind orphan asylum of a critic. Neither has been published.[2] I'd discuss verse and drift and all that sort of thing, but it's too late and I haven't the heart. — Thanks for the Aldous Huxley, which is good enough for universal agreement (including Gosse and Courthope, if not Methusalah). Am wasting considerable time preparing for my weekly Literature lectures and struggling through Giddings' "Studies in the Theory of Human Society."[3] I shall let you manufacture the books of my castle-in-the-air career; while I content myself with Nootka Texts, Sarcee Texts, and a few articles of related interest. I'm not awfully ambitious or, if I am, am too lazy to stay so. And too distracted, I fear. — Watch the Dial. I have a little squib on Elsie's book, which will make you smile. I'm curious to see how she'll take it. You must let me know in due course of time.

Sincerely,
E. Sapir

P.S. I don't envy you your Museum tours. It must be hard on shoe leather.

Ottawa, Ont.
Nov. 15, 1924.

Dear Ruth,

Thank you for the verses, which I have wanted to write you about for some time. I like the two sonnets the best of the five poems.

"Discourse on Prayer" [4] is extraordinarily fine, and poignant. Could you not give it a less drab title than "Discourse on Prayer"? "Lovers' Wisdom" [5] is even better in idea, if anything, and very moving, but seems to me [to] have one or two purely technical shortcomings. The off rhymes (silence — incense, lovers — idolators, relinquishment — argument), with their weight or half-weight on unaccented syllables, do not strike me as happy, though they are perhaps not unsought, and "lovers — idolators" is a technically inaccurate couple because lóvers is a feminine ending, while ĭdólătórs has a weak masculine ending. I should not be professoring if I heard a subtle harmony in these curiously humble rhymes, but I am afraid I don't. Such half lights do not seem to me to go with the great feeling and large seriousness of the sonnet. Then, "idolators of foulness" — is it not a little precious? Finally, "the corrupted urn" does not quite follow up "corrupted under earth the sweet limbs are." I should not be so detailed in my remarks if I did not think so highly of this fine sonnet as to wish you to make it perfect. Certainly these two sonnets show that you can easily master the form if you wish, and that you can inform the outlines with individual feeling and keenness and great beauty is already abundantly evident. I do wish you would persuade yourself to apply yourself more continuously to verse. Your efforts would be more than repaid and you would soon find yourself one of a very distinguished group indeed. — "Wood Paths" [6] seems to me to have idea rather than convincingness of expression. "Armored" [7] too needs revision. The omitted relative after "whispers" is awkward; "implacable to destroy" is a poor line. "In Parables" [8] has splendid passages; I like particularly stanzas 3 and 4, which have that same lightning-like strength that I think I once noted in some of your other work ("Sacrilege," [9] for instance). The last stanza seems obscure to me. . . .

Discourse on Prayer

Never ask God for peace. Have I not thrown
My years as dust upon the wind and cried
For weariness, that it might put aside

One hour the insupportable madness known
Only of men dream-tortured? Beauty has blown
Her fever through me, and every kiss that died
On passionate flesh been flame intensified
Upon the quick in nights I lay alone.

And I have peace. The moon at harvest is
Round jocund laughter on the sky, — no more;
And I have sleepy comfort in your kiss
That is a wind-blown flame to you. Therefore
Set seal upon your lips and make no prayer
Lest you be too a traitor unaware.

Lovers' Wisdom

Lovers have only bitterness of death.
To all beside there is some chancelled silence
In deep grief that still keeps faith with breath;
From loss and loveliness some sudden incense
Drifts voluptuous down their sorrow. Lovers
Have nothing left, the incomparable worth
Of flesh become a shifting ash that covers
Love's utmost grief with characterless earth.

Lovers have nothing left. Thereby they win
Largess of wisdom in relinquishment:
Never to dream that those things which have been,
Imperishable still, are argument
For eyes that fear the present; never turn
From this one hour to the corrupted urn.

Ottawa, Ont.
Nov. 26, 1924.
I was delighted to get the three poems, as you may have gathered
from "Signal," [10] and shall don my professorial robes at once and

discuss them as best I can. It is wonderful to know you are likely to take your poetic gift seriously and get down to serious work. More of that in a moment.

"Toy Balloons" [11] is a splendid poem. I admire your ability to use solid words like "unadulterate" and "perpetuities" with such effect. It is a significant sign. The whole poem is extraordinarily strong. There are just two slight technical points about it that seem to be worth mentioning. "Do nót sell thése to children" seems to me to drift a little, rhythmically. Can't you strengthen that passage? I also feel that "They are too slight . . . finger touch" is a trifle wowzy. What is "they"? Not "children," I presume, though there is that syntactic possibility. It must be "these," i.e. "dreams of men." But you had said that the dreams were "blown each into a perfect sphere;" in other words, the dreams *are* balloons. How then can you say "they" ("dreams" balloons) "are too slight to *hold the globed . . . beauty.*" Is not that like a pair of concentric spheres? Why not rather say something about the children in contrast to your masterly last sentence about the old? I have gone into detail because this should be a first-class poem. — "Profit of Dreams" [12] has the makings but is not as close to complete mastery of form as the other. The octave is by far the better part of it, but I regret that "idols of stone whose gross feet" sounds a little too commonplacely reminiscent of the proverbial "idols with feet of clay." But it is the sestet that needs re-writing the most. I feel that the concrete episode, "Last night . . . quiet things," which is after all not a very original idea nor very originally expressed, takes away from the authority of the more abstract matter that precedes. "That nothingness shall withstand" is unrhythmical. Better would be "That nothing shall withstand" as both more rhythmical and more abandoned. "That leave . . . being" is rubbed, and "thing-being" clashes for my ear. Throw away the sestet and make another more in keeping with the majesty of the octave. — "This Gabriel" [13] has wonderful passages. "Walking the stars, his even pace / Shaped to a crystal citadel?" takes one's breath away for its majestic originality. But I don't, frankly, quite understand "He liked . . . divinity." Who or what besides "this Gabriel" is referred to in "their common scars"? People or stars? Does "a simple tree" roll into one the stars over the tree and the crucifixion? What does "transcience" mean? I feel hopelessly stupid about this finely marching and austere poem. I think I notice in this and other work a certain tendency to use pronouns a little unguardedly.

But these and the previous poems prove beyond all possibility of argument that you have the stuff and the go, a unique feeling for majesty and austere irony, great boldness of conception, and the beginnings, at least, of a very original diction. Rhythm, I suspect, will always be a secondary consideration with you, but perhaps I am quite wrong. I believe rhythm comes to its own only after great experience in handling words and forms. Now to the moral. You must take this business of writing verse far more seriously than you do or pretend to do, Ruth. . . . I should not waste too much time on the sonnet but go clean into the barer and stronger forms, which best suit your temperament and genius. Let the smoke gradually give way to flame. . . .

I am very glad you are drawn to Hopkins. He is very difficult and sometimes needlessly obscure but nearly always worth one's serious while. A poet for poets. . . .

. . . Your copy of "Time's Wing" [14] must be blurred. The last lines read:

> Nor I can rùn
> Befòre your wíng
> Wĭth ă cóolnĕss còme
> And stráight swíng.

In other words, "nor is it I who can escape Time — no more than God himself —, as he comes ["come" is the participle] with the coolness, wing-beaten air, that warns of his impending presence and with the straight, unflinching, measured swing or flap of his wings." Others too find this last stanza difficult, so that I may try to change it, though to me it is so simple and transparent as can be. I had hoped you would like the poem, as it is perhaps the most authentic thing rhythmically I ever essayed. The first two stanzas wrote themselves at once, the third was next day's substitute for another one that seemed unworthy. — No, I did not submit "Lovers of Happiness" [15] and "The Window of his Soul" [16] to Miss Monroe. They happened to be knocking at another door just then; the former has been rejected by The Measure. I doubt if Miss Monroe would care for either. Her taste always leans to the pretty and second best.

I have been disappointed not to get your Religion by now.[17] Let me have read it before I see you in New York. Nor have I yet read Lowie's book.[18] I am planning to be present at the linguistic meeting on the last Sunday in December and shall probably go to Washington. I have sent in a couple of titles for the meeting — quite technical linguistic papers (Kwakiutl-Nootka and Athabaskan). The Cooper Union lecture comes on January 11th.

Signal (To A. S.)

Edward Sapir

Throw fagots on the fire,
  Armfuls of knotted oak!
Let the mad cinders dance
  In the revolving smoke.

Let swirl the mountain cloud —
  Toss it to wind, to sea!
On the horizon wisp
  Let vanish utterly.

Throw fagots on the fire!
  Give the mad tonguing play,
Path for the flame's desire,
  Shoulder the smoke away.

Profit of Dreams

All things fail save only dreams. There only
Profit is unalloyed, a quickened flame
That leaves no forest desolate, a lonely

Pool no cloud can shadow. We defame
Blindly our surest blessings, to pursue
Idols of stone whose gross feet and hair
We surfeit with caresses, to subdue
That doubt of beauty we misname despair.

I shall keep my dreaming. Last night we walked
Under sun-tangled branches hand in hand,
And our two palms made music while we talked
Of quiet things. That nothingness shall withstand
All futile years, that leave no other thing
At crest of being, with unbroken wing.

Ottawa, Ont.
Dec. 12, 1924.

. . . I am very glad you have made up your mind to look seriously
at your verse. You were evidently aching to throw yourself whole-
heartedly into it and needed but an encouraging nudge or two. I
won't be disappointed with the product because I know the ability,
the richness of experience, the boldness of conception, and the
moulding power are there. Do not make the cardinal mistake (for
you) of essaying any but worthy themes. I am becoming still further
convinced (I have just read "Our Task is Laughter" [19]) that you
will do well to give the sonnet a rest. You do it thoroughly well but
its external prettiness does not quite go with good style of matter.
Try severer forms — crisp, angular patterns that will drive you to
your very best, sudden, and sardonic expression. The sonnet has a
linked sweetness about it that forces crisp geniuses to sag every now
and then. It does quite literally demand a filling in. Don't give up
the sonnet, of course, but don't make a religion of it. — "Our Task
is Laughter" is very fine. Again the peculiar gift of using difficult
words rightly and strongly and without strain. "Her dear absurdity,"
"whose wisdom is but by decree" (but note sound clashes: *wis* . . .
is, but by. Beware!), "to wear its farthest implications," "ultimate
drolleries" (this is the real thing, fetched, I suppose, from some
Ultima Thule of Donne-like shades), "cajoles . . . from the rotting

years" — these phrases are mintage. Nobody else is doing just your style of diction. Robinson is crabbed, Bodenheim far less natural. Your great merit, I am beginning to see, is that you are finely in the tradition, even Puritan tradition, but with a notable access of modernity, not flaunted or sedulously nurtured, but slowly, unconsciously grown. Your expression is never stale, yet never exotic. What better could one ask? There are two passages in this last poem I demur to — slightly. "From their conformity" seems worn and also vague — a shop-word from your inventory of protest. And the last line should be strictly iambic for maximum strength, say "Who else inherits the world's hemispheres?" or something cadenced like "Who else can hold the world's two hemispheres?" As it is, the last line seems to stumble a bit.

Now for content. It is dangerous to give advice (!) on anything so intimate, but it strikes me you are banking a little too heavily on the philosophy of prescription and therapeutic protest. One feels a little too much the effect of inhibition and of irritation at this inhibition. Always "Thou shalt not" and "But I will!" Too much of this will bring you to a blind alley. I suspect that what you really need is something like systematic idleness. Are you not allowing yourself to be driven too much? Can't you develop an atrophied conscience? Or rather no conscience at all? Why not let things slide a little and give your fancy a chance? It seems hard to have to say, "Our *task* is laughter." Your verse won't lose edge when you loosen up the psychic machinery, a bit. Don't fear. By the way, you mustn't dare use a *nom de plume*. No tricks of the protective coloration type. Better develop a hide if you're going to lose your conscience. . . .

. . . There is one interesting facet of verse appreciation that we never discussed, but I am driven to it now. I refer to the relation of verse to music. I am passionately fond of certain kinds of music and there is for me just that nostalgia in haunting passages of music that you evidently get from Miss Adams' verse. I strongly suspect that my trouble is that my richest type of expression is potentially a musical one, that my linguistic expression gets its color from rhythms, and the intellectual content of words, but that the subtler feeling value of words and phrases is deficient in me. I believe that an analysis would show that my verse rhythms, both creatively and appreciatively, are musical rhythms transplanted to language, not speech rhythms or idealized speech rhythms. (Incidentally, this may explain why I am not very sensitive to Frost's famous use of speech rhythms.) This I do know — that my rhythmical intentions are often, significantly often, missed, as though I were using words to carry pulses they are intrinsically alien to. And so often I have observed that when I read aloud what I have written the hearer receives the poem as an entirely different thing from what he had heard in his own silence. I speak of this not because I attach importance to my rhythms (they are not individual or compelling enough to warrant any particular pother) but merely to indicate once more that linguistic *art* must be somewhat foreign to me. It results, horribly, that my poetic appreciation is born a cripple. My unconscious loyalty to music is probably a bar to the subtler sorts of poetic appreciation. Perhaps I am all wrong in this, but if the two kinds of aesthetic appreciation are not completely co-congenial (and I doubt if they are), there may be some ground for believing that poetry is a marginal, not a central, expressive medium for me and that what little success I can extort from the Muse is nothing but an extortion, a negligible *succès d'estime*. And all this, of course, must have its counterpart in the appreciative sphere. Have you ever thought of this underground incompatibility of music and rhythmic language? Or is it absurd to theorize, there being as many rhythmical accents in poetry as there are significant individuals with rhythm in their souls, be this rhythm of musical origin or speech origin or both at once? . . .

Our Task is Laughter

Being then branded, do not weep for this.
What have they cherished behind fast-turned key
One-half so precious as this injury
That leaves us still together? Here only bliss
Is for our taking, stripped of the artifice
She wears to guard her dear absurdity

From those whose wisdom is an old decree;
Who cannot know the folly of a kiss.

Our task is laughter. We must learn to wear
Its farthest implications in our souls,
And fashion our years out of the mocking flare
Of ultimate drolleries. Who else cajoles
A greater wisdom from the rotting years?
Who else inherits earth's two hemispheres?

Ottawa, Ont.
Dec. 20, 1924.

. . . I prefer the earlier version of "Lovers' Wisdom" [20] in spite of my former criticism. I should not like to lose "plumb the mockery of God's mirth." In the later version the new image seems rather drab and I find the assonance "characterless earth" somewhat jejune.

I don't see why you need feel discouraged by a run of rejections. Torrence is apparently crotchety in his tastes and Harriet is, of course, still less dependable. I think you'll find it necessary to bombard a considerable number of journals with a long-continued barrage of verse ammunition to score your hits. I am sure that is everyone's experience, though of course it sometimes happens that a particular editor may take a spontaneous fancy to somebody's work. Quality does not count nearly so heavily as most people suppose it does. There are hundreds of reasons for rejecting first-rate poems and dozens for accepting rotten ones. A certain level of quality is of course necessary for consideration — and that matriculation quality you more than possess — but the chances of any particular poem's acceptance are always slim.

I have not done any verse to speak of lately. You have "The Rescue" [21] and "Be not afraid of Beauty," [22] neither of which I am at all sure of. The enclosed, "Star-gazer," [23] impresses me more favorably.

I am sorry to hear you are not going to Washington. With you and Margaret Mead away and Boas only partly present the meeting is sure to seem dull. It is absurd for Boas to leave just before my linguistic papers are due, for I presented them for his especial benefit! Nobody else there will care a ha'penny. But that's always the way with these meetings. They are a perfect symbol of the way life meanders along. . . .

Ottawa, Ont.
Jan. 19, 1925.

Your three poems are splendid. Congratulations. The refrain of "Sirens' Song" [24] is exquisite. I should like to see ever so much more of your blank verse if this is how you are going to do it. It has stride and the noble arch. Lest you be swept away on a Miltonic breeze, however, forgive my pedantry a couple of technical animadversions. Odysseus is trisyllabic, not Ŏdýssĕús. In the last line of the first blank-verse stanza I find the "that" a little taxing because of the two relative clauses preceding ("who knot . . ." and "that leaves . . ."). "For guerdon of gods' bounty," I find a bit dim, and "gods' bounty" is for the eye — the ear apperceives "God's bounty." Finally, my ear finds "that we should refuse" unconvincing metrically; I made a similar criticism, you may remember, of a passage in the toy balloons sonnet, I think it was. But, seriously, I hope you are going in strong for blank verse. "Lordlings of infertile days" has the right go.

The two sonnets do not strike me as too clearly Robinsonian by any means — the thought is too strictly your own. In "Sight" [25] you have achieved a very fine climax. There is latent irony in the "stare-starred" clang (or was this unintentional?) and the last line and a half is strong beyond praise. My only criticism is to wonder whether the two "reality" images ("a heaven-scaling wall" and "those four walls") are not so closely similar as to get in each other's way. — "Genessaret" [26] is my favorite of the three poems. It is finely imaginative, grave, and whimsical all in one. I like the passages "the moon lays down . . . star-shine," "where's refined . . . consigned," "roads ran to stars," and "But what man . . . path?" immensely. The last sentence is tremendously apt and gives that impression of reserved strength which your best verse always gives. I have only very minor points of criticism. "Moon-glitter" feels a little rubbed after "star-shine" and "sea-sparkle." Perhaps "Of roads paved with the moon. He had no need" [27] would do; or some other dodge. "The

Romans lay" bothers me. I suppose "lay" is a generalized present, but it sounds absurdly like a misunderstood past of "lie"! Why not "laid"? But that would make your "streets" too specific, wouldn't it? It's a practically negligible point in any event. — Do send me some more poems. I'm going to read your three last ones to the club at an early opportunity. . . .

Sight

He said, "Reality will be at last
A heaven-scaling mountain on your path,
And you'll ignore it in your puny wrath
And brain yourself still trying to get past.
Is it not anything to you this roof
Will last our life-time, and will keep us warm
On every winter night, that you must form
These dreams of bliss that bide no mortal proof?"

But she could only wonder at his sight
That made of these four walls reality
The equal of her dreaming. Stare as she might
She could not see them for the urgency
Of tortured promises that starred her night
With their implacable transplendency.

Ottawa, Ont.
Jan. 26, 1925.

I was awfully sorry to hear of Dr. Boas' illness. It is with regret that one is reminded that this beloved hero is subject to the frailties of the flesh. But I hope nothing truly serious happens. What a punishment it would be for him to have to discard the pen for any length of time! I have just read his "What is a Race?" in The Nation[28] and found his point on family lines as distinct from races quite illuminating, but I doubt if most people will see much relevance in the article to anything they really care about. My own humble paper[29] will seem such a descent after the first article of the series.

"Any Wife" [30] is a perfect sonnet. "The great winds shook / Their banners, and are gone" is perhaps the most original thing you have done yet. Magnificently and imaginatively precise. You are already getting into your stride. "The Flesh and the Flame" [31] is a good sonnet, but by comparison with the other hardly more than competent. I feel it as a somewhat pale, generalized treatment of several of your other poems. I begin in it to feel an overworking of one line of thought. But the last sentence ("Quick . . . see!") is splendid. Look out for your diction, Ruth! You are beginning to use certain words too often (e.g. wisdom; comfort; comforted; comfortable; dream; mocking). "At crest of being" does not convince me. — Have you ever thought of dramatizing your theme and treating it in a comparatively easy medium like narrative blank verse? I would wager you could do something quite as notable as Robinson (after "The man who died twice," [32] which I have just read, I don't know that this is necessarily a great compliment). I am very eager to see you get away for a while from the sonnet form, for I want an ampler field for your spirit. Even simple quatrains would be worth trying. . . .

. . . "Heaven-scaling barrier" [33] keeps the images better apart but is not intrinsically very strong, because a "barrier" is a *class* of things and only concrete, individual things can be "heaven-scaling." (Do let the pedant babble!)

Good for Margaret! She'll enjoy Samoa, but the thought of a grind of field-work out there somehow makes me yawn. How perverse we can be!

I am wondering if you can rescue 45 poems out of the batch I sent you.[34] I shall be hugely surprised if you do. There really isn't stuff for more than a slender volume of some 40 poems if it's to be the kind of volume you and I will not be ashamed of as soon as the irrevocable cold print does its worst.

Ottawa, Ont.
Feb. 7, 1925.

I hope you will pass "Chronicle" [35] now. "The Circus" [36] was dashed off last night by way of reaction to a fit of depression. I don't know whether this whimsy is worth including in the book or not.

Thank you very much for your very careful reading of the MS. As you may have noticed from my new table of contents, I followed all your suggestions in regard to order of pieces, exclusion and inclusion, and title (I changed "Tearless Memory" to "Quiescence," [37] which is an improvement, I think). Some of the dropped pieces, like "Ballad of a Swan Maiden" [38] and "Charon," [39] I much prefer to some of those included, but I thought it best to consider your more sensitive and objective judgment a point of departure and to have Brooks or anyone else who may pass favorably on the MS adjust the contents by eliminating here and there and perhaps drawing on the alternates. You will notice that I cut down considerably the number of alternates submitted. I thought it best not to water the reaction too seriously. The four poems sent since the MS was made up ("Chronicle," "Epistle," [40] "The Hunt," [41] and "The Soul stands up" [42]) I am adding to the MS, perhaps not wisely in every case. I think "The Soul stands up" is one of the few really decent things I've done but perhaps others would find the thought too obscure or far-fetched and the imagery too strained.

Many thanks for the individual comments, from which I am sure to profit. The "illuminate" — "elate" passage is going to cause me lots of trouble, I imagine, it is so hard for me to get back into the spirit of the poem. I hope to have the final revisions ready very soon so as to be able to send the MS to Brooks without much further delay.

Don't take the new title, "Stars in the Sea," too seriously. It is an interim title and may be changed later. I am not much good at titles and would be glad to get further suggestions from you.

I hope you are not slowing up in writing. I am looking forward to more of your verse and hope you are having better luck with the editors. There's no royal road, just the banal road of the hammering drummer. By the way, what shall I use instead of "R.F.B.," to which you object? Shall I make it "E.B." (Emily Benedict)? . . . Do help me out. Would not "R.F." be better? [43] Have you a report from Knopf on the religion book?

I wonder if you could help me out with a little matter. I left with

Dr. Boas a typewritten pamphlet on the aims of the International Auxiliary Language Association. It had been given me by Mrs. Dave H. Morris and I want to read it over before I give her the memo I had promised to send her from Ottawa. I am afraid Dr. Boas may have forgotten about it and I hate to bother him about so small a matter at this time. Perhaps you could tell Miss Bunzel about it and she could either drop a hint to Dr. Boas or, if he has obviously laid the MS aside and is not planning to read it and comment on it, she might just quietly return it to me.

Are you hearing Goldie and Mrs. Parsons on the feasibility of monogamy? I have sent my 35 cents for the pamphlet.

Ottawa, Ont.
Feb. 27, 1925.

"Lift up your Heart" [44] is difficult and splendid, a poem of high diction. The second stanza is wonderful, and the last sentence. But it's all good, though I should like to see the load of compounds lightened a little, particularly the sequence "dear-bought heaven-p t . . . bright-passionate." Your diction sounds almost like a literal translation, at times, of some difficult Greek poet! Is there, possibly, a slight self-contradiction in "scrawled star-incised," or am I looking for trouble?

Are you having better success with editors? I hope you are. — Not a word from Brooks yet.[45] I am steeled for a rejection. Must be! After a considerable lapse of time I ventured recently to send Torrence some verse and it came back rejected so quickly that I am disposed to take comfort in the theory that he hadn't the time to read the stuff. To such devices are we mortals driven! . . .

Ottawa, Ont.
March 3, 1925.

. . . It is instructive to read Browning as a warning. Here is a man with a perfectly colossal sense of life, certainly as abounding a sense for its graspable texture as any English poet has ever had. But what's the good? Convincingness of form, including, above all, of rhythm, is lacking, hence the poems weary. At least they do me. Moral for both of us: look to your form and rhythm. Let every asperity *which is not the embodiment of the essential feeling* be shunned like the plague. — I should like to see Ransome's books (I believe he published two), particularly the one reviewed in "The Double-dealer." Those two poems I referred to are not entirely satisfying, but there is something about them that gets me at about the same spot as several poems of mine as "Music"[46] and "The Circus"[47] come from — a certain something that your more reverent nature is not altogether glad of. Your "Toy Balloons," say, and my "Epistle"[48] are common ground. Your "Sacrilege"[49] is rather beyond me, unless "The Soul stands up"[50] and "Star-gazer"[51] come from its country — but only superficially so — costume, not heart.

Glad to hear Mrs. Boas does so well.

Ottawa, Ont.
March 6, 1925.

. . . I don't know who is editing The Measure just now but he (or she) can't know much about the art of discovering poets if two such gems as "Toy Balloons" and "Riders of the Wind"[52] have to be returned with a form letter. But don't worry. Somebody will know these poems for what they are — sooner or later. There's the pity of it all. It has struck me very forcibly of late how maudlin our taste in verse is today. For all our talk about irony and astringency and the rest of it, we are arrant cowards of the spirit. We know enough not to take sickly sentimental at its innocentest (yet vide Helen Carns in current "Poetry"), yet hunger for it in any morbid disguise that gives us the feeling that we're devilish courageous, don't you know. Honest to goodness intellectual and emotional strength we won't stand for. We all seem to be remarkably soft in the head. I suppose it's all day work on the adding machine that creates the demand for ingenious lollypops evenings.

"Withdrawal"[53] is magnificent. The imagery is fresh and passionate. What sweep in "thresh their passion on the sky" and "down all its firmament"! I like the curious "what time . . . afresh." It gives the poem a fresh old English flavor that adds to the more modern feeling. But will Harriet Monroe or the current Measure editor take it? I doubt it. Anything but passion. One must know how to write for cowards.

"Moth Wing" [54] is exquisite, Sapphic. I demur a little to "for largess of suffering" which seems too burdensome for the spirit of the poem. To me "frost-patterned" is a little out of drawing, digressive, because "frost" clashes with the moth imagery. There is a nostalgic summer feeling in the poem for me. "Of her most wayward loveliness" and "There is no hour but this hour, nor" are truly beautiful lines. — "Girl Wife" [55] is not as convincing as the other two. "Her eyes . . . sunshine" and "She is . . . confesses loveliness" should set the feeling for the whole poem. "And her hands . . . folly" seems too thought out. "For her, desire . . . gross" is finely startling, but is followed by two stanzas that are somewhat heavy and off center. The contrast between "her" and "us" should be more hinted at than elaborated in so short a poem and we should not so quickly lose sight of the ingenuous "her."

I hope you cared for "Wind Music." [56] "Advice to a Girl" [57] seems of little moment to me. I am strangely, almost blithely indifferent now to Harcourt's rejection. It's a good sign. Am caring more for the work and am less concerned with the reception. I should like to try a longer form but have not quite the elan yet. I'm surer of you somehow.

Poor Margaret! She'll have to stop being driven. Can't you take her in hand and lay down the law? . . .

Ottawa, Ont.
April 1, 1925.

. . . "Spiritus Tyrannus" [58] is a fine poem. I like particularly the first stanza, though I find "that find" rather difficult. Should it not be "they find" for "that they find"? The other two stanzas are a bit abstract, I find. It is not easy for me to get the pronouns spontaneously — "it" for the flesh, and "she" for the spirit, but that's because the soul as feminine is not altogether self-evident to me — I mean I haven't the tradition of English religious poetry in my bones, as I should have. The real difficulty in the poem for me is the line "Thick strewn . . . sea." Does this refer to "flesh"? If so, as it must, I find the image hard to get. . . .

Ottawa, Ont.
April 3, 1925.

Mother is rather better now and it looks as if she had a nervous collapse rather than anything alarmingly wrong with her heart. However, she is keeping to her bed for the present.

I am not worrying the least bit about A. & C. Boni. — Am glad Léonie Adams got her volume accepted by McBride's.[59] It will go well with the critics. . . .

. . . I rather liked Lowie's article in The Century.[60] It is dangerous to know an author, isn't it? — Ogburn's "only son" research? Damn! — . . .

. . . By the way, I had meant to ask you to look at the last of Harold Vinal's 4 sonnets in current "Voices," I mean for March (sonnet no.). Margaret has a copy I'd sent because of the "Ariel" sonnet.[61] Is this of Vinal's good for Anthology?[62] It's fresh but perhaps not quite what we want. I saw nothing else. . . .

. . . I have answered Lowie — and of course I want his notes — but not Paul, whom I shall want to reply to before long.

"Unicorns at Sunrise"[63] is fine intellectual fantasy. It shows greatly increased technical control. Only "hunger-blasted" I somewhat squint at. And "pawing . . . zodiac" is wonderfully felicitous.

Ottawa, Ont.
April 15, 1925.

Thank you for "Preference."[64] It's a splendid poem. When I see you toss off a passage like "where how should the shred / And filament of the air-stepping mist / Be lovely still," I grow envious. That is great diction. I don't particularly care for the word "durance," but that's not a criticism. Are you doing much more verse? I hope you are, for you are in your stride and will go on straight to the mark, without fail. I am anxious to hear what Harriet has to say, but I understand she is away just now. My own poor Muse is discreetly and properly silent. . . .

. . . I've been reading Koffka's "Growth of the Mind" [65] (Margaret's copy) and it's like some echo telling me what my intuition never quite had the courage to say out loud. It's the real book for background for a philosophy of culture, at least $\begin{Bmatrix} \text{your} \\ \text{my} \end{Bmatrix}$ philosophy, and I see the most fascinating and alarming possibilities of application of its principles, express and implied, mostly implied, to all behavior, art, music, culture, personality, and everything else. If somebody with an icy grin doesn't come around to temper my low fever, I'll soon be studying geometry over again in order to discover what really happens when a poem takes your breath away or you're at loggerheads with somebody. Nay more, unless a humanist like yourself stops me, I'll be drawing up plans for a generalized Geometry of Experience, in which each theorem will be casually illustrated from ordinary behavior, music, culture, and language. The idea, you perceive, is that all you really need to do to understand — anything, is to draw a figure in space (or time) and its relevance for any kind of interest can be discovered by just noting how it is cut by the plane (= context) of that interest. . . .

Preference

So I shall live, a ravelling brief smoke
Before the wind, and glut your eyes with brightness.
Let be these words of a poor foolish folk,
Unused to ecstacy, who make of ripeness

Eternal durance, and a paradise
Got by the snakes upon Medusa's head,
Immutable now forever. It's a price
Too great for heaven, where how should the shred

And filament of the air-stepping mist
Be lovely still, or hush itself to blue

Against the wintry sky? 'Twere best we kissed
Before the wind, and went as smoke-clouds do.

Ottawa, Ont.
Aprl. 20, 1925.

I was horrified to hear of Helene's illness. But from your second
letter I infer there is every reason to believe she will pull through,
which I fervently hope she will. The Job game would not be Christian even for a Biblical God. I can picture poor old Dr. Boas and all
he's going through. . . .

. . . I admire greatly "in a slight / And hieroglyphic shadow cast
on dew / Beauty herself is told." The rest of "Counsel for
Autumn" [66] leaves me unconvinced. It seems too little characteristic
to be truly yours. — . . .

Ottawa, Ont.
May 2, 1925.

. . . I am immensely relieved to hear of Helene's recovery. It is
so good to know that the old man can breathe freely and be himself again. How fortunate you are to have a mother who is hale
enough to venture to Europe alone! It is beautiful to reach the
downward slope of one's journey with full enjoyment of the ever
changing prospect. My mother is much better but her left arm is
quite stiff yet. . . .

. . . I am very glad that Margaret has obtained her desire. She
will enjoy the year in the South Seas hugely and will profit greatly
by it, I feel certain. She lives intensely in the outer world and it will
all mean a great deal to her. I hope her neuritis is letting up. She
can't go on indefinitely with it. — Are you not glad to be going to
the Southwest? Will it be Zuñi again? If so, I presume it will not be
mythology only this time, though ritualism has its *longueurs* too, no
doubt. I should quite like to do linguistic work in the Southwest.
It's such a varied field. I always seem to hanker after California
linguistically too. If Chicago proves a fizzle,[67] I may do Hupa after
Summer School, but please don't speak of it at present to anyone. . . .

Ottawa, Ont.

May 14, 1925.

Harriet and her staff did not respond as cordially as I should have liked to your verse. She seems to think the pieces end rather weakly as a rule. However, she likes "Toy Balloons" and is keeping it, asking me to forward the enclosed card to you. She says also: "I like *Moth Wing* up to the last two lines." Would you perhaps care to work at this poem, which I like so much, and get it into "Poetry"? [68] I attribute Harriet's reaction chiefly to her inveterate softness or sentimentality. Difficult or in any way intellectual verse gets past her only with difficulty. She prefers stuff about sweet love and my baby.

I was delighted to learn no less than 3 of your poems are going into The Measure[69] and another to Palms.[70] It's exciting, isn't it, when you actually see your work in print. My copy of The Measure hasn't come yet. Has it been sent out? Perhaps you could tip off somebody (Léonie or Louise or Margaret) in case they overlooked my copy. I've just sent Léonie Adams a batch of verse. I wonder if it's all right to have her send rejected MS back to me *via* Eda Lou Walton, so she can have a squint at the stuff for possible selection for "Palms." Do you mind attending to this or getting busy Margaret to attend? If this sounds impolite, send me Eda Lou Walton's address as editor of "Palms," so I can send her stuff independently.

Will write about your last poem later. I haven't it on hand. — Just got a note from Goldie. Poor boy! He indulges in the soulful vocabulary of an adolescent of the German "Storm and Stress" period who is prepared to sing an ode to Life with the intention of putting a bullet through his brain as soon as he's finished. When do you leave for Zuñi?

Ottawa, Ont.

June 14, 1925.

. . . The new version of "Moth Wing" is splendid and I hope Harriet will have no qualms about accepting it.[71] She doesn't seem to know her own mind sometimes, though. "You have looked upon the Sun," [72] too, is a finely expressed idea, though actually it has not

the lyric significance of the other. And thank you for the extra copy
of The Measure. I've got out of the way of sending people copies of
things I do, but perhaps I can use this to remind some lost sheep
among my friends that I still hear the tinkle of his bell (this meta-
phor is inaccurate, is it not?). . . .

. . . I'm delighted to learn you're to have a secretary next season.[73] Only an idealistic slave-driver like Boas would ever have expected you to do five or six full-time jobs all at once, and you did
famously to chide his incredible faith in the stiffness of the long-
suffering human neck. And now, I presume Elsie is ready for a monument to her munificence, for no doubt she is to cough up the necessary funds for this new secretarial extravagance. (Oh no! I see you
speak of the JAFL paying for it — which may or may not mean
Elsie.) By the way, I hope they are going to have the common
decency to give you a salary for your editorial work on the Journal,
and I also hope your Columbia work has at last been put on a respectable financial basis. I pray you won't disillusion me on either
of these two points, for I do detest cheap labor, particularly where it
calls itself idealism, scientific fervor, or love. . . .

. . . So I . . . dedicate most of my time to the immortal Comparative Nadene (and Athabaskan) Dictionary, which will probably
never be written, and to other pursuits of that order. Poetry I
neither read nor write. Even the Ransome is only half read, so you
see to what abysmal depths I have plumeted. I really think I shall
end life's prelude by descending into the fastnesses of a purely technical linguistic erudition. There is great comfort in withdrawing from
the market-place of so-called human interests and resolutely following a star (a miner's will o' the wisp) so pale, so clear, so remote
it can bring neither joy nor disappointment. I can understand better
than ever before what content there may be in pure mathematics.
Must everybody contribute his share toward the saving of humanity?
That is your faith and an inhuman absorption in a purely intellectual
pursuit will never satisfy you. I have no desire to save or help save
humanity but merely to try to keep myself as systematically busy as
my innate waywardness will allow up to the moment when the
demonstrator in anatomy gets tired of his demonstration. You and
Margaret have more to ask of the hosts of this party, and the en-

tertainment is correspondingly keener (certainly in Margaret's case and I hope in yours too); my main job will have to be to school myself against absurd regrets and against puny disappointments at the non-fulfillment of absurder demands. . . .

Chicago, Illinois
October 3, 1925.

. . . Do send me your verse. My Muse has taken a holiday. She doesn't like to have furniture moved into the house, apparently.[74] . . .

Chicago, Ill.,
Oct. 19, 1925.

. . . I am glad you thought well of the sonnet entitled "He implores her." [75] . . . My own favorite among these poems is "Nostalgic Ditty." [76] Enclosed is a sonnet I wrote last night in bed (it was Sunday and I had decided to take a real rest and try to shake off the miserable cold that had been hanging on to me for over two weeks). I wonder if you could take off a little time and run me off four copies on your typewriter, you to keep one? My own typewriter is not in working trim yet, so I must sponge on somebody. Will you be the spongee, my dear and sweet counselor? And you *must* send me your verses. I can't suffer Anne Singleton to languish into thin air. Zuñi myths are important toys, of course, but your verse, even when you're not pleased with it, is a holier toy. You may quote this to Boas if you like. I have strayed from the paternal roof and no longer fear the Sire's displeasure. . . .

Chicago, Ill.
March 11, 1926.

. . . Congratulations on your eight poems in "Palms"! [77] They are magnificent. "Evening Sky" I had not seen. They will create much admiring comment, I am sure, and "Anne Singleton" will soon be a real name in American verse. I hope you are wise enough to continue writing. It is no secret between us that I look upon your poems as infinitely more important than anything, no matter how brilliant, you are fated to contribute to anthropology. Don't affect an apologetic Muse, dear. Stand up and sing. The few I am enclosing for you are rather innocuous though I rather like the fancy of "Fantasy for a Girl." [78] . . .

. . . You will be interested to know I've seen quite a bit of Clarence Darrow lately. I got to know him through Cole and some lectures Cole got for me which I'm delivering to a so-called Biology Group of which he (Darrow) is the founder. The lectures are called "The Psychology of Culture" and are a miniature (10 lectures) of my college course. Have you read Darrow's "Farmington"? It's very delightful. Anyway, I love the old kindly whimsical cynic. . . .

Chicago, Ill.
March 23, 1926.

I'm so sorry Jean and I can't see you before you go to Europe, but I wish you a pleasant trip both ways and a fine time abroad. But you're not going for quite a while yet, are you? As you no doubt know by now, I'm not going to Columbia next year. Boas wrote to say the Faculty's recommendation was not passed by the trustees. This news stirred me hardly at all. I'm constantly being surprised to see how little matters of ambition of that sort concern me. . . . I have a hunch I'm here for good. I really like it so well that I don't quite see, barring difference in salary, what advantage there would be in my shifting now. . . .

. . . I was rather relieved to hear you hadn't written "Evening Sky." [79] It was so out of keeping with your other verse and I was vaguely puzzled by its carefully sought beauties — "The anointed sun," "airs enameled lawny green" — and somewhat artificial feeling. But it's a good poem, so I said nothing about it. It just isn't your style. . . . You did not say whether you read my review of [Léonie Adams'] book in "Poetry" [80] and whether or not you thought I was just to her. — I rather sympathize with Eda Lou about your pen name. Pen names are an abomination. You know how I feel about even toying with the idea of dissociation of personality. I hate it.

Lie outright if you have to, but for God's sake don't stylize the lie into a pretty institution. . . .

Chicago, Ill.
May 11, 1926.

. . . I was very sorry to learn that you did not get the fellowship after all. Did your being married have anything to do with it? Cole apparently had little or nothing to do with the award. Malinowski said something about recommending your work to the Rockefeller Memorial people, but I don't know whether he did so or not. I suppose, my dear girl, that if you stay around Columbia long enough and learn the noble art of doing things Boas' way perfectly you may, in the fullness of time, look forward to getting a fellowship. Meanwhile, my singular Anne, write your elegiackest and despairingest, so posterity may tell of how she wrung beauty out of tears. I hope, too, you may keep up the standard set by Gladys! And you'll have all that Rome interlude for breathing space, so you'll come to your work fresh and glorious. Oh dear, why can't one laugh at it all *viva voce* instead of in ink?

I am eager to hear how your poetry reading to those doubly elect came off. You must write me all about it, as that is a real event, I take it. Remember you promised verses, too. I am writing very, very little and that little not good. Here is the latest harvest. I rather like "Blowing Winds" [81] but am not sure of it, and still less of the rest. I'm beginning to feel the best thing I can do with poetry is to let it strictly alone. After all, one ought not to write verse when he hasn't the stuff. . . .

Chicago, Ill.
Oct. 21, 1926.

There are your letters of September 26th (from Rome and SS) and October 16th (from N.Y.) to answer. . . .

I'm sorry you found the Congress[82] so dull. Is New York more to your taste? Let me know what's up out there. I'm such a good Chicagoan now that New York seems quite safely remote. And I'm what's called "busy" — two four-hour courses on the campus and a two-hour research course (Ruth Bunzel and a very able Chinaman), also two 2-hr. courses down town (extension). And some private lecturing, for which they at least pay pretty well. Research sits all hunched up, quietly (almost inaudibly) whistling for a wind. . . .

. . . Write me all the news, and as often as you can. The flight of my Muse has been so precipitate that in the confusion of packing up she even took the prose dictionary along. Be good. Lots of luck and good cheer to you. . . .

Chicago, Ill.
Oct. 21, 1926.

. . . You have poetry on hand, have you not? You promised to send me copies before you left for Europe but, Madame, failed to deliver. I am *not* bored with poetry — not yours — so would gladly see your new things. I write practically not at all. Only very short book-reviews for The American Journal of Sociology, of the editorial board of which organ (it sounds like an organ-grinder, doesn't it) I am a member — this privilege is thrown in with my salary.

Oh *dear*, this is slow work — writing a letter. I'd rather talk to you. About everything pretty much. Why don't you come to Chicago and visit Aunt Harriet[83] and us? Is New York the *only* place? She — Harriet — knows who Anne Singleton is, I learned from her. That's as it should be. Air an indiscretion and it settles to earth like any accepted bird. Your reputation is intact, in spite of the horrible revelation. . . .

P.S. I nearly forgot the main purpose of my note, which was to tip you off to apply for a research fellowship to the Social Science Research Council. Merriam told Cole that not many applications were in, at least for anthropology, and that he wished anthropology might get busy. I think Cole will try harder this time to help you get a fellowship. Only, *for God's sake*, don't make it so remote and technical as last year. Pueblo mythology doesn't excite people any more than Athabaskan verbs would. Take your courage in your hands, mutter loving maledictions at Boas, and come across with a live project — and *you'll get* what you ask for. Make it a 3 years' project on something that sounds important — say a study of the declining, or increasing, mentality of Mayflower stock. Do shake yourself. Don't be a fool. Follow your own intuition and your own sense of humor. To be serious — can't you devise some general subject in the American Indian field that outsiders can warm up to? Primitive dream life and its significance for general psychological theory; or Hopi culture as a response (positive or negative) to environment. Talk the jargon in your project, then do as you like when you get the fellowship. Anyway, make the try this time again. Cole feels the chances are distinctly better. Both you and Ruth Bunzel ought to land fellowships. Hurry. . . .

E.

Chicago, Ill.,
March 16, 1927

. . . Have you more verse? And what good reading have you to report? I'm now on the home stretch in Spengler's "Decline of the West." Does the book appeal to you at all? I find it needlessly long and muddle-headed in places but fundamentally sound. . . .

Chicago, Ill.
Sept. 29, 1927

. . . Seeing "The Dirge" in The Dial [84] gave me a momentary feeling of being a poet, but scant reflection showed the unconvincingness of the argument. I've not written a line of verse for a longer span than I remember to have ever let slip by without poetic exercises since the habit came to me ten years ago. That sounds fatal, doesn't it? The age and I don't seem to be on very intimate speaking terms. In the last number of "Poetry," for instance, I find almost nothing that even remotely interests me. I think the ideology of a Hupa medicine formula is closer to my heart than all this nervous excitement of Hart Crane's. Can you tell me what he wants? You spoke of Mark Van Doren's excellence. I've not read his recently published book [85] but the citations in the review in "Poetry" were not very alluring. They sounded more like keen cerebration in verse form than poetry. And I'm utterly sick of intelligence and its vanity. It's the arch disease of the time and the reason for its choking vulgarity and its flimsiness. So I don't feel I have anything to say that anybody would want to hear, even if I had a sufficiently great gift of words to say it with, and I doubt greatly if I have that gift. The experimental excitements of this great modern time do not rouse me, they chill me to loathing. The freedoms we hear about are pinchbeck whims of the body and it is as much as one's accredited sanity is worth to even whisper the word "noble." Well, we're all upset now with moving the first of the month, but when that's over, perhaps I shall take you at your word and send you MS to choose from. I'm weary of approaching publishers. . . .

. . . Your plans for the role of a lady of leisure sound most attractive. I hope to sample your cooking some day. Maybe I can even meet the shadowy Stanley. You must let me see the fruits of your leisure — poem on poem, but I shall not allow more than one Aeschylean compound per poem of 10 lines, make it 14 — remember. And you're not to use the word "ecstacy" except on extreme provocation and even then I implore you to spell it "ecstasy." "Ecstacy" is exceedingly offensive to one's classical taste — the Greeks, who made the word, spelled it with an S. . . .

Chicago, Ill.,
Dec. 17, 1927.

At last I have mustered the courage to look at the poetry MS. I am sending it to you under another cover — just as it was when submitted to Harcourt and rejected, except that I have added to the "alternates" a number of others, chiefly later poems, and have pencilled in "E" to indicate my personal preferences. Have you the sturdy heart to look over this collection of futile poems and nearpoems once again? Ignore the selection, the order, the distinction between "Stars in the Sea" and "alternates," my preferences — everything but your honest conviction. I've put in the "E" merely to help you out here and there where it's a toss-up, for you, between this and that. Please make a rather small selection, things that you really feel would not fade away when imprisoned in a volume. And

use your judgment as to order. I really shall obey your dicta —
impliciter. As to publisher — let's not cross that bridge yet.

And why don't you send me copies of your poems, Ruth? There's
no talk of reciprocity now. I have nothing to send myself. . . .

Chicago, Ill.,
February 7, 1928.

. . . These last poems you send are very fine. Just a few comments, may I? "This Breath" [86] is a high-felt poem, so I wish "We
have for blocks to build with" were out. Is not the image incongruous? — "But the Son of Man" [87] is beautiful, moving. It flows
well too. — "And his Eyes were opened" [88] is a burst of magnificence. Two passages trouble me. First, "for to his hands . . .
shadows to his eyes" seems a little weak for a "for" clause following
up "mad." I mean to say I don't quite get the force of the contrast.
These shadows are hardly black enough to temper "the arc of
heaven." And, secondly, "will as then make bare" bothers me. What
does "as" mean? — "Myth" [89] is a most original and imaginative
poem.

As to my MS, the alternates did not altogether mean preferred for
discarding. Some, like "Yet Water runs again" [90] and "Music brings
Griefs," [91] were composed after the tentative volume was made up, so
found no place in it. Of course you're to include any of the alternates
you think might go in. I'm curious to see what your acceptances and
your discards will be this time.

I'm in the second volume of "The Magic Mt." [92] still. I shall
finish it, but when? Spengler *was* more interesting, I admit it. What
must I read? You are so blamelessly good and give me titles and I
remain as heathen as when I was born.

It will be good to see you, Ruth. Won't you send all your newer
poems? Have you placed your volume?

And his eyes were opened

Suddenly from the sky, lacquered with light,
Light fell, a mask withdrawn, and the gold stars

Stood fixed in austere heaven. It was not night,
For still the jewel of the water lay
Thick-flawed with glitter, its more lovely scars,
And sunshine splintered on the grass all day.

He was not mad, for to his hands the bark
Was harsh as always, and the low-hung fruit
Dripped shadows to his eyes; only the arc
Of heaven, letting fall its casual veil,
Stood intricate-panoplied, all its minute
And jewelled loveliness his holy grail.

After, he went so canopied at noon,
His seeing loosed upon a tameless glory.
He laughed that we who know the stars, so soon
Believe them shattered, day on day, or make
Imponderable light an old wives' story,
An iron curtain that no eye can break.

Secure in sight that held its level way
To tangible barriers, he left to us
The insubstantial fables, that some day
No stone being shifted, suddenly will bare
The world new-minted, the sky luminous
With stars at noonday, timeless on the air.

Chicago, Illinois
Feb. 12, 1928.

Your letter of Feb. 5th and the MS of poems crossed my letter. How can I thank you sufficiently for all the toil and interest? I've just gone over the volume and put "The Jackal" [93] in Group I. I've also put "By the Water" [94] and "Time's Wing" [95] in other places — not out of conviction, for I have almost no feeling about arrangements of disconnected poems, but in order to show you that I have done some thinking about this volume.

I think your choice is excellent and the arrangement splendid. There are only two poems I would question somewhat for the volume

— "Heavenly Message" [96] and "Ariel." [97] Do you think they are
up to the general level? Then I have ventured to append, in alpha-
betical order, a selected list of Alternates, those I like best being
marked E. S. in pencil. What I am thinking of is this: — I want to
abide absolutely by whatever volume you fix up. If, on consideration,
it remains as you've planned it, well and good. That's the volume.
If you find you'd like to tinker a bit, leaving out one or two or adding
a couple or so, well and good. I accept the revision in advance.
Slip in or out as you will, then send me what's left but please don't
bother to return the volume for renewed approval, for you have it in
advance. If you include "The House of Virtues," [98] please add The
Pagan to the prefatory note.

The volume having thus been definitely agreed upon, please decide
on that of the following three titles pleases you best. Frankness com-
pels me to say that neither Jean nor I thought "Diver's Farthings"
(a hard phrase to say! and not my sort of diction), though a splendid
phrase in itself, nor "Witch's Wood" as appropriate as "Stars in the
Sea." Here are the three:

> Stars in the Sea
> Blowing Winds
> Chronicle

Or if, in desperation, you suddenly decide on "Poems," let it be that.
"Chronicle," I think, pleases me almost the best of all. It's dour, and
I like that. — I don't think the volume should be much longer than
you had it. I should not like to see all the alternates go in.

Would you mind getting the MS retyped, with carbon? And
please send me the carbon, you keeping the original. And also send
me the bill, please. Then what?

Have you a carbon of your MS that I could see? I should so like
to read your poems in such connected form as you yourself approve.
Don't fear my pestering you with suggestions as to order or omissions
or additions (though I doubt if I have all your later ones; you've not
been sending me much of your work lately, now that I've stopped
writing and, you think, no doubt rightly, that I'm lost to God!). I
know what a dub I am on fixing things up.

I'm glad you liked "The Unconscious." [99] Most people seem to

think it's nearly all piffle. I shall be very glad to see your reviews.
You know I am always happy to see anything of yours. . . .

Chicago, Illinois
March 4, 1928.

Here's the first poem I have done for about *fourteen months!* [100]
It's not much of a renaissance, is it?

At the last meeting of the Poetry Club, held at my house, I had
read two of your poems — "Ripeness is all" [101] and "Foxes have
Holes." [102] They were much admired, but in the latter the phrase
"taking to breast a stone" seemed to be felt by several as disturbing
because introducing human feeling into an animal situation. I tried
to defend your phrase but they still seemed to feel the justice of the
criticism, which to my mind has nothing in it. I thought I'd mention this because it's one of those "obvious" strictures that might
sway any editor. Not that I should advise your changing the
passage. I am no crank on water-tight images myself and I think
there is something childlikely appealing about the very mixture of
animal and human motive that these technicians — who sicken me
with endless quibbles about diction — object to. By the way, Sterling
North asked me if you would care to publish "Foxes have Holes" (or
rather "But the Son of Man") in "The Forge." I said I'd ask you.
Personally I think the poem is much too good for them. It should
appear in a more important journal, but I'm delivering the question
as I said I would. . . .

Chicago, Illinois
April 16, 1928

. . . I have already told you what I think of your MS volume of
poetry. It is superb and I look forward to its unqualified acceptance.
Jean finished it after her return to Chicago and likes it very much.
It is not easy reading, Ruth, but you would not want it to be that
exactly. . . .   The title[103] still strikes me as too self-revealing; I
should prefer something more discrete and less sad, but I can suggest nothing now. — I have let Lasswell see my "Chronicle" and

I gather he thinks it decidedly intellectual verse, very head-breaking and eye-straining material, mostly. He apparently wishes more of it had the Housman-like punch at the end, like "The King of Thule," also suggests that perhaps it would have been better arrangement to have more of the easier poems come first, so that the poor reader — publisher's reader — might be reassured at the start. And I had thought I was one of the Simple Simon school, and here are you severe and lofty-dictioned Parnassians — you and Léonie and Louise Bogan, whom I for one am certainly not understanding (Louise, I mean) — and where do I come in? Yet my one self-delivered merit is turned into an opposite. Oh dear! And you needn't tell me Harper's have accepted "Chronicle," for I know they haven't. . . .

Chicago, Illinois
April 23, 1928

. . . But it is of *your* book I wanted to write before mailing MS back to you. It is all, or nearly all, of a piece. It seems difficult to say specific things of the single poems, many of which I had commented on before. They all have a richly weighted magnificence, the gold a little dark at times but always gold. I think the one technical thing that stands out is this, that the writer has obviously always known English. The implicit acquaintance with the age-long heritage of English verse that you discover is so little usual today that it almost surprises one, moves one to a nostalgia that I cannot describe. The queenly originality, or rather individuality, that you maintain throughout shows how deep and sincere is the feeling. There are no obvious tricks of style, no whimsicalities, just straight, honest expression. It will make an important volume, tying the present modernities up securely with the older verse as no other volume has done this. . . .

Chicago, Illinois
June 10, 1928.

What a belated answer this is to your last letter! Anything I can say about the points you raise is probably deader than a post-mortem

by now. But first of all, let me congratulate you on Louis Untermeyer's inclusion of your work in his anthology.[104] I take satisfaction
in having my "Signal" come prophetic. I presume "Son of Man" [105]
and the other two you mentioned have already gone forward to
Untermeyer as your choice. They are three splendid poems, and
there are, of course, many others I should have liked to see in too.
You asked why I don't care for "Theseus." [106] I just don't. It seems
too much like a private exercise, I suppose, and then perhaps I mis-
understand it and make applications that are not intended and that
I don't happen to like. It's the only poem in the book I actually
dislike. The "Annunciation" [107] I don't dislike in that sense at all,
merely think it not worthy of the level of most of the book. But
it's wrong to cavil at particular poems, and the book as a whole
so wonderful, and I know your reviews will be enthusiastic and
significant. I presume Harcourt has definitely taken it on by now.
The title, "Ripeness is all," seems much better than "Winter of the
Blood," though I confess it would have meant nothing to me if the
citation had not been made from "King Lear."

Have you anything new in regard to "Chronicle." If it comes back
again, you mustn't be bothered hawking it about any longer. After
all, that wouldn't be fair to you. . . .

Chicago, Illinois
Oct. 6, 1928.

. . . The Congress[108] already seems far behind. What stands out
is the opportunity I had to see you. I was also glad to see more
of Herzog and the Lessers. There's excellent stuff in Herzog, I
think. . . .

. . . The McCann office told me about the same you had said —
they'd be glad to have me resubmit "Chronicle" for a second group
of four later on. So, as you know, I turned the MS over to Lovett
but have not yet heard from him about it. Meanwhile I get a long
and enthusiastic letter, with some interesting criticism of details, on
"Chronicle" from W. Y. Elliot, to whom I had sent the carbon. He
says: "If you do not publish it, you will be acting from a perverted
modesty that will be most unworthy." Es ist zum Lachen! You'd

think I was planting Verboten signs on my preserves to keep the publishers from rushing in and snatching my MS away. Enclosed are a couple of things done since my return. The Dial has accepted "Rain on the Railroad Yards." [109]

I have read your new poems. As usual, they are full of rich substance and are getting more, rather than less, difficult. "Monk of Ariège" [110] is very fine and nicely rounded. I have trouble with two details. I presumed "the shape . . . insult" may be considered some of the subjects of his MS. illuminations (so Jean suggests). If so, I find it hard to see rivers and deserts on the parchment. But if these are only remote metaphors, then they feel a bit purple-patchy in the texture of the whole. And "a dream could be a water cupped" I don't understand. — "This is my Body" [111] is a profound poem. I like particularly the second stanza. — "Resurgam" [112] is neat, if a little gruesome in its imagery. "And nothing . . . perfected" is a fine line. — "Serpents lengthening" [113] is splendid, sure-moving blank verse. It suggests you ought to try a long-breathed form, say imaginative narration, in blank verse. I think you once said rhyme meant little more to you than a pretty task to be got over. You may need an absolutely clean field for the development of your rich imagery. "Ways not Wind's Ways" I had already seen. It is a beautiful poem, easily the best of this group. As I already have a copy, I am returning this to you, for you may be glad to have it.

Are you reading interesting things? I'm at Hamsun's "Women at the Pump." [114] It is interesting, but too episodic in style to be absolutely so, at least so far.

Have you anything new on the religious developments at Columbia? I refer to your plans, not to anybody's soul.

What are you planning in the way of writing? I feel a little up-to-the-neckish with all this promised article-writing and book-writing and wish I had guts enough to plunge into something imaginative. That sort of thing, I fear, needs to come as a habit earlier in life. If the habit delays too long in the forming one pays with a chronic dryness in the mouth. This is only just. . . .

. . . When can we all get together again? I resent these distances and the hasty sketchiness of our meetings. Life should be completer, have more regard for private significances and not leave

so much to silly chances — Congresses and what not. Couldn't you
spend a week here with us some time?

Resurgam

This is the season when importunate rains
Rutting the graves unearth slim skeletons
We buried to corruption, and strong winds
Whip from the ocean where no passing suns
Strike nethermost, the bones we wept beside.
Now is the season of our mourning past
And reek forgotten, the white loveliness
Of ivory ours to play with. Now at last
Our griefs are overspanned, decay played out,
And nothing dead but it is perfected.
Come, of the bones we'll make us flutes and play
Our hearts to happiness, where worms have fed.

This Is My Body

"Unceasingly," God said, remote in heaven,
"This man child beats his head upon the stone
Desiring knowledge; has he not computed
The stride of the wind, the little crumbling ash
Left, at the last, of bone?"

God said, "Let him take his pleasure. Let him fathom
The treasuries of darkness, and unloose
The band from bright Orion; when the last
Sky's charted and Behemoth yoked, what profit
The firmament to his use?

"His feet shall know no resting place, his eyes
Be weary as mine with knowledge; broken, who scaled,
Hands bleeding and his brain sick on its leash,

Dissembling cliffs not nearer to the moon
For all the suns he trailed.

"And all the while, a child curled in the brain,
Quiet lies smiling in a swaddling sheet.
A wise man spoke this riddle to the deaf
Once in Judea, handling the bread and wine:
'This is my body. Eat.'"

April 29, 1929

Your letter of April 26th, with its strange misunderstanding moves
me to an instant reply. But let me dispose of the lower toned matter
first. I sent back the poetry volumes because I found I just wasn't
in the mood to read poetry and wasn't likely to be for months to
come, so there was no use holding on to the books any longer. I
think the climax came one evening when I was feeling rather depressed and hoped Ransome's verse would be a relief. I came onto a
run of what struck me as completely pusillanimous, perverted verse
— a lot of strong blasphemy about items so dead to most of us that
we've forgotten there is still a kick to be got out of the blasphemous
exercise — and tangled, emotionally non-significant rhythm. So I
chucked the book on the floor and picked it up next morning with
the determination to have done with it. I did not finish "The
Tower beyond Tragedy" [115] though I read a little beyond the point
I had reached when I last wrote you. As for the general impression I
fully realize the sweep of Jeffers' verse and the intensity of his feeling and imagery. He is not a minor poet. It's none of his fault that
the thunder rumbles in the far inane for me. . . .

. . . That you would not care for my sex article[116] I took for
granted, hence was not interested in sending you a copy, as I do not
wish to have our relations unnecessarily muddied by irreconcilable
differences, but that you were outraged by a supposed quotation
shocked as few things have shocked me. . . . You will not believe
me — and yet it is the sober truth — when I say that you were never
once in my thoughts when I wrote the paper on sex, which I did,
by the way, rather reluctantly at the request of Harry Stack Sulli-
van. . . .

. . . — Ruth, I don't know why I am writing so much. I had almost convinced myself there was no use writing to you at all, our relations seemed to have become so embittered with misunderstandings, with contrary beats. Oh dear, life is so hard when one tries to be emotionally honest. It is much better to slip on the kind of spectacles that make one see everything consistently cock-eyed and conventionally intelligible. If I don't write more often to you, it is not because I am not interested — you are one of the very few friends I have ever had — it is because I am too greatly interested and am dead tired of receiving and inflicting useless hurts. This is an age of perfectly terrifying loneliness and no wonder we run to the deceptive anodynes of the mob. I am content to be as lonely as my nature demands and as much more lonely as a profound distrust of the temper of intellectual America condemns me to being. What values I possess I hope to keep as clear as I can, even if my doing so is attended by no least ripple in the moving sea of opinion and acclaim. I am too old to learn to be different, too young to be indulgently or wisely indifferent. . . .

Chicago, Illinois
Jan. 8, 1931.

I've just learned from Kidder that I've been reappointed Chairman of the Com. on Field Parties of the Laboratory of Anthropology. The idea seems to be to return to the S.W. Would you like to head the ethnological party next summer? If you do, I'd be glad to urge it on the Com. Please don't mention the matter to anyone just yet.

As you may have heard, I'm going to Yale next year. The title is "Sterling Professor of Anthropology and Linguistics." I do not know if I am acting wisely in leaving Chicago, where they have treated me so well, but it seemed impossible not to accept the offer. . . .

New Haven, Conn.
Dec. 30, 1931

I learned only yesterday that Dr. Boas is seriously ill. If I understand the reports correctly, he will not be able to do any lecturing for quite a while, perhaps not for the balance of the present academic year. If, in the rush of readjustment, I can help out in any way, please don't hesitate to suggest to Dean McBain that I should be glad to come down once or twice a week to fill out with courses, if that seems at all practicable or in any way desired. Even if you may not care to suggest any such arrangement for next semester, when Kroeber is on the scene, you may, for reasons of routine, find it convenient to have somebody fill in some of Dr. Boas' work for the balance of the present semester. Needless to say, I shall want no remuneration beyond traveling expenses. . . .

New Haven, Connecticut
October 27, 1938

I was very glad to get your letter of October 24. I hope you had an enjoyable trip to Nicaragua[117] during the summer. I had a very quiet time in New Hampshire and am now back to a regular academic schedule, though I am giving fewer hours than I normally would.

I have not indicated to Setzler a successor on your program committee for Michelson. I would suggest that you let me know whom you would like to have on your committee in his place and I shall be very glad to drop Setzler a note to make the appointment regular.

I should have liked to prepare a paper for your suggested symposium on current ethnological theories, but I am afraid it will be impossible for me to consider it. As president of the American Anthropological Association I have to prepare an address anyway for a joint evening meeting of our Society and the Linguistic Society of America. If time allows and circumstances seem right, I may wish as chairman to make a few remarks by way of adding to the discussion of papers that you are planning for the symposium, but I should prefer not to have you put me down for anything formal.

With best wishes, . . .

Part III

Patterns of Culture

1922–1934

Margaret Mead

"I want to find a really important undiscovered country," Ruth
Benedict wrote from Cochiti in 1925.[1] She still thought that this
was to be found by learning French or Russian "well enough to be
really at home in the verse." She also wanted to find out whether
she would have felt at home in a different period — in ancient
Egypt, for example. Through her first experience with anthropo
logical materials, she began to find answers to these two basic preoccupations.

In Edward Sapir's work, devoted for many years to primitive
materials, there was a contrasting search as he tried, in what Ruth
Benedict called "his desire to prove that culture doesn't matter," [2]
to find in literature some affirmation of the importance of individuality that would transcend culture.

My generation, which became in many ways her generation because her own seemed to her to follow unintelligible goals, was concerned with the problem of self-consciousness and creativity: would
an individual's knowledge of the unconscious underpinning of an
idea — of its "evil" or "low" origins in sexuality — prevent him from
exercising his creativity? Translating this into cultural terms, we
asked how an understanding of the way in which "pattern" shaped
thought would affect our ability to think. So, in 1928, when Franz
Boas came to dinner with a group, all of whom but myself were
primarily interested in literature, and knew that Léonie Adams would

be there, he prepared an appropriate question to ask her: Did she think that words deriving from Anglo-Saxon had a different emotional tone from words with Latin origins? And when I showed Reo Fortune the anthology which Ruth Benedict had made for my Samoan field trip, he looked up from Amy Lowell's "Patterns," [3] to ask, "Is that why you are always talking about patterns?" Also, I took into the field all the questions about deviance she had raised, and I tried to discipline my perceptions by imagining what would have been the fate of the very definite personalities I knew — Franz Boas, Ruth Benedict, Léonie Adams, Edward Sapir — if they had been born Samoans.

It was out of her own searching for an undiscovered country and for an explanation of deviance, and out of the ways in which the rest of us were wrestling with the problem of the individual and culture, that she began to shape the results of her field work into the theory which has become identified with her name — that cultures could be seen as "personality writ large."

Ruth Benedict stood midway between the older type of anthropology, in which theoreticians — men like Tylor or Frazer, Lang or Crawley — worked with materials gathered by others — with old documents, travelers' and missionaries' accounts, or with notes laboriously written down by native converts — and the kind of anthropology related to living cultures, which grew out of field work in the South Seas and in Africa. Because she wanted vivid materials, she valued old eyewitness accounts of American Indians, such as those found in the Jesuit Relations; because she wanted materials meticulously collected by the rigorous textual methods which Boas insisted upon, she herself was willing to spend long, grueling hours of work among Indians whose cultures, through the erosion of contact with cultures brought from Europe centuries before, had hardened in resistance or were disintegrating before her eyes.

She never had an opportunity to participate in a living culture where she could speak the language and get to know people well as individuals. In her work with North American Indians, she always had to work through interpreters and to seek out the particularly knowledgeable individual who was also amenable to the task of sitting and dictating while, with flying pencil and aching arm, she wrote down verbatim hundreds of pages of translated tales to be redictated when she returned to New York. The materials which she herself collected differed from the fragments which other students of North American Indians had collected in that she had seen the Indians who told the stories, had watched people whom she did not know go through a few ceremonies, and had learned to trust her knowledge of the shape and feel of a culture of which she was recording only a very small part.

Even when she was sitting in a pueblo day after day, she was always, because of the very nature of the problem, straining to see and hear a more coherent culture back of the broken phrases of the day. This made her field work more like reading the work of others and made it particularly easy for her to work over the field materials of her students. Back of their inadequate notes — as also back of her own partial ones and back of the partial insights of a Jesuit missionary, or a Grinnell camping with the Cheyenne, or a Sahagun recording the crumbling glory of the Aztecs — there was a whole, if one could but perceive it. She had begun her work by following separate themes and small items wherever they occurred, and in the conclusion to her study of the Guardian Spirit, she wrote:[4]

> There is then no observed correlation between the vision-guardian-spirit concept, and the other traits with which it is associated, as it were organically, over the continent, and we have found no coalescence which we may regard as being other than fortuitous — an historical happening of definite time and place. The miscellaneous traits that enter in different centers into its make-up are none of them either the inevitable forerunner, the inevitable accompaniment of the concept, but have each an individual existence and a wider distribution outside this complex. In one region it has associated itself with puberty ceremonials, in another with totemism, in a third with secret societies, in a fourth with inherited rank, in a fifth with black magic. Among the Blackfoot, it is their economic system into which the medicine bundles have so insinuated themselves that the whole manner of it is unintelligible without taking into account the monetary value of the vision. Among the Kwakiutl,

their social life and organization, their caste system, their
concept of wealth, would be equally impossible of comprehension without a knowledge of those groups of individuals sharing
the same guardian spirit by supernatural revelation. It is in
every case a matter of social patterning — of that which cultural
recognition has singled out and standardized.

It is, so far as we can see, an ultimate fact of human nature
that man builds up his culture out of disparate elements, combining and recombining them; and until we have abandoned the
superstition that the result is an organism functionally inter-
related, we shall be unable to see our cultural life objectively,
or to control its manifestations.

This statement Radcliffe-Brown took as representing her ultimate
position, namely, that she believed that cultures were made up of
"rags and tatters." [5] But she herself was working steadily to find
some integrating principle that would explain both the disparate
origins of the elements of which a culture was built and the wholeness which she felt was there in each culture.

When one works with a living culture this wholeness is part of
one's everyday experience. The people among whom one is living
speak, walk, talk, sleep, pray, and die within a recognizable and
related pattern. The infant one holds in one's arms shows by pre-
figurative tension in his muscles just how he expects to be carried,
and there is an echo of his particular urgency in the pleading gestures
of the sick and in the trembling touch of the dying. Living among
a people whose skin color is gleaming copper, soft brown, or shining
black, whose hair is straight and coarse as a horse's mane, or falls
in waves, or curls so tight that it can be combed straight up in the
air, it is very difficult both to attend to the ways a people embody
the language they speak and the patterns they are living out and to
remember that this language, which seems to be so appropriate to
these lips, and these feelings may also occur half the world away —
where all the externals are different — with as seeming entire appro-
priateness as one finds here. Watching a tall Sepik native, lime stick
tasseled with records of the human heads he has taken, pounding the
ground with the heavy end of a fallen palm leaf to scare away the

ghosts, it is difficult to see this act, so perfectly integrated into a local ceremony, as "an element," unless one has also stood in a Balinese village and has seen the same pounding, in a setting so different, among a slender, exotic, peaceful, and ritualistic people of another race and with a quite different culture.

Many field workers who in the early twentieth century wrote the first monographs based on the study of living cultures were victims of this illusion of "fit." If they knew enough anthropology to realize that human cultures are human inventions, that they are learned anew by each generation, and that one people can borrow from another, not borrowing all but only a bit — a way of making a pot or of killing an enemy by magic, a form of courtship, or a method of cremating the dead — then the need to account for the coherence, the wholeness, of a culture became even more urgent.

Anthropologists dealt with this problem in different ways. Rivers, after making a vivid study of a single people, the Todas,[6] accepted a totally historical viewpoint and ended his days treating discrete items of behavior as the residues of an earlier integration. Radcliffe-Brown, after having had an opportunity to work on one of the most isolated and integrated cultures in the world, that of the pygmies of the Andaman Islands,[7] discounted all his experience of them as a living people — which would nevertheless sometimes peep out in conversation as he would describe how *they* peeped out, bright-eyed, from their tiny houses — and treated cultures, which afterward he never studied as wholes, as examples for the establishment of universally valid principles. Malinowski, repelled by his first field trip among the Mailu[8] and captivated by the Trobrianders,[9] pushed away all historical and areal considerations to concentrate on the way "elements" of culture were only meaningful within a functioning context. A generation later, Claude Lévi-Strauss, who was for a time entranced by the vivid detail of a living people,[10] also turned to a search for universal principles which run like wires through the material, freezing people eternally into *tableaux vivants*. And those anthropologists who were less firmly grounded took refuge in theories of race or constitution to explain the patterned and consistent differences among peoples of different cultures.

But Ruth Benedict, piecing together bits from the old, sometimes vigorous, sometimes dull descriptions of Indians as long dead as the buffalo they once had hunted, or turning from the recitation of tales which had lost their functioning relevance in the Pueblo of Cochiti, faced no such problem. She never saw a whole primitive culture that was untroubled by boarding schools for the children, by missions and public health nurses, by Indian Service agents, traders, and sentimental or exiled white people. No living flesh-and-blood member of a coherent culture was present to obscure her vision or to make it too concrete, when, in the summer of 1927, she saw with a sense of revelation that it would be possible to explain the differences among the tribes of the Southwest or the Plains — both in what they had taken from one another and in what they had resisted — as one might explain the choices of an individual who, true to his own temperament, organized his life out of the myriad and often conflicting choices presented to him by a rich historical tradition. She had always been interested in Nietzsche, and his contrast between Apollonian and Dionysian seemed ready-made to her hand to describe the contrast between the Pima and the Zuñi. From Pima, she wrote to Boas in 1927,[11] "These people have more in common with the Serrano than with the Pueblos. The contrast with the latter is *unbelievable*."

During the following winter, in 1927–1928, I was writing *Social Organization of Manu'a*,[12] happy in the freedom to write more technically, after my attempt to make the material on Samoan adolescence intelligible to educators in *Coming of Age in Samoa*.[13] We spent hours discussing how a given temperamental approach to living could come so to dominate a culture that all who were born in it would become the willing or unwilling heirs to that view of the world. From the first Ruth Benedict resisted any idea of schematization in terms of a given number of temperaments — Jung's fourfold scheme, for instance. She saw the relationship between a culture, which was "personality writ large" and "time binding," and any individual, who might or might not fit in, as a way of so phrasing all deviation that the unfortunate could be pitied and the world seen as the loser because of gifts which could not be used. She wanted to leave the future open. No attempt to understand human cultures as limited by a given number of temperaments, and so with limited temperamental contrasts, ever pleased her.

Into our discussions there came echoes of Koffka's *The Growth of the Mind*,[14] which I had read and lent to Sapir in 1925, and of conversations between Sapir and Goldenweiser at the Toronto meetings in 1924, when Sapir had been stimulated by Jung[15] and also by Seligman's recent article, "Anthropology and Psychology: A Study of Some Points of Contact," [16] in which he discussed the possibility that certain recognizable pathologies, associated with Jung's types, were given more scope in one culture than in another.

Also into our discussions came my field plans for the next year's work in the Admiralty Islands, where I wanted to test whether one would find among primitive children the kind of thinking that Freud [17] had identified as characteristic of children, neurotics, and primitives, and that Piaget,[18] taking a clue from Levy-Bruhl's[19] discussion of prelogicality, had also identified as primitive. These latter considerations I had hammered out in discussion with Reo Fortune who, before he had begun work in anthropology, had worked on Freud's and Rivers' theories of dreams.[20] Working with Ruth Benedict, I supplied the psychological materials and the concrete experience of participation in a living culture and the way children experienced it, and she tested and retested her emerging theory against her knowledge of the Indians of the Southwest and of the literature on American Indian religion.[21]

Historically, the first written application of her conceptualization was in my chapter on "Dominant Cultural Attitudes," in *Social Organization of Manu'a*,[22] written in the winter of 1927–1928, before she wrote her own first formulation in "Psychological Types in the Cultures of the Southwest." [23] None of her theoretical phrasings were included in my chapter, but every detail of the phrasing was thrashed out between us. The clarity of her concept, which owed so much to the lack of a sensory screen between the field worker and the pattern[24] and to her search for meaning within fragments, was also subjected to the test of living field work as I marshaled a procession of identified Samoan children to challenge or confirm a formulation.

So much has been said and written about the origins of her theories, about her attempt to impose a set of cast-iron types upon all cultures or to see all cultures as expressions of one or another pathology, that it seems worthwhile to document the actual origins

in considerable detail and to include two pages from my monograph,[25] unconfused by the ghosts of German theoreticians to whom
Boas considered it appropriate for her to refer when, four years later,
she wrote her book. It is also important to realize that although she
refers, in a footnote to the paper read before the International Congress of Americanists in 1928, to another one then "in press" with
the *American Anthropologist* called "Cultures and Psychological
Types," which was to present "the theoretical justification of this
position in the study of cultures," [26] this latter paper was never published. "Configurations of Culture in North America," published in
the *American Anthropologist* in 1932,[27] was written only *after* most
of *Patterns of Culture* had been completed.

The whole position is quite clear. I wrote:[28]

> By this emphasis upon conformity to the all important social
> structure, I do not mean here the attempt of a society to make
> all those within it conform to all its ways of thought and be-
> havior. The phenomenon of social pressure and its absolute
> determination in shaping the individuals within its bounds has
> been remarked too often to need laboring here. I mean to stress
> rather the particular implication in the lives of individuals of a
> particular kind of social pattern. As the Winnebago culture
> forced its children to blacken their faces and fast for a blessing,
> goaded them into a search for special experience often beyond
> any natural inclination in the individual child, so the Samoan
> emphasis upon social blessedness within an elaborate, impersonal
> structure influences every aspect of the Samoans' lives.

The chapter on "The Girl in Conflict" in *Coming of Age in
Samoa*[29] had been written in the autumn of 1926, and was already
an organized part of our discussions before Ruth Benedict's summer with the Pima in 1927. That chapter began with a question
which Ruth Benedict had taught me to ask:[30]

> Were there no conflicts, no temperaments which deviated so
> markedly from the normal that clash was inevitable? Was the
> diffused affection and the diffused authority of the large families,

the ease of moving from one family to another, the knowledge of sex and the freedom to experiment a sufficient guarantee to all Samoan girls of a perfect adjustment?

In the chapter, I discussed the cases of those deviants of whom this was not true.

Coming of Age in Samoa was published in the summer of 1928, close to the time of the Congress at which Ruth Benedict read her paper on "Psychological Types in the Cultures of the Southwest." *Social Organization of Manu'a* was not published until 1930. The extent to which my work had been shaped by her preoccupations and both of us had been shaped by Sapir's interests was so little remarked then or later that Ernst Kris could say to me, in 1946, that he thought Ruth Benedict's work showed signs of coming around to my point of view! David Mandelbaum's Introduction to the *Selected Writings of Edward Sapir in Language, Culture, and Personality* contains only one reference to Ruth Benedict:[31] "Ruth Benedict has written [in her obituary of Sapir] that the position in Chicago was one he was uniquely qualified to adorn." In the posthumous volume in his honor, *Language, Culture and Personality, Essays in Memory of Edward Sapir*,[32] three of the people who had profited most from his speculations about personality and culture — Ruth Benedict, John Dollard, and I — are not among the contributors.

Instead, posterity has been treated to reconstructions which give misleading impressions. So, for instance, Victor Barnauw, who had been her student, reconstructed in a long obituary article, which is frequently percipient but in which he ignored both written and living sources of information, the origins of the idea of *Patterns of Culture*:[33]

Willingly Anne Singleton slipped on the rough hair shirt of discipline, took upon herself the exacting Boas regimen of hard work, read endlessly, endured the discomforts of ethnological field work, and finally emerged as "Dr. Benedict." But it is a measure of her individuality that Ruth Benedict never became a mere rubber stamp of the old man's thinking. In fact, her work represents a marked contrast to his. Boas had long ago rejected the "deep" intuitive plunges of German scholarship and philosophy; but in these same dubious sources Ruth Benedict now found inspiration. Under her master's somewhat jaundiced eye she turned to Nietzsche, Spengler and Dilthey, whose ideas she somehow blended with the Boas tradition of intensive field work in a particular area. From this unexpected amalgam she managed to fashion her famous *Patterns of Culture*.

And there is Melville Herskovits' comment in his book on Boas:[34]

Broader uses of psychological concepts, such as those which attempted to assign entire societies to particular categories of mental set, as in the book *Patterns of Culture* by his student and colleague Ruth Benedict, seemed to him to raise methodological questions that had not been faced. Though for personal reasons he consented to write a brief preface for the work, he devoted several paragraphs to a critical discussion of the problem in his chapter on methods of research in the textbook he edited, especially pointed because he takes as his example the Northwest Coast Indians, who had been cited as an extreme case by Benedict. Indicating that "the leading motive of their life is the limitless pursuit of gaining social prestige and of holding on to what has been gained, and the intense feeling of inferiority and shame if even a part of the prestige is lost," he adds, "these tendencies are so striking that the amiable qualities that appear in intimate family life are easily overlooked."

The actual facts are that the theoretical part of the work — the usefulness of viewing the integration of a culture within an area in the light of the way individuals with specific temperaments integrated items from within their cultural heritage — was worked out with reference neither to Spengler nor to Dilthey. Nietzsche had been an old favorite of hers.[35] Boas had approved the early manifestations of the theory.[36] When he read *Coming of Age in Samoa*, which was written under his direct supervision, he made only one objection: "You haven't made clear the distinction between roman-

tic and passionate love." He read Ruth Benedict's paper, "Configurations of Culture in North America," written in 1932, and
discussed it with her on the trip which they took to the Southwest
together, and she went over with him every detail of the Kwakiutl
material in hour-long discussions, which she explicitly acknowledges:[37]

> For the Northwest Coast of America I have used not only Pro-
> fessor Franz Boas' text publications and detailed compilations of
> Kwakiutl life, but his still unpublished material and his penetrat-
> ing comment upon his experience on the Northwest Coast ex-
> tending over forty years.

And in the Introduction Boas writes:[38]

> As the author points out, not every culture is characterized by
> a dominant character, but it seems probable that the more in-
> timate our knowledge of the cultural drives that actuate the
> behavior of the individual, the more we shall find that certain
> controls of emotion, certain ideals of conduct, prevail that ac-
> count for what seem to us as abnormal attitudes when viewed
> from the standpoint of our civilization. The relativity of what
> is considered social or asocial, normal or abnormal, is seen in a
> new light.

As for Dilthey, far from battling for her individuality against
Boas' disapproval of Dilthey, it was Boas who insisted that she must
discuss him, not out of sympathy for Dilthey's ideas but out of the
special standards of scholarship which required mention of those
who had used comparable ideas irrespective of whether or not one's
own ideas derived from them.

From the fresh excitement of the 1927 summer in Pima, when she
saw the basic contrast between the Pueblos and the other Indian
cultures of North America "as the contrast that is named and described by Nietzsche in his studies of Greek tragedy," was a six year
road, in the course of which she published two articles on the subject, both of which dealt with American Indian material. Only in

1932 did she decide that in the book it would be necessary to add a third culture — one which had been studied by a field worker whom she knew well and on which she could trust the material — to set beside Zuñi, where she had her own field work as a guide and a corrective, and the Kwakiutl, where she could test each smallest interpretation against Boas' detailed memory. She chose Dobu. The history of her interest in Dobu and of her choice of this culture is contained in a series of letters exchanged with Reo Fortune.[39]

But between what seemed so obvious to me, writing in 1927 — namely, that a culture shapes the lives of those who live within it — and the views of the literate world of 1934, when *Patterns of Culture* was published, there was a great gap. Her publishers in their choice of publicity materials stressed not what she regarded as its major contribution but rather what we had come to think of as obvious. Through a long and spirited correspondence with Ferris Greenslet of Houghton Mifflin, beginning with a request for a blurb, my writing of the blurb and her revision of it, and the publisher's choices from it, to her rebellious rewriting of the circular for the general reader, she fought for a clear statement of what she felt she had contributed that was new by writing this book. In the copy which she herself prepared for the publisher, she wrote: "In a straightforward style, the author demonstrates how the manners and morals of these tribes, and our own as well, are not piecemeal items of behavior, but consistent ways of life. They are not racial, nor the necessary consequence of human nature, but have grown up historically in the life history of the community."

A Brief Sketch
of Serrano Culture*

THE SERRANO, one of the several dialectic groups of Southern Californian Shoshoneans, live in Riverside and San Bernardino Counties, California. The information in this paper was obtained in 1922 at the Morongo Indian Reservation in the San Gorgonio Pass near Banning. By far the fullest account was given by Rosa Morongo, who was born about seventy years ago at Akavat, north of Beaumont, and who married Captain John Morongo of Mission Creek, chief (*kika*) of the Maronga band.

The Serrano of the San Gorgonio Pass were familiar with the distribution of peoples of their dialect from Redlands east along the northern slope of the pass to Twenty Nine Palms, a distance of about one hundred and twenty miles; three local groups at the base of Mt. San Jacinto along the southern slopes of the pass; and two local groups north of the San Bernardino Mountains, in the southern Bear Valley region. The emphasis in this paper is upon the eastern, or Morongo Valley, Serrano. They are probably the only bands whose life can be reconstructed to any extent today. The western settlements removed almost bodily to the missions, and at the secularization in 1834 there were apparently too few survivors to reestablish tribal life. A very few returned to Akavat, north of Beaumont, Mrs. Morongo's birthplace, but it was in the eastern regions of

* *American Anthropologist*, XXVI, No. 3 (1924), 366–92. This presentation consists of brief excerpts from the original paper.

the pass that native culture survived, though even here some Indians had been at the missions.

Such information as may be gathered among the Serrano today is almost entirely exoteric. No old shaman (*hümte*) or priest (*paha*) survives. The annual fiesta is still kept up in a modified form, and until a few years ago the Morongo Reservation Serrano depended on a shaman of the desert Cahuilla for some of the old dances and shamanistic performances. A great deal of the old meaning, both in social organization and in religious practices, is undoubtedly lost. It is largely by guesswork that they can give the meaning of any of the ceremonial songs; and any religious connotation in such practices as rock-painting, for instance, is now unknown. It must therefore remain an open question in many cases, as for instance the universal animal designations of all local groups, whether the absence of any esoteric interpretations today is the reflection of an old Serrano trait, or is due to a fading of the old traditions.

Descent and Marriage. Descent was patrilineal. Only in cases where the father is white is descent counted through the mother. Residence was always patrilocal.

Marriage was arranged by the parents, sometimes soon after the child was born. When a girl had passed through the adolescence ceremony and it was considered time for the couple to live together, the man's immediate family sent presents to the girl's father; a rich family would send a couple of horses or a couple of cows, and poorer families in proportion. There was no gift from the girl's family.

There was no ceremony at marriage. The girl simply went to live at the house of the man's father. After a time they built a house of their own.

Arrangements for marriage were said to be wholly the concern of the immediate family; neither the tribal nor ceremonial chief was consulted.

Polygamy was rare; it usually occurred in cases where the first wife had no children, or where the husband was an especially good hunter and married his wife's younger sister.

After the death of her husband, a widow stayed in her father-in-law's house unless there was good reason to move. She usually married her husband's elder brother, but this was not obligatory.

Annual Ceremony. The outstanding ceremonial of the Serrano groups is the composite of dances and observances culminating in the mourning ceremony. A fixed number of local groups, including two Cahuilla groups, co-operated in this ceremony. These were, fifty years ago:

The Maringa-Mühiatnim-Atü'aviatum group, of which the Maringa and Atü'aviatum groups were responsible for the ceremony on alternate years, assisted in each case by the Mühiatnim *paha.*
The Wanapüpayam, west of the Maringa.
The Mamaintum, east of the Maringa, at Twenty Nine Palms.
The Kayukuyam, Cahuilla of Palm Springs.
The Pahi'ninayam, Cahuilla of Palm Springs Canyon.
The Pü'viatum, Serrano of Bear Valley.
The Kutcáviatum, another Serrano group of Bear Valley.

Of these the last two have been extinct for many years, and the last representative of the Mamaintum has recently died.

The first group must always lead off in the ceremonial series, in October. I shall describe the ceremony as it was given by this group.

The responsibility for the ceremony of this Morongo Valley group was taken on alternate years by the Maringa, and by the Atü'aviatum. The chief of each group however contributed to the fiesta provisions every year. This is now standardized in the requisition of two bags of flour apiece from the chief of each group. In old times, first-fruits of every harvest were given him for use in this festival. These provisions are turned over at the time of the ceremony to the *paha* of the Mühiatnim group, but this group never contributes, unless on account of a death among its number. For in addition to the meal contributed by the chiefs an equal amount is given by every family which belongs to the group giving the ceremony and which has lost a member by death during the year.

The chief of the group presiding any one year calls the ceremony through his messenger, the *paha.* It begins on Monday morning, and lasts through Sunday morning. The first three days, however, are concerned with providing the materials for the feast. Even today some of the women spend the time in the gathering and preparation of the seeds as formerly, and some of the men hunt rabbits to provide the meat. The rabbits have no ceremonial significance in this connection, but are a customary part of the feast.

The ceremonial house, *kitcatü'atc*, is open during these days, and old stories are told there, and the men may play peon.

The first great event of the week is the all-night ceremony on Wednesday when the feathers are brought to the ceremonial house. These are the most sacred possessions of the Serrano, and are kept during the year under the care of the *paha* in a secret cave in the mountains. The ceremony on Wednesday night begins with a great supper. After supper they sing, led by the ceremonial singer, the *tcaka*, an hereditary officer, a Maringa, until at the direction of the *paha* all lights are extinguished, and the assembled people wait in silence till the feathers are brought. They first know that the feathers have come when they hear the *paha* praying in a peculiar voice in the darkness. The words are indistinguishable, but what he says concerns the beginning of things. This lasts about an hour. Then the fires are relighted, and the feathers are hung around the room. In old times the *paha* and other dancers danced with the feathers at this time, but the last man who could dance this dance died twenty-five years ago. Besides, the feathers are falling to pieces now, and require very careful handling.

The first songs that are sung after the fires are relighted refer to the taking of the toloache drink, *manitc*, though no one now living has any memory of any connection.

> "Musüka [said to be an esoteric word for soul]
> Musüka,
> Take the manitc.
> We shall depart [said to refer to loss of consciousness]
> But we shall not die."

The second:

> "Behold,
> We have drunk the manitc.
> We are restored again."

There were a number of songs for the dance with the feathers the words of which are variants of the phrases:

> "Up and down, up and down.
> We dance with the feathers."

Women dance the first half of this night; men the second.

The feathers are left hung about the ceremonial house for the remainder of fiesta week. They are never brought out on any other occasion. In the late afternoon of any day while the feathers are displayed, a special ceremony may take place. The *paha* swings the bullroarer in the ceremonial house; this is a signal for silence, and no one must look to see whence the noise comes, or by any chance see the bullroarer. If he does, he is tied up with the sacred feathers, and remains so until his family pay to have him released.

On Thursday all children born during the year are brought to be named. Whichever group, the Maringa or the Atü'aviatum, is responsible for the ceremony that year, all children of both these groups and of the Mühiatnim are named each year.

The names are selected out of the stock of personal names belonging in the father's line. They are the names by which the children are commonly known thereafter in the family. There are no secret names.

At the ceremony the members of the immediate family of the child distribute money and lengths of calico by tossing them among the guests. People used to be lavish in these gifts. The ceremony begins with singing and dancing. Then the *paha* takes each child in turn, sings, and in former times danced with it, and just before the child is returned to its mother, the name is called out by the chief of the group giving the ceremony that year.

Thursday night people sleep.

Friday the eagles are killed. Young eagles were formerly taken from the nests, and cared for by the *paha*. Rabbits and other food had to be taken to him for the eagles by men of the group. The birds are strangled at the fiesta, and the feathers used to decorate the images of the dead which are burned on the last night. Other eagle feathers were used for the sacred dancing feathers, but the feathers of the eagles killed at this ceremony are not known to have ever been so used. The men sit in a circle, and the *paha* slowly strangles the birds. The feathers are removed, and those who are making the images of the dead each receive some.

The images or "dolls," *tü-iv* (ghosts), must be made on Friday afternoon. The immediate family may make the image representing the relative who has died that year, but it is more usual to pay some-one outside to make it. There is no restriction on the group-affilia-tions of the person who is paid to do this service. The images are about life-size, and in former times were dressed in as excellent material as the family could afford to make or buy. Ten-cent pieces are sewed on for eyes, and the eagle feathers used to decorate the head.

Saturday was the day for the dance known in English as the Eagle Dance. The Serrano word for it is *tuwituaim*, meaning simply "dance." It has for them at present no association with the eagle. The dance has not been danced by a Serrano for twenty-five years, but a shaman of the Desert Cahuilla used to come to dance it some-times at fiestas until rather recently. In old times the boy who won in the race at the *toloache* ceremonies was supposed to be trained for this dance. It was a whirling dance, and required much skill. The dancer always painted, though with no particular pattern. Much red was used, and also black and white. A feather costume was used, but not the sacred feathers.

Saturday night is the great all-night ceremony. The Wanapü-payam sing their songs the first half of the night; the Kayukuyam the last half. The mourning ceremony proper begins rather more than an hour before sunrise with the distribution of meal to the heads of families in the invited groups. The *paha* is the distributor. It will be remembered that the chiefs of the Maringa and of the Atü'avia-tum, and the heads of all families in these groups and the Mü-hiatnim who have lost members by death during the year, contribute an equal quantity of meal to the fiesta. From each of these quanti-ties of meal the *paha* distributes one panful each into the apron of the leading woman of the principal households of the groups that are ceremonially invited to the fiesta. This is an hereditary privilege. Other families among the visiting groups may be included in this distribution if they have lost a member during the year, but this is a voluntary honor done them by the group which acts as host, and they cannot complain if it is omitted.

The images, *tü-iv*, are now brought out, each by a woman not in the immediate family of the deceased. Usually the woman who dances with the image is a member of the same group, but the family usually pay for this service, and there is no restriction on the social group of the person who takes this place. They march around in procession carrying the life-sized images before them under the arms, and then form a circle outside the ceremonial house. The dance is a bending motion with a rather pronounced resumption of the upright position. It lasts about half an hour. The songs are repetitions of the following:

"Tü-iv [i. e., images; spirits of the dead; evil spirits] will go away in flame;
Tü-iv will go away in smoke.
Tü-iv have departed;
They have gone away in the burning."

At the conclusion of the dance and singing, which was accompanied by wailing, the dancers put the images on a pile of wood which was kindled by the *paha*, and burned. It was the signal for money and calico to be thrown among the guests by the members of the bereaved families. Other things of some value were also thrown upon the fire, but most was tossed promiscuously among the people.

After the burning, the chief, through the *paha*, gave the sacred strings of shell beads, *uk'*, to the chiefs of the local groups which make up the ceremonial unit which is traditionally present at this ceremony. Many of these bands have become extinct, and in 1919 beads were given to the Wanapüpayam, the Mamaintum (Twenty Nine Palms), the Kayukuyam (Cahuilla of Palm Springs), and the Pahi'ninayam (Cahuilla of Palm Springs Canyon). The Mamaintum have since become extinct. The beads, *uk'*, which are given at this time are mentioned as original possessions of the Serrano in the myths and in certain songs. They are also identical with the beads which were formerly used as currency. Such beads were buried in as large numbers as possible with the dead.

If a death had occurred in one of the visiting groups which it was desired to notice with honor, an additional string of beads was given to the chief of the bereaved group, one for every death that had occurred.

The ceremony was now over. This Maringa ceremony was given always in October, and the visiting groups followed in turn in reciprocating as hosts in their own mourning ceremonies.

Food. On the desert mesquite was the standard vegetable food and was highly valued everywhere in the Serrano territory. It was prepared preferably in a deep wooden mortar sunk in the earth. It was first pounded coarsely, then winnowed, then pounded to fine meal. It was stored in ollas on the ridges of the foothills; sometimes also in granaries of willow twigs. To prepare the meal for eating, it was simply mixed with water, and eaten without cooking.

Acorns grew in all the canyons and were gathered by the women, and pulverized either in movable or in bed-rock mortars according to the custom of the district, and leached in large tub-like baskets of willow twigs lined with sand. Hot water was poured through until it ran clear.

Piñon nuts were important in the diet of all these groups. A trip was made over into the Bear Valley region every fall for these nuts. No group could go without its chief and the Maringa-Mühiatnim-Atü'aviatum group went together, under the leadership of the Maringa chief. The two first groups went first to Kupatcam, The Pipes, where the Atü'aviatum lived. From the time they left this place, the party began to *witc-at.* This term refers to communal, that is, ceremonial, eating. When any ceremony whatever was to be undertaken, the requisition for the feast upon the proper heads of families was the *witc-at.* So on this trip all provisions were turned into a common fund by the heads of the families and distributed by the chief through the *paha.* The first piñon nuts were given to the chief by every family, and these were used for his *witc-at* at the annual feast which always followed this trip very shortly.

The cones were thrown into the embers of a fire and raked out when the nuts had loosened. According to one informant they were also roasted under cover. They were then struck against something to loosen the nuts, and these were ground into flour in mortars, shells and all. There was no winnowing.

Many deer were taken during this trip. All night ceremonies were held over each one, and the work of cutting the meat and dressing the skin was the work of the men. What meat was left over was dried in slabs and taken home. To prepare it for eating it was cooked partially, then pounded, and finished off by roasting. The bones were pounded in the mortars while fresh, and eaten in a sort of paste.

They Dance for Rain
in Zuñi*

AGAINST THE terra-cotta house-walls of the plaza, the katcinas are dancing the summer rain dance. For four days they have danced, masked, and bright with feather headdresses, hour in, hour out, in Zuñi. And now the clouds have listened to the insistent measure of the song, to the rhythm of forty dancing feet, to the beat of their turtle-shell rattles. Great desert clouds have loosed themselves from their moorings along the horizon and filled the sky to the zenith. There is a patter of rain; then the prayed-for, delayed deluge of a New Mexican summer afternoon.

No one runs for shelter. On and on the katcinas dance, their bright parrot feathers drooping in the rain, their brilliantly embroidered dancing kilts heavy with the wet, their red and blue and quill-embroidered moccasins splashed and muddy. The song only rises a little louder, and a quiet happiness at heard and answered prayer moves the people of the pueblo. "Our grandmothers have heard us."

For the dance in Zuñi is no idle pastime. It is insistent petition by the gods and to the gods. They bring their supernatural beings themselves into their streets and plazas to make their prayer for them. For in Zuñi the katcinas are the spirits of the dead, their supernatural pantheon, and they live in a sacred lake far out in the desert from which they come whenever a Zuñi man puts on their

* Unpublished paper, undated (probably 1920's).

mask and costume "to play with them, and have happy days." It is a gala time whenever the katcinas are dancing; the pueblo washes its hair, and gives over all drudgery, and troops to the plaza, all in its best necklaces and moccasins and bandas and mantas to watch the dancing for the day.

The dance itself is well calculated to compel the attention of the forces of nature by its almost hypnotic repetitions. It is danced in a long double line of masked and brightly costumed men, their slim bodies bared and painted to the waist, their long black hair down their backs. Hour after hour they dance in place, turning one after the other in half or quarter turns to right or left, marking the rhythm heavily on the right foot, to which is fastened the katcina's turtle rattle. There are breaks, however, in the regularity of the rhythm: sometimes there is a held beat when as one man the forty dancers hold back the insistent foot-beat; sometimes the song slows to half-time and the feet are as if weighted with lead, only to quicken to a double-time.

When the four songs of each series have been danced, and the katcinas troop out of the plaza for the intermission, the delight-makers take the field. They are the clown gods of the Southwest, the grotesque knob-headed "Mud Heads" of Zuñi. They provide the relief of laughter, of human mockery. Sometimes they satirize the dance the katcinas have just been dancing, sometimes they play a kind of pull-away with a wool bag for missile, their "grandmother," sliding and slipping to exhaustion in the mud if it has rained for the dance. Sometimes they hold some village incident up to public ridicule, perhaps a suspected bribery, or a quarrel among the priests. Nothing is too sacred for their jest. Sometimes, and this is most popular of all, they gather in the pueblo great toppling loads of bread and tortillas and roasted corn and pumpkins and watermelons, and lengths of cloth and tobacco from the store, and they have a "throw-away." Every man, woman and child of Zuñi is on the flat roofs of the houses or crowded in the plaza, and great is the rivalry when the delight-makers throw the trophies high in the air. The men and children lean sideways from the very edges of the roof-beams snatching at a single tortilla; on the ground a small boy and a venerable grandmother roll over and over with their fingers deep in a Zuñi bun.

Everywhere laughter, calls, and the shouts of the victors. Suddenly from the passageway the katcinas return to dance; double file they enter, and their feet take up the beat of the dance. The delight in an ordered beauty has taken the place of the riot of the clowns.

Six times during every summer season they dance a rain dance in Zuñi, and each dance may be repeated from two to four days. Each dance may be different, with different songs, different steps, and different katcinas, but there are certain popular dances that are usually brought back more than once in a season. Whatever it is they dance, the great ceremonial background of it is shut away, only the dancing is public. No white man sees the painting and preparation of the masks, the long prayers in the kiva, the planting of prayer-sticks to the spirits. Without these things, the dance would be to them unthinkable, a tinkling cymbal that came to nothing.

At sundown the dance is over. The unmasked high priest who has "made their road" all day, makes a last road for them to the kiva, sifting fine white meal in a line before him on the ground. He goes before them up the high sky-pointing ladder that leads to the kiva roof, and standing beside the hatchway puts sacred meal upon each shoulder as one by one they descend into the kiva. He stands, etched against the vivid evening sky, the bright-colored unbroken line of costumed dancers ascending the ladder from the plaza and below a knotted group waiting for their places in turn against the sky. It is dark when alone at last upon the housetop, the high priest lifts a last pinch of the sacred white meal to his lips, prays once more silently, and follows the katcinas into the kiva. The dance is over. Only after everything is dark and still, each dancer will take his mask out to a sacred place along the river and send him "home" with a prayer and a hope that their days have pleased him.

As in the summer they must dance the summer rain dances in Zuñi, so at each other season they must dance other dances the year around in a calendric ritual. Some of these dances come only at four-year intervals; some of the greatest they have not danced now for many years. Not all of the dances are masked; often the dancers dance in their own proper characters, not as masked supernaturals, and the women dance with them. One of the most popular is a round dance around a hemlock tree planted for the occasion in the plaza. Great is the maneuvering to hold a sweetheart's hand in the four moving circles, for courting is strictly guarded at Zuñi and it is not easy otherwise to accomplish.

There are corn dances, and war dances and solstice dances, and dances of the curing societies, and dances more especially for display; there is no dance that is not popular in Zuñi. Each one has its own movements and song-rhythm, and its own proper name and place in the calendric cycle. It has individuality and a history, and as likely as not a certain priesthood who "owns" it. It makes its own distinctive pattern of beauty and costume and music. But always, to the Zuñi, it is danced for rain.

An Introduction
to Zuñi Mythology*[1]

FOLKLORISTIC STUDIES, since the days of Cosquin and the students stimulated by the collections of the Grimm brothers, have been extensive rather than intensive. Whether the proposed problem was historical reconstruction or a study of creative processes in mythology, the method that has been followed is that of far-flung comparative studies. This method has been used by Ehrenreich and the psychoanalytic students of myth, both of whom are interested in the role of symbolism in folklore, as well as by the modern school of Aarne, which is interested in reconstructing archetypal forms of folktales, and by students like Bolte and Polívka who are committed simply to documenting distribution.

The intensive study of one body of folklore has been scanted throughout the history of folkloristic studies, and little stress has been laid upon its possible rewards. The most valuable studies of this kind have tabled and analyzed the cultural behavior embodied in the tales, and these have been made only in American Indian material, i.e. Franz Boas' "Description of the Tsimshian Based on Their Mythology"[2]; Franz Boas' *Kwakiutl Culture as Reflected in Their Mythology*[3]; and Clara Ehrlich's "Tribal Culture in Crow Mythol-

* From *Zuni Mythology* (2 vols., Columbia University Contributions to Anthropology, XXI; New York, Columbia University Press, 1935), I, xi–xliii. In its present form, the Introduction has been condensed by approximately one-third.

ogy." [4] Such studies show the great amount of cultural material in myth, and stress the value of folklore for an understanding of the culture. This is not the only kind of intensive study of folklore. Boas has defined, and contrasted with other regions, the themes of Eskimo folklore in "The Folklore of the Eskimo." [5] He has indicated the relation of these themes to the cultural behavior and ideals among that people. In addition, there is also the possibility of the study of the native narrator, that is, the literary materials which he has at his disposal and his handling of them.[6]

These problems have seldom been attacked, and several circumstances have contributed to this neglect on the part of folklore students. In the first place, the most striking and obvious result of research in the early days of folkloristic study was always the fantastically wide distribution of episodes and plots, and everyone therefore joined in diffusion studies.

In the second place, there are certain conditions which must be fulfilled before intensive study of one body of folklore can yield any considerable fruits, and these conditions have not often been met in the available collections. For the most profitable study of single bodies of mythology, folktales should hold an important place in the tribal life, not being relegated, for example, to children's amusement or used solely as word-perfect recitations of magical formulae; a large body of tales should have been recorded, and over as long a period as possible; the culture of the people who tell the tales should be well known; and folklore among that people should be a living and functioning culture trait.

These optimum conditions are fulfilled in the folklore of Zuñi, the largest pueblo of the Southwest of the United States. Even compared with other North American tribes, mythology is a highly developed and serious art in Zuñi, and the great number of tales that have been collected by many different persons extend over a period of fifty years. The culture of Zuñi is well known, and in discussing the tales I have been able to use my own first-hand acquaintance with Zuñi beliefs and behavior, as well as detailed accounts by other students. Finally, in contrast to that of almost all other tribes of the North American continent, folklore in Zuñi is not moribund. The processes that can be studied in it are not reconstructed in a kind of folkloristic archaeology but are open to observation and experiment.

When these conditions can be fulfilled, intensive study of a single body of folklore is of first-rate theoretical importance, whether the problem at issue is historical reconstruction, the study of culture, or literary problems in the development of oral traditions. It seems obvious enough that studies in the two latter problems can be carried out best by careful intensive study, and that the students of symbolism, for example, have overlooked in favor of misleading comparative studies a method of work which can yield definite results. Even in the matter of historical reconstruction, which is the chief end of comparative studies of folklore, intensive study has much to contribute. The usual library-trained comparative student works with standard versions from each locality; in primitive cultures, usually one from a tribe. This version arbitrarily becomes "the" tribal tale, and is minutely compared with equally arbitrary standard tales from other tribes. But in such a body of mythology as that of Zuñi, many different variants coexist, and the different forms these variants take cannot be ascribed to different historical levels, or even in large measure to particular tribal contacts, but are different literary combinations of incidents in different plot sequences. The comparative student may well learn from intensive studies not to point an argument that would be invalidated if half a dozen quite different versions from the same tribe were placed on record.

The two problems which I shall consider at the present time from the analysis of Zuñi mythology are: I, the themes which their folklore elaborates and the relation of these to their culture; II, the literary problems of the Zuñi narrator.

I

No folktale is generic. It is always the tale of one particular people with one particular livelihood and social organization and religion. The final form that a tale takes in that culture is influenced, often fundamentally, by attitudes and customs that cannot be discovered except with full knowledge of life and behavior among that people. It has always been obvious to students of every theoretical persuasion that folklore tallied with culture and yet did not tally with it, and the majority of students have agreed upon one convenient explanation of those instances where the two are at odds. Folklore, it is said, reflects not the customs and beliefs of the narrators of the tales, but those of many generations past; cultural survivals of earlier ages are perpetuated in folklore, and these, it is often felt, are the chief reason for the study of oral traditions. Even conditions of barbarism in which fathers are supposed to have eaten their children, and conditions of primal life when man first gained ascendancy over animals, have been said to be embalmed in folklore.

A conservatism that perpetuates long-discarded customs, however, is characteristic of a dead lore rather than a living one, and the great emphasis on the importance of survivals in the interpretation of folklore is evidently due to certain characteristics of oral tradition in Western civilization. European folklore was rescued from the memories of old men and women much as that of the Plains Indians is rescued today. It was recorded by collectors long after its heyday. Grimm's tales are found to reflect the manners and customs of the feudal age, not contemporary contacts with industrialism or with urban civilization, and the belief has become current that survivals of old customs are perpetuated in folklore through great lapses of time. This, however, is to generalize the senescence of folklore into a law by means of which mythology is elaborately interpreted. Folklore often remains current and can be adequately collected when it is no longer a living trait. North American Indians can almost always relate their folktales long after their aboriginal cultural life is in abeyance, and many valuable bodies of mythology have been collected in dead cultures from old men who learned the stories in their youth. The functioning of myth in culture and the processes of cultural adaptation, however, cannot be adequately studied in these cases. Comparison of variants under such conditions indicates mainly how much or how little different informants have forgotten of a dead culture trait, and such comparison is comparatively unrewarding. In Zuñi tales are constantly told, and recounting folktales is an habitual occupation of a great number of the most important members of the community.

A living folklore, such as that of Zuñi, reflects the contemporary interests and judgments of its tellers, and adapts incidents to its own cultural usages. Like any cultural trait, folklore tends, of course, to perpetuate traditional forms, and there is a certain lag in folklore as there is in contemporary statecraft or in morals. But the scope of this conservatism is limited in folklore as in other traits. It is never sufficient to give us license to reconstruct the items of a racial memory; and contemporary attitudes are always to be reckoned with, rather than those that have been superseded in that culture. In the present collection the cultural lag is apparent in many details of overt behavior. In the folktales, for example, except in those recognized by the tellers as Mexican, entrance to the house is by means of a ladder to the roof and down another ladder from the hatchway, yet doors have been common in Zuñi since 1888 and are today universal except in the kivas. Old conditions, therefore, have been equally retained in the ceremonial house and in the folktale. The same may be said of the use of stone knives. Stone knives are still laid upon altars and used in ceremonies; and in folktales also heroes use stone knives instead of the omnipresent contemporary store knife. More elaborate modern innovations are also unrecognized in folklore. At present sheep herding occupies much of the life of Zuñi men, and hunting is in abeyance. In the tales, however, all heroes are hunters, and there is no mention of sheep herding except in tales recognized as Mexican. In like manner men do not now come courting with a bundle of gifts for the girl, but in folklore this is a convention usually observed. Similarly, at the present time the activity of the medicine societies is centered in their great all-night ceremony at the winter solstice, the individual planting of prayer-sticks at full moon, and in not very exacting incidental activities. In the myths, on the other hand, every member goes every night to his medicine society and returns home when others are in bed.

The cultural lag that is represented by these differences between custom in contemporary life and in folktales covers, however, a short period, and by no means gives indication of an early cultural horizon such as can be reconstructed, for instance, from comparative studies of culture, still less from studies of comparative linguistics. The agreement between the conduct of contemporary life and the picture of life in the folktales is very close. The roles of men and women in Zuñi life, the role of the priesthoods, the conduct of sex life, the concern with witchcraft are all faithfully indicated.

Where there is a contrast between Zuñi custom and literary convention, the divergence commonly rests upon other considerations than survival of older customs. Even in the divergences just mentioned, cultural lag is not a sufficient explanation. It may well be, as any native will assure you, that, in times not long past, men spent every night in their medicine society meetings. On the other hand, it is possible that in those times as in these, this was a conventional description of a golden age, and golden ages have often existed only in the imagination. The impulse to idealize must be reckoned with in folkloristic contrasts with contemporary life when it is also possible to set the difference down to cultural lag. Similarly, courting with bundles may not be a survival of an older custom but a borrowed incident which is a folkloristic convention. Stone knives and entrance through the hatchway also have become conventional attributes of a less troubled and ideal age, and from this point of view should be considered along with the fabulous prowess of heroes as runners in the stick race.

This tendency to idealize in folklore has often been pointed out. There is another set of discrepancies in Zuñi folklore that cannot so easily be disposed of. The most striking instance is that of the constant recurrence of polygamy in the tales. Zuñi institutions are thoroughly monogamous. It is of course conceivable that the folkloristic pattern reproduces earlier conditions. Polygamy is allowed almost everywhere in North America outside the Southwest and even polyandry is accepted in certain nearby tribes. The absence of any taboo against multiple spouses is an old and general North American Indian trait. To assign the Zuñi folkloristic pattern, however, to such a reflection of an earlier background is difficult for two reasons. In the first place, all pueblo cultures have the Zuñi taboo on polygamy and pueblo culture is exceedingly old and stable, as one may judge from archaeological evidence in material culture. It is doubtful whether any folklore can be cited from any part of the world that reflects cultural conditions as remote as those before pueblo culture took form, and there is, therefore, good reason for dissatisfaction with this explanation. In the second place, even if it were possible to interpret the Zuñi folkloristic pattern of polygamy as a survival, we should still have to explain why the marriage with eight wives or with two husbands is prominent in Zuñi mythology and not generally over North America. The simultaneous marriage with many wives was culturally allowed over most of the continent, but it does not figure in their tales as it does in pueblo folklore. The presumption that is indicated by a study of the distribution of this folkloristic pattern in North America is that in the pueblos polygamy is a grandiose folkloristic convention partaking on the one hand of usual mythological exaggeration and on the other of a compensatory daydream. Just as the hero of folktales kills a buck every day, or four in a single day, so he also is courted by eight maidens and marries them. When a hero is given supernatural power by his supernatural father, he signalizes it by accepting all eight of the priests' daughters who had flouted him, killing them, and resuscitating them to serve his triumph. It is a grandiose demonstration of power, and of the same nature as the rain-blessing the eight wives bring back to the pueblo after their resuscitation, a blessing so great that the consequent blood fills the whole valley and the people have to escape to the top of the mesa. In the same way the hunter whose sister uses her supernatural power in his behalf marries wives from all the seven towns, and in his witch wife's reprisal she has him abducted by eight Crane girls who keep him as their husband for four years. Marriage with many wives is a Zuñi fantasy of the same order as raising the dead or traveling with seven-league boots in other bodies of folklore. It plays a fairytale role in Zuñi mythology which is automatically rendered impossible in those areas of North America where tales of polygamy and polyandry have bases in fact. What compensatory elements the tale embodies it is hard to prove, but it seems likely that these are present.

Other contrasts between custom and folkloristic conventions must be explained as fundamentally compensatory. The abandonment of children at birth is a constantly recurring theme and is alien to Zuñi custom. In real life it does not come up for consideration at all. Illegitimate children are cared for in their mothers' homes, and present-day gossips, though they specialize in outrageous libels, do not tell of any instance in which an infant has been done away with.

All men and women, not only the parents, give children the fondest care. There is no cultural background for the abandonment of illegitimate children. It is harder to judge about the abandonment of young children in famine. The tales of migrations to pueblos where crops have not failed are based on fact and such incidents may possibly have occurred, where children too large to carry and too young to make the journey were left behind, though actual reminis- cences are always of tender protection of the child. The incidents, however, of the girl in childbed who overtakes her party, leaving the baby in the grinding stone, are regarded as fabulous by contemporary Zuñis, like all tales of women who are able to get up immediately after childbirth as if nothing had happened. The abandonment of the child and the impossible physical recovery are grouped in one category. When the story of babies abandoned at birth is used in explanation of Zuñi custom, the narrator concludes from the in- cident: "That's why girls who become pregnant before marriage con- ceal their condition" — which is true — not "That's why they ex- pose their babies."

The fact remains that abandonment of children is an extraordinar- ily popular theme in Zuñi folklore. The clue lies in the fact that the hearers' identification is with the child, not with the mother. Even women, who would be expected to identify with the mother in telling these tales, comment on the reunion of the abandoned child with his mother from the point of view of the child. "He made her cry all right," a woman said with heat, and, "Oh, she (the mother) was *ashamed*." The plots are all concerned with the supernatural as- sistance and human success of the poor child, and often the whole plot is directed toward the triumph of the abandoned child over the mother or the parents. In the popular tale of the *Deserted children protected by dragonfly* the parents return in poverty and miserably sue their children for favors. The daydream, from the point of view of the child, is completed by the final largess of the children and their appointment to priestly rank. In two versions of the *Twin Children of the Sun*, the twins return, make a laughingstock of their mother, and force her to confess. These two versions, which tell of the children's abandonment at birth, contrast strongly with two other versions, in which the girl does not expose her children but is

killed by a witch or by the priests as a punishment for her uncon-
fessed pregnancy. Her sons therefore do not humiliate her, but
vindicate their mother's memory. The point of the story is entirely
different.

The popularity of the theme of abandoned children in Zuñi has a
psychological significance that parallels the familiar daydreams of
children in our civilization which detail their parents' suffering at
their imminent death. That is, it is the expression of a resentment
directed by children against their parents and worked out into a
daydream of the children's imagined vantage.

Another theme, which also reflects Zuñi culture but with a difference, is that of violent action based upon secret enmity. Grudges
are cherished in Zuñi. They are usually the rather generalized expression of slights and resentments in a small community. In actual
life they give rise to malicious aspersions, but in folklore they are
usually satisfied by nothing less than the death of the offender.
People grudge others their prosperity and set about to destroy them;
they grudge a man his success in hunting and attempt to do away
with him; they are jealous of a supernatural who has brought a new
dance to Zuñi and try to bewitch him; a priest who has not been
paid for instruction kills the delinquent; the child who is scolded
for shirking satisfies her grudge by leaving so that her family fear she
is dead and recover her only after search by the supernaturals;
people are angry because a girl will not lend a dipper and they have
to drink from their hands, therefore a feud starts and two girls are
killed. Men and women both resent any slight in courtship; the
woman tries to kill the man who has refused her a piece of his
game (a usual courtship gesture in the tales), and men kill or
bewitch girls who have laughed at them, or refused them a drink
(a courtship preliminary today as well). The deserted husband
ritualistically causes a drought, an earthquake, or an epidemic, which
threatens to wipe out the whole pueblo. The deserted wife similarly
summons Navahoes or Apaches to demolish the village, or attempts
to kill her husband. Unlike those of the Plains, Zuñi folkways have
no place for an ideal of character which overlooks slights, however
small, and their folktales provide exaggerated fantasies of reprisal.
In a culture in which homicide occurs with such extraordinary rarity

that instances are not even remembered, the compensatory violence of these reprisals is the more striking.

True to the peculiar ideology of Zuñi these reprisals are easily phrased as "teaching people to love you," i.e. to act decently toward you. The despised children, whom the people spit at, throwing refuse and urine into their grandmother's house, get the help of Salt Mother who takes away all the clothing in the pueblo. They tell her: "The people at Itiwana hate us. We want them to learn to love us." The people have to stay in bed all the time and in their shame are brought to the point of begging work from the poor children. The latter remove the curse when the people promise to "love them." The whole story is an excellent illustration of the strange way in which, according to Zuñi notions, you teach people to love you.

Zuñi folklore, therefore, in those cases where it does not mirror contemporary custom, owes its distortions to various fanciful exaggerations and compensatory mechanisms. The role of daydreams, of wish fulfillment, is not limited to these cases of distortion. It is equally clear in the tales that most minutely reflect the contemporary scene. Zuñi folklore differs from most North American Indian mythology in that the usual daydream is little concerned with prowess in warfare. Nor are there in Zuñi accounts of supernatural encounters and the acquisition of power, such as fill the folktales of the Plains Indians. Zuñi folktales are as faithful to Zuñi fantasies in what they exclude as in what they include. Their most popular theme is the triumph of the despised and weak and previously worsted. The poor orphan boy is victorious in hunting, in stick races, in gambling, and in courtship; those who do not have witch power are triumphant over those who have; the stunted ragamuffin Ahaiyute win first place in everything.

There is singular mildness in Zuñi tales, and this mildness is strangely at variance with the compensatory violence we have already discussed in the reprisal stories which have cherished grudges as their theme. In these latter the violence of the daydream is fabulous, and the very fact that it is not a reflection of Zuñi behavior allows the vengeance to take the most extreme forms. In other tales the mildness of actual Zuñi life and institutions are accurately reflected. The idea of trapping all the witches into an ambush from which they could kill Apaches and must therefore have to become bow priests is a curious one. "So A·lucpa caught all the witches in the bow priesthood. They were forced to go into retreat and be purified. They were bow priests. Only one witch had not been able to go out. So one witch was left. That is why there is no witch society any more, because A·lucpa made them all bow priests." This tale in no way calls in question the great prestige of the bow priesthood in Zuñi, nor the fear and hatred of witches. Nevertheless the conclusion is felt as adequate. In a case of personal vengeance, the priest's son who has been distressed at his wife's demonstrativeness calls the Apache to kill him in order to test his wife's faithfulness to his memory. She is merely left to enjoy herself at the favorite yaya dance, by which he proves her affection was too shallow to allow for proper respect for her husband. "He turned into an eagle, and that is why we value eagle feathers."

II

The literary problems which confront a primitive narrator are easily misunderstood. The gap between the traditionalism of primitive mythology and the emphasis upon originality in our own literature is so great that the reader from our civilization confronted by a collection of folktales is often led to false conclusions. Many students have assumed that the fixity of the tales is absolute or almost so, that the individual narrator has no literary problems, and that the tales originated in a mystical source called communal authorship. On the other hand, it would be as easy to interpret the tales as far more fortuitous than they really are, for from the point of view of the outsider the incidents out of which the tale is built might just as well be other incidents, the stylistic elements might as well be omitted or amplified in any imaginable direction. In fact, because of the diffuseness and ease of prose, it is far easier to mistake the problems of the artist in this field than, for instance, in the plastic arts.

There is no more communal authorship in folklore than there is a communal designer in ironwork or a communal priest in religious rites. The whole problem is unreal. There is no conceivable source of any cultural trait other than the behavior of some man, woman or child. What is communal about the process is the social acceptance by which the trait becomes a part of the teaching handed down to the next generation. The role of the narrator in such a body of folklore as that of Zuñi remains as real as that of any storyteller in any civilization though its scope is somewhat changed by the role of the audience.

On the other hand, even more serious misunderstanding of folklore is introduced by the outsider's inability to appreciate the fixed limits within which the narrator works. The artist works within definite traditional limits as truly in folklore as in music. The first requisite in understanding any folk literature is to recognize the boundaries within which he operates.

In Zuñi, tales fall into no clearly distinguishable categories. Even the Emergence story, which is the Zuñi scripture, is not reserved for the priests nor owned by them. It is freely repeated by any fireside by any layman, and all versions differ markedly, not so much in order of incidents as in the details introduced. Incidents of it, moreover, can be lifted and used as the basis of entertaining stories.

Tales of kachinas, also, form no special group. Kachinas are freely introduced even into European tales, and are heroes of romances who marry several wives, contest with witches, and win in stick races. Much of the stock saga of the Ahaiyute has evidently been ascribed to them since Cushing's day, and these little supernatural twins figure as supernatural helpers in tales of every kind. They make themselves a "kapitan" and buy a dog from a Mexican in a patently Mexican tale. In other cases the Ahaiyute tales are direct transcriptions of Zuñi daydreams and represent the wish fulfillments most desired by the people. A variety of stories are attributed to the Ahaiyute in one of several versions, and it seems probable that this tendency is still operative in Zuñi. If that is true, still other stories that were not yet told of the twins ten years ago when these stories were collected may become Ahaiyute stories in the future.

It is in keeping with the fact that folklore is such a living and popular trait in Zuñi at the present time that tales of European derivation are so little differentiated from others. The ones that are popular or have been told for some time or are retold by a good narrator often mirror the details of Zuñi life to the last degree. Cushing fifty years ago published an excellent example of this in his day in the tale of *The Cock and the Mouse*, which adapted an Italian accumulative tale he had himself repeated in Zuñi.[7]

Animal trickster tales, which form so large a bulk of many North American mythologies, are little told.

In all tales, therefore, since the short animal incident occurs so rarely, roughly the same objectives are present to the narrator. Of these stylistic aims, probably the one most relied upon is the endless incorporation of cultural details. In most mythologies the picture of cultural life can be abstracted from the tales, as in the studies of the Tsimshian, Kwakiutl, and Crow, is a comparatively adequate description of most phases of social life, but in Zuñi there is in addition a loving reiteration of detail that is over and above this faithful rendition. The most extreme examples are the long descriptions of ceremonies. These have practically no plot but are strung together on some thread such as that of the Pekwin who grieved for his dead wife and was comforted by each of the three religious organizations of Zuñi, which each brought out a dance in turn, and finally by the great ceremony of the Corn Dance. In one of these ceremonies more than forty participants in the dance are severally invited by the bow priests to take part. In each of the forty retellings the priests go to the individual's house, greet those who live there with the conventional greeting, "How have you lived these days, my fathers, my mothers, my children?" are answered, fed, thank them for the food, explain the part in the dance they wish them to assume and conduct them back to the priests' chamber or leave them to prepare for the occasion. In each case, also, the moment's occupations of the principal occupants of the room are described as the priests enter. Practice for the dancing and the great occasion itself are meticulously described in the same fashion.

The Zuñi narrator, besides this general preoccupation, has a special obligation to relate certain details. The greeting formulas, with the offer of food to the visitor and his thanks, recur constantly. Localization is imperative, and certain places are the scenes of certain kinds of incidents, as Cunte'kaia is the scene of witch tales and Hecokta of ogre tales.

Indication of points of the compass is marked, but is much less of a stylistic necessity than in the pueblo tales from Laguna, for instance. The introduction of helpful animals is marked in all tales where such incidents are relevant. Such animals, according to their abilities, fly, gnaw, or kill, for the hero. Stylistic obliviousness to incisiveness or condensation is obvious in all the tales and if anything is only the more marked in the text translations.

The Zuñi narrator is almost always free to incorporate his special knowledge in a tale. If he has taken part in a Corn Dance, his incidents of the Corn Dance reproduce his own experience, which is then retold by others. Men, as well as women, incorporate accounts of woman's childbirth ritual, or of cooking techniques. The Emergence tale is used as a basis for the incorporation of a variety of ritual with which a narrator is familiar.

Cushing's tale of *The Cock and the Mouse* has already been mentioned. It is a striking example of the extent to which Zuñi stylistic requirements operate to remodel a borrowed tale. He himself told a group of native friends a European accumulative tale and a year later recorded the same tale as he heard it told by one of his listeners. The European tale tells simply of the joint nut-gathering adventure of the cock and the mouse. When the cock had tried in vain to reach the nuts he asked the mouse to throw some down to him, and the nut cut the cock's head. He ran to an old woman to get it bandaged, and she asked two hairs for payment. He ran to the dog for these, who asked bread. He went to the baker, who asked wood, to the forest, which asked water. He went to the fountain, which gave him water, and so he retraced his steps and got his head bound up. The story is bare of all further details. In keeping with Zuñi narrative standards, the adapted version begins with a description of the old woman and her turkey yard, "like an eagle cage against a wall." The cock of the original story has appropriately enough become a Zuñi pet turkey, and the fact that the turkey has a beard while the cock has not is capitalized in the resulting story. The old woman had only the one turkey and she was too poor to give it meat, so that the turkey was always meat-hungry. One day he caught sight of Mouse's tail disappearing in his hole and snapped it up for a worm. Now the mouse's tail was his "sign of manhood" and he vowed vengeance. So far the additions are by way of supplying the traditional literary motivation of the despised and put-upon who set out to overcome their enemies. The mouse, therefore, made friends with the cock, who allowed him to eat crumbs thrown him by the old woman, and finally brought the turkey a nut out of his own hoard. The turkey lamented that he was not free like the mouse to gather such nuts and the mouse offered to gnaw the fastening of his corral. This incident is the familiar *Helpful Animals: rodent (mouse, gopher, etc.) gnaws (ropes, wall, tree roots, etc.)*. When the nut hit the turkey he was stunned, fell "dead" as the Zuñis say, and the mouse avenged himself by gnawing off his neck bristles, his "signs of manhood," in exact compensation for what he had himself suffered. When the turkey could get up he went to the woman to have his head bound and she asked him for four neck bristles, i.e. his signs of manhood. But they had been gnawed off. He therefore went to the dog, etc., until at last he got to the spring to ask for water, and the spring asked for prayersticks which should pay the gods for rain. It came and he retraced his steps and was healed. The story is easily a better story than its original; it has been thoroughly adapted to its new cultural setting by the incorporation of all sorts of observations of Zuñi life, motivation has been skillfully built up, and well-known Zuñi incidents have been appropriately introduced in a thoroughly workmanlike manner.

The second ideal of the Zuñi stylist is the building up of plot sequences out of large numbers of incidents. A Zuñi audience likes very long tales, and the majority of stories combine in different ways several well-marked incidents. These incidents are stock property, and their outlines are known to all the audience. It is impossible to understand Zuñi stylistic problems without this realization of what is traditional material. The collections of Zuñi folklore that are now available do not reproduce all the tales that are told or may be told, but they give at least the elements out of which these would be built up. The study of the different variants indicates the principles of composition, and the way in which these elements, and new ones when they are introduced, are handled by the native narrators.

The principal themes in the service of which these incidents are combined have been discussed above. The narrator's skill is shown in his use of these stock incidents in elaborating these stock themes, and an examination of the tales shows clearly that this is no mean role. The way in which incidents are combined is certainly a main interest of the Zuñi audience, and the skill with which this is done by the narrator can be illustrated over and over again.

Certain of these combinations of incidents are very stable, and such complex stories as the *Box Boat* and the *Sun's Twins* follow the same sequence in Cushing's versions and in the present collection. Cushing's tales were recorded fifty years ago, and from families with quite different ceremonial affiliations and clan relationships. The sequences of incidents in these cases had very likely become popular and fairly fixed long before Cushing's time, and they may well hold firm until folktales are no longer told in Zuñi.

Even in such a tale as the *Sun's Twins*, however, the scope of the narrator in building plot is clearly marked. Version A in this collection reproduces the Cushing tale; it is the theme of the proud maiden magically impregnated by a supernatural, publicly killed because she was about to bear illegitimate children, and vindicated by her two sons at the direction of their supernatural father. The great contrast between these two versions is the cleverness with which the thoroughly non-Southwestern ceremony of the Cushing version (this part of Cushing's story has many Shoshonean analogues) has been transformed into the familiar ceremony of the Zuñi scalp dance in the present tale. This present version, moreover, has dropped the concluding incidents of the Cushing tale. This omission of the concluding incidents consolidates the plot, just as the changes in the ceremony bring it into agreement with Zuñi cultural behavior. The difference between these two versions, however, and versions B and C in this collection is more drastic. The same incidents have been used in these latter versions to elaborate a different theme: that of the sons' humiliation of the mother who abandoned them at birth. This role of the Zuñi narrator in adapting incidents to different themes is apparent in many tales. The narrator must follow out the implications of the new sequence he has chosen.

The freedom with which plots may be built up is made clear also by a consideration of certain incidents which serve as stock introductions or conclusions to a variety of tales. Whenever the plot allows its use, the incident of *Supernaturals are sent to shrines* may be called in requisition. The *Orpheus* incident is popular in a similar capacity, as well as the *Contests to retain a wife* and *Witch contests*. The *Apparition impersonated to punish evildoers or enemies* is used both as introduction and conclusion to several tales. The *Kachinas at Kachina Village provide food or clothing* is requisitioned in almost any tale in which it is appropriate. The *Marriage taught by supernaturals to those who refuse it*, the *Magical impregnations* by Sun or Horned Serpent, the *Famine is caused by misuse of corn in a game* are popular introductions to tales the plots of which differ completely.

It is obvious that where such freedom in handling incidents is expected of a good storyteller, it will often become impossible to trace with assurance a tale's genetic relationship with tales of other peoples.

The Zuñi narrator is also allowed freedom in the use of stock folkloristic devices. The loads made magically light, the runners who carry straws or gourds or feathers to run lightly, the inexhaustible meals provided by helpful animals, the magically surmounted precipices, are all legion. Good storytellers usually incorporate these devices at any appropriate point.

The greatest freedom allowed the Zuñi narrator, however, is in the adaptation of the tale to explanations and origins. Such "that's whys" are a stylistic requirement in Zuñi, and no American Indian folklore presents such a prodigality of explanatory elements. They are seldom standardized, so that the same explanatory elements occur in different versions even of the same tale, and good storytellers often give several to one tale.

The most striking way in which the importance of personal bias and experience is shown in Zuñi tales is in the contrast between tales told by men and by women. There is no taboo in Zuñi which restricts such choice. The differences that exist are the result of unconscious preference on the part of narrators. Men tell the tales which feature extended accounts of the stick races, of gambling, and of hunting. Women tell those which detail cooking techniques.[8] The Cinderella story is told by a woman, and the stories of women assisting in childbirth who discover that the mother has initiated her baby as a witch. Women also tell the only tales of poor little girls who are overworked. "Every day the little girl worked all day long. Her mother said to her, 'There is no water. Go fetch a jar of water.' The little girl cried, she was so tired she could not go for water." A moth takes pity on her and her mother grieves. Even when the little girl is brought back she cannot restrain her tears and so loses her again. The kind of detail that distinguishes the women's stories is characteristic; women give the only account of childbirth observances; women add to a description of a picnic, "The mothers nursed their babies and laid them down comfortably"; to an account of girls grinding for the priests, "Their sweethearts waited to see in which houses the girls were grinding. They drew their shawls over their faces and went in to husk for them." The one case of a mother's regret in abandoning her child at birth and her care of it is in a tale told by a woman. When the baby was born she picked it up. "She liked that baby, but she was ashamed to take it home. She broke the soft leaves off the weeds and made a nest to put it in. She broke the weeds and branches and made a shelter over the baby. She nursed it," and returned next day to renew the shelter and nurse the child again. "The third day his mother went out in the evening to see if the baby was still there. He was gone. She saw the deer tracks. She was sorry."

In two cases tales are told from the point of view of the men actors or of the women according to the sex of the narrator. The version of *The Deserted Husband* told by a woman expatiates on the woman's grievance; her husband did not compliment her on her cooking, "He never said, 'How good!'" It details the wife's determination to cook at other people's feasts and arrange a meeting with a man; it tells how she made herself beautiful, and how she went home to look after her little daughter; "She was making dolls out of rags." It follows through her arrangements with her lover and her handling of her suspicious husband. The men's versions omit all this; they tell the story from the point of view of the man. They begin with the husband's proposal to bring calamity upon the pueblo because of his faithless wife, and relate the details of the kiva conversations, the ritual which causes the earthquake, the friend who informs on him, and the help of the Hopi priests.

In the *Rabbit Huntress,* the woman's version tells how the resourceful girl gets more than a man's good catch in her hunting and expends itself in an account of the making of the sand bed and presentation of the child and role of the father's mother in the birth of the child of her marriage with Ahaiyute. The man's version tells how the girl had no success in hunting and gets only two rabbits; instead of the women's details of the other version, it goes on to describe a second marriage to a human husband and how the latter followed her to the land of the dead.

One minor point remains for discussion in connection with the Zuñi tales, and that is in regard to their accuracy as history. The historical reconstructions of early ethnological students in Zuñi and Hopi were based in large measure upon the statements in folklore. Thus Fewkes interpreted the history of the Hopi as a gathering of diverse groups, now represented by the clans, from the four points of the compass; he interpreted their social organization as a consequence of these originally distinct groups. Cushing similarly, though less insistently, interpreted Zuñi migration legends. The comparison of the different versions makes it clear that the often-repeated migration incident, the *Choice of eggs,* is told with almost as many "that's whys" as any other Zuñi tale and that these explanatory elements are strictly comparable to those in courtship or witch tales. They certainly give no basis for reconstruction of history. In other examples of "that's whys" that have historic reference, the same truth is obvious. Thus the tale of *Tupe kills the Apaches* is given as the origin of the scalp dance, an origin accounted for by half a dozen other tales, and recounts a scalp dance said to have been held two generations before the tale was told to me. Obviously the scalp dance in Zuñi has no such recent origin, and the narrator himself scouted the suggestion. His "origin" was a literary flourish. In the same way a true story of treachery against Navaho visitors which happened two generations ago is told by the grandson of the chief actor as an origin of albinos in Zuñi, yet immediately after telling the tale he named albinos who had been born considerably before the date of the incident. I did not point out to him the inconsistency and he saw none. The tale did not even represent history according to his own personal knowledge.

The lack of historicity in the tales is apparent in other ways than in the explanatory elements. In the albino story a comparison with the historical account of the incident recorded by Dr. Bunzel shows that even in so short a time the tale has been built up to a climax with repetitive incidents and otherwise modified. The story of the battle which took place on Corn Mountain, at which time a friendship pact was made with the Lagunas and the Big Shell cult vanquished the enemy, is told in two historical settings, once as the tale of a quarrel with the eastern pueblos, and the other, the catastrophe of the Rebellion against the Spaniards in 1670. To the latter tale is added the story of the Spanish priest who saved the people and who elected to stay in Zuñi rather than return to his own people. It is obvious that standard literary versions of battles may do service in different connections, and that it is impossible to trust their historical accuracy.

Dominant Cultural Attitudes in Manu'a *

Margaret Mead

CHIEFLY CONCERNED then with their social pattern, the Samoans have time for little else. Pondering upon the exigencies of ordered society, they take small interest in the world of the supernatural, nor are they puzzled and perplexed by the world of natural phenomena. The wavering line which divides the animate from the inanimate, the personal from the impersonal, borders their field of attention instead of threading its way among their preoccupations. For an interest in the intractability of material, the unaccountable tendency of wood to split or gardens to languish, they have substituted an interest in the personnel of carpentering or gardening parties. It is not that they have a clearer knowledge of the properties of material things than the Maori, who must perform long rituals to remove the sacredness from a tree which they wish to cut down. Occasional particular tapus, explicit beliefs in some animate phenomenon, attest to their typical untrained confusion. But their all inclusive social formula gives them no acceptable basis of interest in the mysterious properties of material things or natural phenomena. As the development of a human personality may be expressed in terms of choices made between many interests in an effort to bring all parts of one's character within one coherent picture, so a culture like Samoa may be envisaged also. A diffuse cultural equipment which drew from atti-

* *Social Organization of Manu'a* (*Bishop Museum Bulletin*, LXXVI; Honolulu, 1930), 85–86.

tudes widely distributed in the Pacific has been reshaped to an individual people's emphasis. White civilization, on coming in contact with a primitive people, may teach them that material things must not be regarded animistically or that their gods are false. So the adult's world takes the varied conceptions of the child, pooh-poohs its rituals, ridicules its tapus and insists upon an acceptance of the findings of science. But without definite pedagogic discipline, many children will make some of these selections for themselves in terms of their own temperaments; one child will spend all his strength striving to control the world by means of formulas; another will devote himself to a careful investigation of the properties of material things or the principles of mechanics; a third will throw all his energies in establishing social rapport with his fellows. So human societies, left to themselves, will select parts of their heritage for elaboration, and the original choice will gain in impetus from generation to generation until a coherent individual culture has been developed. A strong religious interest, a premium upon aberrant individual gifts, a permission to love without social sanction and give without stint to that which is loved; all these would disturb the nice balance of Samoan society and so are outlawed. Samoa may be said to have a formal social personality, to be a devotee of a careful observance of all the decreed amenities.

Psychological Types in
the Cultures of the Southwest*

THE CULTURE of the Pueblo Indians is strongly differentiated from
that of surrounding peoples. Most obviously, all aspects of their life
are highly ritualized, highly formalized. No one has lived among
them who has not been struck by the importance of the formal detail
in rite and dance, the intricate interrelations of the ceremonial
organization, the lack of concern with personal religious experience
or with personal prestige or exploit. The emphasis in their all-absorb-
ing ceremonial routine is placed where it was in the medieval Roman
church of certain periods, on the formal observance, the ritualistic
detail for its own sake.

This is so conspicuously true for the Southwest peoples that in
descriptions of their culture we have been content to let the matter
rest with this characterization. Yet in a civilization such as that of
the North American Indians high ritualistic development sets no
group off in any definitive fashion from the vast majority of peoples.
The ritual of the sun dance, the peace pipe ceremonies, the cult
groups, and age-societies of the Plains, or the winter ceremonial of
the Northwest Coast bulk perhaps slightly less prominently in the
total life of these people than the calendric dances and retreats of the
Southwest, but it is not by any such matter of gradation that the
Southwest is set off from other American Indian cultures. There is

* Proceedings of the Twenty-third International Congress of Americanists,
September 1928 (New York, 1930), 527–81.

in their cultural attitudes and choices a difference in psychological
type fundamentally to be distinguished from that of surrounding
regions. It goes deeper than the presence or the absence of ritualism;
ritualism itself is of a fundamentally different character within this
area, and without the understanding of this fundamental psychological set among the Pueblo peoples we must be baffled in our attempts to understand the cultural history of this region.[1]

It is Nietzsche who has named and described, in the course of his
studies in Greek tragedy, the two psychological types which have
established themselves in the region of the Southwest in the cultures
of the Pueblo. He has called them the Dionysian and the Apollonian. He means by his classification essentially confidence in two
diametrically different ways of arriving at the values of existence.[2]
The Dionysian pursues them through "the annihilation of the ordinary bounds and limits of existence"; he seeks to attain in his most
valued moments escape from the boundaries imposed upon him by
his five senses, to break through into another order of experience.
The desire of the Dionysian, in personal experience or in ritual, is to
press beyond, to reach a certain psychological state, to achieve excess. The closest analogy to the emotions he seeks is drunkenness,
and he values the illuminations of frenzy. With Blake, he believes
"the path of excess leads to the palace of wisdom." The Apollonian
distrusts all this, if by chance he has any inkling of the occurrence
of such experiences; he finds means to outlaw them from his conscious life. He "knows but one law, measure in the Hellenic sense."
He keeps the middle of the road, stays within the known map, maintains his control over all disruptive psychological states. In
Nietzsche's fine phrase, even in the exaltation of the dance, "he remains what he is, and retains his civic name." [3]

The Southwest Pueblos are, of course, Apollonian, and in the con-
sistency with which they pursue the proper valuations of the Apollonian they contrast with very nearly the whole of aboriginal America.
They possess in a small area, islanded in the midst of predominantly
Dionysian cultures, an *ethos* distinguished by sobriety, by its distrust
of excess, that minimizes to the last possible vanishing point any
challenging or dangerous experiences. They have a religion of fertility without orgy, and absorption in the dance without using it to

arrive at ecstasy. They have abjured torture. They indulge in no wholesale destruction of property at death. They have never made or bought intoxicating liquors in the fashion of other tribes about them, and they have never given themselves up to the use of drugs. They have even stripped sex of its mystic danger. They allow to the individual no disruptive role in their social order. Certainly in all of these traits they stand so strikingly over against their neighbors that it is necessary to seek some explanation for the cultural resistances of the Pueblos.

The most conspicuous contrast, in the Pueblos, is their outlawry of the divine frenzy and the vision. Now in North America at large the value of ecstatic experience in religion is a cornerstone of the whole religious structure. It may be induced by intoxicants and drugs; it may be self-induced — which may include such means as fasting and torture — or it may be achieved in the dance.

We may consider first the ecstasy induced by intoxicants and drugs. For the neighboring Pima, who share the culture of the primitive tribes of northern Mexico, intoxication is the visible mirroring of religion, it is the symbol of its exaltation, the pattern of its mingling of clouded vision and of insight. Theory and practice are explicitly Dionysian.

> "And I was made drunk and given the sacred songs;"
> "He breathed the red liquor into me,"

are in their songs common forms of reference to the shamanistic experience. Their great ceremony is the drinking of the "tizwin," the fermented juice of the fruit of the giant cactus. The ceremony begins with all religious formality and the recitation of ritual, but its virtue lies in the intoxication itself; the desired state is that of roused excitement, and they accept even extreme violence more readily than a state of lethargy. Their ideal is to stave off the final insensibility indefinitely while achieving the full excitation of the intoxicant. This is of course a form of fertility and health magic and is in complete accord with the Dionysian slant of their culture.

It is much commoner, north of Mexico, to use drugs rather than intoxicants for religious ends. The peyote or mescal bean of northern Mexico has been traded up the Mississippi Valley as far as the Cana-

dian border, and has been the occasion of serious religious movements among many tribes. It gives supernormal experiences with
particularly strong affect, no erotic excitation, very often brilliant
color images. The cult is best described for the Winnebago[4] where
the peyote is identified with the supernatural. "It is the only holy
thing I have been aware of in all my life"; "this medicine alone is
holy and has rid me of all evil." [5] It was eaten everywhere with the
object of attaining the trance or supernormal sensations which the
drug can give. The Arapaho ate it in an all-night ceremony after
which the effects of the drug prolonged themselves throughout the
following day.[6] The Winnebago speak of eating it for four days and
nights without sleep.

The *datura* is a more drastic poison. I have been told by the
Serrano and Cahuilla of boys who have died as a result of the drink,
and the Luiseño tell also the same story.[7] It was used by the tribes
of Southern California, and north including the Yokuts, for the initiation of boys at puberty. Among the Serrano the boys were overcome by the drug during the night and lay in a comatose condition
through the next day and night, during which time they were granted
visions. On the following day they ran a race.[8] Among the Luiseño
it seems to have been the same, four nights of trance being spoken of
as excessive.[9] The Diegueño reckon only one night of complete
stupefaction.[10] The Mohave drank *datura* in order to gain luck in
gambling; they were said to be unconscious for four days,[11] during
which time they received their power in a dream.

None of these alcohol and drug-induced excitations have gained
currency among the Pueblos. The Pima are the nearest settled
neighbors of the Zuñi to the southwest and easily accessible; tribes
of the Plains with which the eastern Pueblos came in contact are
the very ones in which peyote practices are important; and to the
west the tribes of Southern California share certain characteristic
traits of this very Pueblo culture. The absence of these traits in the
Pueblos is therefore not due to the cultural isolation of impassable
barriers. We know too that the period of time during which the
Pueblos and their neighbors have been settled relatively near to one
another is of considerable antiquity. But the Pueblos have defended
themselves against the use of drugs and intoxicants to produce trance

or excitement even in cases where the drugs themselves are known among them. Any Dionysian effect from them is, we may infer, repulsive to the Pueblos, and if they receive cultural recognition at all it is in a guise suited to Apollonian sobriety. They did not themselves brew any native intoxicant in the old days, nor do they now. Alone among the Indian reservations, the whiskey of the whites has never been a problem in the Southwest. When, in 1912, drinking seemed to be making some headway among the younger generation in Zuñi, it was the Pueblo elders themselves who took the matter in hand. It is not that it is a religious taboo; it is deeper than that, it is uncongenial. The peyote has been introduced only in Taos, which is in many ways marginal to Pueblo culture.

Datura is used in Zuñi as it was in ancient Mexico[12] in order to discover a thief, and Mrs. Stevenson gives an account of the manner of its use.[13] Read in connection with her quotations on datura poisoning and the two to four day trances of the Mohave and Mission Indians, it is a classic example of the Apollonian recasting of a Dionysian technique. In Zuñi the man who is to take the drug has a small quantity put in his mouth by the officiating priest, who then retires to the next room and listens for the incriminating name from the lips of the man who has taken the datura. He is not supposed to be comatose at any time; he alternately sleeps and walks about the room. In the morning he is said to have no memory of the insight he has received. The chief care is to remove every trace of the drug and two common desacratizing techniques are employed: first, he is given an emetic, four times, till every vestige of the drug is supposed to be ejected; then his hair is washed in yucca suds. The other Zuñi use of datura is even further from any connection with a Dionysian technique; members of the priestly orders go out at night to plant prayer sticks on certain occasions "to ask the birds to sing for rain," and at such times a minute quantity of the powdered root is put into the eyes, ears, and mouth of each priest. Here any connections with the physical properties of the drug are lost sight of.

Much more fundamental in North America than any use of drugs or alcohol to induce ecstasy was the cult of the self-induced vision. This was a near-universality from ocean to ocean, and everywhere it was regarded as the source of religious power. The Southwest is by no means beyond the southern limits of its distribution, but it is the one outstanding area of North America where the characteristic development of the vision is not found. This experience has several quite definite characteristics for North America: it is achieved characteristically in isolation, and it gives to the successful individual a personal manitou or guardian spirit who stands to him in a definite life-long relationship. Though west of the Rockies it is often regarded as an involuntary blessing available only for those of a particular psychological make-up, throughout the great extent of the continent it is sought by isolation and fasting, and in the central part of the continent often by self-torture. This "vision," from which supernatural power was supposed to flow, did not by any means signify only supernormal or Dionysian experiences, but it provided always a pattern within which such an experience had peculiar and institutionalized value; and in the great majority of cases it was these more extreme experiences that were believed to give the greater blessing.

The absence of this vision complex in the Southwest is one of the most striking cases of cultural resistance or of cultural reinterpretation that we know in North America. The formal elements are found there: the seeking of dangerous places, the friendship with a bird or animal, fasting, the belief in special blessings from supernatural encounters. But they are no longer instinct with the will to achieve ecstasy. There is complete reinterpretation. In the pueblos they go out at night to feared or sacred places and listen for a voice, not that they may break through to communication with the supernatural, but that they may take the omens of good luck and bad. It is regarded as a minor ordeal during which you are badly frightened, and the great taboo connected with it is that you must not look behind you on the way home no matter what seems to be following you. The objective performance is much the same as in the vision quest; in each case, they go out during the preparation for a difficult undertaking — in the Southwest often a race — and make capital of the darkness, the solitariness, the appearance of animals. But the significance is utterly different.

Fasting, the technique most often used in connection with the self-induced vision, has received the same sort of reinterpretation in the

Southwest. It is no longer utilized to dredge up experiences that normally lie below the level of consciousness; it is here a requirement for ceremonial cleanness. Nothing could be more unexpected to a Pueblo Indian than any theory of a connection between fasting and any sort of exaltation. Fasting is required during all retreats, before participation in a dance, in a race, etc., etc., but it is never followed by power-giving experience; it is never Dionysian. Fasting, also, like drugs and visions, has been revamped to the requirements of the Apollonian.

Torture, on the contrary, has been much more nearly excluded. It is important only in the initiations and dances of certain curing societies[14] and in these cases there is no suggestion of any states of self-oblivion. It is interesting that the Pueblos have been exposed to self-torture practices, both in the aboriginal culture of the Plains, and in European-derived practices of the Mexican Penitentes. The eastern Pueblos are in the very heart of the Santa Fé Penitentes country and these Mexicans attend their dances and ceremonies regularly and without hindrance. Much in their practice they have in common with the Indians: the retreats in the ceremonial house, the organization of the brotherhood (priesthood, for the Indian), the planting of crosses. But the self-lashing with cactus whips, the crucifixion on Good Friday, are alien; torture has not penetrated Pueblo life either from these practices or from those of the Plains or of California. Among the Pueblos, every man's hand has its five fingers, and unless he has been tortured as a witch, he is unscarred.

No more than the Pueblos have allowed ecstasy as induced by alcohol or drugs, or under the guise of the vision, have they admitted it as induced by the dance. Perhaps no people in North America spend more time in dance than the Southwest Pueblos. But its use as the most direct technique at our command for the inducement of supernormal experience is alien to them. With the frenzy of a Nootka bear dance, of a Kwakiutl cannibal dance, of a ghost dance, of a Mexican whirling dance, their dancing has nothing in common. It is rather a technique of monotonous appeal, of unvarying statement; always, in the phrase of Nietzsche's I used before, "they remain as they are and retain their civic names." Their theory seems to be that by the reiteration of the dance they can exercise compulsion upon the forces they wish to influence.

There are several striking instances of the loss, for the Pueblos, of the Dionysian significance of specific dance behavior, the objective aspects of which they still share with their neighbors. The best is probably the dance upon the altar. For the Cora of northern Mexico the climax of the whirling dance is reached in the dancer's ecstatic, and otherwise sacrilegious, dancing upon the ground altar itself. In his madness it is destroyed, trampled into the sand again.[15] But this is also a Pueblo pattern. Especially the Hopi at the climax of their dances in the kivas dance upon the altar destroying the ground painting. Here there is no ecstasy; it is raw material used to build up one of the common Pueblo dance patterns where two "sides" which have previously come out alternately from opposite sides, now come out together for the dance climax. In the snake dance, for instance,[16] in the first set Antelope (dancer of Antelope society) dances, squatting, the circuit of the altar, retires; Snake (dancer of Snake society) repeats. In the second set Antelope receives a vine in his mouth and dances before the initiates trailing it over their knees; retires; Snake repeats with a live rattlesnake held in the same fashion. In the final set Antelope and Snake come out together, dancing together upon the altar, still in the squatting position, and destroy the ground painting. It is a formal sequence, like a Morris dance.

It is evident that ecstatic experience is not recognized in the Southwest and that the techniques associated with it in other areas are reinterpreted or refused admittance. The consequence of this is enormous: it rules out shamanism. For the shaman, the religious practitioner whose power comes from experiences of this type, is everywhere else in North America of first rate importance. Wherever the authority of religion is derived from his solitary mental aberrations and stress experiences and his instructions derived therefrom are put into practice by the tribe as a sacred privilege, that people is provided with a technique of cultural change which is limited only by the unimaginativeness of the human mind. This is a sufficient limitation; so much so that it has never been shown that cultures which operate on this basic theory are more given to innovation than those which disallow such disruptive influences. This should not blind us to the fact, however, that the setting in these two cultures for the exercise of individuality is quite different; individual initiative which would be fully allowed in the one case[17] would in the other be suspect, and these consequences are fully carried out in the Southwest. They have hardly left space for an impromptu individual act in their closely knit religious program; if they come across such an act they label the perpetrator a witch. One of the Zuñi tales I have recorded tells of the chief priest of Zuñi who made prayer sticks and went out to deposit them. It was not the time of the moon when prayer sticks must be planted by members of the curing societies, and the people said, "Why does the chief priest plant prayer sticks? He must be conjuring." As a matter of fact he was calling an earthquake for a private revenge. If this is so in the most personal of Zuñi religious acts, that of planting prayer sticks, it is doubly so of more formal activities like retreats, dances, etc. Even individual prayers of the most personal sort — those where corn-meal is scattered — must be said at sunrise, or over a dead animal, or at a particular point in a program, etc.; the times and seasons are always stipulated. No one must ever wonder why an individual was moved to pray.

Instead therefore of shamans with their disruptive influence upon communal practices and settled traditions, the Southwest has religious practitioners who become priests by rote memorizing and by membership in societies and cult groups. This membership is determined by heredity and by payment[18] for though in their own theory serious illness or an accident like snake bite or being struck by lightning are the accepted reasons for membership in certain societies, there are always alternative ways of joining even the curing societies so that no man with interest and sufficient means remains outside. In Zuñi heredity is the chief factor in membership in the priestly groups, payment in the curing societies; in neither is individual supernatural power ever claimed by any member as a result of personal illumination. Those who practice curing in Zuñi are merely those who by payment and by knowledge of ritual have reached the highest orders of the curing societies and received the personal corn fetish, the *mili*.

If the ecstasy of the Dionysian has been rejected in the Southwest with all its implications, so too has the orgy. There is no doubt that the idea of fertility bulks large in the religious practices of the

Southwest,[19] and with fertility rites we almost automatically couple orgy, so universally have they been associated in the world. But the Southwest has a religion of fertility founded on other associations. Haeberlin's study gives a useful summary of the type of ritual that is here considered to have this efficacy.[20] The cylinders the men carry and the annulets carried by the women in ceremonies are sex symbols and are thrown by them into springs or onto ground paintings; or in the women's dance two are dressed as male dancers and shoot arrows into a bundle of cornhusks; or a line of women with yucca rings run in competition with a line of men with kicking sticks. In Peru in a race of exactly similar import, men racing women, the men ran naked and violated every woman they overtook.[21] The pattern is self-evident and common throughout the world, but not in the Southwest. In Zuñi there are three occasions on which laxness is countenanced. One of these is in the retreat of the Tlewekwe society, which has power over cold weather. The priestesses of the medicine bundle of this society (*le etone*) and the associated bundle (*mu etone*) during one night receive lovers, and they collect a thumb's length of turquoise from their partners to add to the decorations of their bundles. It is an isolated case in Zuñi and the society can no longer be very satisfactorily studied. The other two cases are rather a relaxation of the customary strict chaperonage of the young people, and occur at the ceremonial rabbit hunt[22] and on the nights of the scalp dance; children conceived on these nights are said to be exceptionally vigorous. Doctor Bunzel writes, "These occasions on which boys and girls dance together or are out together at night provide an opportunity for sweethearts. There is no promiscuity, and they are never, never orgiastic in character. There is amiable tolerance of sexual laxity; a 'boys will be boys' attitude." It is all very far indeed from the common Dionysian sex practices for the sake of fertility.

It is not only in connection with fertility and sex that orgy is common among the peoples of America. In the region immediately surrounding the Southwest, there is on the one hand the orgy of sun dance torturing to the east and the orgy of wholesale destruction in the mourning ceremonies to the west. As I have said, torture plays a very slight role in the Southwest, orgiastic or otherwise. Mourning is made oppressive by fear of the dead, but there is no trace of abandon. Mourning here is made into the semblance of an anxiety complex; it is a completely different thing from the wild scenes of burning the dead in a bonfire of offered property and of clothes stripped from the mourners' backs that the Mohave practice[23] and that is found in such Dionysian fullness commonly in California, where among the Maidu mourners have to be forcibly restrained from throwing themselves into the flames,[24] and among the Pomo they snatch pieces of the corpse and devour them.[25]

One Dionysian ceremony of wide American distribution has established itself in the Southwest — the scalp dance. This is the victory dance of the Plains, or the women's dance, and the position of honor given to women in it, the four-circle coil danced around the encampment, the close-fitting war bonnet, certain treatments of the scalp, are the same in the Southwest as on the Plains. The wilder abandons of the Plains dance are, as we should expect, omitted, but there occurs in this dance, at least in Zuñi, one of the few ritual Dionysian acts of the Southwest — the washing and biting of the scalp. For the repulsion against contact with bones or a corpse is intense among these people, so that it makes an occasion for horror out of placing a scalp between the teeth, whereas placing a snake between the teeth in the snake dance is no such matter. The woman who carries the scalp in the dance — the position of honor — must rise to this pitch and every girl is said to dread being called out for the role.

Ecstasy and orgy, therefore, which are characteristic of America at large are alien in the Southwest. Let me illustrate this fundamental Apollonian bent in the Southwest by certain specific examples of the way in which it has worked itself out in their culture.

There is considerable emphasis in North America upon the ritualistic eating of filth and it is in this category that the very slightly developed cannibalistic behavior of the Northwest Coast belongs. That is, the emphasis there is never, as so often in cannibalism, upon the feast, nor on doing honor to or reviling the dead. The cannibal dance of the Kwakiutl is a typically Dionysian ritual.[26] It is not only that it is conceived as a dramatization of a condition of ecstasy which the main participant must dance to its climax before he can be restored to normal life; every ritualistic arrangement is designed — I do not mean consciously — to heighten the sense of the anti-natural act. A long period of fasting and isolation precedes the rite, the dance itself is a crouching, ecstatic pursuit of the prepared body held outstretched toward him by a woman attendant. With the required ritualistic bites the anti-natural climax is conceived to be attained, and prolonged vomiting and fasting and isolation follows.

In the filth eating of the Southwest, which is the psychological equivalent to this initiation of the Kwakiutl cannibal, the picture is entirely different. The rite is not used to attain horror, nor to dramatize a psychological climax of tension and release. Captain Bourke has recorded the Newekwe feast he attended with Cushing, at which gallon jars of urine were consumed by the members of the society. The picture is as far from that of the Kwakiutl rite as any buffoonery of our circus clowns. The atmosphere was one of coarse joviality, each man trying to outdo the others. "The dancers swallowed huge decanters, smacked their lips, and amid the roaring merriment of the spectators, remarked that it was very, very good. The clowns were now upon their mettle, each trying to surpass his neighbors in feats of nastiness." [27]

The same comment is true not only of filth eating but of clowning in the Southwest in general. I take it that the true Dionysian use of clowning is as comic relief in sacred ceremonial where the release from tension is as full of meaning as the preceding tension, and serves to accentuate it. This use of clowning seems to have been developed, for instance, in the ancient Aztec rites. Now I have never seen any clowning in the Pueblos that seemed to me remotely even to partake of this character, and I do not know of any description which would indicate its presence. Clowning can be buffoonery with no Dionysian implications, as we know well enough from the examples in our own civilization. It is this same use that is most prominent in the Southwest, but clowning is used there also for social satire, as in the take-offs of agents, churches, Indian representatives, etc., and it is common too as a substitute for the joking-relationship, which is absent here, and its license for very personal public comment.

Another striking example of the Southwest Apollonian bent is their interpretation of witch power. The Southwest has taken the European witch complex with all its broomsticks and witches' animal suits and eyes laid on a shelf, but they have fitted it into their own *Weltanschauung*. The most articulate statement that I know of a widespread attitude is still in manuscript in Doctor Parson's monograph on Isleta. The difference, for Isleta, between witch power and good power is simply that good supernatural power is always removed from you as soon as you have put it to the use you intended; witch power is nonremovable, it rides you for life. Their practice perfectly agrees with this; after every sacred investiture every participant in any rite is desacratized, the unwanted mysterious power is laid aside. Nothing could conceptualize more forcibly their discomfort in the face of mystery. Even the best supernatural power is uncanny.

Their lack of comprehension of suicide is, I think, another specific Apollonian trait. The Pima tell many stories of men who have killed themselves for women, and the Plains made suicide a ceremonial pattern; fundamentally their vows to assume the slit sash were suicide pledges in order to raise their rank. But the Pueblos tell the most inept stories[28] which are obvious misunderstandings of the concept. Again and again I have tried to convey the general idea of suicide to different Pueblo Indians, either by story or by exposition. They always miss the point. Yet in their stories they have the equivalent. There are a number of Zuñi stories[29] which tell of a man or woman whose spouse has been unfaithful — or of priests whose people have been unruly; they send messengers, often birds, to the Apache and summon them against their pueblo. When the fourth day has come — nothing ever happens in the Southwest till the fourth day — they wash themselves ceremonially and put on their finest costumes and go out to meet the enemy that they may be the first to be killed. When I have asked them about suicide no one has ever mentioned these stories, though they had perhaps been told that very day, and indeed they do not see them in that light at all. They are ritual revenge and the Dionysian gesture of throwing away one's life is not in question.

The cultural situation in the Southwest is in many ways hard to explain. With no natural barriers to isolate it from surrounding peoples, it presents probably the most abrupt cultural break that we know in America. All our efforts to trace out the influences from other areas are impressive for the fragmentariness of the detail; we find bits of the weft or woof of the culture, we do not find any very significant clues to its pattern. From the point of view of the present paper this clue is to be found in a fundamental psychological set which has undoubtedly been established for centuries in the culture of this region, and which has bent to its own uses any details it imitated from surrounding peoples and has created an intricate cultural pattern to express its own preferences. It is not only that the understanding of this psychological set is necessary for a descriptive statement of this culture; without it the cultural dynamics of this region are unintelligible. For the typical choices of the Apollonian have been creative in the formation of this culture, they have excluded what was displeasing, revamped what they took, and brought into being endless demonstrations of the Apollonian delight in formality, in the intricacies and elaborations of organization.

Anthropology
and the Abnormal*

MODERN SOCIAL anthropology has become more and more a study of
the varieties and common elements of cultural environment and the
consequences of these in human behavior. For such a study of
diverse social orders primitive peoples fortunately provide a laboratory not yet entirely vitiated by the spread of a standardized world-
wide civilization. Dyaks and Hopis, Fijians and Yakuts are significant
for psychological and sociological study because only among these
simpler peoples has there been sufficient isolation to give opportunity
for the development of localized social forms. In the higher cultures
the standardization of custom and belief over a couple of continents
has given a false sense of the inevitability of the particular forms
that have gained currency, and we need to turn to a wider survey in
order to check the conclusions we hastily base upon this near-universality of familiar customs. Most of the simpler cultures did not
gain the wide currency of the one which, out of our experience, we
identify with human nature, but this was for various historical
reasons, and certainly not for any that gives us as its carriers a
monopoly of social good or of social sanity. Modern civilization,
from this point of view, becomes not a necessary pinnacle of human
achievement but one entry in a long series of possible adjustments.

   These adjustments, whether they are in mannerisms like the ways
of showing anger, or joy, or grief in any society, or in major human

* *Journal of General Psychology*, X, No. 2 (1934), 59–⁎ :

drives like those of sex, prove to be far more variable than experience in any one culture would suggest. In certain fields, such as that of religion or of formal marriage arrangements, these wide limits of variability are well known and can be fairly described. In others it is not yet possible to give a generalized account, but that does not absolve us of the task of indicating the significance of the work that has been done and of the problems that have arisen.

One of these problems relates to the customary modern normal-abnormal categories and our conclusions regarding them. In how far are such categories culturally determined, or in how far can we with assurance regard them as absolute? In how far can we regard inability to function socially as diagnostic of abnormality, or in how far is it necessary to regard this as a function of the culture?

As a matter of fact, one of the most striking facts that emerge from a study of widely varying cultures is the ease with which our abnormals function in other cultures. It does not matter what kind of "abnormality" we choose for illustration, those which indicate extreme instability, or those which are more in the nature of character traits like sadism or delusions of grandeur or of persecution, there are well-described cultures in which these abnormals function at ease and with honor, and apparently without danger or difficulty to the society.

The most notorious of these is trance and catalepsy. Even a very mild mystic is aberrant in our culture. But most peoples have regarded even extreme psychic manifestations not only as normal and desirable, but even as characteristic of highly valued and gifted individuals. This was true even in our own cultural background in that period when Catholicism made the ecstatic experience the mark of sainthood. It is hard for us, born and brought up in a culture that makes no use of the experience, to realize how important a role it may play and how many individuals are capable of it, once it has been given an honorable place in any society.

Some of the Indian tribes of California accorded prestige principally to those who passed through certain trance experiences. Not all of these tribes believed that it was exclusively women who were so blessed, but among the Shasta[1] this was the convention. Their shamans were women, and they were accorded the greatest prestige in the community. They were chosen because of their constitutional liability to trance and allied manifestations. One day the woman who was so destined, while she was about her usual work, would fall suddenly to the ground. She had heard a voice speaking to her in tones of the greatest intensity. Turning, she had seen a man with drawn bow and arrow. He commanded her to sing on pain of being shot through the heart by his arrow, but under the stress of the experience she fell senseless. Her family gathered. She was lying rigid, hardly breathing. They knew that for some time she had had dreams of a special character which indicated a shamanistic calling, dreams of escaping grizzly bears, falling off cliffs or trees, or of being surrounded by swarms of yellow jackets. The community knew therefore what to expect. After a few hours the woman began to moan gently and to roll about upon the ground, trembling violently. She was supposed to be repeating the song which she had been told to sing and which during the trance had been taught her by the spirit. As she revived her moaning became more and more clearly the spirit's song until at last she called out the name of the spirit itself, and immediately blood oozed from her mouth.

When the woman had come to herself after the first encounter with her spirit she danced that night her first initiatory shamanistic dance, holding herself by a rope that was swung from the ceiling. For three nights she danced, and on the third night she had to receive in her body her power from her spirit. She was dancing, and as she felt the approach of the moment she called out, "He will shoot me, he will shoot me." Her friends stood close, for when she reeled in a kind of cataleptic seizure, they had to seize her before she fell or she would die. From this time on she had in her body a visible materialization of her spirit's power, an icicle-like object which in her dances thereafter she would exhibit, producing it from one part of her body and returning it to another part. From this time on she continued to validate her supernatural power by further cataleptic demonstrations, and she was called upon in great emergencies of life and death, for curing and for divination and for counsel. She became in other words by this procedure a woman of great power and importance.[2]

It is clear that, so far from regarding cataleptic seizures as blots upon the family escutcheon and as evidences of dreaded disease, cultural approval had seized upon them and made of them the pathway to authority over one's fellows. They were the outstanding characteristic of the most respected social type, the type which functioned with most honor and reward in the community. It was precisely the cataleptic individuals who in this culture were singled out for authority and leadership.

The availability of "abnormal" types in the social structure, provided they are types that are culturally selected by that group, is illustrated from every part of the world. The shamans of Siberia dominate their communities. According to the ideas of these peoples, they are individuals who by submission to the will of the spirits have been cured of a grievous illness — the onset of the seizures — and have acquired by this means great supernatural power and incomparable vigor and health. Some, during the period of the call, are violently insane for several years, others irresponsible to the point where they have to be watched constantly lest they wander off in the snow and freeze to death, others ill and emaciated to the point of death, sometimes with bloody sweat. It is the shamanistic practice which constitutes their cure, and the extreme physical exertion of a Siberian seance leaves them, they claim, rested and able to enter immediately upon a similar performance. Cataleptic seizures are regarded as an essential part of any shamanistic performance.[3]

A good description of the neurotic condition of the shaman and the attention given him by his society is an old one by Canon Callaway[4] recorded in the words of an old Zulu of South Africa:

"The condition of a man who is about to become a diviner is this; at first he is apparently robust, but in the process of time he begins to be delicate, not having any real disease, but being delicate. He habitually avoids certain kinds of food, choosing what he likes, and he does not eat much of that; he is continually complaining of pains in different parts of his body. And he tells them that he has dreamt that he was carried away by a river. He dreams of many things, and his body is muddied (as a river) and he becomes a house of dreams. He dreams constantly of many things, and on awaking tells his friends, 'My body is muddied today; I dreamt many men were killing me, and I escaped I know not how. On waking one part of my body felt different from other parts; it was no longer alike all over.' At last that man is very ill, and they go to the diviners to enquire.

"The diviners do not at once see that he is about to have a soft head (that is, the sensitivity associated with shamanism). It is difficult for them to see the truth; they continually talk nonsense and make false statements, until all the man's cattle are devoured at their command, they saying that the spirit of his people demands cattle, that it may eat food. At length all the man's property is expended, he still being ill; and they no longer know what to do, for he has no more cattle, and his friends help him in such things as he needs.

"At length a diviner comes and says that all the others are wrong. He says, 'He is possessed by the spirits. There is nothing else. They move in him, being divided into two parties; some say, "No, we do not wish our child injured. We do not wish it." It is for that reason he does not get well. If you bar the way against the spirits, you will be killing him. For he will not be a diviner; neither will he ever be a man again.'

"So the man may be ill two years without getting better; perhaps even longer than that. He is confined to his house. This continues till his hair falls off. And his body is dry and scurfy; he does not like to anoint himself. He shows that he is about to be a diviner by yawning again and again, and by sneezing continually. It is apparent also from his being very fond of snuff; not allowing any long time to pass without taking some. And people begin to see that he has had what is good given to him.

"After that he is ill; he has convulsions, and when water has been poured on him they then cease for a time. He habitually sheds tears, at first slight, then at last he weeps aloud and when the people are asleep he is heard making a noise and wakes the people by his singing; he has composed a song, and the men and women awake and go to sing in concert with him. All the people of the village are troubled by want of sleep;

for a man who is becoming a diviner causes great trouble, for he does not sleep, but works constantly with his brain; his sleep is merely by snatches, and he wakes up singing many songs; and people who are near quit their villages by night when they hear him singing aloud and go to sing in concert. Perhaps he sings till morning, no one having slept. And then he leaps about the house like a frog; and the house becomes too small for him, and he goes out leaping and singing, and shaking like a reed in the water, and dripping with perspiration.

"In this state of things they daily expect his death; he is now but skin and bones, and they think that tomorrow's sun will not leave him alive. At this time many cattle are eaten, for the people encourage his becoming a diviner. At length (in a dream) an ancient ancestral spirit is pointed out to him. This spirit says to him, 'Go to So-and-so and he will churn for you an emetic (the medicine the drinking of which is a part of shamanistic initiation) that you may be a diviner altogether.' Then he is quiet a few days, having gone to the diviner to have the medicine churned for him; and he comes back quite another man, being now cleansed and a diviner indeed."

Thereafter for life when he achieves possession, he foretells events and finds lost articles.

It is clear that culture may value and make socially available even highly unstable human types. If it chooses to treat their peculiarities as the most valued variants of human behavior, the individuals in question will rise to the occasion and perform their social roles without reference to our usual ideas of the types who can make social adjustments and those who cannot.

Cataleptic and trance phenomena are, of course, only one illustration of the fact that those whom we regard as abnormals may function adequately in other cultures. Many of our culturally discarded traits are selected for elaboration in different societies. Homosexuality is an excellent example, for in this case our attention is not constantly diverted, as in the consideration of trance, to the interruption of routine activity which it implies. Homosexuality poses the problem very simply. A tendency toward this trait in our culture exposes an individual to all the conflicts to which all aberrants are always exposed, and we tend to identify the consequences of this conflict with homosexuality. But these consequences are obviously local and cultural. Homosexuals in many societies are not incompetent, but they may be such if the culture asks adjustments of them that would strain any man's vitality. Wherever homosexuality has been given an honorable place in any society, those to whom it is congenial have filled adequately the honorable roles society assigns to them. Plato's *Republic* is, of course, the most convincing statement of such a reading of homosexuality. It is presented as one of the major means of the good life, and it was generally so regarded in Greece at that time.

The cultural attitude toward homosexuals has not always been on such a high ethical plane, but it has been very varied. Among many American Indian tribes there exists the institution of the berdache,[5] as the French called them. These men-women were men who at puberty or thereafter took the dress and the occupations of women. Sometimes they married other men and lived with them. Sometimes they were men with no inversion, persons of weak sexual endowment who chose this role to avoid the jeers of the women. The berdaches were never regarded as of first-rate supernatural power, as similar men-women were in Siberia, but rather as leaders in women's occupations, good healers in certain diseases, or, among certain tribes, as the genial organizers of social affairs. In any case, they were socially placed. They were not left exposed to the conflicts that visit the deviant who is excluded from participation in the recognized patterns of his society.

The most spectacular illustration of the extent to which normality may be culturally defined are those cultures where an abnormality of our culture is the cornerstone of their social structure. It is not possible to do justice to these possibilities in a short discussion. A recent study of an island of northwest Melanesia by Fortune[6] describes a society built upon traits which we regard as beyond the border of paranoia. In this tribe the exogamic groups look upon each other as prime manipulators of black magic, so that one marries always into an enemy group which remains for life one's deadly and unappeasable foes. They look upon a good garden crop as a confession of theft, for everyone is engaged in making magic to induce into his garden the productiveness of his neighbors'; therefore no secrecy in the island is so rigidly insisted upon as the secrecy of a man's harvesting of his yams. Their polite phrase at the acceptance of a gift is, "And if you now poison me, how shall I repay you this present?" Their preoccupation with poisoning is constant; no woman ever leaves her cooking pot for a moment untended. Even the great affinal economic exchanges that are characteristic of this Melanesian culture area are quite altered in Dobu since they are incompatible with this fear and distrust that pervades the culture. They go farther and people the whole world outside their own quarters with such malignant spirits that all-night feasts and ceremonials simply do not occur here. They have even rigorous religiously enforced customs that forbid the sharing of seed even in one family group. Anyone else's food is deadly poison to you, so that communality of stores is out of the question. For some months before harvest the whole society is on the verge of starvation, but if one falls to the temptation and eats up one's seed yams, one is an outcast and a beachcomber for life. There is no coming back. It involves, as a matter of course, divorce and the breaking of all social ties.

Now in this society where no one may work with another and no one may share with another, Fortune describes the individual who was regarded by all his fellows as crazy. He was not one of those who periodically ran amok and, beside himself and frothing at the mouth, fell with a knife upon anyone he could reach. Such behavior they did not regard as putting anyone outside the pale. They did not even put the individuals who were known to be liable to these attacks under any kind of control. They merely fled when they saw the attack coming on and kept out of the way. "He would be all right tomorrow." But there was one man of sunny, kindly disposition who liked work and liked to be helpful. The compulsion was too strong for him to repress it in favor of the opposite tendencies of his culture. Men and women never spoke of him without laughing; he was silly and simple and definitely crazy. Nevertheless, to the ethnologist used to a culture that has, in Christianity, made his type the model of all virtue, he seemed a pleasant fellow.

An even more extreme example, because it is of a culture that has built itself upon a more complex abnormality, is that of the North Pacific Coast of North America. The civilization of the Kwakiutl,[7] at the time when it was first recorded in the last decades of the nineteenth century, was one of the most vigorous in North America. It was built up on an ample economic supply of goods, the fish which furnished their food staple being practically inexhaustible and obtainable with comparatively small labor, and the wood which furnished the material for their houses, their furnishings, and their arts being, with however much labor, always procurable. They lived in coastal villages that compared favorably in size with those of any other American Indians and they kept up constant communication by means of sea-going dug-out canoes.

It was one of the most vigorous and zestful of the aboriginal cultures of North America, with complex crafts and ceremonials, and elaborate and striking arts. It certainly had none of the earmarks of a sick civilization. The tribes of the Northwest Coast had wealth, and exactly in our terms. That is, they had not only a surplus of economic goods, but they made a game of the manipulation of wealth. It was by no means a mere direct transcription of economic needs and the filling of those needs. It involved the idea of capital, of interest, and of conspicuous waste. It was a game with all of the binding rules of a game, and a person entered it as a child. His father distributed wealth for him, according to his ability, at a small feast or potlatch, and each gift the receiver was obliged to accept and to return after a short interval with interest that ran to about 100 per cent a year. By the time the child was grown, therefore, he was well launched, a larger potlatch had been given for him on various occasions of exploit or initiation, and he had wealth either out at usury or in his own possession. Nothing in the civilization could be enjoyed without validating it by the distribution of this wealth. Everything that was valued, names and songs as well as material objects, were passed down in family lines, but they were always publicly assumed with accompanying sufficient distributions of property. It was the game of validating and exercising all the privileges one could accumulate from one's various forbears, or by gift, or by marriage, that made the chief interest of the culture. Everyone in his degree took part in it, but many, of course, mainly as spectators.

In its highest form it was played out between rival chiefs representing not only themselves and their family lines but their communities,
and the object of the contest was to glorify oneself and to humiliate
one's opponent. On this level of greatness the property involved was
no longer represented by blankets, so many thousand of them to a
potlatch, but by higher units of value. These higher units were like
our bank notes. They were incised copper tablets, each of them
named, and having a value that depended upon their illustrious
history. This was as high as ten thousand blankets, and to possess
one of them, still more to enhance its value at a great potlatch, was
one of the greatest glories within the compass of the chiefs of the
Northwest Coast.

The details of this manipulation of wealth are in many ways a
parody on our own economic arrangements, but it is with the motivations that were recognized in this contest that we are concerned in
this discussion. The drives were those which in our own culture we
should call megalomaniac. There was an uncensored self-glorification and ridicule of the opponent that it is hard to equal in other
cultures outside of the monologues of the abnormal. Any of the
songs and speeches of their chiefs at a potlatch illustrate the usual
tenor:

Wa, out of the way. Wa, out of the way. Turn your faces
that I may give way to my anger by striking my fellow chiefs.

Wa, great potlatch, greatest potlatch.[8] The little ones[9] only
pretend, the little stubborn ones, they only sell one copper again
and again and give it away to the little chiefs of the tribe.
Ah, do not ask in vain for mercy. Ah, do not ask in vain for
mercy and raise your hands, you with lolling tongues! I shall
break,[10] I shall let disappear the great copper that has the name
Kentsegum, the property of the great foolish one, the great
extravagant one, the great surpassing one, the one farthest
ahead, the great Cannibal dancer among the chiefs.[11]

I am the great chief who makes people ashamed.
I am the great chief who makes people ashamed.
Our chief brings shame to the faces.

Our chief brings jealousy to the faces.
Our chief makes people cover their faces by what he is continually doing in this world, from the beginning to the end of the year.
Giving again and again oil feasts to the tribes.

I am the great chief who vanquishes.
I am the great chief who vanquishes.
Only at those who continue running round and round in this world, working hard losing their tails,[12] I sneer, at the chiefs below the true chief.[13]
Have mercy on them![14] Put oil on their dry heads with brittle hair, those who do not comb their hair!
I sneer at the chiefs below the true, real chief. I am the great chief who makes people ashamed. . . .
I am the only great tree, I the chief.
I am the only great tree, I the chief.
You are my subordinates, tribes.
You sit in the middle of the rear of the house, tribes.
Bring me your counter of property, tribes, that he may in vain try to count what is going to be given away by the great copper-maker, the chief.
Oh, I laugh at them, I sneer at them who empty boxes[15] in their houses, their potlatch houses, their inviting houses that are full only of hunger. They follow along after me like young sawbill ducks. I am the only great tree, I the chief. . . .

I have quoted a number of these hymns of self-glorification because by an association which psychiatrists will recognize as fundamental these delusions of grandeur were essential in the paranoid view of life which was so strikingly developed in this culture. All of existence was seen in terms of insult.[16] Not only derogatory acts performed by a neighbor or an enemy, but all untoward events, like a cut when one's ax slipped, or a ducking when one's canoe overturned, were insults. All alike threatened first and foremost one's ego security, and the first thought one was allowed was how to get even, how to wipe out the insult. Grief was little institutionalized, but sulking took its place. Until he had resolved upon a course of action by which to save his face after any misfortune, whether it was the slipping of a wedge in felling a tree, or the death of a favorite child, an Indian of the Northwest Coast retired to his pallet with his face to the wall and neither ate nor spoke. He rose from it to follow out some course which according to the traditional rules should reinstate him in his own eyes and those of the community: to distribute property enough to wipe out the stain, or to go head-hunting in order that somebody else should be made to mourn. His activities in neither case were specific responses to the bereavement he had just passed through, but were elaborately directed toward getting even. If he had not the money to distribute and did not succeed in killing someone to humiliate another, he might take his own life. He had staked everything, in his view of life, upon a certain picture of the self, and, when the bubble of his self-esteem was pricked, he had no interest, no occupation to fall back on, and the collapse of his inflated ego left him prostrate.

Every contingency of life was dealt with in these two traditional ways. To them the two were equivalent. Whether one fought with weapons or "fought with property," as they say, the same idea was at the bottom of both. In the olden times, they say, they fought with spears, but now they fight with property. One overcomes one's opponents in equivalent fashion in both, matching forces and seeing that one comes out ahead, and one can thumb one's nose at the vanquished rather more satisfactorily at a potlatch than on a battle field. Every occasion in life was noticed, not in its own terms, as a stage in the sex life of the individual or as a climax of joy or of grief, but as furthering this drama of consolidating one's own prestige and bringing shame to one's guests. Whether it was the occasion of the birth of a child, or a daughter's adolescence, or of the marriage of one's son, they were all equivalent raw material for the culture to use for this one traditionally selected end. They were all to raise one's own personal status and to entrench oneself by the humiliation of one's fellows. A girl's adolescence among the Nootka[17] was an event for which her father gathered property from the time she was first able to run about. When she was adolescent he would demonstrate his greatness by an unheard of distribution of these goods, and put down all his rivals. It was not as a fact of the girl's sex life that it figured in their culture, but as the occasion for a major move in the great game of vindicating one's own greatness and humiliating one's associates.

In their behavior at great bereavements this set of the culture comes out most strongly. Among the Kwakiutl it did not matter whether a relative had died in bed of disease, or by the hand of an enemy, in either case death was an affront to be wiped out by the death of another person. The fact that one had been caused to mourn was proof that one had been put upon. A chief's sister and her daughter had gone up to Victoria, and either because they drank bad whiskey or because their boat capsized they never came back. The chief called together his warriors. "Now I ask you, tribes, who shall wail? Shall I do it or shall another?" The spokesman answered, of course, "Not you, Chief. Let some other of the tribes." Immediately they set up the war pole to announce their intention of wiping out the injury, and gathered a war party. They set out, and found seven men and two children asleep and killed them. "Then they felt good when they arrived at Sebaa in the evening."

The point which is of interest to us is that in our society those who on that occasion would feel good when they arrived at Sebaa that evening would be the definitely abnormal. There would be some, even in our society, but it is not a recognized and approved mood under the circumstances. On the Northwest Coast those are favored and fortunate to whom that mood under those circumstances is congenial, and those to whom it is repugnant are unlucky. This latter minority can register in their own culture only by doing violence to their congenial responses and acquiring others that are difficult for them. The person, for instance, who, like a Plains Indian whose wife has been taken from him, is too proud to fight, can deal with the Northwest Coast civilization only by ignoring its strongest bents. If he cannot achieve it, he is the deviant in that culture, their instance of abnormality.

This head-hunting that takes place on the Northwest Coast after a death is no matter of blood revenge or of organized vengeance. There is no effort to tie up the subsequent killing with any responsibility on the part of the victim for the death of the person who is being mourned. A chief whose son has died goes visiting where-ever his fancy dictates, and he says to his host, "My prince has died today, and you go with him." Then he kills him. In this, accord-ing to their interpretation, he acts nobly because he has not been downed. He has thrust back in return. The whole procedure is meaningless without the fundamental paranoid reading of bereave-ment. Death, like all the other untoward accidents of existence, confounds man's pride and can only be handled in the category of insults.

Behavior honored upon the Northwest Coast is one which is recognized as abnormal in our civilization, and yet it is sufficiently close to the attitudes of our own culture to be intelligible to us and to have a definite vocabulary with which we may discuss it. The megalomaniac paranoid trend is a definite danger in our society. It is encouraged by some of our major preoccupations, and it confronts us with a choice of two possible attitudes. One is to brand it as abnormal and reprehensible, and is the attitude we have chosen in our civilization. The other is to make it an essential attribute of ideal man, and this is the solution in the culture of the Northwest Coast.

These illustrations, which it has been possible to indicate only in the briefest manner, force upon us the fact that normality is culturally defined. An adult shaped to the drives and standards of either of these cultures, if he were transported into our civilization, would fall into our categories of abnormality. He would be faced with the psychic dilemmas of the socially unavailable. In his own culture, however, he is the pillar of society, the end result of socially inculcated mores, and the problem of personal instability in his case simply does not arise.

No one civilization can possibly utilize in its mores the whole potential range of human behavior. Just as there are great numbers of possible phonetic articulations, and the possibility of language depends on a selection and standardization of a few of these in order that speech communication may be possible at all, so the possibility of organized behavior of every sort, from the fashions of local dress and houses to the dicta of a people's ethics and religion, depends upon a similar selection among the possible behavior traits. In the field of recognized economic obligations or sex taboos this selection is as nonrational and subconscious a process as it is in the field of phonetics. It is a process which goes on in the group for long periods of time and is historically conditioned by innumerable accidents of isolation or of contact of peoples. In any comprehensive study of psychology, the selection that different cultures have made in the course of history within the great circumference of potential behavior is of great significance.

Every society,[18] beginning with some slight inclination in one direction or another, carries its preference farther and farther, integrating itself more and more completely upon its chosen basis, and discarding those types of behavior that are uncongenial. Most of those organizations of personality that seem to us most incontrovertibly abnormal have been used by different civilizations in the very foundations of their institutional life. Conversely the most valued traits of our normal individuals have been looked on in differently organized cultures as aberrant. Normality, in short, within a very wide range, is culturally defined. It is primarily a term for the socially elaborated segment of human behavior in any culture; and abnormality, a term for the segment that that particular civilization does not use. The very eyes with which we see the problem are conditioned by the long traditional habits of our own society.

It is a point that has been made more often in relation to ethics than in relation to psychiatry. We do not any longer make the mistake of deriving the morality of our own locality and decade directly from the inevitable constitution of human nature. We do not elevate it to the dignity of a first principle. We recognize that morality differs in every society, and is a convenient term for socially approved habits. Mankind has always preferred to say, "It is a morally good," rather than "It is habitual," and the fact of this preference is matter enough for a critical science of ethics. But historically the two phrases are synonymous.

The concept of the normal is properly a variant of the concept of the good. It is that which society has approved. A normal action is one which falls well within the limits of expected behavior for a particular society. Its variability among different peoples is essentially a function of the variability of the behavior patterns that different societies have created for themselves, and can never be wholly divorced from a consideration of culturally institutionalized types of behavior.

Each culture is a more or less elaborate working-out of the potentialities of the segment it has chosen. In so far as a civilization is well integrated and consistent within itself, it will tend to carry farther and farther, according to its nature, its initial impulse toward a particular type of action, and from the point of view of any other culture those elaborations will include more and more extreme and aberrant traits.

Each of these traits, in proportion as it reinforces the chosen behavior patterns of that culture, is for that culture normal. Those individuals to whom it is congenial either congenitally or as the result of childhood sets are accorded prestige in that culture, and are not visited with the social contempt or disapproval which their traits would call down upon them in a society that was differently organized. On the other hand, those individuals whose characteristics are not congenial to the selected type of human behavior in that community are the deviants, no matter how valued their personality traits may be in a contrasted civilization.

The Dobuan who is not easily susceptible to fear of treachery, who enjoys work and likes to be helpful, is their neurotic and regarded as silly. On the Northwest Coast the person who finds it difficult to read life in terms of an insult contest will be the person upon whom fall all the difficulties of the culturally unprovided for. The person who does not find it easy to humiliate a neighbor, nor to see humiliation in his own experience, who is genial and loving, may, of course, find some unstandardized way of achieving satisfactions in his society, but not in the major patterned responses that his culture requires of him. If he is born to play an important role in a family with many hereditary privileges, he can succeed only by doing violence to his whole personality. If he does not succeed, he has betrayed his culture; that is, he is abnormal.

I have spoken of individuals as having sets toward certain types of behavior, and of these sets as running sometimes counter to the types of behavior which are institutionalized in the culture to which they belong. From all that we know of contrasting cultures it seems clear that differences of temperament occur in every society. The matter has never been made the subject of investigation, but from the available material it would appear that these temperament types are very likely of universal recurrence. That is, there is an ascertainable range of human behavior that is found wherever a sufficiently large series of individuals is observed. But the proportion in which behavior types stand to one another in different societies is not universal. The vast majority of the individuals in any group are shaped to the fashion of that culture. In other words, most individuals are plastic to the molding force of the society into which they are born. In a society that values trance, as in India, they will have supernormal experience. In a society that institutionalizes homosexuality, they will be homosexual. In a society that sets the gathering of possessions as the chief human objective, they will amass property. The deviants, whatever the type of behavior the culture has institutionalized, will remain few in number, and there seems no more difficulty in molding the vast malleable majority to the "normality" of what we consider an aberrant trait, such as delusions of reference, than to the normality of such accepted behavior patterns as acquisitiveness. The small proportion of the number of the deviants in any culture is not a function of the sure instinct with which that society has built itself upon the fundamental sanities, but of the universal fact that, happily, the majority of mankind quite readily take any shape that is presented to them.

The relativity of normality is not an academic issue. In the first place, it suggests that the apparent weakness of the aberrant is most often and in great measure illusory. It springs not from the fact that he is lacking in necessary vigor, but that he is an individual upon whom that culture has put more than the usual strain. His inability to adapt himself to society is a reflection of the fact that that adaptation involves a conflict in him that it does not in the so-called normal.

Therapeutically, it suggests that the inculcation of tolerance and appreciation in any society toward its less usual types is fundamentally important in successful mental hygiene. The complement of this tolerance, on the patients' side, is an education in self-reliance and honesty with himself. If he can be brought to realize that what has thrust him into his misery is despair at his lack of social backing he may be able to achieve a more independent and less tortured attitude and lay the foundation for an adequately functioning mode of existence.

There is a further corollary. From the point of view of absolute categories of abnormal psychology, we must expect in any culture to find a large proportion of the most extreme abnormal types among those who from the local point of view are farthest from belonging to this category. The culture, according to its major preoccupations, will increase and intensify hysterical, epileptic, or paranoid symptoms, at the same time relying socially in a greater and greater degree upon these very individuals. Western civilization allows and culturally honors gratifications of the ego which according to any absolute category would be regarded as abnormal. The portrayal of unbridled and arrogant egoists as family men, as officers of the law, and in business has been a favorite topic of novelists, and they are familiar in every community. Such individuals are probably mentally warped to a greater degree than many inmates of our institutions who are nevertheless socially unavailable. They are extreme types of those personality configurations which our civilization fosters.

This consideration throws into great prominence the confusion that follows, on the one hand, the use of social inadequacy as a criterion of abnormality and, on the other, of definite fixed symptoms. The confusion is present in practically all discussions of abnormal psychology, and it can be clarified chiefly by adequate consideration of the character of the culture, not of the constitution of the abnormal individual. Nevertheless, the bearing of social security upon the total situation of the abnormal cannot be exaggerated, and the study of comparative psychiatry will be fundamentally concerned with this aspect of the matter.

It is clear that statistical methods of defining normality, so long as they are based on studies in a selected civilization, only involve us, unless they are checked against the cultural configuration, in deeper and deeper provincialism. The recent tendency in abnormal psychology to take the laboratory mode as normal and to define abnormalities as they depart from this average has value in so far as it indicates that the aberrants in any culture are those individuals who are liable to serious disturbances because their habits are culturally unsupported. On the other hand, it overlooks the fact that every culture besides its abnormals of conflict has presumably its abnormals of extreme fulfillment of the cultural type. From the point of view of a universally valid abnormal psychology the extreme types of abnormality would probably be found in this very group — a group which in every study based upon one culture goes undescribed except in its end institutionalized forms.

The relativity of normality is important in what may some day come to b' a true social engineering. Our picture of our own civilization is no longer in this generation in terms of a changeless and divinely derived set of categorical imperatives. We must face the problems our changed perspective has put upon us. In this matter of mental ailments, we must face the fact that even our normality is man-made, and is of our own seeking. Just as we have been handicapped in dealing with ethical problems so long as we held to an absolute definition of morality, so too in dealing with the problems of abnormality we are handicapped so long as we identify our local normalities with the universal sanities. I have taken illustrations from different cultures, because the conclusions are most inescapable from the contrasts as they are presented in unlike social groups. But the major problem is not a consequence of the variability of the normal from culture to culture, but its variability from era to era. This variability in time we cannot escape if we would, and it is not beyond the bounds of possibility that we may be able to face this inevitable change with full understanding and deal with it rationally.[19] No society has yet achieved self-conscious and critical analysis of its own normalities and attempted rationally to deal with its own social process of creating new normalities within its next generation. But the fact that it is unachieved is not therefore proof of its impossibility. It is a faint indication of how momentous it could be in human society.

There is another major factor in the cultural conditioning of abnormality. From the material that is available at the present time it seems a lesser factor than the one we have discussed. Nevertheless, disregard of its importance has led to many misconceptions.

Ruth Fulton,
two years of age.

The Shattuck farm at Norwich, New York, about 1900. *Left to right:*
Aunty My (Miss Myra F. Shattuck), Grandpa and Grandma Shattuck.

Dr. Frederick S. Fulton,
1857–1889, Ruth Benedict's
father. Taken about the time
of his marriage in 1886.

Bertrice Fulton,
1860–1953, and her
two daughters, Ruth
and Margery. Taken
in 1894/95.

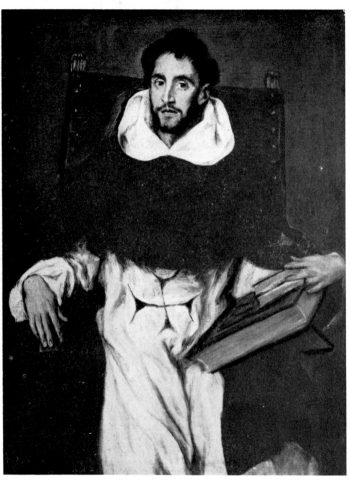

Portrait of Fray Felix Hortensio Paravicino by El Greco, the portrait which exercised such extreme fascination for Ruth Benedict and which her mother said resembled her father more than any photograph. *Courtesy Museum of Fine Arts, Boston.*

Ruth Fulton
in 1913.

Stanley R. Benedict,
1884–1936. Taken about
the time of his marriage
to Ruth Fulton in 1914.

Ruth Benedict,
about 1924.

Stanley Benedict in the later
years of their marriage.

Franz Boas, teacher,
1858–1942.

Edward Sapir, colleague
and critic, 1884–1938.

After her path
was clear.

"If I can just live till
I'm fifty, I'll be peaceful."

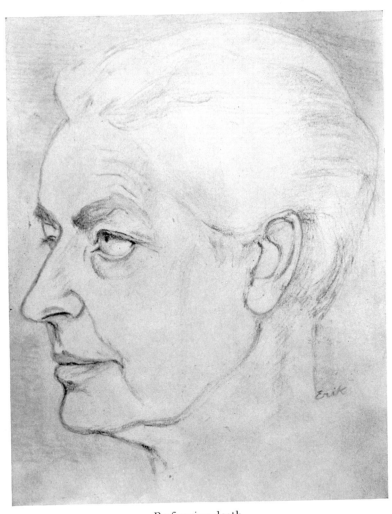

Prefiguring death.
Sketch by Erik H. Erikson, early summer 1948.

The particular forms of behavior to which unstable individuals of any group are liable are many of them matters of cultural patterning like any other behavior. It is for this obvious reason that the epidemic disorders of one continent or era are often rare or unreported from other parts of the world or other periods of history.

The baldest evidences of cultural patterning in the behavior of unstable individuals is in trance phenomena. The use to which such proclivities are put, the form their manifestations take, the things that are seen and felt in trance, are all culturally controlled. The tranced individual may come back with communications from the dead describing the minutiae of life in the hereafter, or he may visit the world of the unborn, or get information about lost objects in the camp, or experience cosmic unity, or acquire a life-long guardian spirit, or get information about coming events. Even in trance the individual holds strictly to the rules and expectations of his culture, and his experience is as locally patterned as a marriage rite or an economic exchange.

The conformity of trance experience to the expectations of waking life is well recognized. Now that we are no longer confused by the attempt to ascribe supernormal validity to the one or the other, and realize how trance experience bodies forth the preoccupations of the experiencing individual, the cultural patterning in ecstasy has become an accepted tenet.

But the matter does not end here. It is not only what is seen in trance experience that has clear-cut geographical and temporal distribution. It is equally true of forms of behavior which are affected by certain unstable individuals in any group. It is one of the prime difficulties in the use of such unprecise and casual information as we possess about the behavior of the unstable in different cultures, that the material does not correspond to data from our own society. It has even been thought that such definite types of instability as Arctic hysteria[20] and the Malay running-amok were racial diseases. But we know at least, in spite of the lack of good psychiatric accounts, that these phenomena do not coincide with racial distributions. Moreover, the same problem is quite as striking in cases where there is no possibility of a racial correlation. Running amok has been described as alike in symptoms and alike in the treatment

accorded it by the rest of the group from such different parts of the
world as Melanesia[21] and Tierra del Fuego.[22]

The racial explanation is also ruled out of court in those instances
of epidemic mania which are characteristic of our own cultural
background. The dancing mania[23] that filled the streets of Europe
with compulsively dancing men, women, and children in mediaeval
times is recognized as an extreme instance of suggestibility in our
own racial group.

These behaviors are capable of controlled elaboration that is often
carried to great lengths. Unstable individuals in one culture achieve
characteristic forms that may be excessively rare or absent in another, and this is very marked where social value has been attached
to one form or another. Thus when some form of borderline behavior has been associated in any society with the shaman and he
is a person of authority and influence, it is this particular indicated
seizure to which he will be liable at every demonstration. Among
the Shasta of California, as we have seen, and among many other
tribes in various parts of the world, some form of cataleptic seizure
is the passport to shamanism and must constantly accompany its
practice. In other regions it is automatic vision or audition. In
other societies behavior is perhaps closest to what we cover by the
term hystero-epilepsy. In Siberia all the familiar characteristics of
our spiritualistic seances are required for every performance of the
shaman. In all these cases the particular experience that is thus
socially chosen receives considerable elaboration and is usually patterned in detail according to local standards. That is, each culture,
though it chooses quite narrowly in the great field of borderline
experiences, without difficulty imposes its selected type upon certain
of its individuals. The particular behavior of an unstable individual
in these instances is not the single and inevitable mode in which his
abnormality could express itself. He has taken up a traditionally
conditioned pattern of behavior in this as in any other field. Conversely, in every society, our own included, there are forms of instability that are out of fashion. They are not at the present time
at least being presented for imitation to the enormously suggestible
individuals who constitute in any society a considerable group of the
abnormals. It seems clear that this is no matter of the nature of

sanity, or even of a biological, inherited tendency in a local group, but quite simply an affair of social patterning.

The problem of understanding abnormal human behavior in any absolute sense independent of cultural factors is still far in the future. The categories of borderline behavior which we derive from the study of the neuroses and psychoses of our civilization are categories of prevailing local types of instability. They give much information about the stresses and strains of Western civilization, but no final picture of inevitable human behavior. Any conclusions about such behavior must await the collection by trained observers of psychiatric data from other cultures. Since no adequate work of the kind has been done at the present time, it is impossible to say what core of definition of abnormality may be found valid from the comparative material. It is as it is in ethics: all our local conventions of moral behavior and of immoral are without absolute validity, and yet it is quite possible that a modicum of what is considered right and what wrong could be disentangled that is shared by the whole human race. When data are available in psychiatry, this minimum definition of abnormal human tendencies will be probably quite unlike our culturally conditioned, highly elaborated psychoses such as those that are described, for instance, under the terms of schizophrenia and manic-depressive.

Selections from Correspondence
to and from the Field
1924–1934

FIELD WORK is central in the life of working anthropologists; they date events in the past as they occurred before, during, or after a given field trip. Sending a student into the field for the first trip is always a major decision for a teacher. Going into a new field or into the field with a new problem remains a major challenge — as it was to Franz Boas who, at the age of seventy-three, at the time when he was President of the American Association for the Advancement of Science, went into the field to use the new technique of motion picture film for a study of gesture.

Because field work involves a very special sort of distance, letters from the field must try to create for the reader a sense of the actual conditions, and anyone who has ever been to the field will write a special kind of letter to someone whom they know is far away in time and space, speaking and thinking in a strange idiom. From the hundreds of letters covering the period from Ruth Benedict's second field trip in 1924 to her last field trip in 1939, I have selected letters in which she first described conditions among the Southwest Indians, letters focused upon my early field trips — as a student to be followed with solicitude, for whom she also tried to re-create anthropological events at home — and the letters bearing most directly upon *Patterns of Culture*.

[From MM in Holicong, Pennsylvania, to RFB in Zuñi]
August 30, 1924

Randolph Bourne's[1] "won battles" seemed to me to be first, distinctly American ones. He seemed to have fought through and conquered his provincialism, bringing with it a release from the little standards of material prosperity a sense of what a real national culture might mean, an understanding of other civilizations untouched by provincial bias. That is an attitude taken for granted by your young intelligentsia today. Then he'd escaped the notion of "Service," which you have made seem such a real bogey — such an effective moist cloth on hopeful activity. Also channeled and expected affections were put in their place without the unpleasant devices of the Electra and Oedipus notions. And he's escaped the insistence on classicism in English literature. Perhaps I've misinterpreted a lot of your description of attitudes prevailing before the war, and when I used them to illustrate Bourne's triumphant recording of what he visions as real victories over very live and vicious enemies, these seem real battles with which my generation has nothing to do, but calmly accept the fruits of victory. He also had achieved tolerance and a sense of the place of Puritanism as a rather puerile accent to Paganism rather than a veritable menace to be assaulted.

I don't like to think of you all alone — though in many ways I suppose it will be less of a conversational strain at least. I wish we could go on a field trip together — only in my present state I'd talk you insane.[2] I don't seem to be able to stop talking any more than I can stop thinking:

> When I am dead or sleeping
> Without any pain
> My soul will stop creeping
> Through my jeweled brain.

Only there I disagree with Elinor Wylie. At present I'm sure my soul won't ever stop. It's discovered perpetual motion in a circle.

I have a few things I've written this summer which I will send you when I have time to type them. They are very bad, but I think it's important for you to see the worst things I'm capable of; you are too encouraging.

[From MM in New York to RFB in Zuñi]
September 8, 1924

This morning's mail brought your letter about my paper[3] and a letter from Sapir — so I've had much food for thought all day though few interstices when thought was possible. I suppose it's a very bad sign that Sapir has time to write letters, but I do enjoy them. It's such a satisfactory friendship, defaced by no tiresome preliminaries (that's thanks to you) and founded on such sure ground of like-mindedness.

If you'll forgive a Jungian reference I think your contention that my protocracy are over-endowed with fitness for the task I'd assign them would be true if they were all of the same type, not introvert vs. extrovert. Of course I am concerned with extroverts, but whether they were all intuitive or not — If they were intuitive enough I suppose one would have to bet on too much boredom for any good achievement, but I am not sure they are. There seem to be some who have the feeling for organization, the crusading spirit (always of course in the interest of an abstract ideal, not for purposes of making others merely conform) sufficiently developed to make them fitted for the task. And likewise I grant you that a husky group of normal people bigoted beyond disturbance — and that in favor of individual freedom — would be the best guarantee of continuance. Maybe, at the back of it all, I have a Puritan desire to make people fight their own peculiar battles. I'm mightily relieved to know you think it is worth saying.

Isabel[4] is back, having taken genealogies for some 1000 children and being most weary of it. She is going to live in New York during the weekends and Passaic during the week coming over only for classes. If you decide not to return to the Kingscote[5] you and Isabel would dovetail perfectly in the occupancy of a room. I am now bending all my energies towards persuading her to try to go to the South Seas with me. It would be far better than going alone.

It's six-thirty and I have only allowed myself half an hour off; there are dishes to collect at least and then I have some thirty letters to get off tonight for the *Journal*.[6]

I shall also try to type my attenuated plans for my thesis and stick them in this letter.

Two tidbits —

(1) At the Marcus Garvey convention they served watermelons. Bless that man for his imagination.

(2) Léonie met the woman who does most of the designing for the Chinese rugs. They find they sell better if the designs are made in America!

[From MM in New York to RFB in Zuñi]
September 13, 1924

Be lazy, go crazy, be lazy, go crazy. I'll finish that charm off. This week when I had planned to accomplish so much, I celebrated by getting a piece of glass in my eye, and as a result got nothing done. Got in on the way to a conference with Goldy too, and finally arrived looking the picture of woe. However, we got on quite well; his method being apparently to make one defend oneself at every point — but he decided that my second plan[7] was best, which was what I thought myself. He wants me to analyze boat building in all its ramifications and show him the analysis before I go any further towards deciding what complexes I will use. I think perhaps if I have an outline worked out and examples of analyzing two or three "complexes" and my Italians[8] finished for Dr. Boas, that won't be quite so bad.

Dr. Boas isn't returning till the end of the month and the world seems full of people who wander disconsolately until his return. Dr. Jochelson, for instance, and the little German boy who thinks maybe he has enough money to last until Dr. Boas comes back, only Jeannette says he doesn't say so with much gusto. Dr. Jochelson is rather like a dog that is half fox — and half some more retiring beast. He is very nice to work with.[9] The tower room is filled with material . . . brought back from Darien. Very uninspiring mostly — but those perplexing wooden pillows. . . .

. . . Your letter sounded about eight times too industrious. Aren't you really awfully tired out? Eleven hours of dictation makes me think of the day I gave thirteen Binets,[10] and the memory is a most unsavory one.

[From MM in New York to RFB in Zuñi]

September 16, 1924

I knew the verse was poor. . . . I didn't quite understand your query about its being an expression of my mood — in your sense. I wrote them rather to be rid of moods that bored me or plagued me. And they were a very diverse picture because of some things I didn't finish which came in between. Most of them conformed to your description of saying "ouch when your corns are stepped on."

[From Franz Boas to RFB in West Alton]

Columbia University

July 16, 1925

My dear Ruth,

Sapir had a long talk with me about Margaret Mead. You know that I myself am not very much pleased with this idea of her going to the tropics for a long stay. It seems to my mind, however, and it has seemed to my mind ever since I prevented her going to the Tuamotu, that it would be much worse to put obstacles in her way that prevented her from doing a piece of work on which she had set her heart, than to let her run a certain amount of risk. In my opinion Sapir has read too many books on psychiatry . . . to trust his judgment; he does not really know the subject and therefore always sees abnormal things in the most disastrous forms. Of course, I know that Margaret is high strung and emotional, but I also believe that nothing would depress her more than inability on account of her physical makeup and her mental characteristics to do the work she wants to do. In my opinion an attempt to compel her now to give up the trip — and that is all Sapir has in mind — would be disastrous. Besides it is entirely against my point of view to interfere in such a radical way with the future of a person for his or her own sake, — unless there is actual disease that needs control. Of course, Sapir takes that point of view, but if he were right, then who should not be restrained? I should like to hear from you, if possible at once. Margaret can be reached until the 25th of this month in Philadelphia.

[From Franz Boas to MM]
July 14, 1925

My dear Margaret,

I suppose the time is drawing near when you want to leave. Let me impress upon you once more first of all that you should not forget your health. I am sure you will be careful in the tropics and try to adjust yourself to conditions and not work when it is too hot and moist in the daytime. If you find you cannot stand the climate do not be ashamed to come back. There are plenty of other places where you could solve the problem on which you propose to work.

I am sure you have thought over the question very carefully, but there are one or two points which I have in mind and to which I would like to call your attention, even if you have thought of them before.

One question that interests me very much is how the young girls react to the restraints of custom. We find very often among ourselves during the period of adolescence a strong rebellious spirit that may be expressed in sullenness or in sudden outbursts. In other individuals there is a weak submission which is accompanied, however, by a suppressed rebellion that may make itself felt in peculiar ways, perhaps in a desire for solitude which is really an expression of desire for freedom, or otherwise in forced participation in social affairs in order to drown the mental troubles. I am not at all clear in my mind in how far similar conditions may occur in primitive society and in how far the desire for independence may be simply due to our modern conditions and to a more strongly developed individualism.

Another point in which I am interested is the excessive bashfulness of girls in primitive society. I do not know whether you will find it there. It is characteristic of Indian girls of most tribes, and often not only in their relations to outsiders, but frequently within the narrow circle of the family. They are often afraid to talk and are very retiring before older people.

Another interesting problem is that of crushes among girls. For the older ones you might give special attention to the occurrence of romantic love, which is not by any means absent as far as I have been able to observe, and which, of course, appears most strongly where the parents or society impose marriages which the girls may not want. . . .

. . . Stick to individual and pattern, problems like Ruth Bunzel on art in Pueblos[11] and Haeberlin on Northwest Coast.[12] I believe you have read Malinowski's paper in Psyche[13] on the behavior of individuals in the family in New Guinea. I think he is much too influenced by Freudians, but the problem he had in mind is one of those which I have in mind.

Good luck. I hope you will let me know soon how you are getting on. I trust that your trip will be successful in every way. Don't forget your health. With kindest regards.

[From RFB to FB]
West Alton, July 18, 1925

Dear Dr. Boas,

Your letter has just come. I agree heartily with your position in regard to Margaret. All these things that have alarmed Sapir I have known for a long time and tried to take into account. Last spring I sent her to two doctors of the highest standing, one a neurologist, and they could find nothing organically wrong. The diagnosis is nervous fatigue and they prescribe rest. It seems to me that it is perfectly possible that the natural relaxation of a tropical climate, and the necessarily rather haphazard character of the work she will be doing, far away from the strenuous setting she is used to, may be the best possible change for her.

The mental condition I think Sapir is unduly alarmed about. There is of course the very great risk of a tropical infection when she has so little physical stamina to fight it with. I know that a letter from you emphasizing the duty of care and avoidance of risks would count very much with Margaret. I suppose that the Bishop Museum sends its staff with some knowledge of treatment of the simpler troubles and probably with individual medical advice after an examination. If not, it has seemed to me that she should have consultations, before leaving Hawaii, with the very best physician familiar with the conditions, and should live up to the advice even if at times it meant interrupting her work. Whatever you write her of such precautions would have great weight.

Sapir has written me his anxiety about Margaret's going, and I am trying to reassure him. It would certainly seem to me disastrous to stop her. She has written me about the offer of the museum for next year, and I think that, coming at just this time, nothing better could happen to allay the attitude Sapir is worried about. She is most enthusiastic. But it is her lack of physical resistance I am really troubled about, and fortunately that is something about which she can be quite frankly warned. I credit her with a great deal of common sense and I know she can carry out any precautions she agrees to, as far as humanly possible. I shall be in New York next week, Tuesday the 28th, and shall come to the office. It will be good to see you.

[From RFB in Zuñi to MM on the way to Samoa] [14]
August 6, 1925
I've discovered in myself a great fondness for this place — it came over me with a rush — We[15] drove in with the rain pouring down in great white separate drops and sunlit clouds, and soft veils of rain sifting and forming against the far off mesas. The red terraced hillock of Zuñi never looked better in any setting.

[From RFB to MM]
Zuñi, August 11, 1925
This mail is the last that will surely catch the boat from San Francisco the 18th. . . . I know I can't make all the beauty you'll be surrounded by, anything but aching pains. . . . And other times you must just love it because you are you and indomitable in the long run. After all this is the only safety in life . . . and we always fight through to it in agony of soul. There is nothing else . . . that is truly safe to build on, and we lay the miserable foundation over and over again. There is only one comfort that comes out of it — unbelievably — the sense that there is that sure something within us, no matter how often it is laid in ruins, that cannot be taken away from us. We're none of us, any of us, able to do without that recurring assurance of it. You will have moments too, even now, of knowing it. Be very good to yourself. Eat all that is stupid and

wholesome, sleep when it seems impossible, experiment with the light touch when it seems treachery. . . .

[From RFB to MM]
Zuñi, August 15, 1925

And this letter goes to Samoa. It seems aeons till I can hear what it's like and what its prospects are. How much change have you already had at language? My heart goes out to you in that, for I shouldn't learn Zuñi in three years . . . but then I compare our memory and our ears and [I] am quite prepared to have you speaking it in three months. It's lucky you never have been on a field trip with me, you'd be outraged at my slowness in language. Nick and Flora[16] both eat out of my hand this summer. Nick is invaluable — if I could only take his "singsongs" in text! The stories he tells which he calls "sacred stories" are as endless in ceremonial details as Flora's, so I guess the general type is established beyond question as far as Zuñi goes. I shall end by being fond of Nick. He told me the emergence story with fire in his eye yesterday through twenty-two repetitions of the same episode in twenty-two "sacred" songs. He'd try to skip but habit was too strong. He would only interrupt, "Zame zing, zame zing" — and go on with the same endless phrases to the end. There's something impressive in the man's fire. He might have been a really great man. And yet I think any society would have used its own terms to brand him as a witch. He's too solitary and too contemptuous. . . . I try to bring you close by the nearest, most routine facts — be thankful I spare you menus and Indian callers. I'm getting a taste of what these three week gaps between letters will be all this year. I shall count off the year with the steamers' coming as the Indians do with their prayerstick plantings. . . . You'll remember my most obsessive quarrel is with life as endless episodes so the pattern is pretty well fixed. If the letters had to be six months apart you'd still redeem life from episodes.

[From RFB to MM]
Zuñi, August 19, 1925

I've been trying to get linguistic help out of a Zuñi dictionary, of the "nice missionaries" next door. There are two varieties in Zuñi, nice and "not." These next door came here twenty-five years ago and have raised nine children here. They left the missionary business for trading almost twenty years back, and they are very companionable people — But this dictionary! It runs through *aggrandize* and *aggravate*; it includes *evolution* and *harlot*; and *idol* is rendered *katanc* or its Zuñi equivalent. It's a silent monument to the difference in interest between two peoples. I don't suppose one word in fifty is common in Zuñi talk, and certainly none of my constantly recurring tale-words are in it at all. . . .

Ruth Bunzel comes day after tomorrow . . . and I leave Monday. I go from there to Peña Blanca.

With this last shifting of priests, all my hopes of really efficient help from them in Peña Blanca have melted. I can only go down, be as tactful as possible, and see what comes of it. It will waste time, but I see no other way. I only wish our Zuñi Father Anthony were there. He's a dear, who makes it a rule to take everyone who comes to Zuñi into his little chapel that they may have a chance of a brief adoration if they wish. When he took me in and went to kneel himself, he blushed like a lover going to his mistress. He has none of the martyrdom of everybody else who lives here — hasn't he been called to his work? Beyond that, he can say that the detail of it "gets his goat" sometimes. He thinks he could have me in the fold if I were exposed long enough. Perhaps he could; I'm smitten with the faith of all such —

[From RFB to MM]
Zuñi, August 24, 1925

This is the last morning in Zuñi. . . . Ruth Bunzel came by Friday's mail wagon. Yesterday we went up under the sacred mesa along stunning trails where the great wall towers above you always in new magnificence. . . . When I'm God I'm going to build my city there.

I've had an excellent piece of luck about Peña Blanca. A Mr. Halseth of the Santa Fe Museum was there with a party yesterday — a very nice young German. He knows Cochiti well and has intimate Indian friends there. He'll drive me down on Friday, and introduce me, and get the informant for Peña Blanca. I can't think of anything that would seem better. I shall enjoy staying the two days in Santa Fe too — loafing.

[From RFB to MM]
Santa Fe, August 25, 1925

I am luxuriating in idleness. I'd much rather stay on than go on to Peña Blanca. . . . I lap this up. Tomorrow I move on, but today is excellent. I went up the arroya today straight into the mountains. There were great radiant clouds piled on top of them and shadows in their laps — I lay down on the bank. . . .

I am glad you know how much of me is shut into your book of verses[17] — I shall delight in having you feel me speaking them to you. Will you do one thing? — jot down the verses you wish you had or the ones that haunt you brokenly, and I'll send them to you. You must have thought of a lot by now. . . . I am glad about the new story. When you get time to copy it, I long to see it. I'll send Louise Nicholls' address as soon as I see a *Measure*.[18]

I wonder, is Samoa seething activity for you, or peaceable? Do you find time or mood for verses? I hope so. I've had bad luck finishing mine up lately, and of course no time. Peña Blanca will be isolation again.[19]

[From RFB to MM]
Peña Blanca, August 29, 1925

I don't have to trouble about betraying Dr. Boas[20] any more; here I am, upholding his hands to the utmost, and foretastes of eternity are thrown into the bargain. Tomorrow, it's true, I expect my Indian from Cochiti, but even that is only six hours a day, and there are twenty-four in a day. Eighteen all mine! I'm living with a Mexican family — a clean room under a tin roof — but the lady of the house is not well and couldn't feed me. They can let me have milk and tomatoes and there was bread and butter at the store so I am glad to be spared the ceremonial of three meals a day. But my repasts won't cut into my leisure.

It's lucky I didn't leave anything to the priest here. The sisters are adorable, and were most anxious to house me, but even that the father superior forbade. Mr. Halseth was worth his weight in gold. He's been chauffeur, guarantor, and introducer. — I wish he could be switched from Hewlitt to Boas, but that's difficult — it's through Hewlitt he got interested in this. His great ambition is to learn and to record Keres, especially the Sia dialect; would anything be more calculated to win Boas' heart? He thinks of getting an appointment as teacher at Sia. He has devoted friends in all these Rio Grande pueblos, and he rather looks down on people who have to pay. On the other hand, he learns shockingly, considering his contacts.

I like this place. The Jemez range facing us across the flats of the Rio Grande is a lesser edition of a one-walled Grand Canyon. The shadows prick new contours every hour just as they did there. It is a quarter horizon's stretch of opalescent colors. And we see it across the green irrigated fields of alfalfa and corn, with a still greener line at the joining where the cottonwoods grow along the river itself. By mid-morning the clouds have formed over the range, still as mountains, and more varied, and with the constant beauty of their shadows heightening the beauty of their range.

One reason I feel so much as if I'd stepped off the earth onto a timeless platform outside today, is because there was not a single scrap of paper in the post office for me. . . .

Don't fail to notice Marguerite's poem in the new *Nation*. It's partly because I know the image and know it is herself that it moved me so much. Her verses in the June *Poetry* were "Clinic" too, but way behind this, I thought. Her verse will never have variety, but if she can air her obsession over and over in verse she approves of, it will be her gain and ours too.

. . . In the isolation of this month . . . three years ago it would have been enough to fill me with terror. I was always afraid of depressions getting too much for me. . . . But that's ancient history now. . . .

[From RFB to MM]
Peña Blanca, September 1, 1925
It looks as if I had to go to Cochiti. My Indian came, but he doesn't know enough. He wants me to come to an old man in

Cochiti and he'll interpret. He seemed entirely oblivious to those taboos everybody talks about in the Rio Grande pueblos. So of course I didn't tell him! He said it would be all right if I wanted "only stories" — imagine that in Zuñi! I never do seem to find the spiked fence Elsie talks about — and Papa Franz for Cochiti too. Well, we'll see. He's going to arrange it this afternoon, and drive me across the Rio Grande in a cart tomorrow. . . .

I'm mailing a *Poetry.* I shall watch for more things from there by Frank Mitalsky; these have quality. For the rest, George Dillon's things seem below the level of his in the *Measure,* though "Compliment to Mariners" [?] is very worth while.— There's mostly no-account verse, as there has been so much lately.— She[21] sent back, at last, the verses I sent her from New York last June. She wouldn't even take her choice "Moth Wing." She liked "You have looked upon the Sun" best.

[From Jaime de Angulo in Berkeley, California, to RFB]
May 19, 1925

My dear Ruth

My Taos stuff is purely linguistic and has no value for folk-lore.

As for helping you to get an informant, and the way you describe it "if I took him with me to a safely American place" . . . "an informant who would be willing to give tales and ceremonials" . . . oh God! Ruth, you have no idea how much that has hurt me. I don't know how I am going to be able to talk to you about it because I have a sincere affection for you. But do you realize that it is just that sort of thing that kills the Indians? I mean it seriously. It kills them spiritually first, and as in their life the spiritual and the physical element are much more interdependent than in our own stage of culture, they soon die of it physically. They just lie down and die. That's what you anthropologists with your infernal curiosity and your thirst for scientific data bring about.

Don't you understand the psychological value of secrecy at a certain level of culture? Surely you must, but you have probably never connected it with this. You know enough of analytical psychology to know that there are things that must not be brought to the light of day, otherwise they wither and die like uprooted plants.

Have you never lived with Indians, Ruth? I really don't know, that's why I ask you. Is your own interest in primitive religion the result of a deep but unacknowledged mysticism? I wonder. You are connected in my mind very strongly with Edna who is still just as present in my life as she was before she died. That's why I talk in this strange way, because I am afraid to hurt your feelings. If it were Mrs. Parsons I wouldn't give a damn. If I ever find her or any other anthropologist ferreting out secrets in Taos or any other pueblo I will immediately denounce her and her informants to the old men. But I couldn't denounce you, and it will break my heart.

Why do you want to know these things? Of course if you promised that you would never publish the *actual* secrets, I would help you all I can. I would tell you a lot myself about the meaning of the whole thing. It is all right to talk about it in a general way, with certain reservations, the necessary care that must be always used in handling all esoteric knowledge. It is as powerful and dangerous as the lightning. Look at all the harm that raw psychoanalysts do to their patients. . . . But the actual details of ceremonies, that must never be told. They are as much part and parcel of the mind of the believer as the pyramidal cells of his cortex. They belong to him. They belong to the secret society. They have a real, actual meaning and value, as secrets, for the members of the society. You must not rob them. You must not sneak into their house. You wouldn't inveigle my child into telling you the secrets of my home.

Don't you see the meaning of it all? In Europe we can go back to our mother the earth through the spirits of our own ancestors. They inhabit the soil, the trees, the rocks. In America the soil is teeming with the ghosts of Indians. Americans will never find spiritual stability until they learn to recognize the Indians as their *spiritual* ancestors. The Sun-father of Egypt is a living symbol yet in the collective unconscious psychology of every European through actual tangible contact with the unbroken chain of organic culture. Only the Sun-father of the American Indian (an entirely different sort of person from that of Egypt) can ever be a father to the white American. That is the legacy of the Indian. But you would lose it by killing the Indian off before that message has been comprehended

by the white Americans. And you kill the Indian as surely by dis-
organizing his spiritual social life as you do with guns.

Well, I have told you what was in my heart. Perhaps it is all
gibberish to you. I would rather you would laugh at it than be hurt.

We start on the first of June, in a kind of prairie schooner built
on a Chevrolet truck chassis. We will visit first some of our friends
among the Pomo. Then the bulk of the summer among the
Achumawis. Then across the desert to Taos. Let's keep in touch.
We might have some time together, perhaps even in Taos, although
I doubt whether they would allow a white man to live in the pueblo,
even with us. I really want to have you with us. I am sure I could
give you a certain slant on their real life of the Indians. I am not
an anthropologist but I am half an Indian, or more.

Don't forget that Cushing killed Zunyi. Mrs. Parsons is doing her
best to kill Santo Domingo, but fortunately the people there are on
their guard now.

[From RFB to MM in New York]

August 13, 1930

Jaime has been here. We sat over whiskey and soda till after midnight one night, and I liked him just as I always have. With all the
ostracism he courts — and gets — he hasn't a trace of a persecution
complex, speaks the kindliest and keenest things of everybody, and
— of all things — cares most in the world about Nance's getting back
to professional achievement, to linguistics, that is. . . . He's on his
way to the congress in Hamburg. . . .

[From RFB to MM]

Peña Blanca, September 2, 1925

I'm waiting for my Indian cart to ford me across the river. It's
7.30, and already desert hot. . . .

Sept. 3 — [Cochiti]

The cart came, and we lunged across the river and up to this quite
charming pueblo. I'm glad I spent so much time with my mountains
in Peña Blanca, for here, being so near them, we can't see them at

all. My house is next door to a half-underground kiva with its ladder
thrust up to the sky. An adobe stairway ascends from one side. It's
quite effective. The houses many of them have twisted acacias to sit
under in front, and porches covered with boughs whose leaves have
turned just the color of the adobe. In Zuñi you would never sit out
unless it was about to rain because no shade is thought proper in
Zuñi.

There are drawbacks in this abode. The menu is somewhat
difficult since neither bread nor milk are known here. I've decided
on rice and raisins as my staple, and there are some canned soups in
the store. Presently the Indians will begin to provide, and I'll be
eating field corn with the rest of them. — The worst is as usual, and
I haven't had time to get them tamed down at all. I'm renting the
house from an old Indian who was an old, old-time graduate of
Carlisle and who speaks English with notable precision. He said
farewell the first night, and then: "Well, friend, you'll be troubled
by bugs *some*. There were none here, but our neighbors kept
chickens in the back yard. We came in a week or two ago —
(they're out "on the farm" now) — and it was awful. At that time
we saw them crawling in lines in the cracks of the floor." Therefore
as soon as he'd left I managed to scramble up an amputated ladder
to the roof with my bedding on my back. It was much better, but
even daytime gives no surcease as yet.

I don't understand the openness with which they give me the
stories. They don't seem in the least secretive before the rest. Dr.
Boas thought I ought not to set foot myself in Cochiti if I were
going to be within a hundred miles with an informant. But there is
no trace of the Zuñi intensity of feeling. Of course I am getting
very unesoteric stories, but if I sit long enough, I don't doubt getting
the other kind. I never do get this sense of the spiked dangerous
fence that Elsie, and Dr. Boas in this case, make so much of.

[From RFB to MM]
Cochiti, September 5, 1925
More stretches of leisure are before me for my old man doesn't
work Sundays. The perverse Catholicity of these Eastern pueblos

turns up at every coming-in and going-out. However, it's quite a different complexion from Peña Blanca's leisure, for I have male callers, mother callers, innumerable children who've heard I have candy, and the family of the house wander in at least every day from the farm across the river. There'll be a dance tomorrow, too; — I don't expect much. "Young Horse Dance" they call it. I see they've set up four posts in the Plaza that are probably the hitching posts!

My diet is expanding. The chief difficulty was that I was wholly unprepared to find flour unknown in these stores. But the keeper of one of these little rows of shelves they call "stores" — there are two — unearthed three little cartons of Aunt Jemima pancake flour, and I am saved. My muffins are excellent, and as for butter, even Peña Blanca butter was inedible, so I'm already at ease about that omission.

My old man is ninety and a great old character. He must have been fair as a white girl in his day — he's known all over this country as "the Fair" (blonde). He speaks excellent Spanish and I can follow a good deal when he talks it — I am angry that I have to bother with interpreters at all, but I do. He hobbles along on his cane, bent nearly double, and is still easily the most vivid personage in the landscape — he has the habit of enthusiasm and of good fellowship. I'll warrant it comes where his fair skin comes from. But he doesn't regard himself as mixed; — my interpreter, he says, is Nambé, his *wife's* great grandmother's mother was Nambé. So if he thinks he's pure, it isn't because he's not interested in genealogies.

I've read *Antic Hay*, I forget if you have or not; I brought it from the Santa Fe library. It was an excellent choice for time and season — perhaps no one should read it who wasn't at a distance from all civilization's amenities and a little desirous of them. Then it's delightful as a purling stream. I don't believe under any circumstances the moral of the book would loom very large; certainly under mine, the virtue was all in the dexterity and sureness with which he rendered the sophistication he wished to hold up as futile.

I brought de la Mare's *Come Hither* along from the same library. Why doesn't somebody I know have a child it would be within the bounds of sanity to give the book to. . . . It's the first collection of verse in heaven knows how long that makes me realize that there are still undiscovered countries even in English verse. Did you know this English Maying song? [22] . . .

. . . But I wish I knew French — or Russian! — well enough to be really at home in the verse. — I want to find a really important undiscovered country. . . .

. . . I wonder so often how you'll be living when *this* letter finds you. I imagine you'll still be wrestling with the problems of Pago Pago society, and eating up the language in trenchers. I hope Naval society has its highlights — or is it only excellent preparation for living native — a foil against which taking care of Samoan babies will be a vivid experience. However it seems, don't forget that you must save yourself for the field work which is bound to need all the physical fitness you can lay hold of. Develop all the expedients you can against weeping — companionship is only one of them. I've had excellent ones: they range from brushing your teeth and gargling your throat with every onset, to playing you're your own daughter for a year. After such samples you'll never ask me for any more like them. But I know there is no clear-sightedness nor course of reasoning that will help — you have that already. God bless you . . . and make life easier for you.

[From RFB to MM]
Cochiti, September 8, 1925

These last few days I've been having excellent samples of what your living native will be like. I imagine the complete gregariousness of it staggers belief in a hermit New Yorker! You won't have — perhaps — the eight hours of paid informants besides, but instead you'll be there in the thick of the herd *all* the time. As soon as I go out for water the men begin to come in. One amorous male I think I have got rid of, dear soul! He's stunning, with melting eyes and the perfect confidence which I can't help believing has come from a successful amour with a white woman. He hopes I'll be another Mabel Dodge; he's all ready to take Tony's part and I will say he's a better catch than Tony.[23] It was when I bribed a little girl to come over and sleep with me under my trees that he took to heart that, if I let him kiss my hand six times with much heat, on departing, I meant nothing that interested him. — There's the gay boy who's married a second time now and just comes here to sit in the room where Madeleine lives in the wintertime — she's my host's unmarried twenty-year old daughter who teaches in the day school. And there's the jolly old man who tells me stories and has the Spanish-American temperament transplanted bodily. — And of course there are women, but they are more of a piece.

Everybody in Cochiti seems to know my occupation and asks how "the old man got on with his stories today?" Now it's "the old woman," for he's been sick these last two days and I like the old woman quite as well. I've had two other offers of informants and I try to squeeze them in — one especially is very promising for the esoteric stories. Of course their great justification is that they aren't telling me anything sacred, and of course it's so far pretty public material but it would be anyway on this acquaintance, and here the great problem is to find the rare person who still knows. It isn't general, as it is in Zuñi. The men Mr. Halseth recommended are both ignorant even of this general lore. Stories aren't told night after night as they are in Zuñi, and societies and priesthoods are reduced to almost nothing. — And I pay so little here I can afford to take the tales as they come — only a dollar a three-hour session.

I ought to assure you that the outward amenities of existence are finding their way here. I still depend on Aunt Jemima, but once a week bread comes from Peña Blanca for my special delectation. My Black Flag arrived and the bed bugs are forced away from certain quarantined areas. I even slept in my bed, after a hard afternoon rain, last night, and managed very well.

I must tell you the blow that fell on me in yesterday's mail — Catherine Russell [24] moves to Portland, Oregon, immediately, for keeps! One beautiful solution that is never to be! — The only solution I've hit on at this distance is to put all the year's money into a five months' fulltime stenographer, and make up the rest myself so that she can take stories for me. But I'm afraid that would be wasteful because she'd have to work quite fast to get away with all I want done, and I could get a non-shorthand person for the *Journal* [25] cheque, I suppose.

[From RFB to MM]
Cochiti, September 13, 1925
— Please overlook that terrible "veery" stanza in the verses I sent you last week.[26] I don't know how it got by me. I suppose Edward would get an echo of his play-girl out of "For Seed Bearing." [27] You don't, do you? I mean diametrically the opposite — not a figure for "the growing anguish of a soul," but of that time after heart-break when one is thrown back upon oneself. I have the figure so vividly in my own mind that I can't make out whether I have it set out clearly in the poem or not. It will be one of this year's crosses not to be able to have your comments on my verses while they are fresh in my mind.

The stories are growing in bulk. I am fairly certain I shall get no esoteric tales this trip. I'll have to come again, but a second time I think it would be fairly easy. Meanwhile the whole village vies to sit with me for a seance. Joe disperses appointments as he would a poor fund and I'm in luck that my old shaman is poor — otherwise he'd be frowned on. One of those who rob the poor working girl, you know! My best interpreter I am forbidden to use for her husband supports her amply! I think I'll go out Saturday and spend Sunday with Katherine [Brenner]. Sundays are never any good in this "Catholic" village. Today they've all been to Santa Domingo to a dance — no whites allowed for there are Katcina. I've stayed in a deserted pueblo. I didn't get up till afternoon, and all day I've been stunning company to myself! . . . I don't know myself any more.
Your last letter came from Hawaii on Thursday's mail. . . .

[From RFB to MM]
Cochiti, September 16, 1925
I'll write you a few minutes before I go to sleep, though it's time for me to turn out my light if I'm to be ready for the sunrise arrivals I get here. My last informant tonight didn't leave me to cook my dinner till eight o'clock — you see I'm no longer indulging in stretches of leisure. I've been taking nine hours dictation right along, except Sunday, for the last ten days — a goodly bulk. But the tales I'm really curious about I don't get — the katcina stories. —

I'm thankful it was Zuñi stories and not these I got my thousand pages of, for those are at least rich and earthy with their manners and their religion, and these are rather the recreation of a people without either. The disintegration of culture has gone further on the Rio Grande than I'd thought. It makes me more appreciative of the privilege of getting at Zuñi before it's gone likewise.

It's Wednesday and I'm leaving Saturday. I'll be glad to be starting homeward. . . .

[From RFB to MM]
B & O Train, near Chicago
September 25, 1925

I spent last evening with Edward, had dinner with his mother and the children and took him off to my hotel where I listened till after midnight. . . . Last night he was tortured by the idea of Nemesis, and I wouldn't let him fall back on it. But it was he who said, "I suppose it's envy — I can't get that out of life, and I want other people to acknowledge it isn't possible." — But he comes back to it again and again as if it were the decalogue. He has many images — life shall be a tree incorporating all into one harmonious growth, it shall cease to be capsules, and many others. It is as deep-seated as you recognized it long ago to be. . . .

. . . He had your letters from the first Samoan boat, so I read the news letter and the sheet about the book of poems. Was the seasickness a long drag after you got to land? . . .

He is looking a little thin, but alert and well. He's very curious to know how he'll like Chicago. Altogether, I've never seen him when I'd more trust him to meet his problems as they could best be met. . . .

I liked your suggestions about the order of Edward's book,[28] but I only read it on the train, so of course I didn't see the accompanying manuscript.

[From RFB to MM]
March 5, 1926

I had such a good time yesterday with Malinowski. He turned up at lunch — no one knew he was here and asked to spend the after-

noon with me. Radin came down for dinner, and afterwards he went
to Radin's "course" and as soon as Radin threw the discussion open,
Malinowski held forth. You'd like him a lot. He has the quick
imagination and the by-play of mind that makes him a seven-days'
joy, and he's discovered as if it were a new religion that acculturation
makes so much difference that it hardly matters whether or not the
trait is invented on the spot or diffused from some outside source. Of
course it's just a swing of the pendulum to right the fantastic ex-
tremes of Eliott Smith and Graebner, but it's intriguing to find an
intelligent person discovering with such force the things we've been
brought up on with our mother's — or Papa Franz's! — milk. Give
him time, and he'll discover with the same force that the little detail
of independent invention or diffusion *does* make a difference in the
picture after all. He starts of course from the premise that there's
really no such phenomenon as an "invention"; it's all a very slow
accretion that hardly, in its slow accumulation, gives more evidence
of human inventiveness than borrowing does. He's right of course;
it's just that he ought to say that for the purposes of his argument
he's laying aside the problem of historical reconstruction from the
distribution of traits, and of the differences between internal growth
and stimulation from the outside — but why expect anyone who's
just got religion to specify the things he's overlooked?

About psychoanalysis he's as skeptical as Papa Franz — nearly.
He feels that no one now flies that banner except the extremists.
The worth of it has been taken up into general psychological positions. Of course that's easy to say and overlooks the fact that they've
been right before when they were outlawed and may be again. But
anyway the orthodox will have nothing whatever to do with his
work, of course. He and Papa Franz could agree to their hearts'
content. Radin fumed all the evening. He's lectured me all the year
about getting the good out of Eliott Smith et al. and of course about
the great god Jung. It was fun to have so excellent an ally. Besides
Radin hated my expositions of Boas. Malinowski liked to hear
though and it was all to the good. He said, "if only I'd known, Boas
was my spiritual father all the time," and "You must tell me what
Boas has been teaching for twenty years about this and that, or I'll
be discovering it as if it had never happened to anybody before."

At the evening session he rather pointedly ignored Radin — whom he very obviously has a fondness for — and we all had a good time. You'd have thought we were all ardent diffusionists, and I'd been expecting to see the whole set run down Boas and his mechanical interpretations. There's rather a lot of the feeling abroad, I think, but I see the younger set, "Jacob's gang" [29] very casually and never to talk anthropology.

The seminar is going to be just as difficult as I thought. We had stupid discussions on the diffusionists' positions, and that included Dr. Boas's work; the point I made was that studies of distribution really had it as their objective to put the problem before us, not to solve any of them. Dr. Boas in some moods would say that himself, but it troubled him just the same. Then this week Klineberg — do you remember the very fair, neat-minded boy in psychology — reported on psychoanalytic treatment of myth. I told him to do it as sympathetically as possible, and he thought at first that with the best will in the world that was impossible. But with the help of Malinowski's work and of suggestions we cooked up, he gave an exceedingly interesting report. I think Boas would accept all of it but the terminology — but that kills it. He won't talk about a repression. He'll say that people have a drive to make fun of their taboos, but to call it compensation for an inhibition — that is beyond the pale. He got very excited and it made a very good discussion; we haven't talked about it since but Goddard says he was really stirred up. It's curious.

[From RFB to MM on the way to the Admiralty Islands]
New York, September 21, 1928

There've been no casualties.[30] Papa Franz has even had a good time since the first day, and nothing has gone conspicuously wrong. Bogoras retails how at the Congress in 1902 they shook the hand of the President of the United States in Washington and were taken out to the desert of the Southwest and given shovels to dig up whatever they should find; it was all "planted" and there was a speech about all that they were being given under the "fresh dust of centuries" — so he says this is a one-horse funeral. But he's otherwise placid, and there seems to be no general demand for the unattainable, like planted potsherds, and Calvin Coolidge's hand. David has been invaluable, and has enjoyed it too, going on the parties and being delightful to the foreign languages.

I've seen a lot of Edward till today when he took a day off. We spent one evening on a bench in the park. It took an hour or two to get him over a discussion of — how would you guess — jealousy. He nearly repudiated me and our conversation because I didn't agree that jealousy was the necessary reverse of any important love and that you measured the size of the love by the size of the jealousy. . . . Finally, to avoid having to give chapter and verse out of my life, I had to pacify him by saying that after all I'd never been tested; but he bore away the resentment at my lack of understanding of his holy point. . . .

. . . I must begin farther back. The formal opening was notable for the fact that, just as Papa Franz had planned, Osborn played second fiddle. That morning a note had come down from Osborn's office saying that the President must make the first and opening address. Up goes Papa Franz and beards the lion in his den, and when they are seated on the platform, sure enough it's Papa Franz that gets up. These occasions when Papa Franz wears Thomas Mott's[31] feathers do not suit me at all. But the formal opening gave one redeeming moment: when Osborn strutted a little extra and said, "and I who can claim to be devoid of a trace of vanity . . ." There was a very excellent tribute to Papa Franz from dear old Professor Penck who is a great beaming child loving all the world and who holds his hand pressed tight against his bow window as if he were feeling for his heart beat; he spoke of the greatest of anthropologists of German birth, Professor Boas, "for we of my country have sent to you our best." It was very good. . . .

. . . But the Bushman played his great role in the formal dinner to the dozen foreign delegates. It went off in great style. I sat next to Bogoras and he talked the revolution and Russian literature to me and I suppose when he's moved he had the most beautiful smile I've encountered. . . .

. . . I've had good talks with Bogoras. He's full of the "new dawn" and sure as a child. From now on man no longer fears circumstance, he is released, a new man. Of course this has put an end to our enjoyment of some of the old classics of literature; even Dostoievsky is a little dated, and Tolstoi and Turgenev are out of the running. But Tchekov is untouched — and who else do you think? I'd give you one hundred guesses. It's Anatole France. I was completely aghast. I instanced the Red Lily and he granted that the Red Lily wasn't a good book to illustrate his side of the point. He says that's general intellectuals' opinion in Soviet Russia. Then there's Thalbitzer who looks old and scarred. He's like a patient academic Christus, and likes to talk to me. . . .

. . . I might get around to the papers too. Koppers is here to talk for Graebner; the only thing I can think of when he talks is that I'd like to go to confession to him. He [is] sure of himself, and probably abominably dogmatic, but he has that authority that we don't know how to come by in this country. Kroeber always gets up after Koppers or Uhle or a paper by Capitan and says a little speech about how we all agree; then up hops Papa Franz and says "But it seems to my mind that there is a fundamental difference," which he proceeds to expound. There was a lot of interest in my paper[32] and it had an excellent place on the program, just before the luncheon at the Heye Museum. Kroeber's question was just, "How does the old man take a paper like that?" Edward said it was a good lecture and a good point, and Kidder came up to say it was illustrated just as much by the pueblo art and material culture as by their religion. Wissler scowled through a great deal of it and I haven't seen him since; Elsie was speechless and rose to make all sorts of pointless addenda when she recovered her breath. Professor Danzel — the one from Hamburg, who's been staying with Gladys — said it was the most important paper of the Congress and agreed with work of his own; the same from Powdermaker. I had to do it all in less than twenty minutes so it had to be too schematic, but for the given length of time I think it was as good as I could have made it. . . .

. . . "Eucharist" is at last in this week's *Nation*,[33] and under list of contributors, what have they but, baldly, "Anne Singleton is a pseudonym." Damn them. Won't an editor ever print a line of mine without knifing poor Anne Singleton? Every time it happens I wonder why it is that I feel so strongly about it — quite as if a murder had been done. Why do they all hang up on that particular point? They don't even know it bothers me. . . .

[From MM on the way to the Admiralty Islands to RFB]
Sydney, Australia
October 18, 1928

Brown is awfully funny. He approves of my work and today, after he had been reading the monograph,[34] he began tea by saying he didn't see how I had gotten away with doing work which was so awfully contrary to the spirit of the American School, the kind of work which Boas didn't believe was possible. I retaliated by saying that Boas had planned my work. He said Lloyd Warner had found the greatest difficulty in being allowed to do such work UNTIL he came out here. I said, strange, he was a student of Kroeber's wasn't he and Kroeber had been so interested in my problem and commented upon how lucky I was to have such a problem. Pause. He also disapproves of Gregory's getting any of it, I've worked him up to that and to tentative suggestions for English publication. I think if he continues to like it, he'll send the whole works to Kegan Paul. The last part could be an appendix and Gregory would have no kick coming for I could use the same argument about leaving his funds free which I used about the Adolescent Girl.[35] . . .

Brown has now gotten to the point where I contrast the institutionalization of kinship in Tonga and Fiji with village institutionalization in Samoa and he is so mad that he was barely civil to me this morning, and didn't introduce me to Elkin who has just come back from the field, and remarked caustically that he'd changed his mind and thought the book shouldn't be published in England, it being the kind of thing which was more appreciated in America. I got the point as disapproval but it wasn't until this afternoon that I knew why. He said, pontifically, that the similarities between Tonga, Fiji and Samoa were much more interesting than the differences. He really is rather insufferable because he is so sulky and rude whenever he is crossed. . . .

I'm worried about that monograph. The rewriting for Gregory is too flat and awful. It's too dull just to make no points at all.

I've a mind to send it all to him and reserve the right to publish any parts which I wish as a book later, and then I would organize a book differently from these first six chapters. Would you be very much disappointed? Gregory is not to publish until I see whether I go to Samoa or not. . . .

Brown identifies himself with every idea he has ever voiced and any disagreement, tacit or uttered, with his ideas he takes as a slap in the face. . . .

[From MM to RFB]
[Sydney, Australia]
October 25, 1928

I am sending you:

(a) *Nation* article with covering letter to Freda Kirchwey[36]

(b) *Mercury* article with covering letter to Mencken[37]

(c) Carbon of two additional pages to be put with the carbon of the Tshi article.[38] Camilla is making the diagram for me and I'm sending it in from here with orders to address all communications to you. This addition I wrote out in a hurry for Papa Franz and didn't type properly. Brown says it's all right though "of course a great deal more could be done with it."

(d) Carbons of a couple of revisions in Chapter I of my monograph.

(e) Two copies of the petition to the Department of Labor which will let Reo into the States. Will you have these sworn to by two witnesses and then send them on to the Department of Labor. The Department sends them back to Australia so you have no more bother with them.

(f) The materials of the application for Reo's fellowship, with the exception of the Dobu manuscript[39] which won't be typed until Monday.

[From MM to RFB]
[Sydney, Australia]
October 27, 1928

I dreamed last night that the book[40] had failed completely, that the publishers had withdrawn it from publication and that the publishers who were doing the monograph had left out the dedication to you. I know what that means — I'm dissatisfied with the monograph.[41] I've not had time to touch it. Brown finally said he had no criticism to offer — probably the most that could be done with the material. . . .

[From RFB to MM]
December 29, 1928

I finished the Dionysian-Apollonian Southwest paper[42] and turned it in. I've a copy for you but I had to leave it this week with Elsie. She went over it carefully and made suggestions. Her comment was that it seemed to her a very good paper, and that her emendations were all further arguments, she thought, along the same lines. Pretty good to fetch conviction to Elsie on so alien a point.

[From RFB to MM in New Guinea]
January 16, 1929

. . . I finished my Century article[43] — on time too — and even had time to show it to Papa Franz. I gave him that and the SW paper[44] and the Animism paper[45] all together, and I trembled when he said he wanted to see me about a point. I'd told him that I thought he'd hate the Century article. But no, "he thought an article like that would do more good than his book. He wished he could write in that way, but he couldn't." — And what he wanted to discuss with me was my point in the Animism article that science couldn't stem from magic! From their point of view he thought it could. He said nice things about the SW paper too. . . .

[From RFB to Reo F. Fortune in the Admiralty Islands]
January 10, 1929

I enjoyed the Dobuan material immensely.[46] After I'd read a couple of hours I'd feel they'd all been sold to the devil. How did you stand it? Did they have sets of subterfuges for eluding the fear they were always institutionalizing? And how did it affect personal relations — at the family hearth did they persist in their picture of an enemy alliance?

I liked your exposition of the kula ring.[47] And the way in which you brought the theories of conception under their general cultural rubric. — For thorough-going difference from our own ways of behavior, you could hardly have hit on a better example.

Yesterday Dr. Boas talked about a plan for not being at Columbia the first half year of 1929–30. It isn't quite time for his next Sabbatical, but he knows he could get it for this October, and he thinks if he takes time by the forelock he could get in another field trip. He's indomitable. I rather guess he'll arrange it so, but it isn't certain. For instance if the new quarters the department is to have in the new Havemeyer Hall are to be ready that semester, he'd stay by to see everything was carried out according to agreement. But it's almost certain that he'll be in time for any move if he's back by the end of January. Margaret said to cable "No Department" if Dr. Boas wouldn't be in charge, but I am quite sure he won't commit himself on the plan for a long while — Not till he's in Europe for the summer maybe.

[From RFF to RFB]
Pere [Admiralty Islands]
May 3, 1929

Thanks very much for your kindness in helping my fellowship.[48] The Dobu material is lacking in much that I'd like to have.[49]

No, there were no sets of subterfuges for eluding the institutionalized fear. They always inferred lack of faith in others, always refused to eat food except from the very few persons trusted (for fear of poison). Maropa, my sorcerer lad, seemed to have a fish with a poisonous gall always to hand concealed in the bush to put in food if necessary (he had while I was there anyway). At the family cook pot the man and wife did not eat together ever that I saw. In resting the man had his place on the house platform, the woman underneath the house. She could never sit beside him on the platform. Inside the house was for sickness only during the day or for sleep. They never ceased to warn me against my going to bathe some twenty minutes before sunset and no one could be induced to accompany me then down the hill to the beach. Fear of the night never lessened — as also fear of neighbours; in bodily form more

in the day, in spiritual form more in the night, though that is no
thorough going distinction.

Thanks awfully for the Hamlet of A. MacLeish. I like it very
well — and better than anything Eliot has written — especially the
seventh, ninth and twelfth passages. The whole thing is so finely
bodied. He feels the matter of the ninth passage more than the
tail of it — which is sorry matter for

> "fight with a shining foil the feigned
> Antagonist for stoops of beer"

But that's a minor point — the poetry is the better for it as a
major point. He conveys philosophic doubt, and cultural doubt
(not his) about sex acutely enough — not enough to keep me
awake at night I might add. But I like his medium and find all
manner of his phrases in my head now and again.

We are looking forward to getting out of primitive society in
overpowering pressure.

[From RFB to MM]
January 30, 1929

Alvin Johnson wrote asking you to do the primitive section of the
article on "child marriage" for the *Encyclopedia of the Social
Sciences* — quite long. I forget the length, to be in the first of
April, for Vol. II. I wrote regretfully declining. If it had been
Education I'd have risked your being late with the contribution
for they could have waited a while, seeing you had such a good
excuse. But I thought it was different with Child Marriage and that
not having library facilities would about rule it out. Anyway there
are plenty more volumes and I knew how you'd hate to be dissatisfied with your first contribution. . . .

[From MM on Omaha Reservation to RFB]
July 21, 1930

This is a very discouraging job, ethnologically speaking. You find
a man whose father or uncle had a vision. You go to see him four
times, driving eight or ten miles with an interpreter. The first time

he isn't home, the second time he's drunk, the next time his wife's sick, and the fourth time, on the advice of the interpreter, you start the interview with a $5 bill, for which he offers thanks to Wakanda, prays Wakanda to give *him* a long life, and proceeds to lie steadily for four hours. This is the more usual procedure interspersed with demands to feast a hundred people before anyone will open their mouths, and one or two cases where people will talk through corruptibility. But they know so little. Practically everything stopped in the days of the old men's fathers. There was no long ritual which would be intact despite disuse. The only interesting points, such as the mechanisms by which a man had the same vision experience as his father, are quite unprovable. If everyone who knew a thing talked, the conditions would still be so aberrant in several cases, and the cases too few to prove anything. There is a belief that death follows divulging sacred things; Joseph La Flesche died ten days after he told Alice Fletcher about the sacred white buffalo robe. And the devil of it is that when they do talk it's nothing. Just little one-line songs. "I'm the tobacco, that's me." It would have been an interesting culture to study with its dynamics because the emphasis on form rather than content would have come out then. But it's no culture to excavate in. What any *one* old man tells you isn't worth beans. . . . They are rich, know very little and fear death if they tell. And anyway, it's not worth getting. The head man of the Marble (Pebble) Society is a Carlisle *graduate*. He's seventy-odd. . . . Would you please write us what you think in terms of worthwhile investment of time and money. The feasts cost a lot to give not only in money, but in time, and spending a whole day at a feast. The conventional thing is to feast everyone from whom you want anything FOUR times. And there is no guarantee that they will tell you anything at the end, no way of checking whether they are telling the truth, and no way of making the stuff coherent and integrated anyhow.

I know you think we are spoiled and will, as you said, be harder too on the conditions than other people will be. But that's a two-edged sword. We are also able to value what we get nearer to what it would be worth gotten in a going culture. If I were going to be an Americanist I would stay in the library most of the time and only emerge to try to verify the most key points after a long search of the literature. For instance there is a place in Texas where the Indians go to pick peyote. If someone who knew a lot like you, could go and camp there for four or five weeks, you'd get informants from every tribe in the middle US, according to the accounts we get here.

. . . I see no way of checking up on material obtained from indifferent, unwilling and frightened informants for money, on what their fathers or grandfathers told them. It isn't the kind of material which ever carries the marks of authenticity on the face of it as verbatim ritual can. It's a case of "You belong to the same society as your father?" "Yes." "Did you have a vision of that society?" "No, no one had visions when I was a boy. The country was all settled and there was no place for a vision." "Who is older, you or SW?" "I am." "Well, SW went out and looked for a vision." No answer from the informant.

This is a culture in which many people refused to give their visions to their own son, but died without giving them; where patients were pledged on pain of death never to repeat the vision which the doctor told them when he doctored them. And they aren't poor enough to be tempted by anything less than $25 or so, and then there is no check on their telling the truth. . . . [It may be] this is what all Americanists are up against, and all of them overcome these insurmountable difficulties and emerge with something, but I am not convinced this is true. And anyway if this is the kind of material they have it is not worth much. After all kinship and social organization can be checked, material culture is tangible if enough survives, but religion of this sort could never have been gotten properly without a mass of detailed evidence, without say a hundred visions of fathers and sons, and material on what they did with them. . . .

Later. More light. Gilmore has been here, financed by Heye, and paid $50 a bundle, insisting on having song and vision. He refused to buy a bundle without the song and vision, so they reckon it is valuable. Now could you see if that information is recorded at the Heye Museum. . . .

Don't think I am a thankless wretch, please. And scold me if you think I still deserve it and am overestimating the difficulties. It costs $100 here to join Peyote. Do you think that is worth doing? It seems dull. We've seen the peyote death ritual. I feel as if I had no sense of values left, when I try to evaluate this work. It has rained after a month's drought. That is one of the mercies.

[From RFB on Apache field trip to MM in New York]
April 14, 1931

. . . He[50] read the AA article[51] and liked it. He only suggested amplifications. He wanted more made of the problem of the individual over against his culture — the range of individual differences and the importance of them. Especially the prime importance in connection with certain problems like those of social control. Then, I take it, the transition at the bottom of page 1 would not be "from these fortuitous omissions" but "from the important problem of individual variability in culture forms to the more elaborate problems of how variously formalized different aspects of culture are in different civilizations, and the method of study in those that are in lesser degree formalized" (or something like that). — Then he suggested that you end the article by drawing up some specific problems to show what is meant — he suggested the problem of social control — for one — how rigid it is and through what channels it is exerted, etc. showing how it can't be done with the old field work.

Is that sensible? My mind is off anthropology and I couldn't honestly tell.

I've been reading Manus[52] with huge delight. And they are clever devils? And it's grand observation. I think an accompanying genealogical table — or tables rather — will make it read more easily and keep one from being so hopelessly lost if one fact has been skipped in the reading. . . .

[From RFB to MM]
New Mexico
Friday, June 12, '31

. . . I've had a good time coming with Papa Franz. He likes to sit around and talk instead of working. He's in Albuquerque today with his Indian, and before we separated on the train he had been talking about what a fool he was not to take more leisure — why, he could come out there on that desert and have his music and a couple of people and do nothing except work up his own material. Why did he go on with Linguistic Journals and Columbia Series? It would only be a few years more before he'd have given them up anyway — why keep them till the last minute? — But it's only a form of speech. . . .

[From RFB on Apache field trip to MM in New York]
El Paso, July 23, 1931

I envy you your chances to talk anthropology with Brown.[53] My two best talkers are Sol and Morris, and they are crass young reformers. I'm glad I got back to school when the pendulum was swung in the opposite direction. The generous enthusiasms of this age group are endearing, but their programs and their great ideas are a weariness to the flesh — the spirit, rather.

[From RFB on Apache field trip to MM in New York]
El Paso, August 8, 1931

I've finished the Reservation Women[54] and it's no end of a good piece of work. I'll send it back Monday, but meanwhile I've let Linton's student, Sol Tax, read it — it's the kind of a problem he thinks he is doing here. . . . And it would be interesting in two generations to have a study of this reservation as it is now — in the hopeful period that for the Omaha is two generations gone. I wonder if any human planning could avert the Omaha tragedy here. I swear every now and again I know it could be done. But I never tell Sol there is a chance — I suppose there isn't. I wish I could *tell* you about it.

[From RFB to MM]
New York, January 20, 1932

First of all I must give my hospital report. Papa Franz is at least well enough to care that he is prone and inactive. At first he didn't even care. Now he cares more when he can't finish a dictation, and he resents not being able to get up or move himself. But of course that is a necessary stage. Some days he works a long time, several hours, but he hasn't strength to move a pen more than a few minutes. However, he's making satisfactory progress, so they say. I told you, didn't I? that the truthful version of his illness seems to be an embolism in the coronary artery (to the muscles of the heart). Of course the condition that causes one blood clot remains and may at any time cause another, but there is very little that can be done to prevent recurring attacks and probably it won't make any great difference even if he works more than he should when he gets stronger. But it is hard to have it always on the horizon. . . .

They're being awfully slow about the Reservation Women MS.[55] Nobody has any money now, and they all hold everything up hoping that if they do the book will come out at a time when more copies can be sold. I sent the Animism article[56] to Seligman for consideration for the JRAI. It's a swell paper. The AA is so desperately slow. My Configurations paper[57] is just out, and the one of yours[58] hasn't appeared yet. . . .

Did you like The Waves? And did you keep thinking how you'd set down everybody you knew in a similar fashion? I did. I suppose I'm disappointed that she didn't include any violent temperaments, and I want my group of persons more varied. I want them to include, not just persons who have a shrug of the shoulders like mine, but persons who haven't, like you and Stanley. . . . It made me realize how Mrs. Woolf's types are circumscribed; she never does anything that isn't essentially mild. This way of setting people down seemed very exciting to me, and I wish a whole crop of authors would try it; then there'd be lots of different sorts of people included. But the talk about The Waves has been mostly about what it means, and it's bored me to death. Well, what is its theme? People have suggested the strangest assortments. To me of course it's just about life's being a wrapping and wrapping oneself in one's own cocoon. What you can spin is all you have to work with, and the result is altogether dependent on that. Don't you think, given the limited types she allows herself, she's done it beautifully? . . .

We've been getting Papa Franz a phonograph. He asked to borrow one, and we've all gone in together to get him a present. I hope he'll like to have it. Anyway he so seldom asks for anything that it's fun to do something when he does. . . .

[From RFB to MM in New Guinea]
July 20, 1932

Tomorrow I am going off to join Mother in the car and I'll be out of New York for a month. It hasn't been bad this three weeks I've been working here. Perfect summer weather. And I've got the library work done that I planned, and written a fair amount, for me. I have to keep your rate of production out of my head, for I can't do anything like it even at my best. But oh how I wish you were here to red pencil and suggest. Do you realize what anthropology is with you and Reo out of the country? Every one of them is either riding some patented horse of his own and only interested in commendations of it, or they are too silly to pay attention to. So I've got out of it by not saying a thing about a book.[59] I'm writing "an article" and then if I get the book done I can say I put some articles together and made a book. They wouldn't need to know that I had to slave to get it together, and that I deliberately did not ask their criticism.

[From RFB to MM]
[Shattuck Farm, Norwich, New York]
July 29, 1932

. . . I'm getting on creditably — for me — with the book, though I can always imagine how much faster you'd have turned it off. It's all straightforward stuff, most of it that I've been over time and again, in lectures and such. But I'm slow and it can't be helped.

Mother is wonderfully peaceable. The two days we spent driving up from the Catskills and visiting college friends of hers were a perfect way of passing time together. The car has certainly been a great addition to our summer. . . .

[From RFB to Reo Fortune]
Shattuck Farm, Norwich, N. Y.
August 2, 1932

Isn't this a nice little review from the *New Republic*? He got the points and said them very well in a paragraph for his readers, don't you think?

I didn't see the one from the *New York Times*. As soon as I get
back to New York I'll go into Dutton's and look over their reviews
and send them to you.

Everybody has liked the book[60] enormously, according to the
measure of his abilities. That means I can like it most! When
small college libraries come asking for accounts of culture they can
buy for the students, I find I tell them Dobu without fail, and give
them choices of others. Those young ever-publishing professors
Schneider and Friess in the philosophy department are getting out
a book on comparative religions for college classes, and they wanted
accounts of three primitive religions. I told them to include Dobu,
and they decided against it because it was an easily available
modern account they could put in the bibliography. So they kept
David looking for a week for a substitute, and I notice they took
Dobu with enthusiasm when they'd looked a little. Their summary
of it in the text I think won't do more than call readers' attention
to your book.

There's a more serious question in connection with my BOOK
I'm writing this summer. Aren't you astonished that I should really
get some 40,000 words already together for a book? . . . It fell
easily into shape, and I'm only seriously dissatisfied because I can't
have you and Margaret read it and hand it back blue pencilled. As
soon as David makes carbons I'll send them on and you can get
your criticisms back before the book is printed.

The theme of course is cultural configurations again. There's a
first chapter on Anthropology Old and New, which is all old stuff
about giving up the concept of THE primitive, etc. It says many of
the same things I said in that old *Century* article[61] about the point
of anthropology. Then there's a chapter on the Diversity of Culture,
how cultures become so different according to the different aspects
of life they capitalize, and how the interpenetration of traits makes
for still more diversity. The next chapter is the Integration of Culture, which is a chapter giving the reasons for thinking that cultures
should be studied as configurations, and speaking of the Germans
who've tried. Then there's a long discussion of the pueblos, contrasting them too with the rest of North America. That's the next
chapter, and long. I'll make there the same points at more length

that are in the Configuration[62] and Abnormal[63] articles. For the
third example I'd choose to use Dobu. The only thing against it is
that you've already put it in shape and said the things that need
saying. It isn't as it is with the Southwest and the Northwest Coast,
a reworking of raw materials. But Dobu is so good, and I feel so
strongly that I wouldn't venture to use a culture that I knew wholly
out of a book without having the chance to talk about it to the
person who knows it — that I've decided to go ahead and write the
chapter. I can make it a discussion that will mostly call attention to
your "sensational material," and direct people to it. And people
need to be told in words of two syllables what contrasting cultures
mean. I wish I knew how you reacted to it. You have said it so well
in your book that I can only sponge. On the other hand I could
use Dobu better than any other as a background for the last chapter
— or I think there'll be two — of the book, which will be an expansion of the Culture and the Abnormal paper, a discussion of the
adjustment of the individual to his cultural type.

If you think it would be awful of me to take the words out of
your mouth this way, cable me collect, just "Don't," and I'll understand. But as this couldn't come till after the chapter was written
you'll get a carbon of my draft anyway. In the chapter on Integration I discuss my reasons for choosing just these three cultures, and
say that I've both been able to talk them over with the persons
who've done the field work, and that the chapters have been read by
the field workers. So I'll get the Dobu chapter off to you for blue
pencilling just as soon as I can.

[From RFB to MM]

August 10, 1932

I wrote a letter to Reo last week when I was turning over in my
mind the choice of illustrative chapters in my book. I've written
him an outline of the book, so stop and read it. If I were properly
forethoughtful I'd have thought the problem all out six months ago
and had his answer by this time. But I hadn't really thought I'd
need to take one of yours or Reo's cultures — because you do them
so well I can only parrot your points. And with the pueblos and the

NWC[64] that isn't so. But there just isn't any assurance in using other people's cultures for a discussion like this (other field workers', I mean). Even in North America I can't do anything but guess. And in Africa it's hopeless. . . .

I've turned over titles and titles. I want the title of the book to clearly indicate that my competence is in anthropology, nothing else. That is, I don't want any psychologizing title. I shall suggest "Primitive Peoples: An Introduction to Cultural Types." Have you suggestions? It can be changed much later.

I hadn't realized till I came to plan this work how all the points I've worked on all fall into the same outline. Did you like the Culture and the Abnormal paper?[65] I haven't placed it in all this time, because I've had some changes I wanted to make and didn't get at. I haven't sent it out at all since I got it back from Schmalhausen. . . .

August 17

. . . You will have a swell book on The Child in Culture.[66] Think of anyone's having five cultures to draw on at first hand. . . . I ought to do something about it, and go myself, but I think it's my cue to stay by the department. You must certainly give a course in Methods — as you say, really *methods* this time. You know Papa Franz has been corresponding with Rhoads about courses that would be required for certain appointments in the Indian Service, and that might someday work out. Any example from English colonial administration is so far above their heads right now that they only sit and stare. But it's a possible field, and would call for another kind of "methods" course. I don't know anyone who could give it half so well as you could.

The whole business of the department is completely guesswork as far as any predictions go. Papa Franz writes that he's walking as spryly as ever, two miles a day. He has made a practice of daily stints, daily increased, and has progressed well. But there's no foretelling. With finances as they are now Columbia will not bring anyone else so long as Papa Franz holds out. Besides, I think they have learned that the proper order of procedure would be to retire him before they brought there a full professor with authority. So all I can see at the present moment is to consolidate my position. Then when the time comes we'll see.

[From RFB to MM]
September 8, 1932

I'm glad you wrote about how strong a commitment you were getting to anthropology — as if you hadn't had it for some time, but then I know the difference too. I've gone in that direction too. You won't know what to make of my seriousness when you get back. . . .

[From RFB to MM]
September 18, 1932

. . . I took the first three chapters of my book and the one on Zuñi down to Knopf's Monday, and told them I thought they could judge from that section whether they could publish it or not. They're sewed up with Goldenweiser's magnum opus, he tells me, and they know they're going to have to take all the punishment that's coming to them on that. So they may not feel like risking any more sheets on anthropology. Anyway I'd like to know what chance there is of publishing it without waiting for the depression to lift.

Has anybody told you that there's still a growing optimism about the return of prosperity.

[From RFB to MM]
October 9, 1932

. . . The first four chapters of my book are ready, and I am holding them till the next boat thinking I can get two more to put with them. It's hard with classes beginning and reviewing and the rest but you'd be amazed at the work I get done. Or I hope you would. It's an improvement anyway. It makes me realize how much energy always went into the mere background of living at all. . . . I don't write verses anymore, but in my present mood I can well do without them. I wonder how you'll like me when you get home, as a quite cheerful and easily pleased matron. It's not worth worrying about yet: heaven knows what I may be by the time you're back. Your comment on my liking bad scrappy ethnology better than good and finished work (La Flesche died last month) came just in time to amuse me while I was doing Kwakiutl. For of course I enjoyed it. Tons of raw material entirely reliable, and a minimum of interpretation or explanation. Of course it's not true that I like it better than Dobu, for instance, or Manus Social Organization,[67] but it's a kind of field work where I don't have to go around to feasts or lay myself out to stupid old women, and of course I enjoy it.

[From RFB to MM]
October 16, 1932

I'm so glad you came to the same conclusion I had about the material I could use for the configuration point. In the AA article[68] I didn't have any sense of attempting to prove the Navaho Diony-sian, but only of showing where their reported burial customs tied up in the general distribution of traits. But of course I can't use them, or even Plains, for a description of the way their culture worked. I'm feeling quite bored with my book just now, for it seems fairly elementary. However it gives reasoned descriptions of SW [69] and NWC [70] and the pictures hang together rather well. Then it gives me a chance to introduce a little sophistication into the dis-cussion of the deviant in a culture. The carbons of the first four chapters go to you on this boat.

You write about the numbers of configuration classifications you might get by going through the cultures of the world, and how help-less we are without stable classifications the psychologists ought to have provided us with. It would make it neater if they had, but I don't know that it would be any guarantee of good anthropological work in cultures. I feel about it just as I do about a novelist's getting down his character with the correct motivations, etc.; it might help him to have had Freud investigate it for him first, but usually all it's done is to take his eyes off the real person he's de-scribing, and it's actually vitiated more character-drawing than it's helped. I know I feel that way about it because what I'm funda-mentally interested in is the character of the culture and the relation of that institutionalized character to the individual of that culture. I can see that there are other problems, but I can't see that we're in a position yet to deal with them. God, though, when I think of all the material you'll be able to control by the time you come back this next time, I think we needn't limit any of our problems — you'll have enough to make a stab at any of them.

I read Sapir's article[71] a little differently from the way you did, and the difficulty lies in knowing what he would have said anyway in the terms of the concepts I was using. I understood him to say that centrifugal cultures (ones with many uncoordinated elements) were spurious, and centripetal ones (well-coordinated) genuine. Then he remarks that genuine cultures are poised, satisfactory, etc., etc., spurious ones muddled, unsatisfactory, etc. Therefore I remarked that homogeneous cultures could be built on basic ideas far from gracious, etc., etc., and that the fact that a society indulged in pretentiousness and hypocrisy might be because it had a most well-coordinated culture which expressed itself in that form. I think you're right that I'd have made my point better if I'd put it the other way around [and] challenged him on his description of centrifugal societies. But I don't feel sure about them.

[From RFB to MM]

November 30, 1932

Sapir has been down for Ethnological,[72] and it was pretty bad. All his charm couldn't carry him to victory in the face of his thinness of material. The speech was on Function and Pattern in modern anthropology, and it was aimed at Radcliffe-Brown. It wasn't a fair statement at all, if your version of his beliefs isn't all poppycock. But there's no reason why it should be fair. And the point of interest was that Edward's got a new way to free himself from the necessity of admitting the role of culture. He analyzed his reactions to football, and he drew the moral that every phase of culture — in all cultures — is all things to all people, and that this concept dissolves Function, i.e. it outlaws Radcliffe-Brown's contentions. Well! All I got out of it was that Edward had satisfactorily phrased his quarrel with the universe again — satisfactorily to himself — and that the next great anthropological contest would very likely be waged between Sapir and Radcliffe-Brown as protagonists.

[From RFB to MM]
Atlantic City
December 28, 1932

What a feebleminded institution these anthropological meetings[73] turn this place into! You've forgotten probably — I had — how bad it can be. And Lowie isn't here, nor Sapir (nor Kroeber). Papa Franz is the one resource. It's not even any good hoping I can trump up any fellow feeling for Radcliffe-Brown. He is condescending to save all our souls, mine with the rest, and he certainly doesn't mince matters. He told me in the first three minutes that he was getting from two students "the first" two studies of American Indian social organization: Sol Tax for the Fox and Eggan for the Hopi. . . . And [Sol] has now spent six weeks with the broken down Fox and can't even control the kinship terminology . . . (let alone knowing anything of the language). Eggan was with this year's laboratory group ("Oh, he just ignored that stupidity and went on his own way independently" R. Brown) and I said something about his having one advantage over Sol in that the society was less broken down (exogamy is completely lost in Fox). "Oh," he said, "They never had exogamy. They have a system that *functions*. If you must talk of broken down cultures there's Dobu.[74] That's broken down for you; they have lost the functioning of their system. But not Fox." I said mildly that it was one of the interesting things in NA Ethnology how many of these missionized Americanized groups had made functioning adjustments in culture. And I let it go at that.

If only he held to a high standard of achievement and required language control, intimacy with total culture, fundamental understanding of kinship, I could understand his scorn of work so far done in America. He could scorn work in broken cultures too. But to thrust this kind of work under my nose as the salvation of the world, it's sad. I asked him if he didn't think Opler's Apache Social Organization[75] was a satisfactory study and he said, "Oh very confused as it came in first, but in the end when I'd whipped it in shape, very good, very good." — And I knew every twist and turn in the preparation of that MS: the one gap that Opler filled in — and proved I was right — on his return trip was the one I had pointed out to him after Chicago had Oked his thesis. Why not?

I know my NA material and Brown doesn't. It's nothing against
him, but it's silly of him to take such a line with me.

Perhaps you'll understand justifications in Brown's remarks that
I don't see. He seemed to me impenetrably wrapped in his own
conceit, and I certainly shan't feel justified in working to have him
appointed at Columbia. Of course my judgment may be premature.
. . . I've got to be shown. As it stands, I don't think Brown is
fighting for good work over against bad, but for work done by disciples over against work done by non-disciples. And that's fatal.

The Radcliffe-Brown speech comes tomorrow. I enclose the
program, and I told you about it in my last letter — about my part
in the "symposium." From Cole's activities here I gather it's to be
a big "get together brothers" gesture. . . .

I wish I could know your and Reo's reaction to my impatience
with Brown. I certainly don't feel like signing up with him against
all other American anthropologists and nothing less, I think, would
make relations endurable. I am terribly disappointed. . . . I am
glad that you and Reo don't have to work just for approbation from
these powers that be, but that we care to satisfy our *own* requirements.

[From RFB to MM]
Atlantic City
December 29, 1932

I'm reneging on Richard Tolman's Physics lecture, it's slides and
I could steal out. . . . The "conference" was all a declination of
combat. Cole told about the field techniques he had used to produce
his invaluable study in the Philippines and Radcliffe-Brown talked
about the interrelation of cultural traits. I at least — in my speech
— did not have interference in my flow of language, and afterwards
Papa Franz made a little speech, and Buck put in a delightful plea
to the effect that if we in authority would provide the wherewithal
the field workers could perhaps live up to the requirements — but
how do it on the money that was available for a piece of work.

The note they all emphasized was that the work could not be
judged by the time invested. Cole advised tearing up one's first

three months' note books. RB was stern with people who stayed short whiles and wrote books. Buck said one must stay *years*. You'd better dig yourselves in the manner of BM in the Trobriands and make yourselves comfortable. It will be counted to you as virtue. *Don't kill yourselves.* RB said he "required" a minimum of two years to a study. What do you make of that? I was altogether hot under the collar.

RB ended on a very weak note, I thought. He rose to dispute my point that change could be reconstructed from distribution, and he went into detail over the t-k shift between Hawaii and N.Z. "But," he said, "that tells us nothing about *how* change occurred. That chance is provided now in Samoa where the same change is occurring today" etc. I didn't call him publicly but afterwards I asked him what observations he would make to give us data on Samoa on how this shift occurred — (that was his point) — and he said: "Oh, but I'm not a linguist. Let them make the tests." "But would you expect to get in the end more than the fact that the change had occurred?" "Oh but you would have observed it." I am quoting but I wish you were here to put sense into it. Privately I think he's a sensationalist who gets a sense of validity only from first hand contact.[76] But more than that is his sense of a category of disciples and non-disciples, of course.

The Papa has come through the meetings very well — he hasn't been dragged down at any time as he sometimes is even after a Columbia lecture. He made his retiring President's speech on "The Aims of Anthropological Research" [77] — one of those close-packed meaty summaries that nobody can read without a key. I'll send you a copy. It's his testament. But nobody will ever do any shouting over it.

[From RFB to MM]
January 6, 1933

I'm distressed about what you write of Reo's reaction to my using Dobu in the configurations book.[78] Of course I haven't had the letter from him, but of course I'd rather not use the material if he has even a lingering objection. I thought you'd both be relieved that

I had come independently to the same conclusion that you had, that points that could only be made by the institutional facts of the case, like Plains, for instance, shouldn't be used. At best they're only suggestive. But I don't see the "dangerous generalization" where you can command both the institutions and the way people use their institutions.

It seems to me too that the same institutions can be used to opposite ends according to the set of the culture, just as you say. But I always had thought that. I wish you'd written more about the nature of the "dangerous generalization." But before long you will have had the chapters of the book and will write your criticism of those. I shall wait for those letters. All the criticism I've had so far is N—'s on antecedents of relative pronouns and conjunctions — very useful — and Otto's on not having authority to quote for every sentence I deliver myself of — it scares him like anything even to see anybody saying something other people haven't said all their lives — and Papa Franz's on substituting "clam" for "mussels." Of course Papa Franz made other points too, but practically nothing. And Lesser, who hasn't read it, bawls at me, "How does it explain coiled basketry?" as if I'd claimed to have a vade mecum. It bores me so that if you call attention to a simple point that hasn't had due notice, they act as if you thought it was the sum total of all wisdom.

I'm awfully off the book just now. I didn't touch it during vacation, and I'm certainly not doing anything on it now. Of course there's very little time, but more than that I'm out of the mood. The mood will come back. But I probably shan't be working on it for the next couple of months.

[From RFF to RFB]
Marienberg, Sepik River, M.T.N.G.
November 21, 1932

Of course use the Dobuan material if it's really good enough.[79] I like it very well that you think it's such, and then like it very well again and then have no different feeling.

Even casually considered — as perhaps for Schneider and Friess, whom I don't know — the more it rises from the dead the better.

I'm much more likely to be elated by your using it, however, than casual, and I'm sure you'll use it interestingly.

I am planning to write something about incest when I emerge — as a first thing. The Encyclopedia[80] hacked my sentences so severely that I am not sure that any idea is apparent in the article they and I wrote for them. What I meant to say about it was that if people kept to themselves they might be disliked and that if they did so obtrusively they might be equally obtrusively penalized. Now on the Sepik[81] I have encountered a more incest ridden place than has yet been described properly, as far as I know. The sanctions are little more than a "free-for-all," and very willing the free for all is. . . . Brothers fight brothers freely, and sons, fathers. The shield is very effective against spears — so much so that the whole contest might as well be that of secret magic for the physical harm done in most cases. Rarely a man gets killed. But the bitterest feeling is within the family. It is very much more pathological than Dobu. Women get killed somewhat oftener than men, as they depend on the men they espouse — not carrying shields themselves. So sometimes a brother kills a sister or a father a daughter for eloping and not securing a male of the family a wife in exchange. A queer society, isn't it? I have a great conviction about societies not yet described that the limits of outrage are not nearly plumbed yet.

I'm looking forward to being back someday — a deal of work here yet though.

[From RFB to RFF]
February 10, 1933

It was awfully good to get your letter cordially serving up your Dobuan material to me. When I wrote you about it I thought that if I put off writing it as long as I have, you'd be back to talk it over and be general mentor. That isn't going to be so, now that all the international complications have conspired to keep you a whole extra year in the field, and I shall be cursing England and its abandonment of the gold standard [82] all the time I'm writing. I'll do it as soon as I can too, so that I can get it off to you and get it back with your criticisms before the whole thing is off my chest and in print.

As a matter of fact I haven't touched the book since last fall when I finished the Kwakiutl. I shall be looking forward to yours and Margaret's criticisms on the manuscript, and when they come I'll go over the whole thing and begin over. I want to do a final chapter on psychological implications, and one on sociological, and I've found the reading for them very discouragingly thin. Not thin in quantity, though, worse luck. . . .

I'm already imagining more details of your scandalous Sepik culture[83] you write of. You know I like them scandalous, and the possibilities you touch on are endless, aren't they? I'm full of curiosity. But the place didn't sound well on paper, and I was delighted when word came that you'd left. I hope this new field [84] has no physical characteristics of the last one, and that you're quite comfortable. I miss you both terribly — think of me with no one to talk anthropology to . . . and I resent the English action in relation to the gold standard! Keep as well and as comfortable as you can. All best wishes, and much gratitude for the Dobu.

[From RFB to MM]
March 10, 1933

I wonder what news of this crazy civilization leaks in to your wilds. What with all the furor over banks, and the poor administration getting office the very day when the whole country closes all its financial dealings, we sound pretty rocky. . . . When the bank holiday is over and we find out how much of depositors' money is gone for good, there may be repercussions, but right now there's a good deal of cheerfulness. . . .

I even got a pretty present this week — for I'd kissed it goodbye and had no idea I'd ever get it again. It's my thousand dollars of Extension salary. Papa Franz made a great gesture of forswearing his, when the University was hard put to it for funds. But I said, No, I didn't think they'd give me extension money another year if they were under economizing pressure, but I'd wait till they acted. Evidently the dean called Papa Franz about continuing mine, and Papa Franz approved, and I get the thousand just as I have before.

This last week the papers carried the announcement of the newly added stars in Who's Who. The list is pretty silly, but there were only three women: two zoologists and me. So we were figured like dancing bears. I'll send the anthropology list. . . . Of course it's an age-group classification, but just the same I had added your name and Bunny's to the list which came to me last winter to vote on, and Papa Franz had added Gladys's. . . . The *Tribune* interviewer was a moron; she asked me about women anthropologists, and in the interests of a bigger and better review she wrote it up about women scientists. And she asked me if I liked domesticity, and what my hobbies were, and palmed me off as remarking on a chief interest in being impersonal. The *Daily Mirror* put in a write up under a column called Caviar, and I'm followed by "Delicatessen in Grand Street" or something like that.

I've been waiting for the *Times* Sunday article[85] to appear. They cut it very intelligently, I thought — the agent left it to them — but they telephoned in considerable perturbation that they thought the article wasn't clear on the point of *why* the men had to keep the women under! I tried to reassure them. That will be another $150 bond to lay aside for you. . . .

I had a letter from the editor of *Man* this week.[86] It's the first indication I've had out of them since I wrote them last September. They said that they had waited to receive an answer from Hart — but I'll enclose the letter. I'll write him that I am sure their summary and expression of regret will cover the case. Do you notice that the letter is dated Jan. 25, and got here this week?

I wrote Lowie sending the note about the changed title of the Omaha book,[87] and saying also that alternatively the reviewer might give the facts. It seemed to me that that would really be best, for then in any clipping or reference the review would give the information, whereas if it were tucked away in a note the person who was interested might not easily find it. . . .

I've had all the work I could do, without accomplishing anything on my own. I've had lots of students' field material to read, and I've worked considerably on the theory course, i.e. "Methods" so-called. I organized it into a consideration of methodology in historical reconstructions; tropical studies (Westermarck Marriage, Beaglehole Property, Boas Art etc.); functional studies. We're in the

middle of the middle topic now. The great excitement is provided
by Al Lesser who comes regularly to get the low-down. . . . It
makes the class realize that these issues are live ones, and it holds
me to greater care, I guess, than if that flock of sheep were all that
were sitting at my feet. They are so lamb-like. . . .

[From RFB to MM]
April 25, 1933

I've waited until the day of the next boat was almost here, hoping
that more letters would perhaps come from you. I feel so much the
need of bulletins. I haven't had any description of the new field [88]
or of conditions one might expect there, and that in itself always
makes me sit on the edge of the chair. . . . Besides I haven't any
way of guessing how long a gap there's likely to be in mail consign-
ments from Ambunti.[89] I comfort myself that even if I had new
letters just off the boat, the effect in a return letter to you would
still be just the same as it is now. At the very best a round trip
letter takes five months, as much water can flow under the bridge in
five months as in seven.

[From MM in Tchambuli to RFB]
March 18, 1933

I keep composing letters to him, as "Dear Brown, We hear that
the Fox and the Ojibwa are functioning cultures, so we have
decided to stay out among the broken down ones, Love and kisses,"
etc.[90] However I just did write him a long letter about Mundugumor . . . and I probably shan't bother. His field work and his
handling of concrete material is beautiful, he's a charming and
stimulating lecturer and he's very good for his students. His fundamental approach I never did think would save the world. I just
thought it was useful in getting field work done more intelligently.
After all he starts with a philosophical premise: society is for the
purpose of enabling people to live together, and all the rest of his
thinking is deductive — just as Malinowski starts with a double
premise, Brown's and also Society must satisfy the inherent needs of

the individual, and then he goes on deductively from there. I am more and more convinced that there is no room in anthropology for philosophical concepts and deductive thinking. Of course Papa Franz has always stood for empirical thinking, but he has never really determined what the data are in social anthropology on which the thinking is to be based. . . . Brown has no tact and no politi- cal sense . . . and needs a nurse.

. . . I am writing this in an interval between dusk and dark, when it is too dark to read my finely written linguistic notes. The lamp is now lit but it is not functioning even as well as the Fox Exogamy. . . . I think my job is safer with me out here, than with me there.[91] It would seem like cruelty to children to fire me alone among the cannibals.

March 21

I am going to send this all off tomorrow. I've had a tremendous spurt of energy and I've gotten the key to this culture from my angle — got it yesterday during hours of sitting on the floor in a house of mourning.[92] Now it's straight sailing ahead, just a matter of working out all the ramifications of my hunch. In fact I think we've both had our big moments[93] in this culture and the rest of the time will be just steady working ahead, verifying, recording, amplifying and learning the dashed language which is really awful. Learning five syllable words and six syllable names is very wearing, and it's a closed community of 540 people, too good a thing not to do in perfect detail, but a fair facer of a job.

We[94] all liked *Year before Last*. I think the reason I didn't like it even better is that she, like the author of *Maurice Guest*,[95] can't put herself in, and she's "Hannah." Therefore one loses mightily. I had to identify with Martin and that's not right. . . . Marian Miller sent me a grand tin box of candy and *Father Malachy's Miracle*. . . . I am saving it against possible illness.

Someone sent me a clipping with a picture of Papa Franz in it and I've put it up in the room-wire mosquito room and I find it makes me very happy to have it there. I am going to write him as soon as I get a minute. Today has not been such a good day, fussing around in the night with canvasses to keep out a storm, a dark rainy morning, failure of scouts to report an event in Kilimbit hamlet,

Tchuikumban so sleepy from staying up all night blowing flutes that he was useless for linguistics, a very horrible yaws sore to dress — half a toe eaten away and a horrible stench, problem of what is to be done about getting some flour now that all our stores are probably burned up [in a fire on the pinnace bringing them from Madang], horrible lot of gnats, etc. etc. But I've been riding such a high horse for the last three days that some come-down was inevitable. . . .

This culture is a very good one, working hard, well rounded and functioning. And it is a lovely place.

[From MM to RFB]
[From the Sepik, undated, 1933]

I'd give anything to have you here so that I could watch your face as I talked, and then perhaps I wouldn't say anything wrong. Because I have a fair number of comments to make,[96] more I think than you ever made on my work which deserves it so much more. But I think that must be taken as a question of temperament. And then I used to bring you the things sentence by sentence. And I keep thinking, that it's so very important that you should write the book and that I've been wanting you to write it for the last five years and that if I should discourage you about it, I'd be miserable. And on the other hand, we're really all you have to depend on to save you from the wolves, and therefore we ought to say everything that we can think of. So here goes, and try to see me saying it, wrinkling my brows and making awful faces to get it clear, and ready to fly if I should say the wrong thing.

The Zuñi chapter is grand. I've written in a few little comments, but they are all routine, mainly concerned with making the stuff intelligible to people who don't know the South West. And that chapter and the Northwest Coast will be the most important, of course. But the order and arrangement of the rest worries me. It's written to some four or five audiences varying from the intelligent man in the street, through the very junior student in the social sciences, philosophers, people with race prejudice which clouds their otherwise existing erudition, etc. And then there are sections sufficiently cryptic to have been written to me, now, after all we've talked. The result has had a bad effect on your style, the texture is all uneven and choppy, sometimes intimate, sometimes heavily formal, sometimes colloquial or journalese, sometimes in the jargon of anthropology and sometimes in the phrases of good literature. I think it's mainly because you have taken old material, written at different times for different audiences — the *Century* article,[97] the *Anthrop.* article[98] and the Broken vessels sketch[99] for instance and strung them together, not really rewriting them from the ground up. If you'll take the whole manuscript and first deciding who you are writing towards, read it straight through from the point of view of that person, stopping to consider at each point his vocabulary, general information, and also his special knowledge. If you do this I think you'll see what I mean and pick the changes which need to be made. It would be a bad accident if your feeling for style and texture were to be spoilt by an accident of assembling of miscellaneous source materials, plus an evident consciousness of trying to write so that Papa Franz and Lowie will approve. Their words, and also Malinowski's words are all wrong in your style, actually all wrong in your thinking. Reo and I have been talking over who to choose. I should think that if you had David read it, mark every passage which seemed to her obvious or worn material, query every point which she didn't understand perfectly, that might be good. . . . I am inclined to think that if you do this, a great deal would fall out as incongruous. Of course I am not sure whether you are writing an essay in social theory, or an essay in the philosophy of cultural temperament, or a book which, under the guise of dealing with this point is to put over a lot of other points also. I am afraid that it is the latter and I don't think it is best. The point is too fine to be muddied about with diffusion and evolution and race prejudice and all the rest of it. I'd scrap the first chapter forever, and I'd put the theoretical discussion like the relationship between your point and diffusion after the three cultures. I'd write a short introduction along the lines of the "arc of human experience and the sounds in language" — but omitting the further illustrations as too slight to carry the point — for it needs a whole culture to do so.

And I'd leave out all the adolescence point and the war point —

for as Reo says it's just a Lowie "they do and they don't point"
while what you want to say is "they do and they don't incredibly"
and it takes a whole culture to do that.

So it would run a brief introduction — all straight theme with no
history and no side lines or morals about race equality or culture
consciousness — *Then* the three cultures — then the theoretical
point — in relation to psychiatry, diffusion, etc. Make it a single
theme essay — all in your own style — scrap all the other articles —
don't ever look at them, and aim at a high audience. It will then
be a fine thing, consistent in itself and with you, with no Boasian-
Lowie-ish-Germanic scraps in it.

You know I think the point is awfully important and I only want
you to do it perfectly — forgetting all the routine things you think
you ought to do — And I do hope this comment is intelligible.

[From RFB to MM]

May 19, 1933

. . . Classes are over and I'm working on the book.[100] I'm distressed that you don't like it, the part you've seen. But I've consulted everybody I can think of about omitting the first two chapters,
and they are strong against it. Even the anthropology people I've
asked about it, like Bunny and Otto, want them kept. God knows
I've tried to put it so they wouldn't give me an answer just to flatter
me. Maybe I can't forestall it. Anyway I've gone over the chapters
and cut and rearranged. I've left out discussion of diffusion and
evolution, for instance. Well, I hope you won't think it's all awful.
I'm distressed that you didn't get the chapter on the Northwest
Coast and the article on the abnormal.[101] I'm sending them both.
The abnormal is coming out this fall in Murchison's journal. . . .

[From RFB to MM]

July 2, 1933

. . . I've been working on the book[102] and on Zuñi Tales[103]
(they're to be published this fall). I wish you'd sent the book MS
with your marginal notes, and perhaps I'd have been able to do

something about it. The blanket disapproval I can't do much with, but I've tried to bring the first chapters closer to my own standards. — I haven't sent you the Northwest Coast chapter, nor the Abnormal article[104] because I've only one carbon of each and I have to use those till I get the discussions in shape. It will be better to send them to you after I'm more nearly satisfied, too.

[From RFF to RFB]
[London, undated; received
by RFB January 5, 1934.]

Your book, Ruth, just to hand.[105] Looks very cheerful and magnificent. I looked at myself in it for a moment being vain and thought maybe we've been building something after all — it's so dull mostly with people being jealous and actively hostile or else indifferent absolutely indifferent — and you so kind the way you believe what is so after all — everyone else just doubting whether one didn't make it all up till one wonders whether one did, or whether one makes them up — these doubters —

It looks fine — and you really are kind the way you take it and you say it all so well — it makes me think of the place and the people and not of my book at all, because that's crudely assertive — and not put with the use of a quick telling style that's possible where one's readily believed and is such an improvement in its ready quick but adequate passage — where putting it down first is lumpy with lumps and bumps of facts in assertion that are a mess — sheer mess in style. . . .

It looks grand and I'm pleased all round.

Part IV

The Years as Boas' Left Hand

Margaret Mead

——————

FROM THE time Ruth Benedict entered Columbia University, in 1921, Boas had shown active interest in and concern for her ability. In a letter to Elsie Clews Parsons, who was at this period giving money generously through an instrument called the Southwest Society, which made the gifts formal but not anonymous, he wrote on February 9, 1923:[1]

My dear Elsie,

I have given further thought to the wish you expressed yesterday of finding someone to help you with your work.

I wonder whether it would not appeal to you to arrange the matter in a somewhat different way; namely to engage someone who would work out such notes as the genealogies to which you referred yesterday and to whom you would at the same time give the task of working out independently one of the big problems of the Southwest which we need to solve and which we do not have time to attend to. I am thinking, for instance, of the question of comparative mythology. The advantage of such an arrangement would be that you would give an opportunity for research work to one of our young anthropologists and in that way help pave the way towards future expansion of our work.

If a plan like this would appeal to you, I should suggest Mrs.

341

Benedict as a possible candidate for the position you have in mind.

Mrs. Parsons replied on the following day:[2]

Dear Dr. Boas,

I like the suggestion about Mrs. Benedict. It doesn't quite meet my personal need, for there is work merely for a copyist which I wouldn't give her, but for that perhaps I can find somebody else. But there is that mythology, also considerable work on kinship terms for a paper I am sending to the Royal Anthro. Institute. And of course other subjects will develop for all of us. If she could get to work at once on the comparative tales, could you not use the references for your Keresan texts.

I wish you would talk over the matter with her — amount of time, pecuniary arrangements, etc.

With this, Ruth Benedict began her first paid work in anthropology.

Her relations with Mrs. Parsons were never easy[3] and usually were mediated through Boas. Their later letters are filled with worries and laments about the complexities of Mrs. Parsons' methods of work and her unfailing but idiosyncratic generosity, to which so many field workers were indebted. Mrs. Parsons always completely rewrote her own work after it was set up in proof, an infuriating habit to the editors of a journal with insufficient funds, most of which were supplied by Mrs. Parsons. Things were made no easier by the circumstance that Mrs. Parsons' approach was uncongenial to Ruth Benedict, even though Mrs. Parsons conceived of it as a faithful following of Boas' methods. All this ran like an undertaste through the review which she wrote of Mrs. Parsons' *Pueblo Indian Religion*.[4]

In the very tight economy of those days jobs were for those who needed money. The wife of a professor at Cornell Medical College did not need money. The position at Barnard College, which would have been the appropriate one for her, Boas was planning to give to Gladys Reichard, who was not married and did need a job. Ruth Benedict was just too old for the fellowships which were opening up — thirty-five years was their upper limit. As Stanley Benedict was fundamentally repelled by the idea of her taking up a profession, communication between them — always difficult, always dependent upon intensity as a medium — became still more difficult. She felt that she must earn a sufficient living to support herself on the days when she stayed in the city to work for anthropology, and not ask Stanley to underwrite this. By 1926, they were even discussing the possibility that she might have to teach in some other city and that they might have to meet for week ends by plane instead of by train as they were then doing. But in Boas' eyes, she was a wife, amply supported and with the obligations of a wife, someone for whose talents he must find work and a little money, someone on whom he could not make extreme demands and for whom he need not be responsible.

In the great network of responsibility in which he lived, carrying in his mind the vanishing materials of the primitive world, the un-published work of dozens of collaborators, the economic needs of the exiled, the irresponsible, and the handicapped, trying to find funds for publication, and making time to edit, time to write up his own great bodies of materials, anyone who could stand on his or her own feet in any way was a relief. I myself did not have half a dozen conferences with him during my whole period as a student or, later, as someone doing research under his inspiration or direction. If he thought we could manage, he turned with a sigh to those who needed help, guidance, and direction. But those for whom he did not have to take such responsibility sometimes felt severely neg-lected.

In her letters to Boas in 1923, Ruth Benedict already shows her growing intellectual relationship to him, the desire to know what he would say about this or that, as she worked over her material. After the field trip among the Serrano in the summer of 1922, she spent the summer of 1923 with Stanley in their summer home on Lake Winnepesaukee. From there she wrote to Boas in September:[5]

> . . . All summer I've worked on the mythology and I don't suppose a day has ever passed that I haven't wished fervently I could ask you some question, or wondered what you thought

of some difficult coincidence in the stories. I've acquired considerable material but I haven't set to work to tabulate it yet,
nor even tried to summarize anything. . . .

I've been acquiring enough Spanish to read the untranslated
tales. You knew I'd have to do it, but I smiled at your tact in
letting me find it out for myself. . . .

She came back in the autumn of 1923, to go on working in the
Columbia University Library on the concordance of mythology,
laboriously and meticulously setting down the occurrence of incidents or themes among different tribes on thousands of little slips,
which are now brown and crumbling and look like this:

O Kanagon   MAFLS11:92

1) Thompson-MAFLS6:56; JE8:229, 338; Shuswap JE2:669
   Fraser Delta-Boas-Sagen 42; Lillovet JAFL25:229 Carrier
   TC15:125
3) Bol & Pol 2:318,516—Quebec JAFL29: 37, 41

When this became unbearably tedious, she turned to working out
half-recorded kinship systems, a task which was rather like reconstructing a chess game in which one had been given only one-third
of the moves randomly distributed. It was during this period that
she sharpened her taste for working with imperfect materials to
which she herself could add the organizing touch.

The department had tiny, cramped quarters in the old Journalism
Building — two offices and a seminar room where all the classes were
held and where students worked between classes. In a letter of
September, 1922,[6] Boas wrote Ruth Benedict not to try to climb
the seven flights of stairs because the elevator was out of order.
Other students began to get used to looking for her in the seminar
room to talk about all sorts of things, and her gentle, faraway accessi-
bility provided a kind of center in a department in which the professor was harried, shy, and abrupt in first contacts. Dr. Marion
Smith tells the story of her first words with Boas, who stopped her

after class, looked at her piercingly from under his bushy eyebrows —
a look which the accident of his weeping eye made much fiercer—
and said, "You should work in primitive art or primitive religion."
No more. Then one went and asked Ruth Benedict what he meant.
And he had very probably already mentioned to her his hopes and
worries about a student. He would walk with her down to the
weekly anthropological lunches at the Stockton Tearoom on West
109th Street, and communication grew apace.

At the same time the atmosphere of the department was being
humanized as first one of his Barnard graduate secretaries, Esther
Schiff Goldfrank, and then a second, Ruth Bunzel, moved from the
close relationship of a secretary to that of a student. Within the
German Jewish ethos which they shared, the remote, frightening
Herr Professor became "Papa Franz" to all of us. There was a period
when he signed his letters to Ruth Benedict "Papa Franz"; later,
with a growing sense of partnership, he again signed them "Franz
Boas."

Although people were to talk a great deal about the "Boas
school," there was actually no such thing, for Boas had neither ador-
ing followers nor uncritical collaborators. The stern training his
students received from him was designed to set them on their own
feet. True, wherever he held control — as an editor or as an adviser
on an expedition or on the granting of funds — he was uncompromisingly strict and brooked no opposition. His influence spread
through American anthropology like an animated veto, seldom exercised but haunting the imagination of those who had absorbed —
almost always by direct contact, for his published work communicated very little — his methodological standards of enough facts
first. When Goldenweiser and Wissler published general books, our
little anthropological world held its breath; we had heard that "Boas
didn't believe in generalizing." But it was a lonely kind of domi-
nance of character embodied in method, and he had remarkably
little close contact even with students who admired and helped him.
In the early 1920's, Pliny Earl Goddard, who had become almost a
dilettante, spending pleasant summers in the Southwest but getting
nothing written up, became conspicuously devoted to Boas, and
Boas accepted this uncritical, sentimental devotion as he might

have accepted the affection of one of the women of his family, with a shy, warm little smile. With Mrs. Parsons his relationship was always a little formal. When he dedicated his Keresan texts to her, she wrote on November 4, 1927:[7]

> Dear Dr. Boas:
> I am delighted with your wish to dedicate to me the Keres texts — who would not be? — and with the expression you give it. As I used to tell you I *do* like compliments, from friends, and from boys, and I don't worry over whether or not I deserve them.

Gladys Reichard, Ruth Bunzel, and Esther Goldfrank came to have the status of daughters over whose affairs, personal and professional, he worried like an anxious father or grandfather.

But Ruth Benedict was never in quite the same category. She entered the department as a stranger, originally neither needing his help nor expecting him to take responsibility for her, and at the same time presenting none of the stiff-necked opposition and occasional disgruntled yielding which he evoked from male students. The quality of their relationship held so many echoes of their unshared past — her image, from her own childhood, of an old man wise and close to death and his frustrated years of seldom seeing his boyhood friends. His elder son had become a physician; his second son was killed in a railway accident in 1925. From his interest in his daughters' husbands, one felt that perhaps, as in European Jewish culture, he was looking not for a son but for a son-in-law as a successor. But though he was always attempting to draw them into his work, their vocations lay along other lines.

From his conception of anthropology, with all its breadth in time and space, as a vast panorama which had only been lighted up here and there, we got a sense that after he died there would be no one who could hold everything together.[8] In each field — linguistics, ethnology, archeology, physical anthropology — there were people working, and he carried on active professional relations with them, finding funds, working on schemes of research, or writing scathing reviews with a clear conscience.

What Ruth Benedict slowly became was a kind of second self,

not in all the diverse realms of his theoretical interests — for she was barred from linguistic work by her deafness and she had scant interest in the studies of physical growth and none in mathematics — but in his sense of responsibility to ethnology, its students, its problems, its methods. He could ask her to give the opening lectures of a course for him, or to talk over a field problem with a student, or to go over a manuscript and see what was to be done with it, or to see to it that the precious little bits of money on which people's lives depended got to them in various strange parts of the world. He could talk over with her the problems which students' behavior presented, express his small vexations, call someone an ass whom he would then review with portentous seriousness in a scientific journal, all without risk of being misunderstood. He entrusted more and more teaching to her, but until 1930, she held only the position of lecturer, which sometimes paid a little and sometimes nothing at all. Hard as she worked, devoted as she was, she still seemed to him — or so she afterward interpreted it — essentially a visitor from afar who might go away.

Then, in 1930, the slow, painful process of estrangement between Ruth and Stanley Benedict came to the point of separation. They had exhausted the various tricks with the calendar by which they had tried to work out the divergence of their interests. They decided to separate.[9] At this time Ruth Benedict presented Boas with a need for professional standing that was accompanied by some reward in money, a need that he recognized. Now when it was necessary, he went to work and got her an assistant professorship which became an associate professorship in 1936. It was now clear that she had come to stay.

Meanwhile the years had dealt hardly with him. His second daughter died of polio in October, 1925, his second son had been killed in a railway accident, and Mrs. Boas was run over and killed in December, 1930. He was in Chicago for the inauguration of the Social Science Building at the University of Chicago, and he came home to sit beside her for just one night before she was buried. Sapir had shared, in an agony of discomfort, the long train journey back from Chicago. In 1931 and 1932 he was very ill. Then almost the whole conduct of the department fell to Ruth Benedict; letters were sent to her on the assumption that Boas was relinquishing his hold on things — that he would never look at this manuscript now, never take up that issue.

Then came Hitler's political success, standing for every evil against which Boas had fought all his life, a concatination of the denial of freedom and of universal human values. Roused by tremendous anger from what might well have been his last months, Boas flung himself back into the world — both that of ordinary anthropological work, now intensified on the subject of race, and that of militant anti-Nazi activities, writing, providing materials for the underground, organizing committees, finding positions for exiled scholars. Tirelessly he devoted what had seemed to be waning strength to the battle which now reversed the problem which had faced him as a German-American in World War I.

This sudden burst of activity presented a new problem to Ruth Benedict, who had never found any great cause worth fighting for except the abolition of war and the protection of individuality. Just when her commitment to anthropology had become strong enough to sustain her as she wrote *Patterns of Culture*[10] and when Boas had at last taken on the preparation of a textbook which might make some of his methods generally available,[11] his interests shifted to this public moral battle. "He has given up science for good works," she complained to me in 1934. "Such a waste!" The contrast seemed especially sharp because all the problems with which she had helped him in the past — finding money for field work and for writing up field work, finding jobs for students and money for publication — were greatly accentuated. In the depression years there was sometimes not a single inquiry in a whole year for a graduate student from the department. Every penny she could spare went to secret supplementation of students' meager funds.

But slowly at first and then more definitely she too was seized by the urgency of the problems facing the world and the obligation as an anthropologist to take part. She never acted as a simple citizen — perhaps here vestiges of her disbelief in causes lingered — but always as an anthropologist within a certain area of competence. In this way the years of active work on the question of race and on the wider questions of democracy began.

Boas was Chairman of the American Committee for Democracy and Intellectual Freedom.[12] Ruth Benedict also worked for this committee and in other organizations of the same sort, some of which had been subtly engineered by Communists in the now well-known tactics of the United Front. Boas believed that he would be able to spot a Communist at once by his lack of intellectual independence which, he felt sure, would show through everything. He remained scornful of attacks on many of the causes with which he associated himself, his uncompromising attitude insulating him from any education on the subject of Communist methods. Ruth Benedict was a little more in touch with the tone of the times. She knew that some of the people with whom she came in contact were Communists, but she too refused to believe that what these doctrinaires advocated needed to be taken seriously. If she had ever had a friend who became a Communist, she would have shrugged her shoulders as she had done when close friends turned to Christian Science or Anglo-Catholicism or psychoanalysis. So she was no less scornful than Boas of the attacks which she herself knew enough to recognize came not from the Right but from the disgruntled and unorthodox Left, which sought to discredit generous human causes by giving them a Communist label. Only after her experience in Washington — after tussles over clearing assistants and briefing sessions on security — could she be persuaded to take even the ordinary sad precautions of the twentieth century, such as writing to a committee for Wallace, which had used her name without her permission, and keeping a copy of her letter of protest. But before the war, in the battles against race hatred, discrimination, and limitations of freedom of speech and of the press, she and Boas marched ahead, hardly vouchsafing a sidelong glance at those who were willing to let a good cause go by default if by chance the "Stalinists" had also espoused it.

In 1937 Boas retired. Given an iron purpose by the continued existence of the Nazi threat, he persisted for the remaining six years of his life in the strenuous combination of campaigning, activities on behalf of displaced Germans, and work on his own materials. The department entered one of those troublesome periods, almost inevitable when a great man who has made a department must be succeeded by younger men. Boas was made Professor Emeritus, and came to his office once or twice a week.

Ruth Benedict now occupied a position made very difficult, on the one hand, by her close identification with Boas and by the long years in which she had administered the department for him and, on the other hand, by problems of adjustment to the new professor, Ralph Linton, who was restive under the burdens of his new status and in the knowledge that in the choice of a successor to Boas, Ruth Benedict had not supported him. Looking at the situation objectively, before his appointment, we had felt that Ralph Linton's thinking and interests were, in certain respects, close to those of Ruth Benedict, whereas sociological and structural emphases were needed to give balance to the department. Letters to and from Boas in this period reflect the anomalies of the situation, which grew worse as long as he lived and were little mitigated by his death, or by Linton's acceptance of the Sterling professorship at Yale University, or by Julian Steward's period as professor at Columbia.

In the summer of 1939, Ruth Benedict directed her second field workshop, this time among the Canadian Blackfoot.[13] She then went on to California, where she spent the year near her mother and sister and her California friends. During this winter she wrote *Race: Science and Politics*,[14] on which she worked with devotion and without delight as if in payment of a moral debt which anthropologists owed a world threatened by Nazism. The book was a more scholarly precursor of the simplified pamphlet, *Races of Mankind*, which she wrote together with Gene Weltfish and which was published in 1943.[15]

In 1940, she returned to New York to resume a life of hurried and harried complexity. The vexations in the department at Columbia, Boas' ebbing strength, the approaching war, the responsibilities for writing and speaking on the race question, which she assumed but never found congenial, all bore down heavily on a strength which was already beginning to fail. Correspondence with students and with her numberless lame ducks and dependents was an ever growing burden. When there were spare moments she sat quietly at home in the apartment she shared with Ruth Valentine and read Shakespeare. She was wearied now not by the old tension between inner and outer life, but rather by an external fragmentation of time resulting from the situation of the moment, the pressure for action, the state of anthropology, the state of her own work.

At this time she found herself once more in the old position of power without patronage. Although she was enormously respected and was consulted by people from many fields, she was leading an encysted life in her own department. In 1941, when she was invited to give the Anna Howard Shaw Memorial Lectures at Bryn Mawr, a signal honor, she had great difficulty in arranging for the necessary leave of absence. These lectures she designed around an organizing idea of *synergy* — studies of the ways in which institutions in a culture either worked together and so released human energy, or else were contradictory and discrepant and so dissipated human energy. The long series of field studies which had been done by students in the 1930's and which still awaited some form of organization provided the materials, and she planned to organize the whole into a book. However, in the end, she kept no manuscript of the Anna Shaw Lectures, and decided to do nothing with the Columbia field studies but instead to let Linton arrange them into the kind of whole in which he was interested.[16]

Meanwhile we were beginning to develop methods by which anthropology could make a contribution to the preparations for the war that was surely coming. The First Conference on Science, Philosophy and Religion was held in the summer of 1939.[17] That same autumn, Arthur Upham Pope organized the Committee for National Morale.[18] In 1941, Lawrence K. Frank, Gregory Bateson, Edwin R. Embree and I started what was at first called the Council for Intercultural Relations and later became the Institute for Intercultural Studies.[19] During this time Ruth Benedict was put on the Committee for the Study of Food Habits of the National Research Council and was called into various other academic councils. She also cooperated peripherally with some of the newly developing activities. In 1941, she wrote a comment on "The Comparative Study of Cultures and the Purposive Cultivation of Democratic Values," which I had prepared for the Second Conference on Science, Philosophy and Religion,[20] and, in 1943, she collaborated in the preparation of a paper for a report "On Supplementing the Regional Training Curriculum by the Use of Material on the Contemporary Peoples, Their Culture and Character." [21]

On the Sunday of Pearl Harbor, while Lawrence Frank, Gregory

Bateson, and I were attending a conference, Ruth Benedict brought me the offer of the job as executive secretary of the Committee on Food Habits. This fulfilled conditions which younger members of the Committee on National Morale had been spelling out — namely, that "we needed a field worker in Washington to find out how the Federal government worked" because we were weary of the errors made by the veterans of the Battle of Washington in 1916, who had never heard of the Bureau of the Budget. She was certain that the proposed job would be a congenial one because I would be working with M. L. Wilson, who was then Chairman of the Interdepartmental Nutrition Coordinating Committee and who saw the task of the National Research Council advisory committee as one of applied social change. When we came out of the meeting at five o'clock, the cloakroom attendant told us about Pearl Harbor. The next stage of work, for which we were already preparing, was now upon us.

One by one those of us who had been working together in New York became absorbed by the war. I went to Washington to work in the National Research Council in January, 1942. Geoffrey Gorer went into the Office of War Information in the spring of the same year. Edmund Taylor, Ladislas Farago, and Lawrence Frank went into various government agencies. Gregory Bateson worked in a wartime film project at the Museum of Modern Art in New York, out of which came the first intensive anthropological analysis of a film, *Hitlerjunge Quex*.[22] Geoffrey Gorer was working on a monograph on the Burmese, using second-culture informants and published materials.[23] In the Committee on Food Habits, Rhoda Métraux was developing a method of qualitative analysis of verbal materials on American culture.[24] In my brief vacation in 1942, I wrote *And Keep Your Powder Dry*.[25] In the summer of 1943, I went to England to lecture for the Office of War Information and to work on further applications of anthropology to cross-cultural understanding.[26] Gregory Bateson joined the Office of Strategic Services to work on Japan. Geoffrey Gorer shifted to the British Embassy wartime staff, and Ruth Benedict replaced him in the Office of War Information.

There she picked up a preliminary study on Rumanian conceptions of history, on which Gregory Bateson, Philip Mosely, and I had worked the year before, and set to work with interviews and published materials to develop a memorandum on Rumania.[27] This she completed in the autumn of 1943. Our discussion of this memorandum, when Mosely came back from his trip to Moscow with Hull, was the precursor of a series of small meetings in Washington in which we tried to pool our growing understanding of ways in which we could use informants and could analyze films and literary plots and other materials to construct models of the cultural character of other nations.

In the Office of War Information, Ruth Benedict then worked on Thailand [28] and, finally, on Japan, for this study drawing on the earlier work of Gorer and Bateson and on the contemporary work being done in other parts of the government by Alexander Leighton, Clyde Kluckhohn, and Kurt Lewin. During this Washington period she made new friends who were later to become part of the big postwar research project, especially Nathan Leites and Nicolas Calas.

Within the wartime security structure, she had an occasional battle — now because *Races of Mankind* was denounced in Congress as subversive (mainly because of a tactical error committed in the writing in stating baldly that some Northern Negroes had scored higher in intelligence tests than had some Southern whites), now because of malicious comments on the suicide, in 1939, of Buell Quain, one of her most valued students, who had killed himself in Brazil and had left her his small legacy to use for other anthropological students.

In the perfervid atmosphere of scarcity and competitiveness of the late 1930's, this legacy had been magnified into a great sum and, in a letter to Boas, she had remarked,[29] "Linton is determined to make me spend the Quain money before I can use any of the department research funds for any of my own students." She described to me with great feeling how, in the security conference in Washington at which her suitability to handle top secret materials was being argued out, she had had to explain in detail the risk an anthropological teacher had to take in sending students to the field. The drama of letting me go to Samoa, the murder of Henrietta Schmerler in

1931, the worries about Jules Henry's trips into the South American jungle — all came back as she had to answer the charge, made verbally by a colleague to an investigator of the Federal Bureau of Investigation, that she had sent Buell Quain down into the jungle to die so that she could get her hands on his meager inheritance. That he was one of the students for whose career she had hoped most had not seemed relevant.

Through such experiences, she began to learn to protect herself a little from the kinds of attack which were made more and more possible in the contemporary climate of opinion as personal spite, greed, and rejected interest became combined with displays of "loyalty" by persons whom she did not know and who had recently been converted from subversive positions.

But although she went to top secret conferences and was engaged in wartime intelligence activities, especially while she was working on European cultures — German, Dutch, and Polish — to help with underground and partisan movements, she also gradually set up her own quiet style of work with one good secretary, a set of younger interviewers, and intensive analysis of materials. The end of the war found her ready to write her book on Japan.

In November 1942, Boas spoke at the celebration of the centenary of the American Ethnological Society, and selected for special emphasis a passionate memorandum by E. George Squier written in 1869, which he quoted in full:[30]

> Statesmen, whether senators or kings, can no longer overlook the profound lessons inculcated by anthropology. The political reorganization of Europe is going on in consonance with its discoveries and results. Religion under its influence is separating itself from a ritualistic dogmatism that has nothing to do with morals or the relationship that exists between men and God and has become all the loftier from the dissociation.
>
> To these grand results we may ask what has the American Ethnological Society contributed. Absolutely, for twenty years, nothing. True, ten of these years have been unfavorable to scientific pursuits in this country. Students having common sympathies and aims have been separated by political and social barriers and investigators weaned or diverted from their pursuits

by imperative requirements in other fields. Estranged co-laborers, however, are returning with that catholic spirit which study for Truth inspires and encourages, to their old associations and researches; and the altered condition of our common country encourages and, indeed, makes necessary a wider and deeper investigation of the character and true relations of the varieties and races of mankind than ever existed before. But this investigation must be made *ab initio*, or rather in a purely abstract scientific sense. It can not be done by men who, for any reason or motive, bring into the study the element of faith, or adhesion to dogmas or creeds of any kind whatever. These subtle elements of depression of scientific inquiry have been, to a certain degree, the ruin of this Society. Your reporter can remember when the question of human unity could not be discussed without offense to some of the members of the Society and when its casual introduction was made a ground of impassioned protest. This allusion is made only to enforce the vital truth that, in scientific inquiry, the item of faith must be entirely eliminated. Not having been so, discussion in this Society has been relatively tame and fruitless.

Boas ended his own summary of the vicissitudes through which the society has gone with the words:

Thus the society has become an active member in anthropological work in our country. Let us hope that it will continue its active participation in anthropological work and contribute by the researches of its members and by its more popular activities to the solution of the difficult social problems of our times.

On December 29, 1942, Boas was giving a lunch for his old friend Paul Rivet at the faculty club at Columbia University. A glass of wine in his hand, he said, "I have a new theory about race . . ." and fell back dead.

There was now no senior person alive to whom Ruth Benedict looked for guidance in the choices she made as to the role which she, as an anthropologist and as a citizen, should play in the world.

The Bond of Fellowship*

WHEN I was growing up in the hinterland of America I did not know any Jews. In the public schools I went to, there were no Jews, and, later, it would not have occurred to me to see anything in common among the few Jews I came to know. There was the daughter of the rich clothing merchant, the threadbare student who kept me on my toes discussing European philosophy, and the itinerant peddler who kept the farmers supplied with store goods and who stayed on to swap words of wisdom with my grandfather. They all fell, in my mind and in their own, into the usual American pigeonholes which have to do first and foremost with money income. The clothing merchant's family in Buffalo consorted with the other rich merchants of the city; they made no common cause with itinerant peddler or with schoolboy living on crusts. There was no issue that drew these Jews together.

Anti-Semitism was no issue in my childhood and we thought it had been outmoded. It has been a cruel teacher, but it has laid the basis in the last decades for a Jewish fellowship which overspans all class and national schisms. Jews have learned the hard way, but they have learned, better than any other group, that outrages on Jews in Germany or on Yorkville tenement-dwellers are ultimately threats to all Jews. They have learned too that discriminations against any minority group, whether it is Irish or Negro, Italian

* Undated manuscript, *circa* 1942.

or Japanese, are potentially threats to the Jewish minority. They have had to recognize from their own experience that they themselves can live decently only insofar as all human beings have opportunity to live without being the butt of outrages and discriminations.

It is an eternal truth for all men, but human beings have to learn it over and over again from their own experience. Democracy has taken this truth as its foundation stone, but the democracies have been halfhearted. It has to be brought home afresh. And in our great need for drastic reaffirmation of this truth in this war and in the peace to follow, Jews can speak clearly and work courageously. More than any other minority group — and all such groups have learned this lesson also in their own persons — Jews are represented among the rich and the poor, business, the professions, and the trades. They therefore span the usual schisms in American life. More than any other group they are international. They therefore span the great modern schisms among the nations. Jews are therefore in a doubly strategic position. It would be tragedy indeed if any timidities, any wisdom of this world, made them turn their eyes away when affronts are perpetrated. Let them not keep silent. There are many Gentiles who have not yet learned the truth Jews know, and that truth must be made clear to them. No other issue in the world today is of greater importance. America desperately needs those who have learned from their own experience that altruism and self-interest coincide in every effort to secure for all human beings the right and the obligation of full and decent participation in our common life. Such efforts are the bond of fellowship which unite in one great crusade, not only Jews of every nation and of every income; it unites also the Jew and the intelligent Gentile.

Race Prejudice
in the United States*

A FEW YEARS ago a friend of mine was returning from a trip in the mountains of the Philippines. He was an anthropologist and the chief of the village in which he lived had gone with him as a guide. As they came along the steep path, they met a tall native carrying a basket of yams on his head. In the village where my friend lived, men carried loads on their backs, so he knew the stranger was from another tribe. The village chief passed the stranger without greeting, and then turned to my friend and said, "Did you see the way he carried his yams? In the old days our village would have killed him for that."

My friend was hardly accustomed to reckoning a different method of carrying yams as a sufficient reason for killing, and he could not help remembering the stranger's graceful, erect carriage and intelligent face. The reason his companion gave for killing this well-set-up stranger sounded barbaric. And then he thought of humiliations he had seen put upon second-class citizens in his own country. For what? Because they spoke Czech or Italian as mother tongues and made bad work of English. Because they kept a different New Year's Day or didn't celebrate Christmas. Because, like the American Indian, they were called red — or yellow — or black. Even the black ones had been, most of them, he remembered, a lighter shade than his own father when he came back from wintering on the

* Radio address, Washington, D.C., 1946.
358

beaches in Florida. Weren't these reasons all uncomfortably close to the reason why the Philippine pagan hated the natives of the next valley? They looked different. They did things differently. It might just as well be the way they carried a basket of yams.

For my friend, who was an anthropologist, knew all the studies on the superiority and inferiority of racial groups. He knew that no scientific study gave any basis for thinking that all the healthy people, the intelligent people, the imaginative people, are segregated in one race or born in certain countries and not in others. He was convinced on the evidence that if you could choose the top third of the human race for their physical stamina, their brains and their decent human qualities, all races of the world would be represented in this top group. Yet the old jealous tribalism of the untutored savage has not died out even in our literate industrial world.

We are always more complicated than we need to be when we explain race prejudice. We justify race prejudice by referring over and over to the poverty, illiteracy, and shiftlessness of the people we segregate — the undoubtedly bad effects of making anybody a second-class citizen. But if the effects of that are so bad, why not try the experiment of offering every American opportunity freely to all Americans, with no ifs and buts? We know from experience that people from every racial group in America and from every country of origin respond to education, become healthy when they have good food and good medical care, and can learn to perform the tasks our civilization offers.

The truth is that when we succumb to race prejudice we don't see the "man from outside" as a person in his own right, with eyes, ears, hands like ours. We classify him like a piece of merchandise by outward signs of color or face or gestures or language. We don't judge him on his personal merits. The cure for race prejudice is as simple as that: to treat people on their merits, without reference to any label of race or religion or country of origin. Some, in every group, will not make good. They don't now either. But there would be one effect: race prejudice would die of malnutrition.

We are more fortunate in the United States than we realize. In many European countries prejudice is harder to eliminate than it need be in our own country. In plenty of European countries the minority groups themselves want to stay outside the common national concerns. They want to wall themselves off. They passionately demand that they be allowed to have their own schools taught in their own languages by their own teachers. They fight to keep their costumes, their saints' days, and their own police. In some countries there are as many national labor unions as there are minority groups, a separate one for each. Each one demands to be a nation within a nation. In other words, it is the minorities themselves which demand segregation.

But in America the cry of the minorities is just as passionate as in these European countries, and it is *against* segregation. Our minorities want to be Americans. To build a strong America we do not have to batter down their resistance to being American citizens. We only have to remove some of the obstacles that have been put in their way. America's real tragedy would be if our minorities were fighting to become little nations within a nation — a weakness no healthy nation can stand. Ironically, in America, it is only the so-called majority which fights for segregation. All the minorities — a vast host — fight for a united America, where segregation and discrimination will no longer threaten our country's strength. Our minorities keep vocal today the dream of equality of opportunity, of "Americans All," upon which the United States was founded. They have great strength in that they are speaking for, and not against, the American tradition. All the more, therefore, a great responsibility rests upon them, lest they, in their turn, raise the cry of inferiority against some other American groups, lest they fall into the temptation of creating scapegoats. For what America needs is no mere shifting of different groups up and down on a ladder; America needs the help of all her citizens to ensure human dignity to all Americans.

Postwar

Race Prejudice *

WAR IMPROVED our domestic race relations. Race riots stopped and lynchings decreased. A million and a half Negroes were employed in the war industries alone, and in some Washington hotels colored men and women got a dinner. White-supremacy editorials became exceptional in Southern newspapers, and the Supreme Court ruled against all-white primaries. It took filibusters to stop the passage of the Federal Fair Employment Act and the repeal of the Poll Tax. Even in the crucial case of the Japanese, America's conscience reasserted itself after the first hysterical act of wholesale evacuation from the Pacific states, and during the four war years efforts to ensure more decent treatment of the Nisei were steadily intensified.

Men and women who cherished the American dream of human decency and of equality of opportunity and of even-handed civil liberties felt in those war years that true Americanism was making permanent gains. They pointed to the fact that not only were there gains for the Negroes but that our Southern and Eastern European minorities were now, in the third generation, becoming American in speech and habit, and that, for instance, popular confidence in Bernard Baruch as a national moderator was hardly touched by the fact that he was a Jew. Many patriotic citizens felt that the better minority relations of the war were a well-earned victory which they had won by hard work; they had educated great numbers of people

* Unpublished manuscript, *circa* 1947.

in the facts of race and they had put their shoulders to the wheel
in local and Federal action programs.

It was indeed a good job. The danger is lest they become disillusioned and cynical when in peace time they find the gains are
not permanent. A friend of mine said to me the other day about a
beautiful Western city where she lives: "We taught the fact of race
in schools and churches and women's clubs. We got some Negro
teachers in the schools and kept down the restrictive covenants and
got Negro tenants in the housing project. And now nobody says a
word when the KKK burns a fiery cross and the Negroes and Mexicans
are fired wholesale from their jobs and white parents boycott the
part-Negro school. What's the use?"

She had not been fore-armed for the conditions of peace, and
it was easy therefore for her to be discouraged. But she could have
been forewarned. Race relations become better when the United
States makes common cause in a war. When the nation is working together toward some goal, a citizen can feel that it is desirable
that some group with which he is not identified ought to be well
fed and healthy and skilled enough to contribute successfully toward
the end they all desire. In peace, we concentrate on our own concerns. We look out for No. One, and we justify it morally, if at
all, by some vague idea that private profit is public gain. As
normalcy reasserts itself, we begin to look askance at personal sacrifices made in the interest of national morale. We look upon our
fellowmen and our minority groups as primarily competitors and
those Americans who resent and fear the achievements and security
of other groups are likely to get the upper hand. Those men and
women who look upon other people as obstacles in their race for a
job or for financial success necessarily fear any strength these others
can muster.

As community ties which were fostered by the war's need for every
individual's output and patriotism weaken, those who easily feel
envy of other groups and who readily speak and act aggressively
against them have less restraint. They are able to recruit their
ranks from among those individuals who are on the borderline between good will and hostility, and the groups who during the war
were willing to subscribe to truly democratic behavior are no longer
active enough to oppose them successfully.

This contrast between war and peace is not a universal social law; it is a cultural fact characteristic of an era of nationalism and especially characteristic of our American individualistic tradition. It is no new thing. During the First World War stories were current among the Negroes which made this contrast explicit. One is a story of two Negro soldiers of the A.E.F. serving in France. One of them says to the other, "When I get back to the States, I'se goin' to march up Sixth Avenue and get me a drink in every white man's joint." And the other one says, "And I'se goin' to walk behind your coffin." He knew that when the war was over, and they were back in America, they would be subject to the same taboos they had known before the war. The old pattern would powerfully reassert itself, and that old pattern vigorously denies social equality to many racial and ethnic groups.

If this were the whole tale of our minority relations in the United States, the picture would be black indeed. But of course it is not the whole story and those who hope for better minority relations need to consider equally, when they think out their strategy, the assets as well as the liabilities. The greatest asset we have in the United States is the public policy of the state. This is not to say that our Federal government, our states, our police forces, and our courts have been blameless; of course they have not. But as compared with the grass-roots discriminations and segregations current in the United States, public policy has been a brake and not an incentive. This would not necessarily be remarkable in a country run, for example, by a benevolent dictator, but in a democracy where the people have a voice in selecting their legislators and their judges, it is something to ponder. The correspondence between popular prejudices and state action has been far from being one-to-one. In states where opinion polls and strong labor unions and powerful industries have been against hiring men without regard to color or creed or national origin, it has still been possible to get Fair Employment Acts passed. In cities where there is a quota for Jewish students in privately endowed colleges, there is no quota for Jews in the tax-supported city colleges. When New York State Negroes protest today that private medical colleges are willing to train such a bare minimum of Negro doctors that the supply is totally inadequate, they unquestioningly propose a state medical college to remedy the situation. In areas where there are restrictive covenants and "Jim Crow" city blocks, city and Federal housing authorities have been able to insist upon and administer housing projects which have both Negro and white tenants. Even in this present postwar year when the record of civil liberties has been deteriorating, Chicago ruled against a "lily-white" policy in its new veterans' homes, and when a mob attacked the houses let to Negroes, the largest police force Chicago had ever called out was stationed to protect them. In Gary, Indiana, when white school children and their parents struck against allowing Negroes in the schools, the mayor broke the strike by the use of the tenancy laws and upheld the city's policy on nonsegregation. On October 30, President Truman accepted as "a charter of human freedom in our times" a strong report on civil liberties for minorities written by the Civil Rights Committee which he had "created with a feeling of urgency," and which recommended laws to end segregation, poll tax and lynchings, the enactment of permanent Fair Employment Acts and of statutes to prohibit Federal or state financial assistance to public or private agencies "permitting discrimination and segregation based on race, color, creed, or national origin."

This state policy is of the utmost importance in the United States. Of course it cannot be fully implemented in a democracy where there is so much free-floating racial and ethnic prejudice. But the fact that public authorities take such stands, often in the face of public sentiment, is a remarkable fact. For the great crises of racial and ethnic persecution have occurred in all countries precisely when the government gave the green light. From the pogroms of Czarist Russia to the mass murder of Jews in Hitler Germany, the constant precondition was a favorable state policy. The government in power was following a policy of eliminating the minority or was at least allowing matters to take their own course without intervention. This importance of whether the state is on the side of racism or is against it is just as true in matters of discriminatory behavior as it is in pogroms and violence. In a democracy or a dictatorship the state can use law and the police to defend the rights of minorities or to abuse them. When, by Federal or city ordinance or by industrial negotiation umpired by the state, a new and less prejudiced situation has become a *fait accompli,* even those who protested most actively against it while it was under consideration tend to accept the arrangement and to become accustomed to it. Certainly in the United States it seems clear that more can be accomplished by these means toward ameliorating job and housing discriminations than by any amount of work by good-will organizations.

This is not to say that informal, private, and nonlegislative efforts to improve social relations and eliminate prejudice are therefore unimportant. In a democracy laws and court decisions must have the backing of interested citizens, or they become dead letters. The ultimate goals of all who work for better race and ethnic relations can never be achieved merely by enforcing laws, which can forbid only the most blatant and overt acts of discrimination. No fiat has ever made any man over so that he can respect the human dignity of a Negro or a Jew if he has lived all his life in a community which acted on premises of white supremacy and anti-Semitism.

Any strategy for lessening our national shame of race and ethnic discriminations before the eyes of the rest of the world must therefore value interracial meetings of the women's auxiliaries of the churches of a Massachusetts town, and the We-are-all-Americans pageants of a Middle Western city. But unless people who participate in such activities see to it that their efforts feed into a demand for Federal and state and city action they are guilty of bad tactics. For it is clear that the state can be used in America as an asset in their endeavors, and if they overlook this they are neglecting a major resource.

Such workers have often been too idealistic to join hands with politicians who want minority votes, but it is by such means that measures are put through in a democracy like ours. If the powers that be are not moved to act for the good of the total community, perhaps they can be prevailed upon to court a substantial group of voters. And these voters may be able to press for enforcement also, thereby gaining first-hand experience in the business of acting as American citizens.

We have a second important asset in the United States in this endeavor to reduce race and ethnic tensions. This asset has to do with the attitudes of our minorities themselves. We should count our blessings. The pattern of behavior of American minorities differs from that of minorities, let us say, in Europe. For we have not one sizable separatist group. In Europe these are constant sources of trouble, from the Irish to the Lithuanians. The Germans in Czech Sudetenland and the Hungarians in Transylvania were separatists. Separatists refuse to be assimilated and are not content with toleration. They cultivate the symbols of a state within a state and have perpetuated sometimes for centuries a form of language and style of life different from those of the dominant group. They demand schools taught in their own languages and often engage in nationalistic movements whose aim is to unseat the government.

In the United States our minorities are quite different. They are assimilationist or pluralist. The universal demand of every group in this country is for the right to "be Americans." They demand their equal opportunity to make sacrifices for their country: to serve in the armed forces on the fighting line, to give their blood for the blood bank. The use of any other language than English has never been an issue in American education. The Catholic parochial schools are the only ones which have been in any way separatist and they have emphasized not native language and symbols of old-country nationalism but the right to educate children in their own religion, a right which the United States freely grants. Above all, they want to be first-class American citizens, and they protest only those discriminations which keep them in a second-class status.

The strategy suggested by such an attitude on the part of our minorities is that we must see to it that minority leaders be given respected roles in political activities which are aimed at civic welfare and responsible Federal government. For if we do not give members of the minorities a place in such movements, the ward boss and the selfish politician will enlist them. They will participate where they are welcomed.

These two assets, the greater likelihood that the state will support civil liberties and equal opportunities more readily than the rank and file, and the assimilationism of our minorities, are resources we cannot afford to neglect. We have other assets, too, which are more often articulately recognized in planning domestic programs for better intercultural relations. Americans have, first, an almost unprecedented faith in nurture as compared to "nature." We do not have an aristocratic society's acceptance of personal destiny which is a mere transliteration of biological inheritance. We have wonderful faith in education and we believe that man is shaped by his environment. We constantly fail to act upon this faith, but we do not have the philosophical doubts about it which are bred in societies with a surviving feudal heritage.

Then, too, we have a knowledge of the facts of race. Anthropology, psychology, history, and biology have all provided scientific evidence to disprove the myth of the master race. There are ample data which have been made available at every level from the most closely argued to the most popular. Such disproof will, of course, not make an upholder of white supremacy into a tolerant democrat, but it is not therefore unimportant. We must remember that when the doctrine of Nordic supremacy was at its height in the fifty years between 1870 and 1920, many people quite simply believed it, even those who knew history and biology and psychology. They could quite honestly plan one kind of world for the racial "inferiors" and another kind for the "superiors," for opportunities would be merely wasted on the inferiors. The evidence that ability and good character and inventiveness vary from individual to individual in all races, and that no race has a monopoly of any virtue is an asset for which to be thankful.

As Americans of the 1940's we have therefore important resources which we can use in our efforts to reduce race prejudice. We shall be the more successful the more realistically we use them and the less we hope for miracles. Only a miracle would enthrone ethnic quality as a daily practice in the United States. However much we hesitate to acknowledge it, race prejudice is deeply entrenched in our routine life and probably, measured by any objective standards, only South Africa goes further in segregation, discrimination, and humiliation. We do not seem, in the eyes of other nations, especially of the Asiatic nations, to be good exemplars of democratic equality. Our race prejudice is the great enemy within our gates, and these postwar years will be a fateful testing ground of how far we will let this enemy advance. We shall be faced with defeats which seem insupportable, and our most reasonable hopes will sometimes seem betrayed. We can only stand our ground if we are willing to make open admission that the patient — our whole country — is very sick, and that the cure is a matter in which we have an incomparable stake. Then perhaps we can use all possible resources wisely and win through to a happier day.

The Natural History
of War *

LIKE EVERYBODY else, we were talking of war the other day. We had all played some role or other in the First World War; some had fought, some had been Wilson idealists, and one had been a thoroughgoing pacifist. They would have cried traitor at one another in 1917–1919, but in 1939 their voices rose together in a chorus of despair. What was the use of discriminating about wars? They had discriminated according to their lights in the last war, and look at the world today. Whatever intelligence had been applied to the last war, nothing had come of it. Everything was worse instead of better. The Wilson idealists had been Three Minute Men and had believed in the Fourteen Points, but the Treaty of Versailles had proved them the dupes of vindictive nationalists. Once bitten, thrice shy. It was better to admit that we were trapped in a world on its way to destruction. The pacifist was still a pacifist, and to touch the pitch with one's fingers was still the sin against the Holy Ghost; it was a sin even to hold an opinion which might prove partial to one contestant or the other. But the pacifist too was hopeless, and he knew this sin could not be eradicated. The clergyman was most desperate of all. Even his religion only made his outlook the darker. He had served with enthusiasm as chaplain in the Expeditionary

* Unpublished manuscript, 1939. *See* letter from RFB to FB, December 3, 1939; from FB to RFB, December 20, 1939; from RFB to FB, December 26, 1939.

Forces, and he had come full circle in his disillusion. "The Western world has been Christian," he said, "for well on to two millennia, and its teachings are against war. If anything could have prevented war, Christianity should have succeeded. Think of the power of the Church for centuries in Europe! But no ethics, no idealism weigh a straw. In the other balance is Human Nature — the old cave man. If we thought man was something else, we were the more betrayed. We must face the truth: the need for war is in man biologically like the need to eat."

I am an anthropologist, and on all these counts I believed they were wrong. It is not usually thought to make one an optimist to study anthropology; the follies of mankind are too obvious and too repetitious to make for utopian faiths. Nevertheless it does put into black and white some facts that are obscured by too great concentration on one decade or one century. Over and above the necessity of sifting the last bit of evidence about the last war, I said, we need a natural history of war. We need to distinguish socially lethal varieties from nonlethal varieties. We need to see what our wars are in contrast to wars in other kinds of civilization. We must get some basis for discrimination which is not just my war against your war, or this war against the war fifty years ago. War is an old, old plant on this earth, and a natural history of it would have to tell us under what soil conditions it grows, where it plays havoc, and how it is eliminated. Control of war cannot be based on anything less than such knowledge, and until our efforts are thus grounded despair is premature.

I am going to put such a natural history of war into as brief a compass as possible, but it means an excursion into far corners of the world and into conditions which Western civilization has long outgrown. We are men in a hurry today, and we are justifiably impatient. But it is worth our while to get a perspective.

A natural history of war must begin by naming the genus. Our dictionary definitions describe only our modern varieties; when they define it in terms of breaking diplomatic relations and of abrogating international law, they are out of date even today. When one defines war as it is both among savages of the Amazon jungle and as it is in England, the common core is that war is homicide that is rewarded with unquestioned acclaim and gratitude by one's fellows. It is homicide in a blaze of glory. Over against the genus War, which always has this characteristic, there stand other aggressions which also bring about an enemy's death and which belong to the genus Murder. Murder is homicide with penalties, and the penalties are always the heaviest of all penalties against aggressions.

When any primitive tribe has no such double standard in homicide, war has not yet loomed upon the horizon. There are some simple primitive tribes which have punitive sanctions for all killing, and these tribes have no idea what war is. Just after the First World War, I was living with the Serrano Indians of Southern California,[1] who had this uncivilized peculiarity. The reverberations of the great struggle had reached them only faintly, but they were bewildered. The expedition overseas, they had thought at first, was like a dangerous journey down into the country of the Gulf of California, and they could understand that a man might lose his life on such a trip. The enemy, too, venturing into such country, might be decimated. But American soldiers apparently killed men, and these Indians speculated that then they would not be returning to their own country after the war. Would not punishment be in store for them? My explanations fell on uncomprehending ears, for they had no double standard which would serve to set apart the Battle of the Marne from a drunken brawl in which men knifed each other in the back after a bottle of firewater.

A primitive tribe in order to judge as these Serrano Indians judged must live in very special conditions. Either they must have a little island all to themselves, or they must have good natural boundaries, or they must live in regions and own possessions which more restless people have not coveted. Most primitive tribes are not so isolated as this or not so poor, and to them the double standard in homicide is upheld by their everyday experience. On the one hand, their own tribe, whether it is little or big, is in their eyes one big family or a number of extended families closely interknit. In economic life, in religion, and in defense against outsiders all the tribe benefit from the activities of all the rest, and the dogma that all are needed by each one is not an ethical aspiration but a fact of experience. Within this group homicide is murder, and a man must face the consequences, which may be that he has a blood feud on his hands, or that he must pay the murdered man's family an often ruinous indemnity, or that the state will demand the death penalty or banishment.

Such a tribe, however, lives surrounded by neighboring tribes with whom it makes no common cause. They are self-sufficient just as my own tribe is self-sufficient, and if my tribe is the stronger and takes from them something we want, we may keep our prize and enjoy it. We must be strong enough to defend it, of course, but since the two tribes are not mutually dependent on one another, my tribe does not suffer from the weakening of my neighbor. To overcome him is an advantage to us, not a disadvantage.

Of course, then, there is popular acclaim for the raider and the warrior. Homicide with glory is as inevitable under these conditions as homicide with death penalties is within the tribal group. The double standard is adjusted, one rule to apply to those who mutually benefit one another, and the other to those with whom one makes no common cause. When this ethic accurately reflects the social facts and the warring groups are actually sufficient unto themselves, war is often an integral part of upstanding, socially healthy societies. The enemies they kill are hunted as animals are hunted, and this is not a figure of speech as it is with us. It is a view of the universe and of human life which is enshrined in the categories of their language and upheld by all tradition and experience. Human beings are merely one's own little tribe; the rest are nonhuman like the animals. Killing animals is of course acclaimed, and nonhuman bipeds of the neighboring tribe are equally objects of prey. Their death proves my strength just as a successful lion hunt does.

This is the picture as the stronger tribe sees it when it judges correctly that it can gain advantages in war. But what of the victim? Until warfare has added to itself conquest and the regimented exploitation of a conquered people, even a victim tribe is not generally disrupted. For many years I had imagined to myself the victims of the swaggering Marindaniṁ, the greatest head-hunters of New Guinea. I had pictured them cringing and panicky, helpless before the brutal aggressions and the superior numbers of the dominant tribe. Some years ago the accomplished British government anthropologist, F. E. Williams, published his intimate study of these people, *The Papuans of the Trans-Fly*.[2] In all New Guinea he had never seen such immaculately tended yam gardens, and the natives of this cheerless country carried out their great display feasts with a confidence and an elaboration greater than that of more secure tribes. They were a mild, inoffensive people, hard-working and ambitious. Of course the head-hunters swept down on settlements and took their bloody trophies; but death comes to all in any case, and death at the hands of the Marindanim was death like any other.

My point is not the callous one that suffering does not matter. It is the realistic one that the kind of havoc war plays today does not occur in all species of war. Before the war two such tribes were as self-sufficient as if they lived on two separate planets, and they remained so after it was over because the object of war was mere hunting and had nothing to do with reducing the conquered to a slave state for the enrichment of the conquerors. The victims of the fierce Marindanim are therefore not abject like natives under a modern system of colonial exploitation; war did not take from them their autonomous way of life and make them the creatures of their conquerors.

This socially nonlethal species of war occurs not only between aggressor and victim but between tribes that are equal in conflict. Most North American Indian tribes in the old days carried on perpetual international blood feuds, and to do deeds of valor in this interminable warfare was the brightest glory a man could achieve. Like a Boy Scout today, each man passed from rank to rank as he had more deeds to his credit, but the Indian deeds were touching a fallen but living enemy, taking a scalp, running off with horses, bringing back one's little war party without loss, and the like. The palm went now to warriors in one tribe, now in the other. But their warfare was not sociologically lethal. These tribes were independent of one another both economically and in obtaining wives, and their warpath corresponded to this social fact. The object of the warpath was to get trophies, not to subjugate other tribes to themselves as masters and profiteers. The idea of conquest never arose in aboriginal North America, and this made it possible for almost all these Indian tribes to do a very extreme thing: to separate war from the state. The state was personified in the Peace Chief, who was a leader of public opinion in all that concerned the in-group and in his council. The Peace Chief was permanent, and though no autocratic ruler he was often a very important personage. But he had nothing to do with war. He did not even appoint the war chiefs or concern himself with the conduct of war parties. Any man who could attract a following led a war party when and where he would, and in some tribes he was in complete control for the duration of the expedition. But this lasted only till the return of the war party. The state, according to this interpretation of war, had no conceivable interest in these ventures, which were only highly desirable demonstrations of rugged individualism turned against an out-group where such demonstrations did not harm the body politic.

These nonlethal species of warfare are quite common among primitive peoples. The proof that they are nonlethal is that they do not drag to ruin the civilization of both tribes that engage in them. They do of course develop ruthlessness and cruelty and the ability to undergo extreme privations. These are character effects, and those who hate these traits will condemn these consequences and those who love them will make the opposite judgment. But in order to have any clarity about war as an institution it is necessary to be able to see beyond these personality traits and to distinguish war that destroys civilizations from war that has no such consequences.

Not all simple, self-sufficient societies wage war even when they recognize a double standard in homicide. This elimination is not so uncommon as one would think from the writings of political theorists on the prehistory of war. Tribes of Central Australia, for example, made warfare practically nonexistent by recognizing self-interests which a considerable number of tribes were willing to pursue in common. Central Australians are the classic example of the simplest savages, but their savagery had in it no "law of the jungle." They shared each other's ceremonies, came together in council, had safe conduct over vast distances, and established forms within which intertribal marriage was as orderly as marriage among blood relatives. They accepted a double standard in homicide and they believed that some foreigner had caused each death in their tribe, but the famous Arunta tribe[3] were so far from taking vengeance upon this alien sorcerer that when they had trodden under heel a bug on the dead man's grave they were content. They said that the man who was responsible would die, but they had eliminated taking any step in a blood feud. The elimination of war in Central Australia was a response to warm ties of interdependence among widely separated tribes and these ties were reinforced by many rites and observances that seem to us bizarre. But they were carried far enough to keep even these classical savages from war.

When primitive societies are not self-sufficient but depend on one another for essential mainstays of their economy, they would be, if they developed no means of dealing with the war situation, test cases of socially lethal warfare. But they have not been resourceless. The arrangements they evolved are among the most bizarre of primitive customs. The area of the Kula Ring in western Melanesia, made famous by Malinowski[4] and by Reo Fortune,[5] have carried their fantastic ceremonial trading to such a point that war between islands is as effectively eliminated as it is in Central Australia. All the islands specialize in certain products used in the whole area; one island makes canoes, another pottery, another polishes greenstone and another carves wood. They do not however trade these goods at a market. Their trade is carried on in two kinds of "money": shell necklaces which are traded clockwise around the ring of islands, and armshells which are traded anticlockwise. These two "moneys" are never brought face to face with each other. The Kula party from one island goes south to get its armbands, and six months later the southern island must come north to get its necklaces in return. But both expeditions carry food and manufactured articles as solicitory gifts. Kula trading is an absurd and time-consuming obsession from the point of view of economic efficiency, but it knits the islands together in a bond which precludes warfare.

In most other parts of western Melanesia trade has not eliminated warfare, but war is nevertheless kept from interfering with their economic realities. Trade is boxed off from hostilities so that it goes on regardless. In some cases the objects a tribe specializes in are ones that are favored by geographical position, but quite as often there is little connection. There are hill tribes who will cook only with salt water and coast tribes who will cook only with fresh water, thereby perpetuating trade in which vessels of salt water are daily carried to a halfway point to be exchanged for vessels of fresh water. No tribe is self-sufficient. But over most of this area there is vigorous head-hunting. The greatest boast of each party to commercial transactions may be the other's skulls which decorate their tribal Man's House, but trade goes on regardless. They do not see nor address one another. One tribe lays down its wares at a given line and retires. Both know the value of the goods exchanged and the other tribe helps itself to no more and no less than the proper equivalent. When this second tribe has in turn retired, the first tribe advances again and shoulders its gains. This is the institution of the Silent Trade, and however naive it may seem to us, it keeps these tribes from reaching such an impasse as that which is overwhelming Western civilization.

In more complex primitive societies conquest was often another way of preventing war from destroying the society. The difference between erstwhile conqueror and conquered was sometimes set up as a traditional and respected caste distinction, and the specialized activities of both tribes were retained and made mutually supporting. Thus in East Africa conquered groups of iron workers and agriculturalists were made an organic part of tribal economy by conquering cattle herders. The farmers were not put off their lands nor the monopoly of the iron workers destroyed. We pity the farmers and iron workers their low status, but war among the occupants of the common territory was nevertheless eliminated and the symbiotic relationship worked well enough to foster a remarkable civilization.

I do not know, therefore, of any primitive tribes which have strong mutual interdependence in the mainstays of life or in the common occupancy of land and have nevertheless carried on among themselves the socially lethal species of warfare. I do not doubt that there have been such tribes, but in the absence of written history the oblivion that covers their folly is complete. Primitive examples of lethal warfare are not in the realm of economic interdependence but in the realm of marriage dependency. Primitive communities have rigid rules about which women a man may marry, and often he may marry no one in his own village. If then each village is at war with every other village, my victim in warfare will be my wife's village-mate or "brother," often even her blood brother and her blood father. If there are no counterbalancing institutions which make for peace, war under these conditions cuts the roots of family life. A woman's existence is passed in divided loyalty; if she is in her husband's village she must celebrate the victory dance for the head of her brother, if in her father's, for the head of her husband. Her children will know their mother's brother as the slayer of their father, and their father as the slayer of their mother's brothers. No economic security can be built up around affinal exchange — the exchange of valuables between marrying families.

In some jungle tribes of South America, such as the Kaingang of Brazil,[6] conditions are even worse. Little food-gathering bands, all of one tribe, wander about the jungle, and in each band a man has relatives who expect him to join their group and help them. He knows, however, that he will do this at the risk of his life, and the hand of every man is therefore raised against his fathers-in-law and brothers-in-law in every other band. Their blood feuds are interminable and treacherous and socially calamitous beyond anything other primitive tribes can show; tribes like this were in the process of destroying themselves when their remnants were herded onto reservations. Such societies have allowed warfare and blood feuds to disrupt the mutually dependent intermarrying groups, and they pay for it in the social consequences of their folly.

The civilized world has reverted today to the war between brothers-in-law. We wage the lethal variety of the genus War and the poisonousness of it comes not from what man is but from what society is. War may root itself deeply and flourish fiercely between truly independent societies, and though individuals die, war does not destroy the social fabric of the civilization. The gains of the victors may be true gains, and the losses of the victims may be taken in their stride or they may be recouped. A weak tribe may be wiped out, but the loss does not weaken the victor. When communities become interdependent, however, gains are not gains and losses can be recouped only by further destruction of both parties to the struggle. Then war becomes a sociological tragedy.

The danger of war to society, therefore, is not just its double standard in homicide. The real threat comes when war flies in the face of social conditions which make it suicidal. The development of modern finance, commerce, production, and art and science had brought the interdependence of nations to a high point before the First World War set a high mark for all times in socially lethal warfare. We have to recognize that waging war under modern conditions is socially disastrous to conquered and conqueror alike, and this is a crucial fact about war in our times that makes nonsense of my friends' fatalism about the world. To me they seemed spectators who had watched a man seeking the health of the right side of his body by mutilating the left. He had used knives and shot and shell, and as he lay in torment they said, "He is trapped. He can't do what he is trying to do. He wasn't made right." Of course he can't do it; an infection on his left side spreads to his right, and when he has put one leg out of commission the other won't carry him forward. But a physician would say, "The man will die unless he stops this behavior. He will be cured only when he recognizes that his life blood circulates throughout his whole body and that all his knifing of one area can end only in his death."

So in the great society which the world has become by technological progress, the economist must say, "Civilization is built today upon mass production and every civilized country wants to sell. It thinks it can sell without buying. It tries to favor one member of its body politic against the other. When it finds that this won't work — as how could it when selling and buying are two sides to the coin? — it goes to war 'to protect its markets' and says it is doomed when finance and commerce are further ruined." The statesman must say, "Modern nations cannot carry out conflicting and cutthroat policies without compromising the interests of all other nations. They cannot divert production from consumption goods to armaments without involving the whole world in a race for armaments. Our policies are creating lethal dislocations which are pulling down our civilization in a common ruin and we cry out that we are betrayed. A civilization which has to live as one whole can save itself only by adopting institutions which allow it to function as such."

For you cannot have it both ways at once. You cannot be an international civilization and reap its benefits, and at the same time engage as a national to destroy other nationals root and branch. War in such a society becomes a case of cutting off your nose to spite your face.

Since this is the fundamental point about war, it is the part of wisdom to admit that no intelligence was applied in the World War, either in the propaganda of the nationals during the war or in the peace treaty that followed it. Every difficulty of the era preceding the World War was intensified between 1914 and 1919, and the results were what any visitor from Mars would have expected. Nations at the close of the war still proposed to themselves goals they could not pursue in splendid isolation, yet not a single nationalistic institution was modified to conform more accurately to the realities of such a world. The elementary change that was needed was an end to international anarchy. We needed an end to national sovereignties in coinage, in colonies, in protectionist policies, and in national defense. What we got was buffer states, "self-determination" to increase the number of little rival cells, restrictions on imports, and a League of Nations to keep the peace when none of those nations wanted to put into effect the conditions of peace. The victor nations set themselves to reap all the profits of international exchange and at the same time laid the ax to the conditions under which international exchange could operate. Of course this bred resentment of the have-not nations, a race for armaments, national aggressions, and eventually the war that was declared on September 2, 1939.

It is a complete misunderstanding to lay this havoc to any biological need of man to go to war. The havoc is man-made. Nevertheless we may soon be involved in the World War. We may be swept along by defense of our American way of life, by our unwillingness to give up profits, by aggressions given and received; whether the reasons are idealistic or not, the cost will be the same. But the price may be paid for nothing as in World War I or it may be paid for something worth the price. But what sort of peace aims must we have if anything is to be salvaged? On that hangs all the issue. Certainly they will not be return to prewar conditions. Those are the conditions of the most lethal warfare in world history. We must work for institutions to implement our modern world necessities. It is necessary to invoke man's real self-interest and to provide a framework within which he can pursue it. For all history testifies that no self-interests operate when social machinery is not provided for them. The human task always and everywhere has been to get this social machinery to conform to social realities. The social realities change, and no change in human history has been more drastic than the change from the tiny self-sufficient tribe to the condition of the industrial world today. Even Aristotle, thinking of Athens in the fourth century B.C., made the distinctive mark of the state, not sovereignty, but self-sufficiency. If there was self-sufficiency, sovereignty flowed from that. His analysis was logical and acute. Today, when this correspondence between sovereignty and self-sufficiency is gone, sovereignty as nations exercise it today has become a suicidal anachronism.

It is international anarchy. Anarchy whether within a nation or among nations is absence of a common government, absence of machinery to insure a *modus vivendi*. Hobbes was right. Anarchy is always in human affairs the one paramount peril outweighing all defects in legislation and administration; in a state of anarchy man's life is "poor, nasty, brutish and short." Hobbes was writing of anarchy within nations as he had seen it in the English Civil War of the seventeenth century; if he had lived today he would have turned his mighty sentences against international anarchy. Not all wars, even in Western civilization, have been followed by cumulative chaos. Between 1780 and 1870 the states at war were as jealous and cutthroat as states today. They seem infinitesimally small to us today, but in proportion to the wealth of nations and the necessities of commerce at that time they were comparable to the world wars of this century. The states that were involved then were Bavaria and Prussia, Baden and Württemberg, Piedmont and Tuscany and the Papal States. The wars that were carried on among these states to prevent consolidation were deadly and left all participants the poorer. Their cost was the price the established order was willing to pay to prevent any readjustment to new conditions, and grinding necessity triumphed only when large sections and huge interests were left powerless by defeat. Since they did bow, and consolidation triumphed, we speak in retrospect of the good these wars accomplished. But the "good" was in the consolidation and not in the wars. In Switzerland, Canada, and the Thirteen Colonies, consolidation was achieved without war among the constituent states, and war was therefore not even a necessary condition.

The federation of these states, however, stopped at boundaries which are no longer large enough for the modern world with its recent industrial and technological advances. These consolidations hardened prematurely after 1870 into units known as Italy and Germany and other European states. Now that the world has contracted still further and still larger areas must pool their claims and recognize reciprocal advantages, we must work for such war aims as we have never worked before. We must create a public opinion in the democracies that will insist on public statement of such aims in Congress and in Parliament before it is too late. We must insist upon it as a condition of aid to Britain. Lethal warfare can be stopped. But it can be stopped only by creating new international arrangements within which all are the gainers because rival sovereignties and cutthroat policies have been eliminated. The idealistic impulses with which all people engage in war are rightly suspect. We shall be idealistic, like everyone else, but we must remember that our good impulses will accomplish no social good for the duration and after the war is over they will accomplish nothing unless they change the rules of the game. Good impulses are necessary because without them the rules may continue as they are, but they really count only when they have revised the rules. There were good impulses abroad in the Thirteen Colonies after the Revolution, but the basis for the growth of our own country was not laid until the rival colonies, after thirteen years of impotence and growing disorder, had pooled their western territorial claims, agreed to a common currency and set up a Federal government to deal with problems which transcended local interests. Our founding fathers had to set up a system under which it was within the realm of possibility that the colonies could pursue common goals at all. They were farsighted, for in 1789 it was not as clear as it is today that technological and commercial and other social forces were operating to make great areas interdependent; it was clearer by 1919 and the havoc was the greater when the task remained undone after the World War.

Ringing generalizations about peace aims are just as suspect as noble impulses are. Even in primitive societies there are horrible examples. We should do well to lay to heart the case of the Iroquois Indians. They were successful warriors who formed a confederacy "to preserve the peace." They talked of their peace aims in many touching metaphors and enshrined them in fine ritual poetry. Their confederacy made them the scourge of all the tribes within reach of their marches; "to keep the peace" they ravaged the lesser tribes and disrupted their own economy. While the Iroquois warriors were away, tribes that had suffered at their hands banded together and fell upon their villages. It reads like a savage version of the Peace of Versailles.

If such peace was a disastrous failure in the simple world of the Iroquois, the chances against its success are infinitely greater in Western civilization in 1941. But there seems no reason to resign ourselves and say that the problem has grown so large that man cannot deal with it if he will. World economic and social conditions today provide the solid bases for international cooperation if we will work to set up the mechanisms which could end our chaos. If we fail it is because we are not sufficiently clear in our analysis and radical in our demands. We cannot trust to police powers and arbitration of conflicts. Penal sanctions do not touch the heart of the problem. We must work for a peace which will provide social machinery which is adapted to modern social realities.

Ideologies in the Light
of Comparative Data *

At the present moment two great ideologies are drawn up in conflict with one another. Wars where the opponents have clear, contrasting value systems or ideologies are not nearly so common as wars where both sides are fighting for the same things, and the great issue at stake is whether one or the other will win the stakes. The Axis, however, has been explicit and drastic in promulgating its value system, and the democracies have countered, producing passionate ideologies of freedom in every day's issues of the press and of books. The Nazi state denounces these milk-sop ideals of freedom and opposes to them ideologies of submission to a leader and of individual sacrifice to a New Order in which lesser breeds will be slaves and servitors to the fittest and dominant conquerors. As anthropologists must we, in this conflict of value systems, take a professional stand of cultural relativity, and no matter how we are involved as citizens write ourselves down as skeptics? It is our traditional position, and we must certainly realize that it is this lesson that all things are relative which the general public has first and foremost learned from anthropology. The phrase "cultural relativity" has passed into currency even among people who have no idea what culture means to the anthropologist. And this "relativity" is today, even in psychological and sociological textbooks which make almost a fetish of cultural causation, hardly more than the generalization made by

* Excerpt from an unpublished manuscript, *circa* 1941–1942.

Sumner in his *Folkways*:[1] that every institutional value is of no value somewhere else and that every institution we do not value is valued somewhere else. Skepticism as to values is therefore the only position possible for a student of comparative cultures.

This skepticism which becomes a commonplace to every anthropologist must be strictly defined. It is a skepticism which doubts the social consequences of any formal cultural institution. Democracy, monarchy, and plutocracy have all been represented in stable and zestful states; democracy has held sway not only in tribes where men pursued their own goals with assurance but in the worst sorcery tribes, too. Democracy is obviously only a political form which *can* be used to promote the individual freedom our ideologies exalt; it does not inherently assure it. Polygamy functions in some instances to make a stable and cohesive family; monogamy in others. Or either one can function to promote a progressively more disrupted family with greater and greater human tensions. It is the same with other cultural traits whether they are divine kingship or bride price or magic; they may function so that people rightly value them as bulwarks of the smooth working of their society, or so that people will say that there is conflict and aggression in *their* society just *because* the divine king kills or exploits at his pleasure, or just *because* the bride price makes it impossible for young men to marry, or just *because* the sorcerer can use his magic against anyone.

As anthropologists I think we would all grant this point as valid, and therefore anthropologists' restatement of many present-day ideologies is drastic. We could not trust political representative government to work automatically and of its own nature to preserve and further the freedom we exalt. Nationalism too is a culture trait which is relative in regard to its functioning. Nationalism is a culture trait which functions in various ways. Our form of nationalism today is disruptive of world order, but the anthropologist cannot be satisfied with "nationalism" as an adequate explanation of that disruption. He knows that in many societies, intense tribal feeling has functioned to maintain loyalty and cohesiveness. Private property figures in certain ideologies today as if it carried with it some inherent kind of functioning. Popular discussions of it are about where anthropological discussions of "communal property" were in the days before Lowie analyzed them in *Primitive Society*.[2] As he showed there, these instances of communal property are not true alternatives to private property; the tribes described as communal had private property too. But it did not function as private property does in some other societies. There is no inherent same-functioning that goes with owning property.

But when we have said all this, we have merely cleared the ground. The fundamental problem before all sciences — physical *and* social — is still to learn the conditions which do bring about a designated outcome. The prime lesson the social sciences can learn from the natural sciences is just this: that it is necessary to press on to find the positive conditions under which desired events take place, and that these can be just as scientifically investigated as can instances of negative correlation. This problem is *beyond relativity*. Durkheim asked questions of this sort in his *Division of Labor in Society*,[3] and though his answers must be challenged today in the light of present-day field work, his phrasing of such problems is important. A major goal of social science is to discover the ways and means of social cohesion — the scientific study of aspects of society which *do* correlate with social cohesion and so with minimizing individual aggression and frustration.

Primitive Freedom*

IN THE 1890's, when Siberia meant to most people only a place to which Csarist Russia sent its political exiles, some of these more enterprising exiles lightened their boredom there by going native. They learned the languages of strange tribes herding mares or reindeer on the frozen tundras, traveled with them from camp to camp, and were taught by the native shamans their mediumistic lore. The most gifted of these involuntary anthropologists was Vladimïr Bogoras, who wrote Russian novels under the name of Tan. His careful account of life among the Chukchee of northeast Siberia is one of the great anthropological volumes.

He was fascinated by his rich, murderous, suiciding Chukchee. Even their routine exchanges of commodities were occasions for knifing. Their language had no word for trading; realistically enough, they called it blood-feuding. Knifing came closer home, too; sons killed their fathers, and brothers their brothers. And with impunity. A strong man was one who could abuse anyone, relative or stranger; and the strong man had his own way and was envied. The father's boast when a child was born was: "Ah! I have created a strong man for times to come, one who will take the property of all those living in the country around us."

Bogoras was not unfamiliar with abuses visited on one man by another; he had been exiled for protesting against them in his own

* The Atlantic Monthly, CLXIX, No. 6 (1942), 756–63.

country. But in Csarist Russia his protests had been directed against the state and its beneficiaries; to protest against abuses meant to protest against the state. And his Chukchee had no state at all. There was no political organization. Whatever men had the strength and means to do they could do. They were rich, too, beyond the dreams of all neighboring tribes. One man might own as many as three thousand reindeer, and that was great wealth. The Chukchee were, therefore, rich and democratic. If a people have no tyrannous state and if they have an abundance economy, ought they not by these circumstances to be free men? Ought they not to feel they were able to pursue and attain their own personal goals?

Nothing was clearer than that the Chukchee knew they were not free. Their word for it was "doom." They were, they said, "doomed to anger," "doomed to death," "doomed to receiving supernatural power." They spoke truly. Anger swept over them like a flood from outside themselves; they showed their teeth, they growled, they lost consciousness of what they were doing. Men — and women too — disappointed in sharing the tag-end of a smoke had killed to get hold of the pipe, and many more had ruined themselves financially because the trader had known they would stop at no price to obtain tobacco without delay. Sons, too, were "doomed" to anger against their fathers, and fathers against their sons. If they killed in their anger, it was nobody's business, and the survivors divided the spoils. They chose to bring about their own death, too. When they suffered from despondency or from physical pain, they preferred, they said, to destroy the self with the suffering. "We are surrounded," they said, "by enemies with gaping mouths [the spirits]," and the worst possible death was the torture these gods were waiting to visit upon them; they preferred to die at their own will. When they ate the fly agaric, a poisonous mushroom for which they had an inordinate passion, they said to it, "Take me to the dead," and some indeed died in the coma the drug induced. Sought death was commoner, though, with a spear thrust. Young men had to rip their own bowels, but older men could vow their own death and require their sons to drive home the spear. It was a solemn duty, for a man who had once announced his wish to die a voluntary death could not take back his vow without disasters striking the whole community.

This picture of Chukchee behavior was not all that Bogoras recorded. He described also the arrangements of their social order. They lived in small encampments which had to be moved as the herd moved. The master of the herd lived in the front tent, and his ownership of the herd meant that he could dispose of all food and skins at his own will; if he chose to put his family on starvation diet, it was his prerogative. His sons or sons-in-law in the camp approached him each morning for his instructions, and he had naked power over them. Even when he became senile he could do with his family as he wished, for they all depended upon the herd. If he was bad tempered and tyrannous, the only way in which they could govern their own lives was to seize wealth and power for themselves — perhaps by killing their father.

At all events sons did not expect benefits from their fathers or from any elders. When they were no taller than their small reindeer, they were herding on the tundra, and if the half-wild animals broke away from them they were responsible like any man. After adolescence they had to obtain a wife, but this meant they had to go empty-handed like any propertyless Chukchee and serve for her. They were systematically humiliated by their prospective fathers-in-law. They slept outside the sleeping tent in the arctic weather and were fed with scraps. They were the butt of the new family's jibes and tyrannies, and if they gave up and returned home their own fathers would receive them with taunts and they had to begin service all over again in another family which had a marriageable daughter. Neither in the matter of getting a wife nor at any other time did a man have any reason to believe that his own family would assist him. If his own family did not, certainly no one else would. If a man lost his reindeer he might become a homeless wanderer, trudging from camp to camp and fed grudgingly with scraps for a day or two before he set out again on his endless tramping.

The Chukchee are a tribe with wealth and with no political autocracy, who made of life a snatch-as-snatch-can. It was not possible to live at peace and without the interference of others. They live, of course, in a punishing environment, but plenty of other preliterate people who live in earthly paradises are as "doomed" as the Chukchee. In such tribes men would laugh at you if you tried to show them that living well and at peace was really a very simple matter because the coconut and the breadfruit tree and the sago grow luxuriantly without human labor. They know that there is no open course toward well-being spread before them to follow at their own will. They know they are not free. They are conscious first and foremost of obstacles in the way of attaining their own purposes. In such societies men are intensely aware that every step toward any goal they have set themselves is at the mercy of others. They are balked at every turn, or else they win through by overpowering others. They know that, whatever they want to do, they must get the better of someone else in the community or they must play the sycophant. They know no other roles than those of aggression and of obsequiousness.

2

A couple of years ago I lived with the Blackfoot Indians of Canada. They too had been rich and they had been democratic, but in addition they were sure they had been free. Even today they could not understand the meaning of being "doomed." They were sure every man had his own personal desires and spent his life realizing them. What else would be a reason for living? Even today, when the buffalo they lived on are gone from the plains, I thought them a people to whom an understanding of liberty was as natural as breathing. How had they achieved a way of life that was so opposite to the Chukchee?

They were full of tales of their great chief Eagle in the Skies, and many early settlers and travelers had also written about him. Eagle in the Skies was chief of an illustrious Blackfoot band and he was rich. All the Blackfoot cared about wealth, and they thought that people without wealth were inferior. Eagle in the Skies was a superior being and he had wealth to prove it. He had been a great hunter and raider of horses. He could provide for a whole coterie of wives who dressed skins for him, made beaded skin garments, dried meat, and made pemmican. As the most successful provider in the band, he was made chief. But a chief among the Blackfoot was not invested with punitive power over his people, and his prestige depended on his band's prestige.

His followers' personal ambitions were Eagle's greatest assets, and it was against his interests to balk them. A young retainer, as yet unmounted, had only to be known as a good horseman to be free to use Eagle's horses in hunting or on a raid. What the young man took contributed to the glory and well-being of Eagle's band, but kudos belonged to the young hunter, even the kudos of distributing the horses or the buffalo meat. The indigent young man's family boasted of his prowess, parading the camp circle and shouting his achievements. The young man himself began looking for a wife among the daughters of leading men who would be glad of such a son-in-law. Without the use of Eagle's horses he would not have been able to make his mark in the tribe's estimation, but such use was no charity; whether the young man brought in buffalo or the enemy's horses, it enlarged Eagle's ego no less than the young hunter's. It was strictly to Eagle's advantage to have a well-fed and well-mounted band. Blackfoot in other bands, dissatisfied with the leaders in their own communities, took occasion to join Eagle's and share in its prosperity. Eagle's band grew. He was well served and so were his followers. When a poor young man lost one of Eagle's good horses on a raid, the chief wrote it off. What was an occasional horse to him when sharing with his followers brought him such large returns? Mutual advantage flowed between the chief and his adherents.

Eagle in the Skies served his own ends by seeing that his people could rise according to their abilities. He served their ends also. Any of his followers, if he had ability, could reach any position in the tribe. If he underwent the training and paid the price, he could have supernatural power. His father-in-law was a principal benefactor throughout his life, and he in turn distributed to his father-in-law a principal part of his take either in hunting or on the warpath. At any step in his career, if he had earned their respect, he could be sure of the praise and active support of his fellows in his undertakings.

There are many such tribes. In these societies the higher a man climbs in status the more responsibilities he must shoulder for his fellows. What else could status mean according to their way of thinking? When any man, on the contrary, is out of luck, it is no catastrophe. Someone with whom he divided his kangaroo meat over and over again, when he brought in game, shares with him as a matter of course. It is tribal custom. When he grows too feeble to be an active hunter, his son-in-law brings him the best cuts just as the old man when he was younger took his best cuts to his own father-in-law. Much of his behavior seems to us to put the interests of others above his own interests, but he would be completely incredulous if you tried to point this out to him. It appears to him that he has always done as he chose to do. Why else did he live?

3

We need to inquire from such societies as these what it is that makes for well-being and a sense of freedom in tribes like the Blackfoot and for the conviction of doom in tribes like the Chukchee. We are fighting today a war which is to preserve freedom, and we need to know its proved strategy. We need a wider range of cases than are available to us from the troubled democracies of our day, and for these we can best go to the anthropologist.

The anthropologist has many instances spread before him, for he studies human societies as different as possible from our own, and specializes in simple societies which have grown up outside the sphere of influence of Western civilization. He can study the strategy by which societies have realized one or another set of values, whether these values have to do with freedom or social cohesion or submission to authority. His tribes serve him as a laboratory serves when we investigate, for instance, the life and death of bacteria. To be sure, the anthropological laboratory is not one the investigator sets up himself; it was set up for him by generations of natives working out their own way of life in all its details over many thousands of years. But the field worker has only to study his own particular tribe to recognize, even if it is in an unfamiliar guise, most of our current issues.

His naked savages do not, of course, talk of social security acts, but they are entirely explicit about the care of the old and the hungry. Some tribes take care of them and some do not, and the anthropologist can study the consequences. Nor do his natives speak of a golden rule, but the working of the golden rule can be studied among natives from Australia to the Kalahari Desert. "Who will feed you if you do not feed them?"; "Who will honor you if you do not honor them?" are themes which are dinned into the young and lived out in detail by adults in native South Sea Islands and under the cold fogs of Tierra del Fuego. There are equally primitive tribes which have no version at all of the golden rule, and the anthropologist can study the consequences of its absence just as well as of its presence. Is it power over people? Some primitive peoples hardly know any other way of handling human relations, and some, on the other hand, have never had occasion arbitrarily to coerce another human being.

So too with liberty. Liberty is the battle standard we fight under today, but we are at odds about the strategy of attaining it. The issue which is relevant to liberty is now, as it has always been, what societies do about the individual's pursuit of his own goals; and some societies are as successful as the Blackfoot in rearing men convinced of their freedom, and some are as unsuccessful as the Chukchee.

The first question we need to ask about such societies is whether they are free because they are democracies. Even a preliterate tribe is democratic if there is no entrenched political autocracy and if social control is ultimately in the hands of citizens. But being a democracy has not by itself guaranteed the blessings of liberty. In many democracies men do not sleep well nights in the confidence that they are safe from the aggressions of the fellow tribesmen. This is unfortunate for them, for their lives become full of violence and frustration, but it is fortunate for us because from their experience we can get information we desperately need.

The mere fact of leaving ultimate social control in the hands of the people has not guaranteed that men will be able to conduct their lives as free men. Those societies where men know they are free are often democracies, but sometimes they have strong chiefs and kings. Whether they are democracies or kingdoms, they have, however, one common characteristic: they are all alike in making certain freedoms common to all citizens, and inalienable. In our

American vocabulary all those things which from time to time society has put beyond the reach of arbitrary interference by other men we call civil liberties. Habeas corpus, equality before the law, freedom of opinion and of assembly, stand or fall according as they are guaranteed to all men. They stand or fall according as it is true that what privilege I have, you have too. Civil liberties are only privileges which men in some societies have agreed to make common property for all citizens.

So too in primitive societies there are civil liberties, the crux of which is that they are guaranteed to all men without discrimination. Wherever these privileges and protections to which all members have an inalienable right are important privileges in the eyes of that tribe, people regard themselves, whatever their form of government, as free men enjoying the blessings of liberty.

4

Every society has a different list of these civil liberties. Some are longer than ours, some are shorter and more restricted. Some are guaranteed by formal law and some are upheld simply by the folkways. The one that is commonest in human societies is the right to hospitality. Any man sets food before his guest, often even without questioning whether or not he is a tribesman. But as a civil liberty within the tribe it goes much farther than days-long hospitality. As in the Blackfoot camp of Chief Eagle in the Skies, no man goes hungry while there is food in the community, and he exercises this right to subsistence not as a claim on charity but as a civil liberty which all tribesmen share. In any season of scarcity, for example, it does not matter who brings in the game or who owns the grain or the herds: the meals are served to all in common, share and share alike, or else through the etiquette of hospitality all those whose supplies are low are guests of those who are well provided. There will be "turn about" someday.

In some tribes, eating from each other's pots becomes a symbol whose value has nothing to do with utility; it becomes obsessive. When the pots boil in the evening before each house, women dish up the food and carry it hither and yon to other houses, receiving in turn the stew from all their neighbors. Each family gathers at last around a pot which contains the cooking of a couple of dozen housewives. There is no measuring of *quid pro quo*; they have elaborated the common and inalienable right to an evening meal till it means to them that all villagers should eat the contents of all pots.

Another civil liberty that is common among native tribes is one which is guaranteed the young when they become physically able to earn their own livelihood. Such tribes regard it as a tribal good that all boys and girls, as soon as they have sufficient strength to do the work of adults, should be provided with tools and fields and herds so that they can contribute to the community food supply. This would often be impossible if they were dependent solely on their parents, and different primitive societies have different ways of solving this youth problem.

Many South American Indian villages which depended on their corn fields for their food had annual reallotments of fields so that each able-bodied man might be responsible for tending the acreage he could actually cultivate. Some tribes in other parts of the world pay youngsters with disproportionate gifts during their apprentice period, so that anyone who is not congenitally lazy can count on having an adult's equipment by the time he is ready to take on a man's responsibility.

In other tribes skills are far more important than the tools of production, and especially in hunting tribes the stress is all upon building up the boy's ability and self-confidence in the exercise of daring feats in tracking the bear or bringing down the buffalo. The child's ability is carefully reckoned against his past achievement, not against some arbitrary or adult standard; he is shown how to hunt by a much older brother or by an uncle, and he is encouraged by village-wide praise when he has taken the initiative and brought in even a tiny rodent. With each larger animal he bags he is again acclaimed. It would be foolish, they think, not to build up a child's self-confidence.

One of the most important of civil liberties in such tribes is the opportunity to enter any profession according to a man's individual ability. When status is thus open and can be freely achieved, any man can weigh the responsibility of important status against its prerogatives and limit his ambitions accordingly. He often accepts gladly the role of follower even though chieftainship has its obvious glamour. A great deal is required of the chief, and many men are willing enough to play a lesser part. A great deal is required of the rich man and the shaman and the priest, of the war leader and the owner of many medicine bundles. Many men choose not to undertake the rigorousness of the training or the responsibilities of the position.

5

When, however, a privileged group can act arbitrarily and without responsibility and still retain its privileges, men's individual goals are threatened. This is not because one group has great prerogatives, for Eagle in the Skies had his great prerogatives too. It is because, as among the Chukchee, these are split off from responsibility and respect for those upon whose labor the advantages depend; it is because under that particular social order men can keep personal advantages without returning equivalents. Then freedom is threatened.

Freedom in all societies therefore must have this ingredient of the exchange of equivalents. Privilege must mean more equivalents returned rather than less. If the king has emoluments, he must be able to use them only so that his people feel he acts for them. If a medicine man has supernatural power, he must not be able to use it to kill others by lingering death, but his prayers must provide rain for the fields, and increase and long life for the people. If the rich are privileged, their possessions must not disallow the subsistence of others or preëmpt natural resources. Otherwise men do not feel confident about their personal goals. They know they are not free of hindrance, and they act with all the furtiveness and the aggression that goes along with serious frustration. They are not free men — not even the privileged. For in societies where advantages can be achieved only at the expense of others, the great and powerful are, if possible, even more vulnerable than the weak. They can never reach a security that cannot be cut at its roots, and "the tallest oak has the greatest fall."

Societies which make privilege inseparable from trusteeship have been able to perpetuate and extend civil liberties. They have been able to unite the whole society into a kind of joint-stock company where any denial of rights is a threat to each and every member. It is the basis upon which strong and zestful societies are built and the basis for the individual's sense of inner freedom.

This analysis of freedom does not sound so alien in Western civilization in times of war as it does in times of peace. War is the one situation in our society when we rally for mutual advantage and call on every man to show group loyalty. It is ironic that nations which exalt personal profit as the one way in which to keep the wheels of industry moving should in wartime eradicate or conceal the profit motive and trust again in group loyalty. In this major emergency we turn away from the competitive motive. In spite of all the declarations of learned writers that working for profit is the only incentive upon which society can depend, in war we know it is too weak and too expensive. We invoke again cooperation for the common good and the defense of our country. And it is a commonplace that men like war. For peace, in our society, with the feeling we have then that it is feeble-minded to strive except for one's own private profit, is a lonely thing and a hazardous business. Over and over men have proved that they prefer the hazards of war with all its suffering. It has its compensations.

The moral is not that war is therefore an inevitable human need, but that our social order starves men in peacetime for gratifications they get only in time of war. Many Indians of the great Mississippi plains, on the other hand, set up war and peace in reverse. Their peacetime dealings with their fellow tribesmen were arranged in joint-stock-company fashion with pooled profits and limited liability. Their primitive guerrilla warfare, however, was a field in which private advantage could be safely sought at the expense of an enemy they did not even count as "human." The Dakota Indians were brave and inveterate followers of the warpath. They were feared by all neighboring tribes. But the state had no stake in their exploits; no armies were sent out for political objectives, and the idea of establishing their sovereignty over another tribe had not occurred to them. Young men on the warpath accumulated long lists of standardized exploits — for getting away with an enemy's horse picketed in his camp circle, for touching a fallen enemy who was still alive, for taking a scalp, for bringing a slain or wounded tribesman from the enemy's lines, for having a horse shot under one. These coups, as the voyagers called them, they totaled up and used for vying with their fellows. The warpath and all that went with it was competitive. A man joined a war party for no reasons of patriotism, but because he wanted to make his mark. When the party got to enemy country, each man put on his finest regalia and the feather headdress, each feather of which was insignia of a coup he had previously taken. When the party returned to its home camp, those who had coups to their credit were extravagantly acclaimed by all those families who could in any way claim relationship to the heroes. To their dying day warriors boasted competitively of their accumulated coups. A hundred or more counting sticks were kept in the council house, and men "won" who had the right to take up the greatest number of sticks and tell their exploits.

Life within the Dakota tribe, on the other hand, and all dealings within the community, rested solidly on mutual advantage and group loyalty. The large family connections, the band, even the whole tribe, was a cooperating group where mutual support brought every man honor. The worst thing that could be said of a Dakota was: "He thinks more of what he owns than he does of people." They took it literally and in great giveaways they showed how much they "cared for people"; obviously, too, giving lavishly raised the giver's own standing in the tribe. *Noblesse oblige* they took literally too. A person who had risen high and who had a strong and prosperous family must be by that token the most generous and the most willing to give all kinds of assistance. It was an essential part of his honorable status. The Dakota had tied group loyalty inextricably to times of peace.

The war against the Axis in 1942 is not Dakota guerrilla warfare which each man can fight out by himself to gain his own personal coup. It is a war between two ideologies about the way to set up human societies. Nazi theory and practice have abjured the strategy of freedom and oppose to it submission to a leader and individual sacrifice to a New Order in which lesser breeds are to be slaves and servitors to the fittest and dominant conquerors. The democracies, with all their shortcomings, base their philosophy upon freedoms which *can* be made common and provide political frameworks which can be used to extend them. Axis oratory uses the word "freedom," but Axis "freedoms" are those which *cannot* be made common, because they imply an underdog. They are the "freedoms" to expropriate from a subject people, to use naked force against the helpless, to drag dissenters from their homes and kill them out of hand. The Axis has made these measures the tools of state administration, and these measures cut civil liberties at their roots. The nation which rules others by terror must extend its reign of terror. It must continue to follow the path it has chosen.

There is solid reason, therefore, in the history of human societies, for the opposition of the democracies to the spread of the Nazi state and of Nazi ideology. But this solid reason is grounded on the social utility of civil liberties, the liberties which can be made common property. Civil liberties in all human societies have always paid their way; they have given advantages to all citizens and all tribesmen. Special privileges, arbitrary power, on the other hand, are boomerangs which return to strike those who wield them, and they bring conflict and often terror into the whole society. Therefore, we in America are willing to pay enormous prices lest liberty be lost on our continent. The only argument is how best to keep ourselves strong and uncontaminated. For this great end we must be clear in our minds that the way to keep ourselves from the taint of our enemies is through the defense of civil liberties. We must be sure that we do not curtail them in the fields already allowed, and we must extend them to other fields not now recognized. For liberty is the one thing no man can have unless he grants it to others.

Selections from the Correspondence
between Ruth Benedict and Franz Boas
1923–1940

To THE end of his life, Franz Boas dictated letters under a sense of constraint, and the copies of his correspondence in the American Philosophical Society are correspondingly unrevealing. However, these letters to Ruth Benedict were written by hand, as were most of her letters to him, and their exchange is revealing of the depth and style of their relationship, for which a common concern for the needs of anthropology and anthropological students and the wider world formed a basis.

West Alton, New Hampshire
September 16, 1923

My dear Dr. Boas,

I'm hoping this will be at least a steamer letter on your way back, but I may be too late even for that. All summer I've worked on the mythology and I don't suppose a day has ever passed that I haven't wished fervently I could ask you some question, or wondered what you thought of some difficult coincidence in the stories. I've acquired considerable material but I haven't set to work to tabulate it yet, nor even tried to summarize anything. There is always something more I need to know before it can be worthwhile to make up my mind about anything.

I've been acquiring enough Spanish to read the untranslated tales. You knew I'd have to do it, but I smiled at your tact in letting me find it out for myself. . . . It was really the European tales that first gave me a real excitement about the problems. I hadn't had sufficient clue till I'd read the stories from the Philippines and from the American Negroes — the Africans too.

I shall be back in New York about the 1st of October, probably just about the time you will be getting back. The summer has gone unbelievably fast. Stanley has spent almost as much time in a new passion for photography as I have on folklore. It's a wonderful hobby. On our days off we've climbed mountains, or driven to the Ocean, or tramped back in the hills. But for all that I've kept a five day week on the stories all summer. And it's much more enjoyable to work out in a canoe than in the Columbia Library.

Give my love to Mrs. Boas. The summer can't have been an easy one, with more insane diplomatic stupidity piling up every day, and suffering growing more and more acute. Have you brought back anything that gives grounds for hope? I shall be enormously glad to see you.

[From RFB to FB in Germany]
June 12, 1929

Dear Papa Franz,

I have thought of you and Mama Franz so often since I heard of her sister's death. It is hard to have a break come in the family when one is away from home.

Ironically enough, I've been working at the college more lately than for a long time before. It seems very lonely without you. Ruth Bunzel has been here so far, but she has her passage reserved for Mexico for next week. I'll be going out to Bedford Hills the end of this week, and the first of next we'll go up to New Hampshire.

Mel and Fan Herskovits have been here this last week. They are both well and full of their coming trip. Fan is going into the bush this time.

Douglas Haring was here a week or so ago. He saw the Sociology Department who seemed to think well in the main of his coming over into anthropology, and he is working this summer to make himself ready. It's still uncertain when he can make it.

I've been much distressed about the winding up of the Folklore business. . . .

It makes me all the more anxious to get together the salary for a real paid worker who'd take over the *Journal*[1] work, and the work on the finance and membership lists of the Folklore Society and the Ethnological. Ruth Bryan sent in a woman to see me who would take $100; she's a little past middle age and wants a permanent job that she could make her own. Ruth says she's an excellent worker. She's a good typist too, so we could use her that way. I shall see Nelson before I go and try to interest him in getting the appropriation from Ethnological. Naturally the woman wants to know whether she could count on the job October 1st, and I shall certainly try hard to garner the salary together. Have you any suggestions.

We made a mistake in not telling Elsie about the Philosophy Department's project in Mexico. Gladys told her, and she was very much interested, and a little annoyed at not having known before. I wrote her how nebulous the whole thing was, and that nothing had really come up yet at all. I don't know why I didn't make a point of speaking to her about it at the very first, but it was always so far ahead and so vague and I see her so little too.

Erna sent in an outline of the Twin Brothers cycle for the whole southwest that was excellent, I thought. She sent it as a model for the revision of the Creation story, and I think it augurs very well indeed. I sent it on to Elsie with a carbon of the letter I'd written Erna, but when she returned it she didn't say at all whether she had liked the abstract or not. I hope she did.

Much love to you and to Mama Franz.

[From FB to RFB]
Mittenwald, Aug. 21, 1929

Dear Ruth,

Your letter of August 6th followed me here and I was glad to hear from you. We have been on the road for nearly a month. We left Berlin on July 26. We spent a delightful week with von den Steinens at their home in the Taunus. I think you know that we have been friends ever since 1885. We both of us like his wife also very much. We talked personal affairs as well as shop. While he is hale and hearty, he is 74 years old and I want to know about the status of his work so as to be able to see to it that it is not lost, if I should survive him. He has very valuable texts from the Marquesas, although phonetically not adequate, but just as good as the old Maori material. It is remarkable how stable these forms are in Polynesia. Some of his songs are almost identical in form with those from Hawaii.

From there we went to Bonn, where the "Burschenschaft" of which I was a member when a student celebrated its 85th anniversary. It was a pleasure to meet after 50 years some of my student friends. There were at least 8 with whom I studied at Bonn and, at least one of them, a man with whom I used to be very intimate. Can you imagine me wearing a red cap and a black, red and gold ribbon walking the streets with students and other old people adorned like myself? I was interested in the general attitude of the young people. It is the same in France and in Germany. The majority are violent nationalists, others extreme nationals. There is little heard from the unorganized middle group. It is sad but only too intelligible (that sounds very German; I mean easily understood). On account of the violence of party feeling and the multiplicity of parties, based partly on economic, partly on religious and local lines they long for a strong discipline to which they are ready to submit. Fundamentally there are two opposed ideas: the need of social readjustment and the enthusiasm for a united nation. Everybody asks for "unity" in all political affairs, but everybody means unity on the basis of his own views — Well, notwithstanding all this we had a few delightful days, a charming trip to the "Aarthal," a trip up the Rhine and finally a walk to the "Siebengebirgen." — From there we went to Stuttgart, just to see an old cousin of Mama Franz and then to München where I wanted to have a look at the anthropological laboratory. Then we went to Linz, again to see a cousin of Mama Franz and then to Carinthia where we stayed a few days with Frau von Luschan. She is just like my sister Hedwig. She lives only in memories of her husband and

all her thoughts center around that one point. If it were possible
to give them a new center of interest! Both have no children and
worked only for and with their husbands — but not independently.
We made a week of delightful trips into the high alps from there
and were favored by beautiful weather. Then in Mittenwald we
wanted to visit the places where we were with Gertrud[2] six years
ago, but the weather is now so unpropitious that we cannot do anything and we are going back to Berlin. I have a few more appointments on the way, but on the 26th we expect to be there.

During these weeks I have, of course, done nothing. I feel very
well and have time to do it when I get back to Berlin.

I had a letter from Herzog yesterday who says that he is getting
interesting points on the selection of language in poetry (music),
although he has not collected songs so far. I worry how we can
keep him over winter.

I trust you are having a good time with your husband in New
Hampshire. You know that we are going to sail from Hamburg on
the 20th of September on the St. Louis.

Mama Franz sends her kindest regards. I wonder if you have
heard by this time from Bunny.

[From FB to RFB]
[Vancouver, B.C.]
Oct. 21st, 1930

Here we are the first lap of our journey completed. Tomorrow
2 p.m. the steamer starts and with good luck we may be in Ft.
Rupert Thursday night, the 23rd. I wonder how I'll find everything. Julia is a pleasant companion, easily satisfied, but much
more interested in matters political than in nature. We had a
beautiful trip across the mountains, clear with wonderful light
effects. I had to think of the lovely trip Mama Franz and I had
eight years ago when we stopped off at Glacier, Lake Louise, Banff
and really enjoyed the beautiful nature. It will never be like that
again.

I trust you received my note from Chicago in which I said that
Jacobs will be glad to come. We ought to get $700 for him con-

sidering the long trip east. He will give the introductory course in
anthropology and modern life. I also wrote about Herskovits who
wants $500 (five hundred) now. You will have to manage that he
gets the rest as early as possible in January. Elsie said she would
pay $3000 on the seventh and the rest soon after. He wants to leave
on the 24th of Jan.

I have deposited my money in the Canadian Bank of Commerce
and shall draw then. I hope the Bursar has sent a draft for $500
to that Bank. You had better ask whether he has done so.

Please, take some interest in Miss Dijour so that she may be well
prepared for next summer. She ought to read all the Thompson
[River] material.

I am really looking forward to the coming week. It will be the
first serious field work I have done for a long, long time. The
Pueblos were always too onesided, because others did the ethnology.

I hope you will write me every now and then and let me know
how things are going.

Kindest greetings to all. Please write to Bunny to write to me.
Stupidly I did not take her address along.

[From FB to RFB]
Fort Rupert, Nov. 9th, 1930

We are getting on quite nicely now. Julia is making friends with
the women and has been learning matting and basket making. Now
she is learning cats cradles of which there are hundreds here. She
is picking up village gossip etc. The language comes pretty hard
to her. I talk with difficulty and understand after I write it. I follow
conversation only partly. It goes too rapidly, but I am getting into
it again. — There are now feasts without end. Day before yesterday I gave a feast to the Indians and according to custom they gave
us presents which make me broke, because I have to return the
value with interest. I have asked Helene to send you a check for
$100 and I wish to use another $100 of our account 19 which I
think I ought to have in order to be on the safe side. Can you get
one draft for the two amounts and send it to the Canadian Bank of
Commerce, Vancouver B.C. I fear I may need that much money.

The question of song and dance rhythm was not complicated.
The feet and hands move with the time beating; but time beating
and singing are a tough problem. There are at least four different
styles of song, text as well as time are of different styles. — I am
getting texts from different informants. The literary style of all
agrees fairly well so far, although there are minor differences. —
Yesterday we had a mourning feast, eating, mourning songs, speeches,
and a song to drive away sadness. There is a Comox Indian here.
I wonder whether you or Ruth Bryan could find in the Salishan
vocabularies in one of the files in my room a Cattotx (or Comox)
vocabulary and texts. If so, please, send it by registered mail. I
might get time to revise it, although I am not sure. He says there
are only 6 Comox left.

Kindest regards to everybody.

[From FB to RFB]
Beaver Harbor P.O. Port Hardy B.C.
Nov. 13, 1930

I telegraphed today in reply to your and Lesser's letters to send
him $150 and to take them temporarily from account 19. I think
this is my best way because I know there is enough money in that
account. I am getting the money for Lucy Kramer from Mr.
Sargent, so that amount will be released.

I am glad you got the $700 for Jacobs. I hope he'll do well and
also that it will help him.

We are getting along quite well. Almost every day brings a feast
with songs and dances. Julia danced last night with the crowd
and has her first formal Dancing lesson to-night. We are getting
quite a little acculturation material. It is marvelous how the old life
continues under the surface of the life [of] a poor fishing people.
I am getting some more rather interesting data regarding the development of the whole modern system. I think even the order
of seats among the bulk of the tribes is less than a hundred years
old. Julia is gradually getting some data on their modern economic
life. So far she has learned blanket work and is still collecting cat's
cradles, the distribution of which is not uninteresting. — I am

getting texts from different informants. The style is partly uniform, although some people have their individual mannerisms. The dance problem is difficult. I hope that the films will give us adequate material for making a real study.[3] In music there are a number of quite distinct styles: summer songs, mourning songs, love songs, winter songs, but I shall not unravel that problem while here. The language has also baffling problems. There is no *good* informant, because all are satisfied with a variety of forms. I rather think this is due to the merging of several dialects into one which is not equal in all individuals. I am mindful that this is an acculturation problem and I hope we shall get enough on that point! Here it is either raining or cold, generally the former. Please remember me to everybody.

[From FB to RFB]
Beaver Harbor, P.O. Port Hardy
Nov. 24, 1930

Please ask Ruth Bryan for Ella Deloria's letter of Nov. 14th. I cannot afford to lose her services just now. There are $1000 in the University which are to hand for her linguistic work this year. I think it would be best to pay her for these coming two months $100 each month extra with the understanding that she is to use full time for the Dakota work. If Harry has made sufficient headway with the Dictionary I should like Miss Bryan to copy a batch of *stems* from his lists — not derivations, send them to her and ask her to give the most accurate translations she can. If this is not feasible ask her to collect more text material and to give me lists which would show what the suffix *-ka* and other similar ones in verbs mean. — ka is I believe a kind of observation, or experience ideas as — sort of —. The question is whether the stem ends in -k or whether the -k belongs to a suffix. I am sorry I have no material here to illustrate but I believe she will understand. I have talked about this question to her. The matter is awkward because it is so hard to tell from here what to do. As I say, if nothing else can be done, ask more material and ask her particularly for personal experiences of old people.

— Yesterday we were again in a feast — dried salmon and fish oil, when a boat from a village about 12 miles off came and invited the whole tribe. They are all gone today except a few old women. I did not want to go because the return is too uncertain and I have my work here pretty well laid out. There will be no interruption. I have already a good deal of material for this style-motor question, but I want some more from different people. Julia is getting the life history of a few women, particularly their marriages. She has more than 50 cat's cradles. She is a pleasant companion.

Please remember me to everybody.

[From FB to RFB]
Beaver Harbor, P.O. Port Hardy B.C.
Nov. 26th, 1930

I am returning by this mail that part of the Comox MS that I do not need, duplicates; also Wagner's MS. I cannot look at it here. I think I wrote Augustin before I left that I should let this matter rest until my return. If I did not, ask Ruth Bryan to write to him to that effect. Will you ask her to make up for me on the model of last year an account of the expenditures for the Com-on-Research in Indian Languages and ask her to get a statement from the Bank. She should send me the financial report, or, if the time is urgent, send it as an advance report and only to Leland. — I did not think I had so many requests. Else I should have written to her myself.

Here everything seems to be going well. Julia is trying to get the confidence of the women. I have so much to revise and fill in that I find it hard to see as much of the individuals as I should like to do. Still there are a few souls with whom I chat now and then, sometimes purposefully sometimes not. Julia dances quite well a few of the dances. She is an expert at cat's cradles. I am worrying now about the style of oratory because I do not yet know how to get it down. Most orators talk so rapidly that I cannot follow except now and then. Anyway I have my troubles with ordinary conversation. Narrative I can understand quite well, if they talk distinctly, but many have the Indian habit of slurring over the ends of their words — whispering — and that makes it difficult. — I heard today from Gladys that Stechert net $1227 for the Folklore journal. That is fine. I presume the Index is responsible for a good deal. I also got the papers for Julia. Will you please tell her? How is Elsie? I'll write to her next time I find time for letters. Life is pretty full here.

[From RFB to FB]
Albuquerque, N.M.
June 28, 1931

I am back again. It turned out to be best to come here and take a night train to El Paso where I ought to be able to get a bus in the morning for Mescalero.

I feel much more like this summer's work[4] than I did when I came across the continent with you. All I wanted to do then was to crawl into a hole and stay there. But that's passed. I'm even looking forward to the party.

We were lucky in our week for our meetings. By Monday morning it was scorching and has been hotter each day since. Hot days have compensations when you go swimming in the late morning and sit out of doors in the early evening, but they have none at all when you are going to meetings. We've been up in the high mountains or at the beach most days and I thrive on such creature comforts.

I was amused at getting acquainted with my young kin. The great row of blond young giants with their boisterous gaiety and huge delight in every hour are very strange to me to find related to myself. . . .

I've planned to come back to New York immediately after the laboratory session is over. And I wonder whether the day has come when you're allowing yourself to make plans for Europe. I hope you're going. And I hope everybody in all your children's families were well when you got back. — It was such a bright spot to me to have come west with you.

[From FB to RFB]
Hamburg, Aug. 1st, 1931

I cannot tell you how shocked and also worried I am by the fate of Henrietta.[5] I am trying to imagine what may have happened and cannot conceive of anything that should have induced nowadays an Indian to murder a visitor. Naturally I am anxious about you and your whole party, — not that I fear any danger for you, but that your whole summer may have been completely upset. I do not know any details and can hardly expect to know anything until the end of next week. I also hope to hear from you not only what has happened, but also in regard to the welfare of yourself and your whole party.

[From FB to RFB]
Jena, Aug. 14, 1931

I had Kirchhoff call on me and asked him for a statement regarding his experiences among the White M. Apache. He found everything normal then. I have sent a copy to Fackenthal and asked him to send you a copy. I am glad to learn from you that the tragedy does not seem to disturb your work. It is a terrible load on my mind. . . .

I hope these lines will find you well and that your crowd is keeping up their enthusiasm. Please, let me hear from you from time to time. I do not feel easy on account of you.

[From FB to RFB]
Jena, August 27th, 1931

Shortly after my arrival here I wrote to you saying that Augustin is anxious to have the Fauset Memoir[6] (Rmk. 3005,90) paid. Conditions here are such that Bank audits are hardly to be had and prompt payment is essential for the conduct of business. Any credits he can get cut 10% interest. I have given him my personal check for $250 and have written to White asking him to send the balance in dollars by cable. Under the circumstances I have guaranteed the correctness of the bill. Will you, please, do what you can to have the matter settled.

I wonder, how your summer has developed. I trust you received my letter in reply to yours. Gladys sent me the first full report about the sad Schmerler affair. It is dreadful. How shall we now dare to send a young girl out after this? And still. Is it not necessary and right? I had a very kindly letter from Rhoads. I must try to see him after my return.

I am sending these lines to New York, because I am uncertain whether this would still reach you at Mescalero.

It is very quiet here. I have taken my sisters along and also a niece. So we live together and I have time for my work. I have also made some progress with von den Steinen's materials. I believe I told you that his widow is staying here with a daughter who is a practicing physician here.

With kindest regards

[From RFB to FB]
Shattuck Farm, Norwich, N.Y.
August 20, 1932

. . . I'm staying here till September 1st unless Ruth Bryan sends for me. Mother is still here, and it has been very pleasant.

I sent Ruth Bryan my chapter[7] for the BOOK last week. She wrote that she hadn't received yours yet, and was free to copy mine. As soon as she returns it I'll send it on.

And what else do you think I've done? I've got 60,000 words of my book on cultural configurations done.[8] You remember I spoke to you last spring about writing it, but I have been afraid to say I was doing it for fear I'd be so slow about it that I'd never get it done. But I only thought I'd make the book about 100,000 words, so at that rate I've some hope. It will be a little longer than I'd planned at first though. It takes me so long to write 1,000 words!

Yes, I'm planning to take Methods first semester, and I'm planning to work at it next month in New York. . . .

I'm so excited about your reports on your walks. I doubt if I could walk two miles! It's wonderful.

[From FB to RFB]
July 13th, 1933
Cornwall Bridge

Thank you very much for your good wishes. I really think that you overestimate what I may have done for you and others. I know myself and my own shortcomings too well. I am not over-modest and want to have my own way when I consider it worthwhile. "Nur die Lumpen sind bescheiden, Wackre freuen sich der Tat." But that too does not prevent a sensible person to know his own limitations.

I hope you will come up here some time while I am still here. I have not done a thing here. I just bask in the sun, sleep, doze and sometimes I pretend to read. How is Bunny getting on?

With kindest regards

[From FB to RFB]
Cornwall Bridge, Conn.
August 23rd, 1934

Many thanks for sending the introduction to your Zuni tales.[9]

I am a little doubtful whether it is justifiable to explain the tales of devoted children and the like entirely on the basis of the play of imagination with possible and real situations. This particular theme is so common in America and so often elaborated in a similar manner that I cannot help thinking that this style of narration may have exerted its influence regardless of cultural patterns — like the bad stepmother in Europe as against the comparative scarcity of the theme of devoted children (like Hansel and Gretl). The final reconciliation is, of course, typical of the Pueblos.

I hope you will have a pleasant time and we'll meet again early in September. I am returning your MS.

[From FB to RFB]
August 26th, 1935
Ridgefield Conn. RFD 3

I fear you selected a bad day to come back to NY. The end of last week must have been fierce.

I am plugging away at the damned book.[10] Just after finishing with Nelson's contribution[11] which is good, except that on account [of] a lot on the history of archeology and mixing in ethnological data that are hardly properly archeological, I took up Lowie's contribution. I confess I had forgotten what he had done to "Economic life." I recall that I asked him after receipt of his MS to add other parts and now I find that the whole thing, almost the whole thing is a history of cultivation of plants and domestication of animals with mighty little economics in it. No discussion of property etc. but a rather truncated discussion of money and trade. And Bunny! I have not got her chapter, I have not got her illustrations. It is damnable. I think I'll throw Lowie's stuff almost all, except the Hunting and Foodgathering stage into inventions and make it a special chapter on Cultivation of Plants and Domestication of Animals. — Of course I am not doing any Kwak[iutl] now.

Did I write that I had to cable $50 to Kirchhoff who cabled that on account of rains he was marooned somewhere?

I sent a report on our Rockefeller money for students to Day. I hope he'll be satisfied, — but what is the future to bring us?

I suppose I wrote to you that my eldest sister died. The poor woman had to suffer terribly. She had cancer of the stomach, so I suppose it is well. She was nearly 81 years old and had a most remarkable power of enjoying what little life could offer her. Music and history were her enjoyment as long as she could enjoy anything. Until two weeks before the end my sister Hedwig read to her every day American history. She wanted to live, the same as Mama Franz who enjoyed and loved life. I do not long for the end, but I shall not be sorry when it is over.

Kroeber's paper[12] is to appear in the October Anthrop[ologist]. I wish Spier had let me know so that I could have answered right away in the same number. What a nuisance. . . .

Next Monday I'll go back to Cornwall Bridge and on the 9th I expect to be back in New York. I'll be so glad to see you again and hear about all you have been doing.

[From FB to RFB]
Cornwall Bridge, Conn.
Aug. 29th, 1938

I trust you are having a pleasant quiet time on the farm. I have been here since July 10th and expect to go back to the City on Thursday the 1st. The summer has not been very good for me, because I have not been feeling well at all for about six weeks. At present I am feeling better, but I cannot do much work without being tired out. I fear old age is beginning to tell with a vengeance. Helene and family are going back on the 11th, but the boys will not be at home. They long to be away and, I think, it will be good for them, — if only they learn to withstand the many temptations that beset young people. — Gladys writes me that she will be in Grenada, Arizona, maybe she has arrived. I am just about through reading the last revises of her proof of the Coeur d'Alène grammar.[13] — The General Anthropology[14] ought to be ready by this time. I finished reading the index before the 10th of July. — I have not heard anything from our South American people. Have you news from them. You know that I expect an Indian from B.C. by November. I made you write several letters for me in regard to him. I hope it will be a success! Do you know that Mac got a civil service position in Albany and will leave me the 1st of Sept. And Paula intends to leave in December. I am glad for them, for their jobs in Columbia held no future. And what else? No doubt you have heard of Michelson's sudden death. Preuss also died. We have to do something about his MSS on which he was working for us. I wish I could tell you some cheering news but I do not know of any. Please let me hear from you.

[From FB to RFB on sabbatical leave in California]
Grantwood, New Jersey
Oct. 24th, 1939

I was so glad to get your letter of Sept. 26th. I ought to have answered long ago, but I am a very poor letter writer now-a-days. You want to know what I think about world affairs? I have given up speculating about it. It seems to me fairly clear that Hitler is now a pawn in Stalin's hands and that Stalin would like western Europe and Germany [to] bleed to death. Only I do not know whether he would like that to happen for the sake of his own power or for the sake of communism. So far as our affairs are concerned we sail under false colors. If we want to have absolute non-interference we have to forbid all trade in any kind of war-material, no matter how innocent it may look. But can we? Our farmers and merchants would raise such a howl that we would be in the war before we knew it. Nobody would be willing to do the reasonable thing and distribute the burden so imposed upon the whole nation. It is no use talking about it, although my fingers itch — to be burnt. The embargo on arms is a purely sentimental affair. I think it would be wise to keep it in view of the future. I remember too well American bombs and bullets being called "Wilson's prayers for peace." I should not mind it, if I had any trust in England's and France's democracy. They do not fight for ideals but to retain power. Under these conditions the whole embargo question as it stands does not seem to me worth all the excitement. What is important is a rigid "cash and carry." I am a little worried about the complaint that nothing is happening at the West front. Obviously they know that an attack would be terribly costly and fruitless. It will be a war of exhaustion. — I am more interested in our own civil liberties and, as you know, I am in that fight. Just now we are attacking the Chamber of [Commerce] of the State of New York, who want to see our free high schools chopped off, religion introduced etc. I wish I had more strength, but I cannot undertake any work that requires physical strength. My heart simply won't stand it.

Anthropology? — It seems your letter to which you refer makes it quite certain that it was suicide. Some of the students here thought — I think without reason — that he[15] was killed. . . . Am I right? The summer certainly was terrible for members of the Department. I am pretty near through with reading proof for my collected papers "Race, Language and Culture." [16] Reading it now I wonder that Macmillan took it. There is too much technical matter in it for a wide sale. I have always general papers followed by technical papers to illustrate methods of my work. — By the way, there is an English edition of Pater Schmidt "The Culture Historical Method of Ethnology." [17] Isn't he a learned fellow — and a conceited ass. Kwak[iutl] moves slowly. Helene is so far advanced now that she practically finishes the language alone so that I can really turn to the ethnology. Gladys' Finnish student who was going to do the Cochiti texts is not here but will be back next term. — It seems that Augustin can finish the volumes that are under way in Glückstadt. I am in trouble about the one Kwak[iutl] volume and the linguistic journal.

I wonder whether Bunny sees all the affairs in the Department without bias. Of course, she is very much troubled. I suppose it is quite true that Linton and Strong have too much undergraduate outlook. I do hope that we may not adopt here the Harvard cosmogony as over against learning how to handle problems. I think we could stand some more positive knowledge, but I should be very sorry, if the main spirit of the Department were changed. Of course, I cannot do anything. I am there on sufferance only.

The students invited me to talk to them next Monday. I think I'll talk about the whole question of scientific approach. — It is very difficult for me to see anyone. I go fairly regularly on Mondays and Thursdays; lunch in the office with Bunny, sometimes with Herzog. There is always a procession of people who want to see me and in the evening I am dead tired. I cannot go to the City to call on people. Whoever wants to see me has to come here. I should be glad to see more people evenings but it is such a long trip for everybody. If Mama Franz were alive we should see more people at dinner, but as it is I do not like to impose the trouble upon Helene and Cecil. — My wife's eldest sister died about two weeks ago. I am now the only of my generation left in that family.

My sister has finally come around to the necessity of living with me. We furnished the little room downstairs next to the stairs for her and I think she feels quite comfortable. — How are your refugees getting on?

Well, I think I have talked enough! Let me hear from you again and do not stay away too long. . . .

[P.S.] I am sending Amelia Susman to the Tsimshian by the end of November. F.B.

[From FB to RFB]
Grantwood, New Jersey
November 17, 1939

I was shocked to hear that you are sick. I trust this will find you well recovered. Please, let me know! Amelia passed her PhD examination yesterday. Next week she will go to British Columbia. I am hoping for good news from you.

[From FB to RFB]
Grantwood, New Jersey
December 20, 1939

I have read your paper on war with much interest.[18] There is one point on p. 9 in regard to which I am doubtful. The cases of "international" marriages do not seem ordinarily [related to ?] destructive social conditions. They are analogous to the same trouble in unilateral societies in which blood revenge may set son against father. They are often outweighed by peaceful relations that are established. However, this is not a serious point. I think your two main points are very good.

This is a Christmas greeting. I hope you are feeling well and will have a happy time with your family.

I cannot give you a very good report regarding myself. I feel that I am aging very rapidly. It began in the summer of 1938. My heart is very irregular and fast and I am physically weak. Walking, even a short distance, makes me short of breath. Attacks of shortness of breath will even come on without any apparent physical activity, and I get tired without cause, I mean without having done any work. I am really concerned about putting all my material in hands that can use it, but I do not know how to do it. Everybody has his hands full. Please, do not mention all this to anyone. If you were told that I was ill that is not quite right. I was tired for a while and feel on the downward grade. — My book of collected papers[19] will come out in January, so they say. The Dakota grammar is slumbering in the Government Printing Office.

. . . It is too bad that things are not going more smoothly. But then, I do not know anything except the somewhat excited reports from Bunny.[20] I have not done anything about transferring the Richardson account to Jules as long as the application to the Fr— Fund is hanging. — Well! Do not feel disturbed about me. I ought to be satisfied, even if my world ended today.

Merry Christmas and happy new year.

[From RFB to FB]
Pasadena, California
December 26, 1939

It was so good of you to read the War article and to write to me so promptly. I have made the point about war between brothers-in-law stronger, I think, by incorporating your objection — you will recognize the Kaingang — and emphasizing that such conditions occur only when there are no institutions which make for peace. I enclose my revision.

Ruth Bryan is typing the RACE half of my Modern Age Book,[21] and the first chapter of the RACISM section. I hate to ask you to read it just as it comes from her typing, for there may be mistakes due to my handwriting. But the publishers are firm that they must have it ready for publication on February 1st and the time for revision will be short. If you can possibly read it now, will you ask Ruth for it in order to save time?

I will type the remainder of the book here, and send these chapters to you within the week. This remainder will include one chapter "Who is Superior?" which is the concluding chapter of the Race section, i.e. it comes before the RACISM section. You will notice too that I have not yet written the part of the chapter which especially discusses race mixture and miscegenation. I didn't think I'd have to bother you with admissions of what isn't done yet, but I'm getting worried about the book's deadline.

Each chapter will have following it as vigorous quotations as I have been able to gather, showing that there is a very great consensus of opinion agreeing with the points I have made about what race is and the evils of racism.

Your physical weakness distresses me daily. I know what great reason you have to be satisfied with your life and your work — far greater than you would ever admit to yourself — but, for the rest of us, you set new goals every year in what one life can stand for and accomplish, and we would give anything in the world to see you strong and able to go on working as you always have. As for me, there has never been a time since I've known you that I have not thanked God all the time that you existed and that I knew you. I can't tell you what a place you fill in my life. It seems paltry to send you good wishes but I send them constantly nevertheless.

[From FB to RFB]
July 19th, 1940
Cornwall Bridge, Conn

I received a note yesterday from Opler telling me that Golden-weiser died. He did not give any details. Isn't it sad to think of the life of a gifted man wasted on account of self-indulgence! He was never able to meet hard facts of life or of science when they ran counter to his mental comfort. — How are you? I am engrossed in the affairs of today, Refugees in France, conditions at home. I do not know whether I am an optimist, or too much an optimist. I cannot imagine that a man like Roosevelt should have changed completely since the year '32.[22] He is a politician and has a hard battle with an unfriendly Congress. How much is due to his willingness to take what he can get and to the attempt not to lose everything by opposing everything that he does not approve of? I do not know, but I feel like giving him the benefit of the doubt.

[From FB to RFB]
Cornwall Bridge, Conn
Aug 30, 1940

I have not heard from you for a long time. I should like to know whether you got Ella's check book. She wrote to me that she had returned it to you; also whether you were willing to write the note about Goldenweiser.

Meanwhile your book[23] came. I hope it will serve a good purpose. Reading it again I find some things that I believe might have a different emphasis. The last chapter I think, is very effective.

When do you intend to be back in NY? I'll probably be back about the 14th.

Franz Boas: An Obituary*

FRANZ BOAS was a great scientist. Though he lived fifty-six years of his life in America, no one who knew him would think of him merely as a great American scientist. He was born in Germany of Jewish parents and was educated in Germany; he passed his adult life in America; but as an anthropologist he took the world for his province. A man of passionate loyalty to both Germany and the United States, he believed that the best good of any country can be attained only through the well-being of all countries. A scientist of immense learning, he probably knew better than any other man the differences among peoples; yet he was convinced that these differences needed only open-eyed and intelligent understanding to become the basis of world cooperation and fair dealing.

Franz Boas brought to the social sciences from his early training in physics and mathematics a mind sensitive to the necessity of framing scientific questions so that they could be answered by investigation. He brought also a conviction that most problems needed new, first-hand investigation and could not be answered by mere

* The Nation, CLVI, January 2 (1943), 15–16. This appreciation of Franz Boas, with its emphasis upon social responsibility, may be compared with an earlier article, "Professor Franz Boas, President of the American Association for the Advancement of Science," Scientific Monthly, XXXII (1931), 278–80, which emphasized primarily Boas' achievements as a scientist. The contrast between the two evaluations of Boas' contributions highlights the change in the direction of Ruth Benedict's own thinking in the intervening twelve years.

examination of existing knowledge. By pressing forward in the social sciences on the basis of these two rules, he laid the foundations of modern anthropology and was himself responsible for many of its greatest achievements. As a scientist he labored indefatigably and his integrity was unquestioned.

It was as a scientist, too, that he took up heavy responsibilities in the world outside the classroom. He never understood how it was possible to keep one's scientific knowledge from influencing one's attitudes and actions in the world of affairs. What he had learned by patient investigation and impersonal research helped him to make up his mind on the questions of the day; and for him it was as much a part of his scientific responsibility to make the application as to publish the detailed research. He collected and analyzed masses of data on the physical anthropology of primitive peoples and of New York City children, but that did not absolve him from condemning publicly the "Nordic nonsense" of Nazi Aryan theories and of race prejudice in the United States. His tireless investigation and recording of the ideas and acts of the Kwakiutl impressed upon him how many different patterns of living can command deep loyalty and enthusiasm from peoples brought up in them. All his studies of other cultures reinforced his conviction that cultural differences are vital and valuable. He believed the world must be made safe for differences.

He spoke out therefore against all efforts by Americans to set themselves up as arbiters of the world. In 1916, when the emotions of the war were running high, he rebuked the American who "claims that the form of his own government is the best, not for himself only, but also for the rest of mankind; that his interpretation of ethics, of religion, of standards of living is right." Such an American, he said, is mistakenly "inclined to assume the role of a dispenser of happiness to mankind" and to overlook the fact "that others may abhor where we worship." "I see no reason why we should not allow the Germans, Austrians, and Russians, or whoever else it may be, to solve their problems in their own ways instead of demanding that they bestow upon themselves the benefactions of our regime."

He made only one condition: "so long as any nation respects the individuality of other nations." A lack of such respect, whether it was shown by the degradation of a people to peonage or wage slavery, or by the humiliation of national groups, or by the arrogance of race prejudice, Boas believed to be a creeping sore that must be healed or it would infect and destroy the whole body politic. In his diagnosis, it was the cause of our ills today; rather than nationalism or capitalism or militarism as such, it was the object of his attack. He believed in the innate dignity of individual men and of groups of men, and he believed that this dignity could be realized when they were not humiliated and pushed about. "I can imagine myself much more at home in a company of sympathetic Chinese, Malays, Negroes, and whites who have interests and ideals in common than in a bigoted or presumptuous company of whites."

As an anthropologist he knew, too, that a fundamental attitude of respect for others is not simply a matter of individual ideals. Under certain arrangements of the social order respect for others cannot become general. He fought therefore against all "laws which favor the members of one nation at the expense of all other members of mankind" — though, as he said, "the very respect I have for the individuality of each nation implies that each has the right to maintain its individuality if it seems threatened by the course of human migration." He fought against all abrogation of civil liberties. He fought against all the conditions in our schools which limit intellectual freedom. Forty years ago he was working to further cultural understanding between the United States and the Far East, between the United States and Latin America. It seemed to him that ignorance of the way of life in other countries was breeding an indifference and callousness among nations which were becoming increasingly threatening as, with modern inventions and modern commerce, the world shrank to smaller and smaller dimensions.

He planned, back in 1902, a school for the study of the cultures of the Far East, a school which should not only conduct research but disseminate information about Asiatic peoples. "Our opportunities in the Far East," he said at that time, "will not become evident to us until we know what we have that is of value to the people in the Orient, and until we learn that they too have accomplished work which may become of value to us." To support the undertaking, he gathered together a group of men among whom were Jacob H.

Schiff and Clarence H. Mackay. One anthropologist, the late Berthold Laufer, was sent to China for several years. But America was not yet ready to maintain such an institution as Franz Boas had hoped for. Unfortunately, the funds were not forthcoming.

In 1908, he tried to organize a center for pan-American cultural cooperation and research, the International School of Mexico. He raised money for it personally and spent a year teaching and doing research under its aegis. But again, the decade was not ready to support a center with this comprehensive scope. A week before he died he spoke of the failure of these attempts to further international cultural understanding. "Some things have been done," he said, "but we are handicapped because they are done so late."

The striking of the eleventh hour, however, was to him no reason for giving up the fight. In these last years he has been proud that his letters and articles were used by the underground in Germany, and he has never been too busy or too weak to help with his counsel. He had faith that among the generation now over forty in Germany there were many who were still democrats at heart, and with these he believed the United Nations could cooperate after the war. But he saw that it was necessary to keep in touch with them, and to let them know that they have strong comrades outside of Nazi Germany.

Throughout a long life Franz Boas kept faith with his ideals. He had an incomparable right to the title of elder statesman in science; yet he evoked more enthusiasm from the younger generation than from those closer to him in years. At eighty-four he had not sold out, or stultified himself, or locked himself in a dogmatic cage. He had set a standard of intensive scientific work in all fields of anthropology which no student could hope to match. After his retirement as head of the Department of Anthropology at Columbia University in 1936 he only felt himself freer to work to preserve those ideals for which we are fighting today. He was a great man, and at this moment we have need of such as he.

Part V

The Postwar Years:
The Gathered Threads

Margaret Mead

WHEN THE end of the war came, Ruth Benedict was fifty-seven. Stanley Benedict was dead. Edward Sapir was dead. Franz Boas was dead. The department at Columbia was going through a phase in which most of the values for which Boas and she had stood were being combated, sometimes more in intent than in actuality; in it she knew she would be somewhat isolated, her students standing a little apart from the rest.

She decided to postpone her return for a year and to write a book that she cared more about than any other of her anthropological writing since perhaps the little essay on Cups of Clay. The beauty of the Japanese tradition, the poignancy of the situation of being a Japanese, the tragedy the Japanese had brought upon themselves, and the danger that Americans, who were now responsible for the next steps, would not handle them wisely, together represented themes which had once been so separate that she had needed separate names for herself and different sets of human relationships to handle them at all. In *The Chrysanthemum and the Sword* [1] they merged in a book that was, as a fellow anthropologist said, "almost too well written — you sometimes get lost in reading it and miss part of the complex thought." In this book there were no ghosts of old-fashioned anthropological scholarship, no demands that predecessors who had not influenced her work must nevertheless be mentioned. There was no one whom she trusted more than herself to say what she should write or how she should write it. The work of her students and younger contemporaries had become so much a part of her thinking, of the air in which she moved, that it was something for which she could give general but not particular thanks. In *The Chrysanthemum and the Sword* she acknowledges the help of her Japanese colleague, Robert Hashima, and of those who were her immediate associates in the Office of War Information or who read the manuscript, but says nothing of Geoffrey Gorer's work, which was the precursor of her own work on national character in general and on Japan in particular.

Her reasons for writing the book were clear in their urgency. In the closing pages there is a warning which has become more pertinent with the passing years:[2]

What the United States cannot do — what no outside nation could do — is to create by fiat a free, democratic Japan. It has never worked in any dominated country. No foreigner can decree, for a people who have not his habits and assumptions, a manner of life after his own image. The Japanese cannot be legislated into accepting the authority of elected persons and ignoring "proper station" as it is set up in their hierarchical system. They cannot be legislated into adopting the free and easy human contacts to which we are accustomed in the United States, the imperative demand to be independent, the passion each individual has to choose his own mate, his own job, the house he will live in and the obligations he will assume. The Japanese themselves, however, are quite articulate about changes in this direction which they regard as necessary. Their public men have said since V-J Day that Japan must encourage its men and women to live their own lives and to trust their own consciences. They do not say so, of course, but any Japanese understands that they are questioning the role of "shame" (haji) in Japan, and that they hope for a new growth of freedom among their countrymen: freedom from fear of the criticism and ostracism of "the world."

For social pressures in Japan, no matter how voluntarily embraced, ask too much of the individual. They require him to conceal his emotions, to give up his desires, and to stand as the exposed representative of a family, an organization, or a nation. The Japanese have shown that they can take all the self-discipline such a course requires. But the weight upon them is extremely heavy. They have to repress too much for their own good. Fearing to venture upon a life which is less costly to their psyches, they have been led by militarists upon a course where the costs pile up interminably. Having paid so high a price, they became self-righteous and have been contemptuous of people with a less demanding ethic.

The Japanese have taken the first great step toward social change by identifying aggressive warfare as an "error" and a lost cause. They hope to buy their passage back to a respected place among peaceful nations. It will have to be a peaceful world. If Russia and the United States spend the coming years in arming for attack, Japan will use her know-how to fight in that war. But to admit that certainty does not call in question the inherent possibility of a peaceful Japan. Japan's motivations are situational. She will seek her place within a world at peace if circumstances permit. If not, within a world organized as an armed camp.

At present the Japanese know militarism as a light that failed. They will watch to see whether it has also failed in other nations of the world. If it has not, Japan can relight her own warlike ardor and show how well she can contribute. If it has failed elsewhere, Japan can set herself to prove how well she has learned the lesson that imperialistic dynastic enterprises are no road to honor.

The book had an enormous effect both in Japan and in the United States. In Japan students of all aspects of Japanese society were stirred to attention and controversy; a whole issue of a Japanese journal was devoted to its discussion.[3]

The Chrysanthemum and the Sword also created a generally favorable attitude toward anthropological work on other modern cultures and a demand for more work of the same kind, as in a review by Erna Fergusson:[4]

One puts down this book feeling that our government should not delay a moment in giving Dr. Benedict another assignment to study other peoples whom we do not understand but with whom we hope to make a livable world.

The need for more work — for the study of Russia, for the study of America — was voiced repeatedly.

Ruth Benedict herself was completely converted to the usefulness, for the safety of the world, of the methods she had used. Certain other expositions of these same methods had antagonized readers because they had so bared their methods of deriving the insights that they reverberated uncomfortably in the minds of the readers. Her own lack of dependence upon psychoanalytic methods — which, in this case, meant a lack of dependence upon the zones of the body, which never made any sense to her — made the book palatable to readers who had resisted, as they now praised, the insights about the Japanese emperor originally developed by Geoffrey Gorer in 1942.[5] Furthermore, her basic skepticism about American culture, which she shared with most liberals of her generation, made it possible for liberals to accept her sympathetic understanding of the virtues of Japanese culture without feeling forced to take a similarly sympathetic attitude toward their own culture, and this removed a stumbling block which stood in the way of anthropologists who did not feel this skepticism so strongly. It was the kind of book that colonels could mention to generals and captains to admirals without fear of producing an explosion against "jargon," the kind of book it would be safe to put in the hands of congressmen alert to resist the "schemes of long-haired intellectuals." The points were made so gracefully, so cogently, that the book disarmed almost all possible enemies except for those who leaned heavily to the Left and those who, through many years, had formed very clear and usually imperfect notions of their own Japanese experiences — the people we used, in another context, to call "old China hands."

The acceptability of *The Chrysanthemum and the Sword* was to mean a great deal to work on national character. But she did not know this when she finished the book and returned to Columbia. She thought she was returning to the old round of small grants, to the laborious search for fellowships, to efforts to eke out insufficient student grants from her own pocket, which had been the way of life before the war. Only this time, instead of the devoted labors — the hundreds of hours spent in putting students' manuscripts into shape and in dispensing meager funds — which she had once shared with Professor Boas, she would be working in isolation in a department which had been sedulously swept bare — though as was later apparent, only temporarily — of any signs of the Boas tradition. She was still only an associate professor, and she felt keenly her inability really to protect and provide for her students. "The trouble with Professor Boas and me," she had said earlier, "is that we have power without patronage." Without her help, her students would have been completely lost, but with it they were little better off. This she minded. A full professorship — long and strenuously resisted on the grounds of sex because "the Faculty of Political Science is a very exclusive gentlemen's club" [6] — came just before her death and, because of what it could mean for her students, pleased her.

In June, 1946, she received the Annual Achievement Award of the American Association of University Women. This sum — twenty-five hundred dollars — was riches indeed. In a world in which grants of two hundred dollars and three hundred dollars were obtained only after weeks of work and in which we were so accustomed to working as volunteers that the first Japanese memorandum had been turned out for the sum of fifty dollars, there now seemed no limit to what could be done. There would be money for some secretarial help, for none was provided by the department; it would make possible little stipends so that one student could go on studying, another could finish her dissertation, another could make a short trip back to the field. All this took me back to the day in 1923 when I had failed to win the Caroline Durer Fellowship, the only graduate fellowship then given at Barnard College, and I received in the mail a handwritten note:

> *First Award No Red Tape Fellowship, $300*
>
> *Ruth Benedict*
>
> (*in charge of fellowships*)

In accepting the award of the American Association of University Women, she said:[7]

. . . I feel that my thanks will be best expressed by describing to you the kind of work which your award will help to carry on.

Three years ago I was asked to come to Washington to help in the war effort, and I am only now returning to Columbia University this fall. I was asked when I came to the Office of War Information to undertake research on civilized nations, both enemy and occupied. I was asked to state in an anthropologist's fashion the problems to be investigated in order to answer the recurring problems with which we were faced, and to use in so far as possible familiar anthropological techniques for solving them. These ways of stating problems of human behavior and these techniques for solving them had been worked out, for several decades, in anthropological studies of small tribes, usually without written language, whose traditional ways of conducting life owed very little indeed to the influences of Western civilization. . . .

I had believed for a long time before the war that the same kind of research could help us to understand civilized nations. I believed that by serious study of learned cultural behavior we could achieve a better international understanding and make fewer mistakes in international communication. Many writers have asked the question of what makes the United States a nation of Americans and France a nation of Frenchmen and China a nation of Chinese, but the answers have either been impressionistic or they have been narrowly historical, economic, or political. The data which the anthropologist finds necessary in order to answer such a question even for a simple primitive tribe were lacking for European nations. They were either unrecorded or they were scattered in a thousand surveys and novels. In my work during the war I had to make the best of a difficult situation. I could not observe daily behavior on the spot in these nations, nor send a trained student. There were, however, plenty of nationals from all parts of the world in this country, and in face-to-face contact and conversation I was able to gather a great deal of material and comment which was essential to my studies.

I worked on the nations of Asia a great part of the time, and my work on Japan I have written up in a book, *The Chrysanthemum and the Sword: Patterns of Japanese Culture*, which will be published this fall. But it is for continued work of this kind in understanding the nations of Europe that I shall use the award you have given me. Next year I shall have a work seminar at Columbia University for students of European background. Some will be holders of fellowships who are in this country to finish their education and will be returning to their home countries immediately. Some will be men and women of European origin who have lived in the United States for some years. I shall give them training in methods of study by arranging opportunities for them to observe American life and having them report on their observations. Their point of view is important in understanding how the United States looks to outsiders, and training will help them to document their impressions or will lead them possibly to revise or rephrase their judgments. They will also report on their own experiences in their native land, and the object of the training will be to teach them techniques of adequate statement and documentation of the conduct of life in their home country.

Such materials must be supplemented later by field work on the spot in the nations selected, but I believe that such a seminar as I have described can be an important contribution. In such a give and take of reactions, accompanied always by training in what satisfactory documentation consists of, I believe we can try out in little some of the problems which face the United Nations. I have the faith of a scientist that behavior, no matter how unfamiliar to us, is understandable if the problem is stated so that it can be answered by investigation and if it is then studied by technically suitable methods. And I have the faith of a humanist in the advantages of mutual understanding among men.

The money award you have given me will go farther in this research than you perhaps think. Every research worker, but especially one in the social sciences, knows how certain opportunities must usually be passed by because in the original arrangements for the research so much is necessarily unforeseen. He knows too how often the university or the foundation may be willing to make an appropriation for one part of the work and not for another; it may be possible to swing the collection of data and then be stymied when it comes to provisions for students to enable them to write up their material. In making this award you have put money at my disposal which has no strings attached to it except that it shall be used to further the work. I can use it at all those places which are otherwise unprovided for or which I cannot foresee before the moment arises. At each such emergency, I shall feel fresh gratitude to the American Association of University Women which has trusted me with this award. You will have an intimate part in the research as it proceeds.

So, in 1946, she returned to Columbia to inaugurate the study of European cultures and to struggle for a recognition of the new methods. Now there was a reversal of the roles played by all of us before the war — when she had been skeptical and we had devoted our best energies to getting the anthropological study of contemporary cultures under way. In 1946, Geoffrey Gorer had returned to England. Gregory Bateson, newly returned from twenty months in Southeast Asia, was devoting his time to the efforts of the atomic physicists to acquaint the public with the new hazards inaugurated by the making of the atomic bomb.[8] Lawrence Frank, at the Caroline Zachry Institute, was deeply concerned with adjustment problems of adolescents. I was still caught in a web of activities assumed during the war, which had gradually to be disentangled.

We all knew, of course, that a study of Russia was vitally important. We knew, equally, that it could be done — if at all — only under government auspices because of the hazards, if not to the senior people, at least to any beginners who ventured to show any interest in Soviet materials.

So the winter started. Then at a party in one of those poor but charming apartments in which the students and poets of the 1920's had lived — but this one much farther west, almost on the river, and in a much more dangerous neighborhood because the little apartments of the 1920's now cost too much for struggling students — Ruth Benedict suddenly announced, "I've discovered where we can get a hundred thousand dollars." She was unaccountably gay and mischievously refused to tell us anything more. None of us took it very seriously. Once, long ago in the early 1930's, there had been a rumor that a great foundation was proposing to give five million dollars to anthropology. When I heard about it, I sat on a mountain top in New Guinea and tried to work out ways in which we could spend it well. But when a second rumor had suggested that the money was to be given in charge to Radcliffe-Brown, some American anthropologists had agreed that no money for anthropology was preferable to money given to Radcliffe-Brown, and the plan had fallen through. Since then we had worked, as we had worked before, for pin money. Even during the war, money for secretaries had been hard to come by.

But the seeming miracle proved to be true. The Office of Naval Research had been allotted funds for basic research in human behavior, and Ruth Benedict had been called in as one of the planning group who were to design the initial projects and she herself was asked to design a study worthy of the size and scope of the problem.

We got out the many old plans which had come to nothing, looked over our resources, which included her Columbia seminar on contemporary European cultures already in progress, and set out to make a new plan. Ruth Valentine, who had been in Washington with Ruth Benedict and had now returned to New York with her, took over the administrative planning. I set to work on the technical design for interviewing, for the protection of informants, and so on, the area in which I had had the most experience. Ruth Bunzel started to build a preliminary manual [9] from the materials which we had all prepared for the Provost Marshal's Office at the beginning of the war [10] and from the Seminar on the Impact of Culture on Personality which Lawrence Frank had set up at Yale under Edward Sapir and John Dollard. Everything we had learned about interdisciplinary research, about organizing teams, about communication, about analyzing films and literature, about interviewing members of one nationality about another nationality, about interviewing specialists at two levels, was to be used. And all the gifted people who had somehow managed in wartime but who did not fit into the peacetime mold — the aberrant, the unsystemic, the people with work habits too irregular ever to hold regular jobs — all of them were to be woven together into a fabric of research. Our plan was to study seven or eight cultures simultaneously in separate research groups, all of which would also meet in a seminar every two weeks so that our insights would resonate and we could work not twice but twenty times as rapidly.

Initially there were endless administrative difficulties. So soon after the war, there was still no space to be had. Columbia University, which undertook to sponsor the project, demanded that it provide funds for rental; this would have required an act of Congress! The people we wanted had to have jobs, and many small projects had to be invented and somehow paid for until the main project got under way. But at last Columbia University Research in Contemporary Cultures was started in the spring of 1947, and in October, 1947, when I had returned from Europe and Geoffrey Gorer had arrived from England, was formally inaugurated at the first seminar held at the Viking Fund (which, in 1951, became the Wenner-Gren Foundation for Anthropological Research).

The all too meager space we had finally uncovered was scattered — one room in the department at Columbia, one room in the Office of the Cultural Counselor to the French Embassy, and three rooms at the Kips Bay-Yorkville District Health Center. At most we could accommodate ten people at any one time. My office at the American Museum of Natural History and Ruth Benedict's at Columbia also sheltered parts of the project. Almost immediately it became apparent that what had at first looked like a very generous budget would not go very far in supporting simultaneous work on seven cultures; so we were very soon working on the basis to which we were more accustomed — money for those who needed it to live, typing help for those who could not type, and neither money nor typing help for those who were in no actual need.

It was necessary to make a design which would, if possible, avoid the kinds of problems of hierarchy and status which are incompatible with anthropological ethos, where each individual from the time he starts to do research must be fully responsible for his own material and for his relationship to his informants. There were in the project a large number of people who had worked for the government and so had been made status conscious, and there were people of many nationalities, each with his or her own notions of dignity. We therefore set up an organizational chart on which RCC (the project) appeared as a circle in the center with the several groups working on specific cultures arranged in a circle around it, and with each important person appearing in at least two different statuses on the chart. Ruth Benedict appeared as Director, with a line up to Columbia University and to the Office of Naval Research, and also as Convener of the Czech group; I was Research Director, Coconvener (with Geoffrey Gorer) of the Russian group, and a member of the French group. In the joint seminar, which included at any one time approximately seventy-five people, every individual — including the secretaries and the youngest graduate student — was regarded as a full member of the group. The small groups working on different cultures met in their members' homes, and people interviewed in their own homes or in their informants' homes, for we never had interviewing rooms. The money from the A.A.U.W. award and from Ruth Benedict's writing and lecturing all went into paying for expenses that could not be handled on a government contract — for such things as Sunday work, flowers for a dowager informant, taxis, and meals in a restaurant which was the only place where a certain kind of interview could take place.

On a grand scale, the project became a kind of actualization of all dreams which for years Boas and Ruth Benedict had had of institutes and coordinated research, which they never visualized as rigid, institutionalized structures but only as frameworks within which work could be done. She herself, of course, took no salary and so was able both to accept voluntary work from others and to criticize and reject the results if they were unsatisfactory. In the history of this interdisciplinary project, in which some one hundred twenty people participated, we never had an important argument about methods or concepts. Our attention was centered on the materials. Each area group was differently constituted, as it was built on the special skills of the people who were available and who then had to work out for themselves how they could best use their assemblage of skills. We never looked for a member of a discipline as such — for "a psychologist" or "a sociologist" — but worked with those with whom some one of us had already worked for years in some other enterprise — so we knew each other's potentialities — or with those who came asking to participate.

A system of keeping records was built into the project, and today all the original interviews, seminar reports, and group discussions are safely housed in my office where they are continually used by students. The long, weary years in which Boas and Ruth Benedict had patiently edited and rewritten their students' and colleagues' work were represented in the provision of someone — Elizabeth Herzog — who, when the time came for writing, helped those who had not yet learned to write.

Out of the first year's work came the basic formulations about Great Russian character, a statement of some central themes in French culture, a recognition that Eastern European Jewish culture must be treated as a single culture that crosscut national lines, an understanding of the methodological importance of infancy — as opposed to an emphasis upon early "child rearing" and on the later years of childhood — and new standards for writing about a culture in such a way that it was humanly intelligible to those who read about it, both the members of the culture described and other readers.

However, by the spring of 1948, it became clear that even if almost all the senior people contributed their time, if everyone who could type did his own work, and if we used our own apartments as bases, nevertheless more money would be needed if the steadily expanding work was to get done. New people with special skills — who had to be paid something — turned up. More graduate students had to be provided for. So Ruth Benedict started negotiations with RAND [11] for a second Russian project and signed a contract with Carnegie to write a book, with a big advance which could go into the project.[12] Money had released a great burst of creative group effort, but it had not essentially changed the style of work which had developed under Boas, in which each person gave as much as he could and was paid as much money as there happened to be —

or nothing if there was none — and each participant was treated fully as a human being, his special skills and defects, his culturally and occupationally defined strengths and weaknesses, his blind spots, his babies, his love affairs, and his psychoanalysis, all taken into account. When people were out of temper, they would say, "Ruth can't tell the difference between research and therapy." In an age when sympathy and a willingness to listen and, if necessary, to agonize with the one who speaks have become highly professionalized, and when most people consider that the proper answers to most problems involve visits to a psychiatrist, Ruth Benedict held fast to the position she had taken long ago — that self-realization through congenial work is vitally necessary and that the teacher has an obligation to help the student find himself.

In May, 1948, when the project was in full swing, Ruth Benedict was invited to go to a UNESCO seminar in Czechoslovakia.[13] This would give her a chance to have first-hand experience of Poland, Czechoslovakia, Holland, and Belgium, countries on which she had worked during the war — from a distance. She had not been to Europe since the summer of 1926. It was an extraordinarily tempting invitation, the more tempting because immediately after the war she had lost a chance to direct some postwar research in Germany when an Army doctor had refused to let her go there on grounds of health.

She was looking frail. Erik Erikson, who had made the lovely line drawing of her in June, 1948, said afterward that he had felt as if he were drawing the face of a very old woman on the verge of death, although that June was her sixty-first birthday. Should she go? Should she, in the middle of the project, take the risk? She intensely wanted to go. All the war years of trying to see through other people's eyes, without field work, had built up a great accumulated passion to find out for herself whether these patterns, so laboriously worked out at a distance, were actually related to a reality she could observe with her own senses. So we said, "Go! If this is what you want to do, do it." For this was what she had said to us during her teaching years.

The summer gave her just what she wanted. The seminar was successful. People all over Europe still talk about it. She felt that her constructs had been accurate — in Poland, where people said things aloud which could only be whispered in Czechoslovakia; in Holland, where she looked at paintings with Netherlanders as guides. She also went to the International Anthropological Meetings in Brussels; later, two young anthropologists reported that there she had been too tired to keep an engagement with them.

Two days after she returned to New York, before she had time to tell us much about the summer and before any of the new project complications were told to her, she had a coronary thrombosis and was taken to the hospital. When the doctor told her that it was her heart and that she must get all anxieties off her mind so that she could rest, she smiled peacefully and said, "My friends will take care of everything." In the five days she lived, she never referred to work again but put all her effort into staying quietly alive until Ruth Valentine got back from California.

When she died, she looked incredibly old, as if the wisdom and suffering of several hundred years was momentarily expressed in a face which, for that instant, seemed more than life-sized. She had always felt so strongly about the beauty of the dead, and we brought our children to see her, giving them a protection which few children have today, in an acceptance that death is a part of life.

Recognition of Cultural Diversities
in the Postwar World*[1]

IN THE United States the serious scientific study of other races and other cultures consciously chosen because they lay outside our own cultural background has ranked as a somewhat esoteric pursuit. It did not have behind it the practical considerations that it had in the British Empire or in Germany; it was far from our national concerns. This war is changing these conditions, and the postwar world will intensify them. Success and failure in our own national economy will hang upon the degree to which we are able to work with races and nations whose social order and whose behavior and attitudes are strange to us.

This strangeness Americans have typically met under conditions little calculated to serve as guides for the postwar situation. Our national experience in Americanizing millions of Europeans whose chief wish was to become Americans has been a heady wine which has made us believe, as perhaps no nation before us has ever believed, that, given the slimmest chance, all peoples will pattern themselves upon our model. This conviction is an integral part of all that is best in our national character, of our moral convictions of rightness, of our unwillingness to use naked force. We do not believe that we shall have to knock people over the head to make them adopt the blessings of our civilization; we are convinced that they will want to.

* American Academy of Political and Social Science, *Annals*, CCXXVIII (July 1943), 101–7.

The postwar world will bring us face to face with a quite different situation; and just insofar as the United Nations succeed in operating through mutual cooperation, the need for cultural understanding will be intensified. Deep-lying cultural diversities were not a matter of intensely practical moment so long as the relationship of Western nations to the rest of the world was authoritarian, whether in political or in industrial enterprises. In such relationships the foreigner deals with the whole culture only tangentially, and needs only isolated bits of understanding of the culture with which he deals. But the cooperation of the United Nations in the postwar world, President Roosevelt has said, is to "lay the basis of that enduring world understanding upon which mankind depends for its peace and its freedom." To realize that goal, we shall have need of the kind of knowledge which results in understanding.

This article presents some of the considerations from my own field of anthropology if the United Nations in the postwar world are indeed to lay such a basis of enduring world understanding. We shall have to deal with all the races of the world, and the stock American reaction to differences of race is a judgment of superiority or inferiority. Scientific work on race, on the contrary, proves that racial physical differences are nonfunctional, and contrast sharply in that respect with physical specializations among animals. In domesticated animals other than man, inherited physiological traits make some dogs fitted for hunting and some for pulling loads; but in mankind, racial differences are hair texture, nose form, cephalic index, skin color, and the like. No one race has a more useful hair or nose or head shape. Very light skin color penalizes some white men in the tropics and they have to take precautions, but many white breeds suffer no difficulty at all.

Scientific work has shown also that no race has a monopoly of superior individuals. Good intellect, good health, and good moral character are distributed in all races and, given propitious social conditions, increase steeply. The arrogance of race prejudice is an arrogance which defies what is scientifically known of human races.

The crucial differences which distinguish human societies and human beings are not biological. They are cultural, and in a cooperative postwar world we shall have to have some understanding of these cultural differences. This is a truism which is often read off to mean that in a reconstruction program we should provide food that the recipients will accept, or plan houses such as they are accustomed to live in. Of course. But the anthropologist does not mean this. He means that in estimating behavior which is culturally our own as well as in estimating that which is alien to us, we must see it as a historical product, man-made and inevitably partial. No one culture has ever developed all human potentialities; it has always selected certain capacities, mental and emotional and moral, and stifled others. Each culture is a system of values which may well complement the values in another. No culture, except as it functions to decrease or increase the happiness of its members,[2] can be ranged on a psychological scale of values. To those who live within each culture, its ways of ordering existence are automatic, and they cannot function efficiently if basic reversals of habit are required of them.

These cultural patterns are coherent within themselves. They are not fortuitous congeries of traits. This is inevitable, since these cultures are carried by living men and women in their habituated bodies and minds. Some cultures are more and some are less integrated, but there is a limit beyond which lack of integration produces catastrophic psychic conflict in individuals and chaos in society. Anthropologists have brought together from small, compact, primitive tribes documentation on extremely coherent value systems, and after such training, the more closely one looks even at modern civilizations, the more systematic and coherent they appear. Crucial cultural situations in early childhood or in adolescence, certain acts the society specifically rewards throughout life, underlie attitudes and behavior that are politically standardized and are basic in class relations and in trade. They hold together, and any one item must be taken in conjunction with the whole structure or it has no relevance. Each item is, as it were, a brick in a total structure; and tearing out the bricks indiscriminately, however inconsequential they seem, may bring the whole structure down in ruins. This does not mean that change is impossible, but that changes have to be adapted to the existing building.

With every occupied country the United States assists in freeing from Axis domination, with every Asiatic country where we operate in cooperation with the existing culture, the need for intelligent understanding of that country and its ways of life will be crucial. These nations will very likely not respond to appeals with which we are familiar, and not value rewards which seem to us irresistible. The danger — and it would be fatal to world peace — is that in our ignorance of their cultural values we shall meet in head-on collision and incontinently fall back on the old pattern of imposing our own values by force.

I have selected one such area of behavior which can be mapped out and in which we could be forewarned. It concerns both the ideology and the practice of democracy itself. Democracy in its cross-cultural meaning is best described by Lincoln's phrase — "of the people, by the people and for the people"; but democracy in different parts of the world has necessarily been additionally defined to include the practices that are in each case relied upon to give the people a voice in their own affairs. Especially in the United States it means extended suffrage, representative government, and the party system. To democracy as thus defined, we have strong ethical commitments and a national loyalty. In our postwar cooperation with other parts of the world these deep loyalties will inevitably lead Americans to believe that adoption of our system is the one trustworthy means to democratic government.

In the United States, political democracy is inseparable from acceptance of the will of the majority and protection of the minority. It is a two-party system which, when there is no issue at stake between the two parties, has by its own logic to carry on the conflict as if there were. This is true because our political system necessarily involves a group which is "in" and a group which is "out," and the "outs" must, if the system is to function, have the right to change places. The "ins" therefore must, within the framework of the system, leave open to the "outs" the possibility of becoming "ins." It is one of our firm cultural dogmas that the majority will be speaking and acting for the common welfare; but from the standpoint of cultures which do not have this system, there seems to be no provision that this will be true. As far as our system goes, there may be little choice as to which speaks more clearly for considered public welfare. All that is basic to our system is that both parties speak and act for themselves and for their own interests.

I have stressed the dangers as they appear to those who are not born and bred to the system, because it is important to realize that only the western fringe of Europe shares with North America and Australia this system of political democracy. Elsewhere it is alien or has been most insecurely poised for certain brief intervals upon different arrangements. The rest of the world has a contrasting arrangement upon which its peoples build the democracy they have. Whereas our democracy is based on a dogma of conflicting interests which must present themselves under any and all circumstances, their democracy is based on a dogma of reconcilability of interests, the key to which can be found in any and all circumstances by men of good will.

Obviously, neither of these dogmas is objectively true; one system chooses and elaborates one ever-present aspect of community relations, and the other a different one. Those cultures which have selected the reconcilability of local interests do not create minorities in order to arrive at social decisions or to carry out group projects. There are no "ins" and no "outs." Social action in regard to their own affairs is taken by the *local community* through a council of elders in close touch with all villagers. This council has great responsibilities: seeing that state taxes are met, naming workers for public projects sponsored by the community, sometimes making all arrangements for calendric festivals, sometimes periodically realloting land according to the needs of families. The elders, in order to maintain their position, must keep their identification, even when they are collecting taxes or rent, not with the state or with the landlords but with the village, and the sanction invoked for social control and activities is rooted in village solidarity.

China is an excellent illustration of this kind of political organization. Its traditional procedures are still basic to its culture, whatever the dislocations of the last few years. We all concede that China has been a great democratic country. But no smallest fraction of its right to be called democratic comes from its national or even its provincial administrations. At these levels there is no representative assembly and no official elected by the people. At these levels the people have no voice. Politically speaking, China is democratic only by virtue of organized local responsibility.

A community has two groups of responsible citizens, the first group made up of heads of all extended families and the other group composed of scholars, large landowners, and especially honored local citizens. Neither of these groups has any voice at the provincial or national level. Provincial and national governments inform the heads-of-families council of the amount of the tax, and these family heads see that the stipulated sums are ready for the tax collector. Local defense, care of waterways and irrigation, provision for calendric feasts and ritual, are the concern of the local councils. To these functions were added by the 1938 government subsidies the highly congenial corporate activities of local agrarian and industrial co-operatives.

Offenders were generally dealt with in the extended family, and Confucian morality demanded that neither the older nor the younger generation denounce the other, but that every effort be made to rehabilitate the person who acted in opposition to the mores. The present Chungking government has legalized the responsibility of the family head, making him liable for violation on the part of any courtyard member. Betrayal of village trust was a different matter; if an official enriched himself unduly from the common funds or accepted a bribe from landlords or state officials, the penalty was banishment. This was not formally decreed, but the community pointed a finger of scorn so that such individuals found it preferable to go to distant provinces for a decade or so.

There is in all this local democratic system in China no place for "ins" and "outs," no elections, no identification of democracy with protecting the rights of minorities.

As Herbert L. Matthews says in a dispatch to *The New York Times*[3] in describing a region with analogous social arrangements in the Punjab: "For a Westerner with democratic and nationalistic ideas, there is something wrong with the picture"; but he insists that in Kapurthala the villagers are well content with their "political and communal peace." Throughout the Punjab, the system of organized local responsibility has operated to weld together into a functioning whole even the caste system, which has often impressed Western observers as the most extreme institution in the world for setting up social separatism. This impression is at least partly due to the fact that our students of political organization have so consistently minimized the coexisting village organization of common community interests and responsibilities. In the Punjab it has been able to operate effectively even through the mechanism of the caste system.

In Russia, councils of local communities, in addition to being organs of fiscal administration, were also responsible for periodic land redistribution among constituent families. Individual use and not individual ownership of farm land was the common privilege of all families, and from the sixteenth century to the middle of the nineteenth, local administration was chiefly directed toward arrangements for sharing the taxes imposed at the capital. The *mirs* combined into larger groups, the *volosti*, which entered into mutual guarantees for settling their tax accounts.

In one or other of these forms, or in still others, these village organizations for local mutual services and joint responsibility are found in Southern and Eastern Europe, as well as in China, India, and Russia.

Poland is an example of conditions found generally in Eastern Europe. Land is entailed in the family, but pasture or wood lots may be village-owned. Biological families have taken the place of large extended families. The cooperative village is still the basic unit. Community affairs are discussed in the village assembly made up of all residents who are more than twenty-four years old and who have lived in the village more than a year. In large villages a council is selected. They act in matters of health and education, moral infractions, crop destruction, theft of means production, fires, expenditure of village tolls, and matters of grievance. Community functions in a tenant village do not differ from those in a village of free landowners. Tenant villages have protested angrily and often effectively against excessive exactions. If letters of grievance and face-to-face personal protests fail, villagers may then attack the landowners' barns or other property and thus carry their point. In 1933, when Poland broke up many large estates in order to create peasant holdings, this land was given to these village councils for distribution to villagers.

Grass-roots democracy was built securely into the folk life of this great area of Eastern and Southern Europe. These village councils were trusted because they were directly responsible to the community, which could make its voice heard in all decisions. But everywhere there were also powerful outside forces whose interests were antagonistic. In some countries these were landlords whose demands might become excessive, in some these were priests, in some these were state officials. At their door the villagers laid their troubles when they could not make ends meet and when it was impossible to meet the village responsibilities.

Military administration in countries of this type, when they are liberated from Axis domination, will be able to utilize for purposes of reconstruction their deeply grounded local solidarity. Broken as these countries will be, they will be capable of local rehabilitation if long folk practice in community cooperation is mobilized. In strongest contrast to America, it is the local village that has had experience in community planning. The local leaders — the *starista*, the *gospodar*, the *wojt* — are the lieutenants in the postwar campaign. We must not fail to recognize them because of our unfamiliarity with their form of democracy.

These political arrangements in these countries are equally important because in their functioning they have created behavior patterns which are also strange in our American experience. Centuries of conviction that individual interests are reconcilable, centuries of experience in mutual help, have given them a character structure which we must learn to understand. This character structure trusts and relies upon joint activity and joint profits as we do not. It regards as simple fact, not as moral precept, the adage that if you help others they will help you. It condemns those who improve their own personal affairs at the expense of common interests. It would not be true to say that they place the common interest above individual interests; they regard their individual interests as best served when they act jointly.

American character structure has been formed from a different set of experiences. Our "rugged individualism" is almost a synonym for resentment of group responsibilities attached to private property; it demands great freedom in the disposition of goods and profits. It is inseparable from the American dream — individual success in economic ventures. The power to fix the conditions under which other people work or carry on their business is one that almost any American would like to wield.

In these European countries, too, strong individualism is often present, but it demands, not unlimited financial autonomy, but a life unpatterned by dominance-submission; men are willing to pool labor and profits, but they find it difficult to work for wages on somebody else's project without a voice in their affairs. Their "rugged individualism" is not identified with free enterprise; it expresses itself in a contempt for a "soft" life, and identifies virtue with lack of the very amenities which reward individual enterprise in our culture.

In all these countries there has been for decades increasing infiltration of the kind of individualism with which we are more familiar. More and more men have had to produce for the competitive market, and more and more men have left their self-sufficient farms for work as laborers. It has produced inevitable change and conflict.

This is a background for the situation with which postwar reconstruction will have to cope. Both patterns of life are known, and the conflict between them is known. Therefore we shall have to understand these areas' traditional methods of dealing with conflict; we shall have to recognize that they lack experience with the two-party system which depends for its existence on guaranteeing to the minority the right to make itself the majority. Their deeply rooted experience has taught them to rely on ostracism when individuals offend the community, and when the persons that are excluded from the group become numerous, this process becomes schism or revolution. It becomes schism and revolution, too, when the opposition of villager and seignior becomes too acute. The traditional commitment of these countries is to the dogma that interests can be reconciled; and when this fails and powerful or numerous groups oppose one another, factionalism and violence are serious social threats.

When one faction in a nation in this area has seized power, we have called these governments totalitarian; but this kind of seizure of power is the inevitable outcome of the folkways of these nations in circumstances of crisis. They are still relying on their old familiar mechanism of ostracism from the community. To Americans, this is the ultimate breakdown of any democratic system; but in their view of life, the crucial point is quite different. They test totalitarian regimes by their old folk test of village democracy: whether or not mutual services are progressively becoming better organized. If the regime accomplishes more and more for the common welfare, by their standards it is democracy. If it does not, it is tyranny. Their test is different from ours, and both are culturally conditioned.

In our dealings with liberated countries of Europe we shall succeed better if we respect their values. Certainly we shall sow only bitterness if we try to impose our own by force. We shall be on firmer ground if we recognize that progress toward a genuine commonwealth will of necessity take different forms in different nations. They have had experience with different social forms and their character structure is different. From the point of view of comparative cultures, the one universal criterion for judging the success of each country's efforts in reconstruction is whether it is progressively furthering the general welfare.

Except in the narrow western strip of Europe north of the Pyrenees and the Alps, which has long experimented with democratic elections, the commonwealth of the postwar world will necessarily be built upon a set of folk commitments which differ from ours. It may well be that eventually they will adopt some of our methods, but it will not be in toto and it will not be immediately. It would be tragic if in the process their cultural values built up by centuries of experience were lost in the shuffle. We shall have to explore the resources they offer — their experience in nonpolitical local representation, their dogma of the reconcilability of interests, their special habits of sharing labor and profits. Whether the problem at hand is a TVA on the Danube or getting in the first harvest after liberation or the care of child waifs separated from their parents, we shall have to be aware of their folkways and of their character structure. We shall need to understand their particular cultural versions of human life.

Child Rearing in Certain
European Countries*

SYSTEMATIC STUDY of national character is an investigation into a
special and paradoxical situation. It must identify and analyze con-
tinuities in attitudes and behaviors, yet the personnel which exhibits
these traits changes completely with each generation. A whole nation of babies have to be brought up to replace their elders. The
situations two different generations have to meet — war or peace,
prosperity or depression — may change drastically, but Americans,
for instance, will handle them in one set of terms, Italians in another.
Even when a nation carries through a revolution or reverses fundamental state policies, Frenchmen do not cease to be recognizable as
Frenchmen or Russians as Russians.

The cultural study of certain European nations on which I am
reporting[1] has taken as one of its basic problems the ways in which
children are brought up to carry on in their turn their parents'
manner of life. It accepts as its theoretical premise that identifications, securities, and frustrations are built up in the child by the way
in which he is traditionally handled, the early disciplines he receives, and the sanctions used by his parents. The study has been
carried on in New York City by a staff of interviewers who have
supplemented their work with historical, literary, journalistic, and
economic materials. The aims of the research have been to isolate

* Presented at the 1948 Annual Meeting of the American Orthopsychiatric
Association. *American Journal of Orthopsychiatry*, XIX, No. 2 (1949), 342–48.
449

exceedingly fundamental patterns and themes which can then be tested and refined by study of local, class, and religious differences. It is believed that such preliminary hypotheses will make future field work in the home countries more rewarding, and such field work in the Old World is already being carried out under other auspices by students who have taken part in this research.

The project has necessarily seen its work as a comparative study of cultures. It has blocked out large culture areas and their constituent subcultures. When a great area shares a generalized trait, the particular slants each subarea has given to these customs is diagnostic of its special values, and the range of variation gives insight which could not be obtained from the study of one nation in isolation. This culture-area approach commits the student, moreover, when he is working outside his own cultural area, to a detailed study of behaviors which, since they are not present in his own experience, have not been incorporated into his own theoretical apparatus. It is therefore a testing ground for theoretical assumptions and often involves a rephrasing of them.

The custom of swaddling the baby during its first months of life in Central and Eastern Europe illustrates well, in the field of child rearing, the methodological value of a culture area approach. It illustrates how the comparison of attitudes and practices in different areas can illuminate the characteristics of any one region that is being intensively studied, and the kind of inquiry which is fruitful. Specifically I shall try to show that any such student of comparative cultures must press his investigation to the point where he can describe *what is communicated* by the particular variety of the widespread technique he is studying. In the case of swaddling, the object of investigation is the kind of communication which in different regions is set up between adults and the child by the procedures and sanctions used.

Because of our Western emphasis on the importance of the infant's bodily movement, students of child care who discuss swaddling in our literature often warn that it produces tics. Or with our stress on prohibition of infant genitality, it is subsumed under prevention of infant masturbation. Any assumption that swaddling produces adults with tics ignores the contradictory evidence in the great areal laboratory where swaddling occurs, and the assumption that it is simply a first technique to prevent a child from finding pleasure in its own body is an oversimplified projection of our Western concern with this taboo. Any systematic study of the dynamics of character development in the swaddling area is crippled by these assumptions. Infant swaddling has permitted a great range of communication.

Careful studies of mother-child relations in this country have abundantly shown the infant's sensitivity to the mother's tenseness or permissiveness, her pleasure or disgust, whether these are expressed in her elbows, her tone of voice, or her facial expression. Communications of these sorts take place from birth on, and when a particular form of parental handling is standardized as "good" and "necessary" in any community, the infant has a greatly multiplied opportunity to learn to react to the traditional patterns. Local premises, too, about how to prepare a child for life will be expressed in modification of procedure in swaddling, and these detailed differences are means of communication to the child, no less than his mother's tone of voice. Any fruitful research in national character must base its work upon such premises and utilize them as basic principles in comparative study.

Swaddling is tightest and is kept up longest in Great Russia. The baby's arms are wrapped close to its sides and only the face emerges. After tight wrapping in the blanket, the bundle is taped with crisscross lashings till it is, as Russians say, "like a log of wood for the fireplace." Babies are sometimes lashed so tight that they cannot breathe, and are saved from strangling only by loosening the bindings. The bundle is as rigid as if the babies were bound to a cradleboard, and this affects carrying habits and the way a baby is soothed in an adult's arms. It is not rocked in the arms in the fashion familiar to us, but is moved horizontally from right to left and left to right.

The swaddling in Russia is explicitly justified as necessary for the safety of an infant who is regarded as being in danger of destroying itself. In the words of informants, "It would tear its ears off. It would break its legs." It must be confined for its own sake and for its mother's. In the 1930's, the Soviet regime made a determined effort to adopt Western customs of child rearing and to do away with swaddling. Young women were trained to instruct mothers that a baby's limbs should be left free for better muscular development and exhibitions of pictures of unswaddled baby care were distributed widely. But swaddling persisted. Informants who have recently lived in Russia say constantly, "You couldn't carry an unswaddled baby." "Mothers were so busy they had to make the child secure." Several hundreds of pictures of babies available at the Sovfoto Agency show the prevalence of swaddling; photographs taken in 1946 and 1947 still show the completely bunted baby with only the face exposed. This physical restriction of the baby is traditionally continued for nine months or longer. It is not accompanied by social isolation. Babies are kept where adults are congregated, and their little sisters and grandmothers act as nurses; they are talked to and their needs are attended to.

In many ways the infant apparently learns that only its physical movement is restricted, not its emotions.[2] The Russian emphasis upon the child's inherent violence appears to preclude any belief among adults that its emotions could be curbed. The baby's one means of grasping the outside world is through its eyes, and it is significant that in all Russian speech and literature the eyes are stressed as the "mirrors of the soul." Russians greatly value "looking one in the eyes," for through the eyes, not through gestures or through words, a person's inmost feelings are shown. A person who does not look one in the eyes has something to conceal. A "look" also is regarded as being able to convey disapproval more shattering than physical punishment. Throughout life the eyes remain an organ which maintains strong and immediate contact with the outside world.

The baby's physical isolation within its bindings appears to be related to the kind of personal inviolability Russians maintain in adulthood. It is difficult for foreigners to appreciate the essential privacy accorded the individual in Russian folk life, for their pattern of "pouring out the soul" would be in most cultures a bid for intimacy, and their expressive proverb, "It is well even to die if there are plenty of people around," seems a vivid statement of dislike of isolation. These traits, however, coexist in Russia with a great allowance for a personal world which others do not, and need not, share. "Every man," they say, "has his own anger," and the greatest respect is given to one who has taken his own private vow — either in connection with a love affair or with a mission in life. Whatever an individual must do in order to carry out this personal vow, even if the acts would in other contexts be antisocial, is accepted. He must be true to himself; it is his *pravda*.

The Russian version of swaddling can also be profitably related to the traditional Russian attitude that strong feeling has positive value. Personal outbreaks, with or without intoxication, are traditionally ascribed to the merchant class and to peasants, but they were characteristic of all classes. Official pressure at present attempts to channel this strong feeling toward foreign enemies, but the uses of violence to the individual psyche seem to be stressed in traditional fashion in this modern propaganda.

Not only is violence in itself a means to attain order, but it is also relatively divorced from aggression against a particular enemy. In Czarist days "burning up the town," breaking all the mirrors, smashing the furniture on a psychic binge were not means of "getting even" or of avenging one's honor; they were "in general." Even the peasants characteristically fired the home of a landowner other than the one on whom they were dependent. This trait is prepared for in the first years of life by the relative impersonality of the swaddling. Even in the villages of Great Russia, moreover, there is constant use of wet nurses and *nyanyas*, older women who are engaged to care for the baby; there is consequently a much more diffuse relationship during the first year of life than in societies where the child's contact is more limited to that with its own mother. It is characteristic of Russia, also, that poems and folk songs with the theme of mother love are practically nonexistent. The Great Russian mother is not specifically a maternal figure; she is quite sure of her sex without having to produce children to prove that she is female — as the man also is sure of his sex.

The Polish version of swaddling is quite different from the Russian. The infant is regarded, not as violent, but as exceedingly fragile. It will break in two without the support given by the bindings. Sometimes it is emphasized that it would be otherwise too fragile to be safely entrusted to its siblings as child nurses; sometimes that the swaddling straightens its bent and fragile legs. Swaddling is conceived as a first step in a long process of "hardening" a child. "Hardening" is valued in Poland, and since one is hardened by suffering, suffering is also valued. A man does not demean himself by retailing his hardships and the impositions put upon him. Whereas an Italian, for instance, will minimize his dissatisfactions and discouragements and respect himself the more for so doing, Poles characteristically tend to prove their own worth by their sufferings. A usual peasant greeting is a list of his most recent miseries, and Polish patriots have exalted Poland as "the crucified Christ of the Nations." From infancy the importance of "hardening" is stressed. In peasant villages it is good for a baby to cry without attention, for it strengthens the lungs; beating the child is good because it is hardening; and mothers will even deny that they punish children by depriving them of dessert and tidbits, because "food is for strengthening; it would be no punishment to deprive them of any food."

Another theme in Polish swaddling has reference to the great gulf fixed between clean and dirty parts of the body. The binding prevents the infant from putting its toes into its mouth — the feet are practically as shame-ridden as the genitals in Poland — or from touching its face with its fingers which may just before have touched its crotch or its toes. When the baby is unswaddled for changing or for bathing, the mother must prevent such shameless acts. Whereas the Russian baby is quite free during the occasional half hour when it is unswaddled, the Polish baby must be only the more carefully watched and prevented. Polish decency is heavily associated with keeping apart the various zones of the body.

Although it was possible to sketch Russian infancy without describing details of nursing and toilet training, which are there warm and permissive, in Poland this is impossible. The high point of contrast is perhaps the weaning. In Russia supplementary food is given early; a very small swaddled baby has a rag filled with chewed bread tied around its neck; this is pushed down on its mouth as a "comforter" by anyone present. The baby is eating many foods long before it is weaned. In Poland, however, weaning is sudden. It is believed that a child will die if it is nursed beyond two St. John's Days of its life — or the day of some other saint — and therefore, when the child is on the average eighteen months old, the mother chooses a day for weaning. The child is not given an opportunity beforehand to accustom itself to eating solid food; the sudden transition is good because it is "hardening." It is further believed that a twice-weaned child will die, and though many mothers relent because of the child's difficulties, it is necessarily with guilt.

Another contrast with Russia is a consequence of the strong feeling about the evil eye in Poland. Only the mother can touch the baby without running the danger of harming it; in the villages even the baby's aunts and cousins fall under this suspicion. Certainly no woman except the mother can feed the baby at the breast. During the spring and summer months the babies are left behind at home with three- and four-year-olds since all older children go to help their parents in the fields. In house after house neglected children are crying and women incapacitated for the fields might advantageously care for them. But this is regarded as impossible.

The Polish child gets nothing from crying. He is hurried toward adulthood, and the steps which reach it are always ones which "harden" him; they are not pleasant in themselves. As a child he has tantrums, but the word for tantrums means literally "being stuck," "deadlocked." He does not cry or throw himself about as the Jewish child in Poland does; he sits for hours with rigid body, his hands and his mouth clenched. He gets beaten but he takes it without outcry or unbending. He knows his mother will not attempt to appease him. His defense of his honor in his later life is the great approved means of unburdening himself of resentments and turning them into personal glory. There are many Polish proverbs which say idiomatically and with great affect: Defend your honor though you die. The long process of childhood "hardening" lies back of their insult contest and their spirited struggles in lost causes.

The swaddling of the Jewish baby, whether in Poland or the Ukraine, has characteristics of its own. The baby is swaddled on a soft pillow and in most areas the bindings are wrapped relatively loosely around the baby and his little featherbed. The mother sings to the baby as she swaddles it. The specific stress is upon warmth and comfort, and the incidental confinement of the baby's limbs is regarded with pity and commiseration. People say in describing swaddling, "Poor baby, he looks just like a little mummy," or "He lies there nice and warm, but, poor baby, he can't move." Swaddling is also good, especially for boys, because it insures straight legs. There is no suggestion that it is the beginning of a process of "hardening" or that it is necessary because the baby is inherently violent. Rather, it is the baby's first experience of the warmth of life in his own home — a warmth which at three or four he will contrast with the lack of comfort, the hard benches, the long hours of immobility and the beatings at the *cheder*, the elementary Jewish school where he is taught Hebrew. In strongest contrast to the experience of the Gentile child, swaddling is part of the child's induction into the closest kind of physical intimacy; within the family the mother will expect to know every physical detail of her children's lives and treats any attempts at privacy as a lack of love and gratitude. The pillowed warmth of his swaddling period apparently becomes a prototype of what home represents, an image which he will have plenty of opportunity to contrast with the world outside, the world of the *goy*.

It is profitable also to relate Jewish swaddling to another pattern of Eastern European Jewish life: its particular version of complementary interpersonal relations. I am using "complementary" in a technical sense as a designation of those interpersonal relations where the response of a person or group to its vis-a-vis is in terms of an opposite or different behavior from that of the original actors. Such paired actions as dominance-submission, nurturing-dependence, and command-obedience are complementary responses. The Jewish complementary system might be called nurturing-deference. Nurturing is the good deed — *mitzvah* — of all parents, elders, wealthy, wise and learned men toward the children, the younger generation, the poor, and the still unschooled. In interpersonal relations these latter respond to the former with deference, "respect," but not with *mitzvah*. One never is rewarded in a coin of the same currency by one's vis-a-vis, either concurrently with the act or in the future. Parents provide for all their children's needs, but the obligation of the child to the parent does not include support of his aged parents when he is grown, and the saying is: "Better to beg one's bread from door to door than to be dependent on one's son." The aged parent feels this dependence to be humiliating, and this is in strongest contrast to the non-Jews of Poland, for instance, among whom parents can publicly humiliate their children by complaining of nonsupport. Among the Jews, a child's obligation to his parents is discharged by acting toward his own children, when he is grown, as his parents acted toward him. His aged parents are cared for, not by a son in his role as a son, but in his role as a wealthy man, contributing to the poor. Such impersonal benefactions are not humiliating to either party.

The swaddling situation is easily drawn into this Jewish system of complementary relations. The personnel involved in swaddling is necessarily complementary; it includes the binder and the bound. The bound will never reciprocate by binding the binder, and the Jewish binder conceives herself as performing a necessary act of nurturing, out of which she expects the child to experience primarily warmth and comfort; she is rather sorry for the accompanying confinement but she regards random mobility as a sign of the baby's being uncomfortable. She is not, like the Polish mother, "hardening" the baby or preventing indecencies, or like the Russian mother, taking precautions against its destroying itself. She is starting the baby in a way of life where there is a lack of guilt and aggression in being the active partner in all complementary relationships and security in being the passive partner.

In swaddling situations the communication which is then established between mother and infant is continued in similar terms after swaddling is discontinued. Diapering of older babies is understood by Jewish mothers as contributing to the baby's comfort, and by Polish non-Jewish mothers as preventing indecencies by insuring that the baby's hands do not come in successive contact with "good" and "bad" parts of his body. In Rumania, where all informants from cities and towns stressed first, last, and always that swaddling was necessary to prevent masturbation, the infant's hands, when he is too old to be swaddled, are tied to his crib, incased in clumsy mittens, and immobilized by special clothing. His nurse or mother spies on him and punishes any slip.

The different kinds of swaddling communication which are localized in Central and Eastern Europe make it clear that the practice has been revamped to conform to the values of the several cultural groups. As in any culture area study, investigation discloses the patterning of behavior in each culture. The diversities do not confuse the picture; they enrich it. And the detailed study of this one widespread trait, like any other, throws light on the individuality of each cultural group, while at the same time it emphasizes the kinship among them.

Anthropology
and the Humanities*

ANTHROPOLOGY BELONGS among the sciences in far more senses than
the obvious one that it sits on the National Research Council and
on the Social Science Research Council. From the moment of its
professional beginnings just about a hundred years ago, it has phrased
the problems it investigated and has adopted conceptual schemes
according to patterns which belong to the scientific tradition of
Western Civilization of the past century. It borrowed some of its
early concepts, such as that of evolution or of the single localized
origin of civilization, directly from phylogenetic concepts of biology,
and it has attempted in all its serious work to arrive at objective,
theoretical, generalized descriptions of reality.

This scientific framework in which anthropology has worked and
developed has not prevented it from falling into error or from ex-
ploring blind alleys. Anthropology, like any science, must constantly
rephrase its questions in the light of new discriminations in its own
field and of new knowledge available to it in the work of other
sciences. It must constantly try to profit by methods and concepts
which have been developed in the physical and biological sciences,
in psychology and in psychiatry. In this present decade we have
every opportunity to do so; we are no longer living in an age which

* Address of the Retiring President of the American Anthropological Association, Albuquerque, New Mexico, December, 1947. *American Anthropologist*, L,
No. 4, Pt. 1 (1948), 585–93.

concerns itself with controversies about how to delimit and to define each self-sufficient science.

The situation is quite different in regard to anthropology and the humanities. They are so far apart that it is still quite possible to ignore even the fact that they deal with the same subject matter — man and his works and his ideas and his history. To my mind the very nature of the problems posed and discussed in the humanities is closer, chapter by chapter, to those in anthropology than are the investigations carried on in most of the social sciences. This is a heretical statement and to justify it I must turn back to the great days of the humanities.

From the Renaissance down to a hundred years ago, the humanities, not the sciences, were the intellectual food of Western civilization. *Humanitas* meant then, as it meant to Cicero, the knowledge of what man is — his powers, his relations to his fellows and to nature, and the knowledge of the limits of these human powers and of man's responsibility. It was in this field of the Study of Man that, after the Renaissance, methods of impartial inquiry were developed. As President Conant has recently written:[1]

> In the first period of the Renaissance the love of dispassionate search for the truth was carried forward by those who were concerned with man and his works rather than with inanimate or animate nature. It was the humanist's exploration of antiquity that came nearest to exemplifying our modern ideas of impartial inquiry.

One has only to read some of Montaigne's essays written in the sixteenth century to realize their kinship to modern anthropology. Montaigne, the humanist, in his accounts of his conversations with his Tupinamba servant, could discuss the economics of daily life and the torture and eating of captives in this great South American tribe from the point of view of his "boy" who had grown up there; the great Frenchman did not apply to the Tupinamba the categories of Western European, Catholic, and French morals and economics. Like any modern anthropological field worker, he used an informant and compared cultures without weighting his argument in favor of

his own ethnocentric attitudes. However slight the attempt he made
in the primitive field, it belongs in the modern anthropological tradition.

This general statement of the common subject matter of the
humanities and of anthropology still does not do justice to their
likenesses. The humanities provided Europeans of that period with
experience in cultures other than their own. Because Greece and
Rome were the prime inspiration of the Renaissance, learning tended
to be justified by the freedom it gave the scholar to move intellectually in a culture different from the one in which he had been
reared. The humanities, in consequence, were an intense cross-cultural experience, and their aims were often couched in the same
phrases as those of modern anthropological investigation of an alien
culture.

Renaissance classical studies often became, as is always only too
likely, authoritarian and formal, but for discerning scholars from
Erasmus to John Stuart Mill their purpose was still to provide en-
lightenment by the study of another culture. Mill put his pleas for
the study of the humanities, organized as they were around Greek
and Latin literature, in exactly these terms.

> Without knowing . . . some people other than ourselves, we
> remain, to the hour of our death, with our intellects only half
> expanded; . . . we cannot divest ourselves of preconceived no-
> tions. There is no means of eliminating their influence but by
> frequently using the differently colored glasses of other people;
> and those of other nations, as the most different, are the best.

It was in this field of the humanities that great men for centuries
got their cross-cultural insights. It liberated them, it taught them
discipline of mind. It dominated the intellectual life of the period.
Then about the middle of the last century the new sciences began
to take leadership out of the hands of the humanists. Until then
science had hardly got a foothold in the colleges and universities,
and it had remained largely a field for amateurs. Its subject matter
for generations had been suspect, not only because scientists had
questioned facts upheld by contemporary religion, but because the

natural sciences dealt with matter and inanimate nature, which stood low in the divine order of the world. They were regarded as enemies of man's higher interests, which were the peculiar field of the humanities.

Professional anthropology had its beginnings during the years which at last recognized in the sciences, at least potentially, the place they have come to hold in Western civilization. The excitement of phrasing the study of man in terms of scientific generalizations instead of in humanistic terms was basic in the whole discipline of anthropology. There were great gains in this new phrasing. But, looking back at it now, there were also losses. Such a great prescientific compilation as that done by Sahagun among the Aztecs was not duplicated by professional anthropologists of the age of Ratzel and Tylor. Instead Spencer collected his huge scrapbooks of meager travelers' items from the five continents and the islands of the seas, and Morgan found it possible to classify his kinship terminologies without ethnological investigation of the significance of the actual relation to forms of marriage or of localized and non-localized residence of kin. Professional anthropologists of this period did not engage in conversations such as those of Montaigne with his Tupinamba boy; they studied marriage or religion or magic in the British Museum without benefit of any informant. William James reports that when he asked Frazer about natives he had known, Frazer exclaimed, "But Heaven forbid!"

With all this in mind, it is tempting to imagine what struggles need never have occurred in later anthropological work and theory if anthropology had originally become a professional study before that turning point in the nineteenth century when the sciences came to dominate the field of intellectual inquiry. It is easy to imagine that anthropology might have then stemmed from and continued the methods and insights of the humanities.

No one is more convinced than I am that anthropology has profited by being born within the scientific tradition. The humanist tradition did not construct hypotheses about man's cultural life which it then proceeded to test by cross-cultural study; such procedure belongs in the scientific tradition. My conviction is simply that today the scientific and humanist traditions are not opposites nor mutually exclusive. They are supplementary, and modern anthropology handicaps itself in method and insight by neglecting the work of the great humanists.

In the early days of anthropology a great gulf divided it from the humanities. As a young scientific discipline anthropology sought to formulate generalizations about social evolution which would parallel biology's phylogenetic tree, or about the psychic unity of man and the vast repetitiousness of his behavior. The basic and unverbalized assumption was that human culture could be reduced to order by the same kind of concepts which had proved useful in the non-human world.

This was a reasonable expectation, and those who sought to realize it had good reason to leave out of account any consideration of human emotion, ethics, rational insight and purpose which had come into being within man's social life. They abstracted, instead, categories of institutions, ranged from the simple to the complex, and discussed them as if they were species in the world of nature. They lifted items of human magic and kinship like blocks out of the cultural edifices where these materials had been relevant in native life, and classified them as a botanist of the time classified the flowers. Even today, when most anthropologists define culture so that it includes human attitudes and behavior, there are some who still exclude the mind and purposes of man, and, indeed, a "science of culturology" and certain kinds of historical reconstruction and of cultural cycles are at present only possible if this exclusion has been made.

The great majority of present-day American anthropologists, however, include the mind of man within their definition of culture — man's emotions, his rationalizations, his symbolic structures. Such anthropologists' theoretical interests have moved strongly in the direction of trying to understand the relation of man himself to his cultural constructs. They have moved in this direction often as a consequence of the vivid material available in this field in anthropological field work, whether their own or others', and they have often not considered sufficiently the difference in training which genuine progress in this field requires.

For if anthropology studies the mind of man, along with his institutions, our greatest resource, it seems to me, is the humanities. By this I mean not all contemporary literary criticism and all contemporary history, but those surviving humanists who are still genuinely in the humanistic tradition. History, literary criticism or classical studies can be written in the humanistic tradition or in the scientific. Scientific method has had unparalleled prestige in the last hundred years, and the humanities, no less than anthropology, have often and sometimes profitably taken over methods of science.

The great tradition of the humanities, from the Renaissance to the present day, is distinguished by command of vast detail about men's thinking and acting in different periods and places, and the sensitivities it has consequently fostered to the quality of men's minds and emotions. History, as a humanitarian art, left out vital economic and political analyses, but it did try to show the deeds and aims of men in a certain period and what the consequences of these were; it might picture men's deeds as vagaries or as destructive but it tied them with consequences; it pictured man as responsible for his successes and his failures. Literary criticism might raise the problem of the spirit of the age or confine itself to the character of one hero; in either case, it was concerned to show that, given certain specific kinds of emotion or of thought, people would act in given ways and the denouement would be of a given sort. The humanities have based their work on the premise of man's creativity and of the consequences of his acts and thoughts in his own world. Their methods of study have been consistent with their premises.

Both method and premise differ from those which have proved valuable in the field of natural science. There the student has to analyze the world of nature, which, as we know, can be described by determinate laws. He has only to find out the law of a falling body or of an expanding gas and he can apply the formula in any context. He can even make large generalizations about animals, since they are not biologically specialized to learn and invent. But man is a species which can create his way of life — his culture. He is not for this reason outside the natural order; rather, natural evolution has, in man, produced an animal who is not merely a creature of circumstance and of instincts but an initiator and inventor. His social life has developed, for good or evil, within a human framework of purposes which he has himself invented and espoused, and the course of evolution, at this human stage, has therefore taken on characteristics which are not present at the prehuman stage. Man is a creature with such freedom of action and of imagination that he can, for instance, by not accepting a trait, prevent the occurrence of diffusion, or he can at any stage of technological development create his gods in the most diverse form. Even granted that many correlations, such as that between technological stage and the character of supernatural beings, have high probability, it is only to the degree that we know concrete and detailed facts about any people — their contacts with other tribes, their location in a cultural area — that we can assume the correlations to hold.

The gradual recognition of these facts has led anthropologists to include the mind of man within their definition of culture. The nature of this anthropological problem has inevitably shown them the common ground they have with psychology and psychiatry. By the same necessity, if they are to interpret their data adequately, they will increasingly find common ground with the great humanists. It is my thesis that we can analyze cultural attitudes and behavior more cogently if we know Santayana's *Three Philosophical Poets* and Lovejoy's *Great Chain of Being* and the great works of Shakespearian criticism. Future anthropological work, too, can reach a higher level if we attract, not only students of sociology, but also students of the humanities. I shall assume that we might better learn from the great masters than from the lesser and I shall try to illustrate what I believe they have to offer.

Santayana, certainly one of the greatest of living humanists, has written in almost all the fields of cultural anthropology. He has not dealt with primitive material, but whether his subject is Greek or Hebrew civilization, or English as in *Soliloquies in England,* or our own as in *Character and Opinion in the United States,* he has dealt with the ways of life men have embodied in their cultures, the institutions in which they have expressed them, and the kinds of emotion and of ideas which have taken root in men so reared. He has constantly illustrated from the side of the humanities and out of his own cultivated sensitivity the truth about culture which he has phrased in one of his books published twenty years ago:[2]

Any world, any society, any language . . . satisfies and encourages the spirit which it creates. It fits the imagination because it has kindled and molded it, and it satisfies its resident passions because these are such, and such only, as could take root and become habitual in precisely that world. This natural harmony between the spirit and its conditions is the only actual one; it is the source of every ideal and the sole justification of any hope. Imperfect and shifting as this harmony must be, it is sufficient to support the spirit of man.

This fine summary of the interdependence of man's cultural institutions and of the personalities of those who live within the realm of their influence is one of Santayana's great themes. He brought all his learning and philosophy to bear against the position, so common among social scientists who were his contemporaries, that a fundamental opposition existed between society and the individual, and that to show man's debt to his cultural tradition was to minimize his claim to originality and free will. Whether Santayana was discussing great artists or great religious masters, his thesis was the same: only those "can show great originality [who] are trained in distinct and established schools; for originality and genius must be largely fed and raised on the shoulders of some old tradition." [3] The worst conditions for cross-cultural understanding, according to Santayana, are present among those who throw over all they regard as established tradition; the best, among those who respect their own canons and dogmas; no matter how dissimilar their beliefs, they have a common ground, and they can best understand each other. When the modern anthropologist says that in any cross-cultural work it is better for the student to be sure of his own ethnic and national position and loyalties, he is echoing Santayana's point, and he can profit by his wisdom.

Santayana's volumes also deal with the topical subject matter of anthropology: social organization, religion, art, and speculative thought. He saw all these arts of man as rooted in the culture of a given time and place. His analysis of Greece and that of the Hebrews, and of the growth of Christianity in Europe, was a part of his *Reason in Religion* which was published in 1905. It is still to my mind indispensable to any anthropologist who is studying religion, and there is no better illustration of the deeper insight the methods of the humanities had achieved than a comparison of *Reason in Religion* with Tylor's *Primitive Culture* — and *Primitive Culture* is a favorite book on my shelves. Tylor performed well the task he set himself, but the humanist's approach to his problem, being holistic and always taking account of context in the mind of man, allows him to investigate problems which have not yet been adequately treated from anthropological material.

In Santayana's *Three Philosophical Poets*, too, he is studying three contrasting cultures, those represented by Lucretius, by Dante, and by Goethe. He is concerned to characterize the "cosmic parables" of these three poets as different ways of viewing life, different ways of conceiving man's fate. They are contrasted studies of the genius of three great civilizations, and I think no anthropologist can read them without profit.

I have stressed Santayana's humanistic studies of culture, but the humanities — even as exemplified in Santayana — do not necessarily deal with culture. Shakespearian criticism is a case in point, and it has nevertheless been most valuable to me as an anthropologist. Long before I knew anything at all about anthropology, I had learned from Shakespearian criticism — and from Santayana — habits of mind which at length made me an anthropologist.

I had learned, for example, from Furness' great Variorum editions, how drastically men's values and judgments are culturally conditioned. The stage versions of Shakespeare's plays rewritten in the eighteenth and nineteenth centuries reflected the temper of the age of Queen Anne, of the Georges, and of the Victorian era. Even the questions critics had asked about the characters in the plays were documentation on the age in which they were writing; for nearly two centuries after *Hamlet* became a favorite play on the London stage it did not occur to any one of them that there was anything particularly interesting in Hamlet's character. With the rise of romanticism this became the central interest of all commentators, and the most bizarre "explanations" were offered.

It was A. C. Bradley who, in his *Shakespearian Tragedy*, first published in 1904, cut his way through this underbrush and emphasized valid humanistic standards of criticism as applied, not only to the character of Hamlet, but of Iago and Macbeth and King Lear and other famous men and women of the tragedies. The core of his method was the critic's surrender to the text itself; he ruled out those "explanations" which sounded plausible only so long as one did not remember the text. Shakespeare was, for Bradley, a dramatist able to set forth his characters with sufficient truth and completeness so that they would reveal themselves to the student who weighed carefully both what was said and what was not said, what was done and what was not done. In the worlds which Shakespeare portrayed, Bradley said, "We watch *what is*, seeing that so it happened and must have happened."

Bradley's canons of good Shakespearian criticism, and his practice of it, are as good examples of fruitful methods and high standards as a student of culture can desire. The anthropologist will, of course, use these canons for the study of a cultural ethos, and not for the elucidation of a single character, but he, like Bradley, knows that he will succeed in his work if he takes into account whatever is said and done, discarding nothing he sees to be relevant; if he tries to understand the interrelations of discrete bits; if he surrenders himself to his data and uses all the insights of which he is capable.

The anthropologist has still more to learn from such literary criticism as that of Bradley. For more than a decade anthropologists have agreed upon the value of the life history. Some have said that it was the essential tool in the study of a culture. Many life histories have been collected — many more than have been published. Very little, however, has been done even with those which are published, and field workers who collected them have most often merely extracted in their topical monographs bits about marriage or ceremonies or livelihood which they obtained in life histories. The nature of the life-history material made this largely inevitable, for I think anyone who has read great numbers of these autobiographies, published and unpublished, will agree that from eighty to ninety-five per cent of most of them are straight ethnographic reporting of culture. It is a time-consuming and repetitious way of obtaining straight ethnography, and if that is all they are to be used for, any field worker knows how to obtain such data more economically. The unique value of life histories lies in that fraction of the material which shows what repercussions the experiences of a man's life — either shared or idiosyncratic — have upon him as a human being molded in that environment. Such information, as it were, tests out a culture by showing its workings in the life of a carrier of that culture; we can watch in an individual case, in Bradley's words, "*what is*, seeing that so it happened and must have happened." But if we are to make our collected life histories count in anthropological theory and understanding, we have only one recourse: we must be willing and able to study them according to the best tradition of the humanities. None of the social sciences, not even psychology, has adequate models for such studies. The humanities have. If we are to use life histories for more than items of topical ethnology, we shall have to be willing to do the kind of job on them which has traditionally been done by the great humanists.

Shakespearian criticism has pressed on in recent years in several new directions which are instructive to the anthropologist. Bradley wrote before the days of modern detailed research into Elizabethan beliefs, events, and stage practices. This is true cultural study in the humanitarian tradition, and all such knowledge is essential for an understanding of Shakespeare's plays. Such research compares, for instance, pirated texts in the early quartos with the texts of the folio collected edition; it studies the diaries and papers of a great Elizabethan theater owner in order to reconstruct the conditions under which the plays were produced. More than all, it describes the current ideas of Shakespearian times in science, history, morals, and religion, both those accepted by the "groundlings" and those aired among the elite. As Dover Wilson has shown in his critical edition of *Hamlet*, such a cultural study is crucial. Only with a knowledge of what the current ideas were about ghosts and their communications with their descendants can one judge what Shakespeare was saying in *Hamlet*; one can understand Hamlet's relations with his mother only with an acquaintance with what incest was in Elizabethan times, and what it meant to contract an "o'erhasty marriage" where "the funeral baked meats did coldly furnish forth the marriage tables."

Carolyn Spurgeon's and Dr. Armstrong's examination of Shakespeare's imagery is another kind of study from which an anthropologist can learn a technique useful in the study of comparative cultures. It can reveal symbolisms and free associations which fall into patterns and show processes congenial to the human mind in different cultures.

In all that I have said, I have emphasized the common ground which is shared by the humanities and by anthropology so soon as it includes the mind and behavior of men in its definition of culture. I could have spoken about what anthropology in its present state of knowledge has to offer to the humanities, but that subject would not be crucial in a talk to anthropologists. It is important, however, for us to be aware of what we can learn from the humanities. Let me emphasize again that the humanities provide only some of the answers to our problems in cultural studies; there are problems in the comparative study of societies with which they do not deal. Because anthropology, as a social science, organized its work to arrive at certain generalized, theoretical statements about culture, it has been able to make and document certain points in the Study of Man which the humanities did not make.

My point is that, once anthropologists include the mind of man in their subject matter, the methods of science and the methods of the humanities complement each other. Any commitment to methods which exclude either approach is self-defeating. The humanists criticize the social sciences because they belabor the obvious and are arid; the social scientists criticize the humanities because they are subjective. It is not necessary for the anthropologist to be afraid of either criticism, neither of belaboring the obvious, nor of being subjective. The anthropologist can use both approaches. The adequate study of culture, our own and those on the opposite side of the globe, can press on to fulfillment only as we learn today from the humanities as well as from the sciences.

Part VI

Selected Poems

1941

Dedication[1]

Haws when they blossom in the front of summer,
Snow-breasted to the sun, and odorous
Of wind-dissolved honey, flaunt their bodies,
Secret and quick, to eyes incurious.

Their fertile golden dust the wind shall scatter,
Surfeited bees maul yet one feast the more,
And all their dainty-stepping petals flutter
At last and publicly to grassy floor.

Still through their roots runs the most secret liquor
No wind shall tamper, no hurrying bee shall sip;
Let the haws blossom, let their petals scatter,
In covert earth wine gathers to their lip.

This Breath

This breath, blown out upon the casual air,
Lost as it passes, formless as the light,
We have for blocks to build with. Mothwings wear
Less brief, less crumbling substance, that take flight
One evening long, and for their instant lift
Darkly and strange, by night a sunlit thrift.

But breath is nothing, though we hold it high;
A simple rhythm pulling at the breast
Having no mark to name it to the eye.
Breath passes lightly, the wave's curling crest
Sucked under lifting oceans, lost and blind,
And all our search a whistling down the wind.

Bind breath no more in sheaves that melt as mist
From sunrise river valleys. Breath's a wraith
No cord shall bind, no dreamer twist
To image of his love, or any faith.
Breath goes the way down which all beauty passes,
Pledged to no goal, wind fumbling in the grasses.

Love That Is Water

Love that is water, love that is a flood
Coming and going, silvering the land,
How shall we say of this, inductile water,
It shall be chiselled by the fragile sand?

Water slips lightly, flawless, from our confines,
Shaped to no permanent feature, fluid as air;
Though we stand hewing till the sword is eaten,
There is no lineament we shall chisel there.

But the Son of Man . . .

Foxes have holes, and in the wintry weather
Save themselves warm at price of breath and bone;
Playing to shortened strength a shortened tether,
Taking to breast a stone.

Their light feet tranced, their blood become as earthy
As sodden marshes when the flood is gone,
They sleep, not knowing bereavement, content, worthy
The ecstasy withdrawn.

So at the winter of the blood we straighten
Our limbs to quiet, crying flesh to find
Oblivion as foxes', sun-forsaken,
Deaf and dumb and blind.

Annunciation

Wide-eyed, O Mary, take the branching lily;
The slant light falls no otherwise today
Than all your quiet days, and if it blossoms
Most lover-like, this god shall disarray

No fold of your slight garments. Therefore go forward
Boldly, your inadvertent maidenhood
Unstirred as yesterday. Draw no curtain
Before this place lest any, passing, should

Spy on the coming of the holy lover;
In likeness of a dove, as casual
As any perching pigeon, he shall settle
In your blue-kerchiefed bosom. He shall dwell

In your girl's body as a prayer chastely.
Though you grow great with god, desire shall be
A song you know not, and sometimes you'll wonder
When, tending sheep, girls tell of ecstasy.

But after, when you have gone in to Joseph,
And borne to him, out of desire, a son,
Will you not pity us, a timid people,
Who confound so the god, the holy one?

Intruder

What's this of breath, a changeling birth that sobs
Distraught in body's hold? Stop fast your ears
And go your way regardless. She's a child
And her tears childish tears.

Body was old what time she was unborn,
And the great rondure of the universe
Confirms its primacy and inert bulk
No spirit shall coerce.

Matter sweeps on, still brother to Orion,
Bound to the wheel, unwitting its frail guest.
O breath, defeated and most futile daughter,
Unhand me, loneliest.

Countermand

Ice when it forms upon the brooks in autumn
Stills their swift feet that ran they knew not where,
Rendered in stone that were but drops tossed seaward,
Splintered to vapor down a rocky stair.

Always a song went up from their white waters,
Yielded obedient to the tug of earth;

Left far behind, the roots that reached to hold them,
And the marshy places, for an alien worth.

Brooks must lay by the summer song they fashioned
Out of a doom that drove them bitterly.
Now it is lifted; silenced is their singing,
All their swift music made a mockery.

It were enough that stone should lie quiescent,
Stone never ran quicksilver in the shade,
Stone never gathered out of doom a singing,
Lost now, forgotten, and its dream betrayed.

Myth

A god with tall crow feathers in his hair,
Long-limbed and bronzed, from going down of sun,
Dances all night upon his dancing floor,
Tight at his breast, our sorrows, one by one.

Relinquished stalks we could not keep till bloom,
And thorns unblossomed but of our own blood,
He gathers where we dropped them, filling full
His arms' wide circuit, briars and sterile shrub.

And all alone he dances, hour on hour,
Till all our dreams have blooming, and our sleep
Is odorous of gardens, — passing sweet
Beyond all, wearily, we till and reap.

Unshadowed Pool

You are a pool unshadowed by cast lustre,
Crystal as air, having no skill to hold
Skies that are cloudy-petaled, and the rushes blowing,
Intricate patterns and sun-aureoled.

Pools should be spread with design caught at heaven,
Laced by near stems and taking the quick bird.
They should be garmented with far-sought garments
Lest any come there and find the pool unstirred;

Lest, at arm's length, pebble to pebble lying,
Life's farthest depths show clear as whitened bone,
Nothing be water-misted, nothing secret,
Past the rent altar-veil, the common stone.

Price of Paradise

And Adam sold Paradise for two kernels of grain.
PERSIAN TALE

Being despoiled, not heir of Paradise,
His senses raw and hungered after long,
He dreamed it worthy the consummate song
The stars sang at its cradle, and its price
The bloody sweat and outstretched sacrifice
Of all his days. The crown of thorns, the thong,
The nails on palm and instep, he was strong
To brook unbroken, spent for Paradise.

He reckoned closer, Adam, who had lived
With Eve in Paradise; it was not worth
The taking. When there came a god with gift
Of two small wrinkled kernels of the earth,
Not valuing Paradise, he sold spendthrift;
But he had lived in Eden from his birth.

Another Theseus

He had been seeking Ariadne always.
Always, abandoned to the Minotaur,

The labyrinth of his soul an empty prison
For that great beast that ravened at its core,

He followed lying omens. Not a lover
But her thread broke and left him helpless there,
And fear would come upon him, turning, turning,
Down those blind mazes, and utmost despair.

Somehow he stumbled to the light of heaven,
By chance conferred another interim,
And you who're sure that you are Ariadne
Have lulled his terrors, and have armored him.

He took your sword and the frail thread you gave him,
Armed now for combat with the Minotaur.
You laughed who thought it was a beast of fable,
Conjured for children, not old enough for war.

You were not Ariadne, notwithstanding,
And your bright sword is broken on a myth.
He could not stand against his spirit's devil;
Better you leave him in the labyrinth.

Eucharist

Light the more given is the more denied.
Though you go seeking by the naked seas,
Each cliff etched visible and all the waves
Pluming themselves with sunlight, of this pride
Light makes her sophistries.

You are not like to find her, being fed
Always with that she shines on. Only those
Storm-driven down the dark, see light arise,
Her body broken for their rainbow bread
At late and shipwrecked close.

For the Hour after Love

Love shall not end except in quietness
And all its tumult hushed against the dark.
He most who mounted heaven as a lark
On bodiless strong wings, most questionless
Shall know this chill estrangement. The largess
Of all our love is a down-curving arc
That ends in sleeping, lest we rouse to mark
How all our fires go out in nothingness.

Love that is so delivered to defeat
Upon the consummation of its bliss,
And all the treachery a trick more sweet
Than any labored virtue, — how of this
Shall we set stars in heaven? or compete
With sleep begotten of a woman's kiss?

Reprieve

Let us not say, dear love, "Lo this! Lo that!
The untoward circumstance of age or birth,
This underpinning of our dear desire,
Shall prove of the earth earth."

And if it chanced, were we the wiser then?
Always who strive with gods shall measure them
At length on the hard ground, and who shall slate
The divine stratagem?

Let us laugh rather when he whispers us
Some sinew's weak to bear his potent hand,
And fall once more upon the wily god
Until the countermand.

Lift Up Your Heart

When you shall lie abandoned to that hour
Scrawled star-incised upon your horoscope,
Do not be comforted. Admit no hope
Warm-lipped upon your breasts, nor folded flower
From any south-turned slope.

I who have loved you leave against that sorrow
Words wise as crickets', tenderer than a sword's,
Lest you feast after at high-fruited boards
And glut yourself with that always tomorrow
There is no man that hoards.

Be desperate in that hour. Lift up your heart
As any cup, and drink it desolate,
A drained and ruinous vessel that no fate
Shall fill again in pity, and no art
Make brim quick-passionate.

Leave not one drop for heart-broke artifice
Against the stricken years. You shall know now
The quiet brooding of the apple bough
Past blossoming, peace of the chrysalis,
The rain upon your brow.

Unicorns at Sunrise

Some night after long loneliness and lack
At dawning down the light they'll come light-hoofed
With gladness, pawing the leafy-hidden track
With forefeet that are slim and velvet-black
And native of celestial ways unroofed
Of zodiac.

Run then, no instant staying, up the hill,
Hot with desire of their curved single horn,
And leap to him, the foremost, no man born
Has mounted to good purpose, and no skill
Made less than unicorn.

Throw slack the reins, and keep no memory
Of foolish dreams we dreamed of ripened corn
In barns, and red fire on the hearth. Be free
As unicorns, that are but fantasy
Unpledged to any truth, a single horn
Against reality.

Withdrawal

All day the rain caressed my straining trees
With slim white hands upon their naked flesh;
And winds there were to lift the boughs and thresh
Their passion on the sky, what time for ease
Love grapples love afresh.

At dusk the wind fell to a whispering,
And rain withdrawn left all the air a clear
And bitter loneliness, wherein I hear
Down all its firmament no echoing
Of that but now so dear.

Sleet Storm

Dusk came grayly with an iron weight
That gathered from the unsubstantial air
Stilly upon the boughs. Upon their spare
And delicate limbs it laid its body straight
And inescapable, an old lust bare
Of joy, and terrible with hate.

All night there was no respite where they stood,
Broken with weight, brittle with agony;
And winds made plaything of catastrophe,
And, for their pain, smote laughter through that wood,
Wherein ice-shackled branches grievously
Cried out for interlude.

O terror of snapped limbs, and dread that night,
At quiet morning had the sun but looked
An hour from heaven, we had brooked
The night its torment. The valley lay to light
A blossoming paradise. And we have looked
In vain, until the night.

Counsel for Autumn

You who have walked the misted meadowlands
And crushed their petaled colors of bright gold
And wine surpassing carmines, on a tongue
Lusting for beauty as new-lighted brands
Lust for the flames they fold,

Dare yet the autumn gladly. Tracery
More intricate-lovely than the June woodbine
Each winter-barren tree shall hold to heaven
And fling on withered meadows. Be glad, who see
Now not a green leaf shine

On any branches; there is come to you
Matter too great to trace in green and gold
Of tangible loveliness, but in a slight
And hieroglyphic shadow cast on dew
Beauty herself is told.

Burial

Had I the green and silver laughter of the birch tree,
The thousand dancing laughters of her lips,

Had I the milk-white fairness of her body,
The quiet of her brooding fingertips,

I should be glad I'd lifted dark sod into the light,
And that the dust of women was sweet again
In me. I pray you then for my burial
Find out a birch. You shall have answer then.

November Burning

Meadows, the harvest done, the kerneled corn
Filched for the granaries, are given to flame,
To flame that fashions of dry useless things
Brief flowers of no name.

But in November the gold broken stubble,
Its sap yet lingering, life waking still,
Shall blossom with no fire; smoke is harvest
Of an autumn hill.

Let be, the bleak long winter, and the field
Guard preciously its stubble; let no shower
Of April mildness stir its roots to life;
Let no stalk come to flower.

Come spring, set torch to tinder, that the flame,
Not hooded now, not clogged with happiness,
Lift clean its strong bright limbs; let the dead find
Life's apotheosis.

"There is no death"

We weary of the earth, its madrigal
Of still-renewing autumns, and the sky
Spread as an azure curtain on the heavens,

Marking our sight its confines. Earth is a child,
Sings but one rondelay.

How shall we dance to her piping, being born
Heavy with memories, and all blown dust
To us decay of limbs; the myriad hours,
Prankt with bright airs, to us the echoing
Of hours that are rust.

I will put memory from me, knowing now
Nothing but the incontinence of breath,
Glitter a moment silver on the grasses,
Love at its noon. I will forget the folly
That there is no death.

At Ending

At ending when the world is done
And the dead air lets fall the ash
Upon the blackened plain no flash
Shall light henceforth forever, none
Of all the wandering breezes kiss
Again to loveliness like this —

There shall be silence always. Riven,
Infertile, charred as any star
Thick-sown at evening, they are
That were mythology of heaven
To our sight: arbutus bed,
And the dark pines, thick-carpeted.

And down the burnt-out air shall come
No hurt upon the night, no cry
Our hearts must stir to satisfy,
No portent of delirium;
A god that kinder, being death,
Set limit to this folly, breath.

You Have Looked upon the Sun

It shall be ended, and no victory
Bind laurel in your hair. Wherefore to you
Should they come bannered with the red and blue
Your eyes are mazed with always? Let it be
Enough for you that never anyone
Unblinded sees the glory that you see,
Enough that you have looked upon the sun.

This Gabriel

He wrought a pitiful permanence
From jagged moments, and dismay,
And tears more purposeless than pain.
He smiled, knowing the gray

And dusty journey for the same
Men saw upwinding through the stars;
Himself no less infinity
Than they. He liked their common scars

The better for their being won
As his upon a simple tree,
Wounding a transience and a flesh
Innocent of divinity.

What comfort had he had in praise
That makes of him this Gabriel
Walking the stars, his even pace
Shaped to a crystal citadel?

Spiritus Tyrannus

This hand that may not lie upon your hand,
These lips that lacking you find nothing worth,

Are so the more deluded, that find dearth
Where is satiety, and ropes of sand
Where is the firm-knit earth.

Flesh when it is a thirst cries out to flesh
Thick strewn as foam-crests on a following sea.
What has it need of preference that we
Should not dip comfort each white day afresh
And drink it royally?

The flesh is weak! It cannot drink at all
Till some strange hour the spirit seal her choice,
It has no passion that it may rejoice
Of its own turbulence; nor mating call
That cries not with her voice.

Earthborn

I have put spirit from me as a cheat
No longer to be borne. Shall flesh be less
Than this impalpable wherefrom I eat
No food of comforting, or ever bless
As once your wandering hands? Put by this boast
That severs our far-faring from the host
Of rooted earthy things that companied
Our hither journeying. Nay! Rather know
I have such need of you as petals shed
Before the wind one burning hour ago.

She Speaks to the Sea

Now would I lay aside the garment of my body,
Lay quite aside its slavery of breath,
For I am smitten to my knees with longing,
Desolate utterly, scourged by your surface-touch
Of white-lipped wave and unquiet azure hands.

Is life no more than this? that always I should come
Unmarked from passion, unbranded from despair?
Shall I come always longing for embrace
Ultimate, irretrievable, complete,
As that you keep far out beyond that last blue bar
For those who come to claim it? Will you have minstrels,
Ocean, when I come, bride to eternal bridegroom,
And save one jeweled chamber for our eternity?

Moth Wing

When you have cast the reckoning
Of her most wayward loveliness,
And thumbed the bright frost-patterned wing
Her laughter lifted for largess

Of suffering, it will be less
Than any rag upon the wind.
Let there be end of weariness
And high endeavor, passion thinned

To songs of her great loveliness.
Weep rather for a crumpled thing
Not any jeweled words shall dress
To beauty sudden-fluttering.

Toy Balloons

He flies the drifting dreams of men
Blown each into a perfect sphere
Of unadulterate color, clear
As moon's gold on the darkness when

The nights grow cold; or poppies robed
With sunlight. Vendor, of your pity,

Do not sell these to children. See,
They are too young to bear the globed

And maddening beauty of this breath
That bursts at finger touch. Frail dreams
Are for the old, whose mirth blasphemes
All perpetuities save death.

Words in Darkness

There will come beauty in a silver rain
Out of the storm-hung heaven of my soul.
Let me remember seasons that have lain
Heavy as this with darkness and the roll
Of the on-coming thunder, and were yet
Distilled to showers crystal-cool and white
Beyond the gift of sunshine; heedless, let
The storm close cold upon me, and the bite
Of sand be on my breasts, nor question why
The silver fingers of the rain are wrought
Out of a maddened tumult and a sky
No man of all would willingly have sought.

In Praise of Uselessness

Let it be useless as the winds at dusk
On river shallows, or the dalliance
Of crimsons in the sunset. Know this husk
Men cast to alien winds and lift no glance
From their plowed harrowed meadows, lovelier
Than any moldering kernels in the loam
Shall lift on delicate breezes. Wherefore stir
The earth to futile pregnancy for whom
We know are futile, and cast forth the brief
Plump grain our day shall grant no more of? Here's

The surety shall garner up of grief
Its loveliness; of love, remembering tears.

Resurrection of the Ghost

Then having died, the knotted coil
Eluded, and the quietude
Only the dead can boast of, being yours,
Cruelly you returned, a ghost the food
Of darkness, laying by
The perfumed garments of the burial.
You freed the linen bands and folded them
As a forgotten heaven folded, full
Of days, God now has lost the clue of, void
And set at naught forever. Nothing housed
In your frail ghost but clarity
Of seeing that espoused
No hope nor love you died for. Now at last
And clear as dew a moment as it holds
To petal of the lily, the round world
Gave up its secret. Death unfolds
Nothing but this, no angel's song,
No beauty at the bone.
Clear-eyed the tenemented ghost stands up
And rolls away the stone.

Mary Wollstonecraft *

THE STORY of Mary Wollstonecraft is that most precious of human documents: the story of a life that achieved an idea. She was one of those few and valuable persons who are born with a pitiless thirst for understanding afresh. For her, life had no axioms; its geometry was all experimental. She was forever testing, probing; forever dominated by an utter unwillingness to accept the pretense, the convention in place of the reality. She reasoned because she must; because a passionately intellectual attitude toward living was her essential tool.

Such a life is perhaps inevitably tempestuous; Mary Wollstonecraft's at least was lavishly romantic. She lived in that incomparable time, intoxicated with its visions of the immanent descent of a new heaven and a new earth — the early years of the French Revolution. She vibrated to every impact of the intellectual excitement of the days. "Life cannot be seen by an unmoved spectator," she wrote somewhere. Her idea did not attain solidity by the congealing of icy and solitary logical processes, like those of her twelve-months' husband, the estimable and frigid William Godwin. She lived life headlong; she lived it with lavish expense of spirit. She

---

* Unpublished manuscript, *circa* 1914–1917. The first reference to a plan to work on "a series of biographical papers" occurs in an entry in RFB's journal, dated November, 1914 (*see* above, p. 132); a foreword to the projected book, written after the study of Mary Wollstonecraft had been completed, dates from 1917.

attained to her idea by the rich processes of living; and the faith
which she had laid hold on, she brought again stoutly to its testing
in her own experience.

Her idea — her painfully evolved, pioneer idea — has been dinned
into our twentieth century ears by one of the most widespread propa-
gandas of this generation and has become one of the great forces that
is shaping our modern world.

Mary Wollstonecraft was born two centuries and a half ago, in
the mideighteenth century, a contemporary of Horace Walpole and
Mrs. Hannah More. History is guilty sometimes of playing off such
little ironies; of filching our logical contemporary from our twentieth
century, and throwing him prematurely forth, an incomparable in-
surrectionist, upon a generation that knows him not.

Certainly the eighteenth century comprehended Mary Wollstonecraft not at all; they had no linear rule by which to take her measure.
She was as incomprehensible to them as the fourth dimension to a
class in fractions. Her name was for her own generation a nine-day
wonder and reproach, and then two centuries forgot her.

Ordinarily it would have ended there. Two centuries of oblivion
leave of the most throbbingly vivid of these lives of our unchrono-
logical contemporaries nothing but an uncertain snatch of story and
a couple of allusions in a musty book. That the intervening centuries did not do the like to Mary Wollstonecraft is due to William
Godwin. At the time he was the leading literary and philosophical
radical of England, and perhaps for all time he is the most consistent
exponent of that obsolete Age of Reason. He married Mary
Wollstonecraft five months before the end of her tumultuous life.
Her death was the one tragedy of his eighty years. However, immediately, with the cold scrupulous detachment that was the very
pillar of his ethical code, he set about the unexpurgated publication
of her most intimate documents — even her passionate letters to
her former lover.[1] And not satisfied even then that he had done his
duty to posterity, he composed and printed an intimate memoir[2]
that stands unexcelled even today among the curiosities of the
nude in literature.

Together with the writings[3] she published during her lifetime,

these give us a vividly complete picture of the life of Mary Wollstonecraft. It is a strange tale of a fight for which the world was not
ready, which seemed worth the fighting only to one soul then living,
to Mary Wollstonecraft herself. She had a startling way of "raising
all the questions at once" — religious, economic, sexual, and philosophic. It is true that she had more than an ordinary justification;
the code of the eighteenth century on the subject of women, which
was always somehow or other Mary Wollstonecraft's basic theme,
was undeniably a study in insanity.

It was a time when Rousseau's banal puppet, Sophia, was the
ideal of the philosophic, and Dr. Fordyce's "soft features, a flowing
voice, and a form not robust" of the conventional. Rousseau had
insisted on the "principle" that "woman is expressly formed to please
the man." "To please, to be useful to us," he continues, "to make
us love and esteem them, to educate us while young, and take care
of us when grown up, to advise, to console us, to render our lives
easy and agreeable — these are the duties of women at all times, and
what they should be taught in their youth." For once Rousseau was
but holding the mirror to his own generation.

Health, education, morals, they were all offered up before this
strange masculine Juggernaut. Dr. Gregory advised every woman to
"feign a sickly delicacy to secure her husband's affection"; Mrs.
Barbauld rejected the idea of a proposed school for women with,
"Young ladies ought to have only such a general tincture of knowledge as to make them agreeable companions to a man of sense, and
to enable them to find rational enjoyment for a solitary hour." And
Hannah More, Horace Walpole's "Holy Hannah," could proclaim
from her worldly pinnacle: "Propriety is to a woman what the great
Roman citizen said that action is to the orator: it is the first, and the
second, and the third requisite."

In the face of such a world Mary Wollstonecraft threw down
her challenge. Truly it seems incredible to claim her for our contemporary. And yet the challenge she flung, the idea she achieved,
even the losses as well as gains that her tempestuous life realized —
they might all be clipped from our twentieth century. For the idea
with which she shocked her contemporaries was only that women
are more than men's playthings, that they have lives and understand-

ings of their own, and that anything short of a full development of their powers is a duty left undone. Her formulation of this modern axiom in her *Rights of Women* would stand today: "The first object of laudable ambition is to attain a character as a human being, regardless of the distinction of sex. And secondary views should be brought to this simple touchstone."

It was her painfully evolved, pioneer idea, and she elaborated it passionately. For her it was no hackneyed program; the pristine glamour of discovery was upon it. With the single exception of an isolated paper of Condorcet's — the one preserved for us by Morley in his *Miscellanies* — her *Rights of Women* is the first expression in any language of beliefs that are today axioms, of ideals of whose evolution no one yet can prophesy.

Mary Wollstonecraft's challenge was not alone in words; there were also the swift, whirling facts of her own life. The faith which she laid hold on, she brought boldly to its testing in her own experience. Of all the elucidations of her "touchstone" which she has left, her own life is the commentary incomparably the most arresting and the most significant.

For Mary Wollstonecraft never spoke her part by rote. She never flinched before the hazard of shaping forth a personality not duly authorized and accepted. She was one of those persons, who, in her own words, did not "rather catch a character from the society he lived in, than spread one about him." She lived with all the alertness of her brain focused upon the abrupt experiences of her life; the knowledge she won, the price she paid, her books may hint to us, but it is her life through which we understand. It is there that we can measure that passionate attitude toward living out of which all the restlessness of modern womankind has grown. It is her life story that makes her our contemporary.

1

Mary Wollstonecraft grew up from babyhood with a cruelly first-hand knowledge of the vulgar tragedies of life. The only thorough education she had was in that most sordid and wanton of all tragedies, a drunken home. Her father had inherited so considerable a fortune that even his large family might have lived all their lives comfortably on the income. But the temptations of a gentleman bred to no trade proved too much for Edward Wollstonecraft. He idled more and more profligately; he drank more and more deeply. He sought to improve his income by gentleman farming, and migrated restlessly from Essex to Yorkshire, even to Wales, in his search for an easy berth. By the time Mary, the eldest daughter of the family, entered her teens, her father was already a poor man. His character became increasingly brutal as his self-pity grew. He beat his wife, he tortured his dogs, he ruled his children by threats and blows. Godwin tells us that the wife was "the first and most submissive of his subjects." Mary took upon herself a childish guardianship over her; she "lay whole nights on the landing place near their chamber door," listening to guard her if "her father should break out into paroxysms of violence." She threw herself between them "that she might receive the blows aimed against her mother." And this mother was only a petty, broken woman, the tyranny of whose husband taught her tyranny toward her daughters.

It was one of those homes which curse society with children poisoned by petty cowardice, small lies, mean subterfuges. It is only the very spirited who survive mentally, the very strong who are clean thereafter. It was fortunate for Mary Wollstonecraft that she had the freedom of a Yorkshire heath, where, she wrote in later life, "we bounded at pleasure . . . in the healthful breeze. To enjoy open air and freedom was paradise after the unnatural restraint of our fireside, where we were often obliged to sit three and four hours together, without daring to utter a word, when my father was out of humor. — My father's orders were not to be disputed, orders which as a mere child I discovered to be unreasonable because inconsistent and contradictory."

It was by a self-reliance pitifully beyond her years that the child Mary Wollstonecraft escaped with her soul. She became her own monitor. When she herself "felt that she had done wrong, the reproof or chastisement of her mother," in Godwin's stiff phrases, "instead of being a terror to her, she found to be the only thing capable of reconciling her to herself." But the arbitrary beatings and caresses of her father, his despotic whims, filled her with contemptuous resentment, which remained all her life through as a ruling passion against all that was arbitrary, all that had the power to compel unreasoned compliance in any relationship — her "pestiferous purple" of despotic rule. It was to her an unjustifiable "insistence on a privilege without being willing to pay the price fixed by nature" — the patient winning of the child's reasonable assent. Parents exact it, she said, "from the same principle that makes a fish muddy the water it swims in to elude its enemy, instead of facing it boldly in the clear stream." Her rebellion against it lay at the basis of her passionate French Revolution faith in democracy; it made her color-blind to convention; it roused her to passion against the bondage of women. And its foundations were laid in a child's resentment at her father's arbitrary blows.

2

The most vivid experience of her girlhood was her friendship for Fanny Blood. Until she was past thirty, it was her only adventure in romance. Mary was sixteen, Fanny but two years older, when they met; and from that time until long after Fanny's death ten years later, this friendship was, in Godwin's words, "so fervent as to be the ruling passion of her mind." It had a momentous influence upon her. "Perhaps it is necessary," she wrote years after, "for virtue first to appear in a human form to impress youthful hearts. Youth . . . deifies the beloved object." With her the stimulus extended to a passionate self-education. She was "a wild but animated and aspiring girl of sixteen" with no education except that of an eighteenth century Yorkshire day school. Fanny seemed intellectually leagues ahead of her; to attain to her learning seemed an impossible dream. Fanny became her guide, her teacher. Mary read the books which her friend had read, she wrote voluminous letters which Fanny corrected for form and style. At home she stipulated for a room alone for certain hours of the day. For the first time she tasted the excitement of using her brain.

It was to her an intoxicating excitement, an excitement which even the inglorious years of her young womanhood could not down — not the two years when she drudged out her teens as companion to the bullying tradesman's widow at Bath, nor the difficult months when for the last time she shielded her mother through her slow, ugly dying.

Through it all, Fanny Blood was her vivid preoccupation. What was at first adoration before an idol became with the years the passionate protectiveness of a mother for her frailest child. For Fanny Blood was only a timid, clinging soul, lovesick through many years for a lover of whom she was never sure. Toward Mary she felt the rather bewildered acquiescence of *l'autre qui se laisse aimer*.

We know from the little memorial story Mary Wollstonecraft wrote of her after her early death that she did not scruple to weigh her idol and find it wanting. "She was timid and irresolute," she wrote of her, "grief only had power to make her reflect. In everything it was not the great, but the beautiful or the pretty that caught her attention." But she had never demanded perfection in Fanny Blood. She had "felt her looks in every nerve," and it was sufficient. Fanny was to her her precious adventure in romance. And on her she lavished all the affection of her youth.

3

It was only another sordid domestic tragedy that made of her quite suddenly a woman full-grown. Her sister Bess had married, when, at their mother's death, their father's house had become an unbearable insult to his daughters. But the marriage was a fresh horror. The husband was a plausible brute, a domestic bully. After the birth of a child, "poor Bess's" mind became deranged, and Mary went to care for her. She saw much, heard much, and wrote often to Everina, the sister in London. For four months she chronicled the "constant fluctuations of reason," punctuated by "violent fits of frenzy." "Misery haunts this house in one shape or other," she wrote. Then Bess grew "better, and of course more sad." It was chiefly from her husband that she had to be protected. There were faults on both sides: "I that know and am fixed in my opinion," Mary wrote, "cannot unwaveringly adhere to it. My spirits are harried with listening to pros and cons; and my head is so confused that I sometimes answer 'no' when I should say 'yes.' — I cannot insult B— (Bess's husband) with advice which he would never have wanted, if he had been capable of attending to it. Miracles don't happen now, and only a miracle can alter the minds of some people. They grow old, and we can only discover by their countenances that they are so." And Mary became convinced that there was no chance of miracles and reformations. "Poor Bess's situation almost turns my brain," she wrote her other sister. "I tell you she will soon be deprived of reason. Those who would save Bess must act and not talk."

Therefore she planned an escape. For an escape it was, clandestine and terror-struck with the fear of the husband's pursuit. There was a stealthy transfer of clothes to the "brushmaker's in the Strand," an excited maneuvering of cabs, and a nerve-racking ride to an unknown goal, poor Bess in a returning frenzy "biting her wedding ring to pieces." By nightfall, Mary Wollstonecraft had her own share of nerve-fagged terror. She sat by the window writing to Everina:

> My heart beats time with every carriage that rolls by — I hope B— will not discover us, for I would rather face a lion; yet the door never opens but I expect to see him panting for breath.
>
> > Yours,
> > Mary.
>
> She looks now very wild. Heaven protect us!
> I almost wish for a husband, for I want somebody to support me.

But even that night did not assail her conviction that the escape was a consummation devoutly to be wished. "The thought of having assisted to bring about so desirable an event will ever give me pleasure to think of," she declared formally. "I knew I should be the Mrs. Brown, the shameful incendiary, in this shocking affair of a woman's leaving her bedfellow; they thought that the strong affection of a sister *might* apologize for my conduct, but that the scheme was by no means a good one. In short, 'tis contrary to all the rules of conduct that are published for the benefit of new-married ladies, — by whose advice Mrs. Brook was actuated when with great grief of heart she gave up my friendship!"

4

So Mary Wollstonecraft began her womanhood. She had challenged her world for the sake of a half-mad sister; she had likewise assumed the responsibility for her support. They were quite penniless. Fanny Blood wrote Everina: "I can not see any possible resource they have for a maintenance; their situation grows ever more and more desperate."

But Mary Wollstonecraft had energy and some knack at succeeding and, with the help of Bess and Fanny Blood, really attained a short-lived prosperity in the school she established at Newington Green. But it became "the grave of all her comforts." Fanny, weak and frail with the long uncertainties of her romance, left her to be married at last to her changeable lover in Lisbon. Expenses at the school increased alarmingly. Bess and Everina proved tactless with the boarders and pupils. And just as difficulties were culminating, word came that marriage had not proved a cure for Fanny's ill health, and that she longed to have Mary with her. We must believe Godwin's words that this friendship for the timid, fragile, lovesick girl was "the ruling passion of her mind." Immediately she began to plan to leave her school with her sisters, to borrow the necessary money for her expenses, and to sail for Lisbon to Fanny Blood. Poor Fanny died less than a week after Mary reached her, leaving a puny son behind her.

So ended the one romance of Mary Wollstonecraft's youth, the devotion on which she had lavished all the powers of her affection. While Fanny lived, the incidents of her life had shaped themselves about her as around some great centrifugal force; with her death they fell into disorder. She entered upon that desperate period of youth that is maddened by its failure to find for itself those inner cohesions, those dominating motives that its soul demands, that feels itself mocked by every hope of purposefulness, by every longing to express itself.

She had outward reasons for her despondency. The school

dwindled and failed. In her extremity she forced herself to become a governess. She dreaded, as she said, "to live without any interchange of little acts of kindness and tenderness." But the forty pounds tempted her; she needed money to settle her debts and to provide for Bess.

So she set out for Ireland and the castle of Mitchelstown. "I entered the great gates," she wrote Everina, "with the same kind of feeling I should have if I were going into the Bastille. There was such a solemn kind of stupidity about this place as froze my very blood." When she was alone, she frightened herself by her apathy and unrestrainable misery. "To tell the truth," she wrote her sister, "I hope part of my misery arises from disordered nerves, for I would fain believe my mind is not so very weak." There was no longer need that she protect "poor Bess," that she cherish Fanny in her weakness; for the moment she had not even those things that "of all the pleasures I relish — rational conversation and domestic affection," so she wrote during that Irish winter.

The episodes of her life succeeded each other without meaning or purpose. She had not yet attained to that strong foothold, that defense against "the casualties of life" which she celebrated in her *Rights of Women*. She summoned all the forces of a religion that for some years had been very real to her, but it did not give her comfort. She attempted to lose herself in the training of her pupils — "wild Irish, unformed and not very pleasing," she had thought them. But here she was balked by the mother's interference.

Her best support was in Mr. Johnson, the prominent Fleet Street publisher, who had published a little pamphlet of hers three years before called the *Education of Daughters*, and who now wrote her that if she would come to London and "exert her talents in writing, she might support herself in a comfortable way."

She would be the "first of a new genus," she wrote her sister under strict pledge of secrecy — a woman regularly employed in writing for her daily bread. "I tremble at the attempt," she wrote. "Yet if I fail, I only suffer; and should I succeed, my dear girls will ever in sickness have a home, and a refuge where for a few months in the year, they may forget the cares that disturb them."

And again: "I have done with the delusions of fancy — I only live to be useful; benevolence must fill every void in my heart." Godwin says she was "the victim of a desire to promote the benefit of others." Yes, but to the Mary Wollstonecraft of those days, her desire was a pillar of strength, the only prop she could lay hold on. She gave herself as freely to her duty as later to her love.

5

Thus she grew calmer. She had come out of those years when she had not dared to think, and had saved her soul alive by a stern invocation to Duty and Benevolence. Poor Mary! All her conscious righteousness could not keep her from being very humanly distraught. It was to the fatherly Mr. Johnson that she wrote most openly:

I have been very ill; Heaven knows it was more than fancy. After some sleepless, wearisome nights, toward the morning I have grown delirious. — There is certainly a great defect in my mind: my wayward heart creates its own misery. Why I am made thus I cannot tell; and till I can form some idea of the whole of my existence, I must be content to weep and dance like a child, — long for a toy and be tired of it as soon as I get it.

We must all of us wear a fool's cap; but mine, alas! has lost its bells, and grown so heavy I find it intolerably burdensome. Good night! — Surely, I am a fool.

Nevertheless, year in and year out, she flung herself into her work. After all, her "dear freedom," her "little peace and independence" was only hack-writing, translating from languages she made acquaintance with for the purpose. Perhaps it was as well; the Mary Wollstonecraft of those early London days held herself upright only by devotion to stern, uningratiating virtues; it does not make stirring reading.

The one original book she found time to write during her first years of translating and reviewing is that curious little volume designed for the moral instruction of children and

Calculated to
Regulate the Affections
And
Form the Mind
to
Truth and Goodness.

It is dominated by the person of Mrs. Mason, that supreme em-bodiment of conscious benevolence and rectitude. She takes her "shamefully ignorant" young charges firmly by the hand, and leads them to call on the minister's wife and the schoolmistress, where they discuss "virtue is immortal" and "the approbation of my own heart elevates my soul," and thereafter the children depart "reluc-tantly, filled with respect." There was never a book that tumbled more ludicrously into all the pitfalls that beset self-conscious preach-ments.

Her life was quite as uncompromising. All the money she could earn she devoted to the support of her family: she sent Everina to Paris, and put Bess as a parlor boarder in a good school; she paid for James' training in the navy; she sent money to her father; she took her youngest brother Charles up to London with her and later fitted him out to seek his fortune in America. On herself she spent almost nothing. She dressed so shabbily that one contemporary at least called her a "philosophical sloven"; she lived so meanly in cheap lodgings in Blackfriars that when Talleyrand called on her, they drank their tea and their wine from the same teacups.

But her uncompromising virtue did not end even in those days with such duly accredited duties as contributions toward the sup-port of her family. It only happened that that virtue was socially approved; others as blatantly in control of her actions did not hap-pen to be common property. The distinction hardly occurred to her; she supported them all with equal ruggedness.

A well-meaning acquaintance undertook to carry to her by proxy a respectable proposal of marriage. It was of the kind that deals naturally more with the amount of financial support offered than with any yearnings of the heart. She answered him, the poor, be-wildered offender — notes blazing with references to his "officious message," his "deliberate insult" — for "what I call an insult is the bare supposition that I could for an instant think of prostituting my person for a maintenance; for in that point of view does such a marriage appear to me, who consider right and wrong in the abstract, and never by words and local opinions shield myself from the reproaches of my own heart and understanding. . . . I tell you, sir, I am *poor*, yet can live without your benevolent exertions." And she wrote to Mr. Johnson: "When I meet him at your house, I shall leave the room, since I cannot pull him by the nose. . . . I will not be insulted by a superficial puppy."

That is rare food for laughter. Evidently she saw no reason to mince the matter. Did she have no inkling that she was wallowing in our nightmare crime, in the very bog of melodrama? And we shrug our shoulders at this very stern moralist who was so uncompromisingly blind to the ethics of humor.

Yet the deadly earnest of her morality was costing her dearer than any shuddering escape from the taint of melodrama. She had disdained "the props of words and local opinions," and the grim effort to hold herself erect unaided was draining her spiritual resources. In her distraught struggle to "form some idea of the whole of her existence," to discover some moral pattern in "the unmarked vacuity of life," she had need of a pre-emptory seriousness.

Besides, this unsmiling moral doggedness, this desperate hunger for principles, was an excellent equipment for the entrée of London literary society of French Revolutionary years. Cynicism and superciliousness had said their say with the Earl of Chesterfield and Horace Walpole; these were the years of Thomas Paine and William Godwin. Their common mainspring was a moral enthusiasm, their watchword, "the rights of man." In the free clashes of opinion at Mr. Johnson's literary dinner parties, the raw angularity of Mary Wollstonecraft's morals became more maturely molded, her intellectual bearings grew clearer.

It was in her third year in London that she made a contribution of her own to this world of radicalism. Burke had published his *Reflections on the Revolution in France*, that high tribute of tears to the overthrow of a mellow aristocracy. Immediately Mary Wollstonecraft threw back her answer: A *Vindication of the Rights of Man.*

"Man preys on man," she challenged him, "and you mourn for

the idle tapestry that decorated the Gothic pile, and the dronish bell that summoned the fat priest to prayer."

It is an answer that is eclipsed for later generations by the classic reply of Thomas Paine in his sturdy *Rights of Man;* but it voices very forcibly at times the same pity for the oppressed, and hatred of rank and power and convention, the same utter confidence in the guidance of reason, the same faith in the perfectibility of man. Already she could state very forcibly the groundwork of her faith in social upbuilding:

> No man chooses evil because it is evil; he only mistakes it for happiness, the good he seeks. — To endeavor to make unhappy man resigned to his fate is the tender endeavor of short-sighted benevolence. But to labor to increase human happiness by extirpating error is a masculine, god-like affection.

A more intimate personal experience was likewise humanizing Mary Wollstonecraft. She, who two years later could write to Imlay with such proud, sweet passion, had not lived already to be thirty-two without discovering her need of love. Godwin tells a very definite story of her friendship with the Swiss painter Fuseli. Since then it has been indignantly denied by her defenders and twisted by her detractors into the story of another Phaedra. But when all is said and done, Godwin's story has all reasonableness on its side.

"There is no reason to doubt," he says, "that if Mr. Fuseli had been disengaged at the time, he would have been the man of her choice." But since he was married — and his wife never ceased to be Mary Wollstonecraft's friend — "she scorned to suppose that she could feel a struggle in conforming to the laws she should lay down to her conduct. She conceived it both practicable and eligible to cultivate a distinguishing affection for him."

At the outset, it was highly stimulating to Mary Wollstonecraft. She went more frequently among people, she surrounded herself with small luxuries, she cultivated the amenities of life.

The affair was still in the experimental stage when she gathered herself together and wrote the *Vindication of the Rights of Women.* She had found her cause.

6

The Rights of Women is Mary Wollstonecraft's main statement of her life idea. She had made her pioneer application of her utter faith in Reason, her magnificent hopes for Democracy. She had a vision of woman, "the companion of man," "placed in a station in which she will advance, instead of retarding, the progress of these glorious principles." As it was, she contended, "women were rendered pleasing at the expense of every solid virtue"; they were "mere dolls," "the toys of man, his rattle, and it must jingle in his ears whenever he chooses to be amused." "To keep the varnish of the character fresh and in good condition was . . . inculcated as the sum total of female duty."

Her warning she put in no uncertain terms: "If woman be not prepared by education to become the companion of man, she will stop the progress of knowledge and virtue. For truth must be common to all." The grand faculty whose cultivation was to make women genuine members of the human species was, of course, that goddess of the French Revolution, the Reason. "The grand source of female folly and vice has ever appeared to me to arise from narrowness of mind." Women have "as the business of life, an understanding to improve"; they are "human creatures who in common with men are placed on this earth to unfold their faculties."

"Their first duty is to themselves as rational creatures; and their next . . . is that — which includes so many — of a mother." Never once, even in the midst of some very plain speaking, does she justify the tradition that has grown up, I suppose, around the strident sound of her book's title and the letters to Imlay — the unfounded tradition that her "rights of women" included emancipation from conventional marriage. "Marriage," she said, is "the basis of almost every social virtue." The domestic ties are its finest fruit; "love always clings around the idea of home," she wrote.

But she never feared that she was upsetting the balance of society by asking a little elbowroom for women; those unheard-of changes she demanded — the study of anatomy and medicine, of gardening, of literature and philosophy, even of business and politics — promised no terrors for her. She knew the world was not so insecurely poised. She had more faith in the love of husband and home and children than those have had since then who have feared to shift an ornament or open a window in the house of love, lest it should tumble in ruins. "Let there be no coercion established in society, and the common law of gravity prevailing, the sexes will fall into their proper places."

As Mary Wollstonecraft's writings always are, *The Rights of Women* is a direct transcription of what she herself had so far found out by living. If she saw in the development of Reason, in the freedom of the intellectual world, the force that was to make great the women of the future, it was because it was that that had already given dignity to her own bewildered struggles. There is a headlong enthusiasm about the whole book that, from Mary Wollstonecraft, could come only when she felt that she had worked through to a solid and reasonable basis in her own life. She no longer sang hymns to Duty and Benevolence in the style of Mrs. Mason and her own early London letters. Nor was she preoccupied with pining after love: "If that is the sole aim of woman," she wondered pertinently, "how they are to exist in that state where there is to be neither marriage nor giving in marriage." For the author of *The Rights of Women*, it is in "the well-stored mind," in those "new sources of enjoyment dependent only on the solitary operation of the mind," in that finer devotion to duty that is the fruit of comprehension, that the possibilities of the future lie. "I do not know of what use is an improved taste, if the individual is not rendered more independent of the casualties of life," and according to her context, those casualties center chiefly about love. In her scheme of life, love is rather the intruder, the upsetter of rational undertakings, the "arbitrary passion that will reign like some other stalking mischiefs by its own authority without deigning to reason."

7

Her "stalking mischief," her uninvited intruder, was pressing closer upon her than she guessed. . . . For almost a year after she launched *The Rights of Women* upon a horrified but very attentive world, she accomplished almost nothing. Her "platonic affection" for Fuseli — it is Godwin's phrase — mainly occupied her. But, as Godwin said further, "she did not in the sequel find all the advantages in the plan that she had expected from it."

Naturally! It is an axiom. We would brush it aside with Horatio's impatient, "Nay, that's certain!" But to Mary Wollstonecraft, as to Hamlet, axioms did not exist. The whole of life was a licensed field of experimentation. . . . And Godwin continued: "She conceived it necessary to snap the chains of this association in her mind."

In September, 1792, she sailed for France alone.

There was little exact knowledge in England of the war to the death that was going on in the streets of Paris. Mary Wollstonecraft wished to see for herself, to be at the crux of events. She arrived in the midst of dramatic proceedings. The month before, the mob of Paris had finally imprisoned Louis and his queen; by the time she reached the city, the National Convention was already sitting, and by December the King was pleading for his life.

"About nine o'clock this morning," she wrote back to London, "the King passed by my window, moving silently along — excepting now and then a few strokes on the drum which rendered the stillness more awful — through empty streets, surrounded by the National Guards, who, clustering around the carriage, seemed to deserve their name. The inhabitants flocked to their windows, but the casements were all shut, not a voice was heard, nor did I see anything like an insulting gesture. For the first time since I entered France, I bowed to the majesty of the people. . . . I saw Louis sitting with more dignity than I expected from his character, in a hackney coach, going to meet his death, where so many of his race had triumphed. . . . I have been alone ever since. Not a distant sound of a footstep can I hear. I wish I had kept the cat with me! I want to see something alive; death in so many frightful shapes has taken hold of my fancy. I am going to bed, and for the first time in my life, I cannot put out the candle."

She was gathering material for what she proposed to make a three-volume publication: *An Historical and Moral View of the Origin of the French Revolution*. But she had not reckoned with her "stalking mischief."

She was living alone that springtime on the outskirts of Paris near the half-demolished barrier, with only a solicitous old gardener for a servant. And it was there that Gilbert Imlay, a tall and likeable American, came again and again; it was there in the woods of the barrier, through the sweet French spring, that their love matured; and, afterwards, when she was fighting most fiercely to keep sacred that first ideal glimpse of love, it was always "back to the barrier with you" that her "imagination chose to ramble — to see you coming to meet me, and my basket of grapes."

It was a lovely idyll, cast strangely ashore by the dark whirlpool of the Terror that swept awfully about them. They had no confident — not even a priest or a magistrate; there was no marriage ceremony. But when, in the summer, the government of the Terror ordered all English citizens to prison until a general European declaration of peace, she obtained a certificate from the American Ambassador as the wife of Gilbert Imlay, American, and they moved to Paris together.

To Mary Wollstonecraft it was an open sesame of happiness; it was her great initiation. Godwin is at some pains to describe the outward change in her: "Her eyes assumed new lustre; her cheeks new color and smoothness and that smile of bewitching tenderness from day to day illumined her countenance which all who knew her will so well remember; and which won, both body and soul, the affections of almost every one who beheld it."

They wrote happy, little, inconsequent love letters, and when, a little later, he had gone to Havre on business, she wrote with "an overflowing of tenderness to you" that someday there would be a little creature "in whom we are to have a mutual interest, you know. . . . Good night! I am going to rest very happy, and you have made me so." She pictured how "you shall read whilst I mend my stockings"; and when he echoed her, she answered swiftly: "What a picture you have sketched of our fireside! Yes, my love, my fancy was instantly at work, and I found my head on your shoulder, whilst my eyes were fixed on the little creatures that were clinging around your knees. I did not absolutely determine that there should be six — if you have not set your heart on that round number."

They are full-blooded, wifely letters, always the expressions of a strong, frank love; and yet already they are shot through sometimes with a hurt bewilderment. The three months before she joined him in Havre seemed a long, unnecessary separation to her. "Of late we are always separating. Crack! Crack! and away you go." "I do not wish to be loved like a goddess, but I wish to be necessary to you." And again she underlined: "Be not too anxious to get money! For nothing worth having is to be purchased."

In February she went to Havre to be with him, and the little snatches of notes of the next six months give tiny peepholes into the happiest of Mary Wollstonecraft's days. She worked on her book — "in truth my life would not have been worth much if it had been found" — and in May, a little Fanny was born.

For the first three months of the baby's life, there are no records or letters. She had smallpox, and her mother was apparently nurse and doctor, until, as she wrote, "our little Hercules is quite recovered." "My affections grow upon me till they become too strong for my peace," she wrote Imlay. "This for our little girl" — she was three months old that day — "was at first very reasonable, — now, she has got into my heart and imagination, and when I walk out without her, her little figure is ever dancing before me."

Her life with Imlay she could still interpret in the phraseology of her love. It was of herself at this time that she wrote in her unfinished novel: "Pygmalion formed an ivory maid, and longed for an informing soul. She, on the contrary, combined all the qualities of a hero's mind, and fate presented a statue in which she might enshrine them." And again: "She was happy — nor was she deceived! He was then plastic in her impassioned hand, and reflected all the sentiments which animated and warmed her."

But it was not for long. In September he went to Paris, and before she joined him, he was off again for London on a business venture that was to have taken but a few weeks. She did not remonstrate. It was three months before she allowed herself to write him of "these eternal projects" that his business was thrusting between them. "To me it seems absurd to waste life in preparing to live." It was the beginning of the end. The separation dragged on for seven months. . . .

She had given herself to the man she loved — simply, completely, permanently. And it was to her the more sacred that it was so un-fetteredly their own. She was the more deceived. To Gilbert Imlay she was but another light woman, a woman valued perhaps above the rest for a certain knack of passionate avowal, but a woman, nevertheless, in the end to be wearied of. To her, the dignity, the distinction of love lay in its dear dream of permanence. But not to him.

And so began that long-drawn tragedy that is preserved for us in her love letters. And through those tragic months she was giving the full measure of her strength to mold to her vision the ugly raw material of life that had been dealt out to her. It was not by aban-doning this relationship that she thought to win through to her ideals. She believed, was disillusioned, and yet again believed that by sheer fidelity she should compel this love to render all that it had seemed to promise of rapture and dignity and beauty.

In the spring she went to him in London. On paper he still offered her love; in reality he was already living with a strolling actress. He was a Tito Melema whose facile repugnance to causing pain plunged into tragedy the lives he touched.

The reunion proved only a time of "too many cruel explanations." To shift the tragedy that was fast becoming unbearable, it was decided that she should go to Norway on some business he wished to have personally attended to, and for three months she traveled there with her baby.

She had one resolution concerning her future and Imlay's: only their common love should bind them. "If you perceive the least chance of being happier without me than with me, . . . tell me frankly that you will never see me more." She catches herself up in her love messages: "But what am I saying? Rather forget me if you can." "I never wanted but your heart; that gone, you have nothing more to give."

It was on her return to London that all compromise came to an end. There came a day when she understood to the utmost what manner of love she had received; she had been to the home of his mistress. Her shamed body shrank from the memory of their dear intimacies; the past was an insult, the future an emptiness unthink-able. The night was raw with a cold rain. She hired a boat for Putney, and there, on the deserted bridge, she walked feverishly up and down that in her drenched clothing she might sink the more readily in the Thames.

She was saved "when the bitterness of death was past, and inhumanly brought back to life and misery." She never wrote an apologia for that night. "I am only accountable to myself. Did I care for what is termed reputation, it is by other circumstances that I should be dishonored." The old Roman's pride in taking fate into his own hands was also hers. But she never repeated the attempt. After that frantic night, her love for her little Fanny forced life upon her. "I shall protect and provide for my child. I only mean by this to say that you have nothing to fear from my desperation."

But the final parting was at hand. The next month Imlay went to Paris with his new mistress. The last letter she wrote him ends: "If there be any part of me that will survive the sense of my misfortunes, it is the purity of my affections. . . . Is it strange that in spite of all you do something like conviction forces me to believe that you are not what you appear to be. I part with you in peace."

She never lamented her love for Imlay. She had hazarded herself on that most dangerous of all the throws of the dice, the throw of love. And she had lost. But it had placed her among those "who know there is such a thing as happiness" — "and what has the future to offer to them?" she could ask even in her letters from Norway in those darkest months of suspense.

Suffering had not blinded her. Suffering much she had learned much. Not only had she permanently cast behind her notions of Duty and Benevolence, but even of the well-stored mind that is a secure foothold against the casualties of existence. She knew now that "principles are unavailing if considered as a breast-work to secure our own hearts." She had cruel reason to understand the fortitude, the unlimited courage, without which there is no success in the crusade of happiness. But she never doubted that her love was in her life the thing absolutely most worthwhile, and therefore rightly claimed the right of way.

8

So she picked up the threads of her life once more and set herself to the task of supporting herself and her baby girl. The months were "but an exercise of fortitude continually on the stretch." "For me there is nothing good in store — my heart is broken." She had not learned that incredible truth, that the one thing life most loves to provide is a chance for a fresh beginning.

Necessity forced action upon her: she had to work unceasingly for support. She had emphatically refused any financial help for herself from Imlay. "I am not yet sufficiently humbled to depend on your beneficence," she had written him. And the bond he settled on their child was never paid.

She prepared her Scandinavian letters for the press, letters originally intended for publication, though they were all addressed to Imlay. They are the most uniformly readable of all her writings. She pictures the fat burghers and their wives, the interminable meals: "a succession of fish, flesh and fowl for two hours . . . coffee immediately following in the drawing room; but that does not pre-clude punch, ale, tea and cakes, raw salmon, etc. A supper brings up the rear, not forgetting the introductory luncheon, almost equalling in removes the dinner. A day of this kind you would imagine sufficient — but a tomorrow, and a tomorrow!" Or she revels in describing the northern summer, "brief, I grant you, but passing sweet," or the pleasure she has had in the little boat she has learned to row on the wild bay. Or she writes of her baby, and of her long-ing for her during a separation: "I never saw a calf bounding in a meadow that did not remind me of my little frolicker."

She dwells with feeling on the lot of the northern women, bound first to their fathers and later to their husbands: "Still harping on the same subjects? . . . We reason deeply when we deeply feel." And there is this that might be an interpretation of her own life: "There are few who do not play the part they have learned by rote; and those who do not, seem marks set up to be pelted at by fortune; or, rather, as sign-posts which point out the road to others whilst forced to stand still themselves amidst the mud and dirt."

Gradually she found her way back into her old literary circle. There had been changes there also. Since she had left for Paris, William Godwin, first with his *Political Justice* and then with *Caleb Williams* had become the intellectual leader of radical circles. He was a remarkable person, a cold, methodical, unimpassioned an-

archist of the study. He was the master of an idealism so unbounded
that he never knew when his logic played with fire. Perhaps no man
who ever lived had such supreme faith in reasonableness — all social
good was to come through it. Emotion only blinded man to his
duties of justice; he requires therefore that his hero shall so far rise
above it that, in his classic example, he may leave his wife or his
mother in the burning building to rescue the superior stranger, for,
as he asks, "what magic is there in the pronoun 'my' to overturn the
decisions of everlasting truth?"

It followed also, since individual reasonableness alone could bring
about social justice, that government was an impertinence. So was
property. "To whom does any article of property, suppose a loaf of
bread, belong? To him who wants it most, or to whom the possession of it will be most beneficial." Also marriage. "Marriage is law,
and the worst of all laws. . . . Marriage is an affair of property, and
the worst of all properties. The abolition of marriage will be attended by no evils. The intercourse of the sexes will fall under the
same system as any other species of friendship."

To himself, he was an inspired prophet filled with all the ardor of
a poet. His millennium, he conceived, "was at no great distance;
and it is not impossible that some of the present race of men may
live to see it in part accomplished. . . . There will be no disease,
no anguish, no melancholy, and no resentment. Every man will seek
with ineffable ardor the good of all."

As for the man himself, he had, in Southey's words, "large, noble
eyes; and a *nose* — oh, most abominable nose! Language is not
vituperatious enough to describe the effect of its downward elonga-
tion." He was already a man of forty, and only once apparently had
he thought seriously of marriage, when he wrote to his sister, asking
her to pick out for him a suitable partner! And she answered, a
serious inventory of abilities in singing, housekeeping and religion,
together with all known facts as to the young woman's expectations.
In due time, Godwin called upon this paragon, but with that the
episode died the death it deserved.

Truly, he was a formidable person to imagine in love. Perhaps the
fascination of his dense ignorance attracted Mary Wollstonecraft,
who knows? At any rate, it was the growing intimacy with William

Godwin that lifted her back to genuine existence. It was "friend-ship," he said, "melting into love." "The partiality we conceived for each other grew with equal advances in the mind of each. . . . When, in the course of things, the disclosure came, there was nothing, in a manner, for either party to disclose to the other."

Nor did they disclose it to anyone else. The situation was difficult. When, finally, the next spring, they announced their marriage, Godwin's disciples reviled him as an apostate, and his sturdily pious, up-country mother wrote him of his "broken resolution in regard to matrimony. . . . You are certainly transformed in a moral sense; why is it impossible in a spiritual sense, which last will make you shine with the radiance of the sun forever." Godwin himself wrote, "Nothing but a regard for the happiness of the individual which I had no right to injure, could have induced me to submit to an in-stitution which I wish to see abolished."

And that "individual's" views she was writing down at about that time in the semi-autobiography she called *The Wrongs of Women*: "Marriage as at present constituted, she (Maria) considered as lead-ing to immorality, — yet, as the odium of society impedes usefulness, she wished to avow her affection to Darnford, by becoming his wife according to established rules — not to be confounded with women who act from very different motives — though her conduct would be the same without the ceremony as with it, and her expectations from him not less firm."

No hint of a delicate situation, however, finds its way into the pleasant camaraderie of the little notes with which they bridged a morning or an afternoon apart:

Should you call and find only books, have a little patience and I will be with you.

Do not give Fanny a cake today. I am afraid she stayed too long with you yesterday.

Today I find myself better, and as the weather is fine, I mean to call on Dr. Fordyce. I do not think of visiting you by the way, as I seem inclined to be industrious. I believe I feel affec-tionate toward you in proportion as I am in spirits. That is a civil speech for you to chew.

I believe I ought to ask pardon for talking at you last night. Faith and troth it was because there was nobody else worth attacking, or who could converse. C— had wearied me before you entered. But be assured, when I find a man that has anything in him, I shall leave my every-day dish alone!

Gradually she won a quiet, pervading happiness that made itself felt among all she knew. It was at this time that Southey met her. "Of all the lions or *literati* that I have seen here," he wrote, "Mary Imlay's countenance is the best, infinitely the best. Her eyes are light brown, and although the lid of one of them is affected by a little paralysis, they are the most meaning I ever saw." Years after her death he harked back to her: "As for panegyric, I never praised mortal being save Mary Wollstonecraft." Godwin dwelt with lingering tenderness on her lovableness: "She had always possessed in an unparalleled degree the art of communicating happiness, and she was now in constant and unlimited exercise of it."

She has left, too, a charming glimpse of her playful intimacy with her little daughter in the Reading Lessons she wrote for her, to be laid aside until she should be old enough to read them. We cannot help wondering what the magnificent Mrs. Mason of the *Original Stories* would have thought of such a pretty equality between a mother and a child of four:

See how much taller you are than William (he was an entirely imaginary baby). In four years you have learned to eat, to walk, to talk. Why do you smile? You can do much more, you think? You can wash your hands and face? Very well, I will never kiss a dirty face.

And you can comb your hair with the pretty little comb you always put by in your own drawer. To be sure you do all this to be ready to take a walk with me. You would be obliged to stay at home if you could not comb your own hair. Betty is busy getting dinner ready, and only combs William's hair because he cannot do it himself.

In March, William Godwin and Mary Wollstonecraft were married. Godwin did not even record it in his minute diary, and the only reference to it in their letters is her little jesting note a day or two later: "Pray send me by Mary for my luncheon a part of the supper you announced to me last night, as I am to be the partaker of your worldly goods, you know."

Godwin's objections to the ceremony, when it came to his own experience, had altered significantly since the days of the *Political Justice*. He had forgotten that marriage is an affair of property. Already he had been initiated into a warmer, more genial world; now his objection lay only in the eternal human wish to keep intimate and sacred the vivid personal relationships of life. It was a travesty, he felt, "to require the overflowing of the soul to wait upon a ceremony."

This intimate reason, however, like the older reasons of property and law, and Mary Wollstonecraft's shrinking from the institution that had bound her mother and sister to a round of sordid days and terror-stricken nights, all were overborne in the expectation of a child. Mary Wollstonecraft felt keenly the position of her little Fanny; she had even wished to give up her home in England altogether that the child might be brought up in the comparatively tolerant freedom of France. Now, with all her hard-won power to estimate the remoter consequences, she desired the marriage ceremony.

On the announcement of the wedding day they took a house together, and Godwin is very frank about her pleasure at this arrangement. Though till then, he tells us, "her mind was visited but seldom by those emotions of anguish which had been all too familiar to her, the improvement in this respect which accrued upon our removal and establishment were extremely obvious. She was a worshiper of domestic life. She loved to observe the growth of affection between me and her daughter, then three years of age, as well as my anxiety respecting the child not yet born."

Still, as Godwin insists — was it to save himself from the appearance of too wholesale conformity? — they did not "entirely cohabit." He took rooms nearby where he did his writing of a morning. "They generally spent the latter half of each day together," he tells us. It does not seem a very startling innovation, rather as if a doctor should take an office downtown, and attribute to that arrangement his domestic happiness. However, with true masculine enthusiasm over his contrivance, Godwin declaims about it to his heart's content; it caused their intercourse to combine, he says, "the novelty and the lively sensations of a visit with the more delicious and heart-felt pleasures of domestic life." So necessary was it to this incredulous scholar to set apart his own great love from the circumstances of common affections; his philosophy could not compass the belief that domestic happiness just as sweet and as bewildering as his has been the lot of generations upon generations of young lovers.

In June, he was away for a couple of weeks, and their letters were voluminous. Hers were very rational. Her love for Godwin was according to her own ideals of the days of the *Vindication*; it never "usurped the scepter which the understanding should ever cooly wield." But for all that, it was a true, sturdy affection.

"If your heart was in your mouth as I felt just now at the sight of your hand," she wrote him, "you may kiss or shake hands with this letter and imagine with what affection it was written; if not, stand off, profane one! . . . I am not fatigued with solitude, yet I have not enjoyed my solitary dinner. A husband is a convenient part of the furniture of a house, unless he is a clumsy fixture. I wish you from my heart to be rivetted in my heart; but I do not desire to have you always at my elbow, although at this moment I should not care if you were."

And he answered: "You cannot imagine how happy your letter made me. . . . We love as it were to multiply the consciousness of our existence, even at the risk of what Montague described so pathetically one night upon the New Road of opening new avenues for pain and misery to attack us." He wondered if this minute Fanny was going "plungity plunge"; and sent her word that he was "safely arrived in the land of mugs," and later that he had chosen her one, "with respect to its beauty you shall set it forth with such eloquence as your imagination can supply."

There was a brief outburst before he arrived at home again; she referred unflatteringly to his "icy philosophy," and told him, "your later letters might have been addressed to anybody." But the little tempest calmed at his return. A few days after, she wrote him again in one of their little comradely notes: "I have designs upon you this evening, to keep you quite to myself — I hope nobody will call! — and make you read the play. I was thinking of a favorite song of my poor friend Fanny's: 'In a vacant, rainy day you shall be wholly mine.' "

It was the calmest season of Mary Wollstonecraft's life. She was writing, though rather laboriously. She was happy with Godwin and little Fanny. She was physically well. There were no premonitions of tragedy. She was come at last into the powers of her tranquil maturity, and the future was before her in which to employ them. So to the end of time we will always reckon, ignoring death.

On the thirtieth of August, she wrote to Godwin: "I have no doubt of seeing the animal today, but must leave Mrs. Blenkinsop to guess at the hour. I have sent for her. Pray send me the newspaper. I wish I had a novel or some book of sheer amusement to while away the time. Have you anything of the sort?"

She had wished that Godwin should not come to the house till she could present him with his son. It was, however, a daughter who was born that day.

At first all was well. After a short period of alarm, it was thought for three days that the danger had been averted. But from that time on, her husband and the doctor were almost constantly at her bedside. Godwin was solicitude itself, but not even the presence of death could tone down his garish literal-mindedness. Until the last hour, he registered details systematically in his abbreviated diary. Once when an opiate brought relief, his wife turned to him with, "Oh, Godwin, I am in heaven!" But as his biographer says, "even at that moment Godwin declined to be entrapped into the admission that heaven existed." "You mean, my dear," he corrected her, "that your physical sensations are somewhat easier." But she understood, and as she sank into her last unconsciousness, she murmured, "He is the kindest, best man in the world."

Her suffering was intense, but for ten days they did not give up hope. She comprehended her danger; she answered Godwin's tentative questions about the children with a quiet, "I know what you mean." But she left no instructions. Why did no prevision of the starved, rebellious life of her two little daughters in the home of a coarse-grained stepmother, no picture of their girlhood escape, Fanny by a piteous self-destruction, Mary at seventeen by an elopement with the poet Shelley — why did not the desperate need of her in their childish lives force her back to life? Her death was not her tragedy; it was theirs.

When all was over, Godwin rose to, perhaps, his one emotional height. "I firmly believe," he wrote Holcroft, "that there does not exist her equal upon earth. When you come up to town, look at me, talk to me, but do not — if you can help it — exhort me or console me." On the day of the funeral, he shut himself away, too prostrated to attend.

So she was laid in Old St. Pancras churchyard, an auburn-haired woman in the prime of her maturity, a woman with whom life had gone hard, upon whom fate had loved to play the full gamut of its ironies, but — let us say it in all honor — one who had come to her last resting bed, "weary and content and undishonored." So was she granted in the end the gift of sleep.

9

In the National Portrait Gallery hangs a picture of Mary Wollstonecraft, a picture of her as she was a few scant months before her death. I remember the child I was when I saw it first, haunted by the terror of youth before experience.[4] I wanted so desperately to know how other women had saved their souls alive. And the woman in the little frame arrested me, this woman with the auburn hair, and the sad, steady, light-brown eyes, and the gallant poise of the head. She *had* saved her soul alive; it looked out from her steady eyes unafraid. The price, too, that life had demanded of her was written ineradicably there. But to me, then, standing before her picture, even that costly payment was a guarantee, a promise. For I knew that in those days when she sat for that picture, she was content. And in the light of that content, I still spell out her life.

Chronology

Notes

Index of Personal Names

Index of Subjects

Chronology

LIFE

Father: Frederick S. Fulton, surgeon (1857–1889).
Mother: Bertrice Shattuck Fulton, teacher and librarian (1860–1953).

1887, June 5	Born, in New York City.
1888–1894	Shenango Valley, N.Y.: lives at Shattuck Farm, home of maternal grandparents, John Samuel Shattuck (1827–1913) and Joanna Terry Shattuck (1827–1909).
1888, Dec. 26	Birth of sister Margery.
1889, March 26	Death of father.
1894–1895	Norwich, N.Y.: mother teaching; home cared for by Hettie Shattuck (mother's older sister); sisters begin school.*
1895–1897	St. Joseph, Mo.: mother teaching; accompanied by Aunt Hettie.
1897–1899	Owatonna, Minn.: mother "lady principal" of Pillsbury Academy; Aunt Hettie keeps house; sisters attend academy.
1899–1911	Buffalo, N.Y.: live in apartment above Ellis family (Aunt Mamie, mother's younger sister, and Uncle Will); mother in Buffalo Public Library.
1900	Death of Aunt Hettie.
1902–1905	Sisters attend St. Margaret's School for Girls.
1905–1909	Sisters attend Vassar College.
1909–1910	Travel in Europe with Katherine Norton and

* All girlhood summers spent at Shattuck Farm.

Elizabeth Atsatt (both from California); Margery marries Robert Freeman.

1910–1911	Buffalo, N.Y.: lives with mother and works for Charity Organization Society.
1911–1912	Los Angeles, Calif.: teaches at Westlake School for Girls; mother goes to live with Margery Freeman in Pasadena.
1912–1914	Pasadena, Calif.: teaches at Orton School for Girls.
1914, summer	Marries Stanley R. Benedict at Shattuck Farm.
1914–	Douglas Manor (Douglaston), N.Y.: first home after marriage.*
?	New York City: one year.
?	Moves with Stanley to Bedford Hills, N.Y.
?	Volunteer work one year for State Charities Aid Association.
1919–1921	New School for Social Research: takes courses with Elsie Clews Parsons and Alexander Goldenweiser.
1921–1922	Columbia University: completes Ph.D. in anthropology in three semesters.
1922–1923	Barnard College: Assistant to Dr. Franz Boas.
1923–1931	Columbia University: Lecturer in Anthropology (a series of one-year appointments).
1923–1924	Columbia University Extension: teaches course in Fine Arts.
1926, summer	Trip to Europe with Stanley; attends International Congress of Americanists in Rome.
1926–1927	Barnard College: Instructor in Anthropology (substituting for Gladys Reichard).
1931–1937	Columbia University: Assistant Professor, Department of Anthropology.
1936	Death of Stanley Benedict. Acting Executive Officer, Department of Anthropology.
1937–1948	Columbia University: Associate Professor, Department of Anthropology.
1937–1939	Executive Officer, Department of Anthropology.
1938, summer	Brief trip to Guatemala.
1939–1940	Pasadena, Calif.: sabbatical leave to write book.
1941	Bryn Mawr College: Anna Howard Shaw Memorial Lecturer (one semester).
1942	Most of Shattuck Farm sold; RFB settles Aunty My (Myra Shattuck, mother's youngest sister) in remodeled farm cottage, where she also spends vacations.

* Summers spent at Lake Winnipesaukee.

1943–1945 Washington, D.C.: Head, Basic Analysis Section, Bureau of Overseas Intelligence, Office of War Information.
1944–1945 Social Science Analyst, Foreign Morale Division, Office of War Information; Lecturer, Washington School of Psychiatry.
1945, August Death of Aunty My.
1945–1946 Pasadena, Calif.: on leave to write book.
1946– Columbia University.
1947– Director, Columbia University Research in Contemporary Cultures (Office of Naval Research Contract for Cultural Study of Certain Minorities of European and Asiatic Origin in New York City).
1948, July 1 Columbia University: Professor of Anthropology.
summer UNESCO Seminar at Podebrady, Czechoslovakia; travel in Europe.
Sept. 17 Dies, New York City.

DEGREES, AWARDS, OFFICES

1909 B.A., Vassar College; Phi Beta Kappa.
1923 Ph.D., Columbia University.
1927–1929 President, American Ethnological Association.
1934 Fellow, New York Academy of Sciences.
1944 Award of the C.I.O. Committee to Abolish Racial Discrimination.
1945 Fellow, Washington School of Psychiatry.
1946 Vice President, American Psychopathological Association.
American Design Award for War Services.
Achievement Award, American Association of University Women.
1947–1948 President, American Anthropological Association.
1947 Fellow, American Academy of Arts and Sciences.
D.Sc., Russell Sage College.
1948 Award of the New York Committee of the Southern Conference of Human Welfare.
1952 Posthumous award of the Institute of Design of Illinois Institute of Technology.

EDITORSHIPS

1925–1939 Editor, *Journal of American Folk-Lore.*
1936–1940 Editor, Columbia University Contributions to Anthropology.

1937–1945 Editorial Board, *Character and Personality.*
1941–1942 Editorial Board, *Frontiers of Democracy*, P.E.A.
1942–1944 Editorial Board, *American Scholar.*
1946 Assistant Editor, *Psychiatry.*
Board of Associate Editors, William Alanson White Psychiatric Foundations.

FIELD STUDIES

1922 Serrano.
1924 Zuñi.
1925 Zuñi and Cochiti.
1926 Pima.
1931 Mescalero Apache, student training direction under auspices of Southwest Laboratory of Anthropology, Santa Fe.
1939 Blackfoot, student training direction under joint auspices of Columbia University and University of Montana.

BOOKS AND MONOGRAPHS*

1923 "The Concept of the Guardian Spirit in North America," *Memoirs of the American Anthropological Association*, XXIX, 1–97.
1931 *Tales of the Cochiti Indians.* Bureau of American Ethnology, Bulletin XCVIII. Washington.
1934 *Patterns of Culture.* Boston and New York, Houghton Mifflin.
1935 *Zuñi Mythology*, 2 vols., Columbia University Contributions to Anthropology, XXI. New York, Columbia University Press.
1940 *Race: Science and Politics.* New York, Modern Age Books. (Rev. ed. with *Races of Mankind*, New York, Viking, 1945.)
1946 *The Chrysanthemum and the Sword: Patterns of Japanese Culture.* Boston and New York, Houghton Mifflin.

* For a full bibliography, see that prepared by Mary E. Chandler for "Ruth Fulton Benedict, 1887–1948," by Margaret Mead, *American Anthropologist*, Vol. LI, No. 3 (1949), 457–68.

Notes

Introduction

[1] "Distant Strumming of Strings," *Canadian Forum*, November 1924, 53.

[2] XXXVI, No. 139 (1923), 104.

[3] See Margaret Mead, "The Role of the Scientist in Society," *Orthopsychiatry 1923–1948: Retrospect and Prospect* (New York, American Orthopsychiatric Association, 1948), 367–73.

[4] *Zuni Mythology* (2 vols., Columbia University Contributions to Anthropology, XXI; New York, Columbia University Press, 1935).

PART I

Search: 1920–1930

[1] Marie Bloomfield (the younger sister of Leonard Bloomfield), who committed suicide in February 1923. See "Diary: 1923," entry for February 8, page 65.

[2] *American Anthropologist*, XXIV, No. 1 (1922), 1–23.

[3] John Dewey (New York, Holt, 1922).

[4] Unpublished poem.

[5] In a letter of February 16, 1937, to Dr. E. V. McCollum of the Department of Biochemistry, Johns Hopkins University, RFB wrote about Stanley:

In his adult life he never had chemicals nor chemical books in his house. All the time outside the office and the laboratory was

527

devoted to recuperating his energies and in these relaxation periods he turned to hobbies which would take his mind off his work. Two of these hobbies were special favorites — engines which he set up and took to pieces, whether they were in pumps, boats or automobiles; and photography where he especially enjoyed playing with different chemical processes in developing and printing.

His summers also were devoted to recuperation so far as his duties as editor of the Journal would allow. He loved the isolation and leisure of a New Hampshire summer; for many years he spent the entire vacation on the shore of Lake Winnepesaukee. Still more he enjoyed traveling and went to the Canadian Rockies or Mt. Ranier Park or took the boat trip to Alaska or to the North Cape. He struggled always, as you know, under the difficulties of an unusually high blood pressure and solved these difficulties as far as he could by leading a regular life with as few intrusions as possible.

6 See "Journal: 1912–1916," where, in an entry for November, 1914, she wrote: "My pet scheme is to steep myself in the lives of restless and highly enslaved women of past generations and write a series of biographical papers from the standpoint of the 'new woman.'" (See page 132.)

7 Letter from a former classmate at Vassar College.

8 The Old Fashioned Woman, Primitive Fancies about the Sex (New York, Putnam's, 1913); Social Rule, a Study of the Will to Power (New York, Putnam's, 1916); Religious Chastity, an Ethnological Study, by "John Main" (New York, 1913).

9 See comment by Franz Boas in his letter to RFB of July 19, 1940, page 418.

10 Alexander A. Goldenweiser (New York, Knopf, 1922).

11 See RFB's obituary of Goldenweiser in Modern Quarterly, XI, No. 6 (1940), 32–33.

12 Memoirs of the American Anthropological Association, XXIX (1923), 1–97.

13 His own position at this time is in part summarized in his letter to The New York Times (January 7, 1916), "Why German-Americans Blame America."

14 From notes on a lecture given by Franz Boas.

15 From notes on a lecture given by Franz Boas.

16 See the list of doctoral dissertations prepared in the Department of Anthropology, Columbia University, for the years between 1901 and 1941, in the Yearbook of Anthropology — 1955, ed. William L. Thomas, Jr. (New York, Wenner-Gren Foundation for Anthropological Research, 1955), 703–5.

[17] Columbia University Contributions to Anthropology, VIII (New York, Columbia University Press, 1929).

[18] New York, Liveright, 1920.

[19] Herman K. Haeberlin, Memoirs of the American Anthropological Association, III, No. 1 (1916).

[20] American Anthropologist, III, No. 2 (1901), 308–36.

[21] An Analysis of Plains Indian Parfleche Decoration (Seattle, University of Washington Press, 1925).

[22] A. R. Radcliffe-Brown, The Andaman Islanders, a Study in Social Anthropology (Cambridge, Cambridge University Press, 1922).

[23] William Fielding Ogburn, Social Change with Respect to Culture and Original Nature (New York, Huebsch, 1922).

[24] The concordance, as such, was never published.

The Vision in Plains Culture

[1] Herman K. Haeberlin, MS. on Indians of Puget Sound.

[2] Rev. J. Heckewelder, An Account of the History, Manners, and Customs of the Indians Who Once Inhabited Pennsylvania (Philadelphia, 1819), 246.

[3] Paul Radin, The Autobiography of a Winnebago Indian (Publications of the University of California in Archaeology and Ethnology, XVI; Berkeley, University of California Press, 1920), 386–87.

[4] William Jones, Ojibwa Texts (Publications of the American Ethnological Society, VII; New York and Leyden, 1917, 1919), 303.

[5] James Teit, "The Thompson River Indians of British Columbia," Jesup North Pacific Expedition, I, Pt. 4 (1900), 318; idem, "The Shuswap Indians," Jesup North Pacific Expedition, II, Pt. 7 (New York, 1909), 558.

[6] A. L. Kroeber, "The Arapaho," Bulletin of the American Museum of Natural History, XVIII (New York, 1902–7), 418.

[7] A. L. Kroeber, "Ethnology of the Gros Ventre," Anthropological Papers of the American Museum of Natural History, I, Pt. 4 (New York, 1908), 222.

[8] Robert H. Lowie, "The Assiniboine," Anthropological Papers of the American Museum of Natural History, IV, Pt. 1 (New York, 1909), 48.

[9] G. H. Pepper and G. L. Wilson, "An Hidatsa Shrine, and the Beliefs Respecting It," Memoirs of the American Anthropological Association, II (1908), 319.

[10] J. O. Dorsey, "A Study of Siouan Cults," Eleventh Annual Report of the Bureau of American Ethnology (Washington, 1891), 390.

11 Prinz Maxmilian von Wied-Neuwied, *Reise in das innere Nord America* (2 vols., Coblenz, 1839, 1841), II, 188.

12 Clark Wissler, "Sun Dance of the Blackfoot Indians," *Anthropological Papers of the American Museum of Natural History*, XVI, Pt. 3 (New York, 1918), 205.

13 Clark Wissler and D. C. Duvall, "Mythology of the Blackfoot Indians," *Anthropological Papers of the American Museum of Natural History*, II, Pt. 1 (New York, 1908).

14 Clark Wissler, "Ceremonial Bundles of the Blackfoot Indians," *Anthropological Papers of the American Museum of Natural History*, VII, Pt. 2 (New York, 1912).

15 Walter McClintock, *The Old North Trail* (London, Macmillan, 1910).

16 G. B. Grinnell, *Blackfoot Lodge Tales* (New York, Scribner's, 1903).

17 G. A. Dorsey and A. L. Kroeber, "Traditions of the Arapaho," *Anthropological Series*, V (Chicago, Field Columbian Museum, 1905), 198.

18 G. A. Dorsey, "Arapaho Sun Dance," *Anthropological Series*, IV (Chicago, Field Columbian Museum, 1903), 184.

19 *Ibid.*, 182.

20 Kroeber, "The Arapaho," *op. cit.*, 419–28.

21 G. A. Dorsey and A. L. Kroeber, *op. cit.*, 49.

22 James Mooney, "The Ghost Dance Religion and the Sioux Outbreak of 1890," *Fourteenth Annual Report of the Bureau of American Ethnology*, Pt. 2 (Washington, 1896), 898.

23 G. A. Dorsey, "The Cheyenne," II: "The Sun Dance," *Anthropological Series*, XI (Chicago, Field Columbian Museum, 1905), 17.

24 G. B. Grinnell, *When Buffalo Ran* (New Haven, Yale University Press, 1920), 79.

25 A. L. Kroeber, "Cheyenne Tales," *Journal of American Folk-Lore*, XIII, No. 50 (1900), 163, 188, 190; G. B. Grinnell, "Some Early Cheyenne Tales," *Journal of American Folk-Lore*, XX, No. 78 (1907), 188; XXI, No. 82 (1908), 282.

26 James Mooney, "The Cheyenne Indians," *Memoirs of the American Anthropological Association*, I (1905–7), 367.

27 *Ibid.*, 361.

28 Robert H. Lowie, "Myths and Traditions of the Crow Indians," *Anthropological Papers of the American Museum of Natural History*, XXV, Pt. 1 (New York, 1918).

29 Robert H. Lowie, The Religion of the Crow Indians, MS.

30 Alice C. Fletcher and F. La Flesche, "The Omaha Tribe," *Twenty-seventh Annual Report of the Bureau of American Ethnology* (Washington, 1911), 591.

31 Personal communication from Dr. Wissler.

[32] J. O. Dorsey, "A Study of Siouan Cults," *op. cit.*, 373.

[33] J. O. Dorsey, "The Cehiga Language," *Contributions to North American Ethnology*, VI (Washington, 1890).

[34] Rev. J. R. De Smet, *Western Missions and Missionaries* (1859), 92.

[35] Maxmilian, *op. cit.*

[36] Lowie, "The Assiniboine," *op. cit.*, 48.

[37] A. L. Kroeber, "Gros Ventre Myths and Tales," *Anthropological Papers of the American Museum of Natural History*, I, Pt. 3 (New York, 1907), 122; George Catlin, *Illustrations of the Manners, Customs, and Conditions of the North American Indians* (London, 1848), 174.

[38] Rev. J. R. Walker, "The Sun Dance and Other Ceremonies of the Oglala Division of the Teton Dakota," *Anthropological Papers of the American Museum of Natural History*, XVI, Pt. 2 (New York, 1917), 68.

[39] Rev. Stephen Riggs, *Gospel Among the Dakotas* (1869), 81.

[40] Rev. James W. Lynd, "Religion of the Dakotas," *Collection of the Minnesota Historical Society*, II, Pt. 2 (1860–67), 164.

[41] Walker, *op. cit.*, 118.

[42] Clark Wissler, "Societies and Ceremonial Associations of the Oglala Division of the Teton Dakota," *Anthropological Papers of the American Museum of Natural History*, XI, Pt. 1 (New York, 1912), 82.

[43] Kroeber, "The Arapaho," *op. cit.*, 419.

[44] Lowie, "The Assiniboine," *op. cit.*, 47.

[45] Wissler, "Societies . . . of the Teton Dakota," *op. cit.*, 81.

[46] J. O. Dorsey, "A Study of Siouan Cults," *op. cit.*, 443.

[47] G. A. Dorsey, *The Pawnee: Mythology* (Publication LIX; Washington, Carnegie Institution of Washington, 1906), 53.

[48] James R. Murie, "Pawnee Indian Societies," *Anthropological Papers of the American Museum of Natural History*, XI, Pt. 7 (New York, 1914), 617.

[49] Clark Wissler, The Pawnee, MS.

[50] Lowie, "Myths and Traditions of the Crow Indians," *op. cit.*, 130.

[51] Jones, *op. cit.*, Pt. 2, 305.

[52] J. O. Dorsey, "A Study of Siouan Cults," *op. cit.*, 443.

[53] Walker, *op. cit.*, 68.

[54] Wissler, "Societies . . . of the Teton Dakota," *op. cit.*, 81.

[55] G. B. Grinnell, *Pawnee Hero Stories and Folk Tales* (New York, Scribner's, 1893), 358; G. A. Dorsey, "Traditions of the Skidi Pawnee," *Memoirs of the American Folk-Lore Society*, VIII (1904), xix.

[56] G. A. Dorsey, *Traditions of the Wichita* (Publication XXI; Washington, Carnegie Institution of Washington, 1904), 312.

57 G. A. Dorsey, *Traditions of the Arikara* (Publication XVII; Washington, Carnegie Institution of Washington, 1904), 164.
58 Washington Matthews, "Navaho Myths," *Memoirs of the American Folk-Lore Society*, V (1897), 165.
59 *Op. cit.*, 639.
60 Wissler, "Ceremonial Bundles of the Blackfoot Indians," *op. cit.*, 276.
61 Wissler, "Sun Dance of the Blackfoot Indians," *op. cit.*, 263.
62 Lowie, The Religion of the Crow Indians, MS.
63 Kroeber, "The Arapaho," *op. cit.*, 436.
64 Robert H. Lowie, "The Sun Dance of the Shoshoni, Ute, and Hidatsa," *Anthropological Papers of the American Museum of Natural History*, XVI, Pt. 5 (New York, 1919), 417.
65 Paul Radin, "Religion of the North American Indians," in *Anthropology in North America*, Franz Boas *et al.* (New York, Stechert, 1915), 305.
66 Lowie, "The Sun Dance of the Shoshoni . . . ," *op. cit.*, 416, 417.
67 *Ibid.*, 418.
68 Radin, *Autobiography* . . . , *op. cit.*, 390; Alanson Skinner, "Social Life and Ceremonial Bundles of the Menomini Indians," *Anthropological Papers of the American Museum of Natural History*, XIII, Pt. 1 (New York, 1913), 104.
69 Rev. J. J. Methvin, *Andele, or the Mexican-Kiowa Captive: A Story of Real Life among the Indians* (Louisville, Kentucky, 1899); Matthews, *op. cit.*, 164.
70 J. O. Dorsey, "A Study of Siouan Cults," *op. cit.*, 393.
71 J. O. Dorsey, "The Cegiha Language," *op. cit.*, 185.
72 Robert H. Lowie, "The Tobacco Society of the Crow Indians," *Anthropological Papers of the American Museum of Natural History*, XXI, Pt. 2 (New York, 1920), 117.
73 Lowie, The Religion of the Crow Indians, MS.
74 G. A. Dorsey, *The Pawnee: Mythology*, 87.
75 G. A. Dorsey, "A Pawnee Personal Medicine Shrine," *American Anthropologist*, VII, No. 2, Supplement (1905), 497.
76 J. O. Dorsey, "A Study of Siouan Cults," *op. cit.*, 381.

A Matter for the Field Worker in Folklore

1 The general tone of the period in work on folklore is given vividly by other articles in the same volume of the *Journal of American Folk-Lore*. So, for instance, in his discussion of "Beliefs and Tales of the Canadian Dakota" (*ibid.*, 36), Wilson D. Wallis wrote:

Nature philosophy should attempt to describe the world as it is apprehended by the individual. The Dakota's world, like our own, is as much one of his creation as it is one of his finding; what we may call his "illusion" is for him the reality deeper than appearance. To give the orientation of the individual in this social, psychic, and quasi-scientific world requires a complete description of that world, its laws and the interrelations of its phenomena. He is no less blind than adventurous who hopes to achieve this; but I am fain to believe that it is a good chart to steer by.

Or, in his introduction to "Two Chinese Folk-Tales" (Edward Sapir and Hsu Tsan Hwa, *ibid.*, 23), Edward Sapir wrote:

> The following Chinese folk-tales were written down by my friend, Mr. Hsu Tsan Hwa, Secretary of the Chinese Consulate in Canada, and corrected by myself. Mr. Hsu heard them in his native Manchuria, and considers them very typical of the tales current among the folk. "Wang Pao Ch'uan" offers points of similarity to our own romantic tales. "Min Tzu Chien" is especially characteristic of the Chinese mentality. Filial piety.

Or, in "Zuni Names and Naming Practices" (*ibid.*, No. 140, p. 171), Elsie Clews Parsons wrote:

> Since information about the naming practices at Zuni is somewhat scanty or confused, the following list of names in the Bear clan, one of the smaller clans, together with my informant's comment, may be of interest. My informant had married into the Bear clan and with at least one of the families, the family of Massalina, he was intimate. A daughter of one of the Bear clansmen, when I asked her for a list of the clan names, refused to give it, although on many subjects I had found her an unusually frank and helpful informant. Our first name is that of Ochochina (w), whose other names are Tsaiutits'a (from father's mother: Turkey), Malia Panchu (Spanish name), Yuneaititsa (Big Firebrand society name).
>
> | | Tsaiutits'a (From father's mother, Turkey) |
> |---|---|
> | Ochochina (W) = | Malia Panchu (Spanish, Maria) |
> | | Yuneaititsa (Big-Firebrand society name) |
>
> Ochochina is a nick-name. Once during the saint's dance it was noticed that one of the girl dancers had curly hair, like the saint, thereafter the girl was called Ochochina from *chinapa*, curly hair, and a word meaning to want to be like another or to have something another has. This is the only nick-name in our list, but nicknaming at Zuni is not uncommon. For example, a man named Kluptsin, Yellow, is said to be so-called from a yellow shirt he once wore. Atsitsana, Little-Blood is a nick-name for the present town crier, a name got from some incident of boyhood. And then there are:

Koluwisi, named for the plumed serpent of the springs, with whom this man's mother had an adventure before his birth; Ne'santu, a man who in boyhood was set up on an improvised altar as a saint by the caricaturing *ne'wekwe*.

Selections from the Correspondence of Edward Sapir with Ruth Benedict: 1922–1923

1 "The Concept of the Guardian Spirit in America," *Memoirs of the American Anthropological Association,* XXIX (1923).
2 Alexander A. Goldenweiser, "Totemism: An Analytical Study," *Journal of American Folk-Lore,* XXIII, No. 88 (1910).
3 T. T. Waterman, "The Explanatory Element in the Folk-Tales of the North-American Indians," *Journal of American Folk-Lore,* XXVII, No. 103 (1914), 1–54.
4 *University of Pennsylvania Anthropological Publications,* II, No. 1 (1909), 1–263.
5 "The Takelma Language of Southwestern Oregon," *Handbook of American Indian Languages* (Bureau of American Ethnology, Bulletin XL, Pt. 2; Washington, 1922), 1–296.
6 *Encyclopedia of Religion and Ethics,* ed. James Hastings (1922), 591–95.
7 *The Nation,* CXV, July 26 (1922), 96.
8 Reviews of *Introducing Irony* by Max Bodenheim: *The Nation,* CXIV, June 21 (1922), 751; *The New Republic,* XXXI, August 16 (1922), 341.
9 C. G. Jung, *Psychological Types,* trans. H. G. Baynes (New York, Harcourt, Brace, 1923).
10 In fact, publication was held up until 1930; see *Proceedings of the American Academy of Arts and Sciences,* LXV, No. 2 (1930), 297–536.

Two Diaries

1 Helen Sapir, Edward Sapir's daughter, then aged 8.
2 W. F. Ogburn, *Social Change with Respect to Culture and Original Nature* (New York, Huebsch, 1922).
3 Unpublished as a paper; incorporated into Chapter II of *Patterns of Culture* (Boston and New York, Houghton Mifflin, 1934). For a passage from this paper, see above, pages 38–39.
4 The Shattuck family farm at Norwich, New York, where Ruth Benedict had lived in her childhood. Aunt Myra — Myra Shattuck, the young-

est sister of Ruth Benedict's mother, Bertrice Shattuck Fulton — took over the running of the farm after the death of her parents. In later years, Ruth Benedict took the responsibility for the care of this, her favorite aunt, while Margery Freeman, her sister, took over the care of their mother in California.

5 "A Brief Sketch of Serrano Culture," *American Anthropologist*, XXVI, No. 3 (1924), 366–92. See above, pages 213–21.

6 Name illegible and verse quotation unidentified.

7 Gladys Reichard had recently been appointed instructor in anthropology at Barnard College. See RFB's diary entry for February 13.

8 Michael Sapir, Edward Sapir's son, then aged 9.

9 To visit the Shattuck family farm.

10 *Tales of the Cochiti Indians* (Bureau of American Ethnology, Bulletin XCVI; Washington, 1931).

11 A local mason, called in to rebuild the fireplace.

12 Ralph Tynkam, an engineer who had passed through Pago Pago while MM was there.

PART II

Anne Singleton: 1889–1934

1 Unpublished poem.

2 Letter of August 18, 1925.

3 Boston Museum of Fine Arts, C–4735.

4 Published as "Dead Star," *Poetry*, XXXV, No. 6 (1930), 306–7.

5 From a dream which she described to me.

6 See "Journal: 1912–1916," entry dated November 1914 (page 132): "For Stanley I shall try to write out the chemical detective stories for which he supplies the plot."

7 There is, however, evidence that she hoped to publish this manuscript, for together with it were found drafts of letters to publishers. In one of these, an undated and heavily revised draft written from Douglaston, she describes the projected book:

> Would you consider for publication a book entitled "Adventures in Womanhood," being three biographical studies of women leaders and pioneers?
> As you will see from the accompanying drafts — of a "Foreword" and of "Mary Wollstonecraft," the first "story" — it is a book to be classified with the feminist literature without being concerned either with *pro* or *con*. A whole library of theorizing can't give half the real conviction that comes from adventuring through the life

of one restless, highly endowed woman. It is from that conviction that I have written this book. Besides the lives of these three women are in themselves splendidly romantic human documents.

To complete my series, I have selected Margaret Fuller (Ossoli) and Olive Schreiner. The selection of a still-living woman of course involves omitting intimate personal matter; still, she is pre-eminently the woman who fits into my plan, and since there is now no study of her in English, I am sure that a sketch of her personality and striking point of view could be made with the help of unpublished notes to fill a real place.

For authorities, I have consulted of course all the published writings of these women and all studies that have been made of them; in the case of Mary Wollstonecraft, the never-reprinted volumes now accessible only in the New York Library Reserve Room; and in the case of Margaret Fuller, the bulky manuscript volumes deposited by her heirs in the Boston Library.

The manuscript found among her papers consists of the completed study of Mary Wollstonecraft, notebooks and dozens of partial drafts. From these it is clear that she was struggling not only with matter but also with style.

[8] The earliest published poems to which there is specific reference and of which there are extant copies appeared under the pseudonym of "Anne Singleton" in *The Measure* (LI, May 1925); the poems are "Withdrawal" and "Sleet Storm." See "Selected Poems," pages 482–83.

[9] *Memoirs of the American Anthropological Association*, XXIX (1923), 1–97.

[10] *Poetry*, XXVII, No. 4 (1926), 177.

[11] *Ibid.*, 175. See above, page 164.

[12] *Voices*, IV, No. 5 (1925), 135.

[13] *Poetry*, XXXI, No. 4 (1928), 194–95.

[14] *Palms*, III, No. 6 (1926), 167.

[15] *Poetry*, XXXV, No. 5 (1930), 253.

[16] *The New Republic*, LXXII, October 19 (1932), 255.

[17] *The Measure*, LII (June 1925), 16.

[18] Letter from Harcourt, Brace to RFB, September 29, 1928.

[19] From a copy of a letter from Léonie Adams to RFB, January 20, 1929, sent by RFB to MM.

[20] Letter from RFB to MM, September 21, 1928.

[21] Letter from RFB to MM, August 5, 1930.

[22] Louis Untermeyer, ed., *Modern American Poetry*, 4th rev. ed. (New York, Harcourt, Brace, 1930). "But the Son of Man" and "Unshadowed Pool" appear on pp. 518–19.

[23] Letter from ES to RFB, December 12, 1924.

[24] Letter from ES to RFB, July 7, 1925.
[25] Letter from ES to RFB, March 23, 1926.
[26] This was a position we shared. I had begun to send out my poems under a pseudonym. *The New Republic* rejected "Absolute Benison" when it was sent to them by "Ellen Morey," but accepted it seven years later when I resubmitted it as "Margaret Mead." With this I gave up submitting poetry for publication.
[27] "Religion," *General Anthropology*, ed. Franz Boas (Boston and New York, Heath, 1938), 627–65.
[28] Letter from RFB to MM, September 21, 1928.
[29] Letter from RFB to MM, Thursday, 5 A.M., October 25, 1929.
[30] Letter from RFB to MM, December 29, 1929.

The Story of My Life . . .

[1] After receiving a copy of her father's publications on cancer research, Stanley Benedict wrote to Ruth Fulton in 1913:

I've been reading your father's papers, — and I do so wish he could have gone on. Your mother needed him, you needed him, and I think the whole world needed him.

He started at the very foundation — the only real way to start — by classifying, looking for relationships. And his handling of the subject matter he had was splendid. If you could only see the large masses of physicians today who with a thousand times the opportunity your father had, are doing nothing at all to contribute anything of value to the profession they've taken as a life work, — if you only saw the multitudes even today when every facility is available to them — you would realize more what it meant for your father to take up the work he did, and in the way he did, nearly thirty years ago.

I am glad that I am doing some work along the line he took up — even though it's a different aspect of it, and the problem is so terrible that I can't keep so closely to it as he did. He was so desperately needed in it. He was willing to start at the beginning and build up a science. And he knew the difficulties and discouragements and wasn't afraid.

[2] Boston Museum of Fine Arts, C–4735.
[3] In one respect — in the education which they received — Ruth and Margery Fulton were protected from the full consequences of their extremely straitened circumstances. In a biographical account, Margery Fulton Freeman describes how, in 1901, when the sisters were in their first year of high school, Miss Mary Robinson — a friend of Bertrice Fulton's younger sister, Mary Shattuck Ellis, and the principal of St.

Margaret's School for Girls, an Episcopal college preparatory school in Buffalo — offered them full tuition scholarships on condition that they win accreditation for the school to Vassar College by doing well on the College Entrance Board Examinations and later by making a good record at the college. Bertrice Fulton was irresolute; she did not wish her daughters to suffer from the kind of social handicaps that had made painful her own life as a student in school with well-to-do girls. But Ruth and Margery "had never been conscious of their poverty, let alone troubled by it. . . . When the time came, the girls steered their bicycles toward St. Margaret's."

Attendance at Vassar College presented an equally difficult financial problem which was solved equally fortuitously. Indirectly, through a teacher at St. Margaret's, the situation of the Fulton sisters was brought to the attention of Mrs. F. F. Thompson, whose husband had been a benefactor of Vassar, and who, in memory of her husband, annually gave full four-year scholarships to several students. During the girls' senior year at St. Margaret's, Bertrice Fulton "received a letter from Mrs. Thompson's secretary, which read: 'Mrs. Thompson has been pleased to place your two daughters, Ruth and Margery Fulton, on her list of Vassar scholarships for September, 1905.' Only that, and nothing more. Nor did they ever hear anything further from Mrs. Thompson. . . ."

The Sense of Symbolism

[1] At the top of the first page, this note is written in:

Begin with Hebrew sym. Child's literal reading. Not till read Greek, understood uniqueness of Heb. sym. Grk. beauty.

[2] This and the two preceding sentences were incompletely corrected by RFB.

[3] The quotation begins a new page; above it, this penciled notation:

Up to these mighty strophes that seem even yet to whirl us to the very gates of heaven with all the one-time glory of that old chariot of flame and the horses thereof.

Journals

[1] For two years, from 1912 to 1914, RFB taught in the Orton School for Girls in Pasadena, California. For a year before this she had taught in another school, also in California.

[2] I.e., the children of her sister, Margery Fulton Freeman.

3 But Stanley Benedict himself thought differently about the question. In 1912, he had refused to come to Pasadena to spend the summer and had gone to Europe instead, but at New Year 1913 he had left his work in New York and made the long trip to California to spend only two days with her. A letter written to her on January 14, 1913, vividly portrays his sense of their possible relationship:

> Your letter came today — amidst a turmoil of excitement and endless worry over our cancer cases. I seem to have lived ten years since our day together. The having of the entire responsibility of several human lives on one's mind night and day is quite different from the thought of it beforehand. . . .
>
> And Ruth your letter didn't altogether surprise me except that you shouldn't have been so sure about Norwich next summer — that was wrong. However, I half expected such a letter as a result of my trip. That was one of the reasons I was unwilling to take it and yet it was the chief reason I did it — it wasn't fair to you not to do it. But it placed both of us under false and strained conditions — our meeting for two days that way — just as happened at Norwich — strong preconceived opinions about people whom we know but very little are not good incentives to a thorough acquaintance and understanding, are they? And it's funny that you're just as sure that a longer time would have made no difference. Perhaps you're right — probably — but really you know nothing about it. It's apt to be quite different after the strangeness of the two people who haven't seen each other for two years wears off — at least they can really come to know each other as they never would in the two days. Especially so with us. I fancy neither of us are easy to get really acquainted with. If you didn't see your own sister for three years you'd find you were partial strangers for a day or two. So I say you know nothing about it — not that I'm urging any "reconsideration," but because I *know* you don't. You know I said it was, at least, beginning all over — and you denied it. Well — it wasn't — I guess our letters — beginning with yours to me in Paris were really about nothing but any chance of our getting acquainted — that — and a two days' trip did it. And Ruth — what's made it worse for me was that I felt that your letters — even the one I received in Paris — were scarcely written to *me* — you've never felt that way in your life, have you? And it made my trip a little harder than you'll ever guess.
>
> As I said that day in the canyon — our acquaintance has depended on such little things — there happened to be a moon the night I first saw you in Buffalo — so we could walk to the Museum — without it we'd not have met again — and so it's gone to the end. And there are two things that are all wrong about it — that

you didn't *tell* me in Pasadena, and that you've been so far away
we could see nothing of each other.

I think that now — perhaps for the first time — we feel much the
same toward each other — probably we're both giving up something. At least I wonder whether it will be — or rather it is — as
hard for you to think of our never having another walk — in the
canyon or elsewhere — as it is for me. But I'm sure it isn't.

. . . I don't know how much this letter of yours will mean later
— I'm too sick with worries of work to tell much about it. It may
be all right. It may not. It *may* make me mad — and if it does
that, Ruth, you'll have a very different person to deal with than
you've yet known. I don't mean that I'll be mean — I mean that
wherever you go I'll be there, and get acquainted, one way or the
other, whether you approve, disapprove, like it, or don't like it.
I'm not altogether sure that I haven't thought too much of you and
too little of myself heretofore anyway. And really, I'm a terrible
person if I get once thoroughly "set" — so look out — it's more
than possible.

. . . Ruth — the real question isn't just how much you think
you can give — the question is *whether we'd be happier together*
or apart. How much it would mean to each of us not ever to see
the other again. The two points I realized most strongly in Pasadena (and they didn't include how much I had to give) were
firstly that it was a great pleasure to be with you — to see you —
and secondly that it would be too hard to be considered, not to
ever see you again. And you must have felt a good deal the same
way, or you wouldn't have made such definite promises about
our meeting next summer — It was settled, and I wouldn't have
gone away without it — and you wanted it too. Why worry Ruth,
about what you can give, or what I can give? It's been too much
of that looking forward which has kept our getting really acquainted
back. But when the time came to finally give up altogether, neither
of us has ever been willing to do it. Except now — you think you
want to do it. You're willing to give up the person who'se tried
so hard to understand you — and who may have succeeded better
than most other people. And Ruth — your mask is getting thicker
and thicker — I could see that it is — and that's all wrong. You
belong somehow where you never have to wear it. You're so wonderful behind it — I believe — I've so often and so long wanted
to get behind it, and I've never done it. You shouldn't *have* to
wear it at all, for it's certain to grow to be a part of you if you do
— and then you'll be altogether alone, and it's so wrong for *you*
Ruth. . . .

You think my work makes it easier for me — my work is a reason

— an excuse — for my living. If I go on at all — it must go on. And do you know that it's *mostly* made up of disappointments, one after the other. . . . How little I've told you about it — except of a few successes. . . .

But Ruth — as I intimated above — you can hardly settle everything by a letter now — your sending a man 6000 miles to Europe and 6000 miles to Pasadena doesn't give him any claim on you I'll admit — but you've had the reins a long time, and you *have* bungled things, haven't you? So it's time I take them I think. You made a good statement our first evening 'make me know you' — and I echo it to you, and I'm going to see that it's done. It *must* and *will* be done. . . .

4 Where she had done social service work for a year, in 1910–11.
5 Her niece, Bertrice Freeman, who was born in 1912.
6 RFB's first home after her marriage in 1914.
7 Only one of these stories, written in 1916, survives in manuscript; for it she adopted the pseudonym "Edgar Stanhope."
8 This is the first statement of her plan, which occupied her for several years, to write these biographical essays. A life of Mary Wollstonecraft, the only one of the essays completed, is reproduced in this volume (see pages 491–519).
9 The type of paper and the handwriting suggest that this may have been written in 1915.
10 Possibly written in 1915. The first paragraph is incomplete.
11 Lake Winnepesaukee, where RFB and SB had a summer cottage.
12 H. K. Webster (New York, Bobbs-Merrill, 1916).
13 A rhythmic dance camp.
14 New York, Huebsch, 1915.
15 Although, in the manuscript, this page follows, there is text missing at this point.
16 Written, as is the final, dated entry, on a leaf torn from a college examination blue book.

Selections from the Correspondence of Edward Sapir with Ruth Benedict: 1923–1938

1 Unidentified poem.
2 Both poems published in *Queen's Quarterly* (October–December 1923).
3 F. H. Giddings (New York, Macmillan, 1922).
4 Unpublished poem.

5 Unpublished poem; the extant version differs from that originally sent to ES, which was several times revised. (See references in later letters, below.)

6 Unpublished poem.

7 No extant poem with this title.

8 *Palms*, III, No. 6 (1926), 165. The central image in this poem derives from the Maori creation myth.

9 Unpublished poem.

10 Edward Sapir, *Poetry*, XXVII, No. 4 (1926), 175.

11 In "Selected Poems," pages 488–89. In the version sent ES, line 8 read: "They are too slight to hold the globed . . ."

12 Unpublished poem.

13 In "Selected Poems," page 486.

14 *The Nation*, CXX, January 21 (1925), 71.

15 *The Nation*, CXXI, July 8 (1925), 72.

16 *Voices*, V, No. 1 (1925), 17.

17 This was the manuscript of a projected book on religion, never published as such.

18 *Primitive Religion* (New York, Boni and Liveright, 1924).

19 The version published in *Palms* (III, No. 6 [1926], 168) differs from that sent to ES.

20 See letter of November 15, 1924, page 160.

21 Unidentified poem.

22 *The Measure*, LIII (July 1925), 6.

23 *Palms*, III, No. 6 (1926), 182–83.

24 Unpublished poem.

25 The published version (*Palms*, III, No. 6 [1926], 166) differs from that sent to ES, in which line 2 read: "A heaven-scaling wall across your path."

26 Unpublished poem.

27 This suggested line was incorporated into the final version of the poem.

28 Franz Boas, "What Is a Race," *The Nation*, CXX, January 28 (1925), 89–91.

29 Edward Sapir, "Let Race Alone," *The Nation*, CXX, February 25 (1925), 211–13.

30 Unpublished poem.

31 No extant poem with this title.

32 See *Collected Poems of Edwin Arlington Robinson* (New York, Macmillan, 1929).

33 A revision of the poem, "Sight." See letter of January 19, 1925, pages 169–70.

34 For ES's projected volume of poetry.

35 *The Measure*, LIII (July 1925), 8.

36 *Double Dealer*, VII, No. 44 (1925), 180.
37 *The Measure*, LIII (July 1925), 8.
38 *Canadian Bookman*, December 1920, 17; reprinted in *Stratford Quarterly*, n.s. I, No. 4 (1924), 46–48.
39 *Poetry*, XXVII, No. 4 (1926), 181.
40 *Voices*, V, No. 6 (1926), 206.
41 *Voices*, V, No. 1 (1925), 16–17.
42 *Voices*, V, No. 6 (1926), 204–5.
43 ES intended to dedicate the poem, "Signal," to RFB (see letter of November 26, 1924, page 161, and that of June 10, 1928, page 192); the initials "A.S." appeared in the published version.
44 In "Selected Poems," page 481. The final version differs from that sent to ES.
45 About his poetry manuscript.
46 *The Measure*, XLVII (January 1925), 11.
47 *Double Dealer*, *op. cit.*
48 *Voices*, *op. cit.*
49 See letter of November 15, 1924, page 160.
50 *Voices*, *op. cit.*
51 *Palms*, *op. cit.*
52 Unpublished poem.
53 In "Selected Poems," page 482.
54 In "Selected Poems," page 488. The final version differs from that sent to ES.
55 No extant poem with this title.
56 *Voices*, V, No. 6 (1926), 203.
57 *Canadian Forum*, VI, No. 68 (1926), 246.
58 In "Selected Poems," pages 486–87.
59 *Those Not Elect* (New York, McBride, 1925).
60 Robert H. Lowie, "Is America So Bad After All," *The Century*, CIX, No. 6 (1925), 723–29.
61 "Ariel (to M.M.)," *Voices*, IV, No. 5 (1925), 135. See above, page 88.
62 I.e. the anthology of verse which ES and RFB planned to edit, but which never got beyond the planning stage.
63 In "Selected Poems," pages 481–82. The final, published version differs from that sent to ES.
64 Published in *The Measure*, LII (June 1925), 13.
65 Trans. R. M. Ogden (New York, Harcourt, Brace, 1924).
66 In "Selected Poems," page 483.
67 The plan to have ES join the Department of Anthropology at the University of Chicago had not yet been settled.
68 "Toy Balloons" was published in *Poetry* (XXVIII, No. 5 [1926], 245), but "Moth Wings" was not published.

[69] "Counsel for Autumn," "Burial," and "Preference," *The Measure*, LII (June 1925), 12–13.

[70] Unidentified.

[71] See letter of May 14, 1925, page 179.

[72] In "Selected Poems," page 486.

[73] To work on the *Journal of American Folk-Lore*. But see letter from RFB to MM, September 8, 1925, below, page 302.

[74] ES had been invited to teach at the University of Chicago and had recently moved from Ottawa to Chicago.

[75] "He Implores His Beloved," *Poetry*, XXX, No. 4 (1927), 194–95.

[76] Unidentified.

[77] "She Speaks to the Sea," "In Parables," "Miser's Wisdom," "Sight," "This Gabriel," "Our Task is Laughter," and "Spiritus Tyrannus," *Palms*, III, No. 6 (1926), 164–69. "Evening Sky," (*ibid.*, 163), also attributed to "Anne Singleton," was a poem by Léonie Adams, who published other poems in the same issue of *Palms*. The correct author is written in by RFB in her file copy of the magazine.

[78] Unidentified.

[79] See above, Footnote 77.

[80] Review of *Those Not Elect* by Léonie Adams, *Poetry*, XXVII, No. 5 (1926), 275–79.

[81] *Poetry*, XXX, No. 4 (1927), 194.

[82] The International Congress of Americanists, which met in Rome in 1926.

[83] Harriet Monroe was a courtesy "aunt" through a friendship which RFB had formed at Vassar College.

[84] *The Dial*, LXXXIII, No. 3 (1927), 208.

[85] Mark Van Doren, *7 P.M. and Other Poems* (New York, Boni, 1926).

[86] In "Selected Poems," page 474.

[87] In "Selected Poems," page 475.

[88] Unpublished poem. In the version sent ES, the last three lines read:

> . . . will as then make bare
> The world new-minted, the sky luminous
> With stars at noontime, laughter on the air.

[89] In "Selected Poems," page 477.

[90] *The Dial*, LXXXIV, No. 6 (1928), 468.

[91] *The Nation*, CXXIII, July 28 (1926), 85.

[92] By Thomas Mann (New York, Knopf, 1927).

[93] *Queen's Quarterly* (October–December 1923), 182.

[94] *Palms*, III, No. 6 (1926), 182.

[95] *The Nation, op. cit.*

[96] Not identified.

[97] *Voices, op. cit. See* above, page 88.

98 *The Pagan*, V, No. 1 (1919), 42.
99 Edward Sapir, "The Unconscious Patterning of Behavior in Society," *The Unconscious: A Symposium*, ed. E. S. Dummer (New York, Knopf, 1927), 114–42.
100 Unidentified.
101 See pages 85–86.
102 "But the Son of Man . . . ," in "Selected Poems," page 475.
103 "Winter of the Blood."
104 *Modern American Poetry*, 4th rev. ed. (New York, Harcourt, Brace, 1930).
105 "But the Son of Man . . ."
106 In "Selected Poems," pages 478–79.
107 In "Selected Poems," page 475.
108 The Twenty-third International Congress of Americanists, held in New York, September 17–22, 1928.
109 *The Dial*, LXXXVI, No. 1 (1929), 42.
110 Unpublished poem.
111 Unpublished poem.
112 *New York Herald Tribune Books*, March 24, 1929.
113 Unpublished poem.
114 Review of *The Women at the Pump* by Knut Hamsun, *The New Republic*, LVI, November 7 (1928), 335.
115 Robinson Jeffers, "The Tower beyond Tragedy," in *Roan Stallion, Tamar and Other Poems* (New York, Modern Library, 1935).
116 ES published two articles on sex problems in 1928 and 1929; undoubtedly that referred to in this letter is "Observations on the Sex Problem in America," *American Journal of Psychiatry*, VIII, No. 3 (1928), 519–34. The "supposed quotation," to which ES refers, has not been identified.
117 RFB in fact went on a vacation trip to Guatemala in the summer of 1938.

PART III

Patterns of Culture: 1922–1934

1 Letter from RFB to MM, September 5, 1925; see page 301.
2 Letter from RFB to MM, November 30, 1932; see page 325.
3 Amy Lowell, "Patterns," *Selected Poems* (Boston and New York, Houghton Mifflin, 1928), 75–76.
4 "The Concept of the Guardian Spirit in North America," *Memoirs of the American Anthropological Association*, XXIX (1923), 84–85.
5 Unpublished statement.
6 W. H. R. Rivers, *The Todas* (London and New York, Macmillan, 1906).

[7] A. R. Radcliffe-Brown, *The Andaman Islanders* (Cambridge, Cambridge University Press, 1922).

[8] Bronislaw Malinowski, "The Natives of Mailu," *Transactions of the Royal Society of South Australia*, XXXIX (1915), 494–706.

[9] See, for example, *Argonauts of the Western Pacific* (London, Routledge, 1922).

[10] Claude Lévi-Strauss, *La vie familiale et sociale des indiens Nambikwara* (Paris, Société des américanistes, 1948); see also, *Les structures élémentaires de la parenté* (Paris, Presses Universitaires de France, 1949).

[11] Unpublished letter, RFB to FB, undated.

[12] *Bishop Museum Bulletin*, LXXVI (Honolulu, 1930).

[13] New York, Morrow, 1928.

[14] Kurt Koffka, *The Growth of the Mind, an Introduction to Child Psychology*, trans. R. M. Ogden (New York, Harcourt, Brace, 1924).

[15] C. G. Jung, *Psychological Types*, trans. H. G. Baynes (New York, Harcourt, Brace, 1923).

[16] C. G. Seligman, "Anthropology and Psychology: A Study of Some Points of Contact," *Journal of the Royal Anthropological Institute*, LIV (1923), 13.

[17] S. Freud, *Totem and Taboo*, trans. A. A. Brill (New York, Moffat, Yard, 1918).

[18] J. Piaget, *Judgment and Reasoning in the Child*, trans. M. Warden (New York, Harcourt, Brace, 1928).

[19] L. Levy-Bruhl, *Primitive Mentality*, trans. L. A. Clare (New York, Macmillan, 1923).

[20] R. F. Fortune, *The Mind in Sleep* (London, Kegan Paul, Trench, Trubner, 1927).

[21] At this period I wrote, out of these discussions, "A Lapse of Animism among a Primitive People" (*Psyche*, IX, No. 1 [1928], 72–77) and "An Ethnologist's Footnote to *Totem and Taboo*" (*Psychoanalytic Review*, XVII, No. 3 [1930], 297–304), adapting Ruth Benedict's emerging conceptualization to psychoanalytic theory and to the possibility that in one culture one part of a universal ambivalence toward the dead might be dominant and institutionalized, so that individuals would have to repress it, while in another culture the reverse situation might occur. With this use of her approach she was never fully in sympathy. Universal mechanisms, whether they were Radcliffe-Brown's "social solidarity by social opposition," or Freudian mechanisms of displacement, sublimation, and repression, or Jungian contrasts within a given set of types, or Kretschmerian attempts to define a set of constitutional types and their psychological correlates (E. Kretschmer, *Physique and Character*, trans. W. J. H. Sprott [New York, Harcourt, Brace, 1926]), the simple applications of learning theory (G. Bateson,

"Social Planning and Deutero Learning," *Science, Philosophy and Religion*, Second Symposium [New York, Conference on Science, Philosophy and Religion, 1942], 81–97), or Erik Erikson's schemata of modal-zonal combinations (*Childhood and Society* [New York, Norton, 1950]), all left her cold because they seemed to her to be both limiting and partial. Each was, it is true, one way of looking at human behavior, but just as such identifications as Apollonian and Dionysian were for her recurrent and useful but partial, so any attempt to set up an exclusive and exhaustive set of categories repelled her.

In this preference she belonged more to the humanities than to the sciences and was more interested in the rich complexity of the real, historically unique situation than in the those types of scientific analysis which, by devising a formula which could be applied to all cultures, stripped the cultures of the very uniqueness which she valued. Some of our most lively theoretical battles were fought over this point — when I would argue for the usefulness of such an analytical method and she would smile and dispose of the carefully constructed analytical scheme as if it were little more than a bit of Zuñi cosmology, as of course from one point of view it was. To satisfy my criteria, as opposed to hers, I had to wait for later formulations, such as that of Niels Bohr in applying the principle of complementarity to both scientific formulations and the value systems of different cultures ("Address to the International Congress of Anthropological and Ethnological Sciences, Copenhagen, August 1938," *Nature*, CXLIII, February 18 [1939], 268).

²² *Op. cit.*, 80–86.

²³ *Proceedings of the Twenty-third International Congress of Americanists*, September 1928 (New York, 1930), 570–81.

²⁴ I found it interesting to remember, as I wrote this chapter, that I had originally written the material which became "A Day in Samoa" (*Coming of Age in Samoa*, 14–19) as the opening section of the chapter on "Dominant Cultural Attitudes" (*Social Organization of Manu'a, op. cit.*), and then removed it as too literary for that context. In the light of the present analysis, I would now say that this was an inarticulate recognition that the sensorily rich memories of real people obscured the clarity of the pattern in which I was then interested.

²⁵ See pages 246–47.

²⁶ *Op. cit.*, 570.

²⁷ XXXIV, No. 1 (1932), 1–27.

²⁸ *Social Organization of Manu'a, op. cit.*, 83.

²⁹ *Op. cit.*, Ch. XI, 158–84.

³⁰ *Ibid.*, 158.

³¹ Berkeley and Los Angeles, University of California Press, 1949, p. ix.

[32] Eds. L. Spier, A. I. Hallowell, and S. S. Newman (Menasha, Wis., Sapir Memorial Publication Fund, 1941).
[33] "Ruth Benedict: Apollonian and Dionysian," *University of Toronto Quarterly*, XVIII, No. 3 (1949), 241–53.
[34] *Franz Boas, the Science of Man in the Making* (New York, Scribner's, 1953), 71.
[35] In a letter of April 1926, Ruth Benedict wrote to me:

> I sent you my copy of Zarathustra to take along on the boat [from Samoa to Europe]. I was still concerned for your eyesight so I thought the marked passages would be to the good. You may find them annoying. Anyway I've often read in it with a pencil so there's no guarantee that the marked passages are the best. There's a gaiety and intoxication about it that nothing else quite achieves. It was newer to me twenty years ago when I first read it than it will be to you — it's in the air we breathe now — but when you read it in Nietzsche it's more clearly the right — poetical way of seeing it than it often is in the people who have learned so much from him.

[36] See letter from RFB to MM, January 16, 1929, page 311.
[37] *Patterns of Culture* (Boston and New York, Houghton Mifflin, 1934), vii.
[38] *Ibid.*, xiii.
[39] See Letters from the Field, *passim*.

An Introduction to Zuñi Mythology

[1] Principal references: F. H. Cushing, *Zuñi Folk Tales* (New York, Putnam's, 1901); M. C. Stevenson, "The Zuñi Indians," *Twenty-third Annual Report of the Bureau of American Ethnology* (Washington, 1904), 1–634; Ruth Bunzel, "Introduction to Zuñi Ceremonialism," *Forty-seventh Annual Report of the Bureau of American Ethnology* (Washington, 1932), 467–544.
[2] *Thirty-first Annual Report of the Bureau of American Ethnology* (Washington, 1916), 29-1037.
[3] *Memoirs of the American Folk-Lore Society*, XXVIII (New York, 1935).
[4] *Journal of American Folk-Lore*, L, No. 198 (1937), 307–408.
[5] *Journal of American Folk-Lore*, XVII No. 64 (1904), 1–13. See also Ralph S. Boggs, "The Hero in the Folk Tales of Spain, Germany and Russia," *Journal of American Folk-Lore*, XLIV, No. 171 (1931), 27–42.
[6] See, for a comparative study, Dorothy Demetracopoulou, "The Loon

Woman: A Study in Synthesis," *Journal of American Folk-Lore*, XLVI, No. 180 (1933), 101–28.

7 Cushing, *op. cit.*, 411.

8 See, however, in tales told by men the bride's teaching cooking to the Ahaiyute grandmother and the good corncakes Lazy Bones makes. These are less elaborate.

Psychological Types in the Cultures of the Southwest

1 For the theoretical justification of this position in the study of cultures, see Ruth Benedict, "Cultures and Psychological Types," *American Anthropologist*. (This article, though contemplated, was never written. — Ed. note.)

2 I have not followed Nietzsche's definitions in their entirety; I have used that aspect which is pertinent to the problems of the Southwest.

3 *Birth of Tragedy*, 68.

4 Paul Radin, "The Winnebago Tribe," *Thirty-seventh Annual Report of the Bureau of American Ethnology* (Washington, 1923), 388–426.

5 *Ibid.*, 392, 408.

6 A. L. Kroeber, "The Arapaho," *American Museum of Natural History, Bulletin* XVIII (New York, 1907), 398.

7 A. L. Kroeber, "Handbook of the Indians of California," *Bureau of American Ethnology, Bulletin* LXXVIII (Washington, 1925), 669.

8 Ruth Benedict, "A Brief Sketch of Serrano Culture," *American Anthropologist*, XXVI, No. 3 (1924), 383.

9 A. L. Kroeber, "Handbook of the Indians of California," *op. cit.*, 669.

10 *Ibid.*

11 *Ibid.*, 779.

12 William E. Safford, "Narcotic Daturas of the Old and New World; an Account of Their Remarkable Properties and Their Uses as Intoxicants and in Divination," *Smithsonian Institution Annual Report for 1920* (Washington, 1922), 551.

13 Matilda C. Stevenson, "The Zuñi Indians, Their Mythology, Esoteric Fraternities and Ceremonies," *Twenty-third Annual Report of the Bureau of American Ethnology* (Washington, 1904), 89.

14 F. H. Cushing, "My Experience in Zuñi," *Century Magazine*, III, No. 4 (1888), 31; M. C. Stevenson, "The Zuñi Indians," *op. cit.*, 503, "All are filled with the spirit of good nature."

15 K. T. Preuss, *Die Nayarit-Expedition* (Leipzig, 1912), 55.

16 H. R. Voth, "Oraibi Summer Snake Ceremony," *Field Columbian Museum, Publication* LXXXIII (Chicago, 1903), 299.

17 See Paul Radin, *Primitive Man as Philosopher* (New York, Appleton,

1927), 257–75, for discussion of the wide limits of individualism among the Winnebago.

18 Except for the war chief's societies where it was necessary to have taken a scalp.

19 H. K. Haeberlin, "The Idea of Fertilization in the Culture of the Pueblo Indians," *Memoirs of the American Anthropological Association*, III, No. 1 (1916).

20 *Ibid.*, especially p. 39 ff.

21 P. J. Arriaga, *Extirpacion de la Idolatria del Peru* (Lima, 1621), 36 *sq.*

22 Information from Dr. Ruth Bunzel.

23 Kroeber, "Handbook of the Indians of California," *op cit.*, 750.

24 *Ibid.*, 431.

25 *Ibid.*, 253.

26 Franz Boas, "The Social Organization and Secret Societies of the Kwakiutl," *Report of the United States National Museum for 1895* (Washington, 1897), 537 ff.

27 John G. Bourke, *Compilation of Notes and Memoranda bearing on the Use of Human Ordure and Human Urine in Rites of a Religious or Semi-religious Character among Various Nations* (Washington, 1888), 9.

28 Elsie Clews Parsons, "A Zuñi Detective," *Man*, XVI (1916), 169.

29 Ruth Benedict, MS.

Anthropology and the Abnormal

1 R. B. Dixon, "The Shasta," *American Museum of Natural History, Bulletin* XVII (1907), 381–498.

2 In all cultures behavior which is socially rewarded attracts persons who are attracted by the possibility of leadership, and such individuals may simulate the required behavior. This is as true when society rewards prodigality as when it rewards catalepsy. For the present argument the amount of shamming is not considered though it is of obvious importance. It is a matter which cultures standardize quite as much as they standardize the type of rewarded behavior.

3 M. A. Czaplicka, *Aboriginal Siberia, a Study in Social Anthropology* (Oxford, Clarendon Press, 1914). A convenient summary.

4 C. H. Callaway, *Religious System of the Amazulu* (Publications of the Folklore Society, XV; London, 1884), 259 ff.

5 G. B. Grinnell, *The Cheyenne Indians* (New Haven, Yale University Press, 1923); E. C. Parsons, "The Zuni La'mana," *American Anthropologist*, XVIII, No. 4 (1916), 521–28.

6 R. F. Fortune, *Sorcerers of Dobu* (New York, Dutton, 1932).

[7] Franz Boas, "The Social Organization and the Secret Societies ᴐ Kwakiutl Indians," *Report of the U. S. National Museum for 10* (Washington, 1897), 311–738; "Ethnology of the Kwakiutl Based on Data Collected by George Hunt," *Thirty-fifth Annual Report of the Bureau of American Ethnology* (2 vols., Washington, 1921); *Contributions to the Ethnology of the Kwakiutl* (Columbia University Contributions to Anthropology, III; New York, Columbia University Press, 1925); *Religion of the Kwakiutl* (2 pts., Columbia University Contributions to Anthropology, X; New York, Columbia University Press, 1930), II; F. Boas and G. Hunt, "Kwakiutl Texts," *Jesup North Pacific Expedition*, III, Pts. 1–3 (New York, 1905).

[8] The feast he is now engaged in giving.

[9] His opponents.

[10] To break a copper, showing in this way how far one rose above even the most superlatively valuable things, was the final mark of greatness.

[11] Himself.

[12] As salmon do.

[13] Himself.

[14] Irony, of course.

[15] Of treasure.

[16] Insult is used here in reference to the intense susceptibility to shame that is conspicuous in this culture. All possible contingencies were interpreted as rivalry situations, and the gamut of emotions swung between triumph and shame.

[17] E. Sapir, "A Girl's Puberty Ceremony among the Nootka," *Transactions of the Royal Society of Canada*, VII (Third series, 1913), 67–80.

[18] This phrasing of the process is deliberately animistic. It is used with no reference to a group mind or a superorganic, but in the same sense in which it is customary to say, "Every art has its own canons."

[19] J. Dewey, *Human Nature and Conduct: An Introduction to Social Psychology* (New York, Holt, 1922).

[20] S. Novakovsky, "Arctic or Siberian Hysteria as a Reflex of the Geographic Environment," *Ecology*, V (1924), 113–27.

[21] Fortune, *op. cit.*, 54–55.

[22] I. H. Coriat, "Psychoneuroses among Primitive Tribes," *Studies in Abnormal Psychology*, Ser. VI (Boston, Gorham, n.d.), 201–8.

[23] J. F. C. Hecker, *The Black Death and the Dancing Mania*, tr. B. G. Babbington (New York, 1885).

Correspondence to and from the Field

[1] A young writer who died *circa* 1920, the author of *The History of a Literary Radical and Other Papers* (New York, Huebsch, 1920).

A comment on the continuing excitement about ideas about psychological types and culture developed in conversations at the meeting of the British Association for the Advancement of Science, held in Toronto in 1924.

3 "The Waste of the Protocracy," an unpublished paper on the role of the deviant, written in 1924. The paper was rejected by *The Nation*; when it was resubmitted in 1940, it was accepted and held for a year but never published.

4 Isabel Gordon, who was working on the problem of common ancestry in a Tennessee mountain community for her dissertation.

5 Where RFB shared a tiny room with a woman who taught in New Jersey and only came to New York on weekends.

6 *Journal of the American Statistical Association*, of which William Fielding Ogburn was the editor.

7 For my dissertation, *An Inquiry into the Question of Cultural Stability in Polynesia* (Columbia University Contributions to Anthropology, IX; New York, Columbia University Press, 1928).

8 Published as "The Methodology of Racial Testing: Its Significance for Sociology," *American Journal of Sociology*, XXXI, No. 5 (1926), 657–67.

9 In the tower of the American Museum of Natural History, where I was writing my dissertation.

10 Given to Italian children for my MA thesis.

11 See *The Pueblo Potter, a Study of Creative Imagination in Primitive Art* (Columbia University Contributions to Anthropology, VIII; New York, Columbia University Press, 1929).

12 Specific publication unidentified.

13 See Bronislaw Malinowski, *The Father in Primitive Psychology* (Psyche Miniature; London, Kegan Paul, 1927).

14 In the summer of 1925, we started out together for our separate fields. RFB went with me as far as the Grand Canyon, which she had never seen. She then turned back to Zuñi, while I went on to San Francisco and sailed for Hawaii on my way to Samoa. Her first letters at this time carry echoes of the discussions about my being allowed to go to the tropics and of her fears that the isolation of field work might end in depression for me.

15 During the Zuñi part of the trip, Katherine Brenner, one of the two girls with whom RFB had gone to Europe after her graduation from Vassar College, visited her. She was now married and had her home in California, but had come to Santa Fe to recuperate from an illness.

16 Two of RFB's principal informants in Zuñi.

17 An anthology which RFB had typed for MM to take to the field.

18 A poetry magazine of the 1920's, of which Louise Townsend Nicholl, Léonie Adams, Louise Bogan, and Rolfe Humphries were editors.

19 Katherine Brenner now returned to Santa Fe.

20 A slang expression we had for spending our time on anything other than anthropology.

21 Harriet Monroe, editor of *Poetry*.

22 Here she copied out "Here we come a-piping" (*Come Hither*, p. 11) and "I had a little nut tree" (*ibid.*, p. 191). Years later, the latter was sung to me by another anthropologist, Scudder Mekeel, who had discovered from his psychoanalysis what it "really" meant.

23 Tony Luhan, a Taos Indian who had married Mabel Dodge. This is a curious echo of Mabel Dodge's first appearance in RFB's life (see "The Story of My Life . . . ," page 109).

24 A friend of William F. Ogburn, who had worked on the "Only Child" study on which Léonie Adams, Louise Bogan, and Louise Townsend Nicholl also worked. She had become interested in RFB's work on folklore and had planned to assist her during the winter of 1925–26.

25 *Journal of American Folk-Lore.*

26 "The Worst is not Our Anger," in which, in the original version (see "Diary: 1923," page 70), these lines occur:

> and weary
> Of all the woodnotes of that veery
> We heard in love's lost countryside.

27 See "Diary: 1923," page 71.

28 I.e. his poetry manuscript. See letters from ES to RFB, *passim.*

29 Melville Jacobs, Alexander Lesser, Gene Weltfish, Thelma Adamson, and Otto Klineberg.

30 At the meeting of the Twenty-third International Congress of Americanists, held in New York, September 1928.

31 This was a slip. Thomas Mott Osborne was a prison reformer.

32 "Psychological Types in the Cultures of the Southwest," *Proceedings of the Twenty-third International Congress of Americanists* (New York, 1930), 572–81. See above, pages 248–61.

33 CXXVII, September 26 (1928), 296. See "Selected Poems," page 479.

34 *Social Organization of Manu'a* (Bishop Museum Monograph, LXXVI; Honolulu, 1930). MM worked under the direction of Radcliffe-Brown, then Professor of Anthropology, Sydney University, on the first Admiralty Island trip.

35 *Coming of Age in Samoa* (New York, Morrow, 1928).

36 "Broken Homes," *The Nation*, CXXVIII, February 27 (1929), 253–55.

37 "Americanization in Samoa," *The American Mercury*, XVI, No. 63 (1929), 204–7.

[38] "A Twi Relationship System," *Journal of the Royal Anthropological Institute*, LXVII (1937), 297–304.

[39] The first draft of Reo Fortune's book, *Sorcerers of Dobu*.

[40] *Coming of Age in Samoa*, which had been published at the end of August 1928.

[41] *Social Organization of Manu'a*, which was dedicated to RFB.

[42] "Psychological Types in the Cultures of the Southwest," *op. cit.*

[43] "The Science of Custom," *Century Magazine*, CXVII, No. 6 (1929), 641–49.

[44] "Psychological Types in the Cultures of the Southwest," *op. cit.*

[45] "Animism," *Encyclopaedia of the Social Sciences* (New York, Macmillan, 1930), II, 65–67.

[46] The first draft of *Sorcerers of Dobu*. This letter was concerned with the problems of RFF's application for a fellowship for Columbia University.

[47] I.e. the denial of cause and effect relationships, from the native point of view.

[48] Written in reply to RFB's letter of January 10, 1929.

[49] Later obtained in a second field trip to Dobu, July 1929.

[50] Dr. Boas, with whom RFB had traveled to the west to attend a Southwest conference.

[51] Margaret Mead, "More Comprehensive Field Methods," *American Anthropologist*, XXXV, No. 1 (1933), 1–15.

[52] Reo F. Fortune, *Manus Religion* (Philadelphia, American Philosophical Society, 1935).

[53] Radcliffe-Brown was teaching at Columbia University in the summer of 1931.

[54] Published as *The Changing Culture of an Indian Tribe* (New York, Columbia University Press, 1932). It turned out that "reservation women" was an army term for prostitutes.

[55] *The Changing Culture of an Indian Tribe*.

[56] Margaret Mead, "An Investigation of the Thought of Primitive Children, with Special Reference to Animism," *Journal of the Royal Anthropological Institute*, XLII (1932), 173–90.

[57] "Configurations of Culture in North America," *op. cit.*

[58] Margaret Mead, "More Comprehensive Field Methods," *op. cit.*

[59] The first draft of *Patterns of Culture*.

[60] Reo F. Fortune, *Sorcerers of Dobu* (New York, Dutton, 1932).

[61] "The Science of Custom," *op. cit.*

[62] "Configurations of Culture in North America," *American Anthropologist*, XXXIV, No. 1 (1932), 1–27.

[63] "Anthropology and the Abnormal," *Journal of General Psychology*, X, No. 2 (1934), 59–82. See above, pages 262–83.

[64] Northwest Coast Indians.

[65] "Anthropology and the Abnormal," *op. cit.*

[66] A projected book, never written.

[67] Margaret Mead, "Kinship in the Admiralty Islands," *Anthropological Papers of the American Museum of Natural History*, XXXIV, Pt. 2 (New York, 1934).

[68] "Configurations of Culture in North America," *op. cit.*

[69] Southwest, i.e. Zuñi.

[70] Northwest Coast, i.e. Kwakiutl.

[71] Edward Sapir, "Culture, Genuine and Spurious," *American Journal of Sociology*, XXIX, No. 4 (1924), 401–29.

[72] For a meeting of the American Ethnological Society.

[73] The annual meeting of the American Association for the Advancement of Science, of which Section H is devoted to anthropology.

[74] When Radcliffe-Brown read the first draft of Fortune's Dobu material, he refused to believe in the accuracy of the account; when he read the second draft and was convinced that the account was accurate, he then said that it was a "pathological culture" and ought not to exist.

[75] Morris Opler, "An Analysis of Mescalero and Chiricahua Apache Social Organization in the Light of Their Systems of Relationship" (Ph.D. dissertation, Department of Anthropology, University of Chicago, 1933).

[76] "Sensationalist" in the Jungian sense of reliance on sensation. I would interpret Radcliffe-Brown's response as coming from a lack of sensory vividness, so that he could argue for a point theoretically which had no reality for him at all.

[77] Franz Boas, "The Aims of Anthropological Research," *Science*, LXXVI, No. 1983 (1932), 605–13.

[78] A misunderstanding of my reference, in a letter, to the proposed use of Plains material in *Patterns of Culture*. On RFF's reaction to the use of Dobu material, see his letter to RFB of November 21, 1932 (page 329), which she had not yet received.

[79] *Sorcerers of Dobu* itself had reached RFF in the field the previous spring.

[80] "Incest," *Encyclopaedia of the Social Sciences* (New York, Macmillan, 1932), II, 620–22.

[81] Actually the Yuat River, a tributary of the Sepik, in the Sepik District, where we were working with the Mundugumor.

[82] The effect of this was to stretch field funds.

[83] Mundugumor.

[84] Tchambuli.

[85] Margaret Mead, "Where Magic Rules and Men Are Gods," *The New York Times Magazine*, June 25, 1933, 8–9, 18.

[86] In reference to C. W. Hart's review of *Growing Up in New Guinea* (New York, Morrow, 1930).

[87] *The Changing Culture of an Indian Tribe, op. cit.* The note concerned the problem of preserving the disguise necessary to protect the tribe discussed in the book.

[88] We had then been in Tchambuli for almost four months.

[89] Ambunti is 250 miles up the Sepik River and at that time was the main government station for the Sepik District.

[90] This letter was written in reply to that from RFB of December 28, 1932.

[91] A reference to the job situation in the depression.

[92] This is the point on sex-ethos reversal; *see Sex and Temperament in Three Primitive Societies* (New York, Morrow, 1935).

[93] A reference to a discussion of RFF's point about cross-cousin marriage, in a part of this letter not reproduced here. The point was published in his article, "A Note on Some Forms of Kinship Structure," *Oceania,* IV, No. 1 (1933).

[94] Gregory Bateson, RFF, and myself. The book is by Kay Boyle.

[95] Henry Handel Richardson, a pseudonym for a woman writer.

[96] On the first draft of *Patterns of Culture.*

[97] "The Science of Custom," *op. cit.*

[98] "Configurations of Culture in North America," *op. cit.*

[99] "Cups of Clay," an unpublished essay incorporated into Chapter II of *Patterns of Culture.*

[100] *Patterns of Culture.*

[101] "Anthropology and the Abnormal," *op. cit.*

[102] *Patterns of Culture.*

[103] *Zuni Mythology* (2 vols., Columbia University Contributions to Anthropology, XXI; New York, Columbia University Press, 1935).

[104] "Anthropology and the Abnormal," *op. cit.*

[105] *Patterns of Culture* (Boston and New York, Houghton Mifflin, 1934).

PART IV

The Years as Boas' Left Hand

[1] Unpublished letter, Boas Papers.

[2] Unpublished letter, Boas Papers.

[3] See "Diary: 1923," entries for February 12–20, pages 65–66.

[4] *Review of Religion,* IV, No. 4 (1940), 438–40.

[5] Letter from RFB to FB, September 16, 1923, *see* pages 399–400.

[6] Unpublished letter, FB to RFB.

[7] Unpublished letter, Boas Papers.

8 This is a fear which may have been premature, *vide* the Wenner-Gren Foundation International Symposium on Anthropology, held in 1952 (Alfred L. Kroeber, ed., *Anthropology Today* [Chicago, University of Chicago Press, 1953]). In the 1920's we had not yet invented the conference method for rapid, many-leveled exchange. Then grasp of a subject meant having the time, the interest, and the knowledge to keep up in a field primarily by reading — possible if one grew up with a new discipline, but much less possible later.

9 Neither one married again. When Stanley Benedict died, he left her his entire estate in a trust fund.

10 Work on the preparation of the manuscript was begun in 1932. See "Correspondence to and from the Field," letters exchanged with MM and RFF, 1932–1934, *passim*.

11 Work on this textbook, *General Anthropology*, ed. Franz Boas (Boston and New York, Heath, 1938), was begun in 1928 and dragged on for ten years.

12 Founded in 1939.

13 Sponsored jointly by Columbia University and the University of Montana.

14 New York, Modern Age Books, 1940.

15 Public Affairs Pamphlet, No. 85 (New York, Public Affairs Committee, 1943).

16 See Ralph Linton, *Acculturation in Seven American Indian Tribes* (New York, Appleton-Century, 1940).

17 See the series of volumes, *Science, Philosophy and Religion*, eds. Lyman Bryson and Louis Finkelstein, published by the Conference on Science, Philosophy and Religion.

18 The Committee for National Morale was an attempt to mobilize what would now be called the "behavioral sciences" for the war effort, with a core of those who had been concerned with the applications of psychology during World War I. Here many of those who were to play a part in psychological warfare and to work on problems of morale came together as volunteers to try to prepare plans which could be put into effect when war came. With Gordon Allport, Ladislas Farago wrote his compendious study, *German Psychological Warfare* (New York, Putnam's, 1942), Edmond Taylor developed some of the interests which he later wrote about in *Richer by Asia* (Boston and New York, Houghton Mifflin, 1947), we tried to work out problems of morale (Gregory Bateson and Margaret Mead, "Principles of Morale Building," *Journal of Educational Sociology*, XV, No. 4 [1941], 206–20), and the committee, together with the Council for Intercultural Relations, sponsored Geoffrey Gorer's pioneering memorandum, "Japanese Character Structure and Propaganda, a Preliminary Survey," some portions of which were published as "Themes in Japanese Cul-

ture," *Transactions*, New York Academy of Sciences, Ser. 2, V, No. 5 (1943), 106–24.

19 Whereas the Conference on Science, Philosophy and Religion stressed an interdisciplinary approach to ethical problems, and the Committee on National Morale stressed applications of social science techniques, the Council for Intercultural Relations began the study of what is now known as "national character." In doing so, we began to develop methods of interviewing highly sophisticated individuals on their own culture and individuals who had lived as outsiders in a culture we were studying; we also developed methods of analyzing films — some of which later were incorporated into studies of culture at a distance (see *The Study of Culture at a Distance*, Margaret Mead and Rhoda Métraux, eds. [Chicago, University of Chicago Press, 1953]).

20 *Science, Philosophy and Religion*, Second Symposium, Lyman Bryson and Louis Finkelstein, eds. (New York, Conference on Science, Philosophy and Religion, 1942), 56–69. For RFB's comments on this paper, see *ibid.*, 69–71.

21 Prepared by Gregory Bateson, Ruth Benedict, Lyman Bryson, Lawrence K. Frank, Margaret Mead, Philip E. Mosely, and Louise M. Rosenblatt for *Suggested Materials for Training of Regional Specialists, Army Program* (1943; mimeographed).

22 *An Analysis of the Nazi Film "Hitlerjunge Quex"* (New York, Institute for Intercultural Studies, 1945; mimeographed). Portions of this analysis were published as "Cultural and Thematic Analysis of Fictional Films," *Transactions*, New York Academy of Science, Ser. 2, V, No. 4 (1943), 72–78.

23 *Burmese Personality* (New York, Institute for Intercultural Studies, 1946; mimeographed).

24 "Qualitative Attitude Analysis — A Technique for the Study of Verbal Behavior." In "The Problem of Changing Food Habits, Report of the Committee on Food Habits, 1941–1943," *National Research Council Bulletin*, CVIII (Washington, 1943).

25 New York, Morrow, 1942.

26 See, for instance, Margaret Mead, "The Application of Anthropological Techniques to Cross-National Communication," *Transactions*, New York Academy of Sciences, Ser. 2, IX, No. 4 (1947), 133–52.

27 *Rumanian Culture and Behavior* (New York, Institute for Intercultural Studies, 1946; mimeographed).

28 *Thai Culture and Behavior: An Unpublished War Time Study Dated September, 1943* (Data Paper, No. 4, Southeast Asia Program, Department of Far Eastern Studies, Cornell University, 1952). Previously issued as *Thai Culture and Behavior* (New York, Institute for Intercultural Studies, 1946; mimeographed).

29 Unpublished letter, RFB to FB.

[30] Franz Boas, "The American Ethnological Society," *Science*, XCVII, January 1 (1943), 7–8.

The Natural History of War

[1] Ruth Benedict, "A Brief Sketch of Serrano Culture," *American Anthropologist*, XXVI, No. 3 (1924), 366–92.
[2] Oxford, Clarendon Press, 1936.
[3] B. Spencer and F. J. Gillen, *The Arunta* (London, Macmillan, 1927).
[4] Bronislaw Malinowski, *Argonauts of the Western Pacific* (London, Routledge, 1922).
[5] *Sorcerers of Dobu* (New York, Dutton, 1932).
[6] Jules Henry, *Jungle People, a Kaingang Tribe of the Highlands of Brazil* (New York, Augustin, 1941).

Ideologies in the Light of Comparative Data

[1] William Graham Sumner, *Folkways* (Boston, Ginn, 1906).
[2] Robert H. Lowie, *Primitive Society* (New York, Boni and Liveright, 1920).
[3] Emile Durkheim, *Division of Labor in Society* (New York, Macmillan, 1933).

Selections from the Correspondence Between Ruth Benedict and Franz Boas: 1923–1940

[1] The *Journal of American Folk-Lore*, of which RFB was the editor from 1925 to 1939.
[2] His daughter, who died of poliomyelitis in October 1925.
[3] These films, however, were lost. RFB described the circumstances of the loss in a letter to me of February 20, 1932:

> The last is that Irving Lerner had borrowed a projector and taken Bunny's Guatemala movies over to Grantwood to show to Papa Franz, and had run off with some of his Kwakiutl pictures, too. On Monday Gladys brought them over in her car, projector, Bunny's pictures and Papa Franz' two copies of his. She didn't want to bring them up to the office by herself, so she left them out in the car Monday and Tuesday, and Tuesday night her car was stolen with everything in it. It's a week later now and nothing heard of anything. Papa Franz takes it very hard that his pictures are gone; he counted on them for a study of rhythm and he even says, "I might as well have stayed at home last winter."

[4] As the director of a summer field training session in ethnological method, on the Mescalero Apache Reservation. These sessions were held under the auspices of the Laboratory of Anthropology, Santa Fe, New Mexico.

[5] Henrietta Schmerler, a field worker, who was killed on the Apache Reservation.

[6] Arthur H. Fauset, *Folklore from Nova Scotia* (*Memoirs of the American Folklore Society*, XXIV; New York, 1931).

[7] "Religion," in *General Anthropology*, ed. Franz Boas (Boston and New York, Heath, 1938), 627–65.

[8] *Patterns of Culture.*

[9] *Zuni Mythology* (2 vols., Columbia University Contributions to Anthropology, XXI; New York, Columbia University Press, 1935). The Introduction is reproduced in part in this volume, pages 226–45.

[10] *General Anthropology*, ed. Franz Boas.

[11] "Prehistoric Archaeology," *ibid.*, 146–237.

[12] Alfred L. Kroeber, "History and Science in Anthropology," *American Anthropologist*, XXXVII, No. 4 (1935), 539–69.

[13] Gladys Reichard, "Coeur d'Alene," *Handbook of American Indian Languages*, Pt. 3, ed. Franz Boas (New York, Augustin, 1933–38), 517–707.

[14] Published 1938.

[15] I.e. Buell Quain, a young anthropologist, who committed suicide on his second field trip.

[16] Published 1940.

[17] Wilhelm Schmidt, *The Culture Historical Method of Ethnology*, trans. S. A. Sieber (New York, Fortuny's, 1939).

[18] "The Natural History of War," unpublished paper, see pages 369–82. RFB's point, discussed in this letter, was that warfare among villages, in primitive societies which practice village exogamy, "cuts the roots of family life. A woman's existence is passed in divided loyalty; if she is in her husband's village she must celebrate the victory dance for the head of her brother, if in her father's, for the head of her husband."

[19] Franz Boas, *Race, Language and Culture* (New York, Macmillan, 1940).

[20] He had formally retired in 1936, becoming Professor Emeritus.

[21] *Race: Politics and Science* (New York, Modern Age Books, 1940).

[22] This was a position on which FB took a public stand. See Albert Deutsch, "Boas Says He'll Vote for FDR because . . . ," *PM*, October 25, 1940.

[23] *Race: Politics and Science.*

PART V

The Post-War Years: The Gathered Threads

1 *The Chrysanthemum and the Sword: Patterns of Japanese Behavior* (Boston, Houghton Mifflin, 1946).

2 *Ibid.*, 314–17.

3 See, in John W. Bennett and Michio Nagai, "The Japanese Critique of the Methodology of Benedict's *The Chrysanthemum and the Sword*" (*American Anthropologist*, LV, No. 3 [1953], 404–11), reference to *Minzokugaku Kenkyu* (The Japanese Journal of Ethnology): Special Issue on *The Chrysanthemum and the Sword*, XIV, No. 4 (Tokyo, 1949).

4 *New York Herald Tribune Weekly Book Review*, December 1, 1946, 3.

5 "Japanese Character Structure and Propaganda, a Preliminary Survey" (1942). A passage from this unpublished report is reproduced in *The Study of Culture at a Distance*, Margaret Mead and Rhoda Métraux, eds. (Chicago, University of Chicago Press, 1953), 402.

6 Quoted by Robert Lynd in *Ruth Benedict: A Memorial* (New York, Viking Fund, 1949), 23.

7 "Remarks on Receiving the Annual Achievement Award of the American Association of University Women" (MS, June 1946).

8 Gregory Bateson, "The Pattern of an Armaments Race," *Bulletin of the Atomic Scientists*, II, Nos. 5–6 (1946), 10–11; Nos. 7–8 (1946), 26–28.

9 *Columbia University Research in Contemporary Cultures, Manual for Field Workers* (1947, mimeographed).

10 Gregory Bateson, Ruth Benedict, Lyman Bryson, Lawrence K. Frank, Margaret Mead, Philip E. Mosely, and Louise M. Rosenblatt, *Suggested Materials for Training of Regional Specialists, Army Program* (1943, mimeographed).

11 This project became Studies in Soviet Culture and was carried out under the auspices of the American Museum of Natural History under the direction of Margaret Mead.

12 This money was returned to Carnegie after RFB's death.

13 Held at Podebrady, Czechoslovakia, July 21–August 25, 1948. See *The Influence of Home and Community on Children under Thirteen Years of Age* (*Towards World Understanding*, VI; Paris, UNESCO, n.d.).

Recognition of Cultural Diversities in the Postwar World

[1] This paper was presented as part of the program of the Council on Intercultural Relations [later, Institute for Intercultural Studies] which was attempting to develop a series of systematic understandings of the great contemporary cultures so that the special values of each might be maintained and enhanced in the postwar world.

[2] Because of the different goals for which people strive in different cultures and the different character structure induced, what happiness consists in differs in different societies.

[3] March 19, 1943.

Child Rearing in Certain European Countries

[1] Research in Contemporary Cultures, government-aided Columbia University Research Project sponsored by the Psychological Branch of the Medical Sciences Division of the Office of Naval Research. The Russian material was collected and organized under the leadership of Geoffrey Gorer and Margaret Mead, and I am especially indebted to Mr. Gorer's skill and insights; Prof. Conrad M. Arensberg directed the group gathering Jewish material, and Dr. Sula Benet organized the information on Poland. Thanks are due to these leaders and to all their coworkers.

[2] In this entire section I am indebted to Mr. Gorer's analysis.

Anthropology and the Humanities

[1] James B. Conant, *On Understanding Science* (New Haven, Yale University Press, 1947), 8–9.

[2] George Santayana, *Platonism and the Spiritual Life* (New York, Scribner's, 1927), 58.

[3] George Santayana, *The Life of Reason* (New York, Scribner's, 1905–6), II, 101.

PART VI

Selected Poems: 1941

[1] This presentation of RFB's poems is a compromise between the manuscripts which she prepared to be books, her great sense that it matters

how a poem looks on a page, and her feeling that if the poems were to be published they should stand on their own or else take a minor place in her life.

The selection is one she herself made in 1941, when she wrote these poems out by hand in a little hand-bound book as a present for me, and it expresses the most recent personal choice of which there is any record of what she liked best. One substitution has been made: "Ripeness Is All," originally included, appears elsewhere in this volume (pages 85–86); and "Resurrection of the Ghost," the latest poem known to have been published (*New York Herald Tribune Books*, August 26, 1934), has been added. RFB frequently reworked her poems; in all cases I have followed the text of the 1941 selection.

Mary Wollstonecraft

1 Posthumous Works, 4 vols. (1798).
2 *Memoirs of the Author of the Vindication of the Rights of Women* (1798).
3 *Thoughts on the Education of Daughters* (1787); *Mary, a Fiction* (1788); *Original Stories from Real Life* (1791); *Vindication of the Rights of Man* (1791); *Vindication of the Rights of Women* (1792); *An Historical and Moral View of the French Revolution*, I (1794); *Letters Written during a Short Residence in Norway, Sweden, and Denmark* (1796).
4 This must have been in 1909–10, when, following her graduation from college, RFB traveled in Europe for a year. She was then twenty-two. — Ed. note.

Index of Personal Names

A.A., *see* Goldenweiser, Alexander A.
A.A.G., *see* Goldenweiser, Alexander A.
Adams, Léonie, poet, xvii, 20, 25–26,
72, 77, 78, 87, 90, 92, 166, 179,
191, 287, 534 *n.*, 550 *n.*
and Boas, 202
book accepted, 176
book reviewed by Sapir, 182
quoted, 91
Adamson, Thelma, graduate student,
78, 551 *n.*
Agnes, *see* Benedict, Agnes
Alexander, Mathilda (Maidie), Louise
Bogan's daughter, 77
Allport, Gordon W., psychologist,
555 *n.*
Angulo, Edna de, first wife of Jaime de
Angulo, 297
Angulo, Jaime de, linguist, 14, 298
letter, 296–98
Angulo, Nance de, second wife of Jaime
de Angulo, 298
Anthony, Father, priest in Zuñi, 293
Arnold, Marguerite I. (M.I.A.), class-
mate of RFB at Vassar, 57, 59,
60–63, 65, 67, 69, 295
A.S., *see* Singleton, Anne
Ashley, Margaret, graduate student of
anthropology, 74
Atsatt, Elizabeth, friend with whom
RFB traveled in Europe, 522

Augustin, J. J., German printer of sci-
entific publications, later in U. S.,
407, 409
Aunt Harriet, *see* Monroe, Harriet
Aunt Hettie, *see* Shattuck, Hettie
Aunt Mamie, *see* Ellis, Mary Shattuck
Aunt Myra, *see* Shattuck, Myra
Aunty My, *see* Shattuck, Myra
Averkieva, Julia, graduate student from
U.S.S.R., 403–5, 407–8

Barbeau, Marius, French Canadian
folklorist and musicologist, 57, 61
Barnauw, Victor, anthropologist,
quoted, 209
Barsky, Hannah Kahn (David), then
in American Museum of Natural
History, Anthropology Department, 307, 320, 336
Bateson, Gregory, anthropologist, 351–
53, 432, 554 *n.*, 555 *n.*
Beckwith, Martha, folklorist, 77
Benedict, Agnes, sister of Stanley Benedict, classmate of RFB, social
worker, 63
Benedict, Clarke, Stanley Benedict's
brother, 56–60, 62–63
Benedict, Mrs. Clarke (Minnie), wife
of Clarke Benedict, 56–60, 62–63
Benedict, Ruth, *see* Index of Subjects

Index of Subjects